The Very Young:

Guiding Children from Infancy Through the Early Years

George W. Maxim
West Chester State College

Wadsworth Publishing Company
Belmont, California
A Division of Wadsworth, Inc.

Education Editor: Roger Peterson
Production Editor: Mary Arbogast
Designer: Carol Kummer
Copy Editor: Carol Dondrea
Illustrator: Patricia Kinley
Cover: Susan Gilmour

Also available:
THE SOURCEBOOK: Activities to Enrich Programs for Infants and Young Children by George W. Maxim. Based on child development concepts, the activities included are designed to fit the particular needs of children at each stage of development. Also provides guidelines for observing children in the classroom and at home. Paperbound. 200 pages. October 1980.

Printed in the United States of America
1 2 3 4 5 6 7 8 9 10 — 84 83 82 81 80

Library of Congress Cataloging in Publication Data

Maxim, George W
    The very young.

    Includes bibliographical references and index.
    1. Child development.   2. Socialization.   3. Education, Preschool.   I. Title.
HQ769.M3695   372'.21   80-10918
    ISBN 0-534-00820-8

Contents

Chapter 5
Establishing a Safe, Healthful Environment   144

Chapter 6
Cognitive Development:
Three Views of the Learning Process   176

Chapter 10
Creative Development:
Encouraging the Spirit of
Wonder and Magic 372

Chapter 11
Involving Parents in the Preschool Program 435

Chapter 12
Putting It All Together: Creating a Challenging
Preschool Environment   459

Chapter 13
Providing for Children with Special Needs   499

A Final Word from Your Author   540

Index   543

Credits   559

Preface

In recent years, the content and methodology of the field of early childhood education has changed drastically. Contributions from psychologists, sociologists, politicians, scientists, teachers, and experts from many other fields have brought changes at a pace never before experienced in our profession. These changes have influenced not only what we know about young children, but also how we help them achieve their greatest potential for growth.

Because of the dynamic nature of early childhood education today, the focus of this book is on decision making. You will constantly be making choices as to the most desirable teaching strategies—choices that reflect your view of the nature of young children. The aim of this book is to help you develop such skills by presenting objectively current information and issues in early childhood education. I have tried to be as comprehensive as possible, although all the information available today could never be presented in any one book. I have also tried to make this information as interesting and meaningful as possible to prospective teachers. As you read the book, you will find a large number of practical suggestions for putting theory into practice. In addition, each chapter includes realistic vignettes designed to stimulate your interest and increase your understanding of the material being presented.

This book covers the early childhood years from infancy through kindergarten. This range of years is a feature that sets the book apart from most others in its field. Since the topic of infant care is a vital one, the information and practical examples related to that crucial period of life should help illustrate the sequential needs of children as they progress through the age of six.

This book was written for those who plan to assume the vitally important career of working with young children. It was constructed to help them (1) understand the growth and development of the early childhood profession, (2) distinguish the characteristics of young children at various stages of development, (3) make informed decisions about the most appropriate teaching methods and materials, and (4) know the key strategies for program development and implementation.

Finally, throughout the book I was confronted with the frustrating dilemma of how to refer to individuals without using sexist terms. Singular pronouns like "it" seem a bit inhuman, as does "one." The plural pronoun "they" seems at first to provide a likely escape, but at times only a singular pronoun is appropriate. So, following conventional practice in textbook writing, I have chosen to use *he*, *his*, or *him* when referring to a single young child, and *she*, *hers*, or *her* when referring to a teacher. Until the day an acceptable neutral pronoun appears, I am stuck with this arrangement.

An instructor's manual is available upon adoption of the text.

Acknowledgments

The process of writing a book is never an individual accomplishment. Although the author's name is prominently displayed on the cover and frequently mentioned in connection with the title, he or she can never take complete responsibility for the completed work. This fact is especially true in my case. The number of individuals who made valuable contributions in helping me complete this book is overwhelming.

My first debt of gratitude is owed to my wife Libby. Her patience was undoubtedly pushed to the breaking point many times, but she never let me know. Her understanding nature, patient approval, praise, and encouragement continually motivated and sustained me throughout many long hours of writing. Without her help, I would never have been able to finish this book. In addition, Libby gave many hours of her own time acting as chief photographer. Her dedication was often an example to me when I began to get "writing-day blues."

Roger Peterson, education and family studies editor at Wadsworth, was of more help than I can say. His insight and knowledge extends not only to writing and publishing, but also to education and human relationships. Roger provided incalculable help in the technical phases of manuscript preparation, as well as in the suggestions for professional materials to include or exclude. Equally important was Roger's concerned, supportive personality. He often served as a pick-me-up whenever things seemed to go not quite right.

Special appreciation is extended to the teachers and administrators who made their exemplary schools and classrooms available for the photographs used throughout this text: Katherine A. Nell, Cramp Child Care Center, Philadelphia, Pennsylvania; Alice Gleockler, Exton Elementary School, Exton, Pennsylvania; Julie Tilson, East Bradford Elementary School, West Chester,

Pennsylvania; Robin Lloyd, Discovery Day Nursery School and Kindergarten, West Chester, Pennsylvania; Joanne Franck, Small World, Kennett Square, Pennsylvania; Pearl Bailes, COPE Program, West Chester State College, West Chester, Pennsylvania; and Sister Eileen Smith, Norwood-Fontbonne Academy, Philadelphia, Pennsylvania.

I am indebted, too, to a number of other people. I want to thank Kathy and Bill Nell for supplying a number of photographs for the book and for making available their darkroom facilities. Jon Wilson, sales representative for Wadsworth Publishing Company, must be cited for his hard work and dedication. Without his perceptiveness and persistence, this book would have remained only a dream. The typing for this manuscript was done by Rae Ricciuti. I am deeply thankful for the hours she spent deciphering my hand-written copy and expertly transforming it into wonderfully typed drafts.

My colleagues in the early childhood area of instruction at West Chester State College provided many suggestions that added to this text: Mary Ann Morgan, Ruth Petkofsky, and Connie Zimmerman. I also appreciate the friendly assistance extended by my department chairperson, E. Riley Holman, and the interest and motivation provided by the assistant chairperson, Robert Herres.

Last, but certainly not least, I wish to express my unending gratitude for the outstanding manuscript reviewers provided by Wadsworth: John Cryan, University of Toledo; Maxine Edwards, Northeastern Oklahoma A & M University; Deanna J. Radeloff, Bowling Green University; Sherrill Richarz, Washington State University; Patsy Skeen, University of Georgia; and Judith Washburn, California State University at Los Angeles. Their careful examination of the manuscript resulted in adjustments that strengthened and solidified this book.

To the Student

1979 was designated as the International Year of the Child. During that time, nations around the world combined in a concerted effort to remind parents, teachers, and other adults of the special needs of the very young. As teachers, we must constantly be aware of those needs so that they, in turn, can be met with our spirit and dedication. The following are aspects of children's needs as identified during the International Year of the Child. Let's be aware of them and use them to guide our work with the very young this year and in all years to come.

A child needs to wonder.
A child needs to taste, smell, and feel.
A child needs to listen.
A child needs to be loved.
A child needs to move.
A child needs to pretend.
A child needs to see.
A child needs to experience.
A child needs parents who care.

This book is dedicated to the loving
memory of two exceptional mothers—
Rose Maxim and Anne Kurlak.
Their devoted love and caring
exemplified motherhood and teaching
in the truest sense.

1

Early Childhood Education: Perspectives on Change

The field of early childhood education has grown and changed over the years. Today, the greatest decision faced by teachers is whether to develop their programs around informal activities such as art and free play or around formal instruction in skills areas such as reading, writing, and mathematics. (Miss Peach courtesy of Mell Lazarus and Field Newspaper Syndicate.)

Welcome to the field of early childhood education. You are one of the rapidly growing number of young men and women entering this expanding professional field. It is a field that requires sensitive, energetic, creative people willing to devote time and effort to the growth and development of young children during their most formative years. What you do with these children during their early years has a great impact on their future lives, their family, their community, and their world. This is an awesome responsibility, for your ultimate influence on the child's growth and development is great—comparable to the control an artist or sculptor has over a painting or a lump of clay. When you plan a child's day, you can draw on all your professional skills and creativity to produce an original masterpiece unrivaled by anything that precedes it. But you are not alone. You are part of a team comprising many individuals—primarily the teacher, the child, and the parents.

As part of this team, you must work with parents to identify each child's needs and to establish the type of program best suited to encouraging the child's fullest potential. Since each young child is a unique individual, subject to many more influences than a sculptor's lump of clay or an artist's canvas, your job is important indeed. Do not, however, be apprehensive about this challenge. At this point in your training you are not expected to be able to create professionally desirable early childhood environments for young children. This text and this course will help you learn the techniques and principles of guiding young children to their fullest potential within a sensitive, creative, loving, and interesting preschool setting. Once you are willing and able to accept this rewarding professional challenge, you will join the thousands of early childhood professionals who experience daily satisfaction in guiding young children through perhaps the most important years of their lives. Your preschool program, which will be based on ideas about young children developed and influenced by philosophers and educators in various cultural contexts throughout history, will reflect the special needs of your children and their families.

THE ROOTS OF EARLY CHILDHOOD EDUCATION

Early childhood programs have not always been part of American education. In fact, they did not exist at all in this country until the late 1870s. Since other areas of the education profession have existed for centuries (almost exclusively for white males from rich families), early childhood education can be considered a fairly new, evolving field.

What explains this late start for such an important aspect of education? Much of the answer lies in the ways children between birth and age six have been viewed in the past. Until the middle 1800s, children were perceived as miniature adults. That is, from the time they were able to control their sphincters and feed and dress themselves, they were seen as individuals capable of performing adult duties. They were placed in the fields or in a craftsman's shop where they worked with other children under the direction of a boss or master to whom they were apprenticed. It was not uncommon to see children under the age of five already helping to support the household.

Not all adults, however, agreed that children were miniature adults. These people began to voice their concerns about the ways youngsters were handled. Elizabeth Barrett Browning summarized these feelings in her poem, "The Cry of the Children":

> The young lambs are bleating in the meadow,
> The young birds are chirping in the nest,
> The young fawns are playing with shadows,
> The young flowers are blowing toward the west—
> But the young, young children, O my brothers,
> They are weeping bitterly!
> They are weeping in the playtime of the others
> In the country of the free.
> They look up with their pale and sunken faces
> And their looks are sad to see
> For the man's hoary anguish draws and presses
> Down the cheeks of infancy.

Although such concern for young children was not widespread, enlightened individuals began to take an interest in their plight, and the concept of

Working in factories for up to twelve or sixteen hours a day was not seen as an unreasonable expectation for young children even at the turn of this century. These "miniature adults" were viewed as having the same capabilities as mature adults, only on a smaller scale. (Culver Pictures)

the early childhood years slowly began to change. Perhaps the greatest motivation for such change came from the pioneer work of early European philosophers. These philosophers were considered radicals during their time, and the concepts of childhood that they introduced were met with a great deal of skepticism. Among them were John Amos Comenius (1592–1670, Czechoslovakia), John Locke (1632–1704, England), Jean Jacques Rousseau (1712–1778, France), and John Heinrick Pestalozzi (1746–1827, Switzerland). They felt that young children should be viewed not as embryonic adults, but as individuals with capacities and developmental characteristics different from those of adults. They often compared young children to plants or flowers; that is, they saw both as living organisms that need special care and support in order to bloom naturally into free, complete individuals. For that reason, the philosophers wanted children removed from adultlike surroundings and provided with a warm, loving environment and child-oriented experiences where they would be free to develop their senses and form their personalities, whether in the home or in school.

Robert Owen

Following the general lead of these philosophers, several educational reformers began to contribute specific ideas on the education of young children. And early childhood programs began to appear. The first of these original programs was designed by a Scot, Robert Owen (1771–1858). Owen was an industrialist who assumed ownership of his father-in-law's cotton mill in 1816. There he became sensitive to the harsh working conditions of young children. He tried to stop this exploitation by refusing to employ children under ten. For these children Owen built an *Infant School*. Here, children received an education appropriate to their age. The school provided a spacious, cheerful, and comfortable environment where the children were free to move and explore as they pleased. One wall was open to nature, and the children were encouraged to play outdoors as much as possible. Inside, the children were exposed to real objects designed to induce questions and encourage activity. Dancing, singing, and other forms of creative play were encouraged, and teachers were admonished not to annoy the children with books or formal lessons—practices commonly found in schools for older children. Patience, love, and understanding characterized the school's atmosphere as children were cared for without fear of punishment.

Owen's Infant School was a happy contrast to the normal environment of early childhood years, but it never achieved the popular acclaim accorded some later efforts by others. One reason for this was that there were no professional journals at the time to spread the word of new educational practices. Another reason was the general lack of interest in making this kind of care available to other parts of the world.

Friedrich Froebel

In Germany, Friedrich Froebel (1782–1852) adopted the tenets of Comenius, Locke, Rousseau, and Pestalozzi, and founded the first popularly recognized school for children younger than eight in Blankenburg in 1837. Because he viewed the child's growth as similar to that of a flower, he called the school the *kindergarten* or "children's garden."

Froebel developed a carefully planned, systematic curriculum that had as its basic elements, "Gifts," "Occupations," "Mother's Plays," and nature study. These elements were considered highly innovative at the time and made the Froebelian kindergarten different from any other educational program in existence. Froebel's "Gifts" consisted of ten sets of manipulative materials (soft cloth-covered balls, puzzle-type wooden cubes, and so on) designed to provide children with hands-on experiences while learning about forms, numbers, and measurements. "Occupations" consisted of small muscle skill activities such as drawing, clay modeling, sewing, coloring, weaving, folding paper, and pasting. "Mother's Plays" were carefully designed songs and games used with the "Gifts." The following song was used in a learning activity involving colorful cloth-covered balls, Froebel's first "Gift":

> Now take this little ball
>   And do not let it fall,
> Balls of yellow, red, and blue
>   Some for me and some for you.

Now take this little ball
   And do not let it fall.
Hold it in your hand
   Then quite still let it stand
Balls of yellow, blue, and red
   You are round just like my head.
Hold it in your hand
   Then quite still let it stand.[1]

Notice how concepts of size, shape, and color were introduced and reinforced through this hands-on, joyful learning experience.

"Nature study" consisted of observing plants and animals and discussing the observations. The children also memorized poems about nature and discussed nature-oriented pictures shown to the class.

Although Froebel's program was a huge success when it was introduced into the United States, the merit of the kindergarten was not recognized during his lifetime. It was banned in Germany soon after it was developed because the Prussian government viewed it as promoting socialistic ideals. This decision severely affected Froebel and led to his untimely death a few years later.

Margaret McMillan

Another trend in early childhood education began in the early part of this century when Margaret McMillan (1860–1931), also building on the philosophies discussed earlier, developed the first *nursery school* in England. McMillan was a vocal member of a group of social activists in England that included such luminaries as George Bernard Shaw. Her concern with the social, political, and economic conditions of the time led to her election to the Bradford school board. In that position, she became aware of the widespread health problems of the children in the city's slum area. Convinced that such problems had already advanced too far by school age, McMillan chose to establish "day nurseries" for children aged two to seven. These nurseries were to make up for the neglect in health and hygiene the children experienced at home. Since a basic educational program was also part of her plan, the "day nurseries" came to be called *nursery schools.*

The concept of physical care was central to the nursery school. Responsibilities in this area included bathing children (a dozen or more children at a time) in waist-high tubs, providing clean clothes and nourishing meals, and planning for adequate fresh air and exercise. Because of her concern for the children's health, McMillan suggested that the school take the form of an "Open Shed," or open-air nursery. Consequently, one side of the school opened onto a garden or play area so fresh air and sunshine were available as children played in herb, vegetable, or flower gardens and cared for a variety of pets. To emphasize her total caring aspect, McMillan called the adult leader a nurse-teacher.

As a means of helping children develop reading, writing, and number skills, McMillan's program first emphasized the training of various muscles of the body. This training was given the label *nurture* by McMillan and centered on the use of clay modeling, coloring, drawing, block play, and the use of other perceptual-motor materials. Rhythmic movement, dramatic play, and musical activities encouraged the children to extend their physical abilities and their self-expression. McMillan expressed her educational philosophy in *The Nursery School*, a book that quickly became popular and influenced preschool educators well into the twentieth century. In fact, the influence of this first nursery school was so great that the McMillan Training College and the nursery school both still exist in London.

Maria Montessori

Maria Montessori (1870–1952), like McMillan, was motivated to start her school in order to meet the critical physical needs of young children. Both of these pioneers stressed that education could operate only in settings that first addressed the health and welfare of the child. When this concern was met, they stressed that early education should take the form of training the muscles of the body through exercise and movement.

Maria Montessori was known throughout her life as a woman of many roles. Her career in education, however, made the name *Montessori* world famous. Her work in education had a strange beginning. As Italy's first female physician, Montessori's first appointment was with the psychiatric clinic at the University of Rome, where she cared for the insane. At that time, no distinction was made between insanity and mental retardation, so Montessori came into close contact with retarded youngsters unmercifully labeled "idiot children." At first she diagnosed and prescribed treatments for all of these children's maladies, but eventually she became most interested in applying educational principles to curing their "idiocy." First, she observed the children to diagnose their weaknesses. Then she created a new activity-centered, sensory method using didactic (self-teaching) materials to educate them. Her program was so successful that all her children passed an achievement test, which they took along with the children from regular Roman schools—not all of the "normal" children passed. While others were admiring the "miracle" she had accomplished, Montessori began to search for the reasons that brought the normal children to such a low level as to allow her unfortunate children to equal or surpass them. Thus she spent several years modifying her method for use with normal children. She got an opportunity to try out her methods when Edoardo Talamo, the director general of the Roman Association for Good Building, asked her to organize a school for young children from families living in Roman tenements. Montessori accepted, and her "Casa dei Bambini," or "Children's House," for children aged three to seven, opened in 1907. The school began opening branches in other locations as her successes became known.

Montessori's method was based on her ideas of child development. She thought that children moved through "sensitive periods"—stages of life during which they were able to learn certain skills or behaviors more easily than they could during others. Based on this idea, she devised an environment with activities and materials designed specifically for the special needs of children during three basic periods of growth: (1) the period of motor education, or practical life experiences; (2) the period of sensory education, or training the senses; and (3) the period of academic education, or teaching reading and writing.

PRACTICAL LIFE EXPERIENCES Montessori saw dressing and undressing as the initial step in caring for the individual. Children were first taught how to button, lace, zip, snap, or buckle their clothing. Similarly, they were encouraged to polish their shoes, wash their hands, clean their nails, comb their hair, brush their teeth, and so on. The second phase of this period involved muscular education. Montessori sought to organize and control the children's natural movements through planned exercises such as walking, marching, running, kneeling, rising, bending, breathing, jumping, swinging, rhythmic movements, and other simple gymnastics. She felt that muscular education was extremely important, not only because of its physiological advantages, but also because of its influence on learning. For example, she considered breathing activities important because they helped the child form correct speech habits. She felt finger exercises were necessary because they readied the fingers for buttoning, lacing, manipulating objects, and, later, for writing. According to Montessori, without such motor coordination, the acquisition of higher mental processes later would not be as effective.

TRAINING THE SENSES Sensory education was designed to help the child develop discrimination in sight, taste, touch, and sound through the use of graded didactic materials (materials designed to teach by themselves). The children were deemed ready to move from the earlier practical life experiences to the sensory materials only when they showed an eagerness to work with these materials. The teacher, following the children's lead, then slowly introduced them to the didactic materials. Each piece of sensory equipment exhibited two important characteristics: *gradedness* and *error control*. The *graded materials* increased in difficulty following the normal cognitive development that Montessori observed. *Error control* allowed the material itself to reveal an error. She considered these two characteristics important because they helped the children become autonomous, or self-motivated learners. The following are examples of didactic sensory materials.

□ *Musical bells.* Two sets of bells, one white and one brown, that are alike in shape, size, and tonal qualities. The children match bells from each set according to tonal quality.
□ *Sandpaper tablets.* Two sets of sandpaper tablets that vary in texture. The children rub their fingertips over the tablets to identify and match textures from each set.
□ *Herb jars.* Two identical sets of jars made of white opaque glass whose tops allow odors to pass through but do not allow the children to see what is inside. The children match pairs of jars according to likeness of smell.

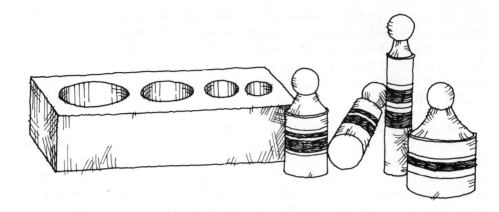

□ *Knobbed cylinder blocks.* Three separate wooden blocks with holes and three corresponding sets of wooden cylinders (with knobs on top) that fit into the holes. One block has holes that vary in diameter only while the depth remains constant; another block varies in depth only while the diameter remains constant; and the third block varies in both diameter and depth. The children remove the knobbed cylinders from the wooden blocks, arrange the cylinders in mixed order, and then attempt to match each to its proper hole.

The lesson technique prescribed to the teacher for each piece of material was to be followed with care and diligence. Montessori characterized her technique as follows:

1. *Isolate the object.* Children are to be exposed only to the object they will be working with. Everything else is to be cleared from the table so there will be no distraction.
2. *Work exactly.* The teacher is to show the children the proper use of the material, performing the activity once or twice so they can develop a complete understanding of its use.
3. *Rouse the attention.* The teacher is to display a lively interest as the object is offered to the children. The goal is to attract their attention to the new material.
4. *Finish well.* The teacher is to show the children how to put the finished material back on the shelf. Children are to carry each item securely in both hands and replace it exactly where it belongs.

This sequence gives some idea of the degree of organization that characterizes the Montessori approach. The sensory materials were not considered just toys, but rather tools necessary to develop the concentration needed for later learning.

TEACHING READING AND WRITING   The final area of Montessori materials involved academic learning. Montessori found that once the children had appropriate early experiences with the sensory materials, they were ready to be led from sensations to the internalization of ideas. An essential component of this process was the use of exact nomenclature as new ideas were presented to the child. The following example illustrates the procedure.

1. The children associate sensations with a letter sound. The teacher says, "This is *b*; this is *a*." Immediately, the children trace these letters, which are mounted on cards. Once they master this skill, they attempt to repeat it with their eyes closed. The goal of the activity is to enhance muscular memory.
2. The children recognize letter shapes when they hear the corresponding sounds. The teacher says, "Give me *b*; give me *a*." If the children recognize the correct letter, they hand it to the teacher. If not, the lesson is ended and begun again on another day.
3. The children recognize the letter and generate its name. The teacher spreads out the letters on the table and asks, "What is this?" They are expected to respond with the appropriate letter name.

Academic concepts were introduced as early as age four through this three-step lesson and the use of a variety of didactic, concrete teaching materials. Some of those materials are as follows:

□ *Geometric insets.* Ten geometric shapes that introduce writing skills. The children choose one alphabet letter inset and trace around it. Then they fill in the letter outline with a colored pencil.
□ *Activity cards.* A set of red cards with an action word printed on each. The children read the word on the card and perform the identified command —jump or sing, for example.

This Montessori teacher guides a young child in a musical activity.

☐ *Sandpaper letters and numerals.* Letters of numerals cut from sandpaper and mounted on individual cards. The teacher uses these letters or numerals in the three-stage lesson just described.

The Montessori method became extremely popular in the United States during the first part of this century. This popularity was short-lived, however, as discontent with her emphasis on academics grew among "child-centered" early childhood educators who believed a higher value should be placed on expressive activities such as play, music, and art. Since the 1960s a revival of interest in academic instruction has led to what many have described as "the rediscovery of Montessori." Since the Montessori program is very specialized and requires at least one year of formal training from Montessori specialists, it is not described in greater detail in this text. Nevertheless, you should become aware of the basic components of the program and of its impact on early childhood education today.

GROWTH OF EARLY CHILDHOOD EDUCATION IN THE UNITED STATES

The Early Kindergarten Movement

In the United States kindergartens and nursery schools were patterned closely after their European predecessors. The first kindergarten was opened in Watertown, Wisconsin, in 1855 by Mrs. Carl Schurz, who had been a student of Froebel's in Germany. This German-speaking kindergarten was originally intended for her own children and those of close relatives immigrating to the United States during the Industrial Revolution, but the school soon became known to others. Schurz's application of Froebel's teaching materials, creative activities, and warm classroom technique attracted other parents, and her school gained widespread interest.

Schurz's professional popularity led her to a meeting with a prominent Bostonian, Elizabeth Peabody, who was especially noted for an exceptional interest in the lives of young children. Peabody was already fascinated with Froebel's theories, which she had discovered through reading, but her conversations with Schurz made her even more so. In 1860 Peabody opened an English-speaking Froebelian kindergarten in Boston. She devoted the rest of her life to this new form of education for young children.

The kindergarten movement spread rapidly. In 1870 less than a dozen private kindergartens existed in the United States, but by 1892 the number of classrooms had risen to approximately 2,500, and involved over 33,000 pupils. This rapid growth was confined mainly to the large cities, where support came from private associations such as mothers' clubs and other philanthropic agencies. Interest in the movement spread to public school systems, too. Encouraged by supporting letters from Elizabeth Peabody, Susan Blow opened the first public school kindergarten in St. Louis in 1873.

By 1900 public school kindergarten enrollments surged to over 130,000 children.

Unfortunately, the development of the Froebelian kindergarten in America was hindered by the fact that the followers of Schurz, Peabody, and Blow were unable to study Froebel's program directly. Froebel had died in 1852 and his program had been banned in Germany. Instead, they studied under proponents of Froebel's theories in the United States, who advocated a more inflexible program than was originally intended. Programs in the United States gradually lost the freedom and activity that characterized earlier kindergartens, and interest in Froebel waned. An example of how formalized the instruction became is illustrated by Joseph Mayer Rice:

> Before the lesson there was passed to each child a little flag, on which had been pasted various forms and colors, such as a square piece of green paper, a triangular piece of red paper, etc. When each child had been supplied, a signal was given by the teacher. Upon receiving the signal, the first child sprang up, gave the name of the geometrical form upon his flag, loudly and rapidly defined the form, mentioned the name of the color, and fell back into his seat to make way for the second child, thus: "A square; a square has four equal sides and four corners; green" (down). Second child (up): "A triangle; a triangle has three sides and three corners; red" (down). Third child (up): "A trapezium; a trapezium has four sides, none of which are parallel, and four corners; yellow" (down). . . . This process [was] continued until each child in the class had recited.[2]

Progressive Kindergarten

Groups of educators in the United States reacted against this rigid formalism, and sought to return to the more flexible, play-oriented settings originally conceived for five-year-old children. Consequently, they turned for the first time to new educational reformers from America rather than directly to the European philosophers and educators discussed earlier. Although these earlier sources greatly influenced American schooling, educators were now searching for a scientific approach to study the characteristics of young children. Such an approach would emphasize formal observation and data collection rather than simple speculation on the uniqueness of childhood. Their interest in scientific information was given great impetus by G. Stanley Hall, commonly referred to as the "father of the child study movement."

Beginning with a formal study of children's thinking in 1891, Hall verified that children were not miniature adults—a concept that was still popular despite the efforts of many educators. Hall's students adopted his point of view and became interested in studying aspects of children's growth and development other than thinking. Arnold Gesell is among the most prominent. He and his coworkers Louise Bates Ames and Frances Ilg extended Hall's original research by observing large numbers of children and describing their intricate development in terms of normal developmental stages. They recorded, averaged, and tabulated physical and behavioral data from large groups of children at various age levels in order to create a "composite" picture of the typical one-, two-, three-, four-, or five-year-old. By describing the early years as the most important, their ideas renewed the enthusiasm of those interested in young children.

> The preschool period is biologically the most important period in the development of an individual for the simple but sufficient reason that *it comes first.* Coming first in a dynamic sequence, it inevitably influences all subsequent development.... This remarkable velocity of mental development parallels the equal velocity of physical growth during these early years.
>
> The character of this mental development is by no means purely or preeminently intellectual. Almost from the beginning it is social, emotional, moral and denotes the organization of a personality.[3]

Gesell's information gave early childhood educators a wealth of knowledge about the uniqueness of children and about the need for developing environmental conditions conducive to optimal growth. Many other theories were developed at this time, some agreeing with Gesell's ideas and others opposed. However, every theory seemed to agree with Gesell on one major point—the early years were the most important.

The theories of Sigmund Freud influenced early childhood education at this time almost as much as Gesell's. Freud felt that the child's early experiences were a major influence on future emotional growth (see Chapter 2). He believed, for example, that the way in which certain key developmental processes such as toilet training were handled had a profound influence on the child's emotional development as an adult. Early childhood educators became greatly interested in this theory. They adjusted their programs to encourage youngsters to express their inner feelings freely through language or behavior, thus preventing negative emotional characteristics from developing. These educators felt that the early childhood setting should stress love, patience, and freedom and that teachers should not thwart the child or cause undue feelings of frustration.

A popular educator, John Dewey, embraced these new views on the value of the early childhood years. He pushed for the immediate application of these findings to school programs for young children. His suggested program, often referred to as "progressive education," emphasized learning through real experiences and an atmosphere that encouraged healthy social and emotional growth in young children. This progressive philosophy was very close to that of earlier European educators—with one major difference. As Martin Dworkin explained, "In education, progressivism brought ... a romantic emphasis upon the needs and interests of the child, in the tradition of Rousseau, Pestalozzi, and Froebel—but now colored and given scientific authority by the new psychology of learning and behavior."[4]

Patty Smith Hill, who became a leader in the "progressive" kindergarten movement, also accepted this new philosophy and dedicated herself to reintroducing the concepts of play and purposeful activity into the kindergarten setting. Hill developed her concept of the "progressive" kindergarten while teaching at the Louisville Free Kindergarten with Anna Bryan. Together, Hill

"Think harder, P.J. I can't hear a thing."

The child study movement during the early part of this century was the first American attempt to explain scientifically the developmental characteristics of children. (*The Family Circus* by Bil Keane courtesy of The Register and Tribune Syndicate, Inc.)

and Bryan proposed a program that used the child's personal experiences as a basis for learning. The program involved concrete, child-oriented activities and classroom play based on the natural activities of childhood, set in a free, informal atmosphere. It was similar to Froebel's original program, except that blocks, dolls, and other toys replaced his "Gifts" and more time was devoted to expressive activities such as housekeeping, art, and music. The basic form of Hill's progressive kindergarten became extremely popular and remained so through the late 1960s. It eventually became known as a *traditional* approach to early childhood education. The types of activities provided during a typical day are shown in the box on page 14.

Dolores Durkin offers this explanation of why Hill's program resisted change for so many years:

> The reason might have been the general tendency of people to resist what is new and different, but it might also have been the tendency to hang on to what was difficult to achieve. Here I refer to the great effort required in earlier years to break out of the Froebelian rut. It is easy to believe that once the new ideas won approval and the new program was accepted, those who worked hard for the approval and acceptance would not be eager to abandon what they had achieved in favor of something else. Further, it is also likely that once the newer ideas became a program, inertia took over. How much simpler to do what was done last year than to try something different![5]

Although the types of programs offered to kindergarten children remained stable over the years, the number of children enrolled in the programs has now risen to over 2½ million. Predictions of future growth are optimistic, especially in light of increased state and federal tax support. Texas and West Virginia, for example, have included kindergartens under state funding, thus making them available to all children. Other states are likely to follow this trend, and provide funds for programs designed for all five-year-olds.

Nursery School and Child-Care Movements

THE NURSERY SCHOOL   Although it too had European roots and its development was subject to many of the same forces, the nursery school movement developed separately from the kindergarten movement. In the United States nursery schools were originally developed to serve three- and four-year-olds, especially children from poor families living in large cities. The first such school was established in New York City in 1915 by a Montessori teacher named Eva McLin. It used Montessori strategies to teach the fundamentals of health care and nutrition. However, because Montessori's

---

TRADITIONAL PROGRAM ACTIVITIES

WORK PERIOD   The children choose their own activity—painting, working with clay, building with blocks, or participating in dramatic play at the housekeeping center.

STORY TIME   The children listen while the teacher reads or tells a story. The story is usually about children their own age or about animals.

MUSIC TIME   The teacher leads the children in singing short, simple songs in which the children are encouraged to move their bodies rhythmically or to experiment with rhythm instruments.

OUTDOOR PLAY   The children spend a generous amount (30–40 minutes) of time on the playground, using equipment such as boxes, slides, swings, tricycles, and digging equipment.

REST TIME AND CLEAN UP   The children return to the room, where they are encouraged to use the bathroom facilities and to wash up. The room is then darkened and the children are encouraged to stretch out, relax, and sometimes take a short nap.

SNACK TIME   The children gather around small tables and have a half-pint of milk or glass of juice along with a cookie or cracker.

REAL EXPERIENCES   Field trips, resource people, and other active experiences help the children acquire information and develop increasingly sophisticated ideas about their growing world.

---

method was felt to be too regimented, her popularity was not great, and soon McLin's school was closed.

In 1919 a nurse named Harriet Johnson opened a nursery school, the *City and County School,* in New York City patterned after the McMillan philosophy. By 1920 a number of teachers trained by Margaret McMillan had come to the United States from England, either to demonstrate her ideas or to set up nursery schools in the United States. One of the first of these trained teachers was Abigail Eliot, who was hired in 1922 by the Women's Education Association of Boston to lead the Ruggles Street Nursery School, which was located in a low-income neighborhood. Before Eliot's arrival the purpose of the school had been group day care. There was no educational program at all. Physical protection, sterile cleanliness, orderliness, and obedience had been stressed. Under Eliot's direction, however, the school's program changed to reflect the educational views of Froebel and McMillan. For example, child-size furniture was put into the main room, and a garden and sandbox were set up in the playground. Health concerns were addressed by watching for contagious diseases and by teaching habits of cleanliness. Large group activities included music, songs, games, and stories; independently chosen "occupations" were performed using Froebelian or McMillan learning materials such as chalk, scissors, and blocks. The children were provided with sound nutrition during a daily lunch and then given about two hours of sleep or quiet rest.

Nursery schools similar to Ruggles Street were soon organized, often by privately funded organizations or departments of home economics in state-supported land-grant colleges. The privately funded Merrill-Palmer Institute in Detroit, for example, was begun in 1922 by a provision in the will of philanthropist Lizzie Merrill-Palmer. She had been concerned about the quality of motherhood in our country and had bequested money to found a school—to be known as the Merrill-Palmer Motherhood and Home Training School—at which young women were to be educated and trained, especially for wifehood and motherhood. The school was first directed by Edna Noble White, who also organized a nursery school so the women could gain first-hand practical knowledge by working with and observing young children. At land-grant colleges, the first program of this motherhood type was offered at Iowa State in 1924.

The nursery school movement in America grew slowly during the 1920s, confining itself mainly to health and motherhood programs, as well as to research projects in child development similar to Gesell's. The programs, which were patterned after McMillan's nursery school program, stressed free play activities such as art, music, block play, water play, and sand play, and self-care skills such as washing, toileting, dressing, and so on. By 1931, however, only 203 such schools were in existence, most affiliated with colleges and universities. The Great Depression changed all this, and during the 1930s the nursery school movement grew significantly. By 1935 alone the number of nursery schools had grown to over 1,900.

One reason for this growth was the *Work Projects Administration* (WPA), an agency established by the federal government in 1933 to combat the prob-

Self-care, habits of cleanliness, and free play were (and still are) major characteristics of nursery schools.

lems caused by the Great Depression. The WPA appropriated money to various groups throughout the nation to create jobs for the unemployed. Nursery schools benefited from this funding, and they became a source of jobs for unemployed teachers. The WPA achieved that objective, and also made it possible for mothers, normally tied to their homes and children, to seek employment and support their families. Most of these schools were day-long nurseries that provided full-day custodial care for parents who either worked or were too poor to care for their own children. Before this time nursery school experiences were mainly provided on a half-day basis.

THE CHILD-CARE MOVEMENT   During World War II, women were forced into the jobs vacated by men entering the armed services, and again day-long child care became a problem. The federal government intervened and passed the Lanham Act, which provided funds for the establishment and staffing of more day-care facilities. Like those in the Depression years, these war-time centers were primarily custodial—they provided children with food, rest, shelter, and a kind, loving, temporary mother substitute. There was little or no desire to go beyond this basic care in most centers by offering educational programs. Day-care provisions spread to industry as some employers sought to provide for the care of employees' children. The Kaiser Shipyards on the West Coast were instrumental in providing quality care. Led by James Hymes, these programs went beyond mere custodial care. They provided attractive school facilities at each shipyard, which were staffed by trained teachers who patterned their programs after the most innovative ideas of the time. This day-care concept was popular during the war years and paved the way for future changes.

Shortly after the war, federal support for child-care services stopped. Local, state, and philanthropic agencies, however, continued to operate many of the facilities. The most significant growth in preschool offerings, though, came through expansion of nursery school programs. Supported by various private funds such as churches or parent groups, nursery school programs steadily grew through the 1940s and into the 1950s.

During this period, nearly all nursery schools, kindergartens, and child-care facilities were identified with health care, play-oriented activities, concern for social and emotional growth, and the teacher as a mother substitute. During the 1960s, however, major changes occurred in nursery school and kindergarten education. In the following section, major contemporary influences affecting the growth of preschool programs in the United States are discussed. Figure 1-1 illustrates the major influences on the growth and development of early childhood education up to contemporary times.

THE EMERGING SCENE: EARLY CHILDHOOD EDUCATION TODAY

At the beginning of this modern period of innovation and growth in early childhood education, most kindergartens were under the auspices of the public schools although a number of private programs also existed. In many parts of the country, kindergartens were the only preschool experiences available. In areas where nursery school and day-care programs were available, they were operated mostly through private funds. In many ways, however, the programs of the kindergartens, nursery schools, and day-care centers were the same.

By 1965 changing views of childhood, along with unresolved social problems, stimulated attention to the young child and ushered in the greatest period of experimentation and growth ever experienced in the field of early childhood education. This period was originally touched off by the launching of the Russian space satellite Sputnik I in 1957. At that time, Americans became overwhelmingly concerned about falling behind the Russians in the technology race; some even predicted disaster and doom for the nation. One of the first areas to be attacked by these critics was the field of education. The public called for a careful examination of schools and demanded new programs to close the gap between the Russians and the United States. Among the areas that received the greatest study were those related to the education of young children and the social problems that directly affected their lives.

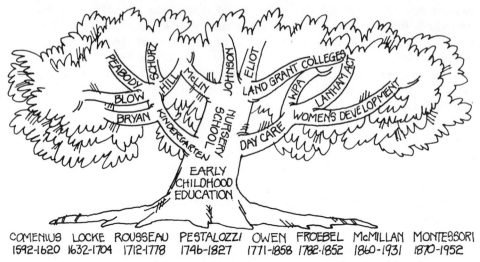

COMENIUS LOCKE ROUSSEAU PESTALOZZI OWEN FROEBEL McMILLAN MONTESSORI
1592-1620 1632-1704 1712-1778 1746-1827 1771-1858 1782-1852 1860-1931 1870-1952

Figure 1-1 The growth and development of early childhood education to contemporary times.

A New View of Children

In 1959 the National Academy of Sciences sponsored a conference in Woods Hole, Massachusetts, to determine how science and mathematics programs could be improved so that the gap in technology between the United States and Russia could be closed. Jerome Bruner chaired the conference and was responsible for compiling and reporting on the group's recommendations. The result was his popular book, *The Process of Education*. One of the strongest recommendations in the book was that science be taught in the early elementary grades. To emphasize why early contact with science was possible, Bruner wrote: "We begin with the hypothesis that any subject can be taught effectively in some intellectually honest form to any child at any stage of development."[6] Orginally the statement was meant to support the request to educators that science offerings in their schools be reexamined and restructured so that even kindergarten children were exposed to very simple science concepts. However, some interpretations distorted Bruner's true intent and led to attempts to teach complex concepts to youngsters without first translating them to their level of understanding. For instance, in some schools two- and three-year-olds were being taught to read and write, and first graders were being asked to deal with fundamentals of economics and algebra. Despite such misinterpretations, Bruner's assumption was a valuable contribution to early childhood education. It renewed interest in the potential of children to learn during the earliest years of development.

J. McVicker Hunt stimulated additional interest in the abilities of youngsters when he published *Intelligence and Experience* in 1961. The book describes and interprets previously completed research studies dealing with optimal early learning environments for young children. Its greatest impact was on the widely accepted contentions of Hall and Gesell, which Hunt attacked with statements such as: "The assumption that intelligence is fixed and that its development is predetermined by the genes is no longer tenable."[7] Hunt explained that learning experiences and academic stimulation were as essential to sound intellectual growth during the early years as play and a loving, understanding adult were to healthy social-emotional growth. He concluded that we should be able to prepare the young children's environment so as to increase their intellectual development (IQ) by up to 30 points. The clue to this growth process is similar to Bruner's—a "match" has to be found between the current level of children's understanding and the new experience to which they will be exposed. Hunt felt that through such a carefully designed, organized plan, young children could gain information and acquire academic skills at an age rarely thought possible before.

Benjamin Bloom also helped focus attention on the significance of the early years. In 1964 he published *Stability and Change in Human Characteristics*, in which he studied the relationship between selected environmental forces, early experiences, and intelligence. Bloom found that "in terms of intelligence measured at age 17, about 50 percent of the development takes place between conception and age 4, about 30 percent between ages 4 and 8, and about 20 percent between ages 8 and 17."[8] Bloom also estimated that the long-term overall effect of living in a "culturally deprived" as against a "culturally abundant" environment to be 20 IQ points, and hypothesized that this effect was spaced developmentally as follows: from birth to 4 years, 10 IQ units; from 4 to 8 years, 6 IQ units; from 8 to 17 years, 4 IQ units.[9] Bloom's conclusions emphasized both the importance of providing suitable learning experiences during children's early years, and the fact that those environments could affect the intelligence of young children.

Other educators of the early 1960s supported the push for early experiences as the key to raising children's intelligence levels during their early years. Martin Deutsch reported that children who attended preschools did better in fifth grade than those who did not.[10] William Fowler rejected the recommendations of early developmental psychologists like Hall and Gesell, who stressed play and social-emotional growth in the early years, and called for specialized teaching methods designed to increase intelligence during that period.[11]

These views on the importance of intellectual stimulation during the early years began a controversy unequaled since Patty Smith Hill began the progressive kindergarten movement in the early 1900s. Supporters felt the preschool years were important for intellectual growth, and advocated more formal academic types of instruction. Opponents believed in continuing an unstructured preschool experience emphasizing social and emotional growth.

David Elkind described the positions of both groups. According to him, the group advocating more structured preschool instruction felt:

(a) The earlier we start a child in the formal academic path, the earlier he will finish and the cheaper the total educational cost; (b) learning comes easy to the

During the 1960s some early childhood educators stressed the importance of the preschool years in the child's intellectual development while others supported time-honored practices, such as play and informal activity.

young child and we should take advantage of the preschooler's learning facility and eagerness to learn; (c) intellectual growth is rapid in the preschool years and instruction will help to maximize that growth while failure to provide appropriate intellectual stimulation may curtail the child's ultimate level of achievement and (d) traditional preschool experience is too soft, too directed towards emotional well-being and too little concerned with cognitive stimulation.[12]

The traditional group reacted with these defenses:

There is no preponderance of evidence that formal instruction is more efficient, more economical, more necessary or more cognitively stimulating than the traditional preschool program. Indeed, while there is room for improvement in the traditional preschool, it already embodies some of the most innovative educational practices extant today. It would, in fact, be foolish to pattern the vastly expanded preschool programs planned for the future upon an instructional format that is rapidly being given up at higher educational levels. Indeed, it is becoming more and more apparent that formal instructional programs are as inappropriate at the primary and secondary levels of education as they are at the preschool level.[13]

This controversy over the role of intellectual development in the preschool setting has continued to grow. During the late 1960s and early 1970s cognitive growth became more important than social-emotional growth (see Table 1-1). During the late 1970s, however, most early childhood educators began to feel that a good balance among all areas of the child's development

—including both the intellectual and the social-emotional—would be desirable. That feeling, popular today, identifies the preschool as an experience designed to address the needs of the "whole" child; that is, programs reflect a balance of activities that lead to physical growth and development, intellectual stimulation, healthy social-emotional growth, and the encouragement of creative potential.

Head Start and Follow Through

In addition to a *changing view of young children,* a second factor that stimulated change in the field of early childhood education was a social concern for *equalizing educational opportunity among children from low-income families.* The ideas of Bloom, Bruner, Hunt, and others made us aware that if youngsters from lower socioeconomic groups did not receive early intellectual stimulation they were destined to fail in public schools. In 1964, therefore, President Lyndon B. Johnson created the Office of Economic Opportunity (OEO) to find solutions to educational inequality. One solution was Operation Head Start, which was conceived as the nation's major weapon in this fight. Head Start funds were sent to community-action agencies throughout the country to establish programs for preschool children from poverty-stricken urban and rural areas to meet the following goals:

Table 1-1 Contrasting the Traditional and Newer Views of Intellectual Growth in the Preschool

Pre-1960s: **Traditional View of** **Intellectual Development**	**Post-1960s:** **Redefinition of** **Intellectual Development**
Intellectual growth occurs in stages that are hereditarily predetermined and sequential in nature.	Intellectual growth depends on both *hereditary* and *environmental* factors.
Growth through stages is exclusively the result of biological maturation.	Growth occurs through experience and practice as well as through biological maturation.
When a child's biological "alarm clock" sounds, he is ready to begin intellectual pursuits.	The environment can be arranged so movement through the developmental stages is accelerated.
Social-emotional development is of major concern because preschool children are not yet "ready" for intellectual functioning.	Intellectual development has the highest priority; social and emotional development are less important.

1. Improve the child's physical health and physical abilities.
2. Help the emotional and social development of the child by encouraging self-confidence, spontaneity, curiosity, and self-discipline.
3. Improve the child's mental processes and skills with particular attention to conceptual and verbal skills.
4. Establish patterns and expectations of success for the child which will create a climate of confidence for his future learning efforts.[14]

The goals were general in nature so local communities could interpret and adapt them to their own special needs. As a result of this leeway, many programs were aligned with the new trend toward intellectual development in the preschool setting, but most maintained a more traditional alignment. Whatever the form, however, all educators were concerned about providing school readiness experiences that would eliminate the disadvantages children from low-income families assumed when they entered middle-class-oriented schools.

During its first summer, in 1965, Head Start programs served over 580,000 children in approximately 2,500 preschool child-development centers throughout the country. Classes were limited to 20 children, although 15 were preferred. Each class had one teacher and at least one aide, both of whom were trained in special Head Start training programs. These first programs were similar to established nursery school and kindergarten routines, although there was a somewhat greater emphasis on labeling and on sensory and academic experiences.

The following schedule describes a typical day in the summer program (8:45 A.M. to 3:30 P.M.):

8:45–9:15	Arrival and independent work time (easel painting, puppets, blocks, dramatic play)
9:15–9:30	Morning group time (story, music, rhythm activities, sharing)
9:30–9:50	Snack and clean up
9:50–11:00	First work period (math, reading, language, cooking projects, and other organized learning activities)
11:00–11:45	Outdoor play
11:45–12:30	Lunch
12:30–12:45	Clean up
12:45–1:40	Rest period
1:40–2:05	Story and snack
2:05–3:10	Second work period (creative dramatics, caring for pets, language activities, and so on)
3:10–3:30	Discussion period and preparation for home
3:30	Dismissal

Social workers, medical personnel, parents, and teachers worked together in this nationwide effort to develop comprehensive programs. Each group assumed special responsibilities. *Social workers* identified the need for clothing, food, toys, and learning materials that were absent from the home. Where child-rearing practices were involved, they were responsible for conducting parent or parent-child counseling sessions. *Medical personnel* examined the children and provided care when needed. In addition, they stressed good nutritional practices. *Parents* did volunteer work in the classroom and helped establish programs and formulate policies for the community preschools. They were also often asked to try learning activities with their children at home. *Teachers* were responsible for planning and providing the high-priority learning activities and for coordinating the efforts of the supporting personnel at Head Start centers.

Early short-range studies of the effectiveness of various Head Start Programs were predominantly positive. The short-range data showed evidence of growing interest in school, gains in IQ scores, better results on reading readiness or language tests, and even growth in initiative, imagination, and expressiveness. Although encouraged, project directors and researchers were, nevertheless, looking for long-range studies; these would give a better idea of the lasting effectiveness of Head Start experiences.

The most prominent early long-range study of Head Start was conducted for the Office of Economic Opportunity from June 1968 through May 1969 by the Westinghouse Learning Corporation and Ohio University.[15] Although the goals of the Head Start program were much wider in scope, the basic question posed by the study was: *To what extent are the children now in the first, second, and third grades who attended Head Start programs different in their intellectual and social-personal development from comparable children who did not attend?*

To answer this question, the researchers studied children from 104 Head Start centers across the country. A sample of children from the centers who had gone on to first, second, and third grades in local area schools (experimental group) were matched with a sample of children from the same grades and schools who had not attended Head Start (control group). Both groups were given a series of tests covering various aspects of cognitive and affective development; parents were interviewed for information on their children's attitudes; and directors and other officials of the Head Start centers were interviewed about the various characteristics of their programs.

The major conclusions of the study were startling to many people.

1. Summer programs appeared to be ineffective in producing any gains in cognitive and affective development that persisted into the early elementary grades.
2. Full-year programs appeared to be ineffective as measured by the tests of affective development used in the study, but were marginally effective in producing gains in cognitive development that could be detected in grades one, two, and three.
3. Head Start children, whether from summer or from full-year programs, still appeared to be considerably below national norms on the standardized tests of language development and scholastic achievement.

4. Parents of Head Start enrollees voiced strong approval of the program and its influence on their children.

Head Start programs, then, did not achieve all that planners had hoped. Nevertheless, rather than give up the planners looked more carefully at the results and prepared a critique of the Westinghouse study. Their basic arguments were:

1. All new programs are bound to have "bugs"—many new programs were growing into large-scale operations, and there was little time to iron out the problems.
2. Very few standards existed for Head Start programs. The Westinghouse study lumped the poor with the good without noting the specific characteristics of successful programs.

These major arguments, together with the mixed results of the full-year findings (conclusion 2), the positive reactions of the parents, the value of the health and nutritional aspects of the program, and the urgent need to remediate the effects of poverty all influenced the planners to recommend the following:

1. Summer programs should be converted as early as possible into full-year or extended-year programs.
2. Full-year programs should be continued but every effort should be made to make them more effective.
3. Since preschool educators are not sure about what constitutes effective early childhood programs, some full-year programs should be set up as experimental programs (strategically placed on a regional basis) for new procedures and techniques.

Project Follow Through, initiated in 1967, was a large-scale program designed to extend Head Start services through grade 3. Its purpose was to maintain and extend short-term gains children made as they continued through elementary school. Both projects had similar goals and encouraged program experimentation to find the best programs for various kinds of settings. Also, Head Start and Follow Through became known for the "planned variation" of their educational approaches. These approaches fell into three categories:

1. *Basic Skills Models.* These programs stressed the acquisition of reading, language, and number skills through programmed teaching with highly structured and sequenced learning activities. (A *product* approach)
2. *Cognitive/Conceptual Models.* These programs stressed the development of concepts and learning processes through activities such as problem solving, observation, and manipulation. (A *process* approach)
3. *Affective/Developmental Models.* These programs tried to strike an even balance among all areas involved in child growth and development:

physical, intellectual, and social/emotional—but with primary emphasis on the last.

Abt Associates, Inc., of Cambridge, Massachusetts, was commissioned from 1969 to 1975 to look at these Follow Through program variations and determine which program model was most successful. The Abt evaluation found, however, that the effectiveness of each model varied from site to site and that no model succeeded everywhere it had been tried.[16] In basic skills development, the report indicated, direct instructional models (Basic Skills Models) had a higher average effect on basic skills scores than the other models. Conversely, the models that put their emphasis on cognitive/conceptual or affective/developmental approaches to learning had more negative effects on basic skills scores. The study also concluded, "It appears that [non–Follow Through] children are receiving educational experiences that teach them the basic skills by third grade more effectively than would the . . . programs offered by Follow Through."[17]

Why did these programs have so many negative effects? The main reason advanced was that the tests used for gathering data were designed exclusively to assess the general goals of schooling, and so did not equally reflect the unique goals of all the models. In addition, the same arguments that had been presented to explain the negative Head Start results were also used to explain the negative outcomes of the Follow Through experimental programs.

Rather than discouraging preschool educators, studies like the Westinghouse Report and the Abt Planned Variations Study have stimulated them to discover more about the relationships between the environment and children's learning. For example, Dr. Irving Lazar of Cornell University recently conducted studies of Head Start children ten years after they had left preschool. He found that there were 50 to 90 percent fewer special education placements among these children than among children from identical backgrounds with no preschool experience, and that significantly fewer children with preschool experience had been retained one or more grades.

Currently, Head Start and Follow Through programs are still receiving support from the federal government through the Office of Economic Opportunity. Although studies indicate the effectiveness of these programs to be mixed, the OEO has to consider their overall educational benefit. Strong community support nationwide has made the government aware that determining the general educational benefit of programs must indeed include consideration of their overall effect on those who are served.

The dynamically changing American society stimulated growth not only in the nursery school and kindergarten, but also in the area of day care. Most of the growth has been stimulated by social factors, including the problems facing children of low-income families, the changes brought by the movement for equal rights for women, the economic need for two-income families, and changing family patterns such as single-parent family units.

During the late 1960s and early 1970s, parents needing child-care services on a day-long basis were not satisfied with available existing facilities.

Child care then was popularly described as "custodial," that is, it simply provided a safe and healthful place for children to stay, and did not consider their total developmental needs. Many child-care centers were unlicensed, private operations whose services amounted to group babysitting at best. M. D. Keyserling described one child-care situation:

> When Mrs. —— opened the door for us, we felt there were probably very few, if any children in the house, because of the quiet. It was quite a shock, therefore, to discover about seven or eight children, one year old or under, in the kitchen; a few of them were in highchairs, but most were strapped to kitchen chairs, all seemingly in a stupor.
>
> Mrs. —— takes care of two families—six children which the Bureau of Children's Services subsidizes. The other children (41, for a total of 47 children) she takes care of independently, receiving two dollars per day per child. She told us that she has been doing this for 20 years and seemed quite proud to be able to manage as well alone, with no help.[18]

And even today such situations may cause tragedy. Here is a recent report adapted from the *Philadelphia Bulletin:*

> Temperatures over 100 degrees apparently killed two infant girls in a Miami apartment that served as an unlicensed nursery yesterday. Police said Louise H—, 32, had been caring for 22 children, ranging in age from 6 months to 10 years, in partially closed rooms with no air-conditioning or fans. Two infants, 6 and 10 months old, died Thursday and charges are pending against Ms. H——.

The quality of child-care programs alarmed those interested in gaining day-long care for young children. They were appalled at the number of centers run by unskilled staff and at the lack of adequate facilities. The 1970 White House Conference on Children addressed the need for higher quality day-long child-care facilities when it called for child-care centers to develop *comprehensive* family-oriented child-development programs. The Conference made 25 specific recommendations, including reordering national priorities to indicate the importance of quality nursery school and kindergarten programs that present "opportunities for each child to *learn, grow,* and *live creatively.*" Gathering support from political groups as well as professional organizations, educators and parents called for the establishment of comprehensive day-long child-care facilities that would meet the *social, emotional,* and *intellectual,* as well as the *physical* needs of children. In other words, they wanted day-long child care patterned after good, half-day preschool programs.

In addition, federal, state, and local agencies began to establish licensing requirements for child-care facilities. However, not all states established such standards of operation, and no national licensing laws have been developed. Newman and Newman explained:

> Requirements for licensing differ in each state. Usually they include specifications about the kind of building, the amount of indoor and outdoor space, fencing

Comprehensive day-care centers are designed to respond to the needs of the "whole child."

for the outdoor play area, a staff-pupil ratio, provision for nutritious meals, and health and safety regulations. These latter requirements usually involve inspection of the site by the health and fire departments of the community. The program of the day-care center and the effectiveness of the center are not subject to direct requirements for licensing or for renewal of the license. As compared to the amount of standardization of the public school curriculum at each grade level, there is enormous variety in the goals and activities of day-care programs even within the same state.[19]

This lack of curriculum standardization is favored by some early childhood educators whose states do have licensing standards for the physical facility. They feel that the variety of children's needs, program philosophies, ways of working, and community desires make national or statewide standardization of programs inappropriate. Thus, most regulatory agencies consider that planning, organizing, and carrying out actual programs is outside their jurisdiction. Many do, however, offer guidelines and models for establishing improved day-care programs. Perhaps the most effective of these aids is a government publication entitled *Day Care: Serving Preschool Children.*[20] Because of the variety of the nation's child-care needs, different types of day-care programs are now widely available in a variety of settings, such as industry, in apartments or condominiums, labor unions, colleges, and hospitals. There is also a growing number of private day-care centers such as those made possible by Head Start and other programs aided by government funds.

Related to this growing availability of comprehensive child-care centers in the 1970s was the problem of finding trained people to run them. A partial answer to this problem came in 1971 when Edward Zigler proposed the Child Development Associate (CDA) program. The program was not designed to replace the college-trained teacher, but rather to train competent professional personnel who understood children, who were able to provide valuable learning experiences, and who reflected the competencies necessary to become good preschool teachers. The CDA program introduced a new dimension to professional training by credentialling people (many of whom were already working in child-care centers) as Child Development Associates based on demonstrated competencies, or abilities, rather than on the completion of college courses or credit hours. Such training is possible through informal, noncredit college-based programs, supervised internship programs, or work-study programs. Preparing sound child-care personnel added trained professionals to the field and increased the availability of quality child-care programs.

In the early and middle 1970s this initial growth in quality preschool services for working women slowed. At the beginning of his administration, President Nixon had made this reassuring statement:

> As I mentioned previously, greatly expanded day-care center facilities would be provided for the children of welfare mothers who choose to work. There is no single ideal to which this administration is more firmly committed than to the enriching of a child's first five years of life, and thus helping the poor out of misery at a time when a lift can help the most. Therefore, these day-care centers would offer more than custodial care; they would also be devoted to the development of vigorous young minds and bodies. As a further dividend, the day-care centers would offer employment to many welfare mothers themselves.[21]

Despite this promise, Nixon vetoed a $2.1 billion Comprehensive Child Development Program bill in 1971. The bill would have provided funds for increased comprehensive child-care facilities throughout the country and would have emphasized a nationwide commitment to early childhood education. It was turned down as fiscally damaging, administratively unworkable, and potentially damaging to the family. Attempts to strengthen the nation's child-care services persisted during the 1970s, but the legal clout necessary for formal action was missing. One attempt was made in 1974 when Albert Shanker and his union, the American Federation of Teachers (AFT), launched a program called Educare, which was designed to provide preschool jobs for public school teachers laid off by declining enrollments and tight budgets. The AFT estimated that 150,000 to 200,000 teachers could be put to work if the nation's 10.4 million children three to five years old were provided quality child-care facilities. Despite strong efforts, Educare has not yet gathered enough support to become a reality. The AFT also endorsed the $1.8 billion Child and Family Services Bill of 1974. The bill, sponsored by Senators Walter Mondale and John Brademas, was designed to provide money for the establishment of comprehensive child-care centers for low- and middle-income families throughout the country. The bill was defeated in Congress because it was seen as too expensive. In 1979, Senator Alan Cranston of California introduced a bill designed to subsidize child-care services for *all* children up to age fifteen, provided the children were enrolled in licensed centers. Cranston's bill was attacked on many fronts—as socialistic, expensive, and administratively unworkable. Those charges led to its demise that same year. Despite the strong support of professional groups, the growth of child-care facilities has been limited by such legislative failures. As a result, most growth in child-care facilities has occurred in the private sector. These private facilities are businesses, and usually provide services only to families who are able to pay.

NURSERY SCHOOLS AND DAY CARE

Early childhood and preschool education are terms that refer to the variety of programs serving young children from *infancy through age eight.* However, programs for six-, seven-, and eight-year-olds are usually considered part of the elementary schools' primary grade structure, and we examine them only indirectly in this text. You will be exposed, instead, to programs for children under age six—that is, programs directed toward the needs of preelementary school youngsters. These programs are usually called *nursery school, kindergarten,* and *day care.* The differences between nursery school and day care are minimal, usually being based on the reason why children are enrolled and the amount of time children spend in them. Similarities between the two are greater—they share goals, values, and emphases. The following is a summary of these similarities and differences.

Similarities
1. They provide similar opportunities and experiences.
2. They furnish the same basic equipment, supplies, and materials.
3. They require nearly the same basic amount of space.
4. The professional training and experience of the staff is similar for both.
5. Both are based on an understanding of children's needs and their stages of development.
6. Both should be geared to promote maximum development in all areas (social, emotional, physical, and intellectual) although some programs may stress one area more than others.
7. They are subject to similar regulations for state licensing and certification.
8. Both may be funded and/or organized through public or private agencies.

Differences

1. The primary function of day care is to provide care and protection for children whose parents must be outside the home; the essential function of the nursery school is to train and develop the child.
2. Day-care centers usually offer services throughout the workday; nursery school programs are frequently offered for half a day.
3. Day-care centers must be equipped to serve meals, in some instances breakfast, lunch, and dinner; preschools usually offer only small snacks.
4. Day-care centers must be equipped so that children spending long hours at the center can nap when necessary.
5. Day-care centers often extend their services to school-age brothers or sisters, through before-school or after-school programs.

You can get a clearer understanding of the similarities and differences between day care and other preschool programs by examining typical schedules for each, which follow. Notice that the activities are basically the same; the major difference is simply the length of time involved during the day.

A Typical Nursery School Morning

9:00–9:20   *Opening Activities.* May include show-and-tell sharing, short songs, or fingerplays.

9:20–10:00   *Self-Selected Activities.* Free choice from among various interest centers such as painting, drawing, water or sand play, puppets, blocks, creative dramatics, toys, or other educational materials.

10:00–10:30   *Outdoor Play.* Vigorous outdoor play, including swinging, running, sliding, climbing, riding tricycles, throwing, and other physical activities.

10:30–10:50   *Bathrooming and Snack.* Toileting and cleaning up in preparation for a short snack of juice and crackers.

10:50–11:20   *Work Period.* Selected activities designed to promote language development and other academic skills. These activities are carried out individually or in small groups, depending on the children's needs.

11:20–11:30   *Dismissal.* Cleaning up and dressing in readiness for parents' arrival.

A Typical Day in a Day-Care Facility

7:00–9:00   *Arrival.* Children arrive at irregular times. Some require breakfast. While some children are engaged with quiet art activities or toys, or with storybooks, others may be taking short naps.

9:00–9:30   *Outdoor Play.* Active play on the playground is first on the schedule. There is much running and use of equipment.

9:30–10:00   *Large-Group Activity.* Music activities, story time, or a special language development program may be offered.

10:00–10:20   *Toileting and Snack.* Children use bathroom facilities and prepare for the snack.

10:20–10:30   *Rest Period.* Children are encouraged to rest on mats or cots.

10:30–11:15   *Special Activities.* Children are free to choose among special activity centers designed to build cognitive skills in math, reading, and language.

11:15–12:00   *Group Project.* This may be a special art or music activity associated with a special holiday, or it may involve cooking, watching television, show and tell, etc.

12:00–1:00   *Lunch.* Children help prepare for lunch by setting up the table. A warm lunch is usually served, followed by clean up.

1:00–3:00   *Sleep.* Children are allowed to sleep on cots during this time.

3:00–3:15   *Snack.* A refreshing snack of juice and crackers or cookies and milk is offered to children as they awaken.

3:15–3:45   *Outdoor Play.* Active outdoor play follows the snack. Some special game or physical activity may be planned.

3:45–4:30   *Free Play.* Children are free to paint, draw, listen to records, play with puppets, and so on.

4:30–5:00   *Going Home.* Parents arrive at irregular times to take their children home.

The job of describing the variety of contemporary nursery school and day-care facilities available and of putting these facilities into a meaningful, comprehensive framework is, at best, difficult. However, personal visits, interviews with program directors and staff members, professional reading, and research study allows me to provide general descriptions of the types of facilities you will encounter when you begin your career as an early childhood educator. Remember this as you examine the descriptions in Table 1-2.

SOME FINAL THOUGHTS

Your professional training will further your understanding of the various early childhood program types as well as the specific kinds of early childhood settings within each category. As you study the approaches discussed in this book and observe their use at the scene, become a critic. Note the positive and negative features of each, weigh them in your mind, and try to choose one (or a combination of several) that seems best suited to a particular group of children. As you do this, consider these basic questions:

1. *Who* should have early childhood programs available—children from low-income families, handicapped children, all children?
2. *What* form should early childhood programs take—what should the content be; what activities, teaching strategies should be used?
3. *Where* should these programs be located—in homes, private buildings, public schools, or separate settings?

Table 1-2   Characteristics of Major Early Childhood Settings

Facility	Characteristics
Home-care center	The belief that the home is the proper place for the care of young children has motivated some parents of infants and preschoolers to seek men or women who offer child-care programs in their own homes. Federal funds are provided for some home-care facilities, but such aid is limited to needy families with dependent children. Such home centers are usually open on a full-day schedule, serving preschoolers during the day and older children after school. Usually, up to ten children can be accommodated in the home setting. If licensed (only about 5 percent are), the home setting must meet minimum health and safety standards.
Day-care center	Located in hospitals, factories, universities, private buildings, public schools, or a number of other settings, day-care centers are designed as full-day programs for children whose parents work. Day-care programs usually offer health, medical, and social care, along with enriching educational experiences. The centers are open approximately 11 to 12 hours per day, from about 7 A.M. to 6 P.M. Most day-care centers cater to preschoolers, but they also provide after-school services for school-age children. Federal funding is normally available for day-care programs serving low-income families.
Nursery school	Nursery schools are usually privately operated programs or cooperatives located in churches, private buildings, some public schools, or homes. They offer half-day sessions providing varied educational experiences for the child. The goals of nursery schools vary widely, ranging from formal education to the open philosophies. Funding is normally not available, so parents must assume the cost of their child's experience.
Parent cooperatives	Formed by parents primarily to save costs, cooperative schools have the dual purpose of providing an

4. *When* should early childhood education begin—in infancy, before age three, in kindergarten?
5. *Why* is early childhood education important—for intellectual growth, social/emotional development, physical development?

The future of early childhood education depends a great deal on your

---

Table 1-2 *Continued*

Facility	Characteristics
	educational program for children and instruction for the parents themselves. Parents share educational responsibilities with the teacher, while they plan and implement the program. Cooperatives are usually nonprofit operations, financed by the parents or by fund-raising projects such as bake sales or auctions.
Child-development centers	These centers, among which are included Head Start centers, offer programs supported by federal, state, or local funds. The purpose of such support is twofold; it allows low-income parents to work and it stimulates employment for teachers. The programs are comprehensive and include health services, nutrition, social services, and parent counseling. Perhaps central to the purpose of child-development centers is a concern for sound educational programs for children from low-income families, programs that will improve their chances for later success in school. Parents are involved to a great extent; they serve as classroom aides or participate on advisory boards.
Campus schools	Commonly referred to as laboratory schools or demonstration schools, these college-based programs are primarily aimed at providing both good education for young children and a good training facility for future teachers. Services range from day care to various nursery school or kindergarten programs. The schools may also be set up as experimental research programs where newer ideas are tested. Because of their strong influence on prospective teachers, campus schools are usually strongly committed to excellence in teaching and programming.
Infant programs	Infant programs have begun to grow throughout the country in recent years. Such programs provide total, continuous care by individuals so close adult-infant relationships can be established.

ability to meet such challenges and to discuss controversial issues openly. Don't shrink from such responsibilities, for your thoughtful contributions are sorely needed.

NOTES

1. Evelyn Osgood Chandler, in Samuel J. Braun and Esther P. Edwards, *History and Theory of Early Childhood Education* (Belmont, Calif.: Wadsworth, 1972), p. 72.
2. Joseph Mayer Rice, "A General Consideration of the American School System," in *The Public School System of the United States* (New York: Century Company, 1893), pp. 39–46.
3. Arnold Gesell, *The Pre-School Child: From the Standpoint of Public Hygiene and Education* (Boston: Houghton-Mifflin, 1923), pp. 2–8.
4. Martin S. Dworkin, *Dewey on Education: Selections, with an Introduction and Notes* (New York: Teachers College Bureau of Publications, 1959), p. 9.
5. Dolores Durkin, *Teaching Young Children to Read* (Boston: Allyn and Bacon, 1976), pp. 12–13.
6. Jerome S. Bruner, *The Process of Education* (Cambridge, Mass.: Harvard University Press, 1960), p. 33.
7. J. McVicker Hunt, *Intelligence and Experience* (New York: Ronald Press, 1961), p. 342.
8. Benjamin S. Bloom, *Stability and Change in Human Characteristics* (New York: John Wiley, 1964), p. 88.
9. Ibid., p. 72, Table 3.6.
10. Martin Deutsch, "Facilitating Development in the Pre-School Child: Social and Psychological Perspectives," *Merrill-Palmer Quarterly* 10 (July 1964): 249–263.
11. William Fowler, "Cognitive Learning in Infancy and Early Childhood," *Psychology Bulletin* 59, no. 2 (February 1962): 116–152.
12. David Elkind, "The Case for the Academic Preschool: Fact or Fiction?" *Young Children* 25, no. 4 (January 1970): 133.
13. Ibid., p. 139.
14. Robert Cooke, Chairman, Planning Committee of Project Head Start, Report to Sargent Shriver, Director, Office of Economic Opportunity (Washington, D.C., no date), p. 2.
15. Westinghouse Learning Corporation–Ohio University, "The Impact of Head Start: An Evaluation of the Effects of Head Start on Children's Cognitive and Affective Development" (June 1960), in *Revisiting Early Childhood Education*, ed. Joe L. Frost (New York: Holt, Rinehart and Winston, 1973), pp. 400–404.
16. Abt Associates, Inc., *Education as Experimentation: A Planned Variation Approach* (Cambridge, Mass.: Abt Associates, Inc., 1977).
17. Emily C. Harris, ed., *Report on Educational Research*, Vol. 9 (Washington, D.C.: Capitol Publications, June 15, 1977), p. 3.
18. M.D. Keyserling, *Windows in Day Care* (New York: National Council of Jewish Women, 1972), pp. 135–136.
19. Barbara M. Newman and Philip R. Newman, *Infancy & Childhood* (New York: John Wiley, 1978), p. 381.
20. D. Cohen, *Day Care: Serving Preschool Children*, Office of Child Development, Department of Health, Education, and Welfare (Washington, D.C.: U.S. Government Printing Office, 1974).
21. Richard M. Nixon, *Weekly Compilation of Presidential Documents* (August 8, 1969), p. 1108.

2

Social-Emotional Development: Learning about Personal Feelings and Acquiring Effective Interpersonal Relationships

*Copyright 1979
The Register and Tribune
Syndicate, Inc*

" . . . and when the flowers are born you'll be
their father."

Helping young children cooperate, share experiences, and get along with one another are important goals of early childhood programs. (*The Family Circus* by Bil Keane courtesy of The Register and Tribune Syndicate, Inc.)

Excitedly, Tommy surged into the classroom with two very special friends. For his birthday yesterday, Tommy had received a pair of frisky, furry gerbils safely contained in a strong wire cage. The teacher quickly recognized the growing interest of the others as children gathered about Tommy and his gerbils. "Oh, how wonderful," exclaimed Mrs. Marsh. "Tommy has brought some visitors this morning." Taking advantage of the situation, she then began to guide a discussion on this experience, which was important enough to be shared by the whole group.

Mrs. Marsh: "Tommy, I think the whole class is interested in what you brought to school this morning. Please tell us about your little friends."
Tommy: "Yesterday was my birthday and I got them for my present."
Mrs. Marsh: "I'd like to know what they are. Please tell us."
Tommy: "They're gerbils. One gerbil is a boy and one is a girl."
Mrs. Marsh: "Have you named them yet?"
Tommy: "Yep. The boy is Mickey and the girl is Minnie."
Mrs. Marsh: "How did you decide on those names?"
Tommy: "Because I like Mickey and Minnie Mouse."
Mrs. Marsh: "That's very interesting, Tommy. Are there any questions that you boys and girls would like to ask Tommy about his gerbils, Mickey and Minnie?"
Gina: "What do they eat?"
Tommy: "Lots of things—sunflower seeds, corn, and I forget what else."
Freddie: "I have some gerbils, too, and they like to eat potato chips."
Julie: "Mine like to eat crackers."
Mrs. Marsh: "My goodness, it sounds like we have quite a few children who have gerbils as pets."
Mary: "Mom says I can't keep mine 'cause they had six new babies. We have to give 'em away."
Todd: "How come?"
Mary: "'Cause our cage is too small for all of them when they get bigger."
Todd: "Can I have one?"
Mary: "Yes, but my mom said that I have to wait until they learn to eat all by themselves."
Mrs. Marsh (sensing the conversation moving away from Tommy):   "Would you like Minnie and Mickey to have baby gerbils someday, Tommy?"

The conversation continued for several minutes as the children asked each other questions and contributed information that clarified many concepts. Tommy beamed with pride at the conclusion of his sharing period when Mrs. Marsh announced, "We liked the way Tommy shared his pet gerbils with us. Would you tell Tommy what you liked best about Mickey and Minnie?"

This short scene illustrates the major role played by interpersonal relationships in nearly all preschool settings. In this example, many communication skills and management approaches supported the children's group experience and contributed to a harmonious environment where everyone was encouraged to express personal ideas and feelings. These types of interpersonal relationships do not happen merely by chance, however. You must work at them. You must understand the child's typical ways of expressing his feelings, relating to new experiences, and adjusting to group activities. These areas are part of the child's *social-emotional development*.

In the past, social-emotional development served as a major focus of American preschools. Those programs recognized the importance of providing experiences that facilitated the expression of feelings and emotions, in addition to facilitating the formation of cooperative relationships among the

The preschool setting provides opportunities for children to interact with one another and to express their personal feelings.

children. Today's programs also reflect this belief, although some disagree as to the extent it should be stressed and as to the techniques by which it should be accomplished. These differences aside, though, the overwhelming majority of preschool educators agree that the major goals of early childhood programs should be to help children express their ideas and feelings freely, acquire reasonable patterns of behavior, and learn to cooperate with others in socially acceptable ways.

Social-emotional growth is influenced by a number of factors, the foremost, many agree, being the family. In all behaviors from toilet training to the refinement of dressing and eating skills, the family has primary responsibility. In our modern society, though, social complexity and diversity has brought about the need for a strong partnership between the family and school in order to address this enormous obligation. The school creates a setting that reinforces and extends the skills learned at home. School also helps the children by exposing them to other children, other authority figures, other experiences, and other levels of expectations. Through a combination of all these influences, children begin to establish themselves as socialized persons. Of course, they are not fully socialized after they leave their nursery schools or kindergartens and enter the primary grades. There are always new people to meet, new situations to face, and new roles to master as they widen their horizons. The nursery school, however, is often the child's first contrasting experience of the world outside the family. Figure 2-1 illustrates some of the factors that enter the child's life and continue to exert a strong influence on his social-emotional development.

Figure 2-1   Factors influencing the social-emotional growth of young children.

The expectations, experiences, and examples provided by each significant factor contribute to an individual's knowledge of social norms and of the conduct that conforms to these norms. Children learn that many people —parents, teachers, neighbors, and friends—hold certain expectations about their behavior. This early awareness of social actions and responsibilities contributes substantially to the gradual acquisition of increasingly sophisticated prosocial behavior.

SOCIAL-EMOTIONAL GROWTH IN INFANTS AND TODDLERS (BIRTH–2½ YEARS)

Infancy

The infant experiences a radical environmental change at birth. It is taken from protective surroundings in which all survival needs were supplied by the mother, and abruptly put into a new world requiring quick adaptations for survival. The infant begins to breathe air; it adjusts to new temperatures; it begins to take in, digest, and excrete food; and it communicates reactions to the environment. It struggles to alter objectionable experiences and takes comfort in an environment filled with love and physical support. Thus, tiny infants receive their first lessons in social behavior as they acquire new behaviors and adjust old ones to satisfy basic needs.

A desirable environment for infants is one that provides not only for their physical care, but also for their strong needs for love, warmth, caring, and trust. Even more interesting than our knowledge of the infant's emotional and physical needs is the growing belief that infants are able to interact socially even during their first days. T.G.R. Bower explained:

One of the more spectacular demonstrations . . . is the fact that babies less than a week old will imitate other people. If the baby's mother, or some other adult, sticks out her tongue at the baby, within a relatively short time the baby will begin to stick his tongue back out at her. Suppose she then stops sticking her tongue out and begins to flutter her eyelashes; the baby will flutter his eyelashes back. If she then starts to open and close her mouth in synchrony . . . the newborn actually seems to enjoy engaging in this mutual imitation game.

. . . And all these [imitative] capacities are bent toward what is clearly, I think, a social purpose. The newborn enjoys social interaction with adults. Imitation at this stage is a social game. The responses are quite specifically directed toward human beings and seem to me to be testimony that the newborn considers himself human too. . . . The newborn baby imitates the facial gestures of the adults around him for no reward other than the pleasure of interacting with them.[1]

Therefore, through an imitative game—interaction with adults—the infant begins to participate in his first socialization experiences (see Figure 2-2).

Emotional expressions become part of the newborn's repertoire, too, but only in very limited ways. Discomfort or distress of any kind—hunger, pain, heat, cold—is usually expressed through techniques such as crying, thrashing, or turning red all over. At about six weeks of age the infant begins to develop a *social smile* in reaction to pleasant stimuli. The social smile can be triggered by a number of pleasing experiences: human voices, faces, famil-

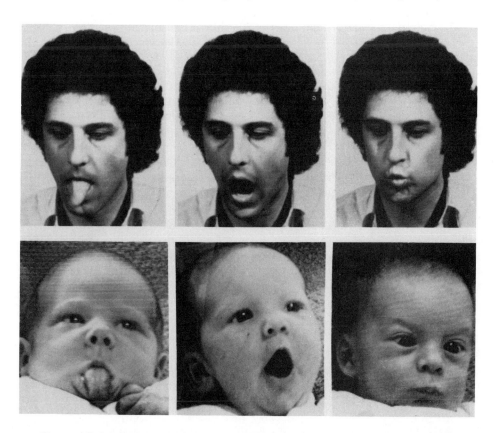

Figure 2-2 Facial expressions imitated by infants. ("Imitation of Facial and Manual Gestures by Human Neonates," Meltzoff, A. N. and Moore, M. K., *Science*, vol. 198, pp. 75–78. Photos 7 October 1977. Copyright 1977 by the American Association for the Advancement of Science.)

iar objects, gentle touches, stroking, tickling, or rocking. Accompanying the smile may be gentle humming or cooing vocalizations and the smooth movement of arms or legs. Parents are usually elated at the emergence of the social smile and its accompanying behavior that the baby directs to them, and they take great pleasure from this interaction. The infant's smile is not only enjoyable for all parties involved, but also socially significant because it is the first obviously positive social response emitted by the newborn. Gradually, during the next two or three months, the child extends the smiling response to other family members and possibly even to some strangers. However, during the sixth to eighth month babies begin to reject the advances of all others and relate only to a loving, mothering person.

This notion of mothering person–infant attachment has received more emphasis today than almost any other area of social-emotional development in infancy. Researchers have found that the period of social attachment between the mothering person and infant is signalled at first by a fear of strangers and anxiety at separation. Bower stated that:

> Smiling is a pleasant social behavior. . . . The second half-year is marked by the emergence of behaviors which are much less pleasant in affective tone. Somewhere around the age of eight months, the baby begins to manifest quite clearly a fear of strangers. At this stage, at the approach of a strange adult, the baby will cry, scream, or otherwise try to avoid the encounter. If the baby is mobile, he will try to crawl away. At a slightly later age, a baby will begin also to show fear of separation from his mother. Separation from the mother will lead to attempts to rejoin her, screaming, stillness, tears, and other signs of distress. Both these behaviors are an unmistakable sign that the baby has formed a critical social attachment.[2]

H. R. Schaffer and P. Emerson call infants' decided fear of strangers *stranger anxiety*.[3] Stranger anxiety, they say, ushers in a phase in children's lives when they reject strangers and form strong emotional attachments only to loving mother figures.

Often, the person who cares for the infant most will become the object of such mothering feelings. That person is able to soothe and comfort the baby when others are unsuccessful; it is to this person the baby turns, gives the most special smile, or stretches out its arms in an appeal to be held. Gladys Jenkins and Helen Shacter feel that, "There are indications that babies thrive best when there is one central mothering person to whom they form an attachment by the middle of this first year. This attachment provides the feelings of security and trust which make it possible for the baby to grow into warm relationships with other people all through life."[4] These authors also feel, however, that other mothering people, including fathers, need to contribute significantly to the child's social growth at this stage in order for subsequent growth to develop optimally.

The intensity of stranger anxiety has become a popular topic for researchers. They have found that its strength seems to depend on how varied the baby's caretakers have been. Schaffer and Emerson found, for example, that babies who have interacted with greater numbers of adults show a

The infant's first social response is usually a pleasurable smile extended to a loving caregiver.

lesser degree of stranger anxiety than those who have had less contact.[5] Bettye Caldwell discovered that children raised in environments where child care is a shared responsibility of many adults (such as the kibbutzim of Israel or some communes in the United States) tend not to show a marked degree of stranger anxiety.[6]

This discussion about stranger anxiety may raise a question in your mind as to whether it is good or bad. L. Joseph Stone and Joseph Church offer an answer to this question:

> It is our hunch that it is good insofar as it reflects a strong emotional attachment which should facilitate cultural learning and may foretell a later generalized capacity for strong affection. It seems to be good, too, in that it shows clear perceptual discrimination among people. On the negative side, stranger anxiety may mean excessively limited social contact or it may represent an attachment so strong as to interfere with the normal weanings from infantile ways.[7]

They go on to stress the significance of stranger anxiety in terms of practical considerations:

> Stranger anxiety is important in practical terms, since it affects leaving the baby with new caretakers while the mother goes outside the home, and because many a visiting grandparent or aunt or uncle has suffered wounded feelings at the hands of a rejecting baby who has been rushed through the process of getting acquainted or reacquainted. The wise stranger keeps his distance, knowing that the

baby's reaction to a novel stimulus has components of both fear and curiosity. With a bit of patience on the visitor's part, the baby's curiosity dominates his fear, and aversion soon changes to friendliness.[8]

Stranger anxiety, then, should be a strong consideration of child-care workers involved with caring for infants. If you find yourself in a professional position working with infants six months and older, keep these ideas in mind as you plan your approach:

1. Proceed slowly as you become acquainted with the baby. Quick movements or sudden talking may cause crying, screaming, or other rejection responses from the child.
2. Encourage the mother-figure to stay at your facility for short periods of time as you slowly gain the baby's approval.
3. Use toys and playthings to capture the child's interest while you slowly allow the baby to become comfortable in the new surroundings.
4. Develop a warm, loving atmosphere reflecting mothering characteristics so that the baby will form trusting, positive emotional attachments to you.
5. Encourage mother-figures to receive their children with warm affection when they are taken back home at the end of the day.

Infants at about the age of eight months normally begin to enjoy the company of other familiar adults. They revel in simple games such as having adults hide their faces behind their hands in a game of peek-a-boo. They enjoy being picked up to exchange nonsense sounds with adults. They always smile and gurgle during their exchanges of "Da-Da," "Ma-Ma," or "Ba-Ba." Infants captivate adults with such social games and quickly learn new behaviors needed to cue their participation—slaps on the high chair tray, fake coughing, or a special smile.

At about the tenth month babies are able to participate in more advanced social games, such as pat-a-cake. (As hard as they may try, though, it is difficult for infants to clap palms together. Their first motion in a pat-a-cake game is clapping their fists together instead of their palms. Eventually, they are likely to clap their palms together, but they won't make clapping sounds.) Slowly, infants begin to understand simple commands and requests, along with special cue words for familiar games and daily routines. These patterns of socialized play indicate a stable pattern of social-emotional growth. Children are fascinated with repetitive play and enjoy duplicating their new experiences many times—to the point where it often becomes monotonous for an adult. Don't lose your patience when this happens, but keep in mind that children behave like this because they are thrilled with their new discoveries. As they are continually encouraged by adults to extend their interests, their growth is stimulated and reinforced.

From about 8 months of age until toddlerhood at about 18 months, infants prefer to strengthen ties with their caregivers, and they make every effort to stay close. They crawl after the caregiver, cry out if the caregiver is elsewhere, clutch an apron or trouser leg, gladly return hugs and kisses, and cuddle comfortably in the caregiver's arms. Infants feel emotionally secure in their newly developed social environment, and they seek to keep close contact with those they trust. This developing confidence encourages further explorations into new relationships.

During the period of infancy, then, children progress through three definable stages of social-emotional development. These stages are summarized in Table 2-1.

The following are suggestions to help you in your social-emotional contacts with infants.

1. Remember that infants understand the language of touch much earlier than the language of speech. As the person caring for an infant, you must be mindful to hold him in a calm, relaxed manner. Handle him confidently, cuddle him, and talk in soothing tones.
2. Don't become overanxious when first handling an infant. Many caregivers are too excitable during their initial experiences with the child and tend to cause anxiety and insecurity within the child. Relax and try to follow the advice in suggestion 1.

Table 2-1   Three Stages of Social-Emotional Development Through Infancy

Stage	Age	Social-Emotional Characteristics
Stage 1	Birth to six months	Infant imitates facial gestures of adults and begins to respond to the mother-figure. The infant enjoys simple imitative games. The social smile begins to appear as the child reacts positively to varieties of positive stimuli. Negative stimuli are usually met by crying or thrashing.
Stage 2	Six months to one year	Infant becomes closely attached to mother-figure. Stranger anxiety ushers in this period. Baby gradually begins to cooperate in social games such as peek-a-boo or pat-a-cake and begins to show greater interaction with those who are trusted.
Stage 3	One year to two years	Infant needs to be close to the caregiver. Babies anticipate expressions of love and gladly return such expressions. Intense positive and negative reactions signal likes and dislikes.

3. Don't become frustrated if your first efforts with the infant are unsuccessful. If the child cries or becomes uncomfortable in your care, give him time. He may require a short time to become familiar with you and your pattern of care. Remain consistent in your behavior—the child is surprisingly flexible and will slowly gain a sense of trust and security from you.
4. Be careful not to overprotect the child. Of course, infants require almost total care in their early months of life, but they should be given increasing independence so they grow naturally into more sophisticated stages of social-emotional development.

Perhaps the key to desirable social-emotional development is establishing an atmosphere of trust. Erik Erikson best explained what is meant by an atmosphere of trust during the period of infancy. Erikson felt that people progress through a series of conflicting crises during their lives. The first of these he labeled *basic trust versus basic mistrust*. If the child's basic physical needs are met during this stage, he sees the world as a pleasant, manageable place to be in; he feels safe in becoming attached to a caregiver, gives and accepts expressions of love, and begins to regulate his behavior to reflect his trusting expectations of others. However, if the child's basic physical needs are not satisfied during this stage, he develops an untrusting disposition characterized by irritability, unpleasantness, and negative emotional expressions. The message to all caregivers, then, from mother-figures to child-care workers, is that it is important to communicate to the child that they are *able* to satisfy his needs and that they *want* to satisfy his needs. In turn, the baby will become more attached to them and will be more willing to regulate his behaviors to reflect his expectations of them.

One additional important matter we must consider concerns questions we all have in our first experiences with infants: "How do I show the infant my love?" "What do I do?" Remember: There is no one way to show your love to a baby. Some caregivers physically demonstrate their feelings with great effusion—we envy their joyful and excitable freedom of expression. Others are soft and quiet in their manner, and tenderly hold and caress the child in a tranquil, nurturing way. Surprisingly, both types of loving expressions probably elicit positive responses from babies. The reason for this is that babies are individuals and need different amounts, as well as different kinds of love. They are responsive and develop trust in you only as you are *reliable* and *consistent* in the types of affection you offer. Be yourself—you, too, are an individual and you have your own special ways of expressing real affection.

Toddlerhood

From about 15 months until about 2½ years, children live in a period commonly referred to as *toddlerhood*. During this time, they become walking, talking individuals full of energy, curiosity, exploration, and discovery. Many of their babylike competencies remain, but new and more childlike behaviors begin to emerge. As children master their own bodies, they begin to strive for

During toddlerhood, children begin to develop a desire to try things out for themselves; but they still cling to a caregiver when they need a sense of protection. (*Hi and Lois* courtesy of King Features Syndicate, Inc.)

autonomy—they want to do things by and for themselves. However, this autonomy does not happen all at once. Toddlers initially alternate between a clinging attachment to the caregiver and an interest in moving away and trying things for themselves. Outdoors, for example, they may toddle off to pet the family cat but suddenly stop short and scamper back to a caregiver's protective hug. At the grocery store, they may eagerly explore the wonders of the packages on each shelf and suddenly burst into tears at the realization that mother has moved out of sight. New tasks, such as riding tricycles, are tried with more confidence if a familiar adult is near and offers a secure finger or hand to cling to. Erikson refers to children as reaching the stage of *autonomy versus shame and doubt*. They must be guided in their desires to try out new things and given encouragement and support in their efforts. If children are made to feel untrustworthy, they may become shy and introverted.

Toddlers are somewhat attracted to other children, but they tend to treat them all alike and hesitate to develop individual friendships. They keep their distance from one another and look on their peers with a sense of wonder rather than of friendship. Social contacts are rarely, if ever, achieved. It is almost as though they were thinking, "You mean there's another one like me?" *Parallel play* is normally a characteristic of peer social relationships by about the age of two years. Toddlers do not know how to actually play with one another, but they are willing to be near each other while playing in a sandbox, or with stuffed animals and dolls. They can sit near each other for extended periods of time and yet remain unaware of what the others are doing. You should remember that it can be hazardous to leave two toddlers alone in these situations because toddlerhood is marked by strong individualism; it is a period during which everything is "mine." Toddlers find it extremely difficult to share and will often bite, push, or hit others who attempt to take something they consider their own. When you do wish to have children share their toys with each other, remember to have a substitute toy ready to place in their hands immediately when they relinquish the other.

Toddlers enjoy taking part in *dramatic play* activities in which they mimic the roles and activities of the adult models to whom they are exposed.

Toddlers enjoy being near other children, but are content to play by themselves.

Beginning dramatic play is extremely simplified, consisting mainly of imitating single social events such as "using" the telephone, "writing" with a crayon, "cooking" a meal, "reading" the newspaper, "drinking" a cup of coffee, or "smoking" a favorite pipe. The child may also follow a family member around the house and imitate the activities or chores being performed by that member. This imitation can lead, in many instances, to the child's actually cooperating in the performance of family duties rather than merely playing at them. Probably the most important contribution you can make at this time is simply to provide many opportunities for such interactions and support the child's experimentation. This type of play strategy seems vital in helping the child toward self-identification and a better understanding of family and societal roles.

Although the toddler period can be very rewarding, it can also be an extremely difficult time for many parents and caregivers. Quiet, easily controlled infants slowly change into individuals who learn to assert themselves and emphatically say no to many requests or "I'd rather do it my way." Toddlers like to do things for themselves, but they have not yet learned to do so safely or responsibly. For example, a child may reach to a shelf for a cookie and knock over a glass of milk instead. Thus, we have to watch toddlers carefully and make sure they don't break a favorite piece of expensive crystal, wander into the street, or eat dangerous things. Our role as caregivers during this stage of development becomes extremely vital. At times we may feel frustrated with the behavior of the toddlers and be tempted to engage in a battle of wills with them. We may lose our confidence and begin to doubt whether we actually have the skills needed of effective child-care professionals. Don't allow such feelings to take over, for your subsequent actions can cause major interpersonal problems and eventually retard the child's social-emotional development. When you are extremely negative and your demands are overly severe, the child may become timid, shy, tense, and negative toward others. Growing up may become very difficult for the child, and uncooperativeness, apathy, or babylike patterns may persist for longer periods of time than normal.

Because toddlers exhibit many difficult-to-control social and emotional behaviors, parents, teachers, and other caregivers frequently ask, "What can I do to control and guide the child?" The following suggestions may prove helpful.

Allow plenty of opportunities for informal dramatic play. Toddlers love to get into everything, and a large part of their day will be spent in cupboards or toy boxes, and with dolls, stuffed animals, adult clothes, household items, or tools. Encourage children to explore these items and to express the feelings that each causes.

Use a happy, positive approach to control. Toddlers respond best to fun and humor rather than to direct interference. Don't attempt to reason with the child—it is not very effective at this age. So, if a problem occurs in a sandbox, simply distract one child with a happy word, place him on your shoulders, and give him a happy "horsey" ride to another activity. Removing the child from the situation and diverting his attention is much more effective than some arbitrary negative punishment can be.

Choose direct, simple statements that can be communicated in positive terms. For example, the statement, "Jimmy is playing with the wagon now, so

Children enjoy mimicking adult roles in their early experiences with play. This girl, for example, applies her makeup just as she saw her mother or older sister do.

you play with the tricycle, Laura," is much more effective than, "You can't play with the wagon, Laura, because Jimmy has it."

A simple, negatively oriented statement designed to clarify consequences of actions may be used if direct interference by the caretaker is necessary. A statement such as, "You shouldn't hit Barry, Fran. It hurts him," helps the toddler realize that her actions affect others. However, stay away from comments such as, "Don't be a bad boy, Bobby. Come over here and behave yourself." Helping children understand the effects of their actions is important in helping them develop moral beliefs, as we shall see in greater detail in Chapter 3.

Establish reasonable, consistent limits and help the toddlers learn to cope with them. Try to keep the child's frustration at a minimum and think of "discipline" as a sensitive guidance skill instead of a form of punishment. Toddlers have a very difficult time understanding why their personal desires need to be compromised in a spirit of cooperation. Punishment may tend to frustrate and bewilder them even more since it is difficult for them to understand your motivations or why it is necessary for them to cooperate and share. Excessive punishment may result in fear, anxiety, or temper tantrums that include head banging, breath holding, or kicking.

Learn to forestall things that are likely to happen. Anticipate the child's readiness to hit another, to wander away from supervised play, or to grasp a dangerous object. We may be able to stop the child beforehand, saying no firmly as we do. For example, suppose a child suddenly darts from an area of supervised play into a parking lot. You bring him back and divert his attention with a tricycle or wagon. After a minute or two, however, the child begins to dart back into the parking lot. You have anticipated his action, though, and you cut him off. Now you have to do something different because the original diversionary tactic simply didn't work. Don't get angry—you'll only make the situation worse. Calmly take the child inside and explain firmly, "When we are on the playground, you must always stay on the grass." The child may cry or kick or pout, but don't feel bad! By the time he calms down and becomes friendly with you again (he will!), he'll have learned a very important lesson: There are certain *limits* he must know, adults are *consistent* in their treatment of those limits, and he must learn to *accept* such limits.

View the child from the proper developmental perspective rather than from an adult perspective. Remember that at this stage children fervently seek independence and do things that often frustrate us, such as refusing to put on a sock while getting dressed. This is not the advent of "bad" behavior, only the beginning of independence. Be patient—wait for the child—give him a chance. A minute later he may be only too happy to put on the sock—only this time he'll do it all by himself!

During this period, as during infancy, children develop as unique individuals, differing in temperament and mood. Some are energetic and bold; others are timid and shy. Some conform readily to behavioral norms; others strongly resist. Some respond to social situations; others do not. Some are serious; others smile a lot.

We must remember that these characteristics only emphasize the fact that every child is different and that our role is to know how to treat each one. Katherine Baker and Xenia Fane expressed this idea well when they stated:

> We help children most when we accept them as they are. We all need to feel that we are loved for what we are. This feeling gives each of us the courage to grow and improve. We are likely to want to change at our own rate and in our own way. It makes us uncomfortable or even unsure of ourselves to be pushed. Being pushed often makes it harder to change. Children feel the same way. . . . Each one wants to be accepted and liked for what he is. Each needs to be helped to grow in his own way and at his own rate.[9]

You, the child's parents, and the culture in which the child is raised each have specific ideas about the kinds of affection, quantity of interaction, and experiences necessary to stimulate individual social-emotional growth. However, the child's own personality will combine with your efforts to become a major force in shaping the eventual socialized individual. How children act in organizing and interpreting the experiences you provide for them accounts for their continued, systematic social-emotional growth.

SOCIAL-EMOTIONAL GROWTH IN YOUNG CHILDREN (3–6 YEARS)

During this period, children begin to extend their primary social base of home, family, or caretaker to include a range of new people, new situations, new roles, and new perceptions. Although the home and family remain the major force in their socialization process, they begin to become aware of other possibilities for role identification and social interaction. The types of people they become and their ultimate relationships with others will have been prominently influenced by the experience, understanding, and guidance they received through these first six years of life. The course of development during this time does not always run smoothly. Children often fluctuate between desirable and undesirable behaviors and between natural impulses to "grow up" and desires to maintain their comfortable childlike status. Temper tantrums, overactivity, and many other extreme behaviors reach their peak of occurrence during the period from age 3 to age 5. Some of the more apparent and necessary behaviors demonstrated by children as they move through a healthy process of maturing are illustrated in the following sections.

Independence

The children are beginning to understand the importance of balancing the newly discovered independence of toddlerhood with certain persistent

The child begins to sense growing independence during his early years, but still realizes that a caring adult will be near when he needs someone to depend on. (*Hi and Lois* courtesy of King Features Syndicate, Inc.)

dependencies. They discover that they don't have to be as totally dependent on adults as they were during infancy, but that there are still certain things that require help and cooperation. In the preschool setting, for example, you will find young children saying, "I want to do it," or "Let me do it myself," when they try new tasks such as putting on their socks and shoes. All may go well until they try tying the laces. If they repeatedly fail at this, they may often say, "I can't do it myself," or "You do it for me." Your task is to provide encouragement and guidance when it is needed, because children attempt many things they cannot do on their own. If such help is not openly given, children may eventually lose their enthusiasm and retreat back toward the easier periods of infancy and toddlerhood when all of their desires were met. Children must learn to trust you. They must know that you will give them opportunities to try things out on their own but still be near should they need someone to depend on. In our shoelace example, the caregiver remembers that tying shoelaces is beyond the capabilities of preschool children and helps them do so, saying, "You did a very nice job of putting on your socks and shoes. It's hard to tie the shoelaces, I know. I'll help you."

Be careful, though, not to encourage children to become overly dependent on you. For example, you've made sure that the children in your preschool classroom have all learned that they must always put away one toy or activity before they can take another. Carla, however, finishes playing with a doll, suddenly drops it on the floor, and heads toward the opposite end of the room to make a picture with crayons. When you ask her about this, she says, "You do it for me." What do you do? Do you (1) pick up the doll and put it back for Carla because you don't want to spoil her enthusiasm for drawing? (2) Pick up the doll and carry it over to Carla, reminding her that the next time she does it, she won't be allowed to go out with her friends to play on the playground? (3) Leave the doll on the floor and say, "The doll is on the floor and you need to pick it up. When you pick it up and put it back where it belongs, then you'll be ready to draw with the crayons"? If you choose the third course of action, you show an ability to encourage children to move from dependency to responsibility. Discuss some of the reasons why the first two courses of action were undesirable.

Jealousy

Between age 2 and age 6, children begin to develop strong feelings of jealousy. Jealousy is a feeling that something very important to one child, especially affection, will be taken and transferred from that child to another child. This strong desire to be the center of attention and the object of an adult's approval may be expressed in many ways, often through statements such as these:

"I can draw better than you."
"My dad can beat up your dad."
"I can jump higher than the school."
"I can count to a zillion."
"I'm a better kicker than anybody in the whole world."

Children may express feelings of jealousy in physical ways, also. They may physically attack a rival—pinching or slapping whenever they get a chance. Or they may demonstrate a false, exaggerated affection for their rival. They may show extreme delight in playing with him, caring for him, or being kind to him. The reason for doing so may be that the jealous child is afraid that any indication of hostility would result in punishment or disapproval from the teacher or other significant person. Another way of expressing jealousy is through reversion to immature behaviors such as baby talk or unreasonable demands for attention. When youngsters are constantly relegated to second place they begin to think of adult love and approval as something that needs to be earned or fought for rather than as something exchanged naturally. The following is an account of the reaction of a three-year-old to the arrival of a new child in a preschool classroom:

When Eve first entered the room, the teacher greeted her with a warm smile and a welcome hug. Dorothy reacted to the situation with apparent disinterest as she first stared at Eve and then at the teacher. However, as the morning developed, Dorothy continued to remain by herself, refusing to join any activity in which Eve was involved.

The situation reached a climax when Eve happened to be momentarily isolated from the others. Dorothy, with a belligerent look on her face, quickly went to her and tried to slap her. The teacher immediately intervened. Dorothy reacted by falling to the floor, kicking her legs, and crying at the top of her lungs. The teacher ignored her behavior, but when she left, Dorothy followed and repeated it. Again, the teacher ignored Dorothy. When Dorothy realized that she would not get attention in this way, she slowly walked over to a corner and sat by herself. After a short period of time, the teacher joined Dorothy, extended a bright smile to her, kneeled down to her level, and gave her a big, loving squeeze. In practically no time at all, Dorothy felt at ease with Eve's presence, and soon both could be found playing cheerfully in the block corner.

It is natural for young children to be concerned about their place in the hearts of teachers or friends. They often become resentful if more time and attention is paid to others than to themselves. Often teachers provoke such unnecessary jealousy by showing partiality or by using one child as an example to improve another: "Why can't you put away your toys as well as Mark does? I never have to tell him to put things away." And thoughtless comments like this serve only to provoke further feelings of resentment: "What a warm jacket Bruce has on. It's a shame you don't have one like it."

You should never allow children to feel that their best method of getting attention or approval is through being "first" or "best." They should be accepted for what they are, regardless of whether they succeed or fail. The following suggestions may help you avoid making unnecessary comparisons between one child and another:

1. *Be patient, trusting, and loving toward all children.* Reassure the children of your feelings frequently.
2. *Deal with all children in a consistent manner.* Do not show partiality or favoritism toward one child. Show all the children that they are loved and cherished.
3. *Make sure there is a special place in your day for each child.* One child may become very jealous when he sees you cuddle another in your lap. However, later, when you give him a big hug and tell him how much you like his drawing, he is reassured of your acceptance.
4. *Minimize excessive competition.* Although children must become aware that life is not constant successes, too many failures may make them feel weak and worthless. Be sure that your children have matured sufficiently to cope with failure and success before you put them into competitive situations.

Fears

At about age 2 to age 5, children begin to demonstrate fearfulness in reaction to situations in which they perceive no apparent or effective means of maintaining themselves. Fears may be realistic or imagined. It is as common for children to be afraid of loud sirens, wind, thunder, lightning, the dark, pain, injury, or animals as it is to be afraid of ghosts, goblins, witches, and the like. Children may panic at the eerie forms of flowing tree branches on a stormy night or at a child who playfully proclaims himself to be a "boogie man" or a mean, hungry tiger on the prowl. Some children are afraid of the dark and insist that a light be kept burning while they take their afternoon naps in the child-care setting. Others, because they have no accurate concepts of size relationships, cry and kick when placed into a bathtub for fear that they may slither down the drain with the bathwater.

Fears tend to increase as children grow in self-awareness and develop a more sophisticated knowledge of the world. For this reason, children at the age of four or five may be more fearful than they were at an earlier age. They realize that some of the misfortunes they heard about may possibly happen to them. Sometimes, unthinking parents or teachers help to build such fears by capitalizing on them to help establish obedience. How many times have

Teachers of young children accept all children and treat them with equal approval.

we heard threatening comments like: "Be a good boy or the boogie man will get you," or, "Stay on the playground or I'll lock you in the dark closet until you're ready to listen to me."

Your role as teacher is very important in helping children cope with their fears. Here are some suggestions for you to consider:

1. *Be careful not to communicate your own fears to a child.* Remember that the mood you establish in certain situations communicates strong messages to the child. For example, your fear of animals may be effectively transmitted to the child when you nervously call him away when a dog is near.
2. *Listen to what the child has to say.* Children learn to cope with certain fearful phases if they have the calm, sensitive support of an understanding adult. By helping the child recognize and admit his fears, we may lessen or eliminate them.
3. *Do not ridicule or shame the child.* By laughingly telling a child that "It's silly to be afraid of the clown," we only force a child to suppress and hide fears.
4. *Protect a child from his fear until he's ready to face it.* Leave a faint light on in the room while the children are napping or present a favorite group activity during a thunderstorm, for example. By doing so, you make children feel more comfortable and secure.

An understanding, loving teacher is essential in helping young children handle fearful situations.

5. *Explain fearful events so that feelings aren't compounded.* For example, many adults explain death to children by saying that it is a deep, deep sleep from which we never awaken. Some children may be terrified of going to bed at night when they hear such an explanation. Children benefit most from such situations when we give them as much information as they can understand and manage. Fanciful explanations only confuse and complicate the child's feelings.

Friendliness

Three-year-olds are much more interested in themselves or familiar adults than in the company of other children. By the time they are four years old, however, their solitary pursuits have lost their appeal and they begin to move more and more toward cooperative ideas of sharing and group play. They begin to reflect a strong need and desire to play with other children and to share toys and equipment with them. Our role is to help children strengthen these traits. They learn some of their most important social lessons during this time.

You already know that *play* emerges in toddlerhood and that it is an important component of the child's understanding of basic social behaviors. During toddlerhood, play normally assumes the form of parallel play, in which two or more children play side by side obviously enjoying each other's presence, but without outwardly exchanging words, feelings, or actions. For example, two children may be playing in the doll corner, one busily preparing tea and cookies for a friend, while the other is putting her child to sleep. Each is oblivious of the other as she pursues individual activities independently of the other.

At about three or four years of age, children engage in *associative play;* during this stage group members may all be doing the same thing—such as cooking, digging in the sandbox, or grouping around the swings. Associative play activities are characterized by children's growing appreciation of others in their group and by their desire to join in and take their place in a group.

The children may talk to each other and notice what others are doing, but they are still content to pursue individual activities. For example, you will often observe one young child busily constructing a model city with blocks; soon he will be joined by two or three "special" friends. They may be very happy in each other's company, but they still probably find it difficult to establish and carry out group plans or to relate their activities to those of the others.

In a short period of time, though, young children move on to *cooperative play.* In this activity, they are much more interested in their friends, more cooperative in their endeavors, more willing to share, more inclined to discuss and assume roles needed to accomplish a joint venture, and more mindful to talk directly to each other. For example, in the classroom's family center, one youngster may assume the role of a parent caring for the baby; another may take the role of a parent preparing the evening meal; a third may play an older brother or sister setting the table. Because the goal of cooperative play is to dramatize an integrated scene, it is more challenging and subject to conflicts or disagreements. Table 2-2 summarizes the four kinds of play children engage in from infancy through young childhood.

Children want and need to play with each other. For that reason, play is perhaps the most potent vehicle in our preschool classrooms for encouraging social-emotional growth. Do your best to ensure ample opportunities for play. Provide plenty of resources and an abundance of space. Specific recommendations for creating play opportunities in the preschool classroom are explained in greater detail in succeeding chapters.

The greatest problems in your child-care facility will involve play-related interpersonal conflicts. Most of these conflicts will be over play areas, sharing or using equipment, or how group projects are to be carried out. You must be able to help children resolve such conflicts and work toward acceptable behavior. The following are examples of typical situations observed in preschool classrooms.

Situation 1

A group of four-year-olds eagerly stands in line to take turns on the playground sliding board. Suddenly, Chuck shoulders in ahead of everyone so that he can be the next to go. Lawrence, Chuck's best friend and the second child in line, blurts out an extreme threat of violence: "You old meanie. Get back or I'm gonna chop your head off!"

Solution

Arguments and fights frequently occur over taking turns. This can happen with playground equipment or with classroom toys. Some children, like Chuck, operate as though they should be first with everything and as though they "own" all the toys and equipment. You must help Chuck realize that he needs to share and take turns. For example, you can say to him, "I understand how much you want to slide, but you've just had a turn. It's now time for Lawrence to go. You wait with me and I'll make sure you get another turn."

Another theme in this situation has to do with children using certain words for their shock value. When confronted with social difficulties, some children resort to intimidating insults that often involve mutilation of a peer's body parts. At the preschool age, children are becoming increasingly aware of their bodies and frequently become concerned with keeping them together. Therefore, when faced with frustrating situations, as Lawrence was, children will react in ways that threaten the body of the aggressor. The reaction of some teachers in this situation might be, "Lawrence, I'm surprised at you. If you can't say something nice, don't say it at all." Such a reaction, however, may not be constructive and,

Table 2-2   Development of Play Characteristics in Young Children

Stage	Age	Characteristics
Solitary play	Birth–2 years	Children like to play by themselves or with familiar adults. Their strong drive for independence at about two years tends to cause them to resist the company of peers.
Parallel play	2–2½ years	Children may enjoy playing near each other, but they still remain independent. Despite conflicts over some playthings, toddlers usually stay to themselves and reject any real exchanges with others.
Associative play	2½–3½ years	Children enjoy playing near each other and participating together in small groups. However, they are still reluctant to share or communicate verbally with each other.
Cooperative play	3½–6 years	Children are more interested in their peers. They learn to share, cooperate, discuss, and assign play roles. They are increasingly aware of the attitudes and feelings of others.

A typical group of preschool youngsters includes children who are willing to play together in groups and children who are content to pursue solitary activities.

in fact, may cause further interpersonal conflicts. Instead, you should simply let the child know that you understand his feelings and that you're willing to listen to him talk about what made him angry or what he thinks can be done about it. "I know how much you like to slide. You don't like it when someone jumps in line in front of you," is a much more effective approach. The child knows you sincerely understand his concerns and that you have confidence in his ability to make appropriate social adjustments.

Situation 2

Three children are busily working together making a snowman after a newly fallen snow. Laura walks over to the area and begins to join in. Alice immediately runs over to Laura and complains, "This is our snowman and you can't play with us. We hate you. We hate you." Laura rushes over to the teacher and tearfully cries, "Alice hates me. She won't let me play."

Solution

Most teachers expect youngsters to allow others to share equipment and to join their play. However, frequently you will find two or three children who enjoy going off by themselves for a period of time to work on a special project in their own way. They cannot tolerate interruptions by their peers, and their emotions often flare when such circumstances occur. You must respect the right of the small group to pursue its goal, and diplomatically divert the offended child's attention to another area.

You may say, "Alice, Cathy, and Betsy are working on a very special snowman. They don't hate you—they are just upset because they wanted to build it by themselves. Let's go over here and ask Jeanie if she'd like to build a snow-man with you."

Situation 3

A group of four-year-old girls enjoys playing with the variety of dolls in the doll corner. When Brad walks over and attempts to join them, Mary Ann complains, "Get out of here, Brad. We're playing with dolls and you can't be-cause boys aren't supposed to. Go away!" Brad runs to the teacher and says, "I want to play dolls. The girls won't let me."

Solution

As you watch this situation unfolding, you may probably begin to ex-amine your own feelings about sexism. You might recall other situations in which girls were excluded—from those "masculine" activities such as working with woodworking tools or digging in the dirt. In this situation, the girls have turned the tables, and, in effect, are protecting "their turf" as fervently as the boys protected "their" trucks and tools in other situations. In essence, the boys and girls have subconsciously established separate territorial rights to activities associated with stereotyped sex roles. What do you do for Brad, who wishes to play in the doll corner?

You must realize that it is perfectly normal for children to explore activities and materials in the preschool regardless of the sex stereotype with which the materials have been traditionally associated. Through their play, they enjoy trying different roles and pretending to be mothers or fathers, or boys or girls, regardless of their sex. A boy may enjoy dressing like the mother, a girl like the father; a boy may enjoy serving tea, while the girl may enjoy sitting on the chair reading the evening paper. This is all very common and very healthy. Allow children to explore and try out these roles.

In this situation, it may be wise for you to suggest to the girls that it is all right for boys to play with dolls. You could say, "Brad would like to play with the dolls. There are enough dolls for everyone. Boys like to play with dolls, too. Let's help Brad find a doll he would like." In the same way, you must make sure the boys don't exclude girls from traditionally male stereotyped activities.

Situation 4

Most children in this room for four-year-olds seem to enjoy playing with one another. One day, however, while a group is busily digging a hole with shov-els, Billy suddenly walks over and hits Amy because she refused to allow him to use her shovel. The teacher intervenes and explains to Billy that he must wait his turn. He lashes out shockingly at the teacher, "I hate you. You're a mean old rotten egg (or worse)."

Solution

You must remember that a frustrating social experience may trigger a personal verbal attack, often with a special vocabulary, sometimes of the four-

Copyright 1978,
The Register and Tribune
Syndicate, Inc.

"Dolly's not old enough to have her woman's
intuition yet, is she, Mommy?"

Play is perhaps the most important factor influencing social development in young children. However, it often results in situations that are difficult to resolve. (*The Family Circus* by Bil Keane courtesy of The Register and Tribune Syndicate, Inc.)

letter variety. Such circumstances are especially common when the teacher has not yet had ample opportunity to build up satisfying social relationships with all members of the group. It is a rare three- or four-year-old, however, who does not develop a friendly relationship with the teacher after a short period of time.

Some teachers react to statements like Billy's with surprise and displeasure, and may express their disapproval by saying something like, "You should never speak to me like that again. You're a naughty boy." Such reactions, however, do not help build positive relationships between the teacher and child, and, in fact, may intensify the child's practice of using such language. The best way to deal with such behavior is to accept it casually—it does not signal the child's moral breakdown, but is merely a frustrated attempt at handling interpersonal conflicts. Often, such language can be ignored and, when the child senses that it has lost its shock appeal, it soon disappears. However, in this instance, Billy's physical action of hitting Amy, combined with his verbal aggression, called for some positive action from the teacher. You should remove Billy from the area and take him to a quiet area. Then you should firmly explain to him, "It hurt Amy when you hit her. You mustn't hit other children. You must remember that other children would like the toys just as much as you do and you must wait your turn." Then, addressing the verbal attack on you, say, "You're angry at me, Billy, but I like you. When you feel better, come back with the others and I'll help you find a shovel. Maybe after a while you'll learn to like me, too."

Situation 5

This classroom for four-year-olds is fairly congenial and a cooperative attitude seems to prevail. Occasionally problems surface, but they nearly always work themselves out. However, one child, James, seems to be always singled out as the object of excessive teasing and taunting. He apparently doesn't have the courage to stand up for what is his and often reacts immaturely to social situations. One day, James falls while running on the playground and tears a small hole in the knee of his trousers. Trying to suppress tiny sobs, James looks embarrassed as some children begin to chant, "James is a crybaby! James is a crybaby!" James runs to the teacher, tears streaming, wounded more by the ridicule than by the small bruise on his knee.

Solution

In almost any group of three-, four-, or five-year-olds, one child will occasionally be singled out for excessive teasing. This child is one who reacts passively or babyishly to many situations. Often, the child comes from a home where he received an overabundance of strong affection, and where his every need and demand were met. As he grew up, he found that continued displays of babyish behavior made him the center of attraction, and adults thought him cute and amusing. Therefore, long after he should have left his immature behavior behind, he continues to entertain and delight those who reinforce such behaviors.

Now, in the school situation, James becomes confused and frustrated when other children react negatively toward behaviors that win him pampering treatment at home. Your role in such situations must be to attempt to help the unassertive child move beyond his babyish reactions, while helping all the children realize that it is their responsibility to treat each other with consideration. Often the immature child presents problems that are almost impossible for teachers to cure. The trouble may have begun very early and may now extend too deeply. You must recognize such handicaps, but be willing to do what this teacher did to help James:

1. *She was a giving person, but she wouldn't allow the child to "push." When she couldn't give James all he wanted, she said no in a firm and assertive way. She didn't lay down the law harshly, however, because it would only have led to further disruptive behaviors.*

2. *She met James's frequent outbursts by removing him from situations and inviting him to return when he was ready not to disturb others. "You must not take another child's crayons while he's using them, James. Wait here until you're ready to share the materials."*

3. *She met his temper tantrums with patient understanding. She stopped him firmly and let him know she meant business. "James, you must stop that," or "When you get done yelling, you can finish your picture," are comments she frequently made. The teacher was careful, however, to stay away from "bribe"*

statements such as, "If you don't stop kicking your feet, you won't be able to play on the playground later."

4. *James's desire to get everything he wanted was allayed somewhat as the teacher helped him share and turned his attention to other things. For example, she would say, "You cannot have the hammer now, James. Martha is using it. I'll help you use the saw while you're waiting."*

5. *The teacher watched James very closely to make sure he would meet situations only when he was ready for them.*

Situation 6

Four children are busily painting in the art center; the teacher is standing by the block corner watching with obvious pleasure. All the children in the room seem thoroughly engrossed in separate little projects and are paying little attention to each other. Richard, who has just completed his picture, turns with excitement to the teacher to share what he has done. Just as he is about to approach her, however, he stumbles into Francine's block city. As her city crumbles, Francine's contentment turns to anger. With tears streaming, she hits Richard with a solid blow and exclaims, "You old creep, I hate you!" Confused, Richard begins to cry and soon tears and sobs from both parties fill the air.

Solution

Accidents frequently cause strong anger and disagreement among young children. In this case, Richard's excitement led to an incident where he destroyed Francine's block city without meaning to. In these instances, the teacher should assume the role of an interpreter rather than that of a disciplinarian. She must help the children understand that the circumstances caused irritating results, but that these results were unavoidable. She must help them perceive the intent of the incident and lead them to respond to it rather than to the actions.

For example, you could have squelched Richard's enthusiasm by rushing to Francine's aid and stating, "Richard, take your time and watch where you're going. You ruined Francine's block city." Instead, you should try to help both children cope with the situation by saying to them, "Francine, Richard didn't mean to knock your blocks down. He was just coming to show me something and forgot all about your blocks. Let's both calm down a little so we can be friends again." Normally, the children will work things out for themselves. As you place Richard's picture in a special area of the room, you can watch him and Francine busily at work rebuilding the block city.

Fantasy

Much of preschool children's play is colored by rich imagery. They are, of course, well aware of the "real" world, but they enjoy associating mystical or magical qualities with the objects and events around them. For example, they will be convinced that cartoon characters are real people, that friendly dragons really exist although they are only seen in dreams, or that Santa

Claus will most certainly arrive on Christmas Eve. Likewise, they may be puzzled about the magical influence needed to make airplanes fly or automobiles go. In a young child's imagination, a block can be a cow; a stick, a train; and a chef's hat can transform him instantly into a cook. Children's thoughts, then, may be directed toward reality, but they are not restrained by its limits.

During the preschool years, one of the most interesting aspects of fantasy begins to appear: the *imaginary playmate*. Stone and Church estimate that the incidence of imaginary playmates may run as high as 50 percent and that most of them are very real and in need of the same care and attention as the child.[10] The playmates are often born of very special needs—needs for models, scapegoats, consciences, best friends, or merely escape from a too dull or frightening reality.

Sometimes the playmates are human, but they can also be animal images. You should recognize the needs and pleasures associated with these flights of fancy. Don't discourage children from talking about their imaginary playmates, but children should know that you know the difference. The young child who rushes to your side followed by a "friendly elephant" should not be told, "Oh, Julie, stop that silliness," or be considered a liar. She can be encouraged to talk about her companion and then be told, "It would be exciting to see a *real* elephant sometime, but I'll bet your friend is a very nice one!"

Imaginary thought develops during childhood and should be considered a very normal part of the growth process. The following are some suggestions for encouraging the use of fantasy (more are made throughout the text).

1. Provide plenty of opportunities for dramatic play, where children can pretend to be firefighters, police officers, grocers, doctors, nurses, cowpunchers, bus drivers, and so on.
2. Make available for their use a wide variety of materials—household objects, books, clothes, playthings, and so on.
3. Establish an atmosphere of comfort and freedom where adults do not always demand standard behaviors of children.
4. Serve as a model and encourage imaginary play. By rewarding children's efforts, you give them the support and encouragement they need and stimulate maximum active participation.

GUIDELINES FOR LEADING YOUNG CHILDREN

Your skill in coping with the variety of situations encountered during play periods and other times of social contact will grow with each year of experience. You will learn to reflect on past experiences and analyze the causes of present situations. You will learn to consider alternative actions based on accepted theories of social-emotional development that will help you handle the feelings of the children involved. Perhaps the most important thing in choosing the proper course of action is to be sure you are dealing with the *primary cause* of behavior rather than the *result*. For example, consider a situation in which Manuel is playing with some clay in the art center when Jennifer intrudes and takes almost half of the clay he was using. Manuel reacts with a sharp slap on Jennifer's arm and the comment, "You're an old *(obscenity)*!"

The *primary cause* of this situation, of course, was Jennifer's intrusion into Manuel's activity. You must learn to address yourself to that component first with a comment such as, "Manuel was using the clay, Jennifer, and I can't let you take it from him. I'll get you some and you can use it at this table." Then you should address the *result* of the confrontation by explaining to Manuel, "I know that Jennifer took some of your clay without asking, but I can't let you hit her and use words like that in our classroom. She made a mistake."

The way you handle situations involving children's feelings is important to the development of healthy personalities and budding social relationships. You must always use constructive methods to cope with the various stumbling blocks that can affect positive growth. The following eleven guidelines, adapted from Baker and Fane, have been designed to help you face or divert potential problems resulting from children's behavior.[11]

Care about the child. You must respect the child and want to help him. Don't let feelings such as "You got what you deserved" enter your thinking or your actions—it will only change the child's behavior for the worse.

Develop a sense of self-respect and a strong feeling of confidence in your ability to help children. By developing a positive view of yourself and of your ability, you radiate confidence when you handle problem situations. You gain the child's respect and make it easier for him to accept your limits when he knows he can trust you, your judgment, and your firm, friendly actions. Don't be hesitant in your dealings with children for fear of making a mistake —we all make mistakes. Remember that mistakes often lead to our greatest learning experiences.

Assume responsibility for seeing that the child does what you expect him to do. Don't assume that all children can regulate their own behaviors and actions entirely. Toddlers, of course, will require more guidance from you than the five-year-old. It is difficult to describe how much guidance you should give different groups of children, because each situation is unique. Perhaps the best advice is to say that experience will be your greatest asset in teaching you how much responsibility is yours and how much is the child's.

Be patient in your response to misbehavior. Remember that children need time to understand the kinds and degrees of behaviors expected of them. They will not change their behaviors overnight, and, while altering certain undesirable behaviors, they may need a great deal of patience from you. Always assume that children are willing to change, even though at times you are convinced there is no hope. Explain rules and acceptable behaviors when needed. Allow children to express their feelings. In general, be an understanding person and realize that young children need time to change behaviors and assimilate rules.

Be consistent in what you say and do. Your smiles, compliments, praise, understanding, trust, and other behaviors are all directed toward controlling the behaviors of children. If children find that you are consistent in your treatment of positive and negative behaviors, they will learn more effectively. However, if you are inconsistent, the children may question your limits and look for any loopholes available. This "limit-testing" behavior is common in young children and seems motivated by their desire to see how consistent you are or can be.

Be firm with your control. State your message to the child in clear, understandable terms. Tell him directly that you liked what he did or that you disapproved of his actions. However, never be negative toward the child ("You are a naughty boy"), only toward his actions ("I can't let you do that").

Use reasonable comments when controlling a child. Remember that your comments should correct a child's negative behaviors, not threaten or psychologically punish him. Ridicule, shame, or criticism—techniques of humiliation—have no place in a young child's environment. Always make your demands reasonable ones. Don't, for example, get carried away and threaten the child with unreasonable comments such as, "If you don't stop hitting Bart, I'm going to make you sit in the corner for the rest of the week." Such techniques may cause resentment, hostility, and excessive fear in many young children. Always use techniques and comments that are reasonable and easily carried through. Comments should be stated positively; that is, you should tell children *what to do* rather than *what not to do.* For example, you should say "Keep your hands on your lap while we listen to the story," rather than "Don't touch anyone while I'm telling you this story."

Give children choices only when you want them to make decisions. Giving children a chance to consider choices and make decisions is a legitimate procedure. However, teachers often give children a choice when they really don't want the children to decide the question at all. A typical example is a neophyte teacher who, during her first day on the job, asked the children, "Would you like to come for snack time now?" Some children wandered to the table, others simply said no, and the rest continued to participate in free play activities, oblivious of the query. What the teacher should have said was simply, "It's time for our snack now." Make sure your questions are legitimate ones before you ask them.

Redirect activity when a conflict is obvious. You will be a more successful teacher if you learn to turn a child's attention from an activity in which there may be a conflict occurring to an activity he finds equally interesting. For example, Sandy is playing in the doll corner with a soft doll. Suddenly she winds up and throws it at Anna. You know that Sandy has been playing in the corner for some time, and you realize that she has lost interest and may want to do something more active. You walk over and suggest, "Sandy, Anna didn't like to have something thrown at her like that. If you want to throw something, there's a ball over here. Come with me and we'll find a safe place for you to play."

Anticipate problems before they happen. This, perhaps more than any other teaching behavior, comes with experience. Learning to prevent problems before they happen is important because children may not always benefit from mistakes. While watching two children playing in the block corner, for example, you may observe that Michael is unknowingly moving closer and closer to Benny's block tower. In another minute, an errant foot may kick over a carefully constructed tower and cause calamity. You carefully appraise the situation, approach Michael, and say, "If you want to play with your truck in the block city, Michael, you should come over here where you won't kick over Benny's tower." If you wait for the situation to unfold before taking action, the children may be unable to learn anything constructive.

Don't become discouraged if your classroom isn't perfect every day. We all have days when things do not go the way we want. Our moods, home situation, the weather, and many other influences affect our routine. When we allow such events to affect our classroom disposition, minor problems tend to compound themselves. Keep a realistic outlook and a faithful confidence in yourself and your children.

The preceding suggestions are basic to the classroom technique practiced by many preschool teachers. Their strategies for encouraging healthy social-emotional growth were originally developed during the early part of this century, and evolved through the influence of two major contributors: Sigmund Freud and Erik Erikson.

THEORIES OF SOCIAL-EMOTIONAL DEVELOPMENT

Psychosexual Theory

Sigmund Freud and his followers pointed out the importance of properly managing the child's socialization during the first five years. By the end of this period, they felt, the basic foundations of social development have been formed and further development is merely an expansion of the early structure. They also felt that many adult psychological problems could be traced back to events that occurred during childhood.

According to Freud, the infant is born with one basic psychological structure—the *id*—which can be described as a primitive framework of instincts and reflexes that drives the child to satisfy basic survival urges such as hunger or warmth. The id is an unrefined personality lacking conscience or rules to govern behavior. Eventually, the child's instinctual urges come into conflict with reality. He finds that some basic biological needs (such as hunger) cannot be fulfilled immediately; mother may be busy elsewhere, for example, and unable to satisfy his hunger urge instantly. He then learns to interpret this *reality*, and realizes that sometimes the gratification of certain needs must be delayed or occasionally denied. Freud used the term *ego* to label this conscious understanding that at times some things are possible and others are not. The developing child, then, learns to balance the id and the ego while satisfying needs in ways that are most profitable for him.

Figure 2-3 Three levels of human personality.

At about age 3 the third component of personality, the *superego*, enters the picture in opposition to the id and ego. The superego moves beyond the mere satisfaction of physical needs and is concerned with social reality; this is the "conscience" that a child develops as he becomes aware of the social and cultural expectations of his behavior. The superego grows and develops as a result of the socialization experiences the child has. Frequently it comes into conflict with the individual's id, or basic biological urges. When such conflict occurs, the reality-oriented ego mechanism surfaces and mediates between the id and superego. Figure 2-3 shows this procedure.

Inevitable conflicts occur among the id, ego, and superego during a sequence of stages that Freud felt all individuals go through. He theorized that individuals at each stage were primarily concerned with sexual desires (that is, desires related to general pleasure seeking rather than to intercourse or other sexual acts), and that satisfaction of these desires was the primary motivation for social behavior all through life. Table 2-3 summarizes the changes in sexual (pleasure seeking) desires that Freud saw, as the individual progresses from infancy through the elementary school years.

These developmental stages reflect Freud's emphasis on sexuality (pleasure seeking) as the major motivator for behavior. During each stage a certain body zone is of greatest importance to the individual. Freud saw the child's development through the stages as accompanied by conflicts with parents and other authority figures over the satisfaction of each need. Shirley Moore and Sally Kilmer explained the significance of such conflicts:

> Freud recognized that the young child has immense love for his parents, but he also rivals them for affection or control and fears their retaliatory power. Authority figures respond to the child's challenge of their authority by exerting control over the child, punishing misbehavior and, in the process, generating guilt and anxiety in the child. While guilt and anxiety were viewed by Freud as necessary components of self-control and the development of a conscience, they were also

regarded as potential sources of later maladjustment. Excessive demands or lack of early fulfillment of [sexual urges] could cause the child to become bogged down at an immature stage of [social-emotional] development or even to regress to an earlier stage of emotional maturity.[12]

Conversely, excessive gratification of sexual impulses at particular stages could result in *fixations*, in which development ceases and no further development of personality ensues. Therefore, excessive control over sexual urges may cause the child to regress to a more comfortable stage of emotional development, while excessive gratification may cause the child to become fixed at a particular stage.

Table 2-3 Freud's Stages of Psychosexual Development

Stage	Age	Behaviors	Character Traits
Oral	Birth– 8 months	Pleasure derived from biological forces of sucking, biting, or swallowing.	Develops feelings of acceptance. Id dominates behavior.
Anal	8 months– 1½ years	Stimulated by retention and expulsion of feces or urine.	Develops traits of punctuality and orderliness. Toilet training creates conflict between self gratification and societal demands. Id and ego dominate behaviors.
Phallic	1½ years– 5 years	Stimulated by the manipulation of and attention given to genital regions.	Becomes aware of love directed toward the parents. Oedipus or Electra complex results from sexual fantasies during this stage.
Latency	5 years– 10 years	Sexual urges are reduced to a minimum during this stage. Sexual stirrings of adolescence not yet evident. Identifies with like-sexed parent.	Looks for love outside the family circle.

Freud's feelings captivated preschool educators during the 1930s and 1940s. Those educators became convinced of the importance of managing the early years in order to encourage proper social-emotional development. And their classroom practices stressed the importance of free play as a socializing force. Through play, they felt, children are able to try on the roles of others as they learn to follow rules and understand the importance of cooperation. Bernard Spodek added that:

> Freud considered play a cathartic activity allowing children to master difficult situations. The child can use the fantasy play situation to act out adult roles, providing him with a feeling of mastery in fantasy situations that allows him to cope with reality situations. The child can use play to act out personally painful occurrences and to master the pain by coming to grips with it in the fantasy of the play situation. The same mastery in fantasy can allow children to cope with the affective elements of more positive life situations as well.[13]

Applying Freudian psychology to the preschool setting, then, involved helping the child in his struggle through psychosexual stages by supporting play activities and by encouraging the child's free expression of thoughts and feelings.

Psychosocial Theory

In the 1950s and 1960s, Erik Erikson proposed a theory of social development that differed somewhat from the pleasure-seeking views of Freud, and provided perhaps an even more relevant understanding of young children. His *psychosocial* theory is based on the premise that all individuals progress through eight stages of development; during these stages they are confronted with unique problems that demand the adjustment of personal needs to the social expectations of the culture involved. Erikson described each stage as comprising a *crisis period*, a time when individuals experience stresses and strains as they attempt to regulate their behaviors to the demands of their particular culture.[14] In each period the crisis is expressed in terms of polar opposites, such as trust vs. mistrust; autonomy vs. shame and doubt. The child's experiences and environment help him resolve each psychosocial crisis successfully. Warm, trusting, understanding adults help the child effectively move toward sound social-emotional maturity. Table 2-4 describes the crises of development from infancy through the elementary school years.

Erikson's ideas helped preschool educators understand the types of environments that would be most effective in producing desirable social-emotional growth. His ideas helped teachers realize that the child must be viewed as a competent being who is motivated by changing psychological needs throughout life. Based on his views, the teacher's role is to help children master specific crises during various life stages. They are to stimulate valued social behaviors and minimize the chances of children failing in essential activities. In essence, teachers are to help children resolve stress during critical developmental periods within an atmosphere of trust and encouragement. Alicerose Barman offered one of the most practical explanations of the importance of Erikson's psychosocial theory:

> What do Erikson's formulations tell the teacher about handling the preschool child? Put in very rudimentary form, they tell her, "Let him trust you as a consistent adult who cares for and about him. Encourage him in his growing independence, avoid shaming him and making him doubt his own worth. Provide him with a climate where new experiences with people and materials challenge his learning and give him goals to reach."[15]

Erikson and Freud, then, offered preschool teachers insight into the social-emotional development of young children and convinced them of the critical importance of trust, love, and play during the early years. However, their philosophies and the techniques they recommended are by no means the only ones known. Gaining some popularity today is the more structured, teacher-centered philosophy of behaviorism.

Table 2-4 Erikson's Stages of Psychosocial Crises

Crisis	Stage
Infancy: Birth–1½ years (corresponds to Freud's oral stage)	*Trust vs. Mistrust:* The baby seeks a loving relationship with those around him. If he finds it, he will learn to trust others and have confidence in them.
Toddlerhood: 1½–3 years (corresponds to Freud's anal stage)	*Autonomy vs. Shame and Doubt:* The toddler has strong needs to do things for himself. The adult must serve as a guide to help him try things out and give support or encouragement when needed.
Young children: 3–6 years (corresponds to Freud's phallic stage)	*Initiative vs. Guilt:* The child wishes to establish his independence. Adults should encourage children to pursue independent goals uninhibited by defeat, guilt, or fear of punishment. Adults should encourage responsibility and courage to pursue goals.
School children: 6–12 years (corresponds to Freud's latency stage)	*Industry vs. Inferiority:* Children learn to earn recognition by producing things. They take pride in their ability to perform new skills and tasks and expect recognition for their efforts. Adults should help children achieve a sense of accomplishment by providing conditions that lead to feelings of worth.

Behaviorist Theory

In some instances, educators have argued that there is a need for more formalized classroom control than has been described to this point. They consider the techniques we discussed as a "soft" approach to managing the classroom and demand that a more formalized system be used with young children, especially those experiencing difficulties adjusting to the classroom routine. These educators are convinced that children need to be guided in a highly structured atmosphere where the teacher prevails—that is, that social-emotional concerns can best be addressed through the direct technique of *behavior modification.* Basic to this approach is the belief that behaviors bringing the child pleasant or rewarding consequences will be strengthened and repeated, while behaviors going unnoticed or unrewarded will diminish in frequency and eventually disappear.

The leading exponent of the behavior modification approach is B. F. Skinner, a psychologist who developed the model of behavior modification called *operant conditioning.* Guy Lefrancois defined operant conditioning in this way: "The simplest explanation of operant conditioning is that a response followed by *reinforcement* will be more likely to recur when the organism finds itself in a similar situation to that which surrounded the behavior's first occurrence."[16] For example, one day Wilma's teacher brought a kitten to school in a cage for all the children to enjoy. Calling the children to the large table, she opened the cage and allowed the kitten to be petted and touched by all who were interested. At the sight of the animal, though, Wilma became alarmed, turned her head, and desperately tried to move away. After calming Wilma down, the teacher sought to find the cause for such behavior. She discovered that the reason Wilma reacted with such fear was because several stray cats had recently been seen wandering near her home, and her fearful parents, seeing her one time playing near a cat and attempting to pet it, quickly ran to her, snatched her away, planted a stinging slap on her behind, and, while tears flowed down her cheeks, had said, "Don't ever go near strange animals again." In terms of operant conditioning, Wilma reacted the way she did because the teacher's kitten was paired in her mind with a similar situation from the past (being near a cat), in which a behavior (petting the cat) was associated with a fear-producing negative reinforcement (the slap and verbal reprimand). In a preschool situation, children will often exhibit strong emotional responses of fear, love, anger, joy, jealousy, aggression, or many other feelings described earlier. Whenever such emotions arise, they are likely to be derived from associated experiences that elicited positive or negative reactions in the past. However, a word of caution should be added here. Behaviorists feel that teachers should focus on the *exhibited behaviors* of the child rather than on those factors that *caused* the behavior. In other words, you should not be concerned with *why* the child acts as he does, only with *how* he acts. George Morrison expanded on this concept:

> This idea usually takes some getting used to on the part of many teachers since it is almost opposite of the way they have been taught to think. Generally, teachers

feel it is beneficial to spend most of their time finding out why the child acts the way he does, and consequently they spend a great deal of time and effort in the process. Johnny, for example, cannot attend to his work in class; he is fidgety all the time and is inclined to daydream. Then he gets up out of his seat and wanders aimlessly around the room. The teacher, in an effort to solve Johnny's problem, spends six weeks investigating the causes. Through the investigative process the teacher finds out Johnny's mother has been divorced three times, is about to leave the man she is living with, and has a tendency to ignore Johnny at home. On the basis of this information, the teacher concludes that Johnny acts the way he acts because of his mother's influence. However, the teacher is no closer to solving Johnny's problem than he was six weeks previously since nothing has been done about Johnny's behavior! A teacher's time and energy should be spent in developing strategies to help children with their problems.[17]

In the case of Wilma, therefore, the teacher would have developed a program to eliminate the exhibited fear rather than trying to interpret the experience Wilma had at home. Obviously the teacher would have been concerned with the underlying causes of such behavior, but simply to gather background information and do nothing about the behavior would be in direct opposition to the basic tenets of behavior modification.

Modifying Children's Social-Emotional Behavior

The first step in modifying a child's behavior is to identify those behaviors you wish to see continued or those you wish to see extinguished. For example, you may want your children to always put their materials away when they are finished with them, or you may wish to extinguish Freddie's habit of pinching the child sitting next to him during group story time. You understand that these behaviors can be promoted or changed if they are reinforced by appropriate methods. But what are those methods?

Reinforcement exists in two broad forms: *positive reinforcement* and *negative reinforcement*. Positive reinforcement includes all those pleasant reactions we've received from others such as money, recognition, and so on; negative reinforcement includes the unpleasant reactions we've received from others such as punishment, ridicule, fines, and so on. Table 2-5 summarizes different types of positive and negative reinforcement.

If you use behavior modification techniques in the classroom, it is important to remember that reinforcement is most effective when it follows an observable behavior as closely as possible. For that reason, teachers employing behavior modification principles often combine positive reinforcement techniques into a reinforcement system that uses *tokens*. In this system whenever a child exhibits a positive social characteristic such as saying "Thank you," he is immediately given a token (a chip or a counter of some kind) and a verbal reinforcement, such as a cheerful, "Way to go. Your manners are super." The child accumulates these chips during the day and uses them to "buy" an activity later in the day. For example, the special art activity may cost him five chips, free play may cost three chips, and so on.

Table 2-5   Positive and Negative Reinforcement
in Preschool Settings

Positive Reinforcers	**Negative Reinforcers**
A. Token reinforcers: Chips, counters, check marks, gummed stars or labels, beans	A. Spanking
	B. Reprimanding
	C. Withholding privileges
	D. Isolating or ignoring
B. Food: Candy, raisins, juice, cookies, peanuts, cheese, fruit, cereal, carrots or celery, milk	*Note:* There seems to be no conclusive evidence that punishment is an effective reinforcer. There is evidence that it can cause temporary suppression of negative behaviors, but that negative social or emotional reactions frequently reappear. Evidence shows that these reactions reappear because punishment techniques are often associated with the punisher rather than with the disapproved behavior. However, it has been shown that isolating the child or ignoring his behaviors will often lead to the extinction of undesired behavior.
C. Manipulatives: Toys, games, puzzles, art activities	
D. Social stimuli: Smiles, hugs, handshakes, pats on the back, verbal priase: "I like the way you did that"; "You're doing a great job"; "Wow! Thanks for helping out"; "Good boy (girl)!"	

A technique often employed to extinguish negative behavior is *time out.* If a child is misbehaving during story time, for example, and begins to disrupt the others in the group to the point where the teacher is not able to ignore his actions, then the child is sent to a special time-out corner in the room where he is isolated from the rest of the group. During this time, of course, the child cannot earn chips and will be unable to collect enough to participate in an anticipated activity. Behaviorists feel that by placing such restrictions on the disruptive child, teachers will be able to extinguish undesired behavior eventually. You probably noticed that the term *ignore* was used to describe the teacher's initial reaction to the situation described. Behaviorists feel that if the teacher gives the child any sort of verbal or nonverbal reaction, the child may be reinforced for his negative behavior since his initial intention anyway was to win the teacher's attention. By accomplishing his goal, the child may be encouraged to duplicate his disruptive behaviors whenever he again wants the teacher's attention. In most preschool situations, teachers use such a combination of techniques: they reward positive behaviors, ignore negative behaviors, and isolate persistent behavior problems.

In summary, preschool classrooms reflecting the behavior modification approach to assisting social-emotional development would employ these basic principles:

1. Identify the behaviors to be reinforced.
2. Determine the appropriate reinforcer.
3. Develop a system of implementation.
4. Reinforce or ignore behaviors as they occur.
5. Periodically evaluate progress toward desired goals.

Social Learning Theory

Some preschool educators prefer to combine strong features from each of these major contrasting philosophies. For example, inherent in the beliefs of both Freud and Erikson is the idea of *identification*. Identification is a method of solving crises or conflicts by emulating an adult model who shows an ability to make successful life adjustments. The young child, for example, first identifies with parents because of their continual presence, but as he grows older, he seeks other significant adults to emulate. As the child's horizons widen further, he has additional opportunities to observe and *imitate* the different people he meets.

A. Bandura and R. Walters concentrated on this imitation feature and formulated a theory of socialization that stressed that the acquisition of prosocial or antisocial behaviors comes about not primarily through internal motives but through behavioristic principles of extrinsic environmental stimuli, especially *modeling*.[18] When children imitate the behavior of an adult model, they frequently are rewarded, particularly if the behavior is approved. If children are exposed to aggressive models, for example, they will likely be aggressive in their behaviors; if they are exposed to helping models, they will likely become helping, caring people. If a child sees that a behavior is successful for someone else, he is likely to try that behavior for himself. And, if the child is rewarded for exhibiting that behavior, he will be inclined to repeat it.

Two examples illustrate this concept. First, consider the child who uses vulgar expressions in your child-care facility. He may have heard his parents and other adults using these words and was looked upon as being cute or amusing when he repeated them. The amused recognition of his vulgar language was a reward to the child and encouraged him to repeat the behavior. He may not have been aware of their meaning, but he repeated them because they were positively reinforced. Second, consider Ricky, who comes from a home environment where help is constantly extended to those in need. When another child spilled his paint on the floor, Ricky was there with a mop to help clean up. The teacher recognized Ricky's effort by giving him a warm smile and thanks for a job well done. In both examples, children repeated model behavior that was rewarded, although the behaviors range from undesirable to desirable in most instances.

The process of imitating behavior is not extremely complex, but it does help to explain further the many influences that account for the social-emotional development of children. Keep in mind, of course, that a portrait of the complex social-emotional world of the child painted by only one artist can be very restrictive and distorted. The key to choosing one method or combination of methods is to understand the children in your care, to establish limits that are fair and reasonable, and to extend firm and consistent intervention whenever any child goes beyond the limits.

Very few persistent social-emotional problems will be solved, however, if you do not develop a plan that is consistent with parents' actions so that the home interaction patterns parallel those of the school. Most parents are willing to cooperate in such a venture and to establish parent–child relationships similar to the teacher–child relationship. This home–school connection is essential to reinforcement of your practices since the parent–child relationship is normally far deeper than the teacher–child relationship.

Strong parent–child ties may at times cause problems, however, for they sometimes prevent parents from perceiving a situation with the same objectivity as you. For example, some parents in your child-care facility may become upset because they want a program stressing group conformity in behaviors while you value individual pursuits more highly. In these instances, you need to resolve the differences by thoroughly discussing them in a professional manner. In other words, explain your philosophy of social-emotional development so that the parents can see the value of your beliefs. They need to understand your position completely so that their strong concerns can be alleviated. Also, remember that your discussion with the parents must be a two-way process. Listen to what they have to say—perhaps their mode of operation is based on deep convictions, such as cultural expectations, very different from your own. In these cases, you must take the time to understand and respect the parents' concerns; a quick resolution is rarely possible. Instead of forcing your beliefs on the parents and risking alienating them and their community, try to empathize with their position and work out an amicable agreement. This takes skill to accomplish, but you won't win them over with a "take it or leave it" attitude, and you can't provide the best situation for their children if you can't offer the type of program you think is most professionally sound—it's a real dilemma. Take the case of young Charles, for example. Charles was brought up in a rough neighborhood, and was taught by his parents to fight whenever possible to protect his possessions. Naturally, when playing in the child-care setting, Charles frequently protected his toys and games with physical force. Concerned for the safety of the other children, Charles's teacher approached his parents. The parents refused to support any of the teacher's suggestions for changing Charles's behavior because they felt it was a necessary quality for survival in their neighborhood. Thoroughly perplexed, the teacher realized that any techniques used in school would not be carried through in the home so she decided that her responsibility would be to do the best possible job at school. Whenever Charles resorted to punching or hitting, she would immediately step in and sternly state, "I cannot allow you to hit other children in school." Respecting the parents' feelings, the teacher did not warn the child that his behaviors were wrong in *all* situations, but she did communicate the limits of his behavior in the classroom in a firm, direct way. Other suggestions for working with parents are presented in Chapter 12. Become familiar with the various techniques of parent–teacher cooperation, for a partner-type relationship between parent and teacher is essential to solving social-emotional problems and helping a child grow.

SOME FINAL THOUGHTS

The move from home to school is a difficult transition for many young children. Learning to become a part of a new group and learning to respond to new adults requires much guidance and patience from the teacher. For many of the children, the new behavior expectations may differ greatly from those they experienced at home. How you handle this home–school adjustment will be important to whether or not children are encouraged to become self-regulating individuals capable of building sound interpersonal relationships and healthy personalities. Whatever method you choose to meet this goal, it is important that you establish an unthreatening environment in which children have guidance and support as they move forward in desired directions.

NOTES

1. T.G.R. Bower, *A Primer of Infant Development* (San Francisco: W. H. Freeman, 1977), pp. 28–30.
2. Ibid., p. 49.
3. H. R. Schaffer and P. Emerson, "The Development of Social Attachments in Infancy," *Monographs of the Society for Research in Child Development* 29, no. 3 (1964).
4. Gladys Gardner Jenkins and Helen S. Shacter, *These Are Your Children* (Glenview, Ill.: Scott, Foresman, 1975), p. 48.
5. Schaffer and Emerson, "Development of Social Attachments," pp. 67–68.
6. Bettye M. Caldwell et al., "Mother-Infant Interaction in Monomatric and Polymatric Families," *American Journal of Orthopsychiatry* 33, no. 5 (July 1963): 653–664.
7. L. Joseph Stone and Joseph Church, *Childhood and Adolescence* (New York: Random House, 1973), pp. 67–68.
8. Ibid., p. 66.
9. Katherine Read Baker and Xenia F. Fane, *Understanding and Guiding Young Children*, 2d ed. (Englewood Cliffs, N.J.: Prentice-Hall, 1971), p. 21.
10. Stone and Church, *Childhood and Adolescence*, p. 280.
11. This list is based on recommendations made by Baker and Fane in *Understanding and Guiding Young Children*.
12. Shirley G. Moore and Sally Kilmer, *Contemporary Preschool Education* (New York: John Wiley, 1973), p. 18.

13. Bernard Spodek, *Teaching in the Early Years* (Englewood Cliffs, N.J.: Prentice-Hall, 1972), p. 204.
14. Erik H. Erikson, *Childhood and Society* (New York: W. W. Norton, 1963).
15. Alicerose S. Barman, "Four-Year-Old Development," in *A Creative Guide for Preschool Teachers*, ed. Joanne Wylie (Western Publishing, 1969), p. 20.
16. Guy R. Lefrancois, *Of Children*, 1st ed. (Belmont, Calif.: Wadsworth, 1973), p. 90.
17. George S. Morrison, *Early Childhood Education Today* (Columbus, Ohio: Charles E. Merrill, 1976), p. 208.
18. A. Bandura and R. Walters, *Social Learning and Personality Development* (New York: Holt, Rinehart and Winston, 1963).

3

Affective Development:
Establishing Values and Attitudes

Helping children understand their behaviors and acquire a set of standards to guide them is a central feature of preschool programming. (*Hi and Lois* courtesy of King Features Syndicate, Inc.)

Affective development is the area of preschool education in which children are encouraged to establish personal feelings, beliefs, values, morals, or attitudes that will serve as guides in the future conduct of their lives. These guiding values may be formed as a result of what they have been taught, what they have experienced, or both. This area of development is closely associated with the social-emotional area and can be considered an extension of it. To show this, let us review the progress of social-emotional development. In Chapter 2 we saw that no infant comes equipped with a system of beliefs to guide his behaviors. His behaviors are responses to the immediate effects of the stimuli with which he is in contact. He reaches for food when hungry and wants to be held and caressed when uncomfortable. The infant is self-centered; his major concerns are himself and his present surroundings. He could not care less about the moral and ethical reasons for his behaviors —his only concern is to receive immediate fulfillment of personal needs.

> For I want what I want when I want it!
> That's all that makes life worth the while.
> For the wine that tonight fills my soul with delight,
> On the morrow may seem to me vile.
> There's no worldly pleasure myself I deny,
> There's no one to ask me the wherefore or why,
> I eat when I'm hungry, and I drink when I'm dry.
> For I want what I want when I want it!
> I want what I want when I want it!

Victor Herbert's lines (from *Mademoiselle Modiste*) give us a succinct description of infants' motivations for their behaviors. As the child moves out of infancy, he slowly learns that his behaviors cannot be determined solely by self-centered demands. Others around him have needs, too, and the toddler begins to understand that certain behaviors can be made only under certain circumstances. He learns some of these expectations *directly*—for example, if he handles the family cat roughly he gets a scratch or if he has a successful potty training experience, he gets a warm hug. He learns other expectations through *verbal techniques*—for example, others within his environment tell him what is good or bad, what is acceptable or unacceptable, what is nice or not nice, what he may do or may not do. The young child, then, either at home or in the preschool setting, often has his behaviors prescribed for him; he is rewarded for compliance to adult demands and punished for noncompliance. All too often, young children reared in this manner progress into the elementary school with little or no opportunity to make choices. In fact, they are virtually helpless when they are asked to make choices because they have been totally dependent on adult sanctions during their early childhood years. In the past, adults guided young children by such rigid verbal means. This is effectively illustrated in the following description:

Master: You must not do so.
Child: And why must I not do so?
Master: Because it is naughty.
Child: Naughty! What is that being naughty?
Master: Doing what you are forbid.
Child: And what harm is there in doing what one is forbid?
Master: The harm is, you will be whipped for disobedience.
Child: Then I will do it so that nobody will know anything of the matter.
Master: O, but you will be watched.
Child: Ah! But then I will hide myself.
Master: Then you will be examined.
Child: Then I will tell a fib.
Master: But you must not tell fibs.
Child: Why must not I?
Master: Because it is naughty.[1]

This method of direct verbal guidance is called *inculcation,* or the process of instilling certain beliefs or virtues in children. Surprisingly, it was taken from the works of Jean Jacques Rousseau. He supported the use of this type of exchange by explaining how the process of inculcation helps to develop beliefs within young children.

Thus, we go round the circle; and yet, if we go out of it, the child understands us no longer. . . . I could be very curious to know what could be substituted in the place of this fine dialogue. . . . To distinguish between good and evil, to perceive the reasons on which our moral obligations are founded, is not the business, as it is not within the capacity, of a child.[2]

For many years, children were seen in this way—as incapable of making their own judgments. They were not considered able to support their judgments in guiding their own behaviors with sound reasoning. Although we respect the overall educational contributions of Rousseau, we can see that his ideas related to affective education deviated substantially from his general educational thoughts. Even today, many preschools that provide excellent cognitive programs for their children still hold fast to the belief that youngsters learn behaviors best through telling, preaching, and providing biased or incomplete information. As a result, some preschool teachers rely on imitation to instill values, that is, they don't play cards, smoke, or drink liquor as all "good" people don't, or shouldn't. They practice the educational system that believes that all the virtues, without exception, should be implanted in the

This method of instruction might have been appropriate for children in the past because of the many commonly held beliefs of that time. However, today's culture is changing more rapidly than ever and contains more conflicting issues than we've ever known. For this reason, the ability to make personal choices is more important than ever. If older children and adults are to make such choices, they should begin making personal decisions as early in their lives as possible, certainly within the preschool setting.

What, then, are some suggestions for strategies other than direct verbal instruction? How can we help young children develop a behavioral guidance system without imposing it on them? How can they be led to make their own decisions? Can special training accelerate this process? At present, we emphasize a child-centered approach to affective education, much as we do to cognitive education. This means that the child interacts with his environment and acquires beliefs and behavior patterns suited to his individual needs—that is, he learns through experience and decision-making techniques rather than primarily through verbal instruction. New theories of affective development have helped us to understand that classroom environments need to provide opportunities for individual experience and growth through which children can develop the capacity to distinguish between right and wrong, and that this ability progressively influences their social behavior. The remainder of this chapter is directed toward two important areas that you should consider in affective education: (1) theories of values acquisition and (2) instructional strategies reflecting those theories.

STAGE THEORIES OF MORAL DEVELOPMENT

In recent years, a number of educators have been guided by various stage theories. Although these theories vary in certain respects, they all share the assumption that moral (affective) development can be categorized in terms of a *predetermined sequence of stages*. Most new stage theories are called *cognitive developmental*. They are cognitive because they recognize that moral education has, as its base, the stimulation of *active thinking* about moral issues. They are developmental because each stage includes elements of earlier structures but expands on them in such a way as to represent a more sophisticated level of reasoning.

Jean Piaget

Jean Piaget developed the first popular developmental theory of moral development. Dissatisfied with Freud's technique of studying deviant adult behavior in order to explain the development of mature thought through childhood, Piaget studied children directly. His results can be broken down into two categories. The first part of Piaget's theory of moral development concerns children's concepts of rules.[3] Piaget found that development progresses along the following lines:

1. *The egocentric stage.* This stage occurs when children do not consciously know or follow rules. The child is self-centered and fails to take other points of view into account. Children view right and wrong simply on the basis of what adult authority figures permit or forbid them to do.
2. *The stage of incipient cooperation.* This level is characterized by the acquisition of a genuinely social character. The child at this stage both cooperates and competes with others, and realizes that rules are made to help solve interpersonal conflicts.
3. *The stage of genuine cooperation.* At this stage, the child completely understands the purposes of rules and enjoys inventing new rules or elaborating on old ones. He even tries to understand all of the consequences that may arise from accepting or rejecting rules.

Children, then, initially pattern their behavior on parental or other adult demands. Later, as they spend more and more time with their peers, they gradually assume greater social awareness. Finally, they learn to make decisions for themselves and do not necessarily accept the authoritative views of others without reflection. In other words, children move from a unilateral respect of authority to a position of consideration of everyone's feelings.

The second part of Piaget's theory of moral development moves from a description of rule-following behavior to accounts of ways in which children judge the goodness or badness of actions in explicitly moral situations. In order to study this, he told the children a pair of stories in which two separate sets of characters differed in terms of both their intentions and the amount of damage they caused by their actions. In one story, the main character performed an act that unintentionally resulted in much damage; in the other, the child caused very little damage, but the act was deliberately improper. The children being studied were to determine which of the central characters was good and which was bad.

This example illustrates the first type of story, in which a child unintentionally caused much damage.

John was playing outdoors when his mother called him for lunch. When he went to the table he noticed his mother was on the phone and that his milk glass was empty. He thought of filling the glass to help his mother, so that she would not need to hurry. But while he was opening the milk carton it spilled and made a big puddle on the tablecloth.

The second story, the one involving deliberate but negligible damage, is as follows:

There was a young boy named David. One day his mother was out shopping and David thought it might be fun to secretly take some cookies and milk. First he got the cookies from the cookie jar and then he poured the milk. But while he was drinking the milk, a few drops spilled from the glass and made a little stain on the tablecloth.

After hearing both stories, the children were asked to explain whether one of the children was naughtier than the other or whether both were equally naughty. Piaget found that until the age of ten, responses fell into two categories:

1. *Moral realism.* In this stage, children argue that the amount of damage caused determines the character's guilt. To them, motives for particular actions do not enter the picture. John, the boy who wished to help his mother, is guilty because he made a large puddle; however, David, the boy secretly taking cookies and milk, is not guilty because the stain was small. Piaget calls this stage "moral realism" because the choice is based on some real, observable result (the amount of damage) rather than on the more abstract cause (the person's intent).
2. *Subjective responsibility.* In this stage, children determine a character's guilt by the nature of intent or motive. To these children, the boy who wanted to help his mother but caused a great deal of damage is less guilty than the boy who participated in an improper act that resulted in little damage. Piaget calls this the stage of "subjective responsibility" since the child takes into account the intents (the subjective state) of the characters in the story.

Piaget determined that the great majority of responses from children of preschool age fall into the category of moral realism. He contended that there are several reasons for this:

1. Parents and teachers are usually realistic themselves. Some adults punish a child more for breaking five glasses unintentionally than for breaking one intentionally. And since adults are respected, so are their rules. An implication of this contention is that if adults (teachers and parents) move away from "realistic" methods of punishing children toward subjective methods, then the children will move more easily toward subjective moral reasoning, too.

2. Children at this preschool age possess egocentric patterns of thought and since they cannot realistically see things from points of view different from their own, they cannot see another's need for truth or for expecting certain behaviors from them. They consequently are not aware of the fact that their "lies" or misbehaviors are deceiving or unpleasant to others.

These two reasons are extremely important for you, the preschool teacher, because they give rise to the classroom interaction that you employ. If we interpret Piaget properly, then we realize that a unilateral respect for the wishes of adults is an unavoidable pattern of moral growth in young children. For this reason, they seek to be guided by adults and wish to have standards of behavior established for them. You must establish those standards of behavior for the children thoughtfully because they cannot understand the rationale behind your regulations. However, this does not imply that these teacher-oriented techniques should continue throughout the child's schooling.

Piaget contends that, while the stages he describes are loosely age-determined, two major factors may alter children's moral orientation: *maturation* and *experience*. Experience can be gained through a guided examination of motives in natural classroom situations involving moral judgments or in fabricated stories like the pair illustrated earlier. There are not many specific suggestions for classroom applications of Piaget's theory of moral development, however, because they were not part of his original research goals. The major purpose of his work in this area was to stimulate further research and experimentation that would culminate in the development of appropriate interaction strategies. To that end, Lawrence Kohlberg has taken Piaget's basic ideas and incorporated them into his own work, which is particularly related to concepts of stage sequence and moral reasoning.

Lawrence Kohlberg

Lawrence Kohlberg became interested in the Piagetian scheme of moral development in 1955. He sought to validate the ideas by carrying out intensive studies throughout the world. Kohlberg found that, despite differences in cultural, social, economic, and religious backgrounds, all individuals move through six stages of moral development:[4]

Preconventional Level: Egocentric in Nature

□ *Stage 1.* To be "well-behaved" means blind obedience to an adult authority figure. The child does not consider underlying moral issues in determining goodness or badness but acts either because of the physical consequences involved (punishment, reward) or because of his view of the physical powers of adults (teacher, parent, and so on).

□ *Stage 2.* The child is basically self-centered at this stage and regards goodness or badness on the basis of whether it satisfies his personal needs. Children begin to consider the feelings of others, but elements of fairness and equal sharing are interpreted in a manner of "you do me a favor and maybe someday I'll do one for you." Children are out to make the best "deal" and do not really consider elements of loyalty, gratitude, or justice as they make their decisions.

Conventional Level: Orientation to Conformity

□ *Stage 3.* Good behavior is that which pleases or helps others. Children conform to what they imagine to be a "good" or "nice" person and begin to see things from another's viewpoint for the first time. Behavior begins to be judged on the basis of intent—"he means well" becomes important. Children are strongly oriented to a good boy–nice girl label.

□ *Stage 4.* The child is again oriented to obeying authority and following fixed rules as in stage 1, but now for reasons of a "law and order" orientation. A good person does one's duty, shows respect for authority, and maintains the given social order for its own sake. One earns respect by performing dutifully.

Postconventional Level: Individual Moral Principles

□ *Stage 5.* Standards critically examined and agreed upon by the whole society guide decisions regarding goodness or badness. Aside from what is constitutionally and democratically agreed upon, right or wrong is a matter of personal opinion. The result is an emphasis on the "legal point of view," but with an emphasis on the possibility of changing laws, rather than freezing them as in stage 4.

□ *Stage 6.* Decisions regarding right and wrong are made in terms of conscience and *self-chosen* ethical principles that are logical, consistent, and universal.

Stage theories of moral development attempt to explain the process by which young children move from self-centered behaviors toward those behaviors that result from a concern for others.

To summarize, preconventional children act because of the physical consequences involved or because their own needs can be satisfied. Children at
the conventional level tend to conform to social order and are motivated to
maintain the rules established by the family, school, group, or nation. People
at the postconventional level tend to reason individually and are concerned
with self-chosen moral and ethical principles. Kohlberg does not assign age
designations to each level, but since his theory is so closely identified with
Piaget's, we can assume that preschool children operate at the preconventional level while most upper elementary and junior high students function
on the conventional level. Kohlberg found that a surprisingly high 80 percent
of the adult population has become frozen at the conventional level, "law and
order."

Kohlberg presents the following considerations concerning individual
progress through each stage:[5]

1. *"True" stages always occur in the same order.* Moral reasoning of the preconventional kind *always* takes place before conventional thought.
2. *All movement through the stages is forward in sequence.* Once a child has
   begun to reason on the conventional level, for example, he or she will
   never return to the reasoning patterns associated with the preconventional level. Of course, many times children will be half in and half out of a
   certain stage and will seem to be moving backward, but this characteristic only indicates a pattern of growth from one stage to the next and not a
   regression.
3. *The stages cannot be skipped.* They represent an "invariant developmental
   sequence," which means that they come one at a time and always in the
   same order.
4. *Some individuals move farther and faster through the stages than other
   individuals.* Differences in achieving various levels of moral reasoning
   can be compared to the differences in achieving various levels of cognitive skills.
5. *The movement from stage to stage is not an automatic process.* Individuals
   may stop at any given stage and apply those reasoning processes to all the
   moral situations they encounter throughout their lives.

Kohlberg's approach to affective education is based on the assumption
that growth through the stages can be stimulated by involving children in
hypothetical "moral dilemmas"—that is, stories in which individuals are
faced with situations involving trust, fairness, or taking advantage. Children
are encouraged to examine such situations and to make judgments about the
various actions the characters may take. Here is an example of a moral
dilemma suitable for children age 4 and up.

*Mark and his brother James were walking in the park one day. As they
skipped by an empty park bench, Mark heard a sad little cry. He looked beneath the bench and called to James, "Look at the sad little kitten. It looks
so skinny and hungry. I think I'll take it home to wash it and feed it."*

Teachers engage children in group discussions of moral dilemmas in order to help them grow through Kohlberg's stages of moral development.

"Don't forget what daddy said," James answered. "He told you never to bring home lost animals because our apartment building doesn't allow pets."

"But look how much it seems to like me," argued Mark. "I would feel awful if I left it here to die."

"Well, you can do what you want," said James. "I feel sorry for the kitten, too, but what will happen to our family if the landlord discovers our pet?"

Ronald Galbraith and Thomas Jones suggest a teaching plan that can be used to encourage children to think about the difficult decision faced by the characters in this moral dilemma.[6] (See the box on page 86).

When the children share their responses to such story situations, they provide you with insight into the levels of moral reasoning at which they are operating. The stages of moral reasoning are not defined by the decision itself, but rather by the *reasons* given for each decision. Here are some examples for the first moral dilemma. (Only the first three of Kohlberg's stages are illustrated because children of ages four through six are not likely to have gone beyond stage 1 or stage 2 in their thinking.)

Stage 1

☐ "Mark and James *shouldn't* take the kitten home because their father told them not to. They'll have to always worry about getting caught. They'll get in trouble."

☐ "The boys *should* take the kitten home because if they let the kitten die, they get in trouble. You'll be blamed for not saving it."

Stage 2

☐ "The boys *shouldn't* take the kitten home because when they get it there it might run back to the park and die anyway. So, going through all that bother might not do Mark and James any good."

□ "Mark and James *should* take the kitten home. If they get caught, they could take it back and wouldn't get much punishment. Besides, if this building won't allow pets, it might be best to go somewhere else."

Stage 3

□ "Mark and James *shouldn't* take the kitten home because the landlord will think they're bad for breaking the rules. After they take it home, they'll worry about how they lied to their father. They won't be able to face anyone anymore."

□ "The boys *should* take the kitten home because their father would understand they did it because the kitten was sick. If they leave the kitten to die, they'll be bad and will never have friends again."

After children are confronted with the moral issue, the teacher should follow these basic suggestions to ensure a smooth discussion:

1. *Focus on reasons.* Final decisions are important, but they are not enough. Children need to examine their reasoning and the reasoning of others as they justify their decisions. This process of stating your reasons and being challenged by others makes children aware of other forms of reasoning and encourages them to move toward the thinking associated with higher levels of moral reasoning.

TEACHING PLAN FOR PRESENTING A MORAL DILEMMA

WARM-UP QUESTIONS (BEFORE THE STORY) How many of you have a kitten? How did you get your kitten? Did anyone find it? How many of you live in an apartment building? Does your apartment building have any rules concerning animals? (or) Did you ever hear of an apartment building that had rules against having animals?

PRESENTATION Explain to the students that you are going to tell them a short story (accompanied by pictures, if you can find them) about two boys who have found a stray kitten and can't decide whether or not to keep it. The boys' names are Mark and James and they need help as they decide what to do. Tell the story to the children.

DISCUSSION (AFTER THE STORY) The purpose of these questions is to clarify the story. Where were Mark and James walking? How did they find the kitten? What problem did they face after they found the kitten?

These questions stimulate the children to make individual responses to the dilemma: What should Mark and James do? Why do you think apartments have rules against keeping kittens? Do Mark and James have a right to break those rules? What is the best thing the two boys might do to help the kitten?

2. *Choose discussion groups.* Mix the stages of moral development within each discussion group so that children at the lower stages of moral reasoning will benefit from exposure to the thinking of children operating at higher levels.
3. *Give direction and guidance.* Allow as many students as possible an opportunity to respond to the dilemma. Sometimes, shy students will be reluctant to do so. In such cases, simply ask them to react to another's comment: "Harold, do you agree with Marge, or do you have another idea?" or "Jane, many of your classmates think the boys should keep the kitten. What do you think?"
4. *Encourage undecided children.* Moral issues can be thoroughly perplexing. Decisions are not always easily reached. Other children may attempt to exert peer pressure on the undecided child to win him over to their side, and it becomes extremely difficult for some children to withstand such pressure. They fear their hesitation may be interpreted as a sign of weakness. To prevent such children from developing a "going along with the crowd" attitude, you should try to convince them that it's okay to remain uncertain until they have had enough time to make up their minds.
5. *Avoid giving your own opinion.* If you are to effectively move children away from stage 1 reasoning, they must not look to you as being the traditionally constant source of "right" answers. They must be encouraged to see right and wrong from a point of view other than that of

---

FOLLOW-UP Once the discussion runs its course, one of several related group activities may be introduced.

Puppetry. Use sock, paper bag, or any variety of hand or finger puppets, and give the children a role to take—for example, Mark, James, and landlord, Mark and James's father, and the kitten. Ask the children to talk for the puppets and decide the best thing for Mark and James to do in this situation.

Story Expansion. If the original story does not present conflict for the children, another aspect may be presented. You may think of an expansion as another chapter in the story.

Here is an example: Mark and James brought home the kitten and secretly hid it in their bedroom closet. One day, the apartment manager knocked on the door and told the boys' father that someone reported to him that they were keeping a kitten someplace in their apartment. The landlord reminded the father that the building rule said that no one was to have any pets in the building and that the family would have to leave their apartment if they did not get rid of the kitten within two weeks. The father goes to the boys' bedroom and asks, "Are you boys hiding a kitten in your bedroom?"

Ask the questions: Is it fair for Mark and James to bring the kitten to the building? Should they tell their father the truth? What is worse, breaking the rule or not telling the truth to their father?

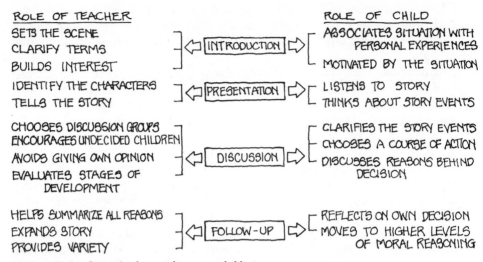

Figure 3-1   Strategy for guiding moral dilemmas.

authority and must be led to understand that the most important products of moral discussions are personal ideas and feelings.

6. *Provide variety.* Preschool children need conditions that vary—especially when considering moral issues. Use a variety of puppetry or other creative dramatic situations to improve and invigorate your program. Children develop a great sensitivity to puppets, for example, as they actually "become" other persons. Their imaginations take over and allow them to verbalize and act in ways that they normally would not consider.

A summary of strategy for guiding moral discussions is outlined in Figure 3-1.

Perhaps the most important role of the teacher is that of identifying the reasoning levels of their children and making sure that the children are exposed to reasoning that is one stage higher than their own. Children easily understand the reasoning that takes place below their own level and reject it as being simplistic. But they grow in their abilities to reason only by listening to the arguments of those reasoning one stage above their own. Children cannot understand the arguments of those who are reasoning more than one stage above their own. Figure 3-2 illustrates these concepts.

Young children enjoy change. Therefore, using stories of moral dilemmas regularly may tend to disinterest them. Look for commercial materials such as films, filmstrips, and audiotapes or records for more variety.

Kohlberg's theory of moral development is doubly important since it implies that the type of arguments to which children are exposed need to be carefully considered in teacher dialogue. Consider for a moment the scene transpiring when two children are sent into the classroom for fighting on the playground. The teacher looks at both children and focuses on the sobbing tears of one child who is wiping away a trickle of red coming from his nose (he is obviously the loser). The first question usually fired at the children in

marked child. "Well, how would you like to have this sort of thing happen to you?" fires the teacher. Her question is met by a slight shrug and downward turn of the eyes. "Look at me when I'm talking!" demands the teacher. "Answer my question."

Tears start welling up in the eyes of the "winner" as he desperately tries to answer the teacher's question. However, the only response he manages is a barely audible "I don't know."

Frantic by this time, the teacher shakes the child and blurts, "Okay, Smartie, you just sit in for one week during your outdoor periods and think about it!"

If we analyze that situation according to Kohlberg's ideas, we might assume that the "winner" was a child operating at stage 1 of moral reasoning. He knew he had done wrong, but only because he had broken a rule established by the teacher, no fighting on the playground. However, in her disciplinary action, the teacher asked the child to reason at stage 3—to put himself into the shoes of another person. Therefore, the child became frustrated and cried because he truly did not understand the type of response desired by the teacher.

An important part of the teacher's use of Kohlberg's ideas is to help children reexamine their actions and their personal reasons for them before they engage in new and different reasoning patterns that require reordering

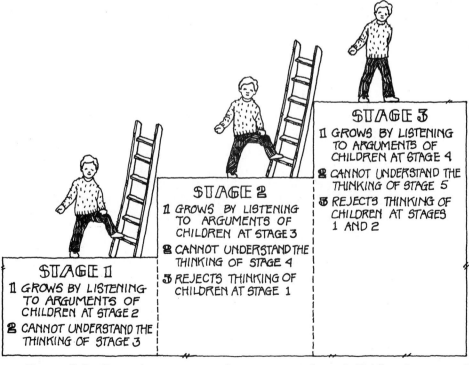

Figure 3-2 Principles accounting for movement through Kohlberg's stages of moral development.

of thinking processes and seeking out new ways of organizing feelings. All children need to be aware that they are members of a group and that they have a responsibility toward the group. For that reason, we usually have only a few restrictions in preschool settings, but they should be rigidly enforced. Those acts usually prohibited are ones that endanger the welfare or restrict the rights of others. Children must be aware that there are things they can and cannot do if the environment is to be safe. You must explain the reasons to them, at the same time understanding that their comprehension of your explanation may be extremely limited. They will usually listen and obey because you are the authority figure in the classroom who has gained their basic trust (stage 1). In many instances, children *demand* your limits.

Children do not automatically respect the rights of their peers at school. You must help them by explaining how others feel when something happens. If it was the "winner" who started the fight, for example, you may want to explain that "He won't want to play with you anymore if you always fight," or "I understand how much you dislike someone who knocks over your blocks, but you don't need to hit him."

This entire area of handling feelings is extremely sensitive. Guiding a child requires a great deal of personal insight. "Overdirection may distort his development; so may lack of direction. He needs time to learn through suitable experiences. He is sure to make some mistakes in the process of learning. . . . If we deal calmly and confidently with unacceptable behavior, we will create the kind of climate in which the child is helped to master his impulses and to direct his own behavior. We will be using authority in constructive ways."[7]

VALUES CLARIFICATION

Values clarification is an alternative approach to affective education. It was designed to help children examine their own values so that they are able to: obtain the values that best suit them and their environment; adjust themselves to a changing world; and ultimately play an effective role in influencing the way the world changes. The values clarification approach is most often associated with Louis Raths, Merrill Harmin, and Sidney Simon, authors of *Values and Teaching*.[8] They believe that children acquire values only as they progress through the three processes of choosing, prizing, and acting. To Raths, Harmin, and Simon, a value is defined when all seven of the following subprocesses are satisfied:

Choosing
1. It must be chosen freely (without coercion).
2. It must come from among alternatives (two or more choices must be involved).
3. It must be chosen after thoughtful consideration of the consequences of each alternative (impulsive choices do not lead to true values).

Teachers encourage children to "open up" and talk more about their ideas or accomplishments by using a clarifying response.

Prizing

4. It must be cherished; you must be happy with the choice.
5. You must be willing to affirm the choice publicly (you want to tell others).

Acting

6. You must do something with the choice (it must give direction to your life).
7. It must be used repeatedly, in other patterns of life.

If the teacher wants to help children develop values according to the values clarification theory, she must keep the definition of values in mind. Raths, Harmin, and Simon state that the teaching process flows naturally from this definition of values. That is, teachers are advised to:[9]

1. Encourage children to make choices, and to make them freely.
2. Help them discover and examine available alternatives when faced with choices.
3. Help children weigh alternatives thoughtfully, reflecting on the consequences of each.
4. Encourage children to consider what it is that they prize and cherish.
5. Give them opportunities to make public affirmations of their choices.
6. Encourage them to act, behave, and live in accordance with their choices.
7. Help them to examine repeated behaviors or patterns in their lives.

The basic technique for achieving these skills through the values clarification approach involves a "clarifying response," a way of responding to children that results in their considering what they have chosen, what they prize, or what they are doing. The comments are not designed to do big things; they merely prod the child to think. Here is a classroom situation illustrating the use of a clarifying response:

Maurice: I just learned how to ride a bicycle for the first time!
Teacher: Oh, how wonderful! How did it make you feel when you first learned to ride it?
Maurice: I felt like a big boy. It was a lot of fun.
Teacher: Did you show anyone else how you learned to ride the bicycle?

Notice that the teacher's response was designed to encourage the child to think more deeply about his accomplishment, but not to start an extended conversation.

Joe Frost and Joan Kissinger supply these additional situations, with suggested clarifying responses that help children examine their ideas.

Ben complained to his teacher that it was too noisy in the classroom. When the class was all together for group time, the teacher guided the discussion as follows: "How do you like our room when you're trying to work?" "What good is it to have our room like that?" "Should it be like that all the time?"

Ann wanted to play in the sandbox and was throwing sand at Jeffrey to keep him out. The teacher sat down at the edge of the sandbox beside her and asked: "What do you think might happen if you throw sand at Jeffrey, Ann?" "What else might happen?" "What can we do about it?" "Do you think you would want to throw sand at someone again?"

One morning, during a group daily planning time, the teacher asked: "When you come to school in the morning, do you know exactly what learning center you want to choose to work in or do you have to look for things to do?" "What do you like best? Why?" "What do you like least? Why?" "Do you like to work alone or with other children? All of the time?"[10]

By now you may sense some criteria for effective clarifying responses. The following are among the essential elements of such responses:[11]

1. Do not criticize or evaluate the child's response.
2. Put the responsibility for looking at his ideas and thinking what he wants on the child himself.
3. Do not try to do big things. The purpose of a clarifying response is to set a mood. Each response is only one of many; its effect is cumulative.
4. Do not intend for the clarifying response to develop into an extended discussion. The idea is for the child to think, and he usually does that best alone. Allow for two or three rounds of dialogue and then offer to break off the conversation with some honest phrase, such as "Nice talking with you," or "I see what you mean now," or "Your idea was very interesting. Let's talk about it again some other time."
5. Do not respond to everything everyone says or does in the classroom.

6. Direct clarifying responses to *individuals* whenever possible. A topic in which Henry needs clarification may be of no interest to Mae. Issues of general concern may warrant a general response to the entire class, but even here the individual must ultimately do the thinking for himself.

7. Use clarifying responses in situations where there are no "right" answers, such as in situations involving feelings, attitudes, or beliefs. They should *never* be used to draw a child's thinking toward a predetermined answer.

Clarifying responses are not to be used mechanically, but rather creatively and with insight. There are several responses, however, that experienced teachers have found very useful with preschool children. Some of these are listed below. As you read through the list, try to elaborate on the items and add to the suggestions.

"Are you proud of that?"
"Do you really like that idea?"
"Does that make you feel good?"
"Are you happy about your choice?"
"How did you feel when that happened?"
"Did you think of any other way to do it?"
"When did you first get such an idea?"
"Have you felt this way for a long time?"
"Did you do it yourself?"
"When might you use that idea?"
"What do you mean?"
"What would happen if your ideas worked out?"
"Would you really do that?"
"What other choices did (do) you have?"
"Should everyone go along with your idea?"
"Is that important to you?"
"Do you do that often?"
"Would you like to tell others about your idea?"
"Do you have a reason for doing (or saying) that?"
"Would you do the same thing again?"
"How do you know it's right? (good?)"
"Is that something that you like very much?"
"Would other people believe that?"
"Is this what I understood you to say?"
"Would you do that again?"

As you progressed through this list, you should have related each comment to the seven components of Rath's valuing process. Those seven criteria are valuable guides in helping you think of other useful clarifying responses. In one way or another, all clarifying responses should be designed to encourage children to choose, prize, or act as outlined by the value theory.

In addition to the clarifying response, Raths, Harmin, and Simon suggest other activities for initiating values discussions.[12] One example is "A Story Without an Ending." In this activity the teacher obtains a short story. She

Children are encouraged to make choices among alternatives through techniques such as Values Voting.

reads it to the children but cuts it off before there is any solution to the problem. (Dr. Seuss stories are especially good for this.) The children then take over and discuss what *should* have been done, how this situation was like something in their own lives, and so on.

Sidney Simon, Leland Howe, and Howard Kirschenbaum offer 79 activities that can be used with individuals or groups from preschool age through adulthood.[13] Each strategy is designed to encourage growth in one or more of the seven processes of valuing. Sample activities from their book, *Values Clarification*, include those in the box on page 97.

In general, the two major approaches to affective education, stage theories and values clarification, agree as to their major overall goals:

1. Giving children experiences in thinking critically about issues
2. Giving them opportunities to share feelings with others
3. Giving them a chance to develop cooperative problem-solving skills
4. Giving them a chance to apply value skills in their own lives

HUMANISTIC PSYCHOLOGY

If neither of these two popular approaches to values education appeals to you at this time, you may wish to approach the development of affective skills from a psychological perspective. Many humanistic psychologists, including Carl Rogers and Thomas Gordon, say that if children are put into a supportive social environment and encouraged to tune into their feelings and the feelings of others, and if they are taught communication skills that maxi-

Infants have operative values—they show preference for one kind of object over another.

mize interpersonal understanding, then they will naturally tend to make wise judgments and will use their experiences to correct judgments that are unwise. A key implication in this theory is that teachers should be honest, warm, and empathetic in the classroom setting.

Rogers explains his theory by pointing out that the term *value* can be used in two general ways:[14]

1. *Operative values:* the tendency of individuals to show preference for one kind of object or objective rather than another. For example, a young child reaches out for a red ball instead of a blue one. The value choice, many times unconscious, is made simply by selecting one object and rejecting another.
2. *Conceived values:* the tendency of individuals to show preference for a symbolized object. Usually the individual employs conceptual thinking as he anticipates the outcome of such a symbolized object. For example, a choice such as "an eye for an eye" is considered a conceived value.

Infants have an operative approach to values: They prefer those experiences that enhance ("actualize") their existence and reject those that do not. For example, hunger is negatively valued but food is positively valued. They are not yet influenced by parents, peers, churches, teachers, or other "experts" in the field. Eventually, they lose this operative approach and move toward actions that bring them social approval, affection, or esteem.

The infant needs love, wants it, tends to behave in ways which will bring a repetition of this wanted experience. But this brings complications. He pulls baby sister's hair and finds it satisfying to hear her wails and protests. He then hears that he is "a naughty, bad boy," and this may be reinforced by a slap on the hand.

He is cut off from affection. As this experience is repeated, and many, many others like it, he gradually learns that what "feels good" is often "bad" in the eyes of others. Then the next step occurs, in which he comes to take the same attitude himself which these others have taken.[15]

The major concern of humanistic psychologists, then, is to determine how preschool teachers can help children develop social awareness while helping them maintain many of the unbridled decision-making characteristics of the child in infancy. Rogers made the following assumptions while suggesting desirable methods of achieving those goals:[16]

1. All children possess a natural valuing system that allows them to adjust their behavior so as to achieve greatest self-enhancement.
2. This valuing system is effective in achieving self-enhancement only to the degree that the individual opens himself to the experiences around him.
3. One way of opening the child to experience is through a relationship in which he is prized as an individual, in which the experiencing going on within him is understood and valued, and in which he is given freedom to experience his own feelings and those of others without being threatened while doing so.

Sarah Leeper et al. used the ideas of Marion L. Leiserson in creating a free, nonthreatening environment for young children. They point out that in a loving environment, the teacher:[17]

1. Looks at each child as a unique person and gives the child opportunities to develop a positive self-concept. She may say, for example, "Erik's feeling very grown-up. His new shirt is size 5."
2. Helps each child feel accepted and that he belongs to the group. She learns the children's names quickly, is courteous, and shows the children that she is happy to see them. For example, she may say, "I'm glad that you are feeling better. We missed you yesterday."
3. Lets children learn by experience, sometimes through mistakes and at other times through successes. The child may say, "My caterpillar crawled out because I didn't have the top on the jar."
4. Helps the child understand that he creates his own emotional environment. She helps him see the effects of his actions on others. The teacher says, "She was knocked down when you bumped her. Is there something you could do to help her feel better?"
5. Listens to children. What the child has to say is important and his comments indicate concepts that he has developed. If the child tears the paper cover of a book, the teacher explains, "After the story you can help me mend the cover." The child responds, "Okay, but can I sit on your lap now and hear the story? Then I can be quiet."

Such openness to experience is said to lead to value directions such as sincerity, independence, self-direction, self-knowledge, social responsivity, social responsibility, and the establishment of loving, interpersonal relationships.

The humanistic classroom, then, is one in which open, flexible teachers, or "facilitators," provide intensive group experiences that allow for freedom for personal expression, interpersonal communication, and exploration of feelings. Each child is encouraged to put aside defenses and facades in such a setting and to relate directly and openly to everyone in the classroom. And once the children feel good about themselves, they are able to develop fuller social relationships in a climate of openness and trust.

Humanistic psychology places primary emphasis, then, directly on the child's development of a positive sense of self. If children lack this positive sense, they will not perceive themselves as worthy persons and will not strive

ACTIVITIES TO CLARIFY VALUES

VALUES VOTING The *purpose* of Values Voting is to encourage children to make public affirmation on a variety of values issues.

Procedure: The teacher reads aloud one by one questions that begin with the words "How many of you . . . ?" Those who wish to answer in the affirmative raise their hands. Those who wish to answer negatively point their thumbs down. Those who are undecided fold their arms.

How many of you: have a pet at home? like asparagus? think school is fun? have a favorite TV show? like to be teased? sometimes tease others? would like your mother to have a new baby? watch Sesame Street? like strawberry ice cream? think it's okay for boys to play with dolls?

PROUD WHIP The *purpose* of Proud Whip is to help children become aware of the degree to which they prize or cherish their beliefs and actions and to encourage them to do more things in which they can take pride.

Procedure: The teacher asks the children to respond with the words, "I'm proud of . . ." or "I'm proud that . . ."

I'm proud that my father (mother) . . . , I'm proud that I keep healthy by . . . , I'm proud when other kids say that I . . . , I'm proud that I once made someone happy by . . . , I'm proud that on my own I can . . . , I'm proud when my teacher tells me . . . .

MAGIC BOX The *purpose* of Magic Box is to help students think about what they value.

Procedure: The teacher shows the children a very special magic box. It can contain anything that the children want it to contain. The teacher then asks the children, "If you came home from school today and found the magic box waiting for you to open, what would be in it?" The children should share their answers with the class.

The teacher then might ask questions like:

☐ What would you want in the box for your mother?
☐ What would you want for your best friend?
☐ What is the smallest thing you would want?
☐ What would you want for poor people?

Humanistic psychologists tell us that the key element in helping youngsters develop a system of values is to open the child up to experiences and to develop a relationship that shows he is prized as an individual.

for further self-actualization. Several commercial programs have recently been designed to implement the goals of the humanists. They focus on furthering these four major sources of self-concept:

1. Impressions received from others
2. Accumulated experiences
3. An ability to internalize experiences into thought processes
4. A capacity to evaluate personal performance realistically on the basis of internalized standards

In 1967 Uvaldo Palomares and Harold Bissell created a humanistic values program designed to enhance a child's ability to develop high self-esteem. They call it the *Magic Circle.*

Magic Circle

The Magic Circle program involves small-group exchange sessions lasting 15 to 20 minutes that encourage group interaction and acceptance of feelings and attitudes. The Magic Circle box (page 99) gives a typical script for the program.

A teacher sensitive to the Magic Circle technique of dealing with children's feelings would plan sharing and discussing sessions such as the following situation described by Mary Olsen:

Teacher: "Some words people use make us feel bad or make us feel happy. Different words make different people feel bad. I don't feel happy when

THE MAGIC CIRCLE PROGRAM

1. Teacher and about seven or eight children sit in a circle.
2. Teacher gives a cue and waits for a child to respond. Cues for discussion are grouped into three categories:
   a. *Awareness:* For example: "Something that made me feel bad," or "What I like about my pet," or "A bad feeling I once had."
   b. *Mastery:* For example, "Some things at school that I can do for myself," or "Something I was afraid of but I did anyway," or "Some things I can't do for myself."
   c. *Social Interaction:* For example, "A time we did something for each other," or "How I made someone feel good," or "Somebody did something that I didn't like."
3. Teacher encourages active listening. Child 1 talks on the cued subject and the teacher feeds back to that child. She may feed back a feeling, such as "How did that make you feel?" or she may paraphrase a child's statement, such as, "When you were telling us about the lake, you mentioned how much you like to swim. You said it as if it made you very proud." As each child talks, the teacher calmly looks at him and nods, smiles, or uses other gestures to indicate interest. When each child is finished contributing, the teacher should thank him for his idea.
4. Teacher begins to vary the procedure.
   a. As conversation slows she may review what each child has said by saying, "Let's see where we've come" and then asking if anyone in the group would review what was said.
   b. She may focus on similarities and differences by saying, "Jim said something that sounds like what Amy was saying. Who can tell us what it was?"
   c. Encourage the shy children through an invitation such as, "Jane, would you like a turn today?" Children should not be forced to speak, however.
5. Teacher leads a roundup. At this point, all the contributions are summarized and the feelings associated with each event are identified. The teacher may say, "Let's go back and tell what each person did," or "Who can feed back just the feeling?"

someone calls me stupid. Did someone ever use words that made you feel bad or unhappy?"

Billy: "My sister calls me 'stinky.' "

Teacher: "How does that make you feel?" *(no response from child)*

Teacher: "Do you like to be called 'stinky'?"

Child: "No. It makes me feel bad."

Teacher: "Would someone else like to share a word."

Susan: "It makes me feel bad when someone says, 'Shut up.' "

Teacher: "I know what you mean; it makes me feel angry when someone says 'shut up' to me."

John: "Big boys say, 'Get out of here.' "

Teacher: "How does that make you feel?"

John: "I don't like it."

Susan: "My sister calls me 'stupid.' "

Chris: " 'You can't play.' I don't like it when they say that."

Teacher: "I can tell by your voice that you feel hurt when someone won't let you play. Alice, you look like you have something to say."

Alice: "My brother calls me 'puny.' I don't like it."

Teacher: "It isn't a nice feeling inside when a brother calls you 'puny.' Did anyone ever say some words that made you feel happy?" *(Two children start to smile but don't respond verbally to the questions.)*

Teacher: "I can tell that you're thinking of something that makes you happy because you're smiling."

Chris: "You get to ride a trike."

Teacher: "How would that make you feel?"

Chris: "I'd say, 'Goodie,' and I'd tell everyone."

Susan (blurts out): "I like you!"

Teacher: "How does that make you feel when someone says, 'I like you'?"

Susan: "It makes me feel good."

Teacher: "It makes me feel happy when my son says to me, 'Mom, that pie was delicious.' John, what did someone say to make you feel good?"

John: "Someone said, 'You're nice.' "

Teacher: "How did that make you feel?"

John: "I liked it."

Susan: "I like it when it's my birthday."

Teacher: "What do you like about your birthday?"

Susan: "The presents make me happy."

Teacher (smiles and nods): "I like presents, too. Words can make people feel happy or sad. Different words can make people feel happy or sad. I'm going to say something that might make you happy. I think you did a very nice job of sharing how you feel."[18]

In this example, then, the teacher encouraged the children to talk openly about their feelings and emotions. You will no doubt have noticed that the Magic Circle guildelines above were not rigidly or mechanically followed, but the teacher's active and friendly leadership helped the children recognize and accept each other's feelings. The Magic Circle program, under the leadership of Palomares and Bissell, has available lesson plans and teacher's guides to direct teachers in improving children's self-confidence and awareness. (Complete teachers' guides and session formats can be obtained from: Human Development Training Institute, Inc., 7574 University Avenue, La Mesa, CA 92041.)

DUSO

Another source recommended for the self-awareness goals of values education is the DUSO kit. Developing Understanding of Self and Others (DUSO) is a program of activities, with an accompanying kit of materials, designed to help children understand social-emotional behavior. The materials are contained in a large metal carrying case and include the following:

1. Teacher's manual—contains a wealth of activities and special guidelines for their use.
2. Storybooks—contain theme-centered stories designed to catch the imagination of the children. Each 10-×-12 storybook contains 41 stories and 200 full-color illustrations.
3. Records or cassettes—songs and stories are done in this form to heighten the children's interest. They contain the "Hey, Duso" and "So Long, Duso" songs that mark the beginning and ending of each story and are loved by all children.
4. Posters—over 30 posters are included in the kit. Each poster summarizes pictorially a major point from each story.
5. Puppets—two puppets make up the central characters in the program, Duso and Flopsie. Other puppets are used in various ways. Duso is an understanding dolphin who helps lead children to a better understanding of behavior. Flopsie is an inquisitive flounder who provides a model for change.
6. Miscellaneous—role-playing situations and puppet plays are designed to help children dramatize real-life situations.

The program follows this cycle:

1. The children hear a stimulating story containing a problem situation.
2. A positive discussion follows the story.
3. A role-playing or puppet activity helps children dramatize a similar situation.
4. Several supplementary individual or group activities are suggested in the manual.

(For more information, write to: American Guidance Service, Inc., Publishers' Building, Circle Pines, MN 55014.)

SOME FINAL THOUGHTS

You no doubt have many questions about values programs. In choosing a values program for your preschool, however, you must first have a clear idea of just what you want to accomplish. Then, in making your choice, find the answers to questions such as these: What kind of individual do you want to help develop? What sorts of goals do you want for your values program? What kinds of learning activities will be available for the children? What skills should you, the teacher, develop in order for your children to develop valuing skills? At what age should your program begin? Once you have found answers to these questions, you are on your way to constructing a sound values program for your preschool classroom.

NOTES

1. Jean Jacques Rousseau, "Selections from Emilius," in *Three Thousand Years of Educational Wisdom*, ed. Robert Ulich (Cambridge, Mass.: Harvard University Press, 1971), p. 397.
2. Ibid.
3. Herbert Ginsburg and Sylvia Opper, *Piaget's Theory of Intellectual Development* (Englewood Cliffs, N.J.: Prentice-Hall, 1969), pp. 100–102.
4. Adapted from Lawrence Kohlberg, "The Claim to Moral Adequacy of a Highest State of Moral Judgment," *The Journal of Philosophy* 70, no. 18 (October 25, 1973): 631–632.
5. Lawrence Kohlberg, "The Child as a Moral Philosopher," *Psychology Today* 2, no. 4 (September 1968): 25–30.
6. Ronald E. Galbraith and Thomas M. Jones, *Moral Reasoning: A Teaching Handbook for Adapting Kohlberg to the Classroom* (Minneapolis, Minn.: Greenhaven Press, 1967), pp. 172–180.
7. Katherine H. Read, *The Nursery School: A Human Relations Laboratory* (Philadelphia: W. B. Saunders, 1971), pp. 108–109.
8. Louis E. Raths, Merrill Harmin, and Sidney B. Simon, *Values and Teaching* (Columbus, Ohio: Charles E. Merrill, 1966), p. 30.
9. Ibid., pp. 38–39.
10. Joe L. Frost and Joan B. Kissinger, *The Young Child and the Educative Process* (New York: Holt, Rinehart and Winston, 1976), p. 293.
11. Based on Raths, Harmin, and Simon, *Values and Teaching*, pp. 53–54.
12. Ibid., p. 117.
13. Sidney B. Simon, Leland W. Howe, and Howard Kirschenbaum, *Values Clarification* (New York: Hart Publishing, 1972).
14. Carl R. Rogers, "Toward a Modern Approach to Values: The Valuing Process in the Mature Person," in *Readings in Values Clarification*, ed. Howard Kirschenbaum and Sidney B. Simon (Minneapolis, Minn.: Winston Press, 1973), pp. 75–91.
15. Ibid., p. 79.
16. Ibid., p. 87.
17. Sarah Hammond Leeper et al., *Good Schools for Young Children*, 3d ed. (New York: Macmillan, 1974), pp. 295–296.
18. Mary Olsen, "It Makes Me Feel Bad When You Call Me 'Stinky,'" *Young Children* 26, no. 2 (December 1970), pp. 120–121.

4

Physical and Motor Development: Patterns of Fitness, Coordination, and Control

A balanced program of physical activity is not only fun, but it also enhances growth in all areas of the child's development. (*Tiger* by Bud Blake, courtesy of King Features Syndicate, Inc.)

Billy, a rather active five-year-old, normally gained great pleasure from outdoor play. He reveled in the variety of available physical activities but seemed to find the greatest satisfaction from participating in throwing and catching games with a partner. Billy's choice of partners was not extremely selective as he basically enjoyed playing with whomever would be willing to join him at the time. There never seemed to be cause for any conflicts as only a few children were interested in such activity, and those children were all generally at about the same ability level. One day, however, Andrew became interested in throwing the ball with Billy and a friend and eagerly rushed to the corner of the playground to join them. Billy willingly tossed the ball to Andrew and watched in surprise as the ball sailed by his rigid arms and rolled away. "Pick it up, Andrew, and throw it back," shouted Billy. Andrew, quite paunchy and slow, ambled toward the ball, fumbled with it for a moment, and finally picked it up. In preparing to toss it back to Billy, Andrew had great difficulty in coordinating his arm and leg movements. Finally, deciding that his left arm would be the best, Andrew awkwardly cocked it back, bent his body at a cumbersome angle, and stepped forward on the wrong foot to give the ball its momentum. It flew off, but landed only a short distance from Andrew's feet, much short of its target. At this time, Billy's original partner began to sense their superiority and soon began to badger and criticize Andrew. "C'mon, Fatty!" he shouted. "My grandmother can throw better than you." "Yeah," others joined in, "I never saw a whale try to throw a ball

103

*before." Crushed beyond words, Andrew shrunk from the area and slowly
withdrew from the active game of ball.*

After this episode, Andrew may feel too rejected and discouraged to continue his "friendships." He may begin spending more and more time alone in
order to avoid the cruel jokes of his peers. Such situations often result in
crying spells and lead to additional rejection, learning problems, or possible
behavioral abnormalities. An ability to throw a ball, as well as the condition
of being overweight, is, of course, a very special attribute. Knowing about
these physical attributes and how they affect the entire realm of behavior and
intelligence is necessary for all early childhood educators, because many
aspects of development depend on children's bodies and their physical
growth. Consider the ability of Andrew to throw a ball, for instance. The act
involves many complex physical tasks and demands the development of
many complex physical systems, beginning with a visual system, which is
necessary for looking at and recognizing a ball. It includes the development
of the hand and arm, including the bones and muscles, all of which allow the
child to grasp the ball in a proper manner. It involves the development of the
brain and nervous system, which are essential for choosing whether to hold
the ball in the left hand or the right and for coordinating precise muscular movements such as opposition of movement between the arms and the
feet; for example, as the throwing arm moves back, the opposite foot moves
forward, shifting the child's weight to the front when the ball is released.
Naturally, as the child grows older, factors such as physical maturity,
appropriateness of experiences, and opportunities for practice determine just
how much better his throwing skills develop. Nevertheless, this one seemingly simple activity paves the way for more complicated tasks involving movement, coordination, and control.

Of course, the ability to throw a ball is a very personal skill, but it
illustrates exactly how much each child's life can be affected by physical
attributes. Throwing a ball well; running fast; jumping high; being tall,
short, fat, skinny, tall, clumsy; having red hair, black hair, or brown—all of
these physical features have a great effect on the way children are treated by
others. "Fatty," "Clumsy," "Canary Legs," "Tubby," "Bag of Bones," and other
tags are often directed at physical attributes and often cause children critical
emotional problems. Sound physical development, then, is important to the
total growth of a child, and the teacher has the big responsibility of providing
maximum opportunities for optimal physical growth.

PRINCIPLES OF PHYSICAL GROWTH

Physical development is usually discussed in terms of what is "normal"
for children at a certain age level. For example, the normal height and weight
of three-year-old boys has been determined to be 38 inches and 32¼ pounds.
These figures were established through a process of carefully measuring and

Physical maturity, opportunity for practice, and appropriateness of experience all determine how the young child's physical skills will develop.

observing thousands of growing children and arriving at an *average* weight and height figure. A "norm," then, is the average for a child at a certain age level, not some *ideal* level of development for that period. Keep these thoughts in mind as "normal" patterns of physical development are discussed throughout this chapter. Table 4-1 summarizes the normal growth patterns for children as they progress through infancy into young childhood.

A number of developmental principles account for the variations in rates of growth in different parts of the body for different individuals. Such principles are classified by researchers in their own unique ways, but they seem to fall into seven basic categories.

1. *Directional Growth:* In general, this principle of physical growth states that growth proceeds from the head down to the toes and from the center of the body outwards. In particular, the principle breaks down into two basic areas:

☐ *Cephalocaudal:* This Latin term meaning "from head to tail" states that the infant's development proceeds from the head to the tail end of the body. For instance, the child's head at birth comprises about one-quarter of its body, the rest being evenly divided between trunk and legs. In contrast, the adult's body is made up of about one-eighth head, one-half legs, and one-third trunk. Likewise, the muscles closest to the head are the first the child is able to control. Therefore, infants placed in a lying position are first able to raise their heads; then, as shoulder, arm, and stomach muscles develop, they become able to raise their shoulders, and eventually they are able to raise the entire upper part of their bodies. Gradually, as leg and thigh muscles develop, the children become able to raise their hips from the surface.

☐ *Proximodistal:* Another Latin term, this one meaning "from near to far," states that physical development proceeds from the center of the body to the extremities. The child first learns to control the shoulders and pelvis; then later, the elbows, wrists, knees, and ankles. For example, infants first use their shoulder muscles when reaching for an object, but, by the end of the first year, they begin to use and control their hand muscles and fingers.

2. *General to Specific Growth:* This principle of development explains that the developing being has a general shape when it is forming in the mother's womb and then it becomes progressively more specific. Likewise, the baby's original reflexive reactions progress from general to specific behaviors. For example, a pin prick to the bottom of a baby's foot may initially result in a general whole-body reaction—kicking, thrashing, and screaming. Later, the same stimulus may evoke a more specific, coordinated response, such as a quick withdrawal of the foot. The overall tendency in physical development is toward minimum, specified muscular involvement: large muscle to small muscle control.

Table 4-1   Average Heights and Weights of Children from Birth through the Preschool Years

	Height (in inches)		Weight (in pounds)	
Age	**Boys**	**Girls**	**Boys**	**Girls**
Birth	20	19¾	7½	7½
6 mo.	26	25¾	16¾	15¾
1 yr.	29½	29¼	22¼	21
1½ yr.	32¼	31¾	25¼	24¼
2 yr.	34½	34	27¾	27
2½ yr.	36¼	36	30	29½
3 yr.	38	37¾	32¼	31¾
3½ yr.	39¼	39¼	34¼	34
4 yr.	40¾	40½	36½	36¼
4½ yr.	42	42	38½	38½
5 yr.	43¼	43	41½	41
5½ yr.	45	44½	45½	44
6 yr.	46¼	45½	48¼	46½

By understanding principles and patterns of growth from infancy through young childhood, you begin to understand the types of experiences appropriate to children at different ages.

3. *Differentiation/Integration in Growth:* As the child moves from large, whole-body reactions toward smaller, specific reactions, he achieves the ability to *differentiate*. Once this state has been reached, the child begins to purposefully combine the random, smaller units of behavior into functional units (*integration*). For example, an infant may use the sucking reflex as a specialized response to hunger. Later, that reflex may be modified and integrated with other behaviors such as using the hands to grasp the food and guide it to the mouth. Physical growth continues as the child learns newer specific behaviors and combines them with others that have developed in the past.

4. *Variations in Growth:* Individuals vary in their growth rates in these two ways: (1) They vary from person to person, and (2) the various organs and systems within each individual grow at different rates. Anyone who has ever observed children recognizes that rates of growth vary from one child to another—some grow quickly; others more slowly. One of the most apparent observations of this principle is that girls are more physiologically mature at all ages than boys. This principle should help us understand what we can expect from children at various chronological ages, but to temper that understanding with a realization that each child is a unique human being and will grow according to his own personal rate.

5. *Optimal Tendency in Growth:* This principle states that individuals seek to reach their full potential for development. For example, suppose growth during a certain period is interrupted by a lack of food or exercise. The child attempts to make up for that lean period as soon as adequate provisions are made available; he soon catches up to normal growth expectancies and then

resumes a characteristic pattern of growth. Only if the deprivation is severe will the child exhibit permanent effects from it.

For children afflicted with some type of physical disability, this principle is especially apparent. Blind children, for example, learn to compensate for their lack of sight by sharpening other senses such as touch or hearing.

6. *Sequential Growth:* This principle, mainly influenced by the work of Gesell, explains that physical growth evolves through an orderly sequence; that is, the child must learn to crawl before he ventures to walk. Sequential patterns of growth have been described for nearly all physical skills including locomotion, use of the hands, and other abilities. Gesell's original work described such sequential growth as a natural "unfolding" process, but the currently popular view is that the child's environment, together with heredity factors, is basic to the process of physical development.

7. *Growth During Critical Periods:* This final principle contends that there are certain key times in a child's development during which the presence or absence of specific interactions can be especially important. For example, the first three months of an infant's life are extremely critical for the development of the eyes, ears, and brain. In order to foster optimal development of these organs, the child should be provided with a rich variety of visual and verbal stimulation. A critical period, then, is the time when certain physical growth can be most readily enhanced.

What does this all mean to you, the teacher of young children in their early years? Consider, for a moment, this scene, which is all too typical of an average day at a preschool center.

Mary and Barbie carefully scoop up dirt with their small trowels and place it in their pails, preparing a neat bed for their seeds. Jeff and James, on the other hand, dig into the soft dirt with their hands and toss it aside, letting it fall where it will. James, suddenly bored with the activity, decides to join other children at the swings and stands up quickly. Unfortunately, the short fence surrounding the garden catches him on the legs and sends the boy sprawling. Unhurt, James runs to his friend Dan at the swings. Meanwhile, Jeff is unaware that James has left, and he continues tossing the dirt about. One of Jeff's tosses inadvertently lands directly on Mary's neat seed bed and partially on Mary, and she gives a loud cry of despair. The teacher's attention is directed to the area at this point and she quickly moves in. The teacher hugs Mary and consoles her the best she can. Eventually, Jeff is directed to another activity and soon all four children are busily involved in new tasks—the garden incidents forgotten by all.

If we examine this situation in depth, we discover several principles of physical growth that have a direct impact on the children's behavior. One principle of growth and development, for example, states that girls mature more quickly than boys (variations in growth). You will note that Barbie and Mary were purposefully scooping up the dirt and placing it into their pails while the boys were tossing their dirt about in an unplanned way. The girls may have been able to control their muscles more effectively than the boys and therefore were able to carry out their work more precisely (general to

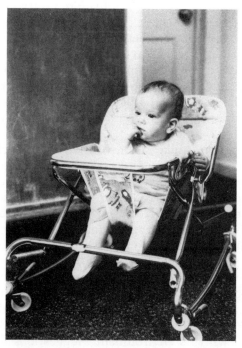

The infant's life is full of many new wonders. "How can I start investigating them all when I still cannot walk or run?"

specific growth). Also, James's fall may have been the result of his lower body not being as well developed as his upper body region (cephalocaudal). If this were so, his center of gravity would be high and would cause him to fall for the slightest reasons. Since his legs are short in proportion to the rest of his body, and he is usually in a hurry to go somewhere, the preschooler often prefers to run rather than walk—oh, for longer legs!

It is important for you to know the patterns of physical growth in young children because there is some general agreement that physical appearance has a major influence on how children view themselves and how others, in turn, view them. Karen Dion found that physical attractiveness plays an important role in how nursery school children are viewed.[1] In the study, women were given reports describing severe classroom problems. Along with one problem, the researcher attached a photograph of an attractive child. A photograph of an unattractive child was attached to a second problem situation. In response to the first problem, the one involving the attractive child, disturbing behavior was excused because "a bad day can occur" and the child's behavior "need not be taken too seriously." However, with the unattractive child, the response was, "I think the child would be quite bratty and would probably be a problem to teachers." Attractiveness, then, seems to be a quality that allows adults to be more tolerant of negative behaviors.

In a study of preschool girls, Kenneth Dion found that young children are well aware of the value of attractiveness—they responded to picture cues with responses such as, "People like you if you're pretty."[2] Clifford and Walster did a study evaluating to what extent physical attractiveness influenced the behavior and judgment of others.[3] Their study showed that teachers thought of attractive children as having greater potential for academic success than unattractive children, even though both groups of children were identical in all other qualities. These studies and others show, then, that we are influenced by the physical characteristics of others—we tend to focus more on the appearance of others than on trying to discover the qualities of the inner person.

Individual differences make it imperative that teachers avoid establishing rigid expectations for physical growth and appearance. Each child grows differently; each is distinguished by body builds, different sizes and shapes, hair color, eye color, skin color, physical abilities, and different levels of physical maturity as a distinctive entity. What are some of the factors accounting for such differences in individual physical growth and development? Basically, these factors fall into two broad categories: *heredity* and *environment*. Our genes help determine such things as body size, build, facial characteristics, hair color, and so on. However, heredity provides only a *potential* for development—the actual growth and maturation process must be considered within an environmental context. We must therefore look back to an old principle of child development: Growth is a product of the interaction of an organism with its environment. Suggestions for creating an environment that encourages optimal physical growth are discussed in the following section.

ENCOURAGING OPTIMAL PHYSICAL GROWTH

Teachers who work with young children have long known the importance of physical growth and maturation in the total development of the child. Recall the concerned efforts of educational pioneers such as Owen, McMillan, and Montessori who reacted most strongly to environmental conditions that related directly to children's physical growth. Their schools contained facilities designed to promote health and physical care. The same is true for schools today. Among the major factors that we now recognize as having a positive influence on physical growth are (1) a balanced program of activity, rest, and relaxation and (2) a safe, healthful environment. Suggestions for preparing and maintaining a balanced program of activity, rest, and relaxation are presented in this chapter. Suggestions for preparing and maintaining a safe, healthful environment are offered in Chapter 5.

All children require active physical experiences in order to exercise their rapidly growing muscles. This muscular growth, referred to as *motor development*, can actually be broken down into two distinct categories: large muscle control (*gross motor development*) and small muscle control (*fine motor development*). Gross motor development involves the use of large muscles such

Varied fine and gross motor activities contribute to the infant's and toddler's muscular growth and encourage increasingly sophisticated explorations of the environment.

as those in the arms, legs, or trunk; fine motor development involves the use of the smaller muscles such as those in the fingers. Both gross motor skills and fine motor skills follow certain predictable patterns of attainment; these are valuable to know because they influence our expectations for young children. Only if our expectations are accurate and result in the preparation of associated experiences can we establish a classroom with a proper emotional tone.

MOTOR DEVELOPMENT DURING INFANCY

Motor development during the period of infancy progresses very rapidly. The child advances in two years from a seemingly uncoordinated individual capable of only reflexive actions to a walking, toddling, exploring wonder (see Figure 4-1 for a summary of infant growth). This development, of course, does not happen simply by chance but is a product of two interrelated factors: maturation and environment. These two influences work together to help children achieve their greatest developmental potential. Some sug-

Figure 4-1 Motor development in infants. (Reprinted by permission of the University of Minnesota Press.)

gested physical activities designed to enrich children's environments during the period of infancy are included in the box on motor activities (p. 114).

MOTOR DEVELOPMENT DURING THE PRESCHOOL YEARS

Although the infant is fairly active during its waking hours, most of its energy is directed toward just growing rather than toward physical activity. This, in fact, is the period of fastest physical growth. Growth in height and weight begins to slow during toddlerhood (at about age 2 children are approximately half their adult height), so the energy required for rapid growth is now redirected toward increasing physical activity. The child is now beginning to walk and feed himself so new experiences and new needs are beginning to surface rapidly. Table 4-2 summarizes the motor skills developing in the youngster between the ages of two and five years old.

Gross Motor Development

Perhaps the most obvious areas of gross motor (large muscle) development during the preschool years lie in the skills of throwing, catching, and kicking a ball; balancing; and jumping.

Children enjoy practicing these skills through frequent repetition. A child stands on a balance board or kicks a ball using many different techniques until he finds one that actually works. It gives him confidence to develop skills through such active self-initiated play. Some of the play activities involving the large muscles with which children may be involved during a normal preschool day include swinging on a swing, climbing on a jungle gym, digging with a shovel in sand or dirt, throwing and catching a ball, jumping with a rope, walking on low balance boards, riding a tricycle, sliding down the slide, pulling a wagon, pushing a small wheelbarrow, painting with water, running through fresh grass, pounding nails, and sawing, planing, or sanding wood.

Katherine Read emphasized the importance of such physical activities: "A child builds self-confidence from control of his muscles. He gains when he is 'in tune' with his own body, able to use it freely following his own rhythms. . . . The child with good motor skills can do more about what he perceives."[4] Verna Hildebrand stated that, "The imaginative games . . . observed during children's [physical] activity challenge the child's creativity, concepts, percepts, and memory. All are part of the child's mental development. Vigorous physical activity stimulates all vital processes, such as circulation, respiration, and elimination. Eating habits improve, and rest is more welcome."[5] Physical activity, then, has values that go beyond mere physical gains—it enhances emotional, creative, and cognitive areas as well.

In order to provide the maximum number of opportunities for such growth through active play, you need to consider several factors.

ADEQUATE SPACE   Children require outdoor play areas that are safe, spacious, and inviting. Space requirements vary according to the source,[6] but generally they fall into the generous limits of 75 to 200 square feet per child.

MOTOR ACTIVITIES FOR INFANTS

GROSS MOTOR ACTIVITIES FOR INFANTS

1. Dress the child in loose clothing so he will be unrestricted in creeping, crawling, turning, or pushing activities.
2. Initiate exercise activities with the infant: move his arms and legs; hold him in a sitting position; encourage him to turn, push, creep, and crawl. Hold the child and toss him gently into the air. Hold him upright while giving him gentle support; bounce and dance to music while giving the child his first feelings of motion.
3. Hold an attractive, colorful toy above the infant as he lies on his back. Keep it steady until you are sure he sees it, then move it slowly from one side to another so that he is encouraged to turn his head and exercise his neck muscles.
4. Use crib toys to attract the infant to new objects and to give him practice reaching and grasping. Toys varying in color, texture, and sounds have great appeal for the infant.
5. Provide a safe, clean area in which the child can freely crawl about. There should be several toys and books in the area for him to look at, explore, and grasp.
6. Grasp the child's hands and pull him from a lying position to a sitting position. After a period of time, the infant will learn to pull himself up as you help by continuing to hold his hands.
7. Pull the infant to a standing position and allow him to feel the weight on his legs. Support him by the hips or waist as he struggles to maintain balance. Later, the infant can be urged to pull himself up by using the rail of his crib or playpen.
8. Place the baby in a walker where he can practice extending his legs and making walking movements without having to support his full weight. Gradually, he will learn to stand by himself. When this happens, squat in front of him, grasp both his hands, and encourage him to step toward you. He may seem reluctant or scared—if he does, don't force him; stop and try again at a later time. Slowly increase the distance as the child gains skill, comfort, and confidence.
9. Roll a ball toward the infant. He will watch it roll and want to roll it himself.

FINE MOTOR ACTIVITIES FOR INFANTS

1. Hold an attractive toy about eight to ten inches from the infant's eyes. After you are sure that he sees it, move it slowly until he follows it with his eyes.

Using the maximum figure of 200 square feet per child, a playground for twenty children would thus be as wide as a football field and as long as the distance from the goal line to the 25 yardline. Naturally, for some child-care facilities, especially those in urban settings, it is nearly impossible to obtain the land necessary for such a spacious playground. In these cases, creative and careful planning is necessary so the limited space can be used to its

---

2. Make a crib gym that gives the infant plenty of practice in reaching and grasping. Stretch a length of heavy gauge elastic across the crib and secure each end. Tie several shorter lengths to the first at intervals, allowing them to hang a short distance. To each of these short lengths of elastic securely attach a rattle, plastic spoon, beads, bells, or other toys too large for him to swallow. The infant will begin to use his gym by hitting the toys and enjoying the bouncing action. Later, he will begin to grasp the objects with his fingers.

3. Give the infant a variety of toys to explore. He will initially select the ones that are easiest to grasp (such as a plastic ring), but will eventually move to ones that require greater finger control (plastic rattles). Vary the toys so that the child will be exposed to many textures, shapes, and sounds.

4. Make squeeze toys from vividly colored fabric stuffed with old pantyhose. A doughnut-shaped toy is probably the most appropriate because babies can easily hold the shape and squeeze it with their fingers. Variety stores sell toys like this with noisemakers inside, but before selecting one make sure that it is safely constructed so the noisemaker won't fall out.

5. Bath time is an excellent opportunity for the child to exercise his fingers. Allow him to pick up and squeeze the sponge or washcloth.

6. Show the infant some pop-beads. Pull them apart and hold the pieces close to each other. The child may at first only look at the two parts, but eventually he will attempt to grasp them and put them back together. Be sure to give the infant constant attention while he is playing with objects that can be easily swallowed. Infants enjoy placing new toys or objects into their mouths and can often swallow dangerous things.

7. Allow the child to use his fingers during feeding time, but remember that he will be messy. This is an important initial step in getting the infant to feed himself.

8. Give the infant a spoon to play with as you feed him. Soon you will be able to help him fill the spoon and put it into his mouth. Naturally, he will miss the target a few times at first, but have patience; he will slowly improve with practice.

9. Let the infant play with an unbreakable empty cup while you are feeding him. When he seems to gain control, fill the cup with a few drops of a favorite liquid and let him try to drink from it. Again, there is bound to be some spilling, so give a small portion at a time and allow plenty of practice.

Table 4-2   Physical Characteristics of the Child from Two to Five
Years Old

At Two Years Begins to	At Three Years Begins to	At Four Years Begins to	At Five Years Begins to
Walk	Jump and hop on one foot	Run, jump, and climb with close adult supervision	Gain good body control
Run	Climb stairs by alternating feet on each stair	Dress self using buttons, zippers, laces, etc.	Throw and catch a ball, climb, jump, skip with good coordination
Actively explore his environment	Dress and undress self somewhat	Use more sophisticated eating utensils such as knives to cut meat or spread butter	Coordinate movements to music
Sit in a chair without support	Walk a reasonably straight path on floor	Walk balance beam with ease	Put on snowpants, boots, and tie shoes
Climb stairs with help (two feet on each stair)	Walk on balance beam	Walk down stairs alone	Jump rope, walk in a straight line
Build block towers	Ride a tricycle		Ride a two-wheel bike
Feed self with fork and spoon	Stand on one foot for a short time		
Stand on balance beam			

---

fullest potential. Some of the most exciting limited space urban play areas have been developed on rooftops or on abandoned lots that were cleaned up and prepared by involved neighborhood groups.

Outdoor play areas should be planned extensions of the classroom. Wide, low windows should face the playground and give the child an uncluttered view of the facilities. If possible, a door should connect the classroom to the outdoors so the children are able to move freely from one area to the other. Some teachers find it desirable to fence in the playground for privacy, safety, and security. High shrubs, evergreen trees, fences, or walls are often used for this purpose. Many child-care facilities have asphalt surfaces as well as grassy or dirt surfaces so that activities can occur in appropriate places: riding a tricycle or bouncing a ball on the asphalt or running with bare feet in the grass or digging in the dirt. Play areas should also provide a good balance between sun and shade. Where large shade trees are not present, teachers have requested that simple overhangs be constructed from the side of the building, have brought in beach umbrellas, and have even tacked up strong cardboard or butcher paper in strategic rest areas. In general, the appearance and formation of the playground stimulate children to explore, to become physically active, to create, and to learn in ways that bring happiness, health, and new challenges to their developing lives.

Classroom space recommendations vary from 35 to 100 square feet per child, depending again on the source. However, how the space is filled and planned is at least as important as how many square feet are available. (The arrangement of preschool classrooms is dealt with in greater detail in Chapter 11.) Indoor play areas must be as inviting to physical activity as are the outdoor areas. Children need room to romp and jump, to push buggies and pedal tricycles, and to move about freely without bumping into one another. They need corners or nooks and crannies to serve as private hide-outs—places that give them a chance to be alone. They need areas for clean up and toileting, for activity and rest. Sufficient space and effective equipment arrangements are a must in providing opportunities for large motor activities both in the classroom and out.

ADEQUATE EQUIPMENT Selecting appropriate indoor or outdoor equipment and supplies is often an expensive experience. However, a resourceful teacher can overcome this obstacle by seeking out used toys or equipment from parents of older children; by contacting parents who know carpentry; and by improvising with boxes, crates, tires, barrels, or planks. Some appealing play areas have been created by innovative teachers and parents using free or inexpensive materials that had been destined for the junk heap. Parents with special materials or skills to contribute are often willing to become involved, especially if their responsibilities are kept to the level at which they feel comfortable.

Most inexpensive equipment also stimulates creativity in young children. For example, they add old buttons or dials to wooden packing crates and turn them into cars, trains, garbage trucks, fire engines, buses, airplanes, boats,

Children delight in activities that involve vigorous movement: pushing, pulling, jumping, running, kicking, and other large muscle play.

and other vehicles. Other equipment is limited only by the child's imagination. The following can also serve as materials for the children:

- □ *Milk crates*—dairies will provide old ones
- □ *Packing crates*—sanded and painted in a variety of bright colors
- □ *Rubber tires*—see your service station manager
- □ *Boards*—large planks 7 to 8 feet long
- □ *Small crates*—orange crates and the like (paint them)
- □ *Telephone cable spools*—make excellent outdoor tables
- □ *Logs and stumps*—excellent for climbing or sitting
- □ *Ladders*—4 feet long with 2-inch boards spaced evenly (Lay the ladders on the ground and watch the children climb, crawl, balance, and walk.)
- □ *Hose*—young firefighters enjoy this important tool
- □ *Barrels*—great for rolling, climbing through, etc.
- □ *Cardboard boxes*—cut holes in the sides to encourage crawling (These also make wonderful, secretive "hiding places.")

If you have to buy any equipment, follow suggested criteria for selection and purchase. Questions such as those on the following equipment checklist should be considered before you buy any new equipment.

Purchasing Equipment for Young Children

1. *Will the children enjoy the equipment?*
   The equipment should be challenging, yet not frustrate or defeat the children.
2. *Are the materials safe?*
   Check the material for sharp corners or edges and exposed nails or screws. Make sure it is constructed of materials that would be injury free when used in normal ways. Check whether the paint, varnish, or other finish is nontoxic. Make sure small pieces are securely fastened so they cannot be swallowed or poked into the eyes or ears.
3. *Are the materials durable?*
   Be sure that the materials are strong and resilient. They should withstand extreme weather conditions and hard use.
4. *Are the materials versatile?*
   Look carefully to see if the materials could be used in a variety of ways. Balls, blocks, wagons, and ropes are but a few of the many items that are appropriate.
5. *Will the equipment provide balance to my collection?*
   Assess the materials you presently have—evaluate whether you are overloaded with one or more of these types of equipment: solitary play vs. group play; creative activity vs. closed-ended activity; motor vs. intellectual vs. social-type equipment.
6. *Is the material attractive?*
   Determine whether the children will be attracted or turned away by the color, form, or sound of the equipment. Equipment should have a high overall appeal for children.

7. *Will the child be actively involved in its use?*
   Many times, equipment is manufactured to appeal to an adult rather than to a child. The simple reason for this is that adults buy the equipment. Therefore, be wary of gimmicky-type equipment that is designed primarily for entertainment and that makes the children passive observers.

8. *Is the material developmentally appropriate?*
   Check to see whether the size is correct and whether it would be suitable for the age level of the children.

9. *Am I buying this equipment because the children need it or because I like it?*
   Be careful to avoid impulse purchases. Decide what your needs are and stick to your purchase plans. Do not be enticed by sharply reduced prices, flashy displays, or smooth sales pitches.

Interesting playground equipment can be made from a variety of different materials.

Many lists of suggested play equipment are available for ready reference. You can consult these lists whenever new equipment is needed. However, the following list of common items will give you a general idea of what is normally found in many preschool centers. Keep in mind that many of these materials can be used either inside or out, depending, of course, on the weather, the space available, and other similar considerations.

Stationary Equipment

1. *Slides.* Standard slides are made of rustproof metal. They come in various sizes so children of each age level will have a safe, appropriate height to negotiate. Some slides are extensions of raised play platforms or tree houses so children can more readily carry their imaginative play over to the equipment. For some children, the slide becomes a firefighter's quick approach to a fire truck, a slipping waterfall, or a parachute jump from an airplane.

2. *Raised play platforms.* These structures are normally 5 to 7 feet in height with a 5 foot square platform surrounded by a safe railing or fence. Many times the play platform is on top of a playhouse in a quiet area of the playground.

3. *Jungle gym.* This is a sturdy arrangement of strong, rustproof steel pipes that presents the child with a maze of climbing and crawling avenues to attempt to negotiate. Wooden gym structures are available for indoor use.

4. *Trapeze.* A rope secured to a sturdy tree branch or other support comprises this uncomplicated piece of equipment. Children can swing on the rope or attempt to climb up its length, hand over hand. Knots should be tied every foot or so to give the children secure footrests for climbing.

5. *Swings.* If the swing area is not properly supervised it can be one of the most dangerous areas on the school playground; some teachers of children younger than age 4 or 5 don't use swings. For younger children bucket swings should have safety straps so the youngsters can be safely placed on the seat with almost no danger of falling out. Older children should have swings made from canvas or flexible rubber strips. If they hit a child, these swings will not harm him as much as a hard rubber, metal, or wood swing could. Children also enjoy tire swings, which are made from old tires hung from tree limbs with sturdy supports. Swings should be placed so that they are away from the direct line of normal play; some advocate placing a barrier such as a hedge in front of the swings to prevent any child from being accidentally injured. Also, soft sand or pine mulch should be placed on the ground around the swings to help protect any child who falls.

6. *Sand areas.* The sandbox should be fairly large (about 10 feet wide on each side). The ledge can serve as a seat or table for various activities, as well as a frame to keep loose sand from spilling over the edges. Other sandboxes are easily made from old tires, plastic wading pools, and similar discarded equipment. A variety of toys and utensils—shovels, pails, plastic containers, old pots and pans, toy cars or trucks—should be kept

Play with dry sand or dirt often fascinates young children and involves them in meaningful physical activity for long periods of time.

in the sandbox to encourage imaginative play and large muscle activity. The outdoor sandbox should always be covered when the sandbox is not being used. This helps prevent contamination from animal elimination, unhealthiness from refuse collection, or problems of excess rain water.

Sand play is a first-rate activity for young children. They fill their containers with dry sand, using scoops or shovels; they can pour sand out of containers into creative piles and make designs with their fingers or utensils. They can mold things with wet sand, using paper cups or pails, and they can pat, shape, and sculpt new designs, or draw lines or shapes with shovels or scoops.

7. *Water play areas.* A washtub or large galvanized container containing 20 to 25 gallons of water to a depth of 8 to 10 inches is suitable for water play outdoors or inside. Protect the children with plastic aprons as they enjoy experimenting with materials such as measuring cups, funnels, egg beaters, medicine droppers, strainers, watering cans, soap, bowls, squeeze bottles, ladles, sieves, sponges, or brushes. Children enjoy using straws to blow bubbles formed with water and mild detergent and revel in activities such as "painting" the slide or playhouse with a paintbrush and water.

Blowing and painting with water are fun, but children often enjoy simply swishing their hands through it, swirling it in circles, stirring it with a spoon, spatula, or strainer, and beating it with a hand-operated egg beater. They love to pour water through a sieve, strainer, funnel, or watering can, to shake it from a clothes sprinkler, or force it from a spray bottle. Children enjoy noting the differences in absorption and other qualities between sponges and different cloth fabrics.

8. *Playhouse.* This structure can provide a quiet retreat for some children and a center of creative play for others. It can be constructed with a

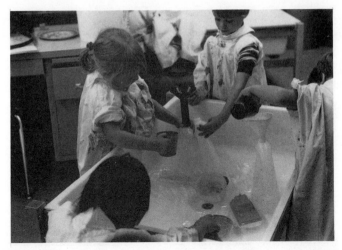

Water play, either indoors or out, provides the children with delightful activity. Careful supervision must be provided to keep clothes dry, but the opportunity to take a cool bath on a hot city playground may be a temptation some youngsters find difficult to resist.

variety of stairs and levels to encourage large muscle development by climbing, crawling, pushing, pulling, and so on. Dress-up clothes and various props help stimulate imaginative play episodes.

9.   *Storage shed.* A small structure convenient to the various play areas is ideal for storing outdoor equipment. Children can be encouraged to put away their equipment when finished or to assist the teacher if a sudden weather problem arises.

Movable Equipment

1.   *Wheel toys.* Tricycles, wheelbarrows, wagons, tractors, trucks—equipment that can be pulled, pushed, and manipulated by the child—are useful both for physical and for imaginative play.
2.   *Gardening tools.* Shovels, rakes, trowels, pails, and similar tools should be available for active digging or raking. Such tools should be durable and child-sized.
3.   *Balls.* Balls of different sizes (8" to 24"), shapes (round, elliptical), and composition (rubber, leather) should be available for throwing, kicking, and catching. Beanbags can also be used for these purposes.
4.   *Carpentry tools.* These hammers, saws, rasps, braces, and so on should be real tools of good quality and appropriate size and weight. The following tools are recommended for an active woodworking area: sturdy workbench with two vises, small, well-balanced claw hammers, saws of good steel with a sharp cutting surface, a brace and bits for drilling holes in soft wood, screwdrivers, assorted nails and screws, C-clamps for holding wood steady during sawing or pounding, a rasp or smoothing plane, sandpaper (wrapped around a wooden block), and soft wood (in many varieties, sizes, and shapes).

5. *Plumbing equipment.* These tools provide many possibilities for large muscle development and dramatic play. The following equipment could be supplied: half-inch pipe in varying lengths, elbows, ells, tees, plugs, couplings, and cotton work gloves.

6. *Blocks.* Blocks are perhaps the most popular raw material for children's play and are available in many sizes and shapes—so many that it's impossible to list them all here. But the three most popular types in preschool classrooms today are described below:

☐ *Unit blocks*—These blocks are made in multiples of a unit (5½″ × 2¾″ × 1⅜″), with increasing size along one dimension only—length—to the size of 22″ × 2¾″ × 1⅜″. Also part of the unit block assortment are pillars

Playhouses give children opportunities to pursue private play activities; storage sheds provide shelter for outdoor equipment.

Scraps of wood and dowels provide interesting manipulative experiences in the carpentry area.

(1⅜″ × 1⅜″ × 5½″), cylinders (1⅜″ or 2¾″ diameter × 5½″), curves (1⅜″ × 2¾″ × 90″), arches (1⅜″ × 5½″ × 11″), and hardwood boards of various sizes (see Figure 4-2).

☐ *Hollow blocks*—These blocks, made of cardboard or wood, come in various sizes and are large enough to make structures the children can actually use, such as a house, barn, store, and so on. Suggested sizes are: thirty-six 12″ × 12″ × 6″ blocks and twelve 24″ × 12″ × 6″ blocks.

☐ *Building blocks*—These blocks come in various sizes and shapes to add inventiveness to construction projects.

7. *Ropes.* Individual jump ropes and longer ropes that can be turned by two people should be available for those children who are able to use them.

8. *Balance boards.* Choose planks of varying widths (4″ to 10″) and lengths (4′ to 8′) for the children to walk along and exercise their sense of balance. You will need about 10 to 12 planks.

9. *Miscellaneous.* Large sewer pipes make fine crawling tunnels; old telephone cable spools serve as play platforms or tables; used tires can become jumping circles, buried halfway into the ground to form a tunnel, made into sandbox enclosures, or bolted together and hung by cables from trees to form climbing or swinging equipment; fallen tree trunks can be sawed into several lengths, anchored vertically in cement (about

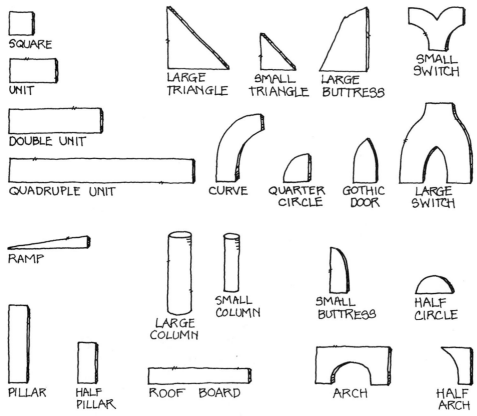

Figure 4-2 Unit building blocks.

two inches apart), surrounded by sand, and used as a walking or climbing area; barrels can be securely mounted on a platform and used as a tunnel, as a quiet retreat, or as a theater, rocket ship, or other prop in a dramatic play. Other miscellaneous equipment includes wooden storage crates, pulleys, air pumps, small ladders, hoses, or nuts and bolts. All these materials tap the child's imagination and encourage valuable physical activity (see Figure 4-3).

Fine Motor Development

Preschool children are given opportunities to refine many school-related skills. In the realm of fine motor (small muscle) activity, they are given experiences to manipulate puzzle pieces, hold paintbrushes to paint lines and circles, use scissors to cut paper, and handle crayons or pencils to color and draw. Nearly all of these experiences are designed to develop perhaps the most necessary of all fine motor skills: precise hand control. Some common developing patterns of hand control are presented in Table 4-3.

Figure 4-3 Miscellaneous play equipment.

Table 4-3   Patterns of Fine Motor Development in Preschool
Children

Age	Fine Motor Abilities
1–2 years	Can hold large pencil or crayon Can pull off shoes and socks Can begin to drink from a cup and feed themselves with a spoon
2–3 years	Can scribble with pencils or crayons Can open boxes and other simple containers Can begin to use knives and forks when feeding themselves
3–4 years	Can use pencils or crayons to copy circles or simple lines Can print large capital letters Can use modeling clay, make cookies, and sew Can feed themselves well and even wash and dry dishes
4–6 years	Can copy some simple geometric figures Can print their names, entire alphabet, and numerals from 1 to 20 Can build crude models from wood and other materials Can bathe themselves, brush own teeth and hair Can dress themselves completely, except for tying shoes

To encourage these fine motor skills, teachers should provide a variety of materials with which the children can experiment. In contrast to infants, who engage in random motor play as a way to develop related skills, preschoolers prefer to use motor activity in ways that help meet general purposes. For example, they may enjoy running barefoot through cool grass simply for the pleasure it brings, but more often they run to catch another child in a game of tag, or twist pipes together to "install" a sink, or dress up to assume the role of a parent or community helper. Because of this functional, purposeful nature of the preschooler's motor play, Maria Montessori was prompted to advise us that *play is the young child's work.*

There are numerous opportunities each day to help the child apply his play orientation to the refinement of fine motor skills. Such activities will be comprehensively discussed in later chapters. The following is only a brief list of some general activities whose primary value is to help develop small muscle skills: pouring, cutting, building (tinker toys), drilling, mixing, printing, constructing puzzles, stapling, pasting, buttoning, screwing bottle tops, manipulating, drawing, zipping, nailing, grasping, painting, lacing, scribbling, and planting seeds.

Equipment designed to foster small muscle control is rich and varied. Some common small muscle equipment is shown in the box on p. 129.

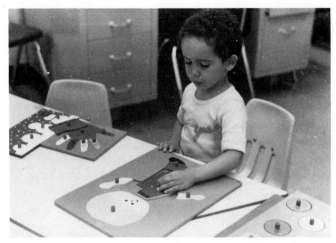

Young children must be provided opportunities to refine skills that help in fine motor development.

In choosing materials for small muscle development, be sure to separate the good buys from the bad. The following checklist should help you when you look for appropriate toys:

Choosing Toys for Small Muscle Development

1. Is it too large to be swallowed, stuck in the ear, or jammed into the nose?
2. Can the detachable parts be swallowed, stuck in the ear, or jammed into the nose?
3. Can little parts easily break off?
4. Are there sharp corners or dangerous points?
5. Is the construction solid and durable?
6. Is the material nontoxic?
7. Can parts pinch or catch hair?
8. Is it possible for long cords to accidentally strangle the child?
9. Can child use the toy independently?
10. Can plastic bags or large containers suffocate the child?

You should be aware of the importance of providing opportunities for refining gross and fine motor skills. As the children experience learning opportunities in curriculum areas, they do so in physically active ways, and children *need* physical activity during the preschool years. You will find that, except for short periods of quiet (as during story time) or rest (as after vigorous play), nearly all learning activities during a typical preschool day involve the children in physical activity. However, it is important that you individualize your program and make it developmental. That is, all children develop at different rates, and so opportunities for muscular exercise should range from the simple (running, jumping) to the more demanding (cutting, printing). Your ability to plan activities based on such considerations will help children develop to their full potential when they are ready.

SMALL MUSCLE EQUIPMENT

STACKING RINGS Children stack the colorful plastic rings in order.

SNAP-LOCK BEADS These colorful plastic beads snap together and pop apart.

PUZZLES Simple wooden or durable cardboard puzzles should be easy enough for the child and not frustrate him. Some suggestions: For two-year-olds use one- or two-piece puzzles with handles. For three-year-olds and older use puzzles of up to eight pieces.

SHAPE TOYS Children put three-dimensional plastic shapes into appropriate openings in a special box.

WOODEN BEADS Children pick up the beads and either string them or plop them back into the can.

DRESSING FRAMES Children refine their skills of lacing, tying, buttoning, zipping, and snapping on small practice frames.

ART SUPPLIES Children can be helped to control their small muscles through creative art media such as fat crayons, fat pencils, felt-tip markers, note pads and paper, glue, clay, blunt-pointed scissors, brushes and paint, and yarn.

SMALL PLASTIC FIGURES Children enjoy manipulating animals, farmers, firefighters, police officers, and other small plastic figures.

PROPER SUPERVISION

Alert supervision implies a system of guiding children that allows them to participate in their active experiences confidently and safely. This means that careful observation of the children and their equipment is necessary at all times. Guidelines for supervising young children follow.

Remember that children develop to different degrees, so some children will feel comfortable in activities that may seem dangerous to adults. Do not discourage such activity simply because you are fearful. In general, children will choose only those activities in which they feel safe.

Supervising for Safety

1. *Keep a constant eye on the children.* Two- and three-year-olds naturally wander off from the play area to explore new wonders. Since they have little idea of what is dangerous, they need firm, positive control. Direct special attention to swing or slide areas and give children directions on the use of this equipment. Don't hesitate to tell children to "Wait until Levi comes down the slide before you climb the ladder," or "Run in the grass, not through the sand box."

2. *Check the equipment to make sure it is safe.* Be sure that the equipment is not faulty and that children can use the equipment safely. For example, if some children still put things in their mouth, postpone activities that involve shells, rocks, sticks, and the like until these children can safely attempt them. Also, arrange the play areas so that effective supervision can be maintained and the possibility of accidents is kept to a bare minimum.

3. *Anticipate possible safety problems.* Position yourself close to a group of children who may be playing with potentially dangerous equipment. If you need to give a group of children special attention, stand facing the other children so you can minimize the possibility of accidents there.

With experience you will learn to anticipate trouble spots and take steps to eliminate problems before they erupt.

The safety and welfare of young children are major responsibilities. Regardless of the quality of supervision, however, accidents are always possible. For that reason, it is wise for every school to carry accident insurance to cover its children and staff.

PERIODS OF PLANNED EXERCISE

Many children enter the preschool setting with good coordination and muscle control. These children benefit from opportunities to improve their skills through continued informal exercise, such as we have been discussing. Others are less proficient and need positive encouragement to achieve greater success. Your role in this process is to structure short indoor or outdoor practice activities in which the children can work on developing their muscular coordination to its full potential. Such activities, combining creativity and physical exercise, can be somewhat informal. Consider the following example.

Careful supervision of areas designed to encourage vigorous outdoor exercise is a must. Encourage parents, grandparents, and other interested adults to join you on the playground to help prevent accidents.

Marge and her friend Terri made an interesting discovery while on the playground one day. They went down on their hands and knees and watched in fascination as a large frog hopped erratically in the tall grass at the edge of the play area. Soon several other children joined the two girls and called to their teacher to observe their discovery. After encouraging the children to comment on the frog's bumpy skin and bulging eyes, the teacher was pleased when the children began to discuss how it hopped and jumped. "Gee, look how far it hopped!" "It jumped so high." Suddenly, Terri kicked up her legs and supported herself with her hands. "Watch me," she called, "I'm a frog. Watch me hop." Soon the other children joined Terri and hopped along with each other. The teacher, alert to the situation, began to lead the children in a rhythmical chant, "Hippity hop, hippity hop, watch us jump and flip and flop. Hippity hop, hippity hop. . . ."

Other activities can be specifically planned by the teacher and therefore will be more formal.

Basic Body Movements

After children are aware of the basic body parts and gain control of them, they are ready to pursue activities that refine rudimentary movement skills and encourage creativity of movement.

Note: Most of these activities are best used along with musical accompaniment such as recordings or simply drums or tambourines.

☐ *Walking:* Walk fast; walk slow; walk backwards; walk on tiptoes; walk on heels; walk sideways; walk with hands on head; walk with hands on hips; and so on. Play games such as Follow the Leader or encourage the children to walk like favorite animals.

☐ *Standing:* Stand on tiptoes for a count of five; stand on right foot for a count of five; stand on left foot for a count of five; stand in each of the previous ways with eyes shut.

☐ *Balancing:* Get a 2″ × 4″ × 8′ board for these activities. First, ask the children to stand on the board to see if they can control their bodies. This ability to balance is basic to other activities. When the child displays good balance, ask him to walk with one foot on the board and one foot on the floor. Then, encourage the child to take short series of steps with both feet on the balance board. Gradually, children will learn to walk forward on the balance board. Then, ask them to walk slowly (forward); walk sideways (first the dominant side leads and then the other leads); walk with a beanbag on their heads; walk slowly (backward); walk slowly backward with a beanbag on their heads.

☐ *Running:* Run fast; run slowly; run on tiptoes; run with hands behind their backs; run with long or short strides; run toward the teacher; and so forth.

☐ *Jumping:* Jump up and down in place; use only one foot while jumping; jump forward; jump backward; jump into the air and make a quarter-turn; jump with eyes closed; and so on. Jump from a low height onto a mat or landing pad. Children can be encouraged to become frogs, grasshoppers, or jumping jacks.

☐ *Galloping:* Help children learn this skill by showing them the correct procedure. Play some background music appropriate for galloping and invite the children to become galloping ponies or reindeer. Then show them how to gallop—step forward on one foot and bring the other foot up beside it. Then step forward on the first foot and again bring the second beside it. Gradually encourage the children to repeat the process to the music until they achieve a smooth, galloping gait.

☐ *Skipping:* Skipping is perhaps the most difficult body movement for young children to master. For that reason, you must spend a good deal of time instructing them in this skill. Tell the children to step forward on one foot while holding the second foot in the air (you may want to hold it up for the child). The first foot then makes a hop and the second foot steps forward. So, the children are led to step and hop on one foot, step and hop on the other, and so on until the step-hop sequence becomes smooth and natural.

Creative Body Movement Activities

Once the children have mastered basic large muscle skills, you may wish to capitalize on their imaginations in order to further refine their capabilities. Some suggested activities include these:

☐ *Simon Says:* The leader gives commands to players, some prefaced by the words "Simon says . . ." and some not. The players must listen carefully and do only those actions prefaced by "Simon says. . . ." The leader tries to see how many times she can catch players who respond to a command not prefaced by "Simon says. . . ."

□ *Freeze:* Play lively music on the radio or tape recorder. Invite the children to move freely as the music is playing. Every so often, quickly turn off the sound and ask the children to "freeze." See if they can hold the position for two or three seconds, and start up the music again.

□ *Shadows:* Two children work together. One child performs a basic body movement and the other child must imitate what was done. They take turns being the leader.

□ *Songs:* Several songs lend themselves to practicing basic body movements. The following song is sung to the tune of "There Is a Tavern in the Town." The children place their hands on the part of the body mentioned in the song.

Head, shoulders, knees, and toes,
Knees and toes.

Head, shoulders, knees, and toes
Knees and toes and—

Eyes and ears
And mouth and chin and nose.

Head, shoulders, knees, and toes,
Knees and toes.

To the tune "Hokey Pokey," encourage the following movements:

Put your right hand in. *(toward center of circle)*
Take your right hand out.
Put your right hand in, and shake it all about.
We'll shake it in the morning or we'll shake it afternoon.
That's what it's all about.

(2nd verse) . . . left hand . . .
(3rd verse) . . . right foot . . .
(4th verse) . . . left foot . . .
(5th verse) . . . head . . .
(6th verse) . . . whole body . . .

Create new words to familiar tunes as children are encouraged to exercise. This is one of many possible variations of the tune "Jingle Bells."

Clap your hands, clap your hands,
Clap them loud and long,
Oh, what fun it is to clap,
And sing this happy song.

(2nd verse) Touch your toes . . .
(3rd verse) Stretch up tall . . .
(4th verse) Walk in line . . .
(5th verse) Row your boat . . .
(6th verse) Throw the ball . . .

□ *Rope Activities:* Place a long length of rope on the floor or ground and use it in the following ways: walk a straight line along the rope frontwards and backwards (for those who are able); make a circle from the rope and ask the children to walk the circle frontwards or backwards; with the rope in a straight line, hop over to the other side of it and then back; make curves in the rope and run or hop so each step will be taken in a new curve; ask the children to invent a new way of moving with the rope.

□ *Tightrope Walker:* Establish a straight line about 10 feet long on the floor of your classroom. Invite the children to walk along the line as far as they can without ringing a small bell held in their hand. For variety, try making a curved line, a circle, and so on, as discussed previously.

□ *Going to the Zoo:* To encourage creative movements of many kinds, gather the children in a group and invite them to go with you on an imaginary trip to the zoo. On this special trip, the children must choose an animal to imitate as their means of getting there. Lead them by saying this phrase: "We're going to the zoo. How is Diana going to get there?" "I'm going to fly like a bird," says Diana. Encourage the rest of the children to follow the child's lead and perform animal movements—fly like birds, hop like frogs, waddle like ducks, swim like fish, crawl like snakes, and so on.

Cognitively Oriented Movement Activities

Use various movement activities to introduce or reinforce cognitive learnings. Here are a few examples.

1. Group the children in a large circle and have them signal how they feel about being there.
2. Have the children use their arms to draw a letter (or numeral) as large as they can in space. Ask them to think about other parts of their body that they can draw with and have them do so.
3. Ask the children to choose partners and form a letter (or numeral) with their bodies on the floor or in a standing position.
4. Form a large letter on the floor with heavy yarn. Then, for example, encourage the children to move around a big "B," "buzzing like a bug" or "bouncing like a ball."
5. Give each child one letter. Then begin this rhyme and ask the first child to make his letter in space as big as he can:

This is what I can do.
Everybody try it, too.
This is what I can do.
Now I pass it on to you.

After the verse is complete, ask the other children to mimic the action and tell what letter (or numeral) was shared. Repeat for each child.

Be aware that many of these physical movements do not come easily to some children. For example, many five-year-olds find it extremely difficult to master galloping and skipping and they should not be made to feel uncomfortable because of it. Help them enjoy such activities and encourage them to experiment until they begin to become more proficient. You may even wish to hold the hand of a child who has a particularly difficult time and help him with hopping, skipping, jumping, or galloping exercises.

It should be apparent that many of the activities suggested for muscular development also involve areas other than physical growth. Physical activity is part of all areas of the preschool curriculum. As such, you will see activities that involve movement of some kind being suggested throughout this book as means to help you teach curricular topics. For instance, Chapter 10 describes physical activities such as marching or walking to music; Chapter 8 explains the language development advantages of fingerplays; and Chapter 7 illus-

GAME ACTIVITIES

1. *Obstacle Course.* Use movable playground equipment, cardboard boxes, barrels, ropes, chairs, and so forth to plan an obstacle course on the playground. Encourage the children to jump over, run around, or crawl under the various obstacles and get through the course as quickly as possible without upsetting the objects.

2. *Red Light/Green Light.* Children line up along side of each other at one end of the playground. A leader stands at the opposite end of the playground with his back to the rest of the children. The leader yells so that all can hear, "1—2—3—green light!" and the players run toward his end of the playground as fast as they can. The leader then calls out "1—2—3—red light!" a signal for all children to stop running. The leader turns around quickly to see if all the players have stopped. Any player caught by the leader must return to the starting point. The first player to reach the leader is the winner.

3. *Cross the River.* Use 8½- × -11 inch construction paper of different colors and paste various geometric figures on them. Arrange them on the floor and explain to the children that they are going to try to cross a river by stepping on stones (the geometric shapes). The teacher guides the children across the river by saying, "Hop to the green square, . . . the red circle, . . . the blue rectangle," and so on.

4. *Red Rover.* Mark off two end boundary lines with lengths of rope. Children stand behind one line while the leader stands facing them between the two lines. The leader calls out, "Red Rover, Red Rover, let (a child's name) come over." The child called must run across to the other side of the other line without being caught by the leader. Any child caught must stay in the center to help the leader. The last one caught is the new leader.

5. *Duck, Duck, Goose.* Arrange the children in a large circle and designate one child who is "It." "It"

trates the valuable role of physical activity in the development of cognitive skills. This is another illustration of the fact that many dimensions are involved in any single activity used with preschool children.

PROPER REST

Strenuous activity is a major cause of fatigue, but there are other causes, including stress, improper nutrition, excessively warm temperatures, or a body constitution that simply requires more rest. Of course, the effects of these conditions vary from child to child, but they are sometimes expressed as crankiness, unreasonableness, shortness of attention span, crying, excita-

---

walks around the circle and touches certain children and says "Duck" with each touch. When he touches a child and says "Goose," however, that child must get up and run around the circle while being chased by "It." If the "Goose" is caught before he returns to his original place in the circle he becomes "It," and the players switch places.

Games should be chosen to help children refine specific physical skills rather than to establish a winner and loser. If excessive competition results from the game, and a child fails constantly, that child's motivation may be killed. For that reason, winning or losing should depend on a child's ability to use effective strategy or on a combination of luck and skill rather than on skill alone. Other suggestions for using games effectively are:

1. Use your time efficiently. As a rule of thumb, young children's attention spans during intensive activities are about one or two minutes more than their age.

2. Keep groups as small as possible. This provides greater opportunity for maximum individual efforts with careful guidance by the teacher.

3. Concentrate on only one or two skills in any game session. More than that number may confuse or frustrate some children.

4. Give clear, simple directions and make sure the children understand how the game is played. You may even demonstrate the actions of the game to give a clear idea of how to play.

5. Do not force each child to play. Try to encourage all to participate, but you will find that the activity will go much better if the children join of their own free will rather than because of the teacher's demand.

6. Keep a watchful eye on the children. Stop the game when their interest wanes and move on to something else. Don't overdo it—too much of a good thing will eventually tire the children of nearly anything.

SMALL MUSCLE ACTIVITIES: FINGER PLAY

Fingerplay activities often involve movements of other body parts as well as the fingers, thereby contributing to the development of both small and large muscles.

Five Little Sausages

(Shared with me by Mary Alice Felleisen.)

Five little sausages frying in a pan. (*extend five fingers*)
One went POP! (*snap fingers*)
And then went BAM! (*clap hands*)

Four little sausages frying in a pan (*extend four fingers*)
One went POP! (*snap fingers*)
And then went BAM! (*clap hands*)

Three little sausages . . .

Two little sausages . . .

One little sausage . . .

No little sausages frying in a pan (*make fist*)
The pan got hot
And the grease went BAM! (*clap loudly*)

Ten Little Firemen

Ten little firemen
Sleeping in a row. (*put all fingers out straight on knees or floor*)

Ding-dong goes the bell (*clap hands*)
Down the pole they go. (*pretend to slide down pole*)

Jumping on the engine (*make fast driving motions*)
WEEE-OOO-WEEE-OOO (*make siren noise*)

Putting out the fire (*pretend to use fire hoses*)
Then home so slow. (*make slow driving motions*)

And back to bed again (*hands form pillow*)
All in a row.

Thumbkin

(Sung to tune of "Frère Jacques")

Where is thumbkin?
Where is thumbkin?
Here I am.
Here I am.
How are you today, Sir?
Very fine, I thank you.
Run away.
Run away.

Repeat, extending a different finger for each verse, as follows: thumbkin = thumb, pointer = first finger, tall man = second finger, ringman = third finger, pinky = little finger.

Bear Hunt

Leader: Let's go on a Bear Hunt.
Children: (repeat above)
Leader: All right?
Children: All right.
Leader: O.K.?
Children: O.K.
Leader: Let's go! (*make walking sounds by rhythmically clapping hands on knees; children repeat each phrase while following all motions and words of leader*)
Oh look! (*children repeat*)
What's that? (*children repeat*)
A big tree!
Can't go under it.
Can't go round it.
Can't go through it.
Have to climb it.
All right? O.K.? Let's go! (*make climbing motions—resume walking motions*)
Oh look!
What's that?
A big field!
Can't go under it.

Can't go round it.
Have to go through it.
All right? O.K.? Let's go! *(swish palms together—resume walking motions)*
Oh look!
What's that?
A big river.
Can't go under it.
Can't go round it.
Can't go through it.
Have to swim it.
All right? O.K.? Let's go! *(swimming motions—resume walk)*
Oh look!
What's that?
A dark cave!
Let's go in it.
All right? O.K.? Let's go!
Ooh—it's dark in here.
The walls are wet. *(make feeling motions)*
Oops—my toe bumped something!
What could it be?
It feels furry!
It has a tail!
A large back!
Two ears!
A big cold nose!
Two eyes!
Ooh—big teeth!
It's a bear!
Let's run! *(clap hands faster—on knees—go through activities backward: swim river, swish through field, climb tree—walk home)*

Ten Fingers

I have ten little fingers and ten little toes, *(point to body parts)*
Two little arms and one little nose,
One little mouth and two little ears,
Two little eyes for smiles and tears.
One little head and two little feet,
One little chin; that's ME, complete!

One Little Body

Two little feet go stamp, stamp, stamp, *(stamp)*
Two little hands go clap, clap, clap *(clap)*
One little body stands up straight, *(stand straight)*
One little body goes round and round, *(turn)*
One little body sits quietly down. *(sit)*

Follow Me

Hands on shoulders, hands on knees, *(follow action as rhyme indicates)*
Hands behind you, if you please;
Touch your shoulders, now your nose,
Now your hair and now your toes;
Hands up high in the air,
Down at your sides and touch your hair;
Hands up high as before,
Now clap your hands, one, two, three, four.

Clap Your Hands

Clap your hands, clap your hands,
Clap them just like me.
Touch your shoulders, touch your shoulders,
Touch them just like me.
Shake your head, shake your head,
Shake it just like me.
Clap your hands, clap your hands,
Now let them quiet be.

Periods of planned physical activity are normally incorporated into the children's day.

bility, and, perhaps, listlessness and inactivity. The following story illustrates the effect fatigue may have on children in your classroom:

Usually Marlene gets plenty of rest and arrives at her school full of vigor and ready to participate in each day's new adventures. However, on this particular morning, she seemed somewhat tired and listless. While on the playground, Marlene is usually one of the most active children—running, climbing, jumping, sliding or swinging. However, on this morning, she was content to sit somberly under a shade tree watching the others. Inside, Marlene spent some time aimlessly leafing through books in the reading corner and eventually she wandered over to the water table. She seemed content to pour water from containers and stayed at this activity until it was time for the children to go to the sinks to clean up for snack break. Miss Jackson, the teacher, walked over to Marlene and said to her, "Marlene, it's time for you to put away your toys and get ready for snack time." Marlene answered with a quick, "No, I don't want a snack today." The teacher answered, "I know you'd like to stay and play, but we have to go now." Marlene, eyes welling, haltingly announced, "I don't like . . . (pause) . . . I don't like . . ." and suddenly burst into tears. Miss Jackson placed her arm reassuringly around Marlene and led her to the area where the sleeping cots were kept. She had Marlene lie down, and then she slowly stroked the girl's back, offering comforting words to soothe her feelings. Slowly, Marlene stopped crying and fell off into a quiet, comfortable nap.

Later on, when Marlene's mother arrived to pick her up, Miss Jackson found out that unexpected company the night before had kept Marlene up for two hours past her bedtime. The resulting overstimulation and lack of sleep had caused behaviors that were not normally part of Marlene's emotional constitution. However, by allowing her to rest during a big part of the morning, Miss Jackson

A program of rest, relaxation, or sleep should be organized on an individual basis so that varying needs can be met.

had recognized the situation and, by allowing her to sleep, had made a proper adjustment for it.

To avoid fatigue, children need an individualized program of sleep, relaxation, and activity. Naturally, not all children need the same kind or amount of rest, so the program should be flexible enough to allow individuals to relax in whatever manner they choose, as long as it is not disturbing to others. Some children may require a long nap in a dark quiet room; others may rest on their cots, read a book, or play quietly with a toy. Whatever the choice, young children should be given an opportunity for rest or relaxation periods, especially if the program is a day-long one. Many teachers arrange a schedule that allows frequent changes of pace. These changes alternate quiet periods with more active periods, and follow concentrated, rigorous activities with more relaxed ones. Some teachers even eliminate rest periods, especially if their children are particularly energetic and need only a minimum of rest.

Day-long programs normally include a period of rest or relaxation in the afternoon, a quiet, relaxed period of about one hour for those children not needing sleep and a longer period of time for those who do. The half-day program normally includes only a short period of relaxation, usually about 15 minutes, during which the children rest from a vigorous outdoor or indoor activity. During this time, the tables may be prepared for a snack while the children listen to pleasant, soft music. The success or failure of any rest period, however, rests squarely on the shoulders of the teacher. It is her responsibility to create the proper atmosphere for relaxation and to help the children settle down whenever a comfortable, quiet interval is needed. That responsibility, as uncomplicated as it may sound, is one of the most challenging teachers face in their daily programs, for although rest is needed by all children it is resisted by many. Often the situation becomes a battle of wills with one side firing, "Do what I say is best for you," and the other responding with, "I dare you to try and make me!"

If you have determined that an extended period of reclining rest or sleep is needed by your children (this case may differ from one preschool setting to another), the following guidelines may be of use.

1. Rapidly growing children need a great deal of sleep. For example, an 18-month-old child needs approximately 16 hours of sleep per day while a two-year-old may need only 12 hours of sleep; a three- or four-year-old may need 11½; a five-year-old, 11. Daytime naps, of course, help children meet these average sleep requirements. Children up to age 3, then, will undoubtedly require additional sleep in the preschool setting while three-, four-, and five-year-olds may have received all the sleep they needed the night before. It must be emphasized that the *amount* of sleep is much less important than the *quality* of sleep. A good rest period, for those in need of one, is a quiet, relaxing period before bedtime, with a comfortable cot, a darkened room, and an emotional climate of comfort and happiness.
2. Make the restless child feel comfortable and reassured. Some children need more time to quiet down than others, so help them along. Walk quietly over to the child and whisper a reminder to him or comment about a particularly enjoyable experience that both the teacher and child can remember with pleasure. Perhaps some gentle stroking on the back will soothe and relax the child. Often a favorite stuffed animal or blanket will help these children to rest.
3. Help the children who are afraid to sleep because of unreasonable fears. Encourage them to talk about what bothers them, and let them know you care. However, be careful not to make comments that will help perpetuate the fears. For example, a child who fears falling asleep because "the monsters will get me" will find his beliefs reinforced by an adult's comment, "Don't worry, I'll stay here and chase them away when they come." Instead, reassure the child that there is nothing to be afraid of, that there are no monsters (or whatever), and that you will be near if he needs you.
4. Allow the children to sleep for as long as they like, but remember that each child has a natural sleep tendency. For this reason, some parents will not want their children to have a long afternoon nap because a longer nap than necessary tends to delay their falling asleep at night. With experience, you will be able to judge each child's needs and adjust their rest times as necessary.
5. Before the nap and immediately afterward, provide for a period of toileting, face washing, and clothing change. After the nap, children often look forward to a refreshing snack.
6. Remember your valuable role as a model for the children. As you supervise the rest time, assume a position of rest yourself. Stretch out on a cot or relax in a chair, but be careful to avoid recordkeeping, busy room

preparation duties, and any other activity that communicates "Do as I say, not as I do."

If you set the appropriate conditions, children will regulate their sleep to the amount they need. But to do this, they must be free from strain, pressure, nagging, and the like. The teacher must find a way to combine freedom, reasonable restrictions, and guidance so that the nap period will be a valued experience for each child. You can do this primarily by getting to know your children and becoming familiar with their needs.

SOME FINAL THOUGHTS

Your knowledge of child growth and development combined with your ability to translate such knowledge into sound teaching practices will help create a comfortable emotional and physical environment in which each child can grow to his full potential. Outdoor and indoor activities, carried out in small groups or individually, offer children opportunities to develop and control large and small muscles. They will then be able to move confidently from the easier large muscle activities to the more demanding small muscle activities that are the forerunners of reading and writing. Some children will be more than willing to move into such activity; others will be reluctant. However, if he is given the proper support and assurance, the child will gain confidence in himself. Such positive feelings will foster greater initiative and trust in himself, and will lead to increased growth in all areas of development.

NOTES

1.　Karen K. Dion, "Physical Attractiveness and Evaluations of Children's Transgressions," *Journal of Personality and Social Psychology* 24, no. 2 (1972): 207–213.
2.　Kenneth Dion, "Young Children's Stereotyping of Facial Attractiveness," *Developmental Psychology* 9, no. 3 (1973): 183–188.
3.　M. Clifford and E. Walster, "The Effect of Physical Attractiveness on Teacher Expectations," *Sociology of Education* 46, no. 3 (Spring 1973): 248–258.
4.　Katherine H. Read, *The Nursery School*, 5th ed. (Philadelphia: W. B. Saunders, 1971), pp. 194–195.
5.　Verna Hildebrand, *Introduction to Early Childhood Education*, 2d ed. (New York: Macmillan, 1976), p. 119.
6.　For example, these figures are recommended by various influential groups in early childhood education—National Association for the Education of Young Children (NAEYC): at least 75 square feet per child; Association for Childhood Education International (ACEI): 75 to 100 square feet per child; Child Welfare League of America: 200 square feet per child is desirable.

5

Establishing a Safe, Healthful Environment

Copyright 1979
The Register and Tribune
Syndicate, Inc.

"That's my little brother's potty train."

Helping children establish health and hygiene routines is one of the most sophisticated skills an effective teacher or parent can have. (*The Family Circus* by Bil Keane courtesy of The Register and Tribune Syndicate, Inc.)

Lois and Evan are four-year-olds who attend a suburban nursery school. They both enjoy playing outdoors—and the messier the activity, the more they enjoy it. After a short swing and a climb on the jungle gym one day, the two youngsters moved to the garden plot where they began to dig excitedly for worms. After uncovering four or five of the wiggly creatures, they decided to place some dirt in a small pail so their new discoveries could be shared with the teacher when it was time to return indoors.

In a little while, the teacher signalled the children to return to the classroom, where they were to remove their wraps and prepare for a short snack. Lois and Evan rushed up to the teacher and shared the worms they had found. The teacher congratulated the youngsters on their fine work and invited them to tell the others about their worms during group time after the snack. But first, she reminded the two, they had to wash their hands. Into the bathroom went Lois and Evan, where they giggled their way through the hand-washing experience, mixing the soap and water to make bubbles. Finding it necessary to use the toilet again, Lois and Evan both stopped to urinate before returning to the classroom. Lois was particularly interested in the fact that Evan was able to stand while urinating, so she watched until he was finished. Turning to her teacher in the doorway, Lois asked why Evan was able to stand and she couldn't. The teacher, realizing that this was not a good time to gloss over the situation, commented, "There is a difference between a girl and a boy. Boys have a penis and they stand up to urinate. You are a girl. Girls have a vagina and they sit down—mommies sit down, too." Satisfied with this explanation, Lois sat on the toilet and completed her tasks in the bathroom.

Lois and Evan returned to the classroom and joined the other children at the tables for a short, healthful snack. Today the teacher had prepared their favorite, milk and oatmeal cookies. When the snack was finished, the teacher invited the children to join her in a group for a short, quiet period of sharing. This group period not only gave the children a chance to express themselves to the others, but it also provided them with an opportunity to relax and regain some of the energy they had expended on the playground. Of course, Lois and Evan beamed as they shared their story of digging up the worms from the school's garden plot.

This brief vignette describing a morning in a preschool illustrates a teacher's ability to arrange a safe, healthful environment. In this case, the teacher met health and safety concerns in the following ways:

1. Outdoor activity encouraged healthful exercise.
2. Proper clothing was worn to meet the demands of the weather.
3. Clean-up experiences were an integral part of the plan.
4. Toileting was encouraged in a warm, accepting environment.
5. Nutritious snacks helped fulfill basic physical needs.
6. A short period of rest helped balance active times with quiet times.

Health and safety education in the preschool is generally informal. It evolves from activities that are basic to daily living rather than from short scheduled lessons or discussions. Safety and good health practices are two important goals that all preschool centers should strive to attain.

PROMOTING GOOD HEALTH

Until the early 1960s many people in the United States were appalled at the idea of placing children up to age 5 together in the same facility, in close contact with each other. This age range is particularly susceptible to illnesses and infectious diseases, particularly common childhood diseases such as measles, chicken pox, and mumps, and many parents at the time felt it would be safer to keep their youngsters at home. Also, medical science was not as advanced as it is today, and if the children did develop such illnesses, medicine was often unable to prevent serious complications. The results were sometimes devastating: hospitalization or death led to grief and great financial burdens, and possible lengthy quarantines led to loss of jobs—and remember that unemployment and other benefits were not available during much of this period. The problem of infectious diseases, then, caused many families to question the value of close situations, such as those found in preschool settings. Because of these strong parental concerns, strict health and safety measures were instituted by the first nursery schools. For example, children were not admitted until they had passed a health examination administered by a physician or nurse. When this was done, and other basic health precautions were followed, it was found that children in preschool groups remained as healthy as those not in contact with other children.

Common Communicable Diseases

Today, immunization programs have drastically reduced the threat of childhood illnesses, but there are some you should still be familiar with. Table 5-1 summarizes these.

Although highly effective vaccines have reduced the incidence of these communicable diseases, the organisms that cause them are still very much with us. For example, a serious polio outbreak occurred in Texas in 1970, and in Connecticut a school suffered a rash of polio cases that left seven children partially or severely paralyzed. Diphtheria claimed the life of a five-year-old New York City girl in 1977 and hospitalized her six-year-old sister and four-year-old brother. During an outbreak of 2,500 reported cases of measles in Los Angeles in May 1977, two persons died and five cases of encephalitis (brain inflammation) set in. The incidence of diphtheria, mumps, whooping cough, and the other communicable diseases has clearly dropped over the decades, but occasional scattered cases arise, and unimmunized children are even more susceptible to such diseases than were the children of the prevaccine generation—and this susceptibility is particularly worrisome. In the 1930s and 1940s communicable disease was so common that some youngsters were able to develop natural immunities. Today, however, children no longer have an opportunity to develop natural immunity, and unvaccinated children are totally open to attack by viruses.

Many educational and health authorities have expressed concern over the growing laxity regarding immunization. They want the laws requiring proof of immunization enforced before children can enter into any child–group situation, including nursery school and day care, rather than only before elementary school. Enforcement of these laws could stimulate interest in getting infants and preschoolers immunized. During the previously mentioned measles outbreak in Los Angeles, for example, the city declared that any child not having proof of vaccination would be barred from school. Lines formed quickly, and eventually 99.9 percent of the school children had been immunized, an incredible figure compared to national immunization figures

Table 5-1   Common Communicable Diseases among Preschool
Children

Contagious Disease	Symptoms	Incubation Period	Isolation Period
Chicken pox	Slight fever; itchy rash; eruptions on face and trunk	14–21 days; usually 14–16	10 days or until disappearance of scabs
German measles	Swollen glands; fever; stiff neck; rash	14–21 days; usually 16–18	4–7 days
Measles	Red, watery eyes; fever; cough; runny nose; rash after third or fourth day	About 10 days	From beginning of symptoms until 4 or 5 days following appearance of rash
Mumps	Swollen glands in front of and below ear; fever	12–26 days; usually 18	7–10 days, or until swelling has diminished
Polio	Fever; headache; stiff neck; sore throat; nausea; vomiting	7–14 days	Duration of the fever or one week following the appearance of symptoms
Scarlet fever	Fever; headache; sore throat; vomiting; rash with flaky skin	1–9 days; usually 2–4	7–10 days
Tuberculosis	Fever; persistent cough; weight loss	6–8 weeks	Until disappearance of infection
Whooping cough	Cold accompanied by hacking cough; followed in 2 or 3 weeks by periodic, sharp, sudden, heavy coughing spells; perhaps vomiting	7–16 days; usually 5–7	3 weeks after appearance of cough

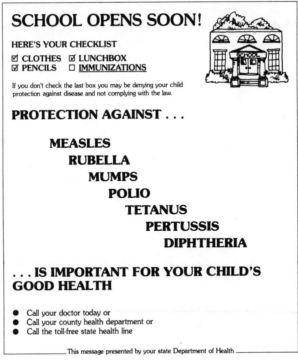

Figure 5-1   Sample poster for an immunization campaign.

of 59.6 percent in nonpoverty areas and 38 percent in poverty areas. This percentage is an ideal goal for the entire country, but even a coordinated community effort involving parents and concerned groups could push up current immunization rates.

Your role, then, should be to become aware of such diseases because their occurrence among children is certainly possible. Be aware of the various symptoms and notify appropriate authorities when a contagious disease is suspected. Help parents become aware of the value of immunizations—if necessary, launch a drive to reach the parents of prospective preschoolers so proper vaccine protection can be provided before the children enter your nursery school or day-care facility (see the poster in Figure 5-1).

Common Skin Infections

Another common health problem for young children is contagious skin infections. Many skin infections are difficult to cure, and you may need a doctor's advice to determine if a child should be kept in school. However, knowing what to look for can help you catch the disease before it spreads on the individual or among other children. Table 5-2 summarizes common skin infections.

Lice infestation is also sometimes found, especially where habits of good hygiene are not regularly practiced. Unwashed hair and unclean bodies make good breeding places for lice—especially the hair and seams of clothing. Symptoms usually include itching and irritation, but proof can best be obtained by examining the child's hair or clothing carefully for signs of the lice. If lice are found, the best remedy is to disinfect, a task that should be referred to and done by proper medical authorities such as the school nurse or your child-care supervisor.

CLEANLINESS AND SELF-CARE

Basic to the prevention of disease and infections is a pattern of cleanliness and self-care. Skills and attitudes related to these areas must be stressed so children develop a positive attitude toward them and begin to look forward to increasing competence in each area. Young children must be taught how to care for their physical selves. They must learn particularly about using the toilet facilities and about washing themselves before and after eating or sleeping and after strenuous activity.

Using Toilet Facilities

Learning to use the toilet facilities is a major accomplishment for children during the preschool years. Most children tend to be nearly fully toilet trained by the age of three, but younger boys and girls cannot, in most cases,

Table 5-2 Common Skin Infections among Preschool Children

Disease	Symptoms	Cause
Impetigo	Yellow, crusted sores filled with pus; usually found near nostrils	Staphylococcus bacteria
Scabies	Itchy, red blotches on the skin	Mites burrowing under the skin and depositing eggs
Ringworm	Ring-shaped, discolored patches of skin, especially found about the scalp; itching	Variety of fungus burrowing beneath the skin
Athlete's foot	Small blisters between the toes; itching	Fungus

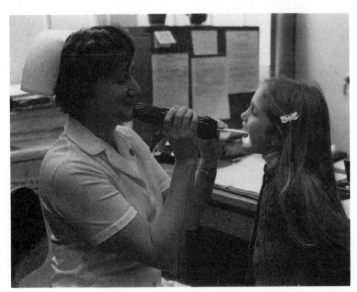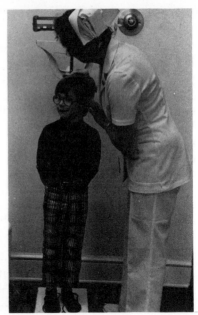

Sound medical information is crucial to the establishment of a healthy preschool environment.

control their elimination, so you must assume a supportive role in caring for them. Such care can become very complicated if all the mechanics are picked up on a trial-and-error basis. The following suggestions are presented so that the tricks of diapering will more quickly become a part of your repertoire and result in more pleasurable child-care experiences.

- To prevent a sore back, change the baby on a waist-high table.
- Wash the baby's bottom with a soapy cloth each time you change him. Rinse it with clear water and pat it dry. This helps control rashes and chafed skin caused by bacteria and the saltiness of urine. This procedure is especially crucial if you are using waterproof pants or disposable diapers.
- Spread baby powder or petroleum jelly on the baby's bottom to prevent rashes or chafed skin.
- Fix a mobile above the baby's head. This will capture his attention and will usually prevent excessive squirming while you are changing him.
- At about nine months, the baby may be changed while standing. Give him a special toy to hold in each hand for balance.
- Sing or talk to the youngster as you clean and change him. Make the situation one in which the baby feels comfortable and encouraged to form better habits of control.

Even when youngsters gain control of their bladders and sphincters, they will continue to experience some accidents. Learn to accept them—they are typical of this age group—and avoid communicating any initial feelings of repulsion at the sight of a child's accidental excretions. If you communicate queasiness or disgust to the child, you may make him ashamed and confused instead of comfortable and secure in the situation. If a child is told, for example, "Change into these dry pants and you'll feel better," instead of, "Oh, you're such a bad boy—aren't you ashamed of yourself?" he will gain self-assurance and learn to control his own needs, knowing that you understand. Under no condition should a child be made to feel ashamed for a toileting accident in school. Such an attitude can only breed conflict and resistance. Meet incidents with a matter-of-fact attitude and direct your attention to the child's successes rather than to his failures.

If you understand the reasons for accidents like this, you may be able to handle such situations with greater insight. The following are some common reasons for accidents.

1. Children are often strained and nervous during the first few weeks of the new preschool year or during other highly exciting times. Reassure the child that it is not bad to have accidents.
2. Some children get so involved in their activity that they fail to heed signs of their physical distress. Remind the child to go to the bathroom at the times you have observed were routine for him. Reinforce him with praise when bathroom experiences are successful.
3. Sometimes a simple relapse occurs. Such regressions will stop with time so try not to draw attention to them. Simply offer the child a change of clothing and reassure him that there is nothing wrong with what happened.
4. An emotional problem may cause a child to have accidents fairly regularly. Confer with the child's parents to see if something at home could be contributing to the problem. Children often have severe toileting problems at home, caused by uncertain adults who set unreasonable toileting standards before the children can comprehend them. In such instances, emotional distress can contribute to several toileting problems, such as wetting the bed for periods of time longer than normal or excessive numbers of "accidents."
5. Kidney or bladder infections may cause toileting problems. If such problems persist and the child appears to be free of emotional influences, a talk with the parents or appropriate medical personnel could be in line.

Regular toileting routines should be carried out in a casual, free atmosphere. You will quickly discover through observation how often each child needs to use the bathroom, and you will be able to make any necessary adjustments. A pleasant "It's time to go to the bathroom," will help the child feel confidence in the teacher's concern for him. After a while, as the child shows increasing ability to regulate his condition, the teacher may simply ask the child, "Do you need to go to the bathroom now?" Slowly the responsibility is shifted to the child, where it must eventually remain. Of course, there will still be accidents, and you must always be on the lookout for them.

The following list of suggestions may be helpful in getting young children adjusted to a sound toileting schedule.

1. Make sure that the bathroom facilities are clean, attractive, and inviting. Maintain a comfortable atmosphere that will help children relax and give them calm confidence.
2. If legally possible, remove the door from the bathroom so toilet provisions can be viewed by the children as part of the normal classroom routine.
3. Allow the children plenty of time to complete their toileting. Being rushed through the process makes it difficult for them to maintain a positive attitude.
4. Be aware of some children who will need help at toilet time, particularly after a bowel movement. Help the child to help himself or to watch others as they gain more skill and confidence.
5. Help those children having difficulty with clothing. Pay particular attention to complicated buttons, fasteners, and buckles, and too tight clothing—this will help prevent accidents. Children often wait until the last moment to use the toilet, so every second wasted by fumbling with a complicated buckle or snap can contribute to the possibility of accidents.
6. Request that parents send a change of clothes for each child so that a proper clean-up operation can be done after inevitable accidents. Some teachers have found, however, that keeping a few sets of unisex clothing on hand is preferable to keeping track of separate clothing for each child.
7. Be constantly aware of the children and look for signs of a toileting accident. Often, the last child to let you know of such incidents is the one who has the problem. If you don't discover it quickly, the other children in the room are bound to do so. And their reactions will often be unintentionally shattering: "Ugh, Kelly just peed in her pants!" If this happens often enough, the child will soon develop feelings of disapproval or shame over her toileting failures.
8. Some teachers of young children believe that toileting should become a specified part of the daily schedule for all children in the room. For instance, all children may be encouraged to use the toilet when they come to school, then after outdoor play in the middle of the morning, and again just before lunch. Those on the full-day schedule will have similar intervals in the afternoon. These teachers believe that such practices encourage the acquisition of greater routine and control. Those who favor a more individualized approach, however, argue that a set schedule ignores the personal needs of each child and that all children must go to the toilet when their personal needs dictate. Others offer a compromise —they establish a schedule to encourage children to develop a routine in their toileting, but it is a flexible one; that is, within the schedule children are allowed to go when they need to. They see this system as being easier to control than the individualized approach but more individualized than the rigid schedule approach.

Since young children of both sexes often share the same bathroom facilities, it is common for boys and girls during the toileting period to begin to show a strong interest in each other's bodies. At about the age of four, they begin to realize that boys and girls are not alike, and this is a confusing discovery. Their faces, arms, legs, and belly buttons look alike—and even their behinds look the same. Now comes the reality that one place indeed looks different—the boy has a penis and scrotum and the girl has a vagina. "Why does Ginny's look like that and mine look like this?" "Why are boys and girls different?" Such questions are not meant to startle adults, but are children's honest efforts to find out about something that is most important to them at this age—their bodies.

What do you tell children when they ask such questions about their new interests? Through your responses, show acceptance and understanding, and explain that all little boys are made with a penis and all little girls are made with a vagina. Avoid substitute names such as wee-wee, tinkler, pee-pee, or ding-dong. If the children pursue your explanation with the question "Why," give them accurate information about sexual matters but without going into a full account of sexual intercourse. Simply explain that when a father and mother want to have a baby, a special fluid comes from the father's body through the penis and joins with an egg in the mother's body where the baby starts to grow. When the baby is born, it comes out through the vagina. Stay away from explanations such as "Daddy plants a seed in mommy." Explanations such as this only confuse young children, as they undoubtedly picture daddy forcing mommy to swallow a peach pit or doing some similar act. Explain that because of these special body functions, it is perfectly natural for boys to stand up to urinate while girls sit down. Remember that young children are not shocked by such explanations. Only when parents or teachers communicate uncomfortable feelings about such information do children feel shock or anxiety. One child, for example, was so surprised when his teacher asked, "Do you need to *urinate* now?" that he immediately blurted, "You used a dirty word!" Keep in mind that young children will react to your unspoken feelings. This is why your attitudes in this area must first be clarified and your feelings of worry and embarrassment modified.

Washing and Keeping Clean

Cleanliness is an important consideration for teachers and caretakers of young children. Of course, the ways in which such care is extended vary with the age groups under their care—infants require specialized techniques that differ from those used with toddlers or young children. The following suggestions are designed to assist you in washing infants.

□ Once the baby loses his umbilical cord (usually at about 10 days), he is ready for his first sponge bath. Wash the baby in a sink or basin. You may want to cushion the bottom of the sink or basin with a towel or sponge and add several inches of warm water (not much warmer than your body temperature).

□ Use a mild soap and soap the baby all over, even his head. Be careful because the baby will become very slippery.

▫   Talk and sing to the baby during the bath—make it an enjoyable time. Say each body part as you wash—this encourages language growth.

▫   Once rinsed and dried, the baby should be rubbed with lotion because skin oils were removed by the water. Some babies will enjoy being rubbed with cooling bath powder, also.

▫   After a few months, the baby will become more and more excitable in the water. At this time you may want to move him to a tub for his bath (oh, your sore back!).

▫   To prevent many fears of children in bathtubs, always make sure you remove the child from the tub before you pull the drain plug. Otherwise, youngsters may fear going down the drain with the bath water. Some children are afraid to have their hair washed, probably because they cannot see what's happening to them. Hold a mirror in front of the child as you joyfully sculpt sudsy forms on his head. He may want to join you after awhile!

▫   Baths are important, but they should not be given each time the infant or toddler becomes soiled. Take comfort, he won't catch a disease simply because he is slightly dirty. As a matter of fact, some pediatricians argue that one of the reasons for the high rate of childhood disease among young children in this country is that they have been kept *too clean* and haven't had a great opportunity to build up natural immunities.

Washing the hands and keeping clean could be encouraged with older children following a toileting routine, but it should not constantly be considered a virtual necessity. It is a habit that young children develop in time, especially if motivated by adults or older children whom they admire. However, in order to maintain an attitude favorable to sound health and hygiene, hand washing should be compulsory before, and in some instances after, eating. In addition, vigorous activity during play, such as digging in dirt or hammering nails, will frequently require a freshening up period, including washing the face and hands. When children awaken from afternoon naps, they have another opportunity to wash. A pleasant, friendly reminder encourages them to refresh themselves after this comfortable period of sleep.

ACCIDENTS AND INJURIES

In addition to childhood diseases, teachers of young children face other common health hazards in the form of accidents, mishaps, and injuries. As the teacher, you will probably be the first adult on the scene in the case of such emergencies. The guidelines in Table 5-3 on how to respond to common accidents explain what steps to take. Diagnosis and treatment of severe injuries should be left to the school nurse or other trained medical personnel, but many common emergencies can be effectively handled with common medical knowledge and basic first aid supplies. Whatever the situation, try to

Table 5-3   Treatment of Minor Injuries

Minor Injury	Condition	Guideline
Abrasion	Oozing blood, as from a scraped knee	Clean out with soap and water; bandage if necessary.
Laceration	Deep cut that bleeds more freely than an abrasion	Apply pressure to wound; clean with soap and water; bandage; notify medical personnel.
Burn	Redness of skin or blistering	Keep under cold running water or wrapped in clean cloth; if blistering, get medical help.
Sprain	Swollen and discolored joint	Keep pressure off the injured joint; apply cold packs; contact medical personnel.
Fracture	Difficulty moving arm or leg; swelling; hard to distinguish from sprain unless bone punctures skin	Do not move the child; summon medical help at once.
Head injury	Sometimes, no apparent signs of injury; bump or bruise often accompanies, however	Calm the child; summon medical help; apply cold pack to minor bumps.
Foreign object in eye	Burning eyes; watery; turning red	Keep child from rubbing eye; wash eye with cool water; summon medical help.
Bee sting	Part of body red, swollen, and warm to touch; if allergic, child may have difficulty breathing, become cold, feel clammy, or even pass out	Apply a cold pack; if allergic, get medical help at once.
Fainting	Loss of consciousness due to insufficient supply of blood to the brain	Keep child lying down and summon medical assistance.
Nose bleed	Trickle of blood from the nose	Keep child quiet; hold head back and apply cold pack; squeeze nostrils together for a few minutes.
Choking	Foreign matter becomes lodged in air passage	Use the Heimlich maneuver.
Convulsions	Child falls unconscious; muscles stiffen, relax, etc. in a series of rhythmical contractions	Make sure breathing passages are open; keep child from bruising self; roll up cloth and place between teeth; place child face down on soft surface.

remain calm and in control—the child will not be reassured by a frightened, tense adult.

Knowing how to handle medical crises is extremely important to the adult working with young children because, as a teacher in a nursery school or child-care facility, you automatically acquire certain legal responsibilities related to what takes place during school hours. Robert Hess and Doreen Croft explain:

> In essence, the administration and staff become liable for the health and safety of the students and, if legally challenged, must provide suitable explanation for the way they met this responsibility.
>
> Nursery school liability is essentially different from that of other schools, because when a young child is injured, there is deemed to be no contributory negligence on his part. If older children are injured, lost, kidnapped, or in some other way harmed while at school, the courts hold that they may conceivably have contributed to their condition. In cases involving nursery schools, however, the law is clear that young children are not expected to take care of themselves. Because caretaking, not education, is interpreted to be the primary purpose of a nursery school, a special burden is placed on the school and its teachers.[1]

Because of this special burden, several remedial steps should be taken to lessen the possibility of costly legal problems:

1. Check the safety of the overall physical plant:
   a. fireproof construction (alarms, extinguishers, fire escapes)
   b. open and free hallways, stairs, or doors
   c. heating plant shut off by fire doors
   d. freedom from chipping paint (especially paint containing lead)
   e. playground free from broken glass, nails, sharp metal edges, and the like
   f. safe and sturdy equipment
2. Provide constant supervision both within and outside the classroom. Children should be constantly supervised by a teacher who is alert to the entire situation.
3. Set realistic limits for the children. Let them know that there are constraints essential for the protection of their health and safety. Make such limits known in simple, concrete terms so they understand exactly what is expected of them: "Walk around the swings to get to the jungle gym." Avoid overly frightening the child with irresponsible comments such as, "If you keep walking so close to the swings, someday you'll get your head knocked off."
4. Report all accidents and injuries to appropriate medical personnel and to parents, regardless of how minor they may seem. Record such accidents on the child's health record.
5. Obtain insurance to cover you if you get involved in a legal suit and to cover the children in case of physical injury.
6. Keep an up-to-date accident report form as a means of pinpointing accidents and avoiding repetitions. Such a report should include the child's

name, time, date, cause of injury, first aid administered, and any recommendations to prevent similar accidents from happening.

Accidents and injuries, then, are sometimes part of a day's unscheduled activities. Since the responsibility for meeting these situations normally falls on the teacher, it is up to you to select and maintain safe equipment and to enforce safety measures in and around the school.

CHILD ABUSE

Nearly every preschool has children with histories of neglect and abuse. This is a very sensitive area and one in which many teachers hesitate to become involved. However, the problem of child abuse is a serious one and reflects some interesting statistics:

Child battering is a major killer of children today.

If no family therapeutic program is initiated, the child once released from a physician's care, stands a 25 percent to 50 percent risk of further permanent injury or death.

Eighty-five percent of the children abused are under six years of age, 75 percent under four years of age, 25 percent under one year, and 16 percent under six months.[2]

Since only a small percentage of child abuse cases are ever reported, these estimates should be considered to be very conservative.

People looking at such statistics often tend to feel that the abusive parent is undereducated, poor, mentally imbalanced, or a basic child hater. However, according to E. F. Lenoski, "Ninety percent of a group of parents reported are married and employed. They come from all walks of life, professions, ethnic groups. They are voters. Eighty percent confess to a religious belief. Only 10 percent are mentally ill. Only 8 percent are drinkers and only 2 percent are drug addicts."[3] Child abusers come from all walks of life. They cannot be classified according to any stereotypes—but one characteristic does seem to be present in most: They were abused themselves as children.

Teachers need to be alert to the signs and symptoms that point to the possibility of neglect or abuse and know the steps they can take to bring help to those children whose needs are not being met at home. Consider the following example.

Jerry was a quiet, withdrawn child who was usually lethargic and listless at school. He very rarely engaged in vigorous activity and seemed to prefer sleeping or daydreaming most of the day. Jerry had a history of missing school regularly—nearly always for flimsy reasons and lame excuses. Despite his withdrawn, passive personality, Jerry often came to school with cuts and welts or in obvious pain. When questioned by his teacher, Jerry always attributed his injuries to accidents incurred while running, to falling off his bicycle, and to similar forms of strong physical activity.

Jerry's teacher was concerned with such inconsistencies. One day he arrived at school with a cast on one arm and a series of swellings and bruises on his face. When questioned, he of course attributed his injuries to falling off his bicycle. But when she examined the injuries closely, the teacher found that the cuts and marks were not the type you would expect in a fall from a bicycle. The teacher was by now confused. She strongly suspected parental abuse and wanted to help the child, but she didn't know what to do.

This situation is not unique—it probably occurs every day in the nation's schools. So that you won't find yourself in the same predicament as Jerry's teacher, carefully examine the following information.

First, Jerry's teacher should be commended on her willingness to do something about the situation. All too often teachers fear personal retribution from angry, raging parents. In addition, many teachers see themselves as having a "righteous" image and fear to come close to situations that are so far removed from their own thinking. In other words, because the situation is so foreign to their backgrounds or views of parenthood, they tend to shy away from it and, in effect, "pretend it isn't there." However, if our concern for the total welfare of children is genuine, we must be willing to confront cases of child abuse and try to do something about them.

Child abuse can be classified into three distinct categories: *physical abuse, mental abuse,* and *sexual abuse.* If children experiencing any of these forms of abuse are identified when they show the first symptoms, they may be helped when their problems can be most readily solved. However, too often problems are not recognized until the conditions of neglect become acute and intolerable. And by then it may be too late to salvage the child or the home. The following is a list of symptoms of possible neglect and abuse that you can look for.

Child's Appearance

1. Does child appear dirty and unkempt?
2. Does child appear hungry, malnourished, or waiflike?
3. Does child have regular swellings, cuts, bruises, burns, and so on?
4. Does child exhibit difficulty or pain when moving?
5. Does child have injuries related to sexual molestation?
6. Does child wear "cover-up" clothing in warm weather?

Child's Behavior

1. Does child have difficulty explaining regular injuries?
2. Does child refuse to admit cause of injuries?
3. Does child appear "afraid" when questioned about injuries?
4. Is child chronically late or absent?
5. Does child explain lateness or absence with flimsy reasons?
6. Is child passive or withdrawn?

7. Does child daydream or seem out of touch with reality?
8. Is child aggressive, disruptive, or destructive?
9. Does child appear to be acting out of need for attention?

Once you have reason to suspect child abuse, it is important to report the case directly to your immediate supervisor or to a child protective agency, depending on the regulations of your child-care facility. Such a procedure is not now simply a humanitarian gesture as it once was, since in several states (including California and Pennsylvania) professionals may be guilty of a misdemeanor if they fail to report incidents of suspected child abuse to the proper authorities.

Teachers who do report such cases rarely, if ever, get involved beyond this point. The protective agencies normally contact the parents, develop the facts in each case, and diagnose the type and quality of service needed to rehabilitate the home without ever bringing the teacher into the picture. This rehabilitation philosophy is based on

> a "reaching out" with social services to stabilize family life. It seeks to preserve the family unit by strengthening parental capacity and ability to provide good child care. Its special attention is focused on families where unresolved problems have produced visible signs of neglect or abuse and the home situation presents actual and potentially greater hazard to the physical or emotional well-being of children.[4]

Many parents, after having their initial anger or resentment calmed by a case worker who convinces them that she is there to help and not to punish, are willing to undergo therapeutic intervention. Strange as it may sound, they are willing to do so because their neglect and abuse was probably not willful or deliberate. The treatment of their children usually results from frustrations associated with their inadequacy or inability to live up to or practice parental roles. And if they are, for example, unable to control their child's behavior, their frustration builds and they may feel that severe physical or mental abuse of the child is the only solution. The role of the protective agency in such a case is to educate these parents and help them become more acceptable and confident in their functioning.

By working together with the proper agencies, you help the child in need of protection. If help is given in time, the emotional impact of serious neglect and abuse can be forestalled and the blocks that inhibit the development of a whole child can be removed.

A SOUND, NUTRITIOUS DIET

Involved in the responsibility of maintaining a healthful environment is providing a program of sound nutrition. Perhaps the most obvious product of an unbalanced program of nutrition is an overweight or underweight child.

The reasons why a child becomes overweight may be either constitutional or environmental (too much exercise with the fork), but many authorities today feel that our affluent society and its wealth of "junk foods" has contributed more to the problem than any other source. Soda pop, candy bars, chewing gum, cakes, cookies, and fast food restaurants (often referred to as "franchised malnutrition") all appeal to children and parents to the extent that America's calorie intake is at an all-time high, but related nutritional benefits have not increased proportionately. Concern about this situation has become so intense today that complaints from special interest groups have pressured food manufacturers and advertisers to soften their hard-sell approach to marketing "junk food" that contains largely starches and sugars. We still have a long way to go, but such public reaction helps to allay somewhat a situation that some authorities view as a major health problem of young children.

Less well recognized are the problems of underweight children. These children, too, need to be understood, for they may suffer as much as overweight children. "Beanpole" or "Stick" and similar taunts can cause children to become shy and sensitive about their condition. Also, they may lack the stamina to engage in some of the more active games.

Both underweight and overweight children have a basic problem with sound nutritional practices. However, in some cases, the underlying problem may be physical. If you are in doubt, check with a physician to see what weight is best for the child and to what extent the condition is physical or psychological.

The need for more effective nutritional practices is noted not only for the physical and behavioral advantages to be gained, but also because there is a relationship between a good early diet and the fulfillment of a child's mental capabilities. R. Lewin has argued that "an infant deprived of nutrition or stimulation will never develop to full mental capacity."[5] Dorothy Rodgers substantiates this claim:

> The infant's brain has reached 25% of its final weight at birth; and by 6 months it is halfway there. By contrast, total body weight at birth is only 5% of its final weight and reaches the halfway mark only by age 10. As a group, severely malnourished children lag behind in language at the age of 6 months. If both *adequate food and supplementary schooling* are provided children by the age of 3½, deficiencies attributed to early malnutrition may be overcome. However, if these children do not get the additional foods until after that age they do not show such gains, because the critical brain-growth period has passed. [Italics are mine.][6]

Similar observations have been made over the years, but only recently have early childhood professionals so strongly stressed the relationship between inadequate diet and reduced learning power. We have become concerned because of our commitment to provide opportunities for optimal development and functioning. Herbert Birch and Joan Gussow report that the *most important* factor in determining the child's growth and functioning is probably nutrition.[7] They go on to explain that "there is no question that the child's ability to respond appropriately to significant stimuli in his environment is retarded during the period of chronic malnutrition; and that continued malnutrition is accompanied by progressive behavioral regression."[8] These are powerful statements—perhaps as important as Bloom's and Hunt's late 1960s research findings (discussed in Chapter 1) that awakened us to the importance of stimulation during the early years for later intellectual functioning.

Mealtime

Child-care centers should recognize the importance of sound nutrition both in their mealtimes and in their educational programs. Although sound nutrition is not fully valued by some, it is as important to the success of a complete early childhood program as any other component. The following guidelines should be carefully considered by child-care facilities catering to infants.

Guidelines for Infant Nutrition

1. Feed infants when they become hungry. They develop many of their feelings of trust by being fed when they are hungry.
2. Hold the infant comfortably during feeding. He will understand that the world is a safe place and that you can be trusted.
3. Smile, chat, and respond to the infant as he is fed. Make the feeding experience a pleasant one.
4. Have a well-trained nursery attendant in charge of one or two infants, and allow each child to determine his own feeding schedule.
5. Ask the mother to bring in the child's formula or to prepare it at the center. However, label each bottle so that formulas cannot be confused.
6. Some infants start on solid food during the first month of life; others start much later. Keep in constant touch with the home so that your practices are consistent.
7. At about six or seven months, the infant can be placed in a high chair for short periods of time.
8. At six to seven months, babies begin to show preferences for food, so it should be selected to agree with individual tastes. Introduce the baby to new foods by encouraging him to explore a variety of foods placed before him—mashed bananas, pears, or apples are especially appealing.
9. Encourage the baby to do things for himself. Reinforce any attempts at self-feeding and provide items such as carrot sticks, bread crusts, and hard cookies to encourage such tendencies. From about age 1 until age 2, the child assumes increasing responsibility for his own feeding.
10. When the child moves toward eating solid foods, a new challenge awaits you—getting him to use eating utensils. Follow these suggestions:

☐ Allow the child to use his fingers during feeding time but remember that he will be messy. This is an important initial step to get the infant to feed himself.

Infants and toddlers in preschool settings need a regular, nutritionally balanced program of meals during the day.

☐ Give the infant a spoon to play with as you feed him. Soon you will be able to help him fill the spoon, and put it into his mouth. Naturally, he will miss the target a few times at first, but have patience, he will slowly improve with practice.

☐ Let the infant play with an unbreakable empty cup while you are feeding him. When he seems to gain control, fill the cup with a few drops of a favorite liquid and let him try to drink from it. Again, there is bound to be some spilling so give a small portion at a time and allow plenty of practice. Perhaps you may want to put a rubber band around the cup to help prevent it from slipping.

Toddlers and young children attending child-care facilities may need one or several mealtimes during the day: breakfast, mid-morning or mid-afternoon snack, lunch, and, in some cases, dinner. These meals should be carefully planned, preferably by a qualified nutritionist, and prepared by capable cooks in clean, sanitary kitchens. The number and kinds of meals, of course, depend on how long a particular child spends at the preschool center. For example, a child attending a center for a half day may be given only breakfast and a snack; a child attending a full day may require each meal. Whatever the case, each menu should be planned around a sound nutritional base, such as the following, which are based on Head Start guidelines. Menus for major meals—breakfast, lunch, and dinner—should include items from each of the four basic food groups plus water:

1. Milk, cheese, eggs, and related dairy products (3 servings per full day)
2. Meat, fish, and poultry (2 servings per full day)
3. Fruits and vegetables (3 servings per full day)
4. Breads and cereals (4 servings per full day)
5. Water (6–8 glasses per day)

Basically, young children require the same foods as adults, but in smaller proportions. Sample food guides for full meals and snacks are given in the accompanying box.

Remember that children this age manage best with small helpings of food and that their appetites vary from day to day. Thus, don't pressure children to eat food they may not feel like eating on a particular day—when they are ready, they will most certainly eat. Conversely, have additional servings ready for children who want them. The following is a list of basic rules of thumb to follow in deciding on a serving size for young children:

- ½–1 cup of milk
- ⅓–⅔ cup of juice
- 1–3 ounces of meat, poultry, or fish
- 1–2 tablespoons of vegetable or fruit
- ½–1 slice of bread
- 1–2 cookies or crackers

It is important that children have their meals in a clean, cheerful environment. Mealtimes should be periods of calmness and happiness for children.

MEAL GUIDES: SHADYSIDE DAY-CARE CENTER

Breakfast
Cereal (½–1 cup)
Milk (½–1 cup)
Cheese cube (1–2 pieces)
Apple (1–2 wedges)

Morning Snack
Orange juice (⅓–⅔ cup)
Bread and butter (½–1 slice whole wheat)

Lunch
Fish pattie (½–1 ounce)
Carrot strips (2–4 raw strips)
Corn (1–2 tablespoons cooked)
Bread and butter (½–1 slice whole wheat)
Pudding (¼–½ cup)
Milk (½–1 cup)

Afternoon Snack
Milk (½–1 cup)
Oatmeal cookie (1–2)

During these periods adults help them establish food habits that are the foundation of good health throughout their lives. Several guidelines should be followed in creating such an atmosphere. They will help teachers and other child-care workers realize the most effective means of facilitating the goals of sound nutrition.

Guidelines for a Good Nutrition Program

1. Children differ in their reactions to food.
    a. Allow them to become acquainted with *new* foods *slowly.* Introducing several new foods at one meal will certainly cause problems.
    b. Allow them to make some choices as to what they eat. For example, let a child who dislikes vegetables choose between two of them—you may get him to eat one.
    c. Keep home and cultural patterns in mind. The foods children will openly accept or reject are those that are likely to be accepted or rejected by their family and culture.
2. A good physical and emotional environment is important.
    a. Provide a bright, clean eating area.
    b. Furnish plates, cups, and eating utensils that can be comfortably managed by small hands.
    c. Have suitably sized tables and chairs so children will be physically comfortable.
    d. Seat four or five children together with one adult at a table, and encourage calm, interesting conversation. Many concepts can be extended during this time by discussing: *yellow* corn, *orange* carrots, or *green* beans; *crisp* vegetables, *soft* pudding; *more* milk, *less* juice; *one* cookie, *two* cookies.
    e. Never withhold foods, such as a special anticipated treat, for punishment.
    f. Try playing soft music at times.
    g. Accept table accidents as a normal part of life. Don't create a fuss by admonishing the child to be more careful—simply assist him in a clean-up operation.
    h. Plan an orderly schedule for mealtimes. However, don't overemphasize regularity to the point of causing emotional concerns. Some children have trouble regulating themselves to a routine and need understanding and guidance from an adult.
3. The way in which food is served to the children may determine whether or not they eat it.
    a. Serve small portions—to a small child a heaping plate may be an impossible challenge. Children respond more positively to a small serving and assurances of seconds than to a huge original portion.
    b. Serve bite-sized pieces of food that may be eaten with the fingers. Even those who can use a fork do so more easily when faced with small pieces of food.
    c. Serve the meal as soon as the children are seated around the table.

Children learn good eating habits and develop a positive feeling for good nutrition if mealtime is conducted in an organized, cheerful manner.

    d. Serve some raw vegetables and some cooked—children may prefer one over the other. Cauliflower, carrots, celery, turnips, and rutabagas provide interesting assortments of this type.

    e. Serve foods with a variety of colors and textures. Cut the food into a variety of sizes and shapes to interest the children—cheese may be cut into diamonds and squares or carrots into strips and circles.

    f. Avoid mixing foods together on the children's plates. Many children avoid eating foods if they even touch one another on the same plate. For this reason, never mix vegetables on the same plate or serve a gravy or sauce that will spill over to another food on the same plate. Many teachers prefer plastic plates that are sectioned off into separate areas.

4. Children should develop a sense of responsibility for establishing good nutritional habits.

    a. Encourage them to wash their hands and faces before each meal. While waiting for others to get ready, children finished early may read books, sit with a friend, or engage in other quiet activities.

    b. Urge children to help set the tables. Napkins, eating utensils, and cups can be arranged by the children and tied into cognitive learning that occurs during other parts of the day. For example, telling the child to "put five napkins at this table," or to "pour a little more juice for Amy," helps to reinforce skills worked on earlier.

    c. Older children (3½ years and up) can pass serving bowls or pitchers to one another as they wish to help themselves to extra portions.

5. A smooth, orderly transition should be made between a preceding activity and mealtime. One teacher, for example, after reading a story filled with animals, had the children move to the eating area one group at a

time—the mice "creeping," the elephants "clumping," the lions "stalking," and so on.

Mealtime in a child-care facility, then, must be organized, clean, and cheerful. Wholesome food, attractively prepared and served, will encourage most children to develop a positive attitude toward eating nutritious meals. However, should eating problems persist over a period of time, it would be wise to consult with the parents, school nurse, or a physician.

COOKING WITH YOUNG CHILDREN

Because of the increased emphasis on nutrition education, cooking programs are finding their way into more and more early childhood programs. Such projects are valuable for two reasons: (1) they involve children with the food and (2) they are meaningful learning activities. Both of these features are illustrated in the following discussion.

When creating a cooking program, keep in mind a principle that weaves its way through nearly every theory of learning: Start with the simple and move to the more complex. Beginning cooking experiences should contain activities in which all young children can participate with a reasonable degree of success. These activities are usually referred to as "precooking" activities, but they can be characterized as tasks that help children become familiar with the various skills necessary for an effective cooking program. The accompanying box describes some "precooking" activities you can have the children do.

PRECOOKING ACTIVITIES

1. Scrub vegetables (carrots, celery) with brushes.
2. Spread peanut butter on ½ slice of bread.
3. Measure and pour dry ingredients (rice, popcorn) from a cup into a bowl.
4. Measure and pour liquids (water, milk) from a cup into a bowl.
5. Blend together two ingredients (water and Jello powder).
6. Shake something (cream to make butter).
7. Roll something with the hands (cookies).
8. Use cooking utensils: table knives (soft to hard foods), hand grinder (peanut butter), hand grater (cheese, carrots), rolling pin (cookie dough), egg beater (pudding ingredients), scraper (peeling carrots or potatoes), hand juicer (oranges), food chopper (nuts).

First cooking experiences should be simple ones that help familiarize children with the basic tools used in the cooking process.

Beginning activities such as these help familiarize children with the cooking process. If they are properly guided, most youngsters become excited about their growing accomplishments and are highly motivated to enter into more complex cooking projects. However, successful cooking projects don't happen just by chance—they must be carefully planned in advance so the maximum learning potential can be derived. Keep the following ideas uppermost in mind as you plan any cooking project with your young children.

1. Allow all children who want to do so to participate actively.
2. Require that children wash their hands and faces before the cooking project starts.
3. Scrub the cooking counter with soap and water before the cooking activity begins.
4. Encourage children to experiment as they work with the food (smell, taste, chop, etc.).
5. Emphasize the many areas of learning as the cooking project evolves:

    □ following directions (pour the milk into the bowl)
    □ listening (pour syrup over the oats)
    □ learning new words (*avocado*)
    □ working as a group member (help to peel the apples)
    □ learning about foods (where they come from, how they grow; their nutritional value)
    □ understanding changes in states of matter (liquid to gelatin)
    □ measuring ingredients (½ cup, 1 teaspoon)
    □ developing muscle control (mixing, pouring, grasping)

Cleaning and scrubbing are important first steps in preparing an area for cooking experiences.

6. Maintain a safe environment:

    ☐ Discuss safety measures for appropriate projects.
    ☐ Use care while working at a hot stove or with hot liquids.
    ☐ Encourage children to respect (not fear) sharp knives and other potentially dangerous kitchen utensils.
    ☐ Provide constant, alert supervision.

7. Allow children the opportunity to have fun and enjoy the cooking experience. The time should be one of pleasant socializing rather than of stony silence or petty arguments.
8. Cooking can be more fun if the children prepare foods they have grown themselves. Beans, spinach, peas, and lettuce are all easily raised in a small garden plot and provide sound, nutritious meals.
9. It is becoming common to hear about doing away with "junk foods" containing sugars, saturated fats, and large amounts of starches. A back-to-nature approach is gaining strength—a program that emphasizes natural fruits, vegetables, nuts, and dairy foods rather than prepackaged foods, cake mixes, pudding, candy, and other sweets. Try to eliminate such "junk food" snacks or meals and move toward more nutritious foods.

Initial cooking projects should be fairly simple—many teachers begin with gelatin, pudding, popcorn, vegetables, and the like. Increased interest and skill will gradually lead to more sophisticated experiences. Be careful, though, to suit the project to the level of the children because if it is too difficult, too long, or has too many steps to follow, children will become distracted and frustrated with the idea, "Here's another thing I can't do!" The following anecdote illustrates how one teacher combined all of these suggestions in creating a cooking experience.

Mrs. Hollister had already done some basic food preparation activities and seen the children respond favorably to them. Now she was encouraged to try making a tossed salad with them. In developing the project, Mrs. Hollister found it useful to complete a planning form [similar to the one illustrated in Figure 5-2]. This task helped her to organize her thinking and kept the project moving along in a confident, constructive manner.

Mrs. Hollister served as the "cooking coordinator," the person responsible for guiding the efforts of four small groups of children, each group working with

---

COOKING PROJECT

Date _____   Project _____

Whole group activity   Small group activity

1. Purpose for the project:

    ☐ New food experience   ☐ Observing texture changes in
                                        cooking
    ☐ Fun experience   ☐ Noting similarities and differences

    ☐ Language development   ☐ Small muscle skills

    ☐ Following directions   ☐ Learning about different foods

    ☐ Cooking skills   ☐ Encourage experimentation

    ☐ Sensory experience   ☐ Listening experience

    ☐ Observing changes in matter   ☐ Social experience

2. Cooking supplies needed:

    _____   _____   _____
    _____   _____   _____
    _____   _____   _____
    _____   _____   _____

3. Ingredients needed:

    _____   _____   _____
    _____   _____   _____
    _____   _____   _____
    _____   _____   _____

4. Step-by-step procedure:

    a. _____   f. _____

    b. _____   g. _____

    c. _____   h. _____

    d. _____   i. _____

    e. _____   j. _____

Figure 5-2 Planning form for a cooking project.

Figure 5-3   Children's recipe guides.

*volunteer "cooking mothers." The groups were located at four separate tables.
Each group used its time to do a specific task leading to the completion of the
salad. At one table children were busily washing and tearing the lettuce and
spinach. Similarities and differences between the two vegetables were brought
out as the cooking mother encouraged the children to observe the dark green
spinach leaves and compare them to the lighter green lettuce leaves. The children
were also asked to compare differences in texture, size, taste, and other features.
As the cooking mother asked questions about the leaves' growth and their other
uses, the children were motivated to hypothesize, and predict answers.*

*In much the same manner, cooking mothers at other tables sparked
conversation about their tasks—at the slicing table, about how cucumbers,
tomatoes, and radishes change in appearance from outside to the inside; at the
grating table, about the smell and texture or appearance of the carrots and cheese
as they are being grated. Meanwhile, a fourth group of children was making a
simple salad dressing that would eventually turn the salad creation into a
masterpiece! The children at each table were guided by the cooking mothers and
a simplified recipe guide in determining just how much of their ingredients were
needed for the salad. [Sample children's recipe guides are illustrated in Figure
5-3.]*

*As the children worked along toward the completion of their separate
projects, Mrs. Hollister and the cooking mothers observed them to determine
levels of motor skill development (eye-hand coordination, manipulation of
utensils, and so on), perception, listening skills, ability to follow directions, and
concept development (quantity, texture, time, and so on). When each separate
table completed its task, the children were brought together by Mrs. Hollister at a*

fifth, central table where all the ingredients were combined. As each table's ingredients were added to a large bowl, the children were asked to talk about what their group did so the whole group could learn to appreciate the efforts of small groups in a large community activity.

When the salad was eventually completed, Mrs. Hollister asked everyone to sit at their tables and then passed out a small bowl of the finished product to everyone. "Yumm, it smells so good" or "This is the best salad I ever ate" were the general comments heard. However, one or two hesitant children couldn't be convinced to try the salad. They were simply asked to, "Please stay and keep the rest of us company." Mrs. Hollister chose to capitalize on the children's pride of accomplishment for this project by developing an experience chart later in the day. In this way, all the experiences were summarized in a meaningful beginning reading activity. Those who wished to do so added illustrations for the story during the quiet time that followed.

Enthusiasm for Mrs. Hollister's project soon reached the children's homes. Parents contacted her and made comments such as, "What kind of salad did you make in school? Billy never wanted to eat salad before and now I can't feed him enough of it." This example illustrates the extent to which teachers can influence good nutrition in the home. Mrs. Hollister decided to take advantage of the parental interest by sending home a recipe letter each time a new recipe was created in her class. The following is a copy of one of her letters.

March 16, 1980

Dear Parents,

We made a tasty tossed salad in school today! We would like to share our recipe with you.

8 cups	iceberg lettuce	¼ cup	diced onions
3 cups	raw spinach	¼ cup	sliced radishes
¼ cup	thinly sliced carrots	¼ cup	diced green peppers
½ cup	sliced cucumbers	2	sliced tomatoes

Wash or scrub all of the vegetables. Tear the lettuce and spinach leaves and place them into a large bowl. Add each of the other ingredients. When all have been added, toss them until the salad is evenly mixed. Store the salad in the refrigerator until it is to be served. Then prepare this dressing and pour it over the top.

Mix

2 cups mayonnaise

1 cup sour cream

4 tablespoons finely chopped green onion.

The salad was delicious!

With love,
Mrs. Hollister's Five-Year-Old Group
Sunnydale Day-Care Center

Teachers can help guide parents, especially low-income parents, in other ways, too. Remember, however, that families with larger incomes often need

Numerous values result from a carefully planned cooking experience.

guidance, but problems of poor nutrition are more commonly confined to lower income levels. Because of greater resources, though, families with larger incomes can afford to make mistakes and still receive an adequate diet for maintaining good health. The following resources can help guide families in need of information on good nutrition:

1. Home visits by nutrition professionals (or teachers if they are specifically knowledgeable in nutrition)
2. Food demonstration classes in which parents are shown methods of preparing food that will preserve the greatest nutritive value
3. Printed materials periodically sent to the home in all forms (pamphlets, leaflets, letters, and so on) and in all languages
4. The U.S.D.A. Home Economist in your area who can help in efforts toward good nutrition.

Thus, two practical approaches to meeting the concern for good nutrition are available to early childhood educators today: (1) providing sound, nutritious meals and snacks in the child-care facility and (2) educating parents about basic principles of good nutrition. It is the responsibility of all of us to be aware of these two major options and to develop innovative, imaginative, practical approaches to nutrition education for young children.

Recipes

The following recipes have been successfully used in various types of preschools around the country. They require only simple mixing and measuring, and varied amounts of cooking time. Other recipes are readily available in special cookbooks for children, in general cookbooks found in the home, or in the activity guide that accompanies this text.

NONCOOKING RECIPES

Waldorf Salad

4 cups diced apples
2 cups diced celery
⅔ cup chopped walnuts
1 cup raisins
1 cup mayonnaise

Mix apple, celery, walnuts, raisins, and mayonnaise; toss. If desired, serve on a bed of fresh lettuce and top with a bing cherry.

Coleslaw

8 cups finely shredded cabbage
½ cup finely chopped onion
1 cup sour cream
½ cup mayonnaise
1 teaspoon salt
1 teaspoon dry mustard

Combine cabbage and onion in large bowl. Blend the remaining ingredients together in a separate container and pour over the cabbage and onion. Mix.

Butter

1 pint heavy whipping cream
½ cup salt
Small baby food jar for each child

Pour about 3 tablespoons of whipping cream and a dash of salt into a small baby food jar. Shake the jars vigorously until butter forms (5–10 minutes). The liquid remaining is buttermilk and the children should taste it.

Three-Bean Salad

1 can green string beans (drained)
1 can yellow wax beans (drained)
1 can red kidney beans (drained)
½ cup chopped green onions
¼ cup chopped fresh parsley
8 oz. Italian salad dressing
1 tablespoon sugar
2 cloves garlic (crushed)
Crisp fresh lettuce

Mix beans, onions, and parsley together in a large salad bowl. Combine salad dressing, sugar, and garlic. Pour over bean mixture and toss. Cover and refrigerate for at least 3 hours, stirring periodically.
Serve on fresh lettuce leaves.

Summer Fruit Salad

3 bananas (sliced)
3 cups oranges (sectioned)
1 cup seedless green grapes
1 cup fresh pineapple (squares)
1 cup fresh pitted cherries
2 cups fresh grapefruit (sectioned)
2 cups pears (squares)
2 cups peaches (squares)

Cut and prepare all fruits. Place into a large salad bowl and leave in the refrigerator to chill. Cover with the following dressing:

Blend 1 cup sour cream, 2 tablespoons honey, and 2 tablespoons orange juice.

COOKING RECIPES

Applesauce

8 apples (pared and quartered)
1 cup water
½ cup brown sugar
¼ teaspoon cinnamon
⅛ teaspoon nutmeg

Heat apples in water until boiling. Reduce heat and simmer 5–10 minutes until tender; stir periodically and add water if necessary. Mash apples with a potato masher and add the remaining ingredients and stir. Heat to boiling and remove from stove.

Oatmeal Crunch

½ cup butter
½ cup sugar
¼ cup dark corn syrup
1 tablespoon molasses
2½ cups oats

Heat oven to 350°. Grease square pan, 8 × 8 × 2 inches with unsalted shortening; line bottom of pan with foil and grease foil. Melt butter over moderate heat. Remove pan from heat, stir in sugar, dark corn syrup, and molasses. Add the oats and stir thoroughly. Press the mixture into the pan and bake 35 minutes. Set pan aside for 10 minutes to cool. Loosen the edges and cut. Let pieces cool completely before serving.

Soft Pretzels

4 cups flour
1 tablespoon salt
1 tablespoon sugar
1 package dry yeast
1½ cups warm water
2 eggs (beaten)
1 cup kosher salt

Combine flour, salt, and sugar. Stir in yeast mixed with warm water. Knead the dough until elastic. Give each child a small ball of dough to form a pretzel in any shape desired. Brush dough with the beaten egg and spinkle with kosher salt. Bake for 20 minutes at 425°.

Apple Crisp

4 cups sliced apples
¾ cup brown sugar
½ cup unbleached flour
½ cup oats
¾ teaspoon cinnamon
¾ teaspoon nutmeg
⅓ cup softened butter or margarine

Heat oven to 375°. Grease square pan, 8 × 8 × 2 inches. Place apple slices in pan. Mix remaining ingredients thoroughly in large bowl. Sprinkle over apples.

Bake 30 minutes until topping is golden brown. Serve warm.

SOME FINAL THOUGHTS

There is much you can do to provide for the health and safety of the youngsters in your care. Try to convince parents that physical examinations and vaccinations are needed before their children enter a group setting. Be prepared to recognize the symptoms of contagious diseases and to care for the children should illnesses or injuries occur while they are under your supervision. Along the same line, help the children understand their role in maintaining a healthful environment by encouraging them to develop desirable health and safety habits.

NOTES

1. Robert D. Hess and Doreen J. Croft, *Teachers of Young Children*, 2d ed. (Boston: Houghton Mifflin, 1972), p. 353.
2. Lola Sanders et al., "Child Abuse: Detection and Prevention," *Young Children* 30, no. 5 (July 1975): 334.
3. E. F. Lenoski, "What's Happening in Child Abuse," workshop comments in "Child Abuse: Detection and Prevention," ed. Lola Sanders et al., p. 334.
4. V. deFrancis, "The Status of Child Protective Services," in *Helping the Battered Child and His Family*, ed. R. E. Helfer and C. H. Kempe (Chicago: University of Chicago Press, 1968), pp. 130–131.
5. R. Lewin, "Starved Brains," *Psychology Today* 9, no. 4 (1975): 30.
6. Dorothy Rogers, *Child Psychology*, 2d ed. (Belmont, Calif.: Wadsworth, 1977), p. 89.
7. Herbert G. Birch and Joan D. Gussow, *Disadvantaged Children: Health, Nutrition and School Failure* (New York: Harcourt, Brace and World, 1970).
8. Ibid., p. 39.

6

Cognitive Development: Three Views of the Learning Process

Cognitive development involves the children's growing ability to conceptualize their ever-broadening world. (*Miss Peach* courtesy of Mell Lazarus and Field Newspaper Syndicate.)

Scene 1

Seated at a table with a small group of children, Mr. Koh enthusiastically announces, "We are really going to have fun today." The children meet his announcement with an approving, "Hooray!"

"I want you all to be good listeners and lookers while I show you a picture. What am I going to do?"

"Show us a picture," reply the children in unison.

"You are all very good listeners today," says Mr. Koh. "Look at the picture and tell me what kind of animal you see."

"Bunnies," offer the children.

"Very, very good," replies Mr. Koh. "Now I will count the number of bunnies in the picture. Follow my finger as I point to each bunny . . . one bunny . . . two bunnies. How many bunnies did I count?"

"Two bunnies!" exclaim the children.

"I like your answers," compliments Mr. Koh. "Now you count the bunnies while I point."

"One bunny . . . two bunnies," count the children in unison.

"Oh, you are so smart today," says Mr. Koh. "Now let me see if I can fool you. Here is another picture—a picture of some kittens. There is one kitten in the picture."

"No!" counter the children.

"No?" questions Mr. Koh. "Show me! I'll point to the kittens and you help me count."

"One kitten . . . two kittens," chant the children. "See, you couldn't fool us."

"You're right," admits Mr. Koh. "You're too sharp for me today."

Scene 2

In another classroom, Ms. Perez is sitting at a table with five of her four-year-olds; the remaining ten children in her classroom have been divided into two other groups, one headed by an assistant teacher and one by an aide. Each group is working on the skill of classifying things according to same *and* different. *Ms. Perez begins this session by stating a rule to the children: "Vehicles are things that take us places." She then asks the children to look at a group of objects (doll furniture, blocks, coins, toy cars, toy trucks) and to select those that take us places by making two groups—vehicles and not vehicles. When the children accomplish the task, Ms. Perez asks them to tell why they grouped the particular objects as they did. Supporting their responses, Ms. Perez says, "Yes. These are all the same, they are vehicles. These are different, they are not vehicles. Please tell me, what is a vehicle?"*

Ms. Perez follows up the vehicle activity with one in which the children are to classify items that are tools *and those that are* not tools.

Scene 3

In this classroom, the children are engaged in several independent activities, either alone or in small groups. Mrs. Field and her assistant do not formally interact with any group, but are nearby to offer encouragement or support when needed. In the science center one child becomes fascinated with a large magnet. Gina finds that by manipulating the magnet and approaching several objects, some materials are attracted to the magnet while others are not. Another child is watching nearby and soon joins Gina. Mrs. Field sees their initial interest growing so she takes a box full of small objects and brings them to the children. "Will these stick to the magnet?" Mrs. Field asks.

"Yes, the block will," says Judy.

"No, it won't," counters Gina.

"How do you think we can find out?" asks Mrs. Field.

"We can touch each thing with the magnet," offers Gina.

"Yes, that would be fun," adds Judy.

"Good idea," Mrs. Field says. "Do it your way and put all the items that will stick to the magnet in the blue box at the table and all the items that will not stick to the magnet in the red box."

Mrs. Field follows the same procedure with other groups throughout the activity period—she creates a problem situation, asks the children to predict an answer to the problem, and encourages them to discover the solutions by themselves.

These three scenes are typical of the ways preschool educators today view the process of helping young children learn. None of the scenes happened by chance; each was carefully planned and developed to encourage and reinforce skills in the academic area of children's development. Recall that such an emphasis began in the late 1960s and, even today, has been part of many preschool programs, especially in Head Start and Follow Through classrooms.

The scenes in the anecdotes reflect the three major philosophies of academic instruction popular today; scene 1 is based on the behaviorist theory of B. F. Skinner; scene 2 is based on the cognitive developmental theory of Jean Piaget; and scene 3 is based on theories of informal learning derived from a combination of Piaget, John Dewey, and Carl Rogers, and can be found in many of today's informal classrooms. These three major theories of instruction are examined in this chapter because such knowledge is essential to help you plan teaching strategies for your own classroom. Grouping the children, choosing classroom materials, deciding on your role, selecting what things to say and how to say them, determining how to evaluate your children, and other key decisions must always be based on a solid theoretical foundation. In short, you should be able to finish this statement for each strategy: "I've decided to try this with my children because . . . ." Answers such as, "They have fun doing it," are not satisfactory. Of course, enjoyment is a major consideration, but a true *professional* early childhood educator should have deeper insight into her teaching repertoire.

The ability to understand learning theory and to apply it in planning the curriculum for their own children is an important professional quality for teachers. Yet, getting teachers to understand or to become interested in such practice is difficult. A great part of the reason for this problem may lie in the way learning theory has been traditionally handled in education courses and/or in professional reading materials. Few attempts have been made to suggest the importance of learning theory to the teacher. Unfortunately, it is often taught as a body of facts to be learned rather than as a strong, applicable tool for teachers. The aim of this chapter, then, is to avoid such common traps and enable you to see how learning theories can help you develop valid, practical teaching practices for the education of young children. The three major classifications of learning theory to be discussed are: (1) the behavioral view, (2) the cognitive developmental view, and (3) the informal view.

THE BEHAVIORAL VIEW

John Watson

Behaviorism began during the early 1900s as a revolt against the explanations of learning popular at the time. John B. Watson began the revolt. He questioned emotion-laden theories that explained learning as occurring through internal forces guiding people to act, such as the psychosexual processes proposed by Freud. Watson insisted that children's education could be

Choosing methods, whether teacher-guided or informal, to foster cognitive skills is an important decision for teachers of young children.

more efficiently guided if their environment were carefully controlled in some way. In fact, he was so convinced that his ideas regarding environmental control were effective that he asserted:

> Give me a dozen healthy infants, well-formed, and my own specified world to bring them up in and I'll guarantee to take any one at random and train him to become any type of specialist I might select—doctor, lawyer, artist, merchant, chief and, yes, even beggar-man and thief, regardless of his talents, penchants, tendencies, abilities, vocations, and race of his ancestors. I am going beyond my facts and I admit it, but so have the advocates of the contrary and they have been doing it for many thousands of years. Please note that when this experiment is made I am to be allowed to specify the way the children are to be brought up and the type of world they have to live in.[1]

Watson's "specified world" was the beginning of behaviorism as we know it today. Basic to his theory was a stimulus-response-reinforcement process for explaining learning that said that a child will tend to repeat acts that are rewarded and avoid repeating acts that are punished or ignored (see Figure 6-1).

Another principle offered by Watson was the principle of *successive approximations*, that is, complicated learning or behavior tasks are learned gradually, in small, carefully planned steps that slowly come closer and

Figure 6-1   The stimulus-response-reinforcement principles of Watson and Thorndike.

closer to a desired level of performance. In other words, any individual can be taught to perform tasks successfully if the unit of learning is small enough and the individual is rewarded for his successes along the way.

Edward L. Thorndike

Following closely on Watson's thinking was the theory of Edward L. Thorndike.[2] Basic to Thorndike's stimulus-response-reinforcement theory were these principles:

1. *The law of readiness.* This law states that when a child becomes interested in reacting to any stimulus, he receives satisfaction when he is allowed to respond and becomes annoyed when prevented from doing so. The term *readiness* implies that previously acquired attitudes, patterns, or reactions serve as a basis for such interest and result in a desire to act. For example, previous enjoyable experiences with a ball arouse within a child the readiness to approach and play with another ball when it is shown to him.

2. *The law of exercise.* Long a basic tenet of education, this law states that learning is strengthened with exercise, provided the learner experiences satisfaction rather than annoyance when involved in the activity.
3. *The law of effect.* This is by far Thorndike's foremost law of learning. It states that those behaviors that lead to satisfying consequences tend to be repeated under like circumstances. For example, giving a child a big hug when he makes his bed in the morning tends to make him repeat the act of making the bed rather than ignoring it.

These principles are illustrated in Figure 6-2.

Thorndike's ideas were well matched with the popular, emerging testing movement begun by Alfred Binet in 1905. Binet's *intelligence tests* provided the advocates of Thorndike's behavioral approach with a valuable tool for measuring and observing the intellectual abilities of children. If the ability to recognize numbers, for example, was regarded as a behavior desirable of children in a kindergarten class, what better way to observe that skill than

Figure 6-2 An illustration of Thorndike's stimulus-response-reinforcement principles: Learning to throw a ball.

through a test? The testing movement gained strong supporters and began to sweep the nation's schools.

John Dewey differed from the behaviorists in that he rejected their structured stimulus-response approach and advocated instead child-centered schools reflecting experiential learning and the *scientific method* of active exploration and direct experience.[3]

Dewey saw the pleas for "training" and "exercising" the child's mind as a reversion to earlier stern, authoritarian notions of learning that were completely out of date with contemporary society's needs. Thorndike, however, whose theory was being particularly attacked, argued that his methods were more "modernized" than those of Dewey because they were so compatible with the popular notions of formalized observation and testing. Perhaps the contrast between the two opposing philosophies can best be seen by labeling Thorndike as someone concerned with a child's *learning* while Dewey was concerned with a child's *thinking;* Thorndike's method can be characterized as "trial and error"; Dewey's, as "learning by doing." Such conflicting philosophical thought attracted a great deal of heated controversy during the 1920s and 1930s. By the mid-1930s, however, Thorndike's ideas had begun to be more widely accepted in elementary schools than those of Dewey, and a 30-year hibernation of Dewey's "progressive" education movement began. By 1935, his ideas had been virtually eliminated from elementary and secondary school teaching practices. However, his ideas of play, exploration, and experimentation remained popular among preschool educators. Dewey's "progressive" education ideas surfaced again during the late 1960s as the force behind the open education movement.

B. F. Skinner

The philosophy of Thorndike and the behaviorists, although the one with the biggest influence on elementary and secondary schools even to this day, failed to affect preschool practices until the late 1960s. By that time B. F. Skinner had emerged as the most respected behavioral theorist. Like Thorndike, Skinner emphasized that reinforcement was the most important factor in learning. He differed from Thorndike, however, in that he assigned less importance to strict stimulus-response-reinforcement (S-R-R) learning, and offered an alternative behavioral theory called operant conditioning.

OPERANT CONDITIONING   Skinner maintained that S-R-R connections accounted for only a small part of learning and that most learning resulted from the immediate reinforcement of behaviors (operants), whatever stimuli may have elicited them. Skinner's theory conceptualized *operants* as any behaviors—singing, hitting, walking, talking, playing, and so on—emitted by an organism. The operant behavior takes on its character not so much because it was elicited by any specific prior stimulus, but because its presence in the environment produced a particular response from a child. For example, when a child presses an appropriate key on a typewriter, a teacher may praise him. Pressing the typewriter key is the operant and the praise is the reinforcer—the stimulus that causes the child to press the key is not important.

The process of education, then, in Skinner's theory, is classified as *operant conditioning*, that is, reinforcing desirable operants so they have a strong chance of occurring again. Thus, the mechanical system by which a child's response is reinforced by the teacher reflects the essential character of Skinner's operant conditioning.

IMPLICATIONS FOR THE TEACHER   When it is applied to the classroom, this philosophy is expressed in terms of programmed instruction. The format dictates that preschool academic instruction be built on three basic principles:

1. identification of the desirable operants (behaviors)
2. careful sequencing of learning experiences from simple to complex
3. use of reinforcers to strengthen and maintain the desired operants when they appear

These ideas became popular among some early childhood educators in the late 1960s—especially because of the strong concern for the education of low-income children. It was felt that these children were handicapped when they entered school because they had lost out on many of the early experiences necessary for success in middle-class-oriented school systems. These experiences had to be provided, therefore, in a short time with a highly efficient, structured, formalized approach. The approach was supported by many, but perhaps the most vocal supporter was Siegfried Engelmann. Educators subscribing to Engelmann's beliefs agreed that time was running out on children from low-income backgrounds and that a structured, highly teacher-directed approach was needed if they were to succeed once they entered the primary grades. Such programs focused on the systematic development of academic and social skills and generally followed this sequence of steps:

1. *Establish terminal behavior.* State the behavior you wish the child to exhibit at the completion of a learning sequence. This must be specified beforehand so that an end point to the sequence is established. For example, one terminal goal would be that children be able to count from one to ten.
2. *Assess entry behavior.* Evaluate the child's present ability (through tests or observation) in the established terminal behavior. Some children, for example, may be able to count to five, others to three, and so on.
3. *Establish a structured, sequential learning system.* Arrange the instructional material in sequential segments and reinforce appropriate behavior at the end of each sequence. Such reinforcement may take the form of *pre-*

ferred activities such as free time or playground time; *tokens* (plastic chips) that can be used much like money to buy candy, school supplies, and so on; *food* such as raisins, cookies, or candy; and *praise.* Reinforcement is most effective when it is presented immediately following a desired behavior, so the teacher must be constantly alert to reward the child so behaviors are effectively strengthened along the way.

The curriculum is normally built around programmed materials that:

1. specify the exact behavior the child will exhibit at the end of the sequence
2. require frequent, direct responding by the child
3. contain clear standards for a "correct" response
4. allow for individual rates of progress throughout the sequence
5. provide for periodic testing of progress toward the desired behaviors

Behaviorally oriented programs usually contain hundreds of learning tasks, each arranged in a hierarchical sequence—skills learned earlier are prerequisites for later tasks. Teachers using such programs are required to follow a strict sequence of instruction. For example, note the following lesson taken from a beginning reading exercise in the DISTAR® program:

Start the Program Here

Objective: Teaching *mmm* as in "him"
Task 1: (Identify new sound)
a. "Everybody, look at the book." *(Praise children who look)*
b. *(Point to letter m in book)* "Mmm. This is mmm. Say mmm. Good."
c. *(Point to picture of ice cream cone in book)* "Is this *mmm?*"
d. *(Wait. Praise the response: "No")* "What is this?"
e. *(Trace m)* "Mmm, say mmm." *(Wait)* "Good."
f. *(Point to letter m in book)* "Look at the book. *Mmm.* This sound is *mmm.* Say it loud. *Mmm.*"
g. *(Wait)* "Good."
h. "Look at the book." *(Point to a picture of an ice cream cone in book)* "Here's *mmm.*"
i. *(Wait)* "You fooled me! What is it?"[4]

Giving the students "Take-Homes" is a reward procedure often used to reinforce those who did a good job during the lesson. Study the following example of teacher instructions for presenting "Take-Homes":

Directions for Take-Home Blending Sheets 1A and 1B

Task 1
a. *(Do not show the picture until the children have blended the word)* "Say it fast and you may keep the picture. Say it fast!" "Ham *(pause)* burger." *(Award the picture to the first child who gives the correct response)*
b. *(Present the word to each child)* "Say it fast! Ham *(pause)* burger." *(Award pictures for correct responses)* "Good. You get to keep the picture and take it home."

c. *(Present either "Motorboat" or "Hamburger" to each child. Alternate the words)* "Say it fast! Motor *(pause)* boat." *(Award the picture of the motorboat for the correct response).* "Say it fast! Ham *(pause)* burger." *(Award the picture of the hamburger for the correct response)*

Task 2

(Hold up the picture of the hamburger so that the line is at the top. Call attention to the line) "Is this how we hold the paper?" *(Wait. Praise the response: "No")* "Show me how to hold the paper. . . . Yes, with the line at the bottom."[5]

Notice the amount of teacher direction involved in the overall strategy. This is what the behaviorists mean when they refer to their teaching strategies as being highly "teacher-directed" rather than "child-centered." Also, the teacher in this program used two types of positive reinforcers during the activity: verbal praise and the "Take-Homes." Other behavioral programs use a system of token rewards as positive reinforcers. As children master various learning tasks, they are given tokens for their progress and improvement. Later, after they have accumulated a number of tokens, they have opportunities to exchange them for events or activities that are valued. The children may, for example, exchange tokens for a favorite puzzle, game, free play toy, or art activity. These activities give the children motivation to learn and to succeed.

Critics have attacked behaviorally oriented programs for several reasons. First, they feel that because children receive their motivation from outside sources (tokens, hugs, candy, and so on), rather than internal sources (feelings of happiness, accomplishment, and so on), what they learn they soon forget. However, the comprehensive study of Follow Through programs completed by Abt Associates in 1977 showed that "highly structured programs that emphasized basic skills were more successful than other education approaches."[6] Second, the behavioral approach is seen by some as stifling a child's creativity and self-direction. However, supporters cite independent research that indicates no significant differences in maladjustment among children in various instructional groups (including behaviorist). Third, some have criticized behavioral programs for not addressing themselves to affective objectives such as helping to foster a positive self-image. However, advocates argue that self-image and self-respect are best developed when children acquire the necessary academic skills to help them compete once they enter first grade.

Jessie Stanton summarized the thoughts of most critics in her stinging 1971 poem, "On Behavior Modification":

> Education works just dandy,
> When you use a piece of candy.
> You don't need to use your brains;
> To help a child make splendid gains.
> You don't need to get involved,
> All your problems will be solved.
> Each time a child does something right,

> Pick out a bonbon colored bright.
> Then tell the child to open wide,
> And pop the pretty piece inside.
> Of course he makes the right connection
> Between the act and the confection.
> It's such a pleasant way of working.
> There is no need for any shirking.
> No play dough, paints or messy clay.
> No cleaning up at end of day.
> The child goes home all full of candy.
> Not weary, Teacher feels just dandy.
> It sounds so simple and so easy.
> Yet somehow it makes me queezy.[7]

James L. Hymes, one of the most popular traditional early childhood educators, attacked both the methodology and the motivation of the behavioral approach when he described the writings of Carl Bereiter and Siegfried Engelmann (two behaviorally oriented educators) as the "best [material] to read to appreciate how devastating a program for young children of the poor can be, once first grade time-panic sets in."[8]

When examining the behaviorist approach, keep in mind that it is a relatively new strategy for preschool education and consequently a candidate for careful review and criticism. Remember, too, that it has been used for over 50 years on the elementary school level and must possess some redeeming qualities in order to last that long. There is no mystery to this new system—its basic principles have been understood and applied for years. Thousands of preschoolers all around our country, though, are now experiencing these behavioral programs and are being exposed to techniques that preschoolers never experienced in the past. Perhaps by choosing one, some, or all of their components, we can apply behavioral concepts to make our personalized programs more effective and enjoyable for the children.

COGNITIVE DEVELOPMENTAL LEARNING:
JEAN PIAGET

The cognitive developmental view of learning is based nearly exclusively on the work of one person—*Jean Piaget*—a name probably more recognizable than any other in formulating educational theory for programs in early childhood.

Jean Piaget's theories are contained in more than 30 books and hundreds of different articles. His theory is broad, and basically too complex to discuss in only part of one chapter. Therefore, our discussion is limited to only the briefest description of those components most directly influencing preschool teaching today. I hope that your basic understanding of Piaget strengthens your understanding and appreciation of children.

Key Concepts

Piagetian notions about the nature of intelligence are based on a combination of biological and epistemological (theory of knowledge acquisition) underpinnings. Piaget talks about intelligence in a broad, biological framework—that some organisms have more complex biological structures, accounting for higher levels of intelligence. For example, "Amoebas do not explore their environment, but dogs, rats, and human babies certainly do. Primates and humans have hands which immeasurably increase the organism's capacity to manipulate and explore objects."[9] Kamii explained:

> It seems more fruitful to put the emphasis on developing the efferent side, i.e., "the capacity to move freely and to act on and manipulate things of the environment." The importance of developing children's curiosity and eagerness to explore and experiment becomes clear. The more curious the child is, the more he will explore and the more knowledge he will gain. The more knowledge he has, the more advanced the nature of his curiosity will be, and the more systematic his exploration will be.[10]

Piaget used this concept of a child's acting on and manipulating things of the environment to eventually form his own general definition of *intelligence*. He said, "Intelligence is a particular instance of biological adaptation,"[11] and that intelligence "is the form of equilibrium toward which all the [cognitive] structures . . . tend."[12] The term *equilibrium* was taken from physics and implies seeking a balance between the person's existing mental structures and those things yet to be understood. To Piaget, this self-regulatory process is the most fundamental of all factors of intelligence. Through this process, the child encounters something that is new to him and actively works toward relating it to something he already knows. As he is able to resolve such discord, he reaches a new level of equilibrium (intelligence).

The growth of intelligence can be viewed as an ascent up a flight of stairs, each stair representing a balanced state of equilibrium. As the person progresses to and through each stair, he is using a process called *adaptation*, a process of adjusting ourselves to our surroundings. Adaptation involves combining two processes: *assimilation* and *accommodation*. Assimilation is the process of dealing with the environment in terms of current intellectual or physical structures. Accommodation is the process of changing existing structures in ways that fit the new situation more effectively. The following example illustrates the process of adaptation.

Suppose an infant is presented with a rattle for the very first time. The infant reaches out and tries to grasp the rattle. He has grasped things like plastic rings and his bottle before, and when he sees the rattle he attempts to pick it up by

ASSIMILATION ✦ ACCOMMODATION ➧ ADAPTATION

SEES A NEW SITUATION IN LIGHT OF PREVIOUS EXPERIENCES	CHANGES THE EXISTING PATTERNS OF THOUGHT OR BEHAVIOR TO FIT NEW SITUATIONS	THE PROCESS OF ADJUSTING TO A NEW SITUATION

EQUILIBRATION

Figure 6-3   Piaget's conceptualization of intelligence.

curving his fingers in one way and then another, trying to use the same grasping patterns he used to fit the shapes of the bottle and rings. The child is comparing the new object with things that he is already familiar with—things that can be grasped. This is the process of assimilation.

The child finds, however, that his grasp must be modified if he is ever to pick up the rattle and hear its pleasing sounds. He eventually curves his fingers in a new way—in a way that fits the long, slender handle of the rattle instead of the more substantive shapes previously experienced. The child has now accommodated *previous grasping reflexes to a shape never before experienced.*

The simultaneous process of assimilation and accommodation, then, is called adaptation. Equilibrium is achieved and the child has grown to a new level of knowledge. Figure 6-3 illustrates this process.

Piaget's feelings about activity, exploration, and direct experience again come to the front as Celia Stendler explains their importance in the process of adaptation:

Self-activity is crucial in the adaptive process; for Piaget, "Penser, c'est operer." If equilibrium is to be achieved at a higher level, then the child must be mentally active, *he* must transform the data. The elements to be incorporated may be present in an experience or the child may be *told* of the error in his thinking, but unless his mind is actively engaged in wrestling with data, no accommodation occurs. Children, like adults, are not convinced by being told they are wrong, nor by merely seeing evidence that contradicts their thinking. They have to act upon the data and transform them, and in so doing, make their own discoveries.[13]

The child's cognitive processes develop in this active way, according to Piaget, within two major areas: physical knowledge and logico-mathematical knowledge.

1. *Physical knowledge.* Physical knowledge refers to the observable properties of those objects within the child's realm of experience. For example, if we pick up a rubber ball, hold it at eye level, and allow it to drop,

Children learn about the physical properties of objects by observing and experimenting. (*Tiger* by Bud Blake courtesy of King Features Syndicate, Inc.)

we find out something about the physical properties of that ball. In the same way, the child learns about the physical properties in his environment through observation and experimentation—looking, dropping, folding, pouring, knocking, watching, and listening are but a few of the actions he can use on objects to find out how they react. Physical activity is seen as a necessary stimulus for mental activity. The objects themselves, not the teacher, tell the child about their properties.

2. *Logico-mathematical knowledge.* This area of knowledge involves five skill areas: (a) classification, (b) seriation, (c) spatial relations, (d) temporal relations, and (e) conservation.

Classification involves the child's ability to group objects based on some common criterion. The emphasis is not on discovering a "correct" grouping, but on the process of independently grouping and regrouping objects in various logical ways. For example, from the following list we may ask the child to "put together the objects that are the same in some way": 3 red plastic dogs, 4 red plastic birds, 3 yellow plastic cats, and 4 yellow plastic chickens.

Logico-mathematical knowledge includes the ability to classify objects according to some common characteristic (*Tiger* by Bud Blake courtesy of King Features Syndicate, Inc.)

These children are involved in a seriation activity: ordering counters from least to greatest.

The objective of asking the child to group these things is not to see whether he can figure out how you want them grouped, but to see whether he can group the objects himself and give you reasons for his actions. A reasonably mature child may create these groupings:

Group 1	**Group 2**	**Group 3**
all the dogs	all the red animals	the dogs and cats
all the birds	all the yellow animals	the birds and chickens
all the cats	(because of their	(fur versus feathers)
all the chickens	common color)	
(because they are		
the same animal)		

Many types of classifications can be made by the youngsters. Preschool children learn to group things according to size, shape, color, texture, taste, sound, and many other physical attributes.

Seriation involves an ability to order or arrange objects according to size (small to large), quality (rough to smooth), or quantity (less to more). The emphasis is on comparing likenesses and differences among objects in the same category and on ordering them according to their relative differences. Figure 6-4 illustrates several types of seriation activities commonly presented to preschool children.

Spatial relations involve the child's ability to understand his relationship to objects and the relationship of objects to one another in terms of direction, distance, and perspective. For example, the teacher may point to the large ball which is *far* from the child and ask him to bring it *near*. The teacher may ask the child to pick up a toy that is *beneath* the table. The child may be asked to point to the boy who is *in* the doll corner or to name the *closest* child to him.

Temporal relations involve the child's ability to perceive time sequences. He learns that events begin and end and that events can be sequentially ordered. Concepts of *first, last, before, after,* and *next* are learned. For example, the teacher may tell the child, "*First*, you will need to put one cookie on each plate and *next* you may pour the milk." At story time, the teacher may say, "I'll *start* the story now and we'll go outdoors to play when I'm *finished.*" Or, during clean-up time, the teacher may promise, "*After* you've put away your toys, we'll *begin* our snack."

Conservation involves the child's ability to conceptualize physical properties of objects. Young children (2–7 years) usually make sense out of the world in terms of the way it looks to them—they focus on only one dimension at a time. They have great difficulty realizing that objects can possess more than one property. These characteristics can be best explained within the context of the following examples:

☐ *Conservation of Substance:* Present the child with a ball of clay, and ask him to observe it. Then roll the clay into a long cylinder. Ask: "Does the sausage have less, more, or the same amount of clay as the ball?" If the child is confused, say, "Was the ball bigger, smaller, or the same size as the sausage?" Ask the child, "Why do you think the sausage was bigger,

SIZE:
THE CHILD IS ASKED TO ARRANGE THE PEOPLE FROM SMALL TO LARGE

QUALITY:
THE CHILD IS ASKED TO ARRANGE THE TOUCH TABLETS FROM ROUGHEST TO SMOOTHEST

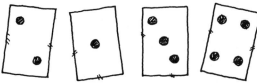

QUANTITY:
THE CHILD IS ASKED TO ARRANGE THE CARDS IN ORDER FROM THE LEAST TO THE GREATEST NUMBER

Figure 6-4 Seriation activities.

smaller, or the same?" This question will provide you with insight into his thinking.

□ *Conservation of Weight:* Now, present the child with two balls of clay and place them on a balance. Ask the child to observe the balance until he's sure that both balls of clay weigh the same. Then remove the balls from the scale and roll one into the shape of a sausage. Ask: "Will the scale stay balanced or will one side be heavier than the other?" Ask the child, "Why do you think so?"

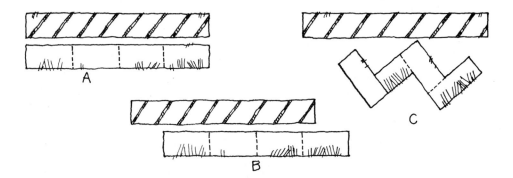

□ *Conservation of Length:* Use two straws, one complete and one cut in sections. Start with the straws lined up parallel to each other (Figure A). Note with the child that both straws are the same length. Move the straws to the position shown in Figure B. Ask: "Would two bugs starting a hike at this end of the straws [*point to one end*] and walking at the same speed, both finish the hike at this point [*point to other end*] at the same time?" If the child is confused, ask, "Would they both travel the same distance?" Justification. Repeat the question. "Would they both travel the same distance? Why do you think so?" Now move the straws into the position shown in Figure C. Repeat the question, "Would the bugs both travel the same distance?" Ask the child, "Why do you think so?"

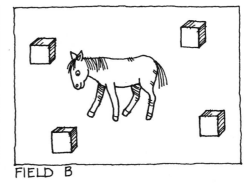

FIELD A   FIELD B

☐ *Conservation of Area:* Present the child with two identical pieces of green construction paper. Tell him these represent fields of grass. Place one toy horse on each piece of paper. Ask the child to compare the fields. Emphasize that they are the same size. Ask: "Since the fields are the same size, would each animal have the same amount of grass to eat?" Tell the child you are going to use blocks to represent barns. Place four barns on each field shown. Leave the animal on the field. Ask: "Now which animal has the most grass to eat? Or will the amount of grass be the same?" Ask the child, "Why do you think this is true?" Continue adding equal numbers of barns to each field. Each time repeat the question, "Which animal will have the most grass to eat?"

Transition from Stage to Stage

The previous material explained a number of key concepts associated with Piagetian theory. These concepts should help you to form an overall idea of what Piaget means when he uses the term *intelligence*. Essential to the development of higher levels of Piagetian intelligence is movement through a series of four developmental stages, each describing an orderly pattern through which the child constructs knowledge. Development through the stages follows a sequential order such that each stage is necessary for the construction of the next. Irving Sigel and Rodney Cocking contrast Piaget's ideas of stage development to the behavioristic philosophies:

> This is in contrast to the behaviorists who do not espouse stage-dependent theories. The distinction is very important. If the stage concept is accepted, it follows that development of knowledge, and learning specifically, is limited by the stage in which the child is at that time. Then, for example, the fact that a young child cannot learn to add or subtract is not necessarily a function of inadequate teaching strategies but rather the fact that the child's level of development precludes his being able to assimilate the necessary information with which to learn arithmetic. For Piaget, development means movement from stage to stage, resulting in changes both in what one *can* understand and *how* one understands.[14]

Piaget identifies four specific stages through which individuals progress: sensorimotor, preoperational, concrete operations, and formal operations. The criteria for defining the characteristics of the child's behavior during each stage are explained in the following descriptions.

STAGE 1: SENSORIMOTOR (0–2 YEARS)   The child begins life capable only of two kinds of *reflexive movements:* (1) those such as knee jerks that are not altered by experience and (2) those such as grasping and sucking that can be altered by the child's experiences. The child, with these reflexes as a base, uses the process of assimilation and accommodation to build higher intellectual structures from that reflexive base.

The child's initial *actions* such as arm waving and sucking appear to be aimless since they appear over and over again as primitive reflexes. However, they soon begin to show purpose as the child learns to grasp objects, hold them, push them, manipulate them, and experiment with them. The infant actively attempts to understand single objects and the relationship among objects as he repeats and alters behaviors in an attempt to adjust to his environment.

One of the more important achievements of the sensorimotor period is the development of the idea of *object permanence.* Early in this stage, if a toy is hidden, the infant acts as if it no longer exists. Only gradually, after experiences in which objects are dropped or rolled out of sight, do infants realize that objects continue to exist and begin to look for them. This is a signal that the youngster is moving away from the concept of "out of sight, out of mind" and toward the ability to form mental images of the people and objects in his environment. Another important concept emerging during this period is the idea of causality—an awareness that other objects besides the child himself can be the source of actions. For example, this cause-effect concept is evident at the end of the sensorimotor period when a child is able to understand that the reason he cannot open a playpen gate is not because he lacks pushing power, but because a piece of furniture may be blocking it.

By the age of two, the child possesses the concepts of object permanence and causality—thus making him quite cognitively different from the infant at birth. The ability to experiment is beginning.

STAGE 2: PREOPERATIONAL (2–7 YEARS)   By stage 2, children have made great progress in cognitive development, but they still have a long way to go. They see the world only from their own point of view (egocentrism) and believe that everyone else sees it the same way.

The child begins to use *words* to represent objects and actions within his environment, perhaps the single most evident development during this stage. However, he describes those objects and actions only in terms of how they look to him. For example, children judge the amount of water in a glass on the basis of the container (a tall, thin glass has more water than a short fat glass of equal volume); a piece of clay rolled out into the shape of a sausage has more clay than that same piece of clay when it was in the shape of a ball.

Because of egocentric thought, basic conservation skills remain undeveloped during this stage.

Rudiments of *classification* and *seriation*, however, do appear during this stage. The child can make collections of things based on some criterion, such as separating red horses and blue horses into two piles. He is even able to shift criteria, that is, first sort the horses into piles of red and blue, then sort them according to size: large and small. The child can also compare two or three members of a set within a series and put them in order.

The child begins to understand basic *temporal* concepts at this stage. He shows a rudimentary understanding of concepts such as *first, next, after,* and so on. However, these terms should always be used only in pairs such as, "*First* wash your hands and *then* you can eat the snack." However, sensing logic among more than two things in a series will cause confusion.

The child *learns* by manipulating objects, recognizing pictures, participating in dramatic play, drawing, and using words or objects to represent thoughts.

STAGE 3: CONCRETE OPERATIONS (7–12 YEARS)   The child now is able to learn some things through mental operations involving symbols (reasoning) rather than through direct physical manipulation (perception). The previously developing skills are becoming refined; as egocentrism fades the ability to *conserve* quantities is beginning to appear. The child understands relationships between the whole and its parts and begins to see things from the viewpoints of others. Logical reasoning brings order to the child's world as he becomes able to understand symbols (reading and math) and is beginning to sense cause-and-effect relationships.

STAGE 4: FORMAL OPERATIONS (12–ADULTHOOD)   The child is capable of learning entirely through verbal and written symbols—the symbols themselves serve to evoke meaningful mental images. He is able to think logically and perform the previously discussed Piagetian tasks with ease. The child is able to construct knowledge independently of concrete experience and now learns to integrate new knowledge while solving problems with meaning, not only for the present, but also for the future.

Implications for the Teacher

Teaching approaches based on Piagetian theory are of two basic types: those that establish a play-game orientation and those that center around a problem-solving atmosphere. Play-game orientations give children ample opportunities to explore and experience objects in their physical environment. The purpose of such exploration is to help children learn about objects by acting on them and by observing the results of such action. Play orientations consist of various "seek and find" games or other ability-challenging tasks. Constance Kamii explains how play-game activities help the young child gain knowledge of his physical world:

In a simple situation like pretending to have coffee with friends, children represent their knowledge of reality in all areas of the cognitive framework. For example, they represent their *physical knowledge* by heating the coffee, pouring it, spilling it, stirring it, and burning oneself with it. They represent the idea of pouring more coffee than cream, or giving a lot of cream and sugar to some people, and less or none to other people (*pre-seriation*). They construct elementary *number concepts* as they get just enough cups, saucers, napkins, and spoons for everybody. They represent the *temporal sequence* of making coffee, getting the cups and saucers out, pouring coffee, drinking it, and then cleaning up. They learn to serve the guests first (*social knowledge*). Sometimes, they invite people by phoning them beforehand. In this situation, some children's temporal sequence has been observed to consist of accepting an invitation first before being invited, or dialing first before picking up the receiver![15]

Such play-game-oriented situations should be kept open-ended. Eventually, the young child's curiosity will be motivated and he will begin a transition to more academically oriented tasks. Ann Hammerman and Susan Morse use an informal classification example to illustrate such a transition activity:

In the course of her play, Judy began grouping objects by color, making a red group and a white group. She noticed a red pencil with a white end. She put it first into the red group and then into the white group. She was noticeably perturbed. Neither solution satisfied her. Finally, she placed the pencil so that the red end was near the other red objects and the white end was near the white objects. The pencil formed a bridge between the two groups. She was experiencing a moment of tension between a more rigid view that an object can belong to only one group at a time and a realization that groups can overlap.[16]

Play-game-oriented activities can lead to more academically oriented tasks if the teacher allows children to explore objects in the classroom freely and perform their own actions on them. When children begin to develop an increasing awareness of the objects around them, the teacher may do some systematic questioning leading to problem solving and a strengthening of logical operations. Hammerman and Morse described the following situation in which a preschool teacher encouraged problem solving.

Teddy approaches the table. The objects available to him are: a rectangular plastic container, funnel, sticks, wooden and plastic discs of different sizes with holes in them, paper and plastic cups of different sizes, aluminum tart tins, different shapes and sizes of blocks (rectangular, cylindrical), marbles, different kinds of paper, beads, spools, straws and plastic airplanes.

Teddy begins making a tower alternating metal tins and paper cups. He is ordering the items in a specific way, as well as testing out the balance of forces. I say, "I'll make a tower too. Let's see if I can make mine taller." I decide to bring in the comparison of heights to see if Teddy will pursue this aspect of tower building. Then he picks up the whole pile of cups to add them to the tower. I ask him, "What do you think will happen if you put all the cups on top there?" Since he is silent, I ask, "Do you think it will fall?" He nods. "Do you want it to fall over?" He shakes his head no. "Well, what could you do so that it will not fall over?" He

Play-game activities, such as this classification task, comprise one type of strategy associated with Piagetian theory.

considers the pile of cups. He takes part of the pile and puts it on the tower. I say, "That's an idea, taking some away." The tower does not fall. He has considered a problem and figured out a solution. He now adds the rest of the cups. The pile topples.

He rebuilds the pile in the same spatial pattern as before. When he is at the point of wanting to add the whole pile of cups, he pauses to consider the situation. He places the entire pile of cups on top of the tower pushing down from the top as he does so to compress the pile. I say, "Another good idea, to press down on the cups." He has considered another solution to the problem. This is a sophisticated solution, intuitively using the laws of physical science.

This time the tower does not fall.[17]

The teacher's role in this problem-solving situation was multifaceted. She:

1. encouraged the child to explore his physical world
2. pointed out logical relationships when they occurred
3. encouraged the child to predict and hypothesize
4. encouraged the child to pursue his own direction in testing his hypotheses
5. verbalized the child's actions so he would direct his major efforts toward thinking
6. asked challenging questions and offered comments that helped the child work toward a solution to his problem

Piaget pointed out the importance of encouraging problem-solving abilities in young children:

The principal goal of education is to create men who are capable of doing new things, not simply of repeating what other generations have done—men who are creative, inventive, and discoverers. The second goal of education is to form minds which can be critical, can verify, and not accept everything they are offered. The great danger today is of slogans, collective opinions, ready-made trends of thought. We have to be able to resist individually, to criticize, to distinguish between what is proven and what is not. So we need pupils who are active, who learn early to find out by themselves, partly by their own spontaneous activity and partly through material we set up for them; who learn early to tell what is verifiable and what is simply the first idea to come to them.[18]

The progression of learning experiences leading toward concept development, according to Piaget's theory, moves according to this pattern:

1. The child physically experiences various materials by sorting or manipulating them in several ways.
2. The child is led to perform various activities with the objects and to perceive their likenesses and differences.
3. The child is encouraged to act both on the physical and mental levels as he associates mental images with physical manipulations of objects.
4. The child can internalize his thoughts and is able to perform operations in his mind rather than in a physical manner.

The teacher using a Piagetian framework, then, must be able to apply Piaget's theories in preparing teaching strategies. She must also arrange the environment so play-game or problem-solving activities involve the children, and help them understand their physical world and develop logico-mathematical operations. The teacher's role can be summarized as follows:

1. Make available concrete, exploratory, sensory experiences and help the children understand the effects of their actions on involved materials. This is, perhaps, the most important single conclusion that teachers can derive from Piaget's work.
2. Allow the children appropriate freedom to manipulate self-selected learning materials.
3. Encourage children to use toys, art materials, and other supplies to symbolize their thoughts and experiences.
4. Use simple language that encourages children to focus on the results of their actions and to predict what might happen next.
5. Maximize the quality of each experience. Help children move from where they are toward the discovery of new concepts and a refinement of concepts already met.

Piaget has never actually applied his own theories to the formulation of teaching strategies so there is no one method of instruction that we can truly associate with him. But educators interested in Piaget's ideas have done so, and their interpretations have resulted in programs either of the structured variety or of the more open type.

INFORMAL EDUCATION

Basic Assumptions

Although viewed by some as a recent educational phenomenon, the basic concept of the informal classroom is deeply rooted in the past. Rousseau, of course, was among the first who argued that schools for young children should reflect an informality that brought forth "natural liberty. . . . Give your pupil no kind of verbal instructions; he should receive none but from experience."[19] Similar feelings about the right of children to grow naturally have been added through the years, through the writings of Comenius, Pestalozzi, Froebel, and others.

Early in this century, John Dewey and William H. Kilpatrick developed ideas of education that urged teachers to form child-centered classrooms. As Kilpatrick said, "Who can question that there are many . . . learnings going on in each child all the time, and that the sum of the . . . incidental . . . [child-centered] learnings may and does overshadow the *specific* [italics mine] school learnings, and may determine what [the child] shall do in life?"[20] Instead of the step-by-step, teacher-directed organization recommended by the behaviorists, these "progressives" reasoned that subject matter would best be learned naturally by the children as they engaged in personally meaningful concrete or play experiences in a socially oriented, child-centered classroom.

Such ideas regarding child-centered learning have been reshaped and molded over the years. Presently, such ideas are called *informal education*, and are espoused by many, Carl Rogers and John Holt being among the most

Informal education stresses the importance of allowing young children to pursue areas of learning in which they are most interested. This child, for example, is spending time observing some newly hatched chicks.

popular. Jean Piaget's philosophy has also gathered support from those advocating informal approaches to early childhood programming. Carl Rogers implored early educators to think of themselves as *facilitators* rather than as *teachers*. He used his "mug and jug" theory to explain the difference:

> The teacher asks himself: "How can I make the mug hold still while I fill it from the jug with these facts which the curriculum planners and I regard as valuable?" The attitude of the facilitator has almost entirely to do with climate: "How can I create a psychological climate in which the child will feel free to be curious, will feel free to make mistakes, will feel free to learn from his environment, from fellow students, from me, from experience? How can I help him recapture the excitement of learning which was his in infancy?"[21]

John Holt's views are similar to Rogers's as he states:

> We do not need to "motivate" children into learning, by wheedling, bribing, or bullying. We do not need to keep picking away at their minds to make sure they are learning. What we need to do, and all we need to do, is bring as much of the world as we can into the school and the classroom; give children as much help and guidance as they need and ask for; listen respectfully when they feel like talking; and then get out of the way. We can trust them to do the rest.[22]

Informal education, then, can best be viewed as a feeling on the part of the teacher that children learn most effectively when they become directly involved in their own learning. It is an attitude that perceives the child as capable of making his own decisions regarding learning. It is a strategy that emphasizes learning as a *process*, not a *product*. Programs based on the informal education philosophy generally hold the following assumptions to be of major importance:

1. Children are naturally curious and are eager to explore their environment freely.
2. Learning is not done "to the child" but "by the child."
3. Active exploration and manipulation enhance learning.
4. Play is the child's form of work.
5. Children have both the ability and the initiative to make certain decisions regarding their own learning.
6. Children learn and develop according to their own unique rates and styles.
7. Learning occurs best as it proceeds from the concrete to the abstract.
8. Most facets of an individual's learning are best evaluated through direct observation of a child at work (play) rather than through paper-and-pencil tests.
9. Learning to interact and cooperate as a group member is essential to the growth of an individual.
10. Education must take place in an environment communicating trust, kindness, warmth, courtesy, respect, openness, and security.

Curriculum and Method

The teacher's role in the informal classroom is to guide and support the child's endeavors by relinquishing the role of authority figure and accepting the role of facilitator. The teacher prepares the environment with a rich variety of materials and informal learning activities rather than with rigid lesson plans that compel children to dispense common sets of skills, content, or responses. She allows children to choose such activities freely, to assist each other, to discuss work freely with one another, and to pursue any one goal for as long as they wish. The teacher encourages children to answer their own questions rather than to respond to hers (à la Piaget) and wants children to look at learning as self-rewarding rather than as dependent on extrinsic rewards or praise (à la Skinner).

It should be emphasized that informal classrooms reflect no single method of instruction, but rather suggest a range of active modes of learning that reflect discovery learning and self-chosen involvement. Basic to all informal education programs, however, is the concept of the *integrated day*. What this means is that the common subject matter distinctions of math, reading, science, and so on are not broken down into separate time slots, but are combined into activities designed to apply involved concepts to everyday life. For example, the teacher might have available a cookie-making project for those children who are interested (see Figure 6-5). The children would measure cups of flour and shortening or tablespoons of sugar, salt, and baking powder. Learning the various measures as well as counting the number of cookies would be part of the mathematics program. Reading the simplified recipe would be part of the informal reading program. Becoming aware of the physical changes occurring during the mixing of ingredients or during the baking process lends itself to direct scientific observation. The verbal exchange during the entire project lends itself well to language or concept development. And the cooperation and interpersonal exchanges necessary for a group project to be completed provide a meaningful social context in the lives of the children. Obviously, the integrated activity becomes the medium for communicating subject matter to young children. This is in contrast to the idea of isolated subjects being taught at different times during the day. The overall goal of such a strategy is to make the children's education as meaningful and purposeful as possible.

In addition to integrating subject matter, some informal classrooms use a variety of learning centers. A *learning center* is an area in which activity-oriented materials motivate and enable children to assume individual responsibility for their own learning. Materials for these centers may include commercial, teacher-made, or "junk" items that can be used in place of workbook assignments or teacher-directed group activities. After analyzing the children's needs and interests, an informal classroom-oriented teacher might decide on several types of independent center activities (see pp. 203–205).

Learning centers can be arranged for a variety of different purposes. Science centers may be established to encourage children to investigate and

Figure 6-5 Learning from a recipe.

study nature; dramatic play centers help children express themselves or interact with others; an art center can help awaken the child's desire to create and discover through a variety of media; sand and water play centers encourage children's imagination and cognitive processes; and woodworking or block centers allow children to construct things. Suggestions that are directly related to planning activities for such centers are discussed in greater detail in Chapter 10. I must caution you not to be misled by this discussion of the physical organization of learning activities; informal classroom philosophy is more than a set organizational pattern or a specific teaching strategy. The pattern of organization and method of instruction are merely vehicles through which a feeling of freedom, trust, and motivation for learning grow. Once this atmosphere is established, children are likely to become productive, positive, and successful learners.

A Sample Classroom

At this point, we're going to look at one variation of the informal classroom in some detail. In this classroom children range from age 3 to age 6. This "multiple-age" grouping, or "family" grouping as it sometimes is called, allows children to form groups as they do outside of school—that is, with siblings or with peers having like interests, abilities, or skills.

READING CENTER

This corner of the room is a very private area. It is a quiet, comfortable lounging area supplied with large pillows, an old, colorfully decorated bathtub, and some small rocking chairs. Interesting books are displayed in the center so children can choose from a variety of different titles. A large table has been set up in this corner with a number of manipulative learning materials on it. Among the activities on the table are:

1. Sticker puzzles. In order to help develop visual discrimination, the teacher bought a variety of gummed stickers in a gift shop, mounted each sticker on a strong piece of cardboard, and cut each sticker in half vertically, horizon-

tally, or diagonally. She then mixed up all the pieces, and put them in a box at the table. The children are to match the two halves to make a complete picture.

2. Palm trace. To "reinforce" letter recognition skills, the teacher provided a paint brush, water soluble paint, and water at the table. The children work in pairs. One child shuts her eyes as the other traces a letter on her palm with the paint brush. The first child calls out the name of the letter and then looks to see if she was right. The children then switch roles.

3. Ice cream cones. To assist children with beginning phonics skills, the teacher cut several cones out of construction paper, pasted one picture on each cone, and placed them into a box at the table. She then cut out a corresponding number of ice cream scoops from colorful construction paper and pasted on pictures that rhymed with the pictures on the cones. She placed the scoops into another box. The children take the cones from their box and arrange them on the floor. Then they put a scoop of ice cream on each cone, matching pictures that rhyme.

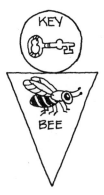
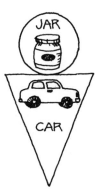

The preschool classroom has one teacher and an aide for fifteen children. The room is large and is organized into many nooks and crannies—messy corners, book corners, display corners, and quiet corners. The children's work, exhibited in many unique ways, is evidence that creative learning activities abound.

As the children enter the room, they move freely to their chosen areas and select the activities they want for this particular time slot. Some children prefer lively activities like painting, woodworking, or puppetry. Others are more passive—they prefer the rug and pillows in the reading corner; this comfortable area is a quiet start to the day.

MATH CENTER

The math corner was prepared with a wide variety of commercially developed and teacher-made materials. Dominoes, an adding machine, number lines, an abacus, catalogs, parquetry blocks, cuisenaire rods, and a variety of other materials were obtained from commercial companies. In addition, the following activities were designed and constructed by the teacher:

1. Number express. The teacher, wanting to help the children develop the skill of placing numbers in sequence and recognizing numbers in a set, cut out an engine, caboose, and ten railroad cars, which she numbered from one through ten. Near these train parts she placed a box containing several buttons. The students are to make a train with the cars numbered one to ten and then place an appropriate number of buttons above each car.

2. Number plants. To help the children recognize the number of objects in a set, the teacher made ten flower pots containing only the stems and bottom leaves of plants from construction paper. On each pot, she drew a number of dots ranging from one to ten. The teacher then glued a small metal washer to the top of each flower stem. She mounted the pots on a strip of heavy tagboard and fastened them to the wall. Next she cut ten flower blossoms from construction paper and glued a small magnet to the back of each. In the center of each blossom, she wrote a numeral from one through ten and put the blossoms into a box at the table.

NUMBER EXPRESS

Children who need more structure are guided by the teacher in deciding what to do, how to do it, and when to do it. A red ticket is given to one child, signifying work is to be done at the reading corner with the teacher's aide. One other child is given a red ticket. Soon three more children join these two voluntarily. The aide helps one child insert a card into the Language Master; the child listens intently as his words are recorded and played back for him. Another child puts on a set of earphones and listens carefully to a prerecorded story on the tape recorder. Two more children become involved with the manipulative letter recognition games located at the reading table. The aide works with Martha on an experience story. As Martha tells her story, the

The children place each blossom on the washer above the stem of the pot in which it belongs.

3. Junk box. To give children practice with relating sets of objects to numerals, the teacher collected a number of familiar objects such as one building block, two erasers, three pencils, four paper clips, five rubber bands, and so on. She placed all of the objects in a large box labeled "Junk Box." She then prepared ten 3 × 3-inch tagboard cards, each with a numeral from one through ten on it.

The children take the objects out of the Junk Box and group them together in sets. Then they take a tagboard numeral and place it with the corresponding set.

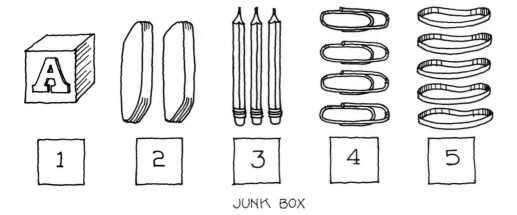

JUNK BOX

Learning center activities characterize many informal-type classrooms.

aide writes it down for her. When the story is complete, the aide reads it back to Martha; then there is a short session during which Martha is asked to locate a few key words. Finally, Martha decides to illustrate her story at the art center.

As the reading corner activity continues, children move freely throughout the room or take up new activities. They write on paper, work with math games, observe the polliwogs, make things, move to music, or simply recline peacefully. Periodically throughout the morning, the teacher helps children in need of special guidance to find activities or tasks that will be valuable to them. Some are directed to the arts and crafts center where children are making butterflies out of construction paper and pipe cleaners. Others join the creative dramatics area where their invitation to a "tea party" is issued with friendly smiles.

Basic to this informal classroom is an outdoor learning area. Flower and vegetable gardens, play equipment, and animals are freely accessible through a door leading from the classroom. On this brilliantly warm day, one child has chosen to bring a book with her and is sprawled in the shade of a large tree. Another child is active on the tire swings that hang from the tree. A small group is digging in the vegetable garden, preparing the ground for a fresh planting of beans. Children move freely from inside to out and excitement and spontaneity flow easily from one area to the other.

Rather than bringing materials from their natural settings into the classroom, this school makes every effort to get the children out of the classroom. The city, the countryside, and the neighborhood all provide exciting opportunities for the children to experience new phenomena. Fresh bakery bread, a newly born baby calf, or a ride on the district fire engine create new situations in which children can ask or answer questions related to newly developed interests. The classroom, therefore, is viewed as not merely an area surrounded by four walls, but as a total living environment in which both teachers and children are discovering novel ways of exploring and learning.

Informal classrooms do not need to be as liberal as the examples used to illustrate the philosophy. Basic to the idea, though, is the belief that learning is most effectively carried out when the child is free to initiate his own learning in an environment rich in materials and activities.

In summarizing the informal classroom concept, then, one realizes that the child comes before the subject matter. The primary goal is to provide a healthy psychological and social climate that allows the child to experience incidental, rather than formal, intellectual education. These ideas lead to an interdisciplinary model that stresses learning centers as the bases for organizing a meaningful presentation of subject matter. Although these principles have been considered highly revolutionary during recent years, in reality they have been around for quite some time. Think back to the ideas of Rousseau, Froebel, Owen, Dewey, and Hill. They all called for child-centered, activity-centered programs for young children. They all believed that subject-centered, teacher-centered programs were contrary to the true nature of children. What do you think? Your ideas and beliefs will form the strong foundation necessary for the effective development of sound teaching practices.

AN ECLECTIC APPROACH

When describing the eclectic approach, I think of the well-meaning student a few years back who reacted in a very concerned voice when a professor announced that he was *eclectic*. "Oh my," said the student, "how serious a problem is it?" Stunned, the professor went on to explain that being eclectic was not a health problem, but an approach to teaching that selects several aspects of different learning theories and combines them into a personalized strategy. Some educators agree that each theory has something valuable to offer and that combining aspects of each approach can be a valuable part of a true child-oriented classroom. They find it difficult to accept the view that any one single learning theory can effectively explain a process so personal and complex as the learning process.

These educators also believe that all teachers are, in a sense, eclectic, and that it is nearly impossible to plan an early childhood program that avoids eclecticism. For example, you may accept the behaviorists' contention that reinforcement of correct responses encourages learning while rejecting their ideas regarding structure and strict teacher direction. You may wish to pattern your basic instructional program, instead, after Piaget's philosophy, and do so within an informal classroom environment. Whether you choose one basic theory to follow or seek to combine the strengths of several into your personalized philosophy, the main thing is to examine the needs of your children and to choose the technique that seems to have the greatest potential for encouraging their success.

SOME FINAL THOUGHTS

To be told that you should pattern your teaching practices after methods that often fail to match your emotional, physical, or philosophical preparation simply because someone else used them successfully does not make much professional sense. Conversely, you should be excited by the possibili-

Table 6-1   Summary of Three Major Cognitive Teaching Philosophies

Behavioral	Cognitive-Developmental	Informal Classroom
Subject matter foremost	Child foremost	Child foremost
Teacher-centered	Teacher and child work together	Child-centered
Subject matter structure	Content and process equally emphasized	Integrated day stressing process
Formalized instruction	Teacher role somewhat prescriptive	Incidental learning
Specific objectives and learning tasks	Activities inferred from Piaget's ideas and theories	"Messing about"
Learning occurs through a process of "conditioning"	Learning occurs through a process of "equilibration"	Each child is unique and learns in his own way
Motivation extrinsic (material rewards)	Motivation may be combination of external and internal rewards, but primarily intrinsic	Motivation intrinsic (self-reward)
Passive learning: pay attention, listen, follow specific instructions	Active learning with adult providing a supportive role	Active learning: exploring, discovering, experimenting
Emphasis on measuring and testing	Evaluating logical thinking processes so new learning can be associated with past experiences	Informal observation and discussion as evaluation
Rigid time schedule for learning activities	Structured as well as informal activity helps to achieve cognitive objectives	Informal atmosphere: children move freely from one activity to another

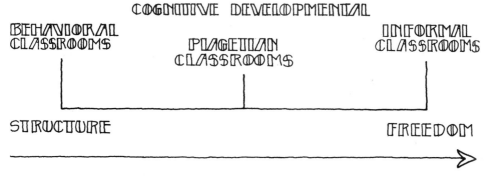

Figure 6-6   Theory continuum.

ties of each style discussed in this chapter and determine which "fits" best into your present orientation—there is room for each kind of teaching style in the field of early childhood education today. Table 6-1 summarizes the major emphases associated with each of the cognitive teaching philosophies discussed in this chapter. Figure 6-6 is a theory continuum; it shows the formal behavioral view at one end, the Piagetian cognitive developmental view somewhere in the middle, and the flexible, informal classroom model at the other end.

NOTES

1. John B. Watson, *Behaviorism* (Chicago: The University of Chicago Press, 1924), p. 104.
2. Edward L. Thorndike, *Educational Psychology: Briefer Course* (New York: Teachers College, Columbia University, 1925).
3. John Dewey, *Experience and Education* (New York: Macmillan, 1938).
4. Robert C. Aukerman, *Approaches to Beginning Reading* (New York: John Wiley, 1971), p. 450.
5. Siegfried Engelmann and Wesley Becker, *Distar Reading I* (Chicago: Science Research Associates [SRA], 1970).
6. Emily C. Harris, ed., *Report on Education Research* (Washington, D.C.: Capitol Publications, June 15, 1977), p. 2.
7. Jessie Stanton, "On Behavior Modification," *Young Children* 31, no. 1 (November 1975): 22.
8. James L. Hymes, Jr., *Teaching the Child Under Six* (Columbus, Ohio: Charles E. Merrill, 1968), p. 14.
9. Constance Kamii, "An Application of Piaget's Theory to the Conceptualization of a Preschool Curriculum," a paper written for presentation at the Conceptualizations of Preschool Curricula conference sponsored by the Department of Educational Psychology, The City University of New York, May 22–24, 1970, p. 9.
10. Ibid., p. 10.
11. Jean Piaget, *The Origins of Intelligence in Children*, trans. M. Cook (New York: International University Press, 1952), pp. 3–4.
12. Jean Piaget, *The Psychology of Intelligence*, trans. M. Percy and D. E. Berlyne (London: Routledge and Kegan Paul Ltd., 1956), p. 6.

13. Celia B. Stendler, "Aspects of Piaget's Theory That Have Implications for Teacher Education," *Journal of Teacher Education* 16, no. 3 (September 1965): 330.

14. Irving E. Sigel and Rodney R. Cocking, *Cognitive Development from Childhood to Adolescence: A Constructivist Perspective* (New York: Holt, Rinehart and Winston, 1977), pp. 17–18.

15. Constance Kamii, "A Sketch of the Piaget-Derived Preschool Curriculum Developed by the Ypsilanti Early Education Program," in *History and Theory of Early Childhood Education*, ed. Samuel J. Braun and Esther P. Edwards (Belmont, California: Wadsworth Publishing Company, Inc., 1972), p. 305.

16. Ann Hammerman and Susan Morse, "Open Teaching: Classroom," *Young Children* 28, no. 1 (October 1972): 51.

17. Ibid., pp. 43–44.

18. Eleanor Duckworth, "Piaget Rediscovered," *Journal of Research in Science Teaching* 2, no. 2 (June 1964): 172–175.

19. Jean Jacques Rousseau, *Emilius or A Treatise on Education* in *Three Thousand Years of Educational Wisdom*, ed. Robert Ulich (Cambridge: Harvard University Press, 1954), p. 398.

20. William H. Kilpatrick, *Source Book in Philosophy of Education* (New York: Macmillan, 1937), p. 422.

21. Carl Rogers, "Forget You Are a Teacher," in *Critical Issues in Educational Psychology*, ed. Meredith D. Gall and Beatrice A. Ward (Boston: Little, Brown, 1974), p. 102.

22. John Holt, *How Children Learn* (New York: Pitman, 1967), pp. 185–189.

7

The Basic Academic Skills: Reading, Writing, and Math

"I made some words, Mommy. Will you tell me
what they are?"

(*The Family Circus* by Bil Keane courtesy of The Register and Tribune Syndicate, Inc.)
Inc.)

"'Would you tell me, please, which way to go from here?' asked Alice. 'That depends a good deal on where you want to get to,' said the cat." This quote from Lewis Carroll's *Alice in Wonderland* illustrates a major dilemma involved in choosing a direction to follow in designing your preschool program. If you are among the group of early childhood educators, for example, who wish to "get to" the development of *intellectual* skills in your program, then you must examine the options of "which way to go." Chapter 6 described three major "ways to go"—that is, behavioral, cognitive developmental, or informal classroom. This chapter discusses the three major academic skills areas that you may wish to "get to"—reading, writing, and math. The ideas examined in Chapter 6 that you feel are most meaningful for the academic preparation of young children must now be more closely examined while choosing a "way to go" and then be tied into actual classroom practice—the place you wish to "get to." In this way, you can see the logical relationship between educational theory and the selection of teaching methods and materials, a relationship that needs to be compatible if it is to be successful.

READING

Whether or not to teach three-, four-, five-, and six-year-olds to read has historically been a subject of great controversy in early childhood education. The controversy began in earnest about the time of World War I when the ideas of Hall and Gesell were gaining widespread popularity. These ideas considered children's development as evolving through a series of predetermined, unalterable stages, and explained that all reading instruction should be delayed until the natural stage for learning to read was reached, that is, after the child had entered first grade. Proponents of this view used the following logic:

1. Development occurs in stages that are sequential and age-related.
2. Growth from one stage to another is solely a result of biological maturation (internal ripening of neural systems) that occurs *only* with the passage of time.
3. The ability to read occurs only when the child naturally reaches one of these stages.
4. Many children do not naturally reach this stage until late first grade and, therefore, are not ready for reading until then.
5. The message for preschool and kindergarten teachers, then, is to postpone all reading instruction until increased age allows the children to benefit from such efforts.

These ideas were accepted by some early childhood educators during the early 1900s. Grace Owen, one of the great pioneers in nursery school education during that era, explained why academic instruction had no place in her classroom: "No mention has been made of instruction in the Nursery School because in any formal sense it has no place. No reading, no writing, no number lessons should on any account be allowed, for the time for these things has not yet come."[1]

Exposing children to formal reading instruction during their early years (before age 6½) was seen as unnatural and sure to create unreasonable pressures leading to certain failure and discouragement.

During the 1960s, educators began vociferously to question the traditional Gesell-oriented concept of reading readiness and began looking more at the influence of the environment on learning. Chief among these, you will recall, were Jerome Bruner, Benjamin Bloom, and J. McVicker Hunt. Their views centered on these basic concepts:

1. Readiness to learn is influenced at least as much by environmental factors as by movement through stages of development.

2. Appropriate experiences during the child's early years (preschool–kindergarten) have special consequences for later success in learning.

The emerging view of *readiness*, then, proposed that very young children can be exposed to reading activities if those activities are appropriate to the developmental levels and experience backgrounds of the children. It was felt that, by analyzing the skills inherent in the reading process, learning experiences could be arranged hierarchically so that each new task could be built on the mastery of the previous one—and some of these tasks could be appropriately placed in the preschool setting rather than in the elementary school. A new definition of reading readiness began to reflect these thoughts: (1) "that every experience both takes up something from those which have gone before and modifies in some way the quality of those which come after,"[2] and (2) that readiness is the "adequacy of existing capacity in relation to the demands of a given learning task."[3]

At present, the view of reading readiness has changed from a belief that any planned program to develop readiness skills before age 6½ is entirely unnecessary to the belief that each child can profit from some planned program of readiness development while participating in a number of prereading activities. This prevailing view of readiness for reading is illustrated in Figure 7-1. It shows that both heredity and environment affect the child's potential for reading, and that his potential can be fully realized only if instruction is matched to the child's developing needs.

HEREDITY + ENVIRONMENT

POTENTIAL TO READ

⇧

TYPE OF INSTRUCTION PROVIDED FOR THE CHILD

Figure 7-1 The prevailing view of readiness for learning.

What experiences are necessary before a youngster is able to move from interest in learning to recognizing the first printed word?

Reading Prerequisites

Since the position has been taken that readiness is basically a planned period of experiences, activities, and instructional procedures designed to bridge the period between nonreading and reading, you may reasonably ask: "What, then, should I be aware of in planning a program to develop areas of growth in which the child is deficient and, thus, move him toward stages of maturity necessary to becoming a reader?"

Educators have identified many behaviors and skills purported to be essential to developing a basic readiness for reading. However, in general, reading readiness involves development of the following competencies:

1. Physical abilities
   a. *Large muscle skills*—running, jumping, hopping, skipping, crawling, balancing, throwing, catching, and so on
   b. *Small muscle skills*—buckling, zipping, hooking, lacing, tying, tearing, folding, pasting, painting, drawing, cutting, holding a pencil, and so on
   c. *State of health*—hearing and seeing well, being generally in a state of good health
2. Social-emotional maturity
   a. *Social growth*—sharing materials, participating in organized activities, playing well with peers, adapting to routines

    b. *Emotional growth*—exhibiting self-control, displaying even temperament, respecting others, assuming responsibility, showing self-confidence
3. Intellectual abilities
    Thinking skills—gaining meaning and understanding (after hearing a story, for example) by remembering main topics or information
4. Language skills
    a. *Language production*—exhibiting normal vocabulary growth and patterns of sentence formation
    b. *Listening*—analyzing and comprehending what is heard
5. Experience background
    a. *Direct experiences*—taking part in in-school and out-of-school trips, watching and participating in demonstrations, observing and interacting with guest speakers
    b. *Vicarious experiences*—listening to stories, viewing films or filmstrips, sharing pictures, watching television, and so on
6. Perceptual skills
    a. *Visual discrimination and visual memory*—differentiating among letters of the alphabet or words and recalling such differences after time has passed
    b. *Auditory discrimination and auditory memory*—detecting differences in sounds among letters or words and recalling such differences after time has passed
    c. *Kinesthetic-tactile skills*—discriminating among qualities of objects (rough, smooth; heavy, light; hard, soft) using senses other than seeing or listening

Many of these categories of essential reading readiness competencies are discussed in other sections of this book, because they are as important for other academic areas of instruction as they are for reading (physical abilities, Chapters 4 and 5; social-emotional maturity, Chapters 2 and 3; intellectual abilities, Chapter 6; language skills, Chapter 8; experience background, Chapter 9; perceptual skills, next topic in this chapter).

Perceptual Skills

Perception is defined as an individual's ability to receive sensory input, interpret it in some way, and then respond to it. The sensory input channels having the greatest impact on reading skills are the visual, the aural, and the kinesthetic-tactile. Development of these three sensory input channels is directly influenced by *neural development* and *experience background.* That is, when a child receives an impulse from any of these channels, he interprets it and responds to it on the basis of his neural capabilities and his experiential background. If both areas have prepared him adequately, the child forms accurate perceptions of the new sensory impulses, and the reading process should develop normally. If, however, either area is inadequate in some way, sensory impulses may be incorrectly interpreted and the reading process most probably will be delayed. (See Figure 7-2 for an example of how neural development can affect reading efficiency.) To see how a child's background of experiences can affect the ability to read, consider these questions: Did you ever read a popular book before you saw a movie based on that book? Which did you like better? If you said that you liked the book better, you responded in much the way most people would. The reason is that as you read the book, you associated *past experiences* with the plot and, as the events unfolded, those experiences caused you to picture the characters and settings in your own unique way. The same is true for each individual reading the same book, ultimately including the movie director. Of course, the director's experiences probably were much different from your own, thus causing disharmony—those movie scenes just weren't the way they happened in the book! Likewise, children call on past experiences when they learn to unlock the printed word —reading is a process that includes not only *word recognition* but also *word meaning.* The only way a child can get meaning from that printed word is to associate it with some past experience. Of course, the lack of or abundance of those past experiences can influence a child's progress either positively or negatively.

Because of this central role of perceptual development in the total reading process, many preschool programs are designed to enhance and nurture specific, related skills. Techniques for doing this range from highly formalized programs to unstructured, informal programs. Whatever technique is chosen, however, the major goal of perceptual instruction remains fairly constant: to develop visual, aural, and kinesthetic-tactile skills within the context of appropriate experience.

Visual Skills

1. *Visual discrimination:* the ability to differentiate among visual patterns —to see likenesses and differences, usually in size, shape, or color. Because children in a readiness program usually have difficulties distinguishing between an *o* and an *a,* a *d* and a *b,* an *n* and an *h,* they need to be provided with opportunities to observe likenesses and differences among the various stimuli in their environment that are more apparent.
2. *Visual memory:* the ability to observe visual stimuli and, when the stimuli have been removed for a period of time, to recall them from memory. Because learning to read involves the recall of letters, combinations of letters, and whole words, the readiness program is designed to help the child first remember simple items in the environment and then to move systematically to the more complex items such as letters of the alphabet or words.

Aural Skills

1. *Auditory discrimination:* the ability to differentiate among sounds— usually detecting likenesses and differences in tone, rhythm, volume, or source of sound. Since reading involves hearing the difference between *an* and *and,* or *gain* and *gang,* and telling which of the four words *ball, big,*

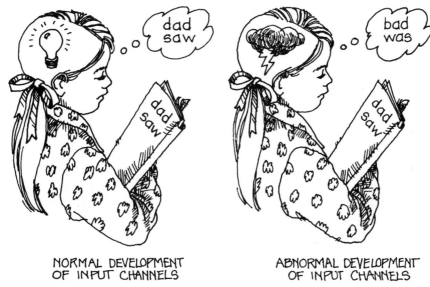

NORMAL DEVELOPMENT OF INPUT CHANNELS   ABNORMAL DEVELOPMENT OF INPUT CHANNELS

Figure 7-2 The importance of perceptual development in the reading process.

pin, and *bone* begin with the same sound, auditory discrimination activities are vital in reading readiness programs.

2. *Auditory memory:* the ability to remember sounds and to recall them after a period of time. The child must not only perceive differences in sounds but he must also learn to remember them.

Kinesthetic-Tactile Skills

The ability to receive and interpret stimuli from outside sources through sensory channels other than the eyes or ears are referred to as kinesthetic-tactile skills. Body movement and the senses of touch, taste, and smell are especially attended to in this area of reading readiness. Some experts believe that the involvement of all the senses in the readiness phase strengthens the teaching of reading.

These three areas of perceptual skills can be developed in a readiness program through dozens of different techniques. To give you an idea of some of the popular approaches to reading readiness, we will examine the techniques of two opposing philosophies: the informal program and the formal program based on behavioral concepts. Both theoretical foundations were presented in Chapter 6; here, we examine their educational implications more deeply.

The only theoretical framework that will not be discussed in great depth is that of Piaget. Piaget is not unimportant—but he is more concerned about *when* reading should begin than about the type of reading readiness program that should be used. According to Piagetian scholars, the time for reading occurs naturally just before the period of concrete operations begins (around seven years). They, like the followers of Gesell, doubt that children are ready to read before that time, for reading involves a level of conceptualization and abstraction far beyond that of the younger child. According to Piagetian scholars, therefore, any formal reading instruction should be postponed until the child enters first or second grade. This does not mean, however, that we "tread water" until the child reaches the concrete operations stage. As you learned from Chapter 6, it is important to develop two major categories of knowledge during the child's preschool years: *physical knowledge* and *logico-mathematical knowledge*. If this is done through observation and experimentation, the child will have reached an appropriate level of cognitive maturity (readiness) by the age of seven and specific reading instruction can be initiated. For Piaget, then, reading readiness means providing experiences designed to encourage overall intellectual growth, especially in physical and logico-mathematical knowledge.

Informal Approaches to Reading Readiness

Some preschool educators feel that an unstructured, informal program where children are free to explore and manipulate objects within their environment is the best way to provide reading experiences. This philosophy reflects the belief that learning is something done *by the child* rather than *to the child* through a series of activities that progress from the concrete to the abstract.

Perhaps the most widely used technique of the informal teacher is *play*. Toys and games are provided in an unstructured, informal setting to capitalize on the child's natural inclination to explore, manipulate, and experiment. As the child becomes involved with play-oriented materials suited to his level, he may use the material over and over again because of his great feeling of accomplishment. In this way, he solidifies his skills and becomes more expert at them. This sense of accomplishment and personal expertise motivates the child to approach new tasks with greater confidence and inspiration.

The teacher's role in such play activity is that of informal interaction and stimulation of thought. Children learn a great deal by themselves, but often require help in putting those learnings together to form increasingly sophisticated concepts. Help is usually offered in two different ways: (1) by guiding the child and (2) by verbalizing the key characteristics of the learning situation. For example, you may wish to encourage the child to be able to discriminate among objects on the basis of color. To achieve that goal, you show a child a box full of small toys and say, "Look at all the toys in this box. Let's dump them on this rug and see what we have." Allow the child to play for a time with the toys, then invite him to join you in a game: "Let's play a sorting game with these toys. We'll put the red toy on this red rug (sample) because it is the same color, the blue toy on the blue rug, and the yellow toy on the yellow rug. Ready? Show me a toy. Where will you put it? Good. The blue toys all go together. . . . You sorted all the toys by color. Very good! Please tell

This child learns the alphabet at a learning station in an informal, child-oriented classroom.

me the names of the colors we sorted. You did very well. Let's mix the toys and play the game again." Analyzing this teacher's strategy we find that she:

1. arranged a special set of manipulative, play materials
2. encouraged the child to play freely with the materials
3. demonstrated an activity with the materials that leads to understanding
4. invited the child to perform the same action until mastery was achieved
5. continued the activity until the child lost interest

Remember that this sequence is only a recommendation and doesn't need to be followed rigidly each time an informal activity is offered. The exact amount of teacher involvement as well as the number and order of play experiences should always remain open so they can more readily match the child's changing interests and needs.

One of the most popular ways of arranging play experiences in the preschool setting is to use *learning stations*. Basically, a learning station is an area containing one distinct developmental activity to which the child may move in order to become individually involved in a reading readiness activity. In any classroom there may be as many as fifteen stations or as few as one. At a learning station, the child usually performs tasks by himself or with assistance from the teacher. The boxes on visual, auditory, and kinesthetic tactile skills illustrate activities that have been popularly used by teachers in learning stations.

In addition to planned visual experiences, you should also be constantly aware of the informal opportunities you have to further related readiness skills. The following are examples of teachers taking advantage of these opportunities.

VISUAL SKILLS

VISUAL DISCRIMINATION ACTIVITIES Visual discrimination activities generally fall into the following basic types.

☐ *Sorting objects:* Children identify objects that are alike and different. For example, sorting all the toy cars into one box and all the plastic horses into another.

☐ *Sorting by color:* Children identify different colors of objects and sort them by color.

☐ *Sorting by size:* Children identify big and little objects and sort them by size.

☐ *Sorting by shape:* Children identify basic shapes of objects (that is, round, square, triangle, and rectangle) and sort them according to likenesses.

☐ *Sorting by pattern:* Children observe a pattern on stimulus objects such as a bead arrangement or other pattern source. They then attempt to match or duplicate that pattern.

Some examples of these general categories of activities for visual discrimination follow.

1. Ask the children to use the separate compartments in the egg container to sort buttons by size, shape, color, or other criterion.

2. Cut 3″ × 3″ squares from fabric or wallpaper samples (two squares from each sample). Mount the squares on heavy tagboard, and mix them up well. Then ask the children to match pairs that are the same.

3. The children place the appropriate geometric shape cutouts into their corresponding holes on a frame.

4. The children duplicate a pattern by stringing together beads of appropriate color, size, and shape.

VISUAL MEMORY ACTIVITIES

1. Show the child a geometric shape; then take it away and ask him to pick one just like it from a group of various shapes.

2. Show the child a simple, uncluttered picture. Then, take the first

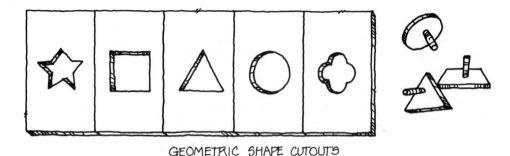

GEOMETRIC SHAPE CUTOUTS

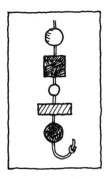

PATTERN CARD   BEAD STRINGING

picture away and show him a second picture that has a simple addition or deletion. Ask him to tell you what is different about the second picture.

3. Show the child a series of three or four picture cards in random order. Then have him arrange the cards in order of their probable sequence and tell you the story as he goes along (see the cards below).

Similar card sets can be made for seeds sprouting, seasonal scenes, chicken hatching from an egg, and so on.

4. Place three objects in front of the child and ask him to name them. Then ask him to close his eyes while you take one object away. Then ask him to tell you what is gone (or what is new if you wish to add an object rather than take one away).

PICTURE CARDS

1. One teacher varied the shapes of cookies during snack time and asked: "Who has square cookies? Who has round cookies?"
2. A teacher noticed several children wearing the same color clothing to school and commented, "Betsy has on a pretty yellow scarf today . . . and, look, Carlos has on a handsome yellow shirt. Everyone else who has yellow on today, please raise your hand and say, 'I.'"
3. In organizing her class for a field trip, one teacher asked all the children with black hair to line up first, brown hair second, and so on.
4. At the end of the daily session, one teacher asked the children to close their eyes and try to remember who wore brown slacks, a red shirt, and so forth.

AUDITORY SKILLS

AUDITORY DISCRIMINATION ACTIVITIES

1. Play a "mystery sound" game. Have the children close their eyes while you make a mystery sound such as knocking on the table, crumpling a sheet of paper, clapping your hands, snapping fingers, pouring water, and so on. The children then attempt to identify the sound.
2. Collect ten small plastic, metal, or glass containers such as juice cans, baby food bottles, or film containers. Cover each container with a colorful design and fill pairs of containers to about one-quarter full with five different noise-making materials—one pair with sand, another with water, a third with marbles, and so on until five pairs are filled. Make sure each pair of sounds is distinct, then have the children shake the containers and match those with similar sounds.
3. Fill several jars or heavy glasses with different amounts of water. Have the children strike each container with a spoon and listen to each resulting sound. Have them try to put the containers in order from the lowest pitch to the highest pitch.
4. For children who are able to count: Have them turn their backs; then you tap on a table, strike a piano key, drop a marble in a pie tin, or hit a drum. Ask the children to tell

5. Focusing on multiple attributes, a teacher asked the children on the playground to find "the smallest red ball," "the biggest brown block."

In addition to these planned aural experiences, you should also be constantly aware of the informal opportunities you have during the day to further hearing skills. The following are examples of teachers taking advantage of such opportunities.

1. Calling Barry to a table where a variety of objects were displayed, the teacher said, "Your name is Barry. Can you find any objects on this table that begin with the same sound as your name?"

---

you how many times they heard the sound from a single source. Then, vary the game by making a series of sounds from two or more sources, for example, two taps on the table and one piano note.

AUDITORY MEMORY ACTIVITIES

1. Read or tell a short story to a child. Then have him put picture cards of the story events in order, and tell the story back to you as he does.
2. Ask the children to listen carefully as you say three or four colors, shapes, names, numbers, and so on. Then have them repeat the words back to you in the same sequence. For example, "Red, blue, green, yellow," or "Billy, Joan, Stan, and Jennifer."
3. Make a series of sounds by hitting a drum, by clapping, or by tapping on a table. Ask the children to repeat the pattern back to you.
4. Create a group story with a group of children. You start the story with a few interesting sentences. Have a child pick up from where you left off and continue the story by adding a few sentences of his own. Then have him turn it over to another child. Continue in this way until all children have had a chance. This activity works best if you choose stories that are familiar to the children.

2. During snack time, the teacher asked Marcie to fill the juice glasses of all the children whose names began with the same sound as Marcie's name.
3. On a trip to a farm, one teacher asked the children to do the horse's neigh, the cow's moo, the chicken's cluck, and the dog's bark.
4. One teacher asked her assistant to go behind a partition and sound a musical instrument (drum, triangle, xylophone, and so on). The children were to guess what each instrument was.

Sometimes in an unstructured approach, teachers prefer to supplement their informal activities with worksheets or workbook pages. Although the use of workbooks is questioned by some preschool educators, the exercises do

---

KINESTHETIC TACTILE SKILLS

1. Use five pairs of empty soup cans and fill each pair with a different amount of a heavy material such as plaster of paris. For example, one pair would be empty; the second pair would be one-quarter full; the third, half full; the fourth, three-quarters full; and the last pair would be filled to the top. Cover the cans with a lid and decorate them with colorful construction paper. Begin the activity with one set of five cans of varying weight. Have the children first choose from among three cans the heaviest, the lightest, and the one in the middle. Then, add the two other cans in the set and ask the children to order the five cans from heaviest to lightest. Finally, introduce the second set of five cans and have the children make finer distinctions by matching pairs of containers that weigh the same.

2. Take ten small containers about the size of baby food jars and make five containers one color and five containers another color. Select five items with distinctive odors that can fit into the containers—

---

provide additional practice in the skills that were introduced in more informal, activity-centered ways. Figures 7-3 and 7-4 are examples of worksheets taken from the *Readiness Experiences Workbook* of the *Bank Street Readers*.[4] Notice the skill area identified at the bottom of the page and the type of activity designed to enhance that skill area. Figure 7-5 is a sample workbook exercise taken from another popular readiness program, *About Me*, published by Holt, Rinehart and Winston.[5] This exercise is designed to enhance the children's ability to identify objects by taste and smell, as well as to encourage the use of words to describe tastes and smells. After spending some time actually tasting and smelling real items in a variety of games and activities, the teacher could use the workbook page as a springboard for further discus-

---

cinnamon, pickle juice, liquid detergent, lemon extract, and mint, for example. Fill one container of each color with each item. You can place cotton balls into the containers to absorb the odoriferous materials, especially those in liquid form. When you finish, you should have five pairs of containers, each pair with one distinct odor. Begin by placing three different containers in front of a child and asking him to smell the different odors. "Can you smell the lemon . . . the pickle juice . . . the liquid detergent?" Then, introduce the three matching containers and see if the child is able to match each to its partner. Finally, for more sophisticated distinctions, ask the children to match all five pairs.

3. Choose four common materials such as wood, styrofoam, carpet, and sandpaper. Make eight tablets —four identical pairs—all of the same size (2" × 3") by gluing the materials to quarter-inch plywood. Have the children cover their eyes with a blindfold and run their fingers over each of the four different surfaces until they become aware of the distinctive feels. Then, ask them to match pairs of tablets according to texture.

4. Fill each of four baby food jars with one of the basic taste sensations (sweet, salty, sour, and bitter). Use sugar for the sweet taste, table salt for the salty taste, vinegar or pickle juice for the sour taste, and unsweetened chocolate for the bitter taste. You may wish to dilute each of the foods with water to avoid overloading your children's taste buds. That is, they can taste the different foods without being affected by the aftertaste of the previous one.

   Line the four bottles in front of a child and explain that each bottle contains a food representative of the four different taste groups. Dip a plastic spoon into the sugar solution and have the child taste it. Comment that: "This food is sweet." Continue with the other three solutions, emphasizing the taste sensation each time. Then, using a fresh plastic spoon, select a taste jar at random and ask the child to name the taste it contains. A word of caution: Use a different plastic spoon and a fresh set of jars for each child participating in this activity.

35

My name is _____ My class is _____

VISUAL DISCRIMINATION: Matching and recognizing shapes

  Have all of the pictures identified. "Find the things on this page that are triangles; color them green. Find the rectangles; color them yellow. Find the circles; color them red." (Experience 9)

Copyright © 1972 The Macmillan Company

Figure 7-3 Worksheet from *More About Readiness Experiences.* (From *More About Readiness Experiences* by Irma S. Black. Copyright © 1972 Macmillan Publishing Co., Inc., New York, N.Y. Used by permission of Macmillan Publishing Company, Inc.)

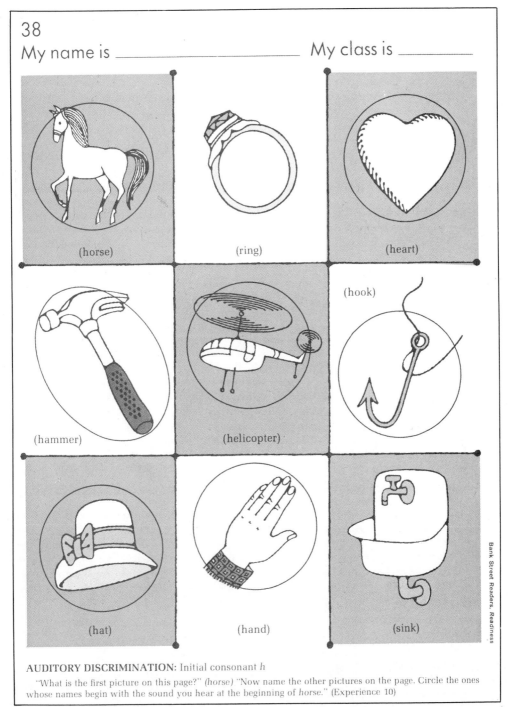

38

My name is _____ My class is _____

(horse)

(ring)

(heart)

(hook)

(hammer)

(helicopter)

(hat)

(hand)

(sink)

Bank Street Readers, Readiness

AUDITORY DISCRIMINATION: Initial consonant *h*

"What is the first picture on this page?" *(horse)* "Now name the other pictures on the page. Circle the ones whose names begin with the sound you hear at the beginning of *horse*." (Experience 10)

Figure 7-4 Worksheet from *More About Readiness Experiences.* (From *More About Readiness Experiences* by Irma S. Black. Copyright © 1972 Macmillan Publishing Co., Inc., New York, N.Y. Used by permission of Macmillan Publishing Company, Inc.)

sion of tastes and smells. The teacher's guide for *About Me* recommended the teacher use the following questions to guide an open-ended discussion, with the page as a stimulus:

1. Name the objects pictured.
2. Which things on this page would you smell but not taste? (Soap; rose; perfume.) Which things could you taste and smell? (Cake; lettuce; lemon; fish; butter; ice cream cone; banana.)
3. Discuss each item in terms of its taste, smell, or both.
4. Which things on this page would you most like to taste? Why? Which would you most like to smell? Why? Which things would you not enjoy tasting? Why? Which smells would you not like? Why?
5. If you were allowed to have any one thing on this page, which would you choose? Why? What would you do with that thing? (Answers will vary. Accept any which are justifiable.)
6. Which foods on this page would taste sweet? (Cake; ice cream cone; banana; maybe butter.) What pictures show things that smell sweet; but you would not care to eat? (Soap; rose; perfume.)[6]

Several supportive activities were recommended for use following the discussion; among these were:

Extension. Have the children select a smell or taste they either love or dislike and make up a story about it. Ask them questions to help them get started, such as, "What if you went to a land where the only taste or smell was. . . ."

Ask each child to act out either smelling or tasting an imaginary thing. For example, picking a flower and smelling it, or eating corn on the cob. Their classmates will try guessing what the imaginary thing is that is being smelled or tasted. Ask them to describe in words the taste or smell of the thing being demonstrated.

The children may enjoy composing a group story about the sense of smell. Ask them to imagine a young boy or girl who smells smoke in his or her house and is able to warn whoever is cooking that something is burning.

Reinforcement. Give each child a piece of 12" × 18" manila paper and have him or her fold it in half vertically. On one side, write "Things I Like to Taste" and draw a picture of a mouth. On the other half, write "Things I Like to Smell" and draw a nose. Ask the children to cut pictures out of magazines and paste them on one side or the other. Make similar column headings on another sheet of paper. These headings should read: "Things I Don't Like to Smell" and "Things I Don't Like to Taste."[7]

Behaviorally Oriented Reading Readiness Programs

Those who advocate a more structured approach to reading readiness insist that the informal, natural type of program leaves too much to chance —that what the child needs is *intensive, systematic training.* Traditionalists at first reacted to such thoughts with great concern, envisioning the preschool classroom becoming a strict, formalized, cold place with little time for play or socialization.However, most current structured preschool readiness pro-

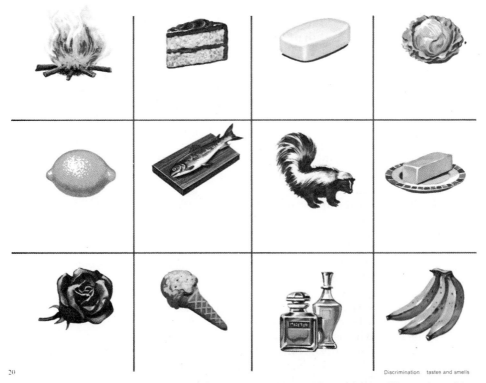

20   Discrimination   tastes and smells

Figure 7-5 Workbook exercise from the *About Me* program. (Reproduced by permission of Holt, Rinehart and Winston, New York, N. Y., from *About Me*, Level One by Evertts, Weiss, and Cruickshank, 1977.)

grams are not as they were originally envisioned by their detractors. They are approaches that involve taking ten minutes to half an hour each day for well-chosen readiness activity—thus leaving adequate time for normal routines of play and socializing.

We examine two behaviorally oriented, structured reading readiness systems in this section. The first, the *Sullivan Reading Readiness Program*, is a series of formalized exercises, drills, and lessons designed to lead the child from simple letter discriminations to more sophisticated word decoding skills. These materials, described as "orally programmed," present small pieces of information at a time, and elicit an immediate response—for example, "This is the letter *A*. This is the letter *B*. Now tell me, which one is *A*?" The teacher is advised to wait at this stage until she is sure she does receive the desired response: "This is *A*." Then she is directed to move on to the next letter ("Now, which is *C*, this one or that one?") and wait for the correct response. At every step, the correct response is immediately reinforced through verbal praise.

These "orally programmed" presentations are given several times each day in short exercises. The basic structure of the program is to cover six letters at a time, beginning with the capital letters. The letters are grouped as follows: A–E plus Z, F–J plus X, P–T plus Y, and U–Z.

Sample dialogue and drill techniques follow.[8] The teacher accompanies these with a long paper strip illustrating the letters of the alphabet.

> *(Point to the capital-letter strip.)* All the letters on this strip belong to the alphabet. Every letter belongs to the what? (Alphabet)
>
> All the letters belong to the alphabet. The alphabet is the name of the whole group of letters. Each letter in the alphabet has a name. Just like you, every letter has a name.
>
> *(Point to A.)* This is the first letter of the alphabet. Who knows its name? *(If you have divided the group into naive and advanced groups, elicit this type of response from the advanced group.)* (A)
>
> A is the name of the first letter of the alphabet. *(Point to Z.)* This is the last letter of the alphabet. Who knows its name? *(Elicit response from the advanced group.)* (Z)
>
> Z is the name of the last letter of the alphabet. What is the name of the first letter of the alphabet? *(Naive group.)* (A)
>
> And what is the name of the last letter of the alphabet? *(Naive group.)* (Z)
>
> *(Point to B.)* This is the second letter of the alphabet. Who knows its name? *(Advanced group.)* (B)
>
> Its name is B. The second letter of the alphabet is named B. *(Point to C.)* What is the name of this letter? *(Advanced group.)* (C)
>
> *(Point to A.)* What is the name of this letter? *(Naive group.)* (A)
>
> *(Point to Z.)* This letter? *(Naive group.)* (Z)
>
> *(Point to B.)* What is the name of this letter? *(Naive group.)* (B)
>
> *(Point to C.)* This letter? *(Advanced group.)* (C)
>
> What is the name of the first letter of the alphabet? *(Naive group.)* (A)
>
> *(Point to D.)* Who knoes the name of this letter? *(Advanced group.)* (D)
>
> *(Still pointing to D.)* This is D. *(Point to E.)* Is this E? *(Advanced group.)* (yes)
>
> *(Point to D.)* What is the name of this letter? *(Naive group.)* (D)
>
> *(Point to E.)* What is the name of this letter? *(Naive group.)* (E)
>
> I shall point to one letter at a time. Let me hear you say the name of the letters all together.
>
> *Ordered progression:*

Point to A. (A)	Point to C. (C)	Point to E. (E)
Point to B. (B)	Point to D. (D)	Point to Z. (Z)

> *Random progression:*

Point to D. (D)	Point to Z. (Z)	Point to E. (E)
Point to A. (A)	Point to C. (C)	Point to D. (D)
Point to E. (E)	Point to A. (A)	Point to B. (B)
Point to B. (B)		

When children progress through the structured activities comprising the readiness program, they are given a reading readiness test. If they respond correctly to 80 percent of the questions, they move into the beginning reading phase. If they score below 80 percent, they continue with a series of review activities.

Another popular behaviorally oriented reading readiness program is Distar®. Siegfried Engelmann, one of the major developers of this approach, states, "Our motto in trying to work out a successful reading approach was simply, keep the baloney out of the program."[9] The Distar® program was developed by determining exactly what skills should be learned, and then creating direct instructional strategies to develop them. Some educators saw this approach as a regression to methods of the past, but Engelmann saw it as an imperative, especially for children of low-income families.

Short, 10- to 15-minute drill sessions in which the teacher leads children in intensive, rhythmic instruction get them enthusiastically involved—like the student body being led by a cheerleader at a feverish pep rally. The group is expected to respond to the teacher in a loud, rhythmic, whole-group response. It is a fast-paced experience with the oft-repeated direction "Say it fast" filling the air. Praise is a major reinforcer in this program; the teacher's instruction book offers these positive responses: "That was good remembering"; "You are smart; I can't fool you today"; "That was hard work, but you did a good job." See the sample lesson of the Distar® technique that follows.[10] It deals with shapes the children in the activity have already studied.

> The teacher draws a circle and a square on the chalkboard, the square partly hidden by the circle. The children, who are seated in a row facing the chalkboard, talk freely among themselves and to the teacher until she has completed the drawing and turns toward them. They then quiet down and attend to the figures on the chalkboard.
>
> *Teacher:* Is the circle in front of the square?
>
> *Children:* *(in unison, rhythmically)* Yes, the circle is in front of the square.
>
> *Teacher:* How do you know?
>
> *Several children:* *(ad lib)* Cause you can't see the whole square. . . . Cause it cover it up.
>
> *Teacher:* Is the square in front of the circle?
>
> *Children:* *(ad lib)* No. . . . In back. . . . No, circle in front.
>
> *Teacher:* All right, give me the whole statement. Is the square in front of the circle? "No, the square is _____"
>
> *Children:* *(in unison)* The square is *not* in front of the circle. The square is *in back of* the circle.
>
> *Teacher:* *(to James, who has stumbled through the last statement)* James, where is the square?
>
> *James:* Back.
>
> *Teacher:* That's right. You're getting it. Now try to say the whole thing. "The square is *in back of* the circle."

After about four minutes devoted to elaborations of this task, the teacher switches to another activity.

Judging Reading Readiness

You can judge the levels to which your children have attained readiness for reading in programs such as those described to this point through either informal observation or the results of a reading readiness test. On the basis of these results, you will usually be able to determine if additional readiness skills are necessary for continued growth and what they should be, or whether some introductory reading activities can be planned.

Many experienced preschool teachers can judge readiness by undirected observation, as the children are playing or participating in various activities. However, most teachers who prefer this method use some type of informal checklist to help them. The observation checklist in Figure 7-6 illustrates one form in which these can be constructed.

Some teachers prefer to combine observation techniques with standardized reading readiness tests. Many factors are involved in readiness to read, and these readiness tests offer a broad selection of items and materials for testing purposes. Some contain manipulative devices; others, kits of activities; while still others involve only paper-and-pencil items. Some address only a single dimension of readiness, such as intellectual development or letter recognition; others cover several areas, including social awareness. Of course, some are much more effective in measuring readiness for reading than others—and most, by themselves, are far from adequate in giving the total readiness picture of the child. You may wish to examine and compare the following three popular readiness tests:

1. *Gates Reading Readiness Test* (Arthur I. Gates) Published by Teachers College Press, Columbia University, New York City.
   Subtests include Picture Directions, Word Matching, Word-card Matching, Rhyming, and Reading in Letters and Numbers.
2. *Lippincott Reading Readiness Test* (Pierce H. McLeod) Published by the J. B. Lippincott Company, Philadelphia.
   Subtests include Identifying Capitals Shown, Identifying Upper Case Letters Named, Identifying Lower Case Letters Named, and Writing Letters Dictated at Random. A useful Readiness Checklist is included.
3. *Metropolitan Readiness Tests* (Gertrude H. Hildreth, Nellie L. Griffiths, and Mary E. McGauvran) Published by Harcourt, Brace and World, Inc., New York City.
   Subtests include Word Meaning, Listening, Matching, Alphabet, Numbers, and Copying. Also included is a Draw-A-Man Test with implications for reading readiness.

After you have assessed a child's readiness to read through informal observation procedures and a standardized reading test (if desired), you should try to reinforce areas in which the child is weak or to begin reading instruction if the child is ready. Most children are not ready for formal beginning reading instruction until the kindergarten year; their intellectual, physical, social-emotional, and perceptual development shows they are not normally ready for it until then. All four areas must mesh—the child may suffer harmful results if he is pushed into reading instruction before he is ready. An exchange of letters between a concerned mother who was not sure that her

Reading Readiness Checklist

(Child's Name)   (Date)

		Yes	No
I. Physical Readiness The child is . . .			
A. healthy and free from persistent illnesses?			
B. able to hop, skip, jump, run, etc.?			
C. able to manipulate blocks, scissors, puzzles?			
D. able to grasp pencils, crayons?			
E. able to dress and care for self?			
II. Social-Emotional Readiness The child is . . .			
A. willing to share with others?			
B. able to work with others?			
C. eager to listen to stories and look at books?			
D. apparently enjoying school?			
E. able to see a task to completion?			
III. Intellectual Readiness The child . . .			
A. knows the basic colors and shapes?			
B. can count to 20?			
C. recognizes his name?			
D. knows own address and phone number?			
E. orients himself in space, i.e., understands relative terms near, far; up, down; big, small; etc.?			
IV. Language Readiness The child . . .			
A. understands simple directions and requests?			
B. pronounces words accurately?			
C. likes to talk about books?			
D. speaks in complete thought units?			
E. enjoys discussions of stories and pictures?			
V. Perceptual Readiness The child . . .			
A. recognizes likenesses and differences among letters of the alphabet?			
B. can hear likenesses and differences among sounds?			
C. can repeat series of objects, pictures, sounds, etc.?			
D. notices signs, labels, etc.?			
E. can remember rhymes, jingles, story sequences, etc?			

VI. Recommendation

From my observation of _____ during

the daily routine, I presently feel that this child is

ready   not ready   for formal instruction in reading.
(underline one)

Figure 7-6 Sample of an informal observation form for assessing reading readiness.

son was ready for reading instruction and Dr. Louise Bates Ames, a prominent authority at the Gesell Institute of Child Development, illustrates this point.[11]

> Dear Doctor:
>   We recently moved to this state. And I learned immediately from well-meaning friends that my son, Tabor, who will be six in December, is eligible for first grade. I was completely taken back as he would not have been eligible in our home state and I have never considered a five and one-half year-old ready for the work of first grade.
>   I couldn't bring myself to register him for the first grade, even though all our friends and neighbors urged it. Instead I started him in kindergarten. To begin with, Tabor is not ready for a full day of school. And in the second place, he is still very babyish. He still enjoys a two-hour nap each afternoon. Still likes to sit on my lap. Is just beginning to show an interest in coloring and cutting out, and his interest span is very short.
>   I don't mean to imply that my boy is not real bright because he is—bright but babyish. But what have I to lose by waiting? Next year will be quite soon enough for him to go to school all day and to cope with the pressures which first grade brings.

Before you read the response of Dr. Ames, think of how you would react to such a letter if it were sent to you. Make a list of your points and compare your ideas to those of Dr. Ames. Her response was the following:[12]

> Go to the head of the class, Mother. Your good letter needs no elaboration from us. Would that the day might come soon when all mothers see things as you do and no babyish nap-taking little five-year-old boy is forced to attempt the work of first grade, regardless of what antiquated state and local laws may permit.

Tabor was *babyish, immature,* not *physically ready,* he had a *short attention span*—all factors that could be easily observed by his mother (or a teacher). However, if he were assessed only by a standardized intelligence or reading readiness test, this youngster might have been proclaimed "ready to read." The point is that *you* are an important source of determining the child's readiness to read—that readiness should be viewed as the *total preparation* for moving from one level of learning to another.

At some point, then, usually between the ages of five and seven, many children become ready to move from readiness programs to beginning reading instruction. Such instruction varies from program to program—in fact, some skills identified as beginning reading skills by one program are considered readiness skills by others (identifying letters of the alphabet, for example). To draw a line in a sound, developmental program and say where readiness ends and reading begins is difficult, but for this discussion, readiness activities will be considered all those experiences that precede teaching children to recognize and understand the letters of the alphabet, words, and combinations of words. Beginning reading, then, will be characterized as that period during which young children are exposed to a planned program

Learning the names of letters and recognizing their proper order is considered a readiness skill in some programs; others view it as a beginning reading skill.

of activities leading to the recognition and understanding of letters of the alphabet, words, and combinations of words.

Beginning Reading

The *reading process* has been defined by educators in many ways, but all the definitions include two things: (1) ability to recognize printed symbols (words) and (2) understanding the recognized words. The relationship between these two components of the reading process is effectively illustrated by Rudolph Flesch: "I once surprised a native of Prague by reading aloud from a Czech newspaper. 'Oh, you know Czech?' he asked. 'No, I don't understand a word of it,' I answered. 'I can only read it.'"[13]

We may all have seen children learn to pronounce words without completely understanding them. Those children were only name calling and not truly reading, according to present-day theories that *word recognition* and *meaning* together comprise the reading process.

Beginning reading programs can be broken down into two major categories, each reflecting an opposing view of how children should be introduced to words. On the one hand are those who structure instruction in ways that closely resemble natural language learning. Instead of focusing on sounds or letters, these theoreticians stress the teaching of whole words or complete thought patterns through labeling, experience stories, and play-type activities. On the other hand are theoreticians who view reading instruction as the process of helping children acquire separate, identifiable skills, beginning with the sounds of letters through structured, carefully sequenced activities. In this latter context, reading occurs after children learn patterned responses and develop sequentially presented skills with a great deal of teacher direction or with programmed materials. There is conflicting evidence as to which approach is superior, so you should base your choice on two important criteria: (1) the ways you feel best explain how young children learn, and (2) the prevailing needs of the child's culture.

INFORMAL APPROACHES TO BEGINNING READING   Educators who use informal approaches follow the basic tenets of the humanists (Rogers) or cognitive developmentalists (Piaget). Their instructional techniques involve practicing whole words and sentences in contexts where children are able to use and understand them. Several types of techniques are used in preschool

LABELING ACTIVITIES

1. On the first day of school, you may want to construct name tags for each child. Cut silhouetted shapes (of fish, birds, kittens, and so on) out of construction paper, print each child's name on one, and pin it to the child. Children take great pride in their name tags and enjoy looking for likenesses and differences among their own tags and those of their friends.

2. Label each child's storage box, locker, or coat hook with his name. On the first days of school, you may want to take each child's photograph with an instant camera, mount it on durable tagboard, print the child's name under it, and scatter all the labeled pictures on the floor. Ask the children, one at a time, to find their own tag, and take it to the locker where an aide can hang it. This procedure can be extended by informally including other reading skills—for example, "Jana did a wonderful job finding her name. Now, let's have someone whose name begins just like Jana ...J...J...find his or hers. That's just great, Jimmy, you really did fine."

3 Write the child's name on a piece of finished artwork. Repeatedly exposing the child to his name is sure to help him in recalling it, and the child takes pride in seeing his name on something he created. When labeling, try to put the name in the upper left-hand corner so the child will become used to looking at that part of a page whenever he begins to read.

4. Label objects in the classroom, but only when these objects have the most meaning. For example, if new gerbils are brought into the classroom and the children's interest in the new additions is high, you may wish to print the word *gerbils* clearly on a bright piece of paper and attach it to the shelf on which the gerbil cage is placed. Discuss the word with the children. If the children decide to name the gerbils, you may want to print their names on a label and place it, too, near the cage. Labels like this can be made for a flower, the fish, the book area, and so on. Instead of simply placing the labels on the wall and seeing them receive no further attention, you may periodically take them

or kindergarten classrooms to provide informal experiences for the children, but perhaps the most popular are labeling activities, experience stories, and play-type activities.

Children are thrilled when they begin to recognize words, especially if the first word they recognize is their own name. You can help children recognize their names as well as other key words through a variety of *labeling activities* —such as those given in the box.

The *language experience approach* is often initiated with four- and five-year-olds. In this approach the teacher capitalizes on a direct experience and writes about it as it is dictated by a child or group of children. When children begin to recognize their spoken words in print, the experience chart becomes

away and see if your children are able to find out where each should be returned.

5. At times, children in a dramatic play area may ask you to provide certain labels for them as they try to make their play a bit more realistic. For example, one group of children set up an ice cream store and were about to open for business when they realized they needed a name for their store and a listing of the available flavors. So the teacher made a sign for the shop and listed the flavors: chocolate, vanilla, strawberry, and butterscotch. This variation of a labeling activity had real meaning for the children involved.

6. For snack time, use placemats made from wallpaper samples and label each mat with a child's name. Change the location of the placemats daily and encourage the children to find where their own is located. As the children begin to recognize each other's names, they may (one or two at a time) take turns arranging the placemats for the entire group.

their first reading experience. The basic reading skills of word recognition and comprehension can be taught through follow-up activities to an experience story. The sequence shown in the experience story box is recommended for use in the preschool or kindergarten classroom.

As the children gain experience with language charts, they will begin to recognize more and more words. Many preschool and kindergarten teachers use this approach because:

1. It is firmly based on each child's background of direct experience.
2. It uses familiar vocabulary and sentence patterns—the child's own.
3. It introduces the printed word as "talk written down."
4. It encourages the child to think.

Detractors argue that the language experience approach has several limitations; among these are:

1. It lacks sequential skill development procedures.

EXPERIENCE STORIES

1. The teacher provides a direct experience that interests the children and stimulates them to talk informally.

2. The children dictate their ideas and feelings to the teacher, who writes them on chart paper (18" × 36") exactly as they were spoken.

3. As each child's words are recorded, the teacher reads them back to the group, emphasizing left-to-right progression.
4. After each child has had an opportunity to contribute, the teacher reads the entire story back to the group.
5. The teacher may ask the children to read from the chart. Some may

---

2. It is too unstructured for an inexperienced teacher to use as a main approach.
3. It may introduce vocabulary that is too difficult or irregular.
4. It relies heavily on a variety of direct experiences—which many schools are unable to provide.

Teachers using informal approaches to reading instruction often supplement their programs with varieties of *play-type* instructional materials. The teacher's basic role is similar to the role explained earlier in the reading readiness section but within a context of actual reading rather than of readiness. The idea behind this type of program is that through active involvement with manipulative activities the child will naturally draw out understandings from the materials. The teacher, of course, draws on every opportunity to ask the child questions and to help the child verbalize patterns and relationships he intuitively learned but was unable to clearly define. Some examples of the countless numbers of manipulative reading materials are given in the play-type activities box on p. 240.

---

read only the title or a word. Others may be able to read the entire sentence they contributed as the teacher points to each word.

6. The teacher may use follow-up activities:
    a. "Find the sentence that Sharon told us."
    b. Hold up a card containing a key word in the story and see if anyone can recognize it on the chart.
    c. Ask questions to check on comprehension; for example, "What color are the hamster's eyes?"
7. Some children may like to illustrate the story when it is complete. The teacher should write the story title and the child's name at the top of the paper.
8. Some children may want to tell a related story as a result of the illustrating experience. Write down the words as the child says them on the

space below the illustration or on a separate piece of paper.
9. Illustrated experience stories, from either the chart paper or individual illustrations, make attractive and interesting "library books" when they are given attractive covers and placed in an area where they are readily available to the children.

OUR HAMSTER

James said, "We have a pet hamster. His name is Fluffy."

Joan said "He has brown fur and big brown eyes."

Carmen said, "Fluffy is a funny hamster."

Jackson said, "He always scratches and digs."

Faith said, "We love Fluffy."

As a means of extending the children's reading interests to books, pre-school teachers often arrange books and children's magazines in a special area of the room. Usually, the area is in a quiet section of the room where the children may go to comfortably look through the available reading materials. You may wish to arrange such an area where the lighting is especially good —near windows, if possible. If windows do not allow enough light into the area, consider bringing in old table or floor lamps to add a homey touch. Along that same line, some teachers arrange the reading corner similar to a cozy room, with carpeting, sofas, lounge chairs, rockers, tables, pillows, and so on. One enterprising teacher bought an old bathtub at an auction sale, painted it bright red, threw in a few cushions and stuffed animals, and placed

PLAY-TYPE ACTIVITIES

WORD JARS: Collect a number of objects small enough so that each fits easily into a baby food jar (coin, toy car, yarn, marble, eraser, paper, and so on). Place one object in each jar. Make a word label for each jar from heavy tagboard and encourage the children to place the appropriate word card in front of each jar.

COLOR WORMS: Make a worm such as the one illustrated with each white construction paper segment having a color word printed on it. Make matching segments from colored construction paper so that they can be matched to the color names.

WORD MATCH: Rule two pieces of tagboard into nine squares each. Draw or paste a picture in each square of the first sheet. For each picture, print a word on the second sheet. Cut the first sheet into separate squares, mix them, and encourage the children to place the pictures on the appropriate words.

WORD MATCH: Make a 6-inch wheel from tagboard and place pictures of familiar objects around it. Laminate the wheel so that it is more durable. Print the word for each object on clothespins and mix them in a box. The children match the clothespins to the appropriate pictures.

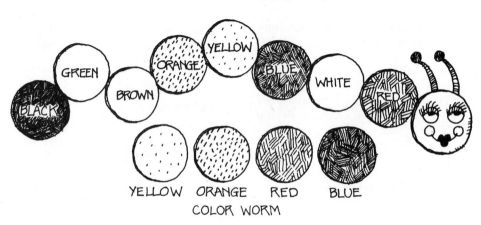

BLACK GREEN BROWN ORANGE YELLOW BLUE WHITE RED

YELLOW ORANGE RED BLUE
COLOR WORM

it in the reading corner. You can imagine the attention this lounging device received. Plants, aquariums, brightly decorated walls, or soft music add a comfortable touch to the area. All of this aside, though, the most important component of a reading area is a selection of good books. The following are some guidelines for choosing books.

1. Check the illustrations. They should be attractive, colorful, and simple in detail.
2. Examine the plot. It should be uncomplicated and directed toward things that interest young children, that is, repetition, catchy phrases, humor, action, rhyme, and a great deal of conversation.

WORD MATCH SQUARE

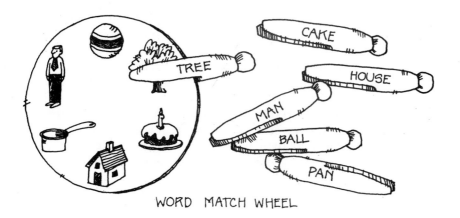

WORD MATCH WHEEL

Children are thrilled when they recognize their first word—usually their own names.

3.   Make sure the books are easy to handle. They should be easy for th children to hold, of good quality paper and binding, and the pages should be easy to turn.

By making a reading area readily accessible to young children, the teacher following an informal approach extends the learnings acquired through other activities and helps the child to develop interest in books and reading.

BEHAVIORALLY ORIENTED APPROACHES TO BEGINNING READING   Structured, programmed approaches to preschool reading instruction are new, but they are receiving a great deal of attention, especially from teachers of children with learning problems. These approaches are based on the behavioral philosophy proposed by B. F. Skinner. The application of his theory is called *programmed learning.* Through teaching machines or books, reading skills that are to be learned are subdivided into small units and organized sequentially, proceeding from simple skills to more complex ones (usually starting with letters, moving to combinations of letters, and eventually to words).

An example of one reading system using a programmed approach is the Sullivan-Buchanan programmed material published by the Webster Division of McGraw-Hill Book Company. This program was designed especially for children who were able to respond to a programmed sequence in booklet form. The material consists of a series of sequenced workbooks through which the children move at their own individual rates of speed, beginning with the readiness material and progressing through beginning reading activities.

Beginning reading instruction starts when the children have demonstrated these identified readiness skills: (1) a knowledge of the alphabet and

Children enjoy seeing their words appear in print as the teacher writes down their comments in an experience story activity.

an ability to print upper and lowercase letters; (2) an ability to associate sounds with the letters, *a, f, m, n, p, t, th,* and *i*; (3) the ability to recognize the words *yes, no, ant, man,* and *mat*; and (4) the ability to read the sentence *I am an ant*. These capabilities are required because the child progresses independently at his own rate with the first programmed booklet, and he must be able to make word choices about pictures of a *man, mat,* and an *ant* in order to begin. Figure 7-7 shows the first two pages of the programmed reader.[14] The material increases in difficulty as the child adds new words to his vocabulary in much the same way as illustrated.

A growing interest in books is often a clue that the young child is approaching a point where reading instruction may begin.

Figure 7-7 First pages of the Sullivan-Buchanan programmed reader. (Reprinted from *Programmed Reading,* Book 1A by C. D. Buchanan, copyright 1973, with permission of Webster/McGraw-Hill, New York, N.Y.)

2

Another behaviorally oriented early reading program is the teacher-guided Distar® instructional system, published by Science Research Associates, Inc. The authors, Siegfried Engelmann and Elaine C. Bruner, started with the idea that children will learn those concepts and skills which they should know, only if those concepts and skills are directly taught. In groups of four to ten children, the teacher is responsible for carrying out the direct instruction leading to the development of effective reading skills. Engelmann and Bruner advise the teacher that their direct approach can best be carried out if the following techniques are used:

1. Act as if you are having fun. Show off: "I can do it. Watch me. Don't you wish you could do it like that?"
2. React to the children. Act as if their accomplishments are big deals, because for the children they are: "Did you see the way Irma did that? I didn't think she could do it, but she sure fooled me."
3. Give the children who are working hard some form of reinforcement. If praise does not seem sufficient, introduce privileges or tangible reinforcers: "John worked so hard today that he's going to get to erase the board. Good work, John. That's the rule: If you work hard, you get a handshake."
4. When children are working on difficult tasks, use tasks that are more fun as contingencies: "Tell you what: if you do a good job on this task, I'm going to let you do one of those stories where you get to see the pictures."
5. Treat the Take-Homes [homework assignments] as payoffs: "John worked so hard today that I'm going to give him a Take-Home. Tell me what it says, John, and you can take it home. I've never seen so many children get Take-Homes. You really work hard, don't you? And are you ever lucky, getting to take this home and show your mother."
6. Use a change of pace in your presentation: "Let's do it again, this time with great big voices.... Again.... Again.... Wow, what big voices! Now shhhhhhh. Listen." Pause. "Listen." Pause. "Let's rhyme with man.... What are we going to rhyme with? ..."[15]

Each reading lesson is highly teacher-directed and involves a great deal of verbal interaction between the teacher and the child. In the beginning phases of reading instruction, nine basic sounds are taught. The first is *a* (as in *and*), which is followed by *m, s, ē* (as in *eat*), *r, d, f, i* (as in *in*), and *th* (as in *this*). Here is an example of the technique the teacher uses to teach a combination of sounds to the children:

"Say it fast and I'll show you the picture. Listen." The children are inattentive. The teacher surreptitiously turns the page and looks at the picture. She laughs. "I like that picture. Who wants to see the picture?" Some of the children raise their hands. "O.K., everybody listen." Most of the children attend. "Listen." All the children are attending. "Listen." The teacher pauses and slowly raises her index finger. All the children are attending. "Now you're listening. Listen: mmmaaa (pause) nnn. Say it fast! I can do it: man. Listen again: mmmaaa (pause) nnn. Say it fast: man. Your turn. Listen: mmmaaa(pause) nnn. Say it fast!" Some of the children say mmmaaannn. The teacher smiles at them. "Say it fast!" Some of the children again say mmmaaannn. Somewhat more demandingly, the teacher says,

"Say it fast!" Again some of the children say mmmaaannn. The teacher says, "I can do it. Listen: mmmaaa (pause) nnn. Say it fast: man." She says the word *man* very fast. She acts pleased. That's saying it fast. "That's right. mmmaaannn. Say it fast: man." She turns to one of the children who had trouble with the response. "Did you see the way Irma said it fast? Watch, Irma, listen. This is for you: mmmaaa (pause) nnn. Say it fast!" The child produces the correct response. The teacher applauds and addresses the child who had trouble with the task. "Wasn't that good? Irma and I are the only ones here who can do that. We're really smart." Some of the other children object, saying that they too can say it fast. "Let's see. Everybody listen." Pause. "Listen: mmmaaa (pause) nnn. Say it fast!" Almost all the children respond correctly. "Yes, that's saying it fast. Let's do it one more time. Listen: mmmaaa (pause) nnn." One of the children interrupts saying "man." The teacher holds up her hand. "Wait! Don't tell me until I say 'Say it fast!' Listen: mmmaaa (pause) nnn." Pause and smile. "Say it fast!" Children respond loudly, "Oh, that was tough. I made you wait a long time. Let's see if you can wait a real long time. Remember—don't say the word until I say 'Say it fast!' Listen: mmmaaa (pause) nnn. Say it fast!" All the children respond appropriately. "Oh, that was so good."[16]

The Distar Reading program differs greatly from most preschool or kindergarten programs, in its step-by-step approach to acquiring basic reading skills. Results from research studies across the country have reported outstanding gains in reading effectiveness for children exposed to the Distar instructional system. Teachers who have used the Distar Reading program are highly enthusiastic about its results and are convinced of its value, especially when used with the mentally retarded, learning disabled, and children with other special needs.

Educators advocating a structured approach to beginning reading instruction support their methods as having these advantages:

1. It works directly with the skills that need to be mastered and eliminates the time wasted on extraneous skills.
2. It can stimulate the learner to elicit an automatic response.
3. It leads to self-direction.
4. It saves teacher time.

Those who oppose behavioral-based instruction present these arguments:

1. It can be confusing if the program is not well developed.
2. It puts an emphasis on the child's mechanistic performance.
3. It assumes that if the child merely pronounces a word, he will automatically know its meaning.
4. It presupposes that all children need to go through the same sequence of learning experiences.

ECLECTIC APPROACHES TO BEGINNING READING Some teachers, especially those who have taught for a few years, have had ample opportunity to experience the strengths and weaknesses of the popular methods discussed in this chapter. Thus, they have generally been able to capitalize on the desirable qualities of each approach while creating a personal approach to teaching beginning reading. This personal, or *eclectic*, approach literally means that the teacher picks and chooses among several systems and combines her choices into her own approach, designed to meet the unique needs and interests of her children. Some educators look at eclecticism and say that teachers who choose this direction are fickle and lack organization as they go from one approach to another depending on their whim of the moment. Others view eclectic teachers as intelligent professionals, capable of making the highly mature judgments necessary to incorporate the good qualities of a variety of approaches. Whether or not you agree with eclecticism or any of the previously mentioned approaches, the responsiblity for establishing and maintaining an effective beginning reading program is squarely on your shoulders. It is up to you to make the decision regarding reading readiness and beginning reading. Examine your children, the present situation in early childhood education, and the demands being placed on your school. Consider these factors as you make a truly professional decision by answering these questions: "Do you teach threes, fours, fives, and sixes to read?" "If so, how can you best do it?"

HANDWRITING

"Writing in the preschool?" asked a horrified teacher. "Goodness, preschool children aren't ready to learn how to write—save it for the primary grades." Teachers like this base their negative reaction to handwriting in the preschool on the idea that young children just aren't ready to examine meaningfully parts of a letter, to recognize letters, or to discover the straight lines and curves required by most formal handwriting programs.

Spontaneous Writing

However, others view writing in the preschool in a different light. Maria Montessori wrote:

Why . . . should we not write independently of such analysis . . . ?

It would be sad indeed if we could *speak* only *after* we had studied grammar! It would be much the same as demanding before we *looked* at the stars in the firmament, we must study infinitesimal calculus; it is much the same thing to feel that before teaching an idiot to write, we must make him understand the abstract derivation of lines and the problems of geometry!

No less are we to be pitied if, in order to write, we must follow analytically the parts constituting the alphabetical signs.[17]

A sensory period during which young children are provided activities to strengthen small muscle control is necessary before an effective handwriting program can begin.

What Montessori envisioned in place of analytical writing was handwriting instruction based on the *natural* growth characteristics of young children: "If I had thought of giving a name to this new method of writing, I should have called it . . . the *anthropological method.* Certainly, my studies in anthropology inspired the method, but experience has given me, as a surprise, another title which seems to me the natural one, "the method of *spontaneous writing.*"[18] Montessori's method of *spontaneous writing* involved planning a period of sensory experiences prior to the actual handwriting activity. During this prewriting phase, the children experienced repeated activities in which they exercised their hands in preparation for writing. Prewriting activities included sewing, weaving, and the manipulation of learning materials —all activities requiring children to use their fingers in ways similar to those used in writing. Once the children gained control over their large and small arm and hand muscles, Montessori introduced them to the writing process with only one special technique: "Seeing that I had already taught the children to touch the contours of . . . plane geometric insets, I had now only to teach them to touch with their fingers the *forms of the letters of the alphabet.*"[19] This procedure of tracing the forms of textured letters with the fingers, according to Montessori, led to *muscular memory* and superior penmanship because the correct letter forms were fixed within the child's neural framework. From this point on, says Montessori, "Writing is very quickly learned, because we begin to teach it only to those children who show a desire for it by spontaneous attention to the lesson given by the directress to other children, or by watching the exercises in which the others are occupied."[20] In general, Montessori found that by advancing through this procedure, *all* children by *four years* of age were intensely interested in writing and *some* children began

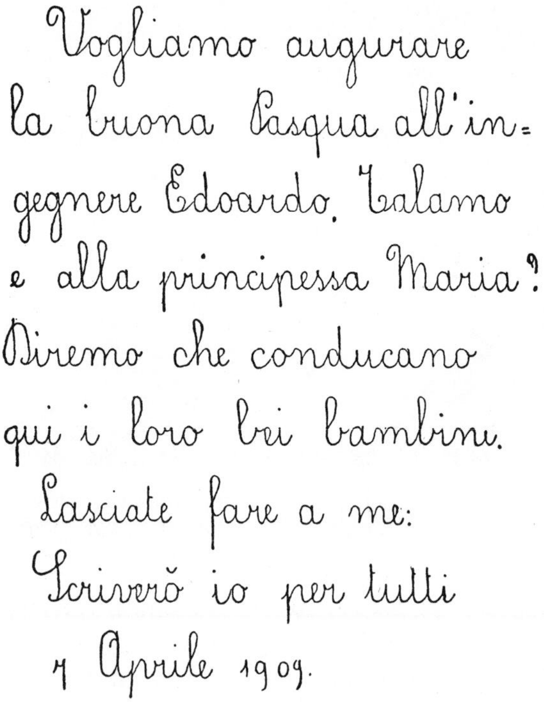

*Vogliamo augurare
la buona Pasqua all'in=
gegnere Edoardo. Talamo
e alla principessa Maria?
Diremo che conducano
qui i loro bei bambini.
Lasciate fare a me:
Scriverò io per tutti
7 Aprile 1909.*

Figure 7-8   Example of writing done with pen and ink by a child of five years. Translation: "We would like to wish a joyous Easter to the civil engineer Eldoardo Talamo and the Princess Maria. We will ask them to bring their pretty children here. Leave it to me: I will write for all. April 7, 1909." (Reproduced by permission of Schocken Books, Inc., New York, N. Y., from *The Montessori Method* by Maria Montessori, 1964.)

to write by the age of *three and a half*! An example of writing done in pen and ink by a child of five years is shown in Figure 7-8.[21]

Writing Readiness

Montessori described that period during which the child exhibited a spontaneous interest in writing as a *sensitive period*. This means that previous experiences have developed the prerequisite skills and motivation necessary for making a new learning task a successful, anticipated part of each child's life. In much the same way, we use the term *readiness* to describe the point at which previous experiences have resulted in the development of appropriate skills and attitudes necessary for beginning handwriting instruction. Some children may possess the prerequisite skills for handwriting when they enter the preschool classroom but others may not. For those who are ready for writing, we must know the types of learning activities considered appropriate for beginning writing; for those who are not ready, we must know the kinds of activities considered most appropriate to making them so. The following checklist contains key criteria that should be observed while judging whether or not any particular child is at the point where he can benefit from writing instruction:

Handwriting Evaluation Checklist
1. Uses crayons, scissors, brushes, and pencils easily?
2. Copies simple shapes?
3. Demonstrates established handedness?
4. Demonstrates interest in reading and writing?
5. Exhibits large and small muscle coordination?
6. Perceives likenesses and differences in sizes and shapes of objects?
7. Displays an attention span necessary for persisting at a new learning task?

Because some educators perceive handwriting as a *graphic art* (drawing letters) as well as a *tool of communication* (expressing ideas), the skill a child attains in drawing is often used as a second source of predicting whether or not he will have success when he begins handwriting. Figure 7-9 shows crayon drawings done by kindergartners at various stages of mental and physical development considered appropriate for beginning handwriting instruction.[22] It is advised that handwriting instruction be delayed until levels *d* and *e* are attained. Some children, of course, will be at those levels when they are four years old, and some won't be even in the first and second grades. Whatever the specific case, however, handwriting instruction should be delayed until the child has reflected the maturity characterized by levels *d* and *e*.

For the child who is judged *not* ready to write, and the great majority of your children will not be ready by the end of kindergarten, a planned program of activities can contribute to the development of skills prerequisite to handwriting. These prewriting activities usually parallel other areas of the curriculum that stress perceptual skills and muscular control. See the prewriting activities box on p. 253.

Keep a watchful eye for relevant scribbles in the children's work and be sure to make appropriate comments that focus on special significant movements. For example, "You spent a lot of time on your drawing—I liked the way you made the lines go up and down." Or, "You drew some very nice circles—I'm so proud of you because that's very hard to do." The scribbler gains a great deal of pride by listening to such comments and begins to develop secure feelings about his growing muscular control and his various lines or shapes. As the children gain more and more experience and become increasingly interested in language, they will soon begin to attach names to their scribbles. For example, one little girl came up to her teacher with marks like these on her paper: *[handwritten scribble]* . "I can write!" exclaimed the girl. "Please tell me what you wrote," requested the teacher. "That's how my dad writes his name," said the girl. Although the girl certainly did not actually "write" her father's name, she was beginning to show a transitional progression from random scribbling toward purposeful handwriting instruction.

a

Only a suggestion of form is evident; many details are missing; control of crayon is erratic.

b

Lack of perception of the relationship of the parts to the whole is apparent; details are missing; some details are overelaborated.

c

Keener observation of form is noticeable; significant details are included, such as ears, arms, hands; hair placement is more accurate.

d

An awareness of the relationship of the parts to the whole is shown; many details such as eyebrows, fingers, neck, and shoulders are included; broad strokes of the crayon are used consistently.

e

An understanding of body proportions is revealed; a variety of details makes a realistic picture; good crayon manipulation is evident.

Figure 7-9 Forms drawn by children at various stages of maturity. (From *Handwriting in Kindergarten,* Seattle Public Schools, Seattle, Wa., 1978. Used with permission.)

Initial Handwriting Experiences

When children begin to show such interest in handwriting and are sufficiently mature in other significant areas of development, they are probably ready to write. The first word that most children want to write is their own name. The primary reason for this, of course, is that their names have such

PREWRITING ACTIVITIES

1. For development of perceptual skills and fine muscle control, collect a variety of sizes of nuts and bolts. Encourage the children to choose a bolt and find the matching nut. Then have them screw the nut onto the appropriate bolt.

2. Also for the development of perceptual skills and fine muscle control, select wooden inlay puzzles with small knobs on each piece for the children to grasp as they pick them up. These knobs encourage the children to coordinate the use of the two fingers and thumb in much the same way as they must be coordinated to hold a pencil properly.

3. Other manipulative experiences include:
   a. playing with building blocks
   b. working with clay or play dough
   c. painting, drawing, cutting, pasting, and coloring
   d. working with pegboards, Lincoln logs, tinker toys, and so on
   e. all of the physically oriented activities described in other sections of this book

4. Assist the children to develop sound overall language skills. Read them stories, show them pictures, label objects, create language experience charts. Ask them to describe objects, play games that require speaking and listening, retell stories, and, generally, play with their language. Specific suggestions for such activities are explained earlier in this chapter and in Chapter 8.

5. Encourage children to scribble at the art corner with crayons or paint. While scribbling, children often use strokes that are basic to letter formation even though they may not truly be making the letter itself. Children enjoy making large scribbles—either circular or up and down—that cover a whole paper when they paint or draw. You should see most of the nine basic strokes of writing (Figure 7-10) in the child's painting on p. 254.

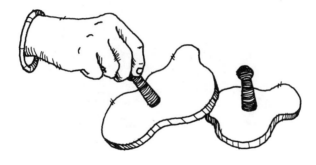

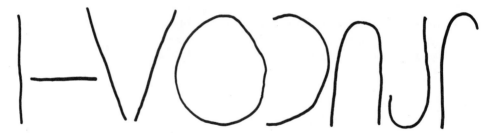

Figure 7-10   Nine basic strokes of manuscript writing.

strong personal meaning. But we must remember too that the child sees his name more than any other word. You put it on his art work, his storage locker, on his belongings, and on anything that goes home—so he also begins to copy it because it's familiar.

Steven, a fairly advanced kindergartner, was especially busy at the painting easel this morning. Using a paintbrush, he was studiously observing his name and reproducing each of the letters with green paint. Working slowly and methodically, Steven dipped his brush, studied a letter, and copied it onto his drawing. Letter by letter he was doing a reasonably good job of copying his name

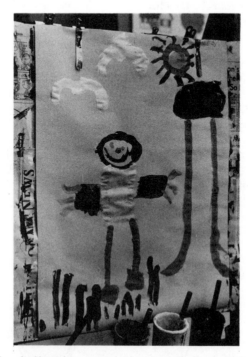

Notice the circles, half-circles, straight lines, and diagonal lines contained in this child's drawing. Such figures are basic to beginning letter formation.

from another drawing of his that had been labeled by the teacher. Carefully, he plodded along: ʔtɘvən . As is often the case, Steven's beginning effort had some letters pointing backwards (reversals) and some of the other letters weren't exactly true to form.

These kinds of problems are very common and are simply indicative of most beginning efforts. The child has not yet learned the individual letters in his name—he is just copying from a model by reproducing its shape, and his visual skills may not be developed enough to allow greater accuracy. This manipulative and exploratory stage is an important part of beginning writing instruction. From such experimentation, handwriting is effectively born.

As children gain additional practice, these errors should gradually disappear. The type of initial practice provided, though, should be directed toward experimentation and manipulation rather than toward formal worksheets or handwriting guides. Since the child developed his interest in writing in a free and natural manner, it logically follows that initial handwriting experiences should follow a similar path. Initial experiences should involve a great deal of large muscle movement (in easel drawing or similar pursuits), which doesn't cause strain as does the sudden demand for small muscle control, which is necessary for writing with crayons or pencils. Such a transition should be gradual and carefully planned by the teacher. Some suggestions for beginning experiences are given in the box labeled "Initial Handwriting Experiences." Remember that in all cases, the visual image of the letter or word must be present so the child will have a model to reproduce, although the model need not be reproduced exactly.

INITIAL HANDWRITING EXPERIENCES

1. Let the children mold letters from modeling clay.
2. Provide smooth fingerpaint as a manipulative, sensorily stimulating writing medium.
3. Cut letters out of sandpaper and encourage the children to run their fingers over the shapes. Such feeling helps the children to remember the shapes of the letters when they draw them.
4. Spread colorful terrarium sand on the bottom of a shoe box lid. Encourage children to print words by running their index finger through the sand.
5. Ask the children to complete letter puzzles. Cut the letters comprising a child's name into two separate pieces. Ask the children to put the pieces together.

6. Provide many opportunities for the child to experiment and explore with a wide variety of writing materials: paint, chalkboard, large pencils, large crayons, fingerpaints, unlined 12″ × 18″ writing paper, and so on.

These children are learning the basic letter shapes by matching one set of letters to shapes on a set of cards.

As motivating experiences are provided for the beginner, he will develop a deeply satisfying feeling toward handwriting. This initially positive feeling is extremely important since the attitudes children develop at this early age strongly affect the degree to which they will meet related challenges later in their schooling.

As the children meet words other than their own names, especially in labels and experience stories, they will want to write them.

A group of five-year-olds had just completed an experience story about their trip to the zoo. The teacher, sensing the children's interest, asked each child who had contributed a thought to the chart to draw a picture of their idea. All children began working busily except Judy. The teacher was puzzled, and walked over to Judy to assess the situation. Judy informed her teacher with determination, "I think I'll write what I said instead of draw it." The teacher, pleased with Judy's enthusiasm, took her to a table near the completed experience story and gave her an 18" × 24" sheet of newsprint paper and a large, soft lead pencil. Judy grasped the pencil, looked at the first word of her statement, and began to write her first sentence.

Judy took parts of a previous meaningful experience and personally joined them into a new learning experience. Children like Judy tend to spend large amounts of time sitting and copying when they are motivated at this stage.

Be careful to praise children for efforts such as Judy's. It is only too easy to approach a child at the beginnig stages of handwriting development with statements like: "Your *m* looks like an *n*" or "Your capital letters should be bigger than your small letters." Remember that the child is only *beginning* and that such problems will disappear with time. Be patient with your guidance. Focus on correctly formed letters rather than on mistakes. If these problems persist over a period of time and do not improve with your concerted efforts, then you may wish to initiate remedial instruction—but don't panic with the four-, five-, or six-year-old.

You must realize that some letters are more difficult to make than are others. This is why your children may be having more difficulty with certain letters. Edward R. and Hilda P. Lewis conducted a study to determine which letters caused the children most difficulty. The following list, which combines capital and small letters, shows their results.[23] The letters are listed from most difficult to easiest.

1. q	14. U	27. K	40. F
2. g	15. M	28. W	41. P
3. p	16. S	29. A	42. E
4. y	17. b	30. N	43. X
5. j	18. e	31. C	44. I
6. m	19. r	32. f	45. v
7. k	20. z	33. J	46. i
8. u	21. n	34. W	47. D
9. a	22. S	35. h	48. H
10. G	23. Q	36. T	49. O
11. R	24. B	37. x	50. L
12. d	25. t	38. c	51. o
13. Y	26. z	39. V	52. l

As you can see, the letters that descend—q, g, p, y, and so on—are the most difficult. The easiest letters seem to be those that are either straight lines or circles. Primarily for this reason, you may see children use capital

After children have shown basic readiness for handwriting instruction and have indicated an interest in learning how to write, formal teaching of handwriting can begin.

letters only in some words, mix capitals and smalls in others, or use all small letters in other words: LOVE, cAt, it.

In addition to providing a comfortable, accepting environment as they guide children's initial handwriting efforts, teachers are also models for good handwriting habits. Many teachers fear this responsibility because they are apprehensive about their own handwriting skills. This is an unfounded fear simply because all writing done by the teacher for experience charts, labels, thank you notes, and so on is manuscript (printing) writing. Figure 7-11 illustrates model upper and lowercase manuscript letters.[24] You will notice that they are all formed from the simple basic nine strokes described earlier in this section: The first five letters are a combination of circles (or circle parts) and straight lines. Make five circles like this: ○○ ○○○ and then add the line segments or subtract the circle segment to form the first five letters: a bc de. The other letters can be easily made with similar rudimentary strokes. With only a few hours of practice on a tablet or on large chart paper, you should become skilled enough to be a good model for your children.

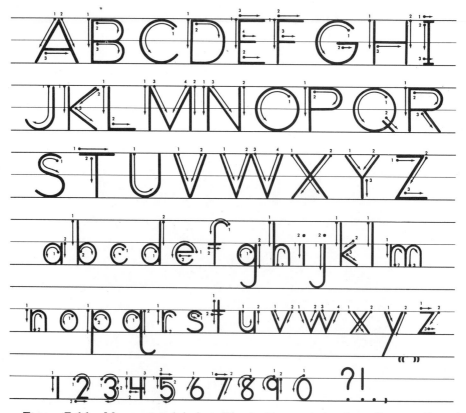

Figure 7-11   Manuscript alphabet. (Used with permission from *Creative Growth With Handwriting*, Second Edition. Copyright © 1979. Zaner-Bloser, Inc., Columbus, Ohio.)

This kindergarten youngster has begun to use the basic letter strokes in forming a series of capital letters. Notice the way she printed her name at the top left-hand corner of the paper.

In summary, handwriting experiences should be provided only for those children who demonstrate a readiness for it. Instruction should initially encourage large, free strokes in which the child attempts to copy a word of particular significance to him. Practice and reinforcement of this skill should be given through a variety of concrete, sensory experiences. Gradually, the child will begin to develop increased coordination and skill and will begin writing with crayons or large beginners' pencils on writing paper. Capital and small letters may be mixed, letter proportions may be off, and words and letters may be scattered over the paper—but remember that the children are still at a very early stage of developing a very difficult skill. Give careful guidance by praising the child for good efforts and not stifling motivation with undue criticism or nagging corrections.

Finally, you assume a key responsibility as a model for good manuscript writing. Much of what the children write (their name, labels, experience charts) will be copied from something you wrote. Therefore, you will want to develop a skill and ease in manuscript writing so your children will have a proper model to imitate.

Most children, at least by the end of kindergarten, will be able to write their names and a few other meaningful words. They will do so with great differences in individual ability and interest but, for those children who are willing and able, the preschool or kindergarten is a good place to start.

MATHEMATICS

Children will say and listen to mathematical terms at home and in the classroom long before they understand their true meanings. To illustrate this

"Why does 'quarter to' mean FIFTEEN min-utes? I thought a quarter was TWENTY-FIVE cents."

Mathematics concepts are frequently used around young children—and this often leads to confusion. (*The Family Circle* by Bil Keane courtesy of The Register and Tribune Syndicate, Inc.)

point, imagine that you are touring a preschool setting and are listening for all the comments related to the field of mathematics. You may hear comments like these:

"My new ball cost *sixty cents*."
"We start school at *nine o'clock*."
"It snowed *yesterday*."
"We have *two* hammers, Arnie, *one* for you and *one* for Ginnie."
"My little sister is *two-and-a-half* years old."
"I want the *square* block."
"*One, two* buckle my shoe. *Three, four* shut the door. . . ."
"My car needs gas—give me a *hundred dollars'* worth."
"My glass is only *half* full."
"My teacher is *bigger* than me."
"*Tomorrow* is Charlene's birthday. She'll be *five* years old."
"Good boy, Charlie. You put *two* glasses on the snack table."
"My mommy gave me a *dime*."

If the preschool setting observed used only this *incidental* type of mathematics activity—commenting on spontaneous events to teach math concepts rather than developing a planned sequence of activities—it would be following the informal philosophy of teaching. This philosophy came under strong attack during the late 1960s and early 1970s, primarily because of its use of unplanned learning in key subject areas such as math and reading. Critics felt that these skill areas were just too important to be left to chance—that if teachers waited only until some significant event in the environment occurred that could be capitalized on for its mathematics worth, too much precious time would be wasted. Therefore, many of the newer programs developed during this era of change emphasized the planning of specific lessons, materials, and experiences with definite developmental goals in mind. Instead of waiting for natural events in the classroom, teachers began to develop mathematics programs based on carefully planned and organized learning experiences. It is important to caution at this point that this new emphasis on planned mathematics instruction did not automatically mean that teaching became highly formalized for the preschool youngster. Of course, some programs, especially behaviorally oriented programs, emphasized a great deal of teacher direction and many recitation sessions, but for the most part, the newer programs stressed student-centered, individualized involvement activities reflecting a concern to help children *understand* mathematical concepts.

Perhaps the most effective way to explain this thought is to describe what the newer programs wanted to *prevent*. This illustration depicts what may be happening in some children's minds when their teachers do not emphasize the understanding of mathematical concepts:

Mathematical Concepts

COUNTING   A sure understanding of mathematics concepts develops slowly because children need a lot of time to comprehend inherently abstract ideas in a meaningful way. So, although some children may enrapture their parents by counting, "One, two, three, four . . . ten" or adding, "One and one is two," they may be simply parroting phrases heard over and over again and are not really counting or adding with understanding. They may be reciting with as much meaning as trick horses pounding their hooves at the signal of a trainer. To prevent situations like this from happening, you must provide many organized experiences to help the children develop the desired mathematical concepts. One teacher met this challenge by preparing a series of activities intended to build these counting skills:

1. Recognizing the amount of objects in a set *(number)*
2. Recognizing the number names *(numeral)*
3. Recognizing the proper ordering of the numerals *(sequence)*

Miss Kramer, a kindergarten teacher, realized that the best vehicle for developing the concept of number *was the* set *(a well-defined collection of objects), and she planned her first experiences with sets of concrete objects. She decided that the best way to begin would be to have the children make collections of things that were alike. Miss Kramer gave each of four children one paper clip and two rubber bands and asked them to separate the objects that belonged together. The children separated the items like this:*

With the goal of comparing objects in a set, Miss Kramer asked the children questions designed to help them observe which group had "more than" and which group had "less than." At this point, the children were not yet ready for counting, so she asked them only to compare sets of different objects with one another. Gradually, Miss Kramer added sets of three erasers, four pencils, five crayons, and so on and asked the children to group the objects accordingly. Through one-to-one matching and comparison activities, the children's concept of number grew as they grouped objects and determined which set had more (or fewer) elements than another.

After Miss Kramer had provided numerous activities of set comparison, she introduced her children to number names (numerals). *To prevent rote memorization of the numerals—1, 2, 3 . . . —Miss Kramer decided to select numbers randomly to present to the group. For the sake of discussion, let us say that she selected the number* three. *She then proceeded through this sequence of activity:*

1. *Ask the child to place the same number of objects in front of him as you have in front of you.* (visual *recognition/matching*)
2. *Present the child with a card containing three squares. Ask him to "place* three *counters on the card—one in each square."* (visual *and* verbal *stimuli*)

3. *Present the child with a card containing three squares and the numeral. Ask him to "place three counters on the card." (numerical symbol introduced)*

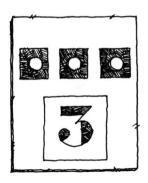

4. *Present the child with the symbol only and ask him to place as many counters on the table as indicated. (numerical symbol only)*
5. *After each numeral is introduced, give the child a card on which the numeral is cut in sandpaper. The teacher and child use the sandpaper numerals in three ways:*
   a. *The teacher shows the card to the child, asks him to move his fingers over the numeral, and says to the child, "This is three," or "This is four," and so forth.*
   b. *The teacher places the cards in front of the child and has him say, "Give me the three," "Give me the four," and so on.*
   c. *Still using the sandpaper numerals, the teacher asks, "What is this?" The child generates the number game.*
6. *For reinforcement, the teacher arranges the classroom with several center-based follow-up activities. For example, the children count the number of objects in each picture and match it to the appropriate numeral strip.*

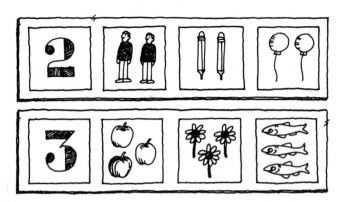

    As a final step in the counting procedure, Miss Kramer moved to the ordering of numbers. While she was establishing the number names for the numbers, Miss Kramer had stimulated exploration of size relationships between numbers (more than, less than, and so on). Now she sought to encourage finer

Informal, enjoyable early counting experiences give children a feeling of accomplishment, as well as a desire to refine and extend their skills.

discrimination among sets by developing the concept of "one more than." She began by asking the children to stack blocks and order number sticks such as cuisenaire rods. She started with one block and asked the children to make a stack that had one more *block than* she had. *Then, she asked them to look at the stack of two blocks and make another stack with* one block *more than* two. *When the children had ordered the objects in sequence, she asked them to place a numeral card below each set. A number of creative, individual reinforcement activities were organized into learning stations for use following this initial introduction. Among these were the activities in the mathematics activities box.*

As you have perceived, the major concern of Miss Kramer was to develop *meaningful* counting skills in an environment where the children are involved with concrete, manipulative materials and where they explore and experiment while making new discoveries. Her basic strategy followed this organizational plan:

1. Compare and contrast sets: "more than," "less than," and "same as."
2. Introduce number names (numerals).
3. Order numbers in sequence.

Techniques like this that involve the children are recommended by most early childhood educators today. Dissenters align themselves with a behavioral philosophy, supporting expository, teacher-centered approaches to learning. (See page 276.) Besides understanding numbers, other areas are covered in most preschool mathematics programs.

UNDERSTANDING TERMS OF COMPARISON   Understanding basic mathematical concepts evolves from the acquisition of relative terms that help young children describe their experiences meaningfully. Some of the more commonly used terms are given in the following list to help you as you begin to select materials and activities for your classroom:

alike—different
big—bigger—biggest
more—less; most—least
larger—smaller
above—below
before—after
here—there
near—far
few—fewer—fewest
fast—slow
thick—thin

in front of—in back of
inside—outside
up—down
top—middle—bottom
high—low
tall—short
close—closer—closest
first—next—last
all—none
hot—cold
big—little

As an illustration, to extend the concept of *more than* and *fewer than*, one teacher placed three crayons on the table in front of a small group of children. She had them look at the crayons carefully; then she asked the children to close their eyes and she secretly placed one more crayon with the set. She then had the children open their eyes and tell if there were now *more* or *fewer* crayons *than* there had been before. Think of creative ways to teach the terms of comparison as you read down the list.

MATHEMATICS ACTIVITIES

The child hooks each railroad car (made from half-pint milk cartons) in numerical order from 1 through 10 and places the appropriate number of counters into each car.

The child counts the number of dry beans that goes into each cup, drops them in, and arranges the cups in numerical order.

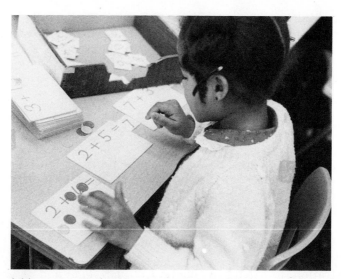

Young children require hands-on practice activities in order to reinforce their understanding of number concepts.

GAINING PERSPECTIVES OF SHAPE   Young children as early as three years of age can learn to recognize basic geometric shapes. They can identify and compare *circles, squares, triangles,* and *rectangles.* As with the introduction of any new idea, though, children should experience shapes directly in various ways during their daily activities. Educators feel that the best way to do this is to informally call attention to shapes within the immediate environment and to use words describing shapes whenever referring to those specific objects. For example, instead of asking the child to put the crayons "into that box," say, "Please put the crayons into the *square* box." Normally, when beginning to start formal shape lessons, you should introduce only one new shape to the child at a time. You can do this by holding up a circle in front of a group of children and saying, "This is a circle," and then asking the children to say the word. You may also have several other geometric shapes cut from construction paper, among which the circle predominates. You can ask the children to all search for a circle. When they have all found one, you may ask of each child, "Tell me what you have." The children may respond, "I have a red circle," or "I have a blue circle," and so on. Once one shape is understood well, others can be presented. However, you should remember to always review a familiar shape before the new one is introduced. You can then encourage children to make discriminations among the familiar and the unfamiliar by asking, "How are these shapes alike?" and "How are these shapes different?"

Naturally, children need enjoyable follow-up activities to reinforce their ability to recognize and compare geometric shapes. Some classroom activities directed toward that goal are described in the geometric shapes activities box.

GEOMETRIC SHAPES ACTIVITIES

1. Have the children sort through cards containing pairs of geometric figures—some matched and some not matched—and decide whether the pairs are the *same* or *different*. If they are the same, have the children place them on the right side of the answer board (over the two geometric figures that are the same form). If they are different, have them place them on the left side (over the two geometric shapes that are different). At first, you may wish to vary the objects by shape only, but as the children gain experience, you may vary them in shape as well as other dimensions (color, size, texture).

2. Cut out a large assortment of each of the four basic shapes. Create four characters based on each of the shapes, that is, Ms. Circle, Ms. Square, Mr. Triangle, Mr. Rectangle. Mix all the shapes on the table and have the children sort the forms by placing them in front of the appropriate person. It may be valuable for the children to name the forms as they sort them.

3. Ask the children to look around the classroom for items or objects with the form of the four basic shapes —items like clocks, boxes, toys, utensils, blocks, and so on.

4. Provide a container through which the child can poke his hand, but which he can't see inside of. Have the child feel the shape within and identify the form felt.

Figure 7-12 Time concepts are nearly impossible to teach in a concrete manner.

ESTABLISHING CONCEPTS OF TIME   Anyone experiencing a situation like the following can certainly verify that concepts of time are very difficult for young children to develop.

The Jones family, during an automobile trip to visit relatives, stopped at a diner for a quick lunch. Returning to the car, five-year-old Clarice inquired of her father, "Daddy, how much longer to grandma's?" "Only three more hours, Honey," replied Mr. Jones. Five minutes after resuming their driving, Clarice suddenly questioned, "Is it three hours yet?"

Since waiting three hours is incomprehensible for young children, we cannot reasonably expect them to grasp significantly time-related concepts of minutes, hours, days, weeks, months, and years when we teach them in a preschool classroom. These concepts are very difficult because they represent one major area of the preschool curriculum whose subject seems impossible to make concrete—the passage of time cannot be seen or felt. When they are learning to read, the children's original experiences involve them in associating words in print with real objects through labeling or experience stories. In learning numbers, children compare sets of concrete objects with numerals, as skills are developed and refined. But with time, we are faced with a monumental task of helping children conceptualize an abstract phenomenon with the use of abstract materials, such as clocks and calendars (see Figure 7-12). Thus, asking preschool children to read clocks and calendars is an unrealistic expectation. Most are not ready for that type of instruction until they approach Piaget's stage of concrete operations (7–8 years).

This does not mean, however, that the topic of time should be avoided by preschool teachers. There is more to time than knowing how to read a watch or interpret a calendar. Children often hear references to time and must be led to sense its importance in their growing worlds—yet they are just beginning to understand. They are reminded: "It's time to get up to go to school. . . . It's time to go outdoors to play. . . . Snack time. . . . Time for a story. . . . Time to go home. . . . Time for lunch. . . . Just a minute and I'll be with you." How long is a minute to a four-year-old? It may be a fleeting moment if spent frolicking outdoors in an enjoyable game or it may be an eternity if spent in line awaiting a turn on a playground swing. How much is an hour? a day? a month? a year? As we grow and mature, even *our* (adult) concepts of time constantly change. For example, when you were five years old, ten years old was old to you—to a ten-year-old, fifteen is old. But, to a fifteen-year-old, perish the thought of becoming an old timer of twenty! Time concepts are interesting and challenging. Someone once said that old is always five years older than your present age, and that person may be right. The point is that time is a difficult concept not only for preschoolers but for all of us. However, it dominates our daily lives, and there must be some value in teaching it. Some of the time-related vocabulary terms usually dealt with in preschool settings are:

yesterday	minute	next week	never
today	hour	next time	always
tomorrow	clock	day	now
morning	calendar	week	early
afternoon	last night	month	late
tonight	long ago	year	birthday

Some ideas for teaching these concepts are given in the time activities box on p. 270.

DEVELOPING MEASUREMENT SKILLS The preschool classroom should provide many opportunities to experience linear measurement (length, width, height), volume, and weight. Such beginning experiences should be informal and should deal with *arbitrary measurements* rather than with formal terminology such as *inch, foot, meter, gram, ounce, pound, pint, liter,* and so on. Some arbitrary measurements that often come up during water or sand play, for example, are "the *big* bottle," "the *small* spoon," "the *long* stick," "the *short* shovel," "the *tall* pile," and "the *heaviest* pail." The measurement program should begin with such simple arbitrary comparisons and proceed to informal measurements with meaningful *nonstandard units.* An example of measurement with a nonstandard unit is to give a child a piece of string (the nonstandard unit) and ask him to sort from a group of objects those items that are *longer than, shorter than,* or the *same* length as his string.

When planning a program designed to foster skills in nonstandard measuring, it is important to begin with simple comparisons such as the one just illustrated and use concrete materials. With such a basic background, the child will form a sound foundation upon which more formal measurement with *standard units* can be introduced later in the primary grades (see Figure 7-13).

The development of measurement skills in the preschool years, then, is based on the idea of *comparison*; the child makes simple, direct comparisons among objects through linear measurements, estimates of volume, and weighing various objects in his environment. Some suggested activities for each of these areas are given in the measurement activities box on p. 272.

Outlined in this section were five basic areas of mathematics skills usually contained in programs for preschool children: (1) *counting skills*, (2) *understanding terms of comparison*, (3) *gaining perspectives of shape*, (4) *establishing concepts of time*, and (5) *developing measurement skills*. The teacher should take advantage of informal environmental experiences, as well as plan organized classroom activities, to foster growth and development of these skills. These varieties of experiences help preschool children build a foundation of understandings that will later support and reinforce the more sophisticated expectancies of the primary grades. The concepts and skills should be taught in a developmental sequence appropriate to each group of children involved. Some teachers may prefer a structured *behavioral* approach to such instruc-

---

TIME ACTIVITIES

1. Use time vocabulary during your daily dialogues with the children. Look at your watch or clock occasionally and show the children where the hands will be when it is time to go home, for example. Help the children plan events with you —for example, a special birthday party *later in the day* for Tammy's birthday, or a special field trip *tomorrow*, or Santa Claus's arrival *next week*. Ask the children to identify the television show they will want to watch *tonight*. These beginning time descriptions should first be given in terms of day and night and tied into routine activities, such as mealtimes, naps, or time to go home. They will soon begin to tell the difference between school days and weekends, school days and holidays, afternoon and morning, and so on.

2. Display a large, colorful calendar for each month and include days of special significance to the children —birthdays, holidays, special events, weekends, and so on.

3. Make a large clock with movable minute and hour hands. Set the hands to indicate what the real room clock will look like when it is time for a story, snack, nap, or any other special event.

4. Keep time records of special activities in your classroom. Count the days that pass between the time a seed was planted and when the sprout first appeared. Keep track of how many days must elapse before it is time to water the plants again. Observe the time it takes for a chicken egg to hatch. Count the number of days until Christmas or Halloween. Use a cooking timer to guide the children in estimating how long it will be until a batch of cookies is ready. In similar ways, teachers have put to good use various timekeeping paraphernalia such as hourglasses, stopwatches, or old alarm clocks.

"TANYA, YOU MAY HAVE THE LONGEST ROPE."

"THIS BOOK IS TWO STRAWS LONG."

"THE BEANS WEIGH 50 GRAMS."

FIRST...

NEXT...

EVENTUALLY...

DEAL WITH <u>ARBITRARY</u> MEASUREMENTS.

PROVIDE EXPERIENCES IN MEASURING WITH <u>NONSTANDARD</u> UNITS.

THE CHILD WILL PROGRESS TO THE USE OF <u>STANDARD</u> MEASURES.

Figure 7-13 A developmental strategy for teaching concepts of measurement.

tion; others may choose a more flexible *informal* technique. Still others may choose a somewhat middle-of-the-road technique to mathematics instruction: the *cognitive developmental* approach. Some preschool programs are directly patterned after one of these three positions although most mathematics components seem to include aspects from all of them. The general philosophy of each approach was described in detail within Chapter 6; their corresponding views of the role of mathematics in early childhood education will be discussed at this point.

The Cognitive Developmental Position

The cognitive developmentalists base their teaching practices on the ideas of Jean Piaget. The bulk of Piaget's research was concerned with mathematical concepts of number, length, weight, volume, and so on. Piaget believes that the way in which children develop logico-mathematical structures influences not only growth in mathematics skills but in all cognitive abilities. Piaget identified several types of logico-mathematical thinking skills that can be expected of children during different stages of development. Those that can be developed during the stage corresponding to the child's preschool years are:

1. classification
2. seriation
3. spatial relations
4. temporal relations
5. conservation

Piaget believes that all reasoning powers are supported by the development of these skills and that all mathematical learning, in particular, is based on an ability to conserve number. Figure 7-14 illustrates conservation of number. The number of items in a set remains three regardless of change in size or position. If the child realizes this characteristic, he demonstrates an ability to conserve number.

Piaget found that children learn to conserve number sometime between the ages of about five and seven, and developmentally progress to the conservation of length, weight, and area. He emphasized that an overall concept of number develops not only from conservation skills, but also primarily from classification and seriation tasks, as well as from other skills. Sample mathematics activities were described for each area in Chapter 6, but additional examples are given here for the sake of clarification. See the box on Piagetian mathematical concepts (p. 275).

MEASUREMENT ACTIVITIES

LINEAR MEASUREMENTS

1. Compare the height of several children. Have them compare feet to see whose are longest or shortest.
2. Compare the length of different objects in the room. Have them guess which would be longer—for example, two straws laid end to end or five paper clips. Their guess can be verified by actual experimentation.
3. Have the children walk heel to toe from one area of the room or playground to another area and count the number of steps. Have them guess which of two objects is farthest from where they are standing, and then pace off the distances to see if they were correct.

4. Have the child use the width of his index finger to measure the length of a crayon, book, toy, or any other handy object.

VOLUME MEASUREMENTS

1. Give the children a spoon with which they can scoop sand from a small sandbox. Have them spoon out the sand from the box into a cup, glass, and jar while counting the number of spoons necessary to fill each.
2. Have the children try to arrange four different containers in order by capacity. They can test their guess by pouring small cups of liquid or sand into the containers and count-

Many new programs were inspired by Piaget's theories. These programs are activity-based approaches that emphasize the manipulation of and experimentation with concrete materials as illustrated throughout this section. They emphasize a *set* approach similar to the one used by Miss Kramer (see pages 262–264), as well as the discovery of relational concepts such as "more than," "less than," and "the same as." All these programs believe that the selection of content and teaching methodology should be based on the logical structure of thinking proposed by Piaget.

The Informal Position

Supporters of this position view the child as the center of the curriculum and the teacher as an arranger of the environment. As an arranger, the

---

ing which container held the most, which the next, and so on.

3. Have the children use a small cup as a measure and find out how many cups of rice, beans, and sand it would take to fill the same pot.

WEIGHT MEASUREMENT Make a simple balance scale from two lengths of wood, some string, and a pair of pie tins. Comparison activities can be carried out on this simple scale.

1. Children often will judge the larger object to be heavier when asked to distinguish between two items. They believe that the bigger the object is, the heavier it will be. Have the children use the scale to compare the weight of a large styrofoam ball with a smaller ball of clay. They will find that the clay is heavier than the styrofoam and that weight cannot always be determined by visual estimates.

2. Fill five cans with varying amounts of sand. Have the children use the

scale to order the cans from lightest to heaviest.

3. Have the children experiment to see how many metal washers balance a cup, how many beans balance a crayon, how many nails balance a block, and so on.

4. Have the children measure one object in comparison to a number of other objects. For example, a block compared to nails, pencils, chalkboard erasers, washers, etc.

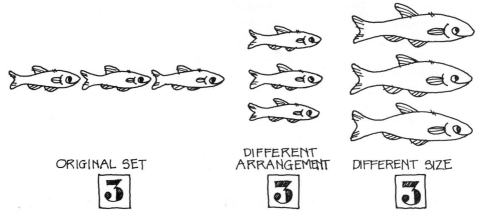

Figure 7-14   The ability to conserve number.

teacher needs to create interesting phenomena that will stimulate the child's curiosity. Once stimulated, the child attacks a problem and seeks to solve it for himself. Martin Johnson and John Wilson explain further:

> While some modern proponents of this position . . . must be viewed as extreme, the common thread found . . . is that the curriculum for the child . . . should be developed from the interests of the child. In the case of mathematics, this approach has at different times in history given support to the "incidental learning" theory of arithmetic. That is, the introduction, development, maintenance, and extension of mathematical content and skills were a function of the incidental need for them in connection with what was usually an activity unit.[25]

The method of incidental learning is to teach mathematics skills in the context of the child's own play activities and not to structure learning objectives or plan specific mathematics lessons. At the snack table, for example, the teacher may say, "There are four chairs, one for each of you." She may singly count the cups or cookies as they are passed out to each child. Children at the sandbox or water table may fill containers, empty them, and experiment with how much more sand or water is needed to fill a larger container than it takes to fill a smaller one. Cooking activities give the children practice in measuring ingredients with cups and measuring spoons. Size relationships are begun as the teacher asks the children to cut the pieces of celery "just as big as this one." During an informal tea party in the kitchen play area the children match the number of cups and saucers to the number of children participating. Boys or girls at the woodworking area plan to "measure" a piece of wood and saw it so that it is the same length as another piece. Block construction leads other children to choose the *biggest* block for the base of a building and the *smallest* block for the top. Separate shelves are provided for blocks of different shapes, so the children practice shape recognition as they remove and replace blocks used for construction projects. Weight relationships are discovered on the playground as children experiment to find which two children can make a seesaw balance. Number concepts are developed as children look for "one more piece to finish my puzzle."

Dozens of daily experiences can be capitalized upon for their informal mathematical value. The philosophy contends that the teacher (or other arranger) should take advantage of these opportunities because every child is naturally curious and eager to find out things for himself. These advocates believe that, with the guidance and support of an alert teacher, the day's normal activities can be exploited for their contribution to mathematics learnings and can form the basis for the entire curriculum. They admonish educators who use more formal approaches to mathematics teaching that their artificial structure and limitations can serve only to stifle open thinking abilities and lessen interest for natural exploration and experimentation.

PIAGETIAN MATHEMATICAL CONCEPTS

BY SIZE   BY SHAPE

CLASSIFICATION   The teacher uses shapes of squares and circles cut out of red construction paper to provide two ways of classifying (size and shape). To begin, the teacher and children identify the shapes, sizes, and color. Then, she tells the children, "Put together the ones that are the same." The children may decide to classify by size or by shape. The teacher asks the children to explain why they grouped the circles and squares the way they did.

SERIATION   The teacher and children make a card set to be used for a variety of seriation purposes. The teacher asks the child to "find the card that shows one dot." The children find the card and say, "This card shows one." The teacher then gives further instructions, for example, "Find another card that shows one," or "Let's look for the number that comes after one." Then, when three or four cards have been sequenced, the teacher may ask the children to identify groupings by number ("How many dots are on that card?") or to state which card contains *more, less,* or the *same* number of dots.

Adults may work directly with young children in small groups while specific skills are being systematically taught.

The Behavioral Position

Behavioral theories, of course, are translated into learning by exposing children to teachers and materials that are designed to *teach* skills and concepts through a carefully planned sequence of tasks supported by a system of reinforcement and reward. Like reading, behaviorally oriented mathematics programs for young children can be divided into two major types: (1) those that are highly teacher-directed, and (2) those that utilize programmed materials. Perhaps the most popular teacher-directed program reflecting the behavioral philosophy is the Distar® Arithmetic program, written by Siegfried Engelmann and Doug Carnine and published by Science Research Associates (SRA). The program is based on *counting* objectives, beginning with rote counting tasks rather than set identification described earlier in this section. The philosophy behind the teaching approach is stated in the teacher's manual:

> Distar Arithmetic I teaches the basic rules about arithmetic that are needed if the children are to have a solid basis for remembering and classifying facts. The children take a step at a time. They do not move on in the program until they have mastered the steps that are needed for the operations that are to come. They are systematically taught the symbols, conventions, and operations that enable them to solve a broad range of problems.[26]

The following is an example of an arithmetic exercise introduced fairly early in the Distar program. The stress is placed on counting as the basic skill needed before more complex concepts and skills can be introduced. In this exercise, on "object counting," the children learn to count to five while the teacher follows the instructions in the teacher's manual exactly:

Group Activity

a. *(Point to the trees.)* These are trees. What are these? *(Wait).*
b. Let's count all of the trees. What are we going to count? *(Wait.)*
c. I'll point, you count. *(Touch the objects from left to right. Do not count with the children unless it is necessary. Encourage all the children to count.)*
d. How many trees? *(Wait.)*
e. Let's count them again.
f. *(This time, touch the objects from right to left.)* Yes, how many trees? *(Wait.)*

Individual Activity

g. *(Call on individual children to count the objects as you point to them. After a child has counted all the objects, ask him)* How many trees? *(Wait.)*

Programmed mathematics materials are normally organized into workbook formats and follow the same basic patterned presentation found in programmed reading materials.

If you choose behaviorally oriented ideas to support your mathematics program, you must be sure to:

1. specify the skill you want the child to develop
2. organize a sequential program aimed at developing that skill
3. establish a pattern of frequent verbal or written response
4. provide for positive reinforcement of successful responses
5. establish a program of periodic evaluation of goals

SOME FINAL THOUGHTS

You have examined several alternative approaches to teaching "the 3 R's: Reading, 'Riting, and 'Rithmetic." Some programs are *product*-oriented, others are *process*-oriented, and still others combine both orientations. As you begin to choose the goals and teaching methodologies that will make up your personal program, this situation may cause you to ask yourself questions like those in the following list. Now that you have been exposed to some of the major considerations for making those decisions, how would you answer each of these critical questions?

1. Should programs stress *product* or *process*?
2. Can programs integrate both *process* and *product*?

3. Is the main goal of preschool programs to develop *factual knowledge* or is it to develop *general understandings*?
4. What is the role of the teacher in *discovery* teaching? In *expository* teaching?
5. How much is really learned by a child who is taught through an expository approach?
6. Can preschool children actually organize their thinking to the point of "discovering" concepts for themselves?
7. Is it possible for me to integrate techniques from an expository approach along with techniques taken from a discovery approach to form my own personal strategy of teaching?

The answers you provide will tell much about you as a teacher. In spite of all the commercially produced teaching materials and teacher's activity guides, it is still *you* who determines whether or not a program will be successful. Within the framework of your knowledge you are constantly put into the role of decision maker—and the decisions you make are a vital and meaningful influence on children and their future years of schooling.

NOTES

1. Grace Owen, *Nursery School Education* (London: Methuen and Company, 1920), p. 25.
2. John Dewey, *Experience and Education* (New York: Macmillan, 1938), pp. 38–39.
3. David P. Ausubel, "Viewpoints from Related Disciplines: Human Growth and Development," *Teachers College Record* 60, no. 5 (February 1959): 246.
4. Irma Simonton Black, ed., *More About Readiness Experiences* to accompany *Bank Street Readers* (New York: Macmillan, 1972), pp. 10, 35, 38–39.
5. Eldonna L. Evertts, Bernard J. Weiss, and Susan B. Cruikshank, *About Me*, Level 1 (New York: Holt, Rinehart and Winston, 1977), p. 20.
6. Eldonna L. Evertts, Bernard J. Weiss, and Susan B. Cruikshank, *About Me*, Level 1: Teacher's Guide (New York: Holt, Rinehart and Winston, 1977), p. T–72.
7. Ibid., pp. T72–T73.
8. Cynthia Dee Buchanan with Barbara Dodson, *Programmed Reading: Teacher's Guide to the Primer* (St. Louis: Webster Division, McGraw-Hill, 1973), pp. 8–9.
9. Siegfried Engelmann, in Robert C. Aukermann, *Approaches to Beginning Reading* (New York: John Wiley, 1971), p. 449.
10. Carl Bereiter and Siegfried Engelmann, "Observations on the Use of Direct Instruction With Young Disadvantaged Children," *Journal of School Psychology* 4, no. 3 (Spring 1966): 56–57.
11. *New Haven Register*, September 11, 1968, quoted in Clifford L. Bush and Mildred H. Huebner, *Strategies for Reading in the Elementary School* (New York: Macmillan, 1970), p. 34.
12. Ibid., p. 34.
13. Rudolph Flesch, *Why Johnny Can't Read* (New York: Harper & Row, 1955), p. 23.
14. Cynthia Dee Buchanan, *Programmed Reading Book 1A* (St. Louis: Webster Division, McGraw-Hill, 1973), pp. 1–2.
15. Siegfried Engelmann and Elaine C. Bruner, *DISTAR Reading* I and II: *Teacher's Guide* (Chicago: Science Research Associates, Inc., 1969), p. 14.

16. Ibid., p. 15.

17. Maria Montessori, *The Montessori Method* (New York: Schocken Books, 1964), p. 259.

18. Ibid., p. 260.

19. Ibid., p. 261.

20. Ibid., p. 293.

21. Maria Montessori, *The Montessori Method* (New York: Schocken Books, 1964), p. 309. Reprinted by permission of the publisher.

22. From *Handwriting in Kindergarten*, Seattle Public Schools, 1978.
    Dorothy C. Petty, and Marjorie Becking, *Experiences in Language*, 2d ed. (Boston: Allyn and Bacon, 1976), p. 214.

23. Edward R. Lewis and Hilda P. Lewis, "Which Manuscript Letters Are Hard for First Graders?" *Elementary English* 41 (December 1964): 855–858.

24. From *Creative Growth with Handwriting*, 2d ed., 1979. Zaner-Bloser, Inc., Columbus, Ohio.

25. Martin L. Johnson and John W. Wilson, "Mathematics" (Chapter 6) in Carol Seefeldt, ed., *Curriculum for the Preschool-Primary Child* (Columbus, Ohio: Charles E. Merrill Publishing Company, 1976), p. 169.

26. Siegfried Engelmann and D. Carnine, *DISTAR Arithmetic I: An Instructional System*, Teacher's Guide (Chicago: Science Research Associates, 1969), p. 7.

8

Exploring Language Growth in Young Children

"Remember when we were anxious for her to learn to talk?"

(*The Family Circus* by Bil Keane courtesy of The Register and Tribune Syndicate, Inc.)

Chris, a three-month-old girl, lies quietly in her crib during one of her frequent daily nap periods. Suddenly she begins to sense a feeling of growing hunger and seeks to find a way to communicate her needs to an understanding adult. Initially, Chris's method of communication consisted of thrashing her arms and legs, but since her efforts met with no response, she adopted a more direct form of exchange—she started to cry. Suddenly an adult's footsteps start toward the nursery and Chris stops crying, knowing that help is on the way. Chris's mother lifts her up and comforts her with a series of cheerful words: "Oh, you sound like you're very hungry. Don't worry, Mommy will take care of you." Chris begins to take comfort in the security of her mother's arms, and soon she finds herself advancing through a procedure experienced many times before. "I have your favorite food, Chrissy. Open your mouth wide—oh, that's a good girl.

Don't these peas taste good? Yes, yes—Chrissy likes peas. Here's another spoonful."

　　Her stomach now full, Chris delights in being held over her mother's shoulder while being gently patted on the back. Her mother's accompanying humming and singing give Chris a very warm feeling indeed. She responds in ways that communicate her strong feeling of security: as tiny bubbles of gas that developed during feeding burble up, Chris smiles, gurgles, and babbles with delight.

　　Through the entire experience, an observer could have easily detected effective patterns of two-way communication that transmitted feelings of love and trust between mother and baby.

PATTERNS OF COMMUNICATION DURING INFANCY

From these and similar patterns of communication during infancy, the difficult task of learning a language begins. The first months of an individual's life are spent in "self-imposed" practice—the baby listens to sounds and learns to discern their likenesses and differences. Long before he can say words himself, the infant learns how to interpret what others are saying: his caregiver's voice, the sound of his own name, or tones of voice all cause him pleasure or frustration. The infant also expresses feelings of pleasure and discomfort during these early months. Loud crying or quick arm and leg movements help communicate a certain need for relief of discomfort. Soft babbling, cooing, and smiling communicate strong positive feelings of comfort and satisfaction. How infants grow beyond these initial phases of communication to acquire and retain formal language is a complex and varied process. You notice how valuable it is for the baby to be with an adult who

A caring adult who warmly vocalizes the child's routines contributes immeasurably to language growth.

warmly and pleasantly vocalizes during routines. This gives the baby comfort and a feeling of trust, and also motivates the baby to try to "talk" himself. Beginning speech flourishes under these pleasurable conditions.

If such experiences are not provided during infancy, language development either fails or is seriously arrested. Consider, for example, the case of Kamala, the "wolf girl," found in Midnapur, India, in 1920. According to Arnold Gesell, who originally reported the story, Kamala was a lost or deserted child who had been separated from human life as an infant and raised among the animals.[1] When she was found, she was brought back to human surroundings, and after six years, Kamala had learned only forty words. Also, she never used sentences of more than two or three words, and she never initiated conversation. She spoke only when spoken to. The child's language had never developed because the impulse to vocalize experimentally during infancy had been outgrown without being exploited. M. C. L. Green supported the value of language play when he said that of all the skills mastered by the child during the early years, "learning to talk is by far the most difficult and most marvelous. Unlike learning to sit, to crawl, and to walk, which baby will do when he has sufficient motor control of his body and with very little if any outside help, baby will not learn to talk without much patient teaching from the adults who surround him."[2]

The wise parent or caregiver should be encouraged to spend time with the child in verbal interaction. The child should be given many opportunities to "practice" his growing ability to communicate, and he should receive continuing reinforcement from his parents. Before long, the infant delights in vocalizations and begins to experiment with volume, pitch, and different sounds. He begins to listen more intently to words spoken by others and tries to repeat them. After the first six months, the child is crudely naming things with word labels. It is at this time, when verbal sounds are associated with objects, people, or activities, that the first true language is spoken. Robert Armstrong and W. J. Gage say that "from that time on, from a linguistic point of view, he never looks back. He listens and tries to imitate what he hears. He receives responses in the form of warm milk, dry diapers, or approval. He modifies his speech, listens again, adds words and structures, and when success seems obvious, a pattern of language becomes habitual."[3]

Table 8-1 presents patterns of normal language growth during infancy. You should be aware of these patterns for they will help you anticipate normal development at different stages, and help you create an appropriate language program for each child in your care.

Of all factors affecting the child's growth during these stages, then, the most important one appears to be the quality of interaction and experience found in the family or child-care environment. Parents and other significant adults, as the child's first teachers, therefore assume primary roles in establishing the child's ability to cope with language. This is not meant to imply that such responsibility ends when the child enters school, but that a good start followed by continuing talking and listening experiences encourages language facility. The following suggestions are offered for parents or child-care workers who are in primary contact with the child during infancy.

Table 8-1   Patterns of Normal Language Growth during Infancy

Age in Months	Listening	Speaking
1–2	Is calmed by familiar voices Listens to voices Listens to noises made by toys	Exhibits undifferentiated crying as a reflexive response to discomfort Makes throaty vocalizations while crying Coos and babbles—undifferentiated vocalizations
2–4	Looks toward sound Moves head and eyes to follow sound	Differentiates cries for different types of discomfort, such as hunger cry or pain cry Babbles in repeated sounds of two syllables: "ba-ba," "goo-goo" Begins loud laughter
4–6	Distinguishes between friendly and angry sounds	Vocalizes, somewhat randomly, over a sustained period of time Imitates the sounds of others Repeats vowel sounds ("a-a-a")
6–12	Responds to hearing own name Looks at other familiar objects when they are named Enjoys listening to own voice Responds to requests ("Give me the rattle.") Understands commonly used words	Begins to say "mama" or "dada" Imitates words or syllables Begins to expand vocabulary to one or two other words
12–24	Follows simple verbal instructions; points to parts of object when named Listens to simple stories of a few sentences, especially about self	Begins to acquire more words by imitating the sounds of others (at 12 months has 10–15 word vocabulary; at 24 months 20–50 words) Begins to use personal pronouns "I" and "me" or own name Asks for objects by name: "ball" or "cookie" Begins to string two words together into simple sentences ("Me go.")

At about six months of age, children begin to name things crudely by attaching word labels. (*Hi and Lois* courtesy of King Features Syndicate, Inc.)

Play sound games with the baby. Let the child know you are interested in his babbling or gurgling. Imitate his sounds for a little while and encourage the baby to alternate his sounds with yours. Eventually, you will become so engrossed in the game that it will be difficult to tell who is leading whom. After imitating sounds for a little while, change your pronunciation of the sound. For example, if the child says "da, da, da" (as in "daddy") change it to sound like the *da* found in "*da*rk."

Babies enjoy playing with their fingers and toes, and this opens the way for many more games. "Ten Little Indians," "This Little Piggy Went to Market," "Thumbkin," "Peek-a-Boo," and other games are fun for infants or toddlers.

Talk to the baby. Don't speak baby talk, but use short, simple sentences. Speak slowly so the child can follow your pattern of speech and repeat key words or phrases when appropriate. Be sure to use the child's name repeatedly in the conversation.

Your normal routines offer excellent opportunities for you to speak to the baby. You can hum or sing to accompany the caregiving experience, but more often you will probably talk. You can tell him simple stories of a few sentences about what he is doing. If you repeat the same story during the same activity each day, it helps him learn about language.

Billy is getting dressed now. Now I'll put on his shirt—put this arm through here and that arm through there . . . slip it over your head, peek-a-boo! Now Billy's pants—one leg goes through here and the other leg goes through there. Now his socks—one on this foot and one on that foot. Now, we're almost done. Whoops—we forgot Billy's shoes! One for this foot and one for that foot. Now Billy's all dressed!

Similar language experiences can be shared during bath time ("Now I'll wash Billy's tummy. Billy laughs so much when I rub his tummy with soap."), feeding ("Here is Billy's bottle. Oh, Billy looks so hungry today."), toileting ("Time to use the toilet, Billy. You did such a nice job. Billy's a *big* boy now."), or other routines. The key thing is to try to put all the child's actions into words.

A word of caution, however: Don't feel strange about talking to babies. Many beginning child-care workers, especially those who are not parents, sometimes feel peculiar talking to babies. Because babies do not "talk back," these caregivers see infants as being essentially like plants—unresponsive to their talk. But remember, through increasing meaningful interaction, you *are* helping the infant move from simple, random vocalizations to more effective means of communication.

Share books with the baby. Hold the baby comfortably in your lap and turn the pages of a book that has large, simple pictures. Point to different objects in the picture and name them for the child. Tell the child something about the picture, such as, "Look, Billy, here is a doll. It looks just like your doll." Do so in a pleasant voice so that everything will add up to a comfortable experience. Remember that the baby's listening vocabulary is much larger than his speaking vocabulary, so, long before he is able to say the name himself, he will be able to point to a picture if you say the name for him. For example, if you say, "Billy, show me the kitty," he will proudly point to the picture. By the time the baby is about a year old, he will be able to turn the pages of appropriate-sized books or magazines as he "reads" all by himself. Babies find books containing large pictures of familiar single objects, animals, or people most stimulating.

Sing to the baby. Babies love being sung to, especially if the songs are accompanied by activity. Many caregivers hesitate to sing because of a lack of confidence in their voices. Don't worry about your voice—infants don't care if you sound like Barbra Streisand or a worn-out fog horn; they simply love to hear you sing. Also, don't worry about finding a known song for every situation. Make up a tune and lyrics as you do whatever you happen to be doing at the moment. Sing to the baby as you feed him, change him, dress him, play with him, bathe him, and so on. Look directly at the baby while you sing; smile and try to get the baby to "sing" along with you.

Songs help the child learn to associate word labels to his body and to familiar objects in his surroundings. For example, the simple tune "Pat-a-Cake," although old and tired for an adult, is met with enthusiasm time and again by the infant.

> Pat-a-cake, pat-a-cake, baker's man *(clap baby's hands together)*
> Bake me a cake as fast as you can.
> Roll it *(roll baby's hands)*
> And pat it *(pat baby's hands)*
> And mark it with a *B (or baby's first initial) (make initial on baby's tummy)*
> And put it in the oven for Billy *(or baby's first name)* and me.

Mother Goose rhymes and other action songs or games are both stimulating and enjoyable for children of this age.

Provide a variety of experiences for the baby. Allow the child to accompany the caregiver to the supermarket, to the park, or on any special trip. He will enjoy the stimulation of new experiences, especially if they are accompanied by explanations by the caregiver ("Let's try the swing, Billy.").

Infants enjoy listening to adult conversations. Some become excited when such communication takes place, many to the point of trying to join the conversation. Let the infant listen to adult conversation and encourage him to sputter and gush as he tries to talk along.

Don't be frustrated if your efforts fail to result in immediate success. It takes much repetition and practice before a baby acquires language. Don't always expect the baby to do something correctly the first time or to remember today what he was able to do yesterday. Don't rush him—he loves to experiment, but only in a relaxed, trusting, accepting environment.

LANGUAGE GROWTH IN THE PRESCHOOL CHILD

By the time the child is two years old, he is beginning to experience a rapid growth in vocabulary and is starting to combine two or three words into rudimentary sentences. Kornei Chukovsky, a famous Russian writer and linguist, wrote: "It seems to me that, beginning with the age of two, every child becomes for a short period of time a *linguistic genius*" (italics mine).[4] Children begin to feel comfortable with words and use them freely. By the time they are 2½, children's vocabulary is likely to explode to the point where it includes 400 words or more. At this age they are beginning to ask endless questions, and their favorite word seems to be "Why?" Although these questions may bother some adults, they do help the child clarify his understandings and feelings.

By the age of 2½, the child has mastered vowel sounds and many consonant sounds, but still has some difficulty with articulation (speaking distinctly); he often says words like "birfday" (birthday) or "wowed" (loud). Table 8-2 lists the latest ages considered normal for the child to have developed the ability to articulate various consonant sounds.

Table 8-2 Normal Ages for Articulation of Consonant Sounds

Age (Years)	Consonant Sounds
3	m, n, ng, p, f, h, w
3½	y
4	k, b, d, g, r
4½	s, sh, ch
6	t, th, v, l
7	th (voiced), z, zh, j

Also by 2½ years the child has moved from one-word noun utterances to simple combinations of nouns with verbs. His first combinations take place at about age 2. The following list shows some word combinations commonly uttered by children during this early phase of language acquisition:

Sit chair	Pretty dolly	There doggie	See baby
Timmy go boom	Papa work	It choo-choo	He go out
Me go	Shoes off	Cars go bye-bye	No nap now
Janie hungry	More play	Where mitten?	Cookie allgone

As children learn to pronounce words, build a vocabulary, and form sentences, they often attempt to imitate adult speech. Much that initially happens between an adult and child during verbal exchange can be characterized as *reduction*, that is, the child eliminates all other parts of speech from the adult's sentence and ends up with a simplified sentence. For example:

Adult's Sentence	**Child's Imitation**
"It's time for you to take your nap."	"Take nap."
"That is a big dog."	"Big dog."
"We'll sit here and take a rest."	"Billy sit."

Although many words are left out of the adult's original sentence, the child makes a strong effort to retain important nouns, verbs, and adjectives. You will notice that although he eliminates over 50 percent of the adult's original words, the basic meaning of the thought is unchanged; only burdensome words of low informational value were eliminated.

A process used by many teachers and parents to encourage children to acquire more complex sentence patterns is *expansion*. This procedure is the opposite of reduction. When the child says a sentence fragment, an adult expands it, adding appropriate elements. For example:

Child's Fragment	**Adult's Sentence**
"Joey eat."	"Joey is eating his breakfast."
"Doggie bark."	"The dog is barking."
"Daddy cookie."	"Daddy has a cookie, too."
"No more play."	"Joey doesn't want to play any longer."

Children love to experiment with language throughout their preschool years in these and similar ways—they are acquiring increased skills in sentence formation through such interaction. The practice they receive often results in a highly creative and imaginative use of the language.

By three years of age, the child's speech patterns have gone beyond the simple two- or three-word phrases uttered earlier. Now they begin to form four- and five-word sentences such as "The dog is barking." By the age of 4 or 5, most children have acquired all of the basic, common sentence structures of the English language. Although we do not know when and exactly in what

Verbal exchange between an adult and young children helps to promote increasingly mature speech patterns.

order these sentence patterns are learned, we do know that most young children are fairly sophisticated linguistic beings by age 3. Table 8-3 shows some of the common sentence patterns mastered by most children by the age of 6.

Young children vary these basic sentence patterns as they expand sentence meaning by forming *combinations*. For example, a child may take two basic sentence patterns, such as "Mommy sang. She laughed, too," and combine them into one complete sentence: "Mommy sang and laughed."

Table 8-3   Common Sentence Patterns Acquired
by Children before Age Six

Type	Example
Noun-verb	Doggy bark
Noun-verb-noun	Jerry ate the cookie
Noun-verb-noun or pronoun-noun	Bobby gave me a ball.
Noun-linking verb-noun	Mrs. Collins is my teacher.
Noun-linking verb-adjective	The kitten is cute.

By the age of four and later, the children are using more adjectives and adverbs to help them expand meaning through a process of *modification*. For example, a basic sentence pattern may be expanded in the following manner:

Basic sentence: "The boy ran."
Modified sentence: "The *big* boy ran *fast*."

The basic sentence form has not been changed; it has simply been modified by the addition of colorful, descriptive words.

As the children gain experiences, as they become exposed to appropriate speech models, and as they receive recognition and praise for steady progress, they begin to develop increasing sophistication in their sentence structures.

Vocabulary growth increases steadily during the preschool years. By the time children are three years old, they are able to use about 900 words. Vocabulary continues at this rapid rate during the next two years, but begins to tail off slightly at about age 5 or 6, dropping from 350–450 word gains per year to gains of only 200–250 words per year by age 6 and 7. What factors account for such a drop? Some authorities agree that formal schooling experiences contribute a degree of artificiality to the previously natural process of language acquisition and begin to create barriers to verbal experimentation. Pose Lamb explains:

> These early nursery years of the twos, threes, and fours bring rapid growth in language skills. Funds of knowledge and ranges of interests broaden to include real conversation and social interaction, resulting in an ever-widening range of interests and skills. The nursery school child is bright-eyed at the wonders of his world. He explores, he looks, he feels, he hears, he tries it all on for size, and, curiously enough, the healthy child takes off and discards the parts that don't fit.
>
> Still wide-eyed with the wonder of it all, the child comes to kindergarten. Here he lives in a world that too often resembles the more formal scene that will come next year upon entry to first grade. The days are too short, the room too small to contain his enthusiasm and exploratory activity.[5]

Chukovsky's "linguistic geniuses" somehow slowly lose their momentum and, as he stated, "beginning with the age of five or six, this talent begins to fade."[6]

The formality of the child's language learning, then, often increases upon entry into first grade. This learning is often characterized by the use of restricted vocabularies in basal readers and by a need to "Sit in your seat quietly so that others aren't disturbed." (This order is especially threatening since children of this age find it frustrating to remain seated quietly for periods of more than 5 to 10 minutes.) It is difficult to determine a true cause-and-effect relationship between the decline of language growth during the primary grade years and the growing formality of the classroom environment, but evidence has clearly indicated a positive relationship between meaningful personal experience and guidance during the preschool years and the acquisition of rapidly growing language skills.

To summarize, children move through infancy and into the preschool years according to the language acquisition patterns illustrated in Figure 8-1.

Because the most crucial language learning seems to take place before the child is six, most educators feel that it is the role of the preschool to create programs to facilitate growth in language skills for those children who are somewhat behind normal speech development levels and to enrich the skills of those children who have no problems. What helpful advice can be given by early childhood educators and students of language? Alvina Burrows says that "one admonition leaps out beyond most others: *Use the oral efficiency that children bring to school as the means of developing [further] efficiency in [language].* To extend, refine, and enhance the oral arts and skills children already possess is the first obligation."[7] To achieve this goal, children must be given opportunities to practice language. They must be able to speak in a variety of situations, and they must be exposed to good language as it is spoken by a good model. The following sections discuss activities that can be used to achieve these goals.

TECHNIQUES FOR ENHANCING LANGUAGE GROWTH

Storytime

Stories, either told or read aloud, have an extremely important place in the language arts program of preschool classrooms. Storytelling is one of the most effective ways of exposing children to rich and varied language; this procedure is basic to the effective development of speaking vocabularies. Children enjoy listening to stories—they discover new words and meanings, develop understandings, and engage in imaginative thought.

STORIES CHILDREN LIKE   Of course, the foremost source of stories for children is good literature. It is important to know what kinds of stories appeal to young children so the stories you choose will meet their developmental interests. Preschool children delight in hearing many kinds of stories, but they especially enjoy stories about things they are already familiar with. Make-believe, humor, new places, animals, family, Mother Goose rhymes, fables, and fairy tales, however, are also favorites. It is difficult to generalize about the type of story enjoyed by all young children since they demonstrate such a wide breadth of interest in stories. They can easily identify with H. A. Rey's lovable monkey *Curious George* or Maurice Sendak's *Little Bear.* They empathize with Dr. Seuss's imaginative Horton as he faithfully attempts to hatch an egg; and their hatred changes to love as Seuss's dreaded Grinch nearly steals Christmas from the citizens of Whoville. All children figuratively hitch up their belts and join the fight with the courageous operator and his brave machine in *Mike Mulligan and His Steam Shovel.* They discover new adventures as they are led through the trials and tribulations of characters in

Reading and telling stories exposes children to new adventures as well as to rich, new language patterns.

accepted guidelines that are helpful in planning and reading or telling a story.

The physical setting should be comfortable and relaxing. Usually all the children will be together in a special area away from other activities and distracting materials; the possibility of inattentiveness can, thus, be minimized. However, there will be times when some children do not care to listen, so they should not be forced to join the group—such coercion often results in unnecessary behavioral problems. These children should be given an opportunity to play quietly in other areas of the room or playground, perhaps in the company of a teacher's aide or volunteer.

When a quiet, comfortable nondistracting area has been selected for the story, you should establish some sort of special technique, or gimmick, to arouse the children to join you. Many creative gimmicks have been used by innovative teachers over the years:

1. Play a special little tune on the piano indicating to the children that story time is at hand.
2. Use a favorite hand puppet to announce that story time is ready to begin. Then, a simple little dialogue between teacher and puppet can introduce the story to be shared. For example, a simple message from Ellie the Elephant encourages the children to listen, and also helps develop interest in the forthcoming story: "Hello, boys and girls. It's so nice to see you again today here at the story time corner. Miss Alley is going to tell us an exciting story today about a brave little boat named Little Toot. Let's all listen carefully to Miss Alley because I think she's about to start." Miss Alley may then thank Ellie and begin the introduction to the story. When using puppets in this manner, look at the puppet when *it* is "speaking" and look at the children when *you* are speaking.

3. Capitalize on the children's creative imagination by engaging them in a simple role-playing experience. For example, the children can be asked to pretend that they are all taking a walk in the woods. Point out some interesting features and have the children imagine that they are actually seeing them: "Oh, look at that tree—it's so tall. Look at how tall it is. Let's all stretch ourselves and try to be as tall as that tree" or "There goes a little rabbit—watch it hop through the grass. Let's all hop like the rabbit." After sharing three or four such experiences, you may all pretend to be getting tired from the long walk and decide that it would be a good time to find a safe, cool place to rest. Ask everyone to pantomime looking for a place to rest. As the children look around the "forest" for a suitable place, you find a little meadow in the trees that would be a good spot. So no dangerous bears or lions will hear them, encourage the children to gather as quietly as they can into a compact group and sit in the meadow. After the children are quietly gathered in their safe little area, you may begin to tell them the story. Depending on the type of story to be told, the children can be similarly led to swim across a river to a safe island where a story is told, build a safe treehouse, and so on.

Children will want to be as close to you as possible while the story is being told so you will need to organize them in a way that is satisfactory for all. Perhaps the best arrangement is an informal semi-circle facing you. The children may be comfortably seated on chairs, on individual rugs, or on the floor, but the most important consideration is that they can easily see your face and any pictures or illustrations to be shared.

Selecting the story is particularly important. Once the children are properly seated and in a mood to listen, the telling or reading of the story may begin. Although a seemingly uncomplicated task, the storytelling or reading process is nevertheless one that involves a great deal of careful preparation and thoughtful presentation. The following questions may be helpful as you select a story that is appropriate both for the children and for you and prepare to tell it:

Selecting Stories for Preschoolers

1. Is the plot simple and uncomplicated?
2. Are the situations presented in generally familiar contexts?
3. Does the plot evolve around a great deal of direct conversation, or dialogue, among story characters?
4. Is the story written with carefully chosen words that will mostly be familiar to the children?
5. Are the story characters interesting and easily identifiable to the children?
6. Is the story free from ethnic, racial, or sex-role stereotypes?
7. Does the plot include catchy phrases, rhymes, and repetition that can catch and hold the children's interest?
8. Can the story be easily related to the experiential background of the children?

9. Can the story be completed in one short reading or broken up into short, distinctive parts?
10. Is the story accompanied by uncluttered, colorful illustrations of animals, people, or objects that are easily identified by the children?
11. Does the story appeal to the teacher?

Children are very insightful into your feelings for a story and can easily detect whether or not you are sincere in your desire to share it with them. The children will deepen their respect for good literature only when they know you want to share it with them.

Make sure the story is one that you *can* tell or read. Some teachers have personalities that do not match the mood or content of a story. If this is true in your case, either choose other stories, or be extremely careful to practice the story so you communicate a feeling of comfort to the children rather than one of confusion or insincerity.

Choose an appropriate method of presentation. Both reading and telling have a valuable place in the preschool classroom. Reading stories helps children gain respect for books and helps them realize that reading can be an enjoyable experience. Telling stories can be especially helpful in these situations:

1. If you want the children to focus on a large number of pictures while the story is being told
2. If the illustrations or pictures are not particularly appealing. In this case, you may need to use your own drawings, puppets, or flannelboard characters to supplement the story. Reading the story and sharing visual aids is difficult, so storytelling may best be used in such situations.
3. If the story is of value to your group but is too long for their attention span

Flannelboard characters help illustrate story events and make a story more appealing to the children.

If you decide to tell the story rather than read it aloud, do not try to memorize it word for word. Memorized stories are usually presented mechanically and thereby lose their appeal. If certain key words or phrases are repeated throughout the story, however, you may want to know them—those words should be carefully learned or the story will be spoiled. It should be emphasized, though, that to tell a story well, you should know it and make it a part of you—carefully organize the sequence of events in your mind.

Be sure to *prepare for each story you read or tell*. Even a story that you have read or told several times should be carefully reviewed in order to ensure accurate recall of details and events. In preparing for your story, consider the following suggestions:

1. Read your story silently to get an overall idea of the plot.
2. Read the story aloud so you can develop a "feel" for its mood. Read it two or three times on a tape recorder and analyze each of your readings. Be especially watchful for "uhs" and "and-uhs."
3. Sit or stand in front of a mirror. Try to communicate openly a feeling of comfort and interest while reading aloud.
4. If you possibly can, practice your story in front of a friend and request honest criticism of your technique.
5. Determine how long the story will take to read or tell. Children's attention spans vary from story to story, but a good rule of thumb is to stay within a time limit of five to fifteen minutes.

Develop your own personal style of telling or reading a story. Successful teachers seem to weave a magic spell during story time and you might be tempted to emulate good storytellers you observed in the past. However, what worked for that individual may not work for you. It is important to be yourself—personality and charm are made part of the story only if the children know that the storyteller is the same person who is with them during other parts of their day; periodic personality changes only confuse and unnerve the children. These suggestions for telling and reading stories may be helpful:

1. Plan a good introduction so children are able to get an idea of what the story is going to be about. Be careful not to get too involved with highly detailed descriptions of characters or events, but give the children an idea of the main story characters and what their major situation will be.
2. Use your voice effectively. Speak naturally, but be aware of the ways in which loudness or softness and fastness or slowness can affect the mood of a story. For example, suspenseful parts may call for a soft, slow, mysterious tone while happy parts may call for livelier, louder, joyous tones. Your voice can be used to add surprise, sadness, question, or fear to the story, but remember not to get overdramatic. If you do, you will shift the focus from the plot to the storyteller, and you will interrupt the children's interest and concentration.

3. Keep good eye contact with the children. A good storyteller looks directly at his audience in order to gain and hold their interest. A few gestures will add to the vividness of the story being told.

4. Anticipate questions and minor interruptions during the reading or storytelling period. Handle children's questions or comments tactfully so the trend of the story is not interrupted. For example, one child became so absorbed in a story that he blurted out just before the climax, "Oh, I wonder how the kitten will be saved." Another child insightfully offered the actual solution, "I know—the mama cat will save her." Although the storyteller could have become flustered at the revelation of the story's ending, she remained composed and simply commented, "Your idea was very good, Robin, but let's all listen and see if you were right." The children, in this case, were drawn right back into the story. Often, teachers themselves cause unnecessary interruptions by throwing out questions or explaining new words along the way. Such digressions add nothing to the story and mainly serve to lessen interest or to interrupt continuity of the plot. Never interrupt the flow of a story yourself except in case of extreme necessity.

5. Share pictures throughout the story if they help clarify or illustrate the evolving sequence of events. By sitting on a low chair or on the floor, you will be in perfect position to hold up the book for the children to see. Hold the book open all the way in a steady position. Some teachers, when reading a story, prefer to hold books at either side; others find it more comfortable to hold them in front. Whatever the position, be sure that all children can see the picture without having to crane their necks or move unnecessarily. If the children are seated in a semi-circle, you may have to move the picture so they all can see. In these cases, it is important to hold the book and pause so the group seated to your left can focus their eyes on the picture; hold and pause at the center; and hold and pause to your right. Some teachers share poorly by holding the picture so the children on the left are able to focus and then slowly sweeping to the right without stopping the picture along the way. It is difficult for the children in the center to focus on the moving picture, and they may not be able to see it properly. Short sweeps and pauses are necessary so the focal point can remain fixed for a short period of time.

6. Use flannelboards and other aids to help illustrate a story being told or read. Some supply companies are now producing attractive flannelboard characters and scenery that help to illustrate time-tested favorites such as "Goldilocks and the Three Bears," "Three Billy Goats Gruff," or "Henny Penny."

7. After the story is completed, the children may enjoy discussing the main characters or plot for a short period. This will not always be the case, but if you find that the interest is high, guide the discussion with questions like these:

☐ Tell us what you liked (or didn't like) about the story.

- ☐ If you had been (story character) how would you have felt when _____ happened?
- ☐ In what other way could (character) have solved his problem?
- ☐ Which character from the story would you most like to meet? Why?
- ☐ How do you think (character) felt when _____ happened?
- ☐ What story character would you most like to be? Why?
- ☐ Why do you think (character) did what he did?
- ☐ Did someone in the story change his mind about something? What was it? Why did he do it?
- ☐ What do you think happens to (character) now after the story ended?
- ☐ Have you ever had a problem like (character)? What did you do about it?
- ☐ Did you like the story? Why? Why not?
- ☐ Which picture did you like the most? Why?
- ☐ What things happened in the story that could really happen? That could not really happen?
- ☐ What would you change about the story?
- ☐ Did you know another story like this one? What is it? How are the stories alike?

Not all these considerations will need to be examined before each story time. However, they must all be emphasized because your ability to plan and execute storytelling is so important to the success or failure of the children's total language program. Your preparation is central in making story time a delightful and rewarding experience both for your children and for yourself.

Picture Discussions

Large, colorful, uncomplex pictures stimulate verbal exchange in the preschool classroom by motivating children to discuss what they see or by inspiring them to make up related stories. However, simply holding a picture in front of a group is not enough to move the children to discuss it. A carefully planned sequence of questions must be designed to move the children from the simple enumeration of objects observed in a picture to higher levels of interpretation. For example, asking a general question such as "What is this picture about?" will lead only to a response such as "A kitten," or "A kitten and a butterfly." Children will very rarely move beyond responses of this listing type unless you encourage them to do so with appropriately stated questions.

Basically, children respond at three levels when they read and interpret pictures: a *low level*, where they are able to identify the objects in a picture; a *middle level*, where they are able to describe what is happening; and a *high level*, where they are able to communicate personal feelings and establish relationships among objects or events (see Figure 8-2). Most preschool children operate on the low level, but occasionally there will be children who are able to answer questions on the middle or high level. The bulk of your discussion questions should be directed at low-level interpretation, but, because your goal is to encourage increasingly mature patterns of thought and language, you will want to insert higher-level questioning periodically. Thus, the children can experience challenges and successes at individual levels of ability while, at the same time, being exposed to higher levels of thought through the comments and observations of their peers.

Help the children look for a variety of things in discussion pictures by guiding their observations along the lines of these questions:

Low Level

"Tell how many. . . ."
"Tell me what you see. . . ."
"Tell me about the picture. . . ."
"What color is the _____?"
"What _____(animal)_____ is in the picture?"

Middle Level

"What is _____ doing?"
"What kind of _____ do you see?"
"What color is the _____?"
"How far from the _____ is _____?"
"How large is the _____?"

High Level

"What will _____ do next?"
"What kind of _____ do you think _____ is?"
"Why did _____ happen?"
"What title can you give this picture?"

Preschool teachers usually draw from several sources when choosing pictures for discussion times. Many good books written for young children can be used for their pictures alone. Excellent picture books often contain a variety of appropriate illustrations—animals, community workers, children at play, cowhands, imaginary characters, and so on.

A second major source of pictures for young children is commercial teaching materials manufacturers. These companies organize picture collections around central themes such as "seasons" or "feelings" and arrange them in sets especially designed for study and discussion. These study prints are normally mounted on durable, attractive backings and are indexed for easy reference. A teacher's discussion and activity guide usually accompanies these sets, either as a separate manual or as a chart on the backs of the pictures. The second method is perhaps the most useful for teachers since the picture can be held up for the children to observe while the question and discussion guide is conveniently in front of the teacher. A separate manual can, at times, cause irritating problems as the teacher shifts back and forth from manual to picture while leading a group discussion.

Still a third major source of classroom discussion pictures is the teacher's own picture file. Developing your own picture file for preschool children is a valuable project you should try to start as soon as possible. Search through

Figure 8-2 Levels of picture interpretation abilities.

magazines, newspapers, old calendars, advertisements, or discarded books to find pictures illustrating subjects of interest to young children. Be sure the pictures are clear and free from confusing details—think of the developmental characteristics of the children. A good source of free or inexpensive pictures for your own picture file is business, industry, or special interest groups like the American Dairy Council.

Once suitable pictures have been discovered, you will need to back them with protective construction paper or tagboard. If possible, run the mounted picture through a laminating machine or cover it with clear adhesive plastic so it will be more attractive as well as more resistant to damage. You may wish to organize your pictures into a permanent file with headings that are attractive to preschool youngsters: animals, food, jobs, play, and so on.

As a method for encouraging language growth, children should be encouraged to make up stories for a small series of pictures. They may not be able to do this for only one picture, but a series of three or four pictures relating to a subject in which they are intensely interested may encourage many excellent stories. Some special place should be available for such experiences—a place where the story could be told to the teacher, to a few select friends, or to the group as a whole. One child, after a trip to the farm, selected several pictures from a group provided by the teacher (some children may like to draw their own) and told this story:

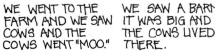

WE WENT TO THE FARM AND WE SAW COWS AND THE COWS WENT "MOO."

WE SAW A BARN. IT WAS BIG AND THE COWS LIVED THERE.

THE FARMER MILKED THE COWS IN THE BARN.

HE GAVE US A GLASS OF MILK.

Photographs taken by the teacher during such direct experiences provide great opportunities for creative storytelling activities, too.

Children's conversation, then, can be stimulated in a variety of ways by the skillful use of picture discussions in the preschool classroom. Children think of many ways to respond to pictures, and your understanding of them will make related conversation highly original and interesting.

Fingerplays

You have read about the usefulness of fingerplays for promoting physical growth, but this form of verbal and physical play also assumes a valuable language role, too. When verses, rhymes, or short stories are shared for the pleasurable repetition of words and for the free use of children's voices in joyous play activity, the children are provided with a strong motivation to speak. Fingerplays may be enjoyed by the entire group at once or by only a few children, but remember that any fingerplay should be matched to the coordination level of your children. For example, the popular fingerplay "Here is the church and here is the steeple" is much too complex for four-year-olds—they usually feel defeated as they try to lock their fingers into the positions suggested within the verse. The fingerplay time should be one of confidence building and fun-filled word play, so situations that frustrate or defeat the children should be avoided. Suggestions for the use of fingerplays in the preschool setting follow.

1. *Use fingerplays in a variety of situations.* Teachers have found that, besides serving as a simple fun-time language activity, fingerplays are a very good means for getting children's attention for a special group announcement, gathering them for storytime or any other large-group activity, or keeping them occupied during potentially restless times—toileting,

awaiting the arrival of a special guest, or any other time the children must be unexpectedly kept waiting. However, a word of caution: *Never* use a fingerplay to calm overly excited or restless children. One instance that sticks out in my mind vividly involves a student teacher who, for the first time in her career, was asked to organize a group of about ten children and guide them down a hall to a place where their restroom facilities were located. Partway down the hall, the children became extremely restless and began to misbehave. Perhaps remembering that fingerplays hold great potential for organizing children during toileting, or perhaps from her own frustration, the teacher began to sing, "Where is thumbkin . . ." and tried to encourage the children to join her. Naturally, by this time, the children were fidgeting, jumping, talking, and pinching —any chance of getting them to join the fingerplay was lost. This unfortunate teacher, desperately attempting to lure the children to join her, continued singing, "Here I am. . . . Here I am. . . ." while most of the children went along totally oblivious of her efforts. The only ones in the entire group who participated in the activity were the teacher and one or two of the children. The true value of fingerplay activities was gone for this time.

Fortunately, this student teacher grew from her failure. During a self-evaluation of her day's experience, she focused on the toileting incident and recognized her mistake. Her recommendation for improvement was that she should have stopped the fingerplay immediately upon recognizing that the children were not going to respond. Then, speaking in a firm, clear voice, she should have involved them in more active pursuits where they could have released energy in fuller, freer, and more purposeful movements. What alternatives would *you* suggest?

2. *Know the fingerplay before you use it.* Many teachers memorize a small number of highly interesting fingerplays before their first experiences with young children. Thus, they have a number of appropriate fingerplays at hand and can use them comfortably whenever unforeseen situations arise. However, if memorizing on your part results in an overly mechanistic presentation, you may wish to consider printing the fingerplays on sheets of oaktag and placing them on the wall or on some fixture near a strategic area in the classroom, for example, the story time corner, file cabinet, or toileting area. In this way, you have a ready reference when your mind needs a little stimulation to help it remember a key word or phrase. Placing the fingerplays on index cards and keeping them ready when needed is not recommended because your shifting from the card to the children during the fingerplay may be extremely distracting.

3. *Choose appropriate fingerplays.* Be sure the fingerplays are the type children like. Often, fingerplays are chosen for their literary quality or because of their appeal to adults. Remember, however, that fingerplays must interest the *children* if they are to be useful, and what appears "cute" or "funny" to an adult may be totally disliked by a child. Also, fingerplays need not reflect high literary standards—in fact, most are of poor literary quality. The purpose of fingerplays, however, is not to teach literary

appreciation, so the poetic accuracy should not be as important as the fun and interest a fingerplay generates. Some traditionally favorite fingerplays for young children are found in the fingerplays box (p. 304).

Informal Conversation

During most of the day, children should be encouraged to speak freely to the teacher and to one another as they plan and execute their daily activities. When we observe four- and five-year-olds, we are often astounded at how free and open they are with their verbalization. They talk to themselves, verbalize to others and listen to their ideas, make up stories or rhymes, and generally participate in a variety of give and take. Through such practice, children steadily improve their vocabularies, sentence patterns, and clarity of expression. The importance of such free, informal talk will be established later in this chapter. For now, we will say only that the key element in fostering linguistic expression is to provide children with genuine things to talk about.

First attempts at having children speak in more controlled situations —for example, before a group—should be somewhat informal. In sharing-type situations, children are encouraged to bring to the group a book, toy, souvenir, or any object that is of general interest to the entire group. These "props" help the boys and girls feel at ease; the props become the center of the group's attention and help focus attention on the words of the speaker.

In order to make such sharing periods a worthwhile part of the day, however, you should always make sure that they involve more than simply allowing each child in the class to "have his say." In this latter situation, the teacher asks the children to each bring in something special for a 15-minute "Show-and-Tell" period or, for example, for a Friday morning. During the period, one child gets up to tell about his object while the others are expected to listen; then a second child does the same; then a third; and so on. Nothing can be so boring and time wasting as a period of this type—children either don't listen, or they wait in fear (or anticipation) of being called on next.

An alternative to the "Show-and-Tell" period is the informal group-sharing time. Perhaps the best way to describe an informal sharing period is to provide this illustration:

When she arrived at school this morning, Belinda was smiling brightly and clutching a colorful stuffed toy hippopotamus. Mr. Roberts noted the pride with which Belinda shared her new toy with him:

"His name is Hippo," offered Belinda.

"He's cute," said Mr. Roberts. "Do you know what kind of an animal Hippo is, Belinda?"

"A hippopa . . . hippopapa . . . a 'potamus," stuttered Belinda.

"Oh, yes," replied Mr. Roberts. "A hippopotamus. You're a lucky girl to get a nice friend like Hippo. Please show everyone what a nice toy you have."

"Daddy gave him to me. Daddy was away yesterday and when he came home he gave me Hippo," said Belinda.

FINGERPLAYS

Let's Make a Ball

A little ball, *(Make a circle with pointer finger and thumb.)*
A bigger ball, *(Make a circle with both pointer fingers and thumbs.)*
A great big ball I see; *(Make large circle with arms.)*
Now, let's count the balls we've made;
One, two, three. *(Repeat action of first three lines.)*

The Apple Tree

Away up high in an apple tree, *(Point up.)*
Two red apples smiled at me. *(Form circles with fingers.)*
I shook that tree as hard as I could; *(Pretend to shake tree.)*
Down came those apples,
And Mmmmmm, were they good! *(Rub tummy.)*

Open, Shut Them

Open, shut them; open, shut them;
Give them a clap.
Open, shut them; open, shut them;
Lay them in your lap.

There Was a Little Turtle

There was a little turtle, *(Make circle with hands.)*
He lived in a box. *(Form box with hands.)*
He swam in a puddle, *(Make swimming motions.)*
He climbed on the rocks. *(Make climbing motions with hands.)*
He snapped at a mosquito, *(Make grabbing motion.)*
He snapped at a flea, *(Make grabbing motion.)*
He snapped at a minnow, *(Make grabbing motion.)*
And he snapped at me. *(Make grabbing motion.)*

He caught the mosquito, *(Clap hands.)*
He caught the flea, *(Clap hands.)*
He caught the minnow, *(Clap hands.)*
But he didn't catch me. *(Start to clap, but stop short.)*

—Vachel Lindsay

Choo-Choo Train

This is a choo-choo train *(Bend arms at elbows.)*
Puffing down the track. *(Rotate forearms in rhythm.)*
Now it's going forward, *(Push arms forward; continue rotating motion.)*
Now it's going back. *(Pull arms back; continue rotating motion.)*
Now the bell is ringing, *(Pull bell cord with closed fist.)*
Now the whistle blows. *(Hold fist near mouth and blow.)*
What a lot of noise it makes *(Cover ears with hands.)*
Everywhere it goes. *(Stretch out arms.)*

Rabbit Song

In a cabin in a wood *(Draw cabin with hands.)*
A little man by the window stood *(Shade eyes and look around.)*
Saw a rabbit running by, *(Make rabbit hopping with hands.)*
Knocking at my door. *(Knock.)*
"Help me! Help me!" the rabbit said. *(Throw hands in air.)*
"Or that farmer will shoot me dead." *(Point fingers like gun.)*
"Little rabbit, come inside,
Safely you'll abide." *(Wave imaginary rabbit in, and stroke him in your arm.)*

(At end of each verse, leave out the words for one motion and do the motion in silence, until whole song is pantomimed.)

> *Mr. Roberts: "Hippo is a nice gift, Belinda. Let's see if anyone can think of another animal that looks like Hippo."*
>
> *"An elephant," volunteered James. "He's as big as an elephant—I saw one at the zoo."*
>
> *"That's right, James," commented Mr. Roberts. "I see you remember our trip to the zoo last week."*
>
> *"I think it looks like a rhino," declared Sally.*
>
> *"Yeah," "Me too," chimed in the others.*
>
> *"Does anyone have a toy rhino or toy elephant?" asked Mr. Roberts.*
>
> *"I think I have a toy elephant—I'm not sure," said Warren. "It's almost as big as Hippo."*
>
> *"I have a toy elephant," exclaimed Marty. "I can wind him up and he wiggles his ears!"*
>
> *Mr. Roberts saw that the interest was still high and allowed the children to talk for several minutes. Then, when he sensed it was time to bring the informal conversation to a close, he simply stated, "Hippo was a wonderful gift for you, Belinda. Thank you for bringing him to school today for all of us to see."*

The principle of developing good language experience through informal conversation is apparent in Mr. Roberts's technique. He allowed Belinda to talk about her toy, but not in the context of a formal presentation. She simply responded to his questions about Hippo. The other children were asked to contribute their own individual experiences as Belinda's toy was shared so their interest level would be maintained. In a few short minutes, then, Mr. Roberts succeeded in involving several members of the group in the conversation rather than forcing them to listen to the often incohesive patter of only one child. The experience was a valuable one, not only for its conversational value, but also for its contribution to intellectual growth.

Informal conversation of this type is often fueled by common experiences shared by the class. However, there will be times when differing backgrounds will influence the way in which those common experiences are interpreted and verbalized. Consider this example:

> "Class, look at the picture, and tell me what you see," said the teacher.
>
> Hands went up, but the teacher called on Peter, whose hand had not been one of them.
>
> "Peter, what is it?"
>
> "It looks like a rat."
>
> The class laughed. Someone said, "Peter is so stupid. He doesn't know a rat from a rabbit."
>
> The teacher said, "Peter, what's the matter with your eyes? Can't you see that it has long ears?"
>
> "Yes," said Peter weakly.
>
> "It *is* a rabbit, isn't it, Peter?"
>
> "Yes," he said.
>
> "Today's story is about a rabbit," said the teacher, pointing to the picture and then the word. It's a story about a *hungry* white rabbit. What do you suppose a rabbit eats when he's hungry?"

"Lettuce," said Mary.

"Carrots," said Suzy.

"Meat," said Peter.

The class laughed. Someone said, "Peter is so stupid. He doesn't know what rabbits eat."

"Peter, you know very well that rabbits don't eat meat," said the teacher.

"That depends on how hungry they are," said Peter. "When I'm hungry, I'll eat anything my mother gives me, even when I don't like it."

"Don't argue, Peter," said the teacher. "Now, Class, how does a rabbit's fur feel when you pet him?" asked the teacher.

"Soft," said Suzy.

"Silky," said Mary.

"I don't know," said Peter.

"Why?" asked the teacher.

"'Cause I wouldn't pet one. He might bite me and make me sick, like what happened to my little brother, the time a hungry one got on his bed when he was sleeping."

The class laughed. Someone said, "Peter is fibbing. He knows his mother doesn't allow rabbits in bed."

After the class had read the story and had their recess, the teacher said to the supervisor, "I hate to sound prejudiced, but I'm not sure that this busing from one neighborhood to the other is good for the children."

The supervisor shook his head sadly and said to the teacher, "Your lesson lacked one very important ingredient."

"What was that?" asked the teacher.

"A rabbit," said the supervisor.[8]

Children who bring divergent viewpoints to discussions often gain an unfavorable reputation. They become confused about their thinking and this, in turn, makes them soon feel self-conscious about talking in group settings. This attitude may spread to a refusal to speak with the other children—a situation leading to social neglect or rejection. You *must* accept the child where he is and embark on a program to move him forward—a belligerent attitude toward children who may talk in extraordinary ways has no place in the preschool setting.

Dramatic Activities

Pantomime, role-playing, puppetry, and other forms of dramatic play help children make sense out of their environment and allow them to express such awareness through body movement and language. Young children are willing and eager to express their thoughts, ideas, moods, and feelings through dramatic activity, and the truly creative teacher will provide many opportunities for them to do so. Young children love to experiment with new words, new ideas, and new ways of doing things as they enter the world of "truckers," "pilots," "doctors," or "housekeepers." In this imaginative way, they gain new understanding of the life around them—all in a spirit of excitement and fun. Because this part of the curriculum is so important in all areas

By using a real telephone, youngsters capitalize on their imaginations and, at the same time, extend their language skills.

of the child's development—social, emotional, physical, and cognitive (language)—it will be treated in greater depth in Chapter 10.

Games and Other Informal Activities

Language expression grows and develops as opportunities for interesting experiences are provided within the classroom. Attractive first-hand experiences and appealing audio or visual materials play a major role in stimulating language growth. Teachers provide opportunities for such experiences through formal, large-group instruction or through informal, individual means. Whatever the choice, however, the activities described in the language growth activities box (p. 308) go a long way toward enriching the language growth environment.

THEORIES OF LANGUAGE ACQUISITION

Nativistic Theory and Application

The strategies described to this point are found in nearly all programs for preschool children, but are particularly essential components for educators

LANGUAGE GROWTH ACTIVITIES

TELEPHONE TALKING   Real telephones, connected by wire and powered by battery, can often be obtained free from your local telephone company for an extended period of time. Place these phones in your classroom and encourage the children to talk to one another or to act out imaginative roles.

FOOLER GAME   Choose a set of words that all belong together—for example, colors, shapes, food, animals, rhyming sounds, clothing. Have the children listen carefully as you begin to say one list, and have them say "Stop!" when they hear you make a mistake. For example, you start out slowly, saying "Red, blue, yellow, green, square ("Stop!")" or "Boy, big, Billy, boat, ball car ("Stop!")."

CLASSIFICATION   CHARTS Draw, cut from magazines or old workbooks, or buy commercially, pictures of fruits, vegetables, animals, colors, toys, and so on. Have the children classify,

name, and describe the pictures on a large pocket chart. Place one card in each row and ask the children to sort out the other cards, placing the corresponding pictures in the appropriate rows. As they place the card in a slot, ask the children to explain their reasons for doing so.

STORY SEQUENCE CARDS   This exercise builds on the idea of ordered sequence in communicating ideas. Cut out three or four pictures that tell a story when they are placed in proper sequential order. Mount the pictures onto heavy tagboard so they will be more durable. Mix up the cards and ask the children to examine them and put them into an order that tells a story. Then, ask them to tell you the story.

GUESS WHAT I HAVE   Hide an object inside a colorfully decorated box with a lid. Then begin to describe the object—its size, weight, use, composition, color, and any other distinguishing

characteristics. Children try to guess what is in the box.

With experience, the children will be able to choose their own familiar objects and provide the descriptions for the other children. Toys, tools, foods, school supplies, and familiar household objects are highly recommended for this activity.

FLANNELBOARD STORIES   Use a flannelboard, a large snowman, and a variety of cut-out birds. The birds may all be cut from the same pattern and varied according to color, size, and design. Pass out one bird to each child in a group of five or six children and ask them to put their bird on and take it off the flannelboard in the appropriate spot of the story. Then read this story:

Once there was a nice, big snowman who grew tired of being all alone in the backyard. So the lonesome snowman wished and wished with all his might, "I'm so lonesome. I wish someone would come and play with me." All of a sudden, a plain red bird flew into the yard and landed at the snowman's feet. "I'll play with you," said the red bird." "I'm coming, too," chirped a white bird with large yellow dots, and it landed right on top of the snowman's head. "Wait for me," sang a checkered bird as he flew right beside the snowman, "I want to play, too." Just as the snowman flashed a big, wide smile on his face, the biggest bird of all flew up and perched next to the snowman's head on his big, round shoulder.

"Oh, my! Oh, my!" said the snowman. "Maybe it's not so bad to be lonesome after all." So, he shuffled his feet and the red bird flew away; he wiggled his head and the white bird with large yellow dots left; he waved his arm and the checkered bird scurried away; he jiggled his shoulder and the biggest bird of all sailed into the sky and flew away, too. "There," said the snowman, "now I'm so tired, I think I'll just go to sleep."

Use your imagination to create imaginative flannelboard stories to suit your needs. Just remember to keep the stories short and full of action and repetition—all with rich, colorful language.

TAPE RECORDER   Explain and demonstrate the use of a tape recorder to a small group of children. Ask each child, in turn, to say something, such as his name, and then immediately play it back. Then, encourage him to talk until he wants to stop—play it back immediately. Children are fascinated by hearing their voices on a tape recorder and will be highly motivated to keep such activity going on their own.

A word of caution: Some children are too shy to do this activity. In these cases, don't force the children to talk; simply wait until they are ready to do so on their own. This is one good way—if it is used properly—of getting children who usually do not talk much to open up and produce more speech.

subscribing to the *nativistic view* of language acquisition. This view was originally described by Noam Chomsky, who holds that language development is an instinctive and natural process.[9] This view purports that the child is born with internal mechanisms that give him the power to understand and produce words and sentences *naturally*. Eric H. Lenneberg talked of an "innately mapped-in *program* for behavior."[10] David McNeill agreed with both and speculated on a set of "templates" in the neural system, called a "language acquisition device" (LAD), that allows the child to develop language naturally. He said, "It is as if he were equipped with a set of 'templates' against which he can compare the speech he happens to hear from his parents."[11] Courtney Cazden explains the nature of such abilities:

> When we say that a child knows a set of rules, of course we don't mean that he knows them in any conscious way. The rules are known non-consciously, out of awareness, as a kind of tacit knowledge. This way of knowing is true for adults too. Few of us can state the rules for adding /s/ or /z/ or /iz/ sounds to form plural nouns. Yet if asked to supply the plurals for nonsense syllables such as *bik* or *wug* or *gutch* . . . , all who are native speakers of English could do so with ease. Most six-year-old children can, too.[12]

Figure 8-3 summarizes the process by which nativistic language acquisition takes place. The language acquisition device (LAD) helps the child analyze the language that surrounds him and produces a developing rule system that becomes the basis for mature speech.

The LAD receives input from the child's environment, probes this input, and helps the child naturally organize words already a part of his vocabulary into a verbal statement (Figure 8-3A). Initial attempts at duplicating adult speech result in shortened versions of the adult's language (see the discussion of reduction on page 287), but the basic sentence and thought forms remain the same (some function words—articles, prepositions, conjunctions, and so on—are eliminated) (Figure 8-3B). With increased exposure and practice, the child gradually acquires an ability to use different forms of verbs and nouns, prepositions, pronouns, and other function words (Figure 8-3C).

This process does not always evolve without pitfalls, however. When children first begin to use some common verb or noun endings, for example, they will often overgeneralize rules they had applied to their earlier speech. You will often hear threes and fours using "digged" instead of "dug" or "mouses" instead of "mice" until they gain further exposure to mature grammar from adult models. However, we must be aware of just how difficult it is for children to move away from their natural tendencies to overgeneralize regular language rules and adjust to the exceptions. Consider the following example of a conversation with a four-year-old:

Child: "We goed to the farm today."
Parent: "You went to the farm today?"
Child: "Uh-huh."
Parent: "What did you say you did?"
Child: "We goed to the farm!"

Figure 8-3   The mechanics of the language acquisition device.

Preschool children often continue to use their own constructions even after hearing the acceptable form used by an adult. They understand what has been said, but are unable to produce sentences using the exception. Irregular plurals and verb tenses often become "regularized" into their own natural linguistic systems. Deliberate attempts to teach children exceptions to general rules that do not yet fit their present system of language result in unacceptance or frustration. Attempts to systematically teach children word forms not fitting into their present rule systems will result in a "filtering" process. McNeill provides this illustration of a child using a filtering process:

> *C:* Nobody don't like me.
> *M:* No, say "Nobody likes me."
> *C:* Nobody don't like me.
>   *(eight repetitions of this dialogue)*
> *M:* No. Now listen carefully; say "Nobody likes me."
> *C:* Oh! Nobody don't likes me![13]

Nativists state that mature speech behavior develops best when teachers or parents talk freely with their children about topics of interest within a context of meaningful experience. As this process unfolds, the child's language begins to approach that of the significant adults in his life and "incorrect" language evolves into more and more mature speech.

According to the nativists, then, mature language is produced when children (1) hear appropriate language from those in their environment, (2) interpret the language with their innate language acquisition device, and (3) form language patterns based on the rule system naturally contained in their language acquisition system.

Nativistic theories have influenced many preschool language programs, particularly those associated with "traditional" or "informal" classrooms. In programs of this type, the teacher (1) interacts with the child while *modeling* good language forms and (2) provides varieties of experiences designed to stimulate language use in a *social context*.

Two other suggested methods for encouraging the child's language skills to grow and develop once he enters into the preschool setting are the cognitive developmental and the behavioral. The first method emphasizes a relationship between intellectual growth and language development; the second argues that rewards and reinforcement of appropriate behavior constitute the major factors involved in language development.

Cognitive Developmental Theory and Application

The *cognitive developmentalists* view language development as an outgrowth of intelligence rather than as a natural, intuitive phenomenon as described by the nativists. They stress the importance of active learning in developing fairly sophisticated thinking abilities as a prerequisite to the child's being able to master the abstract demands of a system of language. Therefore, rather than examining sentence patterns, cognitive developmentalists look at ways in which the experience backgrounds and growing intelligence of children affect their ability to communicate.

Cognitive developmental theory emphasizes that the child's ability to speak grows and develops only to the extent that he has been able to experience things within his environment actively. These direct experiences are then "coded" as concepts within the child's mind and his discoveries are gradually transformed from real experiences into their verbal representations. According to the cognitive developmentalists, language develops only to the extent that the child's intelligence develops through direct, concrete experience.

Perhaps the leading proponent of the cognitive developmental view today is Jean Piaget. Before we examine Piaget's notions regarding language, however, quickly review his concepts of cognitive development in Chapter 6. In Piaget's framework, language ability is generally determined by the level achieved in cognitive growth—its functional use is limited to the level of sophistication achieved in cognitive development.

In addition to the technical vocabulary used to describe Piaget's theory of cognitive development, you must also understand certain of Piaget's language-related terms if you are to attain a basic comprehension of his theory of language acquisition. The most inclusive of all Piagetian language-related expressions is the term *signifier*. A signifier may refer to any of the three levels of representing something in the environment:

1. *Index:* the child has a pure visual perception of an object. When an individual views a pencil, for example, his perceptive abilities operate on it, that is, eyes focus on the pencil, perceive its form, detect its color, and so on. The mental image formed from such a process is a true picture of something directly observed, and meaning comes only from such direct observation.
2. *Symbol:* the child deals not with the object itself, but with representations of objects. Piaget refers to this process as "internal imitation." For example, the child may signify his driving of a car by imitating the sound of a honking horn, or may use tempera paint to symbolize his idea of a flower. The child does not need the real object, but forms an intellectual construction of it.
3. *Sign:* the most abstract representation of an object; this level relies on systems of words and language to communicate ideas. Index and symbol representations are considered *personal* signifiers because they communicate individual interpretations of objects, while sign representations are considered *social* signifiers because they utilize abstractions (words) that must be mutually agreed upon in order to have meaning. Sign signifiers are more abstract, of course, because the word *pencil*, for example, bears no resemblance to the real thing.

These three key Piagetian terms are illustrated in Figure 8-4.

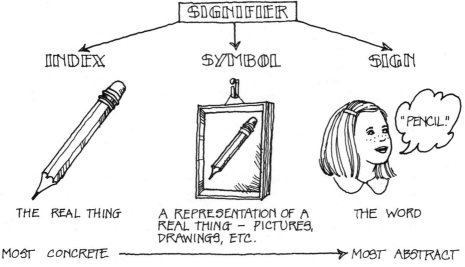

Figure 8-4 Basic terms related to Piagetian language development.

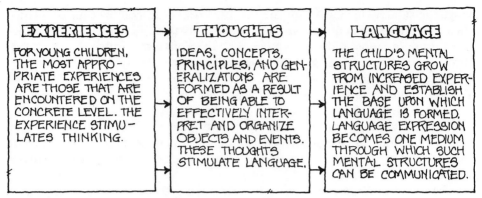

Figure 8-5   Pattern of thinking-language relationships.

To summarize, internalization of real things (*index*) or experiences allows the child to create *symbols*. The child then assimilates the objects and their symbolic representations into his mental schemes, and these eventually grow into the most mature expression of thought—the *word* (*sign*). See Figure 8-5.

Before about the age of two, the child forms only mental images of real objects. He looks at things, handles them, and assimilates them into growing mental schemas, but he has not yet developed an ability to translate these symbols into words. He simply acts on the environment in this important period before he begins to verbalize. By the age of two, the child has moved from an organism possessing basic reflexive and survival characteristics to one who is beginning to think. He begins to attach word labels to those things he interacts with in his environment as he hears the words used by those who surround him. The words he says, though, are used in ways that are often strange or inexact. Remember that the child's background is not nearly as sophisticated as an adult's, and his ability to associate past experiences with a verbal label is much more limited. For example, "doggie" may refer to all four-legged animals, and "cookie" may refer to crackers, bread, or other similar foods. But, since language grows from accumulated experiences, we must remember that such imperfect expression results only from a limited association with objects or events.

Once the child begins to associate objects to words or simple combinations of words, he then begins to progress through several varieties of language. The first variety, *noncommunicative speech*, is considered egocentric in nature and is divided into three types:

1. *Repetition:* the child repeats or mimics something he has heard. Often, he uses words that he does not understand, but repeats the phrase for the mere pleasure of doing so.
2. *Monologue:* the child talks aloud to himself, often at great length. It seems as though the child is thinking aloud when this monologue appears. For example, the three-year-old may busily play alone at the sand box: "My truck goes br-r-r-m . . . I'm building a road. The truck helps me . . . Br-r-r-m."

3. *Collective monologue:* the child talks aloud when other children are present, but the others do not listen to what he says. The speaker may think that others are listening, although he does not expect them to answer or respond in any way. In effect, the child is still talking to himself but his remarks are directed toward a listener. You can expect to hear the same type of monologue as that described in item 2.

Preschool teachers can expect to hear some of each of these types of noncommunicative egocentric speech from young children. In fact, Piaget is convinced that egocentric language characterizes most children's speech up until age 6 or 7. M. M. Lewis, who is interested in collective monologue, said about the ways children carry on in egocentric speech while engaged in this activity: "this self-addressed speech is more than an accompaniment to action . . . it is part of the action, which is thus both non-linguistic and linguistic. The words are a means by which a child is helped to direct his attention, to regulate what he is doing, to 'think aloud.' "[14]

Up to about the age of six or seven, then, children seem to use language as a means of thinking aloud. They do so as they gain increasing knowledge of things through experience and observation. They experience things directly in their environment and they construct mental images of them. These mental "imitations" provide the child with symbols (representations—other than verbal—of some real thing). The symbols then eventually are transformed into words, both symbols and words becoming personal interpretations of real objects or experiences within the environment. Words are eventually combined into meaningful combinations and used in noncommunicative, or egocentric, ways to express growing mental images. During this stage, the children love to play with words, to repeat them, to exercise them. New experiences continuously create and reconstruct mental images, resulting in increasingly sophisticated language patterns.

Working with children at ages 6 and 7, Piaget observed a move from egocentric speech toward *socialized* speech—communicative speech intended to facilitate interaction with others. In socialized speech, the child considers the listener and tries to transmit thoughts to him. For example, he may tell another child about the tempera paint, "Mix red and yellow together if you want orange." The child may also criticize the work or behavior of others, ask questions of others, and answer the questions or commands of others. However, children may not be able to explain *why* things are as they seem ("Why does yellow and red make orange?") and tend to focus on events rather than their causes. An illustration of the various levels of language development is presented in Figure 8-6.

How does the child best move from one level to the next—from less mature language to highly mature language? Piaget does not answer these questions directly and he has never offered practical teaching suggestions for carrying out his theories. However, he does say that language maturity evolves most effectively if the child first has had opportunities to explore and interact actively in his surroundings. Through those direct experiences, the child is able to develop a foundation of mental structures or concepts,

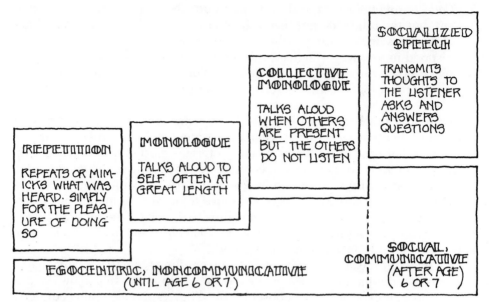

Figure 8-6 Levels of speech development according to Piaget.

although he may not be able to express all such concepts in words. This foundation is important, though, because "Piaget defines teaching as the creation of situations where structures can be discovered, not the transmission of structures which may be assimilated at the verbal level only."[15] Once these structures have been acquired, they may be readily translated into language. According to Piaget, "Mainly, language serves to translate what is already understood: or else language may even present a danger if it is used to introduce an idea which is not yet accessible."[16]

Piaget is warning us to allow children to have opportunities to form mental structures through activity before we begin expecting effective language to develop—activity precedes language. Also, he warns us that by presenting concepts to children verbally rather than through activity in which the structures are first developed, we keep the child from building a firm language foundation (see Figure 8-7).

Several authorities have applied Piagetian language theory to preschool programs. Such adaptations have been generally organized according to the following framework:

1. Helping the children develop logical modes of thought by actively involving them in their environment. Activities and direct experiences should be planned to encourage children to act on their environment and to develop the basic Piagetian skills described in Chapter 6:
    a. *Physical knowledge:* observing the physical properties of objects within the child's environment
    b. *Logico-mathematical knowledge:* (1) classification, (2) seriation, (3) spatial relations, (4) temporal relations, and (5) conservation.

These skills help children organize the complex world around them and form the foundation necessary for increased language growth. Examples of activities appropriate for the development of these skills are given in Chapter 6.

2. Providing verbal stimulation to help children associate language with their experiences. Language is not taught directly, but the teacher capitalizes on spontaneous, self-directed activities to verbalize the physical properties of objects and the relationships among objects in the environment.

Eugene was at the art corner busily working on a watercolor painting. "You are doing a very nice job, Eugene," commented the teacher. "I like your picture. Please tell me more about it." When Eugene had done so, the teacher added, "Your dog is so big he fills up the whole paper." *The teacher made further comments focusing on the other physical characteristics of the painting:*
"You made some nice red circles."
"Look at that big yellow line."
"How nicely you've drawn the small circle inside the bigger one."
"Oh, it's nice how your thick red paint flows across your smooth, yellow paint."
"That long curvy line is just above the small blue dot."

Figure 8-7 The importance of providing direct experiences rather than verbal instruction.

Such comments help stimulate the child's thinking and help him to experience concretely physical features, comparison, contrasts, and various relationships. Through such informal methods, the child gains new names or labels for things, as well as increased concept formation; both are essential to the acquisition of language.

3. Arranging some structured lessons through which the teacher wishes to teach specific concepts and to encourage the child to describe or label objects. The teacher serves as a model for the child to imitate. For example, the teacher presents the child with two cardboard squares, one covered with sandpaper and the other covered with smooth cloth. The teacher asks the child to run his fingers over the sandpaper, and comments, "This is *rough*." She does the same thing with the smooth cloth square and says, "This is *smooth*." She then moves to the next step by asking the child to point to the *rough* square and then to the *smooth* square. The child is encouraged to use the terms himself as the teacher asks, "Tell me about this square." If the lesson had a good effect, the child would say, "It is *rough* (or *smooth*)." In this final stage, the child has generated the word by himself after the initial modeling procedure. You should recognize that, although the lesson was fairly well sequenced, the child moved from direct, active manipulation of the objects in his immediate environment to the use of words to describe those objects—this process is essential to the Piagetian scheme of language acquisition. As further reinforcement, the teacher could follow up the lesson by having the child sort various cards into two piles: rough and smooth.

A Piagetian language program, then, is designed to offer many verbal stimulation techniques to help enrich language skills. Such techniques may be combined with the types of informal activities described earlier. Regardless of the approach, however, teachers must view the learning process as a natural one filled with concrete experiences.

Behavioral Theory and Application

The third prominent theory of language development during the preschool years, behaviorism, emphasizes the importance of imitation and reinforcement in the acquisition process. According to this theory, the child acquires language by modeling what he hears from others and being rewarded (or not rewarded) for his efforts. Verbal behavior is viewed as no different from other behaviors and is acquired in much the same way as other behaviors are acquired. It might be best to review some of the basic principles of behaviorism (Chapter 6) before proceeding.

The behaviorists totally reject the ideas of the nativists and cognitive developmentalists on the basic principle that language development occurs not through some internal mechanism but only through the external reinforcement of imitated speech sounds. The idea that children are able to acquire speech through a natural maturation of innate linguistic mechanisms (nativistic theory) or through the development of increasingly sophisticated thought processes (cognitive developmental theory) is discounted. The behaviorists explain that the only internal mechanism related to behavior of any kind, including language, is the ability to form stimulus-response bonds. The leading proponent of this school of thought is B. F. Skinner.[17] Skinner identified three ways in which the stimulus-response technique can be used to encourage language development:

1. *As an echoic response:* When a child repeats the exact spoken word of a parent, that parent may reward the child for his efforts (see Figure 8-8A).
2. *As a mand:* When the child attempts to express a need and uses words that closely approximate the fulfillment of the need, the parent may reward the child by satisfying that need (see Figure 8-8B).
3. *As a tact:* When the child makes a preferred verbal response to a specific stimulus within his environment, he is immediately rewarded for his accomplishment (see Figure 8-8C).

Skinner, of course, views language development as a growing number of verbal responses acquired solely through the process of conditioning.

In recent years, psychologists and educators have questioned this mechanistic, behavioral view of language development. Even though they may agree with some of its principles (such as imitation or rewarding appropriate behavior) they reject the passive role the child plays as he is involved in language learning. Supporting their critical ideas, ironically, is the Russian "father of behaviorism," Ivan Pavlov. Late in his life, Pavlov began to realize that human beings actually possessed two "signal systems." *First signals* are all the stimuli to which animals *and* humans can respond (hunger, sleep, pain, and so on). Pavlov felt that his stimulus-response principles best applied to shaping behaviors of this type. *Second signals* are mainly *verbal* stimuli. Pavlov felt that this second signal system was the major feature separating humans from animal life. This dimension, according to Pavlov, has its own structures and functions, and, therefore, the established laws of classical conditioning were not applicable. Slobin quotes Pavlov thus, "The word created a second system of signals of reality which is peculiarly ours. . . . It is precisely speech which has made us human."[18]

Although behaviorists have gradually "softened" their stand on the use of pure behavioral techniques for stimulating language development in young children, they remain strongly committed to the principles of imitation, reward, and structured learning experiences as essential components of effective language growth.

The Distar® program offers an example of curriculums for teaching language that are based on behavioral techniques. This program structures its language lessons in small-step instructional units that are carefully broken down to offer the children a systematic introduction to standard English. Lessons proceed in complexity from simple word recognition to the development of complete sentences. Teachers work with small groups of five to six

Figure 8-8   Skinner's three methods of encouraging language growth.

children for about 15 minutes per day; during this time a great deal of repetitive drill—through either choral or individual responses—is carried out. Immediate rewards in the form of praise ("You did it right!") or teacher approval (smiles, shaking hands, and so on) are essential when the children provide correct answers. Tokens or other forms of external reinforcement (food, toys) may be necessary if the teacher approval reward system seems to be initially unsuccessful.

The program is an intensive, fast-paced, highly structured pattern of instruction. The basic presentation pattern—using *circle* as an example—is as follows:

1. Identification
    Teacher: "This is a circle."
    Child (repeats phrase): "This is a circle."
2. Question
    Teacher: "Is this a circle?"
    Child: "Yes (*or* no) this is (*or* is not) a circle."
3. Selection
    Teacher: "Show me the circle."
    Child (child selects the proper geometric shape): "This is the circle."
4. Origination
    Teacher: "What is this?"
    Child: "This is a circle."

The goals of such dialogue are (1) to expand the child's use of word labels, (2) to increase his knowledge of word meanings, and (3) to help him master the use of increasingly mature sentence patterns.

Along with this heavy stress on speaking correctly, the children are required to listen carefully. To enhance listening skills, the teacher periodically attempts to "fool" the children. Consider the following example of a lesson containing a strong emphasis on both speech patterning and effective listening. Remember that the dialogue is carried on in a fast-paced manner that generates the excitement of a football cheering section. Highly structured teacher's guides furnish word-by-word instructions that admonish the teacher to remind the children to "Say it fast" whenever the intensively paced drill seems to falter.

First comes a quick review of a previously learned—and popular—class concept.

Teacher:　Tell me something that is a weapon.
Children (ab lib):　A gun . . . A rifle . . . A sword . . . Bow'n arrow . . .
Teacher:　What's the rule? If you use it . . ."
Children (in unison):　If you use it to hurt someone, it's a weapon.
Teacher:　Can you use a stick to hurt somebody?
Children (ad lib):　No . . . Yeah . . . You can hit 'em . . . You can throw it . . . If it's a big stick . . .
Teacher:　If you use a stick to hit somebody, then what do you know about it?
Children (more or less in unison): It's a weapon.
Teacher: Tell me something that is *not* a weapon.
    After a review taking less than two minutes, the teacher then moves immediately into the presentation of a new concept—part:
Teacher (pointing): This is Tyrone. Now listen. (*Holding up Tyrone's hand and speaking slowly and methodically in a way that the children have learned to recognize as a signal that something new is being presented.*) This is a *part of* Tyrone. This part of Tyrone is a . . .

Children: Hand.

Teacher (pointing to Tyrone's nose): And this is a part of Tyrone. This part of Tyrone is a . . .

Children: Nose.

Several other parts of Tyrone are introduced in this way and then the teacher alters the presentation to require the children to provide more of the statement.

Teacher (pointing to Tyrone's ear): Is this a part of Tyrone?

Children: Yeah.

Teacher: Yes, this is a . . .

Children: Part of Tyrone.

Progressively the children are led to the point where they are supplying the entire pair of statements. Negative instances are introduced.

Teacher (pointing to Marie's nose): Is this a part of Tyrone?

Children: No, this is not a part of Tyrone.

Consideration is then shifted to parts of a chair and parts of an automobile (using a picture in a picture book). At the end of six minutes the children have achieved a tenuous mastery of the concept but have started to become restless and to make thoughtless errors. The teacher then shifts to a concept that had been introduced the day before—vehicle. She will return the next day to further work on the concept, part. During the closing minutes of the period, when some of the children are becoming inattentive, the teacher says, "Try real hard to get this, and then we'll have time to do some more jungle animals." This enticement serves to pull the group together for the final exercise on vehicles.[19]

This example shows that behavioral programs are exclusively interested in using reinforcement techniques to establish imitative, patterned verbal responses to various stimuli within the child's environment. The Distar® program, of course, is only one application of the behavioral concept to preschool language instruction. Some preschool educators reject such total formality as detrimental to creativity, but they still value the principles of imitation and reinforcement. However, they practice these principles more loosely than the behaviorists.

SOME FINAL THOUGHTS

Educational research abounds with data backing each of the three major theories of language development and their classroom applications. Such seemingly contradictory evidence may support those who feel that all three approaches contain some element of truth, and that a combination of theories best explains such a multidimensional accomplishment as language development. Could it be that some aspects of acquiring language are innate (nativists), others are learned (behaviorists), while still others depend on the child's level of cognitive development (cognitive developmentalists)? Perhaps it could be safely argued that, with our present state of knowledge of language development, all three theories have value in the preschool classroom. The needs and interests of the children in any classroom should be the major determiner of whether any single approach should be used or of whether any of hundreds of possible combinations of the three approaches should be used. Such a choice is a sophisticated professional judgment and should be made only after careful observation, effective planning, and concerted study. Whatever the final choice, however, many activities are possible for use in your program.

The entire school environment should provide opportunities for interesting activities that help children communicate to their fullest extent. Such a program has three components: (1) guiding the children to acquire basic speech skills as discussed earlier in this chapter, (2) creating a climate that promotes free, honest, use of words, and (3) using stories, games, and other activities to encourage optimal language growth. By wisely arranging your classroom environment to include these three components, you will move a long way toward fostering growth and creativity in language usage.

NOTES

1. Arnold Gesell, "The Biography of a Wolf Child," *Harper's Magazine* 182 (January 1941): 183–193.
2. M. C. L. Green, *Learning to Talk: A Parent's Guide to the First Five Years* (New York: Harper & Brothers, 1960), p. 14.
3. Robert D. Armstrong and W. J. Gage, quoted in Lillian M. Logan, Virgil G. Logan, and Leona Paterson, *Creative Communication: Teaching the Language Arts* (Montreal: McGraw-Hill Ryerson Limited, 1972), p. 9.
4. Kornei Chukovsky, *From Two to Five*, trans. M. Morton (Berkeley, Calif.: University of California Press, 1968), p. 7.
5. Pose Lamb, ed., *Guiding Children's Language Learning*, 2d ed. (Dubuque, Iowa: William C. Brown, 1971), p. 11.
6. Chukovsky, *From Two to Five*, p. 7.
7. Alvina Treut Burrows, "Children's Language," in *Linguistics in the Elementary School Classroom*, ed. Paul S. Anderson (New York: Macmillan, 1971), p. 90.
8. Eugene Grant, "The Tale of Peter and the Rabbit," *Phi Delta Kappan* 44 (November 1967): back cover.
9. Noam Chomsky, *Aspects of the Theory of Syntax* (Cambridge, Mass.: M.I.T. Press, 1970), pp. 30–33.
10. Eric H. Lenneberg, "The Capacity for Language Acquisition," in *The Structure of Language*, ed. J. A. Foder and J. J. Katz (Englewood Cliffs, N. J.: Prentice-Hall, 1964), p. 600.
11. David McNeill, "Developmental Psycholinguistics," in *The Genesis of Language*, ed. F. Smith and G. A. Miller (Cambridge, Mass.: M.I.T. Press, 1966), p. 36.
12. Courtney B. Cazden, "Suggestions from Studies of Early Language Acquisition," in *Language and the Language Arts*, ed. Johanna S. DeStefano and Sharon E. Fox (Boston: Little, Brown, 1974), p. 43.
13. McNeill, "Developmental Psycholinguistics," p. 69.

14. M. M. Lewis, *Language and the Child* (The Mere, Bucks, Eng.: National Foundation for Educational Research, 1969), pp. 32–33.

15. James A. Smith, *Adventures in Communication* (Boston: Allyn and Bacon, 1972), p. 10.

16. Jean Piaget, quoted in Eleanor Duckworth, "Piaget Rediscovered," *ESS Newsletter* (June 1964), Elementary Science Study, Educational Services, Inc., Watertown, Mass., p. 15.

17. B. F. Skinner, *Verbal Behavior* (New York: Appleton-Century-Crofts, 1957).

18. D. I. Slobin, "Soviet Psycholinguistics," in *Present-Day Soviet Psychology*, ed. N. O'Connor (Oxford: Pergamon Press, 1966), p. 112.

19. Carl Bereiter and Siegfried Engelmann, "Observations on the Use of Direct Instruction with Young Disadvantaged Children," *Journal of School Psychology* 4, no. 3 (Spring 1966): 57–58.

9

The Child's Physical and Social World: Science and Social Studies

"Sugar is real loud when you walk on it."

Children learn about their physical and social worlds when they are able to investigate and experience the daily wonders surrounding them. *(The Family Circus by Bil Keane courtesy of The Register and Tribune Syndicate, Inc.)*

SCIENCE

Whoever first suggested the process of inquiry must have developed the strategy after observing numbers of young children exploring their physical environment in an attempt to answer questions about the natural wonders around them. Children are fascinated by their dynamic new world and naturally delight in manipulating, observing, touching, trying out, and handling everything. The young child is curious—he wants to know: "Why?" "What is it?" "How does it work?" "Where does it come from?" And he has hundreds of similar questions. He is, in effect, the *natural inquirer*—spontaneously and ingeniously using all his senses as he acts on his environment while searching for answers to questions that perplex and mystify him.

The Informal Science Approach

The preschool science curriculum has a major role in building a foundation to support these "natural scientists" and to encourage their active investigations into scientific pursuits. In such a program, preschool teachers use *process* approaches—strategies intended to capitalize on the children's natural tendencies to question and investigate. Such strategies emphasize and value the involvement of children in direct experiences and active exploration. A process approach can be contrasted with a *product* approach in which the attainment of knowledge or specific skills is emphasized and valued more highly than scientific, investigative thinking. In a process approach to teaching science in the preschool classroom the teacher uses several basic strategies.

One thing a teacher can do is to *capitalize on informal happenings during the school day.* Be aware of the numerous opportunities that allow children to use the questioning methods of a scientist. For example, this event occurred one day on the playground of a private nursery school:

On a bright, warm morning the children were allowed to spend a great deal of time pursuing outdoor activities. They moved from one play activity to another and seemed to enjoy the inviting comforts of the weather. After a while, three children moved to the shade of a large tree for a short period of rest. When the teacher noticed that the children had remained in the shade for a longer amount of time than usual, she moved to the area to see if a problem had arisen. One hadn't. The teacher found the three children concentrating intently on the busy efforts of a swarm of ants. "Look at that hole—that's where they live," said Jana. "They live under the ground?" questioned Will. "Yep, and that's where those ants are dragging the food," offered Carrie. "Mrs. Long, do the ants really live *underground?" asked Will. Mrs. Long, in an effort to maintain the scientific curiosity already so effectively raised, simply answered, "Let's watch them carefully and see if Jana and Carrie are right."*

To capitalize on this incidental experience, Mrs. Long later went to another area populated by ants and dug up a shovelful of dirt and ants. She placed the mixture into a gallon jar, secured the lid carefully, and wrapped the jar with construction paper so that no light would be allowed inside. The darkness was necessary so that the ants would sense that they were underground and safe to begin digging a new pathway of tunnels. When the dark paper was removed, Will, Carrie, and Jana all became enthused about the passageways constructed by the ants. From this excitement, others began to ask: "What do they eat?" "Can we feed them?" "Do they drink water?" and other questions that extended their understandings.

The project continued throughout the year. Children fed the ants in small quantities: dead insects, food scraps, and almost any other organic substance. They also occasionally provided small amounts of water.

The teacher's task is to help children place their informal experiences into meaningful contexts so that this background of accurate information can

Petting a newly hatched baby chick is an unforgettable experience for preschool youngsters. This teacher capitalized on such fascination by encouraging her youngsters to question and experience.

help form higher-order concepts and generalizations. This is an important professional task, because random exposure to unrelated events with little or no guidance from the teacher is not sufficient—children must be led to discover that phenomena just don't happen. Skillful leadership is essential to encourage children to observe, question, and make discoveries leading to these higher-level concepts and generalizations.

The teacher can *guide scientific thinking through the use of skillful questions and comments.* Children have a limited background of experiences—thus, their foundation for examining and making sense out of new physical phenomena is also limited. For this reason, they may often misinterpret their new experiences. One child, for example, after observing a chick break through its shell, commented, "My cat is going to hatch some kittens real soon." Carol Seefeldt offered additional thoughts on this subject:

> Observing young children, talking to them, asking them questions about how they think engines work or why they think clouds move reveals to the adult the level of their scientific thinking. Often the children have misconceptions that need clarification and revision. They may believe, for example, that the wind moves because it is happy or the shadows move to get out of their way.... Engines, air, the clouds, according to the young child, move because they want to. Often the young child's egocentricity influences his concepts: He may believe that the sun sets because he goes to bed or that the rain is falling because it does not want him to go outside.[1]

Skillful guidance during science experiences can be an effective weapon against the formation of such misconceptions. Examples of some pertinent questions and comments that can be used during scientific experiences include:

"I wonder if the ants will eat this cracker crumb. Let's try it and see what happens."

"Let's try it again and see if the same thing happens."

"Maybe we can find out if we watch it carefully."

"How can we find out?"

"Martin's snail ate a piece of lettuce. Do you think we should feed lettuce to these snails, too?"

"How can we find out for sure?"

"Which worm is longer?"

"What food does the rabbit eat?"

"What's wrong with the plant?" "It's drooping."

"How many little hamsters were born?"

Several of the questions, of course, were designed to help the children observe an object or event; others were designed to encourage higher thought processes such as predicting and finding relationships. Through such questions and comments, the teacher helps the children to evaluate and extend their experiences.

The teacher can *convey a positive attitude toward the children's interests*. The children's world is filled with items and experiences that fascinate them. However, they do not always receive reinforcement and encouragement from the adults around them as they explore these new wonders, simply because those adults may either frown on certain types of active exploration or lack interest in a particular area in which the child is interested. For those reasons, you may often hear comments or see reactions like the one described in this hypothetical situation:

> *Digging in the garden, Marcianne and Dennis uncovered two small, white, wiggling, wormlike creatures. Calling to their teacher, the youngsters each picked up one of the Japanese beetle grubs, held them in their hands, and asked what they were. Her face turning ashen, the teacher drew back and commanded, "Put those things right back where you found them and get inside to wash your hands right now."*

Although you cannot treat every area of the children's interest with equal time and enthusiasm, you should be prepared to make new experiences pleasant for them. If you cringe at the sight of worms and other crawling creatures, either don't introduce them at all to the children or ask someone else to do it for you. Your queasiness in these situations will, of course, be sensed by the children and have an effect on their enthusiasm for future explorations. When these situations arise by chance, you should exhibit enough insight and self-control to show interest in the child's discovery.

On the other hand, your own interests can be capitalized on and enthusiastically shared with the children. Such strong positive feelings are sure to be contagious and result in new and exciting interests for the youngsters. You may have a "green thumb" and work well with plants. Your interest in machines may result in many valuable simple experiments. Whenever your own personal interests are brought to the classroom, however, remember to

Young children enjoy investigating living creatures of all different shapes and sizes, including these earthworms. Be careful not to stifle this curiosity by communicating negative feelings about spiders, bugs, or other creeping, crawling animals.

be aware of where the children are experientially—we don't want to over-whelm them with too much, too soon.

The teacher should *be knowledgeable about basic scientific concepts and able to communicate those concepts to the children in appropriate terms.* It is not necessary for you to have complete command over every scientific concept handled in the preschool setting, but you should have enough knowledge to be able to help the children whenever they need your support. G. Craig emphasized that "the teacher need not be appalled by the extensiveness and complexity of science as a whole, for she is responsible for imparting only a small portion of the total scientific knowledge, namely that portion pertinent to a group of children at a given age level."[2]

That portion that is pertinent for your age group can be gathered from many sources. It is both enjoyable and informative to leaf through children's reference books in the library, for example. These books are well illustrated and contain the basic information you need. Films, filmstrips, pictures, magazines, and other sources serve the same purpose. Often, the major problem with such self-education is finding the time to do it. However, once you have convinced yourself that such a project is needed, the experience will be, without doubt, a delightful one. Many teachers who have experienced nature themselves, for example, find it easy to pass on their new enthusiasm to their young children.

Having the basic scientific knowledge required to talk with children is only one part of the teacher's responsibility; the other part is to develop skill in communicating that information to the children when necessary. Often, children's observations, questions, and experiments will need to be enlarged and verbalized by the teacher. But note that sometimes the teacher's comments can be too involved, as in this case:

Karen: "Why did the puddle go away?"
Teacher: "The heat from the sun's rays made the water disappear into the air. That's called evaporation."

Instead of this difficult answer, the teacher should have offered a simple explanation:

Karen: "Why did the puddle go away?"
Teacher: "The heat from the sun dried it up."

Teachers sometimes cause problems, too, when they fabricate stories in an attempt to explain scientific concepts. Examine this situation, for example:

Richard: "What happens to our dead gerbil?"
Teacher: "He goes to gerbil heaven—where all the good little gerbils go."
Richard: "Is it nice there?"
Teacher: "Oh yes. He will have a clean, comfortable home and plenty of food to eat. And, even better, our gerbil will see his mother and father along with many of his friends who died, too."

Obviously, there is a better approach:

Richard: "What happens to our dead gerbil?"
Teacher: "The gerbil died because it was very old. If we keep it here it will start to smell. Let's get the shovel and bury it outdoors."

Interpretations of scientific events by the teacher to the children should be free of intricate explanation and mystical description. Your role is a challenging one—to find the balance and sensitivity needed to make a preschool science program uncomplicated and fascinating. Anything that goes beyond these characteristics causes misunderstandings and frustrations that may be difficult or impossible to eradicate later on. Remember simply to stick to the scientific facts and keep fantasy in its proper place, otherwise children may think of physical science as "magic" rather than as a description of the physical environment.

Planned Science Activities

When the teacher plans to enrich scientific discoveries by creating an environment ripe for scientific investigation, a great deal of careful planning is involved. Choices must be made regarding appropriate materials and equipment suitable for the children's interest and developmental levels. Lists of supplies are available from many sources; none are included here because they can be overwhelming to education students who have not yet taught young children. Instead, we will discuss various equipment and materials under topics of investigation popularly experienced in the preschool setting.

Constant care and supervision must be extended to the animals or serious consequences may result. (*Tiger* by Bud Blake courtesy of King Features Syndicate, Inc.)

ANIMALS   Young children are fascinated by all kinds of animals—from imaginary storybook animals with human characteristics to real animals with cold, wet noses so exciting to touch. They can be observed watching in surprise and wonder, mouths agape, as a mother robin feeds and cares for her young. They are captivated by the industriousness and strength of ants as they gather food or materials for their growing colony, and can watch for long periods of time.

The preschool environment should reflect these childhood interests and provide for many experiences with all kinds of animals. In addition to becoming aware of the physical characteristics of living organisms other than human beings, young children acquire strong feelings of importance as they feed the classroom animals and provide for their care. Rarely do young children have opportunities to practice themselves the care and treatment they receive at home from their parents. With animals, however, young children

Children are fascinated by animals of all kinds—including this enjoyable hermit crab, appropriately named, "Hermie."

become directly involved in caring for other living beings and soon develop an awareness of the value of good diet, cleanliness, and protection.

The animals described in the animals for young children box are appropriate for the preschool classroom. With the best of care, they should become interesting and valuable science materials in your classroom.

To obtain the greatest value from having animals in the preschool classroom, you must constantly watch out for their health and safety. Lack of concern in this area only serves to develop a feeling of disrespect in the children; this often leads to abuse of the animal, followed by its injury, sickness, or death. If the children are to respect animal life, they must learn to understand and appreciate suitable environments and patterns of care; they must understand that all living things depend upon each other for survival.

PLANTS   Plants are often used in the preschool program for three main purposes: (1) to beautify the classroom, (2) to involve the children in caring for and nurturing them, and (3) to help children learn about plant life through experimentation and observation. Plants can brighten the preschool environment and make it an attractive and pleasant place for the children. However, because plants are often placed in hanging baskets or on tall shelves, the children rarely have opportunities to look at them closely. They become, unintentionally, the *teacher's plants* as they blend into the environment and become ignored by the children. To be *children's plants* and, therefore, to become a more meaningful part of the children's environment, they must be brought down to the level of the children—where they can be watched, touched, and cared for by the children themselves. Children's initial experiences with plants will undoubtedly involve accidents: overwatering, breaking off of leaves or branches, pulling up the plant with the roots, or even destroying a plant. However, if the children are going to learn to treat plants properly and to respect them, they must be taught to do so. In any event, most of the accidents will occur, not from mischievousness, but from lack of knowledge about how to treat and care for plants properly. A child's actual experiences while caring for and observing plants go a long way toward helping him understand why it is important to protect the environment around him. Some good plants to have in the preschool classroom include:

☐ *Spider plant:* large clusters of flowing grasslike leaves, usually with dark- and light-green tones. Plant reproduces by sending out small plantlets. Ideal for hanging basket.

☐ *Philodendron:* a durable tropical vine with small, waxy leaves. Can be a climber or can be put in a hanging basket. Small, versatile, and hardy.

☐ *Wandering Jew:* attractive vinelike specimen for a hanging basket. Delightful purple leaves with silvery bands. Very fast growing. Branches easily. Roots quickly in water or damp soil.

☐ *Geranium:* a flowering plant with red, white, or pink petals. Cuttings root very easily.

ANIMALS FOR YOUNG CHILDREN

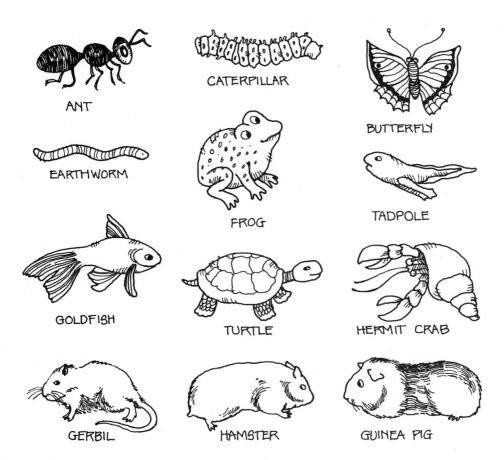

ANT

CATERPILLAR

BUTTERFLY

EARTHWORM

FROG

TADPOLE

GOLDFISH

TURTLE

HERMIT CRAB

GERBIL

HAMSTER

GUINEA PIG

ANTS Ants provide long periods of entertainment for young children as they tunnel through the soft dirt in a jar or purchased ant farm. Ants require no special care except for periodic feeding (they will eat almost anything) and watering.

CATERPILLARS AND BUTTERFLIES Caterpillars or their cocoons can be found in the autumn clinging to the leaves of bushes, trees, or weeds. If a caterpillar is found, be sure to pick a large amount of leaves of the type on which it was feeding and give them to the caterpillar until it spins into a cocoon. If the cocoon is found, keep it attached to the branch or twig and carefully bring it into the classroom to be stored in a cool, relatively moist area until the butterfly or moth emerges. The Monarch butterfly caterpillar or cocoon (chrysalis), found on milkweed, is an exceptionally good insect for the children to observe.

Cocoons occasionally have surpris-

(continues)

ing contents, however. One child brought a cocoon she had found to school. When the cocoon opened sometime later, the room (luckily empty since it was recess time) filled with grasshopper-like insects—lots of them. So you may want to keep caterpillars and cocoons in a covered aquarium.

EARTHWORMS   Earthworms can be purchased at a fishing supply store or can be readily found in soft soil, especially after a rain. They can be easily kept in an aerated container filled with a mixture of loose earth and coffee grounds. Children can watch them tunnel into the dirt and create passageways similar to those of ants. Let the children handle the earthworms if they want to —the rough texture and squiggly feelings in their hands delight many youngsters.

TADPOLES AND FROGS   Tadpole eggs look like small marbles of clear jelly with a tiny dark dot in the center. They are found along the edge of a pond and are easily scooped up and placed into a container of water. When the tadpoles hatch, they eat either the algae and microscopic organisms formed in the pond water or goldfish food. Young tadpoles spend all of their time completely submerged in the water, but as they grow and develop legs, they need to get out of the water. A large rock or floating piece of wood serves this purpose. Be careful to cover the top of the container with a mesh screen or you will have trouble keeping the tadpoles inside. When the tadpole completely loses its tail, it becomes a frog and requires different food: tiny bits of fish, meat, or leafy vegetables; and especial-

ly live flies, gnats, or worms. A frog is nearly impossible to keep in the classroom so it might be best to return developed frogs to the pond in which they were found.

GOLDFISH   The goldfish is perhaps the easiest fish to care for in the preschool classroom as it requires much less special care than tropical fish. Goldfish, or any other kind of fish, rarely survive for any length of time in a small goldfish bowl, so it is recommended that you use a balanced, aerated aquarium for any fish you plan to keep.

When setting up the aquarium, be sure to wash it clean with plain water (no soap!). Add successive layers of sand and coarse gravel to the bottom and secure some live plants into this base. Put a small jar or plate on the gravel so that excessive dust does not stir up as you slowly add water. Hook up an aeration and filtration system for proper balance. Allow the aquarium to set for a few days while the chlorine and other harmful chemicals dissipate. Snails, catfish, and other scavengers help to control algae and waste materials. If all precautions are heeded, very little additional care is needed.

TURTLES   Until recently, turtles were found in nearly every preschool classroom. However, it has been discovered that some carry salmonella, a serious intestinal disease. Some turtles, though, can be successfully kept in your classroom. The best way to determine whether or not the turtle you choose is a safe one is to check with a reputable pet shop.

Turtles are very easy to care for.

They eat worms, ground meat, some vegetable greens, and small insects. Turtles must eat in the water, so it is important that all foods be placed in an area where the turtle is able to submerge its head while eating.

HERMIT CRABS The hermit crab is an increasingly popular classroom animal mainly because it requires so little care and is so fascinating for young children to observe. These tiny creatures can be bought in a pet store or large department store. They use abandoned shells for their homes and to watch them carry their homes on their backs as they move from place to place is a joy for the children.

Keep your hermit crabs in a well ventilated enclosure. Spread coarse gravel at the bottom of the container and scatter a few empty shells on the surface. Except for a diet of almost any type of food scraps, these amusing creatures need little or no care.

GERBILS All children enjoy these small, furry, friendly animals. They are clean, playful animals requiring little care, so they make almost the ideal classroom pet. Gerbils are usually kept in a wire cage lined with newspaper and cedar shavings. These materials form a hygienic bed for the gerbil's wastes, which are nearly nonexistent. Gerbils gnaw on the shavings and shred the newspaper; then they completely cover themselves with the shredded newspaper and shavings mixture as they sleep. The gerbil cage should include a special hanging water bottle, an exercise wheel, and an aluminum can for moments of privacy. Be sure to avoid a gerbil cage and any accessories made of plastic.

Gerbils gnaw and chew almost any materials that are not metal or glass.

Gerbils reproduce readily and often have a litter every month or two. Children delight in watching the mother and father care for the tiny pink babies, but the frequency of reproduction often results in extreme crowding.

Feed the gerbils a mixture of grains, cereals, breads, or vegetables such as carrots or lettuce. Special treats such as potato chips are especially appreciated.

HAMSTERS Like gerbils, hamsters can be purchased very reasonably at pet stores. An old aquarium fitted with a wire mesh screen at the top makes an ideal home for hamsters and gerbils alike. Hamsters are similar to gerbils and require the same basic care. The main reason some teachers select gerbils rather than hamsters is that hamsters are nocturnal animals, and usually sleep during the hours when the children are in school. The gerbils, however, are often awake and active during the hours of the normal school day.

GUINEA PIGS In contrast to the active gerbils and hamsters, guinea pigs are quiet, docile animals who are content to cuddle and snuggle in a person's arms. Their cage should be similar to the gerbil cage, but should contain a bit more shavings or straw to absorb greater amounts of moisture. Because guinea pigs eliminate greater amounts and do so with greater frequency, their cages must be cleaned more often. Guinea pigs are vegetarians and especially enjoy eating lettuce, apples, grass, or commercial food from the pet store.

- ☐ *Snake plant:* long, spearlike leaves grow up to four feet tall. Attractive bands of dark and light green on the succulent leaves.
- ☐ *Asparagus fern:* ideal for a hanging basket. Foliage is delightfully airy with billows of soft green lacy stems.
- ☐ *Umbrella tree* (Schefflera): a good looking, fast-growing tree that reaches a height of six feet or more.
- ☐ *Jade plant:* looks like a miniature tree. Leaves are full and succulent, and look like little mittens extending from branching stems. Grows from 18 to 30 inches.
- ☐ *Rubber plant:* popular treelike plant. Broad, shiny leaves extend from a center stalk that grows to five feet or more.
- ☐ *English ivy:* a good hanging or climbing plant. Typical bushy, ivy-leaf foliage on many branches. Hardy plant that can survive in nearly any environment.

All of these plants are very easy to grow and care for. Their light and temperature requirements cover a wide range of conditions but are not unnecessarily exacting. Once these plants have adjusted to your room—to the light, temperature, and humidity—they can be fed and watered routinely by the children with your guidance. Most of these plants are extremely hardy; the wandering Jew and philodendron, for example, can grow in water as easily as they can grow in soil. Several of these plants, especially the vinelike ones, can be rooted simply by cutting off a shoot and placing it in water. Roots, the part of the plant nearly always hidden from the children, will soon appear. Children enjoy taking these cuttings to start new plants of their own. When deciding upon the collection of plants for your classroom, you may wish to follow this guideline and include at least one *flowering plant*, at least one *vine*, one or two *hanging varieties*, at least one *fern*, and at least one *treelike plant*. When you choose plants for the classroom, be especially watchful that you select nonpoisonous varieties. Toddlers frequently put things into their mouths, and a poisonous leaf or stem is not beyond their interests.

Preschool teachers can add to the child's experiences with plants in the late winter or early spring through various planting activities, either indoors or outdoors. Bean seeds, melon seeds, pumpkin seeds, grass seeds, radish seeds, and the like germinate very easily. You can handle experiences with growing plants from these seeds in one of two ways: (1) you can plant the seeds in wet soil and wait for the sprout, or (2) you can place folded wet paper towels in the bottom of glass containers and lay seeds on each pad. In the second method, the children see not only the sprout, but the formation of the roots as well.

When the plants begin to mature, the children can move some of them to a garden plot outdoors if the space is available and the climate appropriate. Flowers and vegetables offer variety and excitement as they are grown for their aesthetic appeal or simply to be eaten. The digging, weeding, and watering responsibilities add to the children's awareness of life within their environment and to the concept of what plants need to grow.

Many creative activities can follow up direct planting experiences. For example, fingerplays can help children understand the essentials of good gardening:

My Garden

This is my garden. *(spread arms outward)*
I'll rake it with care. *(make raking motions)*
Here are the seeds
I'll plant in there. *(plant each seed)*
The sun will shine. *(make circle above head with arms)*
The rain will fall. *(make fluttering motions with fingers)*
The seeds will sprout
And grow up tall. *(stretch arms above the head)*

Also, planting activities can turn into creative art-related construction projects. For example, try the potato activity described in the box.

In the experiments with plants box (p. 338) are scientific experiments involving plants that are appropriate for young children. They are used most effectively after the children have already had some opportunities to grow their own plants from seeds or cuttings and to transplant the seedlings.

THE CLIMATE   Science experiences dealing with the climate are normally very welcome in the preschool classroom because young children are curious about the climatic features of *weather* and *seasons*. Children are

POTATO HEAD

Start with a large potato (A). Scoop off the top and line the shallow hole with a wet paper towel, sponge, or blotting paper. Stand the potato in a large dish of water. Sprinkle the wet paper towel with grass seed (B). Keep the towel moist at all times. In a short while, the seeds will begin to sprout and the "potato head" will begin to grow "green hair." Furnish cloves to the children so they can add eyes, nose, and mouth to their potato creature's face.

greatly affected by these features as they adjust their play and dress to seasonal demands. Experienced parents and teachers also attest to the fact that the children's emotional states are strongly affected by changes in weather and climate; they agree that children sometimes seem like "human barometers"—some adults can even predict rain or snow as the children's restless behavior increases. When it is too warm, children may become lethargic; when it is too cool, they may become irritable. Two or three snow or rain days in a row may cause increased behavior problems because the children will be unable to release physical energies through vigorous outdoor play. The teacher can capitalize on atmospheric changes during the planned and unplanned preschool science program. Consider these climate concepts as you

EXPERIMENTS WITH PLANTS

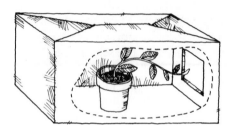

PLANTS GROW TOWARD THEIR SOURCE OF LIGHT Plant bean seeds in soil and water them daily. After the seeds have sprouted, place one plant in a box with a window cut out of one end. That window should be the only light source for the bean plant. Have the children observe how the plant bends toward the window and continues to grow in that direction.

LIGHT IS NECESSARY FOR PLANT GROWTH Plant bean seeds in two separate containers and allow the plants to come through the soil. Keep one pot in direct sunlight on the windowsill and cover the other pot with a paper bag. Keep the plants like this for about two weeks, removing the bag for observation purposes only. After that time, the uncovered plant should be green, robust, and healthy (A) while the covered plant is stunted and pale (B).

WATER IS TAKEN FROM THE SOIL, THROUGH THE ROOTS, AND INTO THE STEM OF A PLANT Have the children stir some food coloring into a glass of water. Take a piece of celery and slice it across the bottom. Allow the children some time to examine the stalk. Let the celery stand in the tinted water for about one hour. The celery stalk will change color as it travels upward. Take the celery out of the water, slice it, and examine the stalk again. Try the same experiment with a carrot or white carnation.

SOME PLANTS DO NOT GROW FROM SEEDS Have the children carefully wash a fresh sweet potato and arrange it so that it is about one-half to two-thirds suspended in a jar of water. The potato can be supported with toothpicks. Have the children observe the emergence of an attractive new plant.

develop your science program—but keep in mind the climate of your own region.

Weather

☐ The weather changes daily and is influenced by the sun, clouds, and winds—"The dark clouds are coming near. Let's go inside because it will rain very soon."

☐ The weather influences the clothing we wear—"It's raining today so you will need to put on your raincoats before you go home."

☐ The weather may influence how we feel—"Come here and lie on the cot for a while, Jerry. Sometimes the rainy weather makes us sleepy."

☐ The weather influences our choice of play activity—"Today is so sunny and warm. We'll be able to use the water table for the first time."

Each *season* has its own set of characteristics.

Fall

☐ Leaves change colors and drop from the trees.
☐ Animals gather food for the winter.
☐ People harvest food from gardens and farms.
☐ The first frost follows increasingly colder nights.
☐ Apples, pumpkins, and squash are characteristic fall foods.
☐ The days become shorter and cooler.
☐ Rakes and harvesting tools are characteristic of the season.

Winter

☐ Trees are bare, except for the evergreens.
☐ Snow, ice, and sleet accompany the cold weather.

Stimulate your children to observe and experience the wonders associated with seasonal changes throughout the school year.

- ☐ Heavy coats, mittens, hats, sweaters, and boots help us feel warmer.
- ☐ Some animals sleep through the winter.
- ☐ Building snowmen and sliding on the ice are but two of the many special winter play activities enjoyed by children.
- ☐ Hot soup and hot chocolate are enjoyed during a particularly cold day.
- ☐ Days become short—the sun sets much earlier.
- ☐ Heat from furnaces keeps us warm inside buildings.
- ☐ Snow shovels, snowplows, and winter tires are characteristic of the season.

Spring

- ☐ Days become warmer, windier, and rainier.
- ☐ Snow and ice begin to thaw.
- ☐ People are busily cleaning up after winter.
- ☐ Flowers, leaves, and plants begin to emerge.
- ☐ Many animals break out of their long winter sleeps or return from their southern migration.
- ☐ Longer, warmer days mean more hours in the sun playing in the sandpile, on the tricycle, and so on.
- ☐ Berries begin to ripen and are enjoyed as one of the fresh foods of that season.
- ☐ Garden tools, construction equipment, and construction workers are characteristic of the season.

Summer

- ☐ Hot, humid, active days call for light clothing, water, and plenty of rest.
- ☐ Many animals are active.

The natural environment is rich in exciting, new discoveries for young children. The teacher who capitalizes on the child's curiosity by arranging the classroom with items to stimulate their thinking, such as this bird's nest, encourages continuous inquiry into scientific wonders.

- □ Plants are actively growing and in full bloom.
- □ Many schools do not continue through the summer.
- □ People relax and have fun during summer vacations.
- □ Swimming and baseball are enjoyable summer pastimes.
- □ Lawnmowers, outdoor grills, garden tools, and refreshment stands characterize the season.

These suggestions are offered only as directions into which you can guide the children's thinking as the days go by through the school year. You must remember that three- or four-year-olds in your classroom are relative newcomers to this world and may be experiencing the first seasons that have any significant meaning for them. As a result, they seek answers to the seemingly magical wonders around them. And you can stimulate their thinking by providing opportunities to observe and discuss the characteristics of all these interesting climatic conditions.

OTHER AREAS OF INTEREST IN THE ENVIRONMENT Plants, animals, and climate are the scientific areas that are most interesting to young children, but other areas stimulate their powers of inquiry, too. "What is it?" "Why did that happen?" and "How does it work?" are questions that reflect the children's curiosity about the many other remarkable things found in their ever-growing world. The children are not seeking technical answers —in fact, they are satisfied with a direct demonstration of a phenomenon. For example, during one particularly warm day in the winter, one group of children showed a great deal of interest in a large sheet of ice that was beginning to melt. They were puzzled at this phenomenon and wanted to know why it was happening. They seemed satisfied with an explanation that the sun was out and the resulting warmth melted the ice. However, their

This child is being assisted by the teacher after he suggested that his roller skates might turn better if they were oiled. The teacher capitalized on his interest and helped the youngster decide how to proceed.

continued interest in the melting snow and in dripping icicles led the teacher to think of a classroom activity that would help demonstrate the effect of heat on frozen water. Back inside, the teacher brought out a tray of ice cubes and placed it on the table. She asked the children to observe the tray carefully and to guess what would happen if it were allowed to stay outside the refrigerator. Then, the teacher left the tray on the table and asked the children to check on it periodically to see what happpened. At no time during the experience was an explanation given other than that ice melts when it gets warm and freezes when it gets cold.

There is no one recommended guide for preschool teachers to follow in determining exactly *what* and *how many* other scientific concepts or topics should be handled in the preschool classroom. You must use the children's interests and your professional judgment in deciding what else should be experienced. The scientific areas described in the box entitled "Other Areas of

---

OTHER AREAS OF SCIENCE ACTIVITIES

AIR

☐ Have the children blow into a container of water with a straw. Call their attention to the resulting air bubbles in the water.

☐ Place a deflated balloon beneath a book on the table. Blow up the balloon and have the children observe how the air makes the book rise.

☐ Discuss how the wind makes a pinwheel turn, the leaves flutter, or a kite fly.

☐ Have the children observe each other's breath on a cold day. Explain that they can see the air that comes from their body.

MAGNETISM

☐ Allow the children to manipulate a bar magnet and/or horseshoe magnet freely as they experiment to see which objects can or cannot be picked up.

☐ Ask the children to separate the objects that are attracted by a magnet from those that are not by sorting a variety of objects into two separate boxes.

☐ Have the children decide which of a group of magnets is strongest by comparing the number of tacks or pins they can each pick up.

☐ Put some iron filings on a paper plate. Ask the children to move a magnet around beneath the plate and observe what happens.

MACHINES AND TOOLS

☐ Take your children to a farm, construction site, factory, or any other place where a large number of tools or machines are used so that they can observe their operation firsthand.

☐ Make a carpentry or plumbing area within your classroom. Encourage the children to manipulate and construct with the tools there.

☐ Discuss with the children how the wheels of their wagon make it easier to transport heavy objects than pushing or pulling the objects.

☐ Call attention to the adjustments made on a teeter-totter as it accommodates children of different weights.

Science Activities" (p. 342) have been taught as separate units or as individual activities in preschool classrooms throughout the country.

It must be re-emphasized that the science areas on which the preschool curriculum draws are so all encompassing that it is impossible to identify the specific informational, observational, and experimental projects that comprise regular parts of instruction. Therefore, to recommend what every "four-year-old should know or do" cannot be done. However, you should capitalize on those facets that interest your children and turn them into activities that meet the general, overall goal of science in the preschool classroom: *to interest the children in their world and help them develop meaningful concepts by involving them in active experimentation.*

SOCIAL STUDIES

Often, when preschool teachers are asked to describe the social studies component of their preschool curriculum, they respond with statements such as the following:

> Social studies? Gosh, we don't teach social studies. Why, our children are just too young to learn about Washington, Columbus, King, and all the other important people in history.

> How can we teach social studies? Our children can't read maps or books. How in the world can you expect them to learn about our land or other countries?

> Our day is too full already—we can't fit it in. You just can't schedule it into an already full day.

> We are sure to take field trips to all the major community helpers—the firefighter, doctor, police officer, and mail carrier. Other than that, I guess there's nothing special. Besides, the first-grade teachers are more concerned about whether our children are good in reading and math than they are about social studies.

After comments like this, you may wonder if the social studies field is important or useful enough to be an integral part of the preschool curriculum. These comments reflect the attitudes of teachers who have, however, misinterpreted the role of social studies in the preschool curriculum. They may be remembering some of their own common social studies experiences as youngsters: memorizing capitals, dates, events, or places; reading from a textbook and answering the questions at the end of the section; copying reports from the unstimulating encyclopedia; going on trips to the stations of various community helpers. Social studies, of course, is much more than that. But, it has been primarily because of these negative personal experiences that social studies has been a neglected part of the preschool curriculum for years.

"Look! That's where they make clouds."

The "hows" and "whys" of a child's world should be capitalized on by the teacher and turned into meaningful experiences that help youngsters understand their surroundings. (*The Family Circus* by Bil Keane courtesy of The Register and Tribune Syndicate, Inc.)

In addition, the social studies field is such an enormously broad area that teachers are just not sure of exactly what should be taught to preschool youngsters. Teachers don't have that problem with curricular areas such as math or reading—the content of these areas is fairly clear-cut from school to school. For example, if you were to observe a mathematics lesson in a kindergarten classroom in Maine and another in Oregon, chances are that both would be working on number sequence or set recognition. However, the social studies area is so complex and all-encompassing that the same kind of conformity would be nearly impossible to find. This lack of a defined body of content has frustrated many teachers and caused great difficulty in planning teaching goals and methods.

The basic content of the *social studies*, though, is drawn from six separate *social sciences:*

☐ *History*—inquiry into what has happened in the lives of people in the past
☐ *Geography*—the study of natural resources and how they affect human life
☐ *Civics*—investigating and experiencing the rights and responsibilities of citizenship
☐ *Economics*—study of the production, distribution, and consumption of goods and services, including occupations and career education

□ *Sociology*—inquiry into the development and organization of people living together in groups such as families, neighborhoods, and communities

□ *Anthropology*—study of the customs, myths, and institutions of various cultures and ethnic groups

You may, at this point, feel certain anxieties about these subject areas: "These social sciences are so broad!" "What do I teach about them?" "What can the children understand?" Don't look at such concerns as problems, but as strengths. You have the whole world from which to choose and, assuming that Bruner is correct, if any appropriately chosen concept is communicated *at the child's level*, we can use it as a source of instruction. Additional examples and illustrations will be shared throughout the rest of this chapter, but, for the sake of clarification at this point, consider the following information about the social sciences listed above.

History

Young children have extremely poor concepts of time, so the introduction and development of ideas related to history are very difficult. Their problems with time were explained in Chapter 7. Such problems create learning limitations that prevent concentrated exposure to concepts in history. This does not mean, however, that all concepts related to the study of history should be ignored. History deals not only with specific names, dates, and events of isolated times of the past, but it also deals with the concept of *change* and the forces that cause it. To develop a good sense of chronology, children must first understand the consequence of the passage of time: change. Change permeates the child's environment—seasons change, friends change, clothes change, weather changes, and skills change. As children learn how change affects us all, focus their attention on such events and characteristics.

1. *Encourage children to observe the changes they are personally experiencing.* "I couldn't do that when I was littler," is a prideful comment heard from youngsters when they learn a new skill or task. "The fairy gave me a quarter for my baby tooth," or, "I got new glasses. The doctor said my eyes were weaker than last year," are comments that afford you opportunities to talk about the physical changes that accompany the passage of time. In addition to seizing on informal opportunities such as these, you may wish to introduce simple comparison activities to help the children focus on other changes in their physical appearance. Ask the parents to send to school with each child a picture of the child as a baby. Have the children compare their appearance then and now. Or, bring in items of clothing that are normally worn by babies. Have the children examine them and discuss why they do not now wear clothing like this. Finally, keep a growth record on one classroom wall; mark the children's height at the beginning of the year, the middle of the year, and the end of the year. After marking each child's height at the beginning of the year, ask

each child to predict what his height will be at the end of the year and mark that height. At the end of the year, discuss the change: "Did you grow? As much as you thought? Why? Why not?"

2. *Help children observe the changes that occur in things in their environment.* "Look, the leaves are red," is a child's comment that gives the teacher an opportunity to help children observe changes that occur throughout the year. "Yes, aren't they beautiful?" asks the teacher. "Do you remember what color they were in the summer?" "What will happen to the leaves in the winter?" By helping children focus on seasonal changes in clothing, plants, and animals (discussed in the science section of this chapter), the teacher helps them understand environmental change.

3. *Emphasize that change can be regular* (as experienced in the previous examples) *or sudden and unplanned.* Excellent opportunities to help them learn this occur, for example, when "Big Bird came to talk about conservation so our story time must be cancelled today," or "We won't be able to play outdoors today because of the rain—what would you like to do now?" or "The police officer is sick and will not come today. She will be here tomorrow." Through such experiences, children learn that things are constantly changing whether or not we anticipate those changes.

In addition to *change,* the historical concept of *long ago* is often introduced by some preschool teachers. Although children find it impossible to conceptualize "long ago," they are nevertheless interested in the characteristics of past times. They love to hear stories of the past and to handle or observe objects from other eras. K. Wann, M. Dorn, and E. Liddle tell us that we must allow children to experience such activity even though they may not yet be ready to put such experiences into a realistic time framework. The authors state: "This dipping into the past without concern for a logical development of chronology from the past to the present does not violate basic principles of learning. To wait until they can handle true chronology is to deprive children of one of the most important learnings of early childhood."[3] Many resources can be used to provide experiences for young children related to the past:

1. Invite resource persons, especially senior citizens, to come to your school to tell stories, share objects, or demonstrate skills that were used in the past.
2. Bring in objects from the past (butter churns, toys, clothes, and so on) and place them in an interest center or in any area where you can demonstrate their use. Encourage the children to manipulate the objects and to talk about their experiences.
3. Take the children to a local museum or old building where they can observe things as they were long ago. Of course, the youngsters cannot comprehend the time period in which the objects from the past were most popularly used, but they will be able to compare the use of such objects with their newer versions.

Discussing seasonal changes helps young children understand the effects of the passage of time.

4. Read or tell children stories about things that occurred long ago. Through such listening experiences, young children learn about games of the past, occupations, jobs, challenges, or accomplishments.

Geography

Like history, geography has a reputation for encouraging only memorization of meaningless facts. Most of us remember classroom exercises that were aimed solely at recalling place locations, land formations, capital cities, major exports, population figures, and so on. Little attention was paid to going beyond these facts and examining the influence of humans on their physical environment and vice-versa. Because schools used to accept this factual recall view of geography completely, the subject has been traditionally viewed as inappropriate for the curriculum of young children. However, with the contemporary view that geography is concerned not only with the characteristics of the *earth's environment* but also with the relationship of that environment to the *people* who live in it, preschool educators have begun to have renewed interest in making it an integral part of the early childhood curriculum. There is great danger in introducing geographical concepts to young children before they are ready for them; consequently, the preschool teacher faces a challenge in designing meaningful activities. Some popular activities designed to promote geographic understandings are included in the geography activities box on page 348.

Civics

Civics deals with the rights and responsibilities of good citizenship, and especially with understanding the governing process—that is, the relationship between authority figures and those subjected to authoritative power. According to John Jarolimek, three concepts are basic to an understanding of this process:[4]

☐ the methods of establishing and maintaining order
☐ the power exerted by an authority figure over the people subjected to it

---

GEOGRAPHY ACTIVITIES

REPRESENTATION Maps are abstract representations of real places on the earth's surface. Because they are so abstract, their use may be beyond the capabilities of preschool youngsters. Nevertheless, readiness experiences that help children understand that certain objects or symbols can be used to represent others should be an important part of every preschool program. Several activities designed to promote this representation aspect of initial map readiness instruction follow:

☐ Encourage free play in the sand or water play areas with trucks, cars, boats, and the like. As children "build" roads, bridges, canals, and other geographic features, they begin to understand how their miniature environment simulates the larger world.
☐ Take a class trip around the neighborhood and photograph the buildings as you go along. Mount the pictures on blocks of wood and encourage the children to use them in much the same way as they would use regular blocks in their play.
☐ Use photographs of the children to illustrate that familiar things can be represented by scale models: "The picture shows you, but the picture is very small and you are really much bigger." Take photographs or draw pictures of a variety of classroom features and ask the children

to point to or pick up the real object. In this way, the children can be led to understand that symbols represent real things or real places, but in much smaller ways.

PHYSICAL FEATURES Present knowledge of child growth and development seems to indicate that focusing on the children's immediate environment is a logical place to start examining physical features. Encourage the children to look not only for the physical appearance of the geographical features around them, but also to discuss the ways in which each feature influences their activities and the activities of others:

☐ If your playground comprises several different surfaces, that is, sand, dirt, grass, asphalt, concrete, and so on, you may want to have the children observe each carefully and decide which is best, for example, for riding a tricycle. Discuss why the hardest surface is easiest and why the softest is least desirable. Ask the children to find the area that would be best for digging, for tumbling, for resting, or for any other activity.
☐ Sand and water play can be used to help children build model rivers, lakes, roads, mountains, farms, cities, and the like. Toy vehicles add additional fantasy to free play and help develop an awareness of the

□ the behaviors expected by individuals who are living within the particular governing framework

Naturally, the preschool curriculum would not initiate a formal study of the local, state, or national government to further these understandings. Children are exposed to concepts of government, however, at various times in

---

different types of geographical features on the earth's surface and of how people use those features in their daily lives.

□ Take a walk outside the school and locate various physical features. The children can identify churches, houses, apartment buildings, trailers, row homes, stores, parking lots, and parks. You should lead discussions designed to help the children compare and contrast the ways in which these neighborhood features are used.

□ Take a trip to an area more remote than the one in which your school is located—to a rural area, for example. Encourage the children to look for different land formations and buildings such as rivers, ponds, mountains, valleys, fields, farm houses, or barns. Lead a discussion of the ways in which this environment differs from their own, especially in terms of the people's clothing, work, play, and living arrangements.

THE EARTH   A complete understanding of the earth and its features is certainly impossible for young children. Consider, for example, the youngster who busily burrows with his shovel because he wants to "dig all the way down to the bottom of the world." Despite such maturational limitations, it is important for children to participate in ex-

periences that focus their attention on some apparent features of the earth's surface:

□ When standing in the sun, ask the children to look carefully and find their shadows. Explain that the sun's strong light makes the shadow. Move into the shade and talk about the differences.

□ Digging in the dirt and playing with water introduce the children to the two basic features of the earth. Take the children to a lake or pond to help them more fully understand large bodies of water covering the land surface. Have the children classify objects or pictures that belong primarily on *land* or on the *water*.

□ Have the children look at the sky (away from the sun) to explore the many varieties of cloud formations. They will learn that large, puffy, white clouds mean fair weather, while large, dark, thick clouds warn of rain or snow.

□ Point out the nature of wind. On a particularly windy day, for example, ask the children to run into the wind and then turn away from the wind and run. Discuss the differences in effort expended.

□ Observe seasonal changes—for activities, refer to the preceding section dealing with science in the preschool classroom.

their daily lives. Teachers, parents, other adults, brothers, sisters, peers, and a host of other significant human beings make and enforce rules that govern each child's actions in the home, at school, and throughout the neighborhood and community. This exposure offers many excellent opportunities to demonstrate the importance of rules for governing personal and group behaviors. See the box on civics activities.

CIVICS ACTIVITIES

THE CLASSROOM GOVERNING PROCESS "Mrs. Jackson is the boss," said Valerie, "and she said to put the puzzle away." Valerie obviously identified her teacher as the classroom authority figure and interpreted the role of authority figure as one that allows the person to "boss" others around. That kind of "boss" is seen by some children as the only or primary control over their actions and behaviors. They view teachers as power figures who rule over all children, and they view the child's role as one of being bossed by others. A basic knowledge of the democratic process cannot be developed if the child lives in an environment that perpetuates such beliefs, for authoritative environments prepare children not for life in a democracy, but for life in a dictatorial form of government. Therefore, to expect the child to respond positively toward you simply because you are the "boss" is a type of expectation that fails to help children become self-disciplined, responsible members of a group. To achieve the goal of classroom democracy, the following suggestions may be of use:

☐ Establish rules that are necessary for the care and protection of your children, and help children realize that those rules are made to protect them and others. In all types of governments, including a democracy, citizens have a certain amount of responsibility to follow rules. For example, three-year-olds must real-

ize that city streets present certain hazards, and that certain restrictions are necessary when the group is on the street. Katherine H. Read presents a good argument for such considerations:

Because we feel confidence that cars on the cross streets will stop when the light is green for us, we are free to drive through an intersection. The child who feels confidence that his parent will stop him is likely to act with less hesitation, to explore more freely. He feels safe when he can feel sure that he will be stopped should his impulsiveness lead him in dangerous directions. If the stopping or the limiting is done with love and without humiliation, he is helped to trust himself, to develop as a spontaneous, creative person. . . . He is free because he has parents who take responsibility. . . . They are setting a pattern which he can follow as he takes over the task of setting and maintaining limits for himself. They give him a model to follow when they act as responsible people.[5]

So, a first step in establishing the democratic classroom is to create an atmosphere in which the children understand (1) that some rules are necessary for their protection and the protection of others and (2) that each child has the eventual responsibility to guide and adjust his own behaviors on

Economics

The ear shattering cry of a youngster appealing to his parents for a new toy during a shopping trip or the round-eyed gaze that accompanies: "Mommy, I wanna new ball for my birfday," all remind us of the many ways in which economics concepts permeate the daily lives of young children. Many

---

the basis of those rules.

☐ Invite the children to participate in democratic decision-making activities. "Our new pet hermit crab needs a name. Does anyone have a suggestion?" After the names Herman and Harry were suggested, the teacher asked the children to vote for the name they liked best. Another class was asked to vote for making either popcorn or Jello for a snack. Such voting experiences give the children opportunities for group decision making and for following the will of the majority. Learning to live in a democracy also involves the ability to choose individual pursuits, so children may be asked, for example, to decide between two activities. "Those of you who want to swing may follow Mr. Adams and those of you who want to play Red Rover come with me to the grass area." Similarly, choices can be made concerning classroom learning activity, amounts of food during snack time, nap requirements, and so on.

THE GOVERNING PROCESS OUTSIDE THE CLASSROOM Many of the concepts related to this phase of understanding are taught in an informal manner:

☐ During dramatic play, the children may be encouraged to use miniature street signs similar to those normally found around their home or school. Make favorable comments when the signs are properly used, "Very nice, Robert. You stopped your car at the stop sign and allowed Becky to cross the street."

☐ While on a field trip, make it a point to call the children's attention to safety rules. "We must go to the next corner in order to cross the street. There is a sign to tell us when it is safe to go."

☐ Invite police officers to visit the classroom. They can explain their duties and help the children understand the importance of following rules. Also, be sure to strengthen the knowledge that certain rules exist for the benefit of members of a group by guiding children's behavior when needed. State what the rule is and explain the limits. Accept the child's questioning of the rule—this helps them understand why the rule is necessary.

☐ Help the children recognize some of the symbols and ceremonies that represent our country without expecting them to memorize passages or understand their underlying meanings completely: Display the flag and explain what it means; play the national anthem before a special event; sing patriotic songs or read patriotic stories; have police badges or caps available for dramatic play; attend patriotic parades or special civic observances.

of today's critical problems are related to economics, so this subject should be made a part of the preschool curriculum. Seefeldt pointed out that "if all people had everything they wanted, then knowledge of economic concepts would not be so critical. But today there are critical differences between people's needs and the things they can have. The concept of scarcity—the difference between the unlimited wants of people and the limited goods,

---

ECONOMICS ACTIVITIES

After taking a trip to the bakery, you can develop these concepts:

☐ *Production.* Bakers use goods furnished by other people: milk, flour, sugar, shortening, and so on. The bakery is a source for many goods: bread, rolls, cakes, cookies, and so on. The work in the bakery is divided into specialized tasks for more efficient production.

☐ *Distribution.* The bakery sells some of the goods it prepares in its own store and distributes other goods to other stores. Many different workers help to get the baked goods from the bakery to the stores. Packaging, handling, and transportation are important elements of the distribution process.

☐ *Exchange.* The dealer uses attractive displays and advertisements to encourage people to buy his goods. Some dealers sell baked goods at lower prices than others. The price people pay is directly related to how expensive it is to produce the goods and how badly the people want them. Dealers make profits when they sell the goods to buyers.

☐ *Consumption.* We buy what we want after deciding what is wanted and needed most. We buy some things because they satisfy basic needs and others because they bring us enjoyment. We examine the goods carefully so that we can select those that give us the most for our money.

These concepts can be expanded on during most trips or other experiences that involve monetary exchange or the use of a person's services. For example, trips to grocery stores, toy stores, drugstores, construction sites, gasoline stations, train stations, farms, and dairies can all be used to develop economic concepts, along with related concepts in many other curricular areas.

Arrange the classroom environment into different areas that help children participate in activities involving the responsibilities of people who produce, distribute, exchange, or consume goods. For example, experimental play with plumbing equipment helps children understand the services rendered by plumbers. Woodworking activities involve the children in real work—similar to the type grown-ups do. A classroom ice cream store, clothing store, shoe store, grocery store, and so on place the children in the creative roles of customer and seller. Vivian Todd and Helen Heffernan illustrated one creative teacher's approach to this suggestion:

One day [the teacher] has individual cans of fruit juice and drinking straws for the children to purchase at the store at juice time. Another day, she provides the store with fresh carrots that are sold to feed the guinea pig and also to proservices, and materials available—is a major concern of economic education."[6]

The field of economics examines and describes the ways in which people produce, distribute, exchange, and consume goods or services. Although children have many opportunities to experience these concepts, a lack of explanation, continuity, or guidance may have left them with false understandings

---

vide carrot sticks at refreshment time. The day she reads from *I Want to Be a Storekeeper* [Carla Greene (Chicago: Children's Press, 1958)], the store has boxes of cereals for sale, and the children have refreshments of cereal flakes in a sandwich bag. When she uses the flannelboard to talk about good things to eat, she makes the children aware that their store does not sell candy. In short, she makes the store an integral part of the school program and the roles of the store personnel a reality to the children.[7]

Illustrate the advantages of division of labor as you assign two children the responsibility of preparing tables for snack time. The children can be led to understand that their work will probably go more smoothly if one child places all the cups and pitchers on the tables while the second child arranges the placemats and plates.

The understanding that our immediate wants and needs cannot always be immediately satisfied can be effectively communicated through creative classroom experiences: "I know you would like to use the shovel now, Chelsea. But Rhonda is using the only one we have. You will have to wait until she is finished." Similar comments can be shared with the children as economics-related experiences evolve in the classroom.

Also, you can make attractive gift package outlines from colorful construction paper. Encourage the children to search through catalogs or magazines and pick out the one or two gifts they would most like to have. They could then cut out their choices and paste them on the package outline. Stimulate discussion of the gift packages as the children complete their work.

Help the children appreciate the contributions of various workers within the community by capitalizing on the workers' eagerness to come to your classroom. Most telephone companies are willing to send a telephone installer to explain how the telephone works and to give the children an opportunity to talk to each other on real telephones that are connected and workable. Some companies even allow classrooms to keep these phones for short periods of time. The wee-ooo of a fire siren when the firetruck comes to the school brings excitement and motivation to learn about the responsibilities of a firefighter. If a delivery person brings your milk, ask him to arrange his schedule so that he and his truck can be seen by the children as the delivery is made. The ice cream vendor is another source of economic learnings. If possible, obtain some cash from the petty cash fund and give each child a quarter. Arrange one day for the vendor to stop at your school during snack time and sell the children some ice cream for which they will pay with their own money

Division of labor is experienced as one child rolls the cookie dough and the other stamps out the shapes.

or fragmented information. For example, many children resent being told no by a parent when they want a particular toy; they cannot understand why these unending fountains of cash refuse their important requests. To help them gain such basic understandings, a planned, organized presentation is essential. See the box on economics activities (p. 352).

Sociology

Sociology involves the study of people's apparent natural tendencies to live together in groups. Such group orientation is one of the foremost characteristics of human beings. Dorothy Skeel stated that the sociologist investigates the characteristic aspects of human groups such as "the family, school, church, and government. . . . He attempts to determine the influence of these groups upon their members—to recognize the behavioral changes . . . exhibited by the members. . . . He attempts to explain why members of a group behave as they do."[8]

Although forming groups appears to be a natural tendency in human behavior, young children start out in this world as anti-group-oriented beings. They are extremely self-centered—the only existence they are aware of is their own. Gradually, they seek contact with others in their environment, and, once they begin to develop language, they gain enough understanding to realize that they are not, indeed, alone in this world. Initial dependencies are directed toward the parents, but, by about three years of age, most children are spending less and less time with their parents and more and more time with other people, especially other children. From that point on, group orientations begin to have increasingly important control over their behavior. (Review Chapter 2 for a more complete discussion of this topic.)

Children need to be helped toward gaining an awareness of group membership and of the behaviors necessary for attaining effective group relationships. They must be led to do so through a great number of direct interpersonal experiences in all areas of the preschool curriculum. The best types of experiences are those that include a rich variety of play. Children's play can be characterized as a hierarchical, developmental process in which children gradually expand the quality and quantity of social interaction with other children. Mildred Parten's time-honored view of the developmental levels of socialized play are described below:[9]

1. *Solitary play.* The child plays alone. Even if other children are present, the child will play as if no one else were there.
2. *Onlooker play.* The child appears interested in the play of others as he watches them play. However, he continues at his own activity without actually joining the others. The only aspect of socialized behavior in this activity is a seeming interest in the activity of others.
3. *Parallel play.* The child is content to play near another child with similar toys or materials, but with no personal interaction. Occasionally, one child will look at the activity of the other, but they will not join together. The acts of sharing and taking turns expand the child's social orientation.
4. *Associative play.* The child plays along with another and shares play materials. The children are more aware of each other and talk to one another as they play. The social significance of this level lies in the fact that children are now beginning to speak and listen to each other for a purpose.
5. *Cooperative play.* The children are beginning to cooperate with one another and assume special individual roles in the activity. Specific rules may govern the activity expected of each child, and group—rather than

By sharing responsibilities for setting the lunch table, young children learn positive attitudes about an individual's contribution to the success of a group.

individual—goals guide their actions. The major social growth during this stage is the desire to work along with others toward a group goal and to participate within a framework of agreed-upon rules.

Some popular activities that can lead to effective membership in social groups are described in the sociology activities box.

Anthropology

Children begin to learn about anthropology when they experience the practices and traditions of various cultural groups: their art, music, institutions, beliefs, celebrations, and so on. Although the preschool child's world centers around himself, his home, and his school, and he demonstrates a strong interest in learning more about those who are close to him, he is also beginning to indicate a budding fascination for the lives of other people, people from backgrounds similar to his own as well as those whose backgrounds are quite different. Such motivation may come from exposure to a diversity of backgrounds within the preschool center or from within the child's own neighborhood. Regardless of its cause, however, the important consideration is that the interest is beginning to grow from within the child.

SOCIOLOGY ACTIVITIES

☐ Give children opportunities to share, either in pairs or in larger groups, common classroom chores: setting the table for a snack, feeding the animals, watering the plants, or filling the paint jars. In this way, they develop strong feelings of their own self-worth, and positive feelings about helpful contributions to the group.

☐ Create a climate that encourages peer cooperation—praise or reward behaviors that contribute to the welfare of the group. A pat on the back and warm words of praise, for example, for Matt and Marty when Matt helped Marty turn a screw into a block of wood encourage similar group-oriented behaviors in the future.

☐ Help the children accept each other into various play activities within the classroom. Comments such as, "Let's go to the doll corner and see if they need a doctor to look after the sick baby," can help some children approach others.

☐ Arrange periods during the day in which children work together toward the completion of a group activity. Examples of activities requiring group cooperation include: (1) playing group games such as Duck, Duck, Goose; (2) completing murals or other large art projects; (3) cooking projects; (4) planting and keeping up a garden; (5) singing songs, telling stories, or doing fingerplays; and (6) building with blocks.

ANTHROPOLOGY ACTIVITIES

- Read or tell stories that describe the lives of people in other cultures. The following books are only a few of the many excellent stories for young children: *Homes* by Virginia Parsons, *Little Leo* by Leo Politi, *Meet Miki Tabino* by Helen Copeland, *The Little House* by Virginia Lee Burton, *Nine Days to Christmas* by Marie Hall Ets and Aurora Labastida, *The Story About Ping* by Marjorie Flack, *Wee Gillis* by Munro Leaf, and *Crow Boy* by Taro Yashima.

- Invite guest speakers into your room. Special information and great enthusiasm can be generated by an effective speaker who has a great deal of information and/or concrete materials to share. Often, cultural or ethnic community centers provide speakers for such purposes.

- Visit museums, cultural or ethnic centers, or historical societies that offer concrete experiences with other cultures. Large cities, especially, have museums where children can learn about the lives of people from many backgrounds.

- Introduce games and toys that represent the types of recreation enjoyed by children in this country and throughout the world. This popular game from the Congo is a good rhythm and movement activity. Gather the children into a circle and designate one child who is "It." Begin clapping rhythmically and encourage the children to join you. While everyone is clapping, "It" stands in front of someone and does some steps in rhythm to the clapping. The person he faces must then imitate the exact foot movements of "It." If he fails, he becomes "It" and proceeds in the same manner with someone else. If the child imitates "It" exactly, "It" must move on to someone else and repeat the procedure until he defeats someone.

- Encourage children to sample a variety of foods associated with various cultures. Preparing such foods will often interest children to try them, especially if the foods from different cultures are experienced each day in a natural setting. Stay away from the temptation of treating the children as if they are going to eat something that is strange or different. Try tortillas, bagels, fry bread, and so on.

- Celebrate popular local or national holidays. Some days during the school year are *especially* noteworthy (although *each* day in the preschool should be noteworthy) because of their significance to the child. By being given opportunities to observe such important days, young children are provided with the most popular means of sharing cultural customs and traditions within their preschool setting. Special songs, stories, food treats, poems, or art projects add to the observance of special days; parents or volunteers can serve as resource persons or additional supervisory help for special projects. Some special days and their customary traditions are given in the following sections. In order not to offend any single cultural group, only those special days having general national exposure are used for illustration. Of course, the suggestions can easily be applied to other observances.

Therefore, it becomes the teacher's responsibility to develop a system of instruction in which the various contributions of cultural groups, including those represented in the preschool setting, can be recognized. The cultural heritage of all children should be handled in a natural way as an integral part of each day's activities. Suggestions for initiating such instruction are given in the anthropology activities box on page 357.

HALLOWEEN   The popular tradition of dressing in costumes and masks should be approached extremely carefully with preschool children because they often have a great deal of difficulty separating reality from fantasy. Therefore, the well-meaning teacher who "surprises" the children dressed as

HALLOWEEN-RELATED ACTIVITIES

☐ Visit a farm having apple or nut trees or grapes ready for harvest. Have each child pick enough to fill a small bag. Share their collections at snack time.

☐ Visit a cider mill and bring back a fresh gallon of cider for snack or mealtime.

☐ Bring to the classroom a large pumpkin suitable for decoration, or visit a pumpkin farm where the children can select their own. Have the children cut open the top of the pumpkin, reach inside, and scoop out the slimy seeds. Making pumpkin pie from the meat or drying out the seeds for spring planting (or for eating) can be valuable follow-up suggestions, depending on the level of your children. Tempera paint can be used to decorate the pumpkin shell as a group activity.

☐ Read or tell stories of Halloween or pumpkins.

☐ Bake cookies in the shape of pumpkins. Children may cover them with orange frosting and decorate them with chocolate chips or raisins.

☐ Make orange gelatin and serve for a snack.

☐ Arrange the dramatic play center with a variety of Halloween costumes or accessories.

☐ As a visual discrimination activity when children are dressed in Halloween costumes, ask each child to say a simple phrase such as "trick or treat." The other children must guess the identity of the speaker.

☐ Use orange and black paint at the easel or finger-painting table.

☐ Make paper plate masks for those children who may feel uncomfortable with a traditional mask. Attach a popsicle stick to a decorated plate so the children can cover and uncover their faces whenever they feel like it.

☐ Make trick or treat bags as large group art projects. Use orange and black paper (either with plain or fringed edges) and crayon-drawn cats, owls, or pumpkins to decorate a shopping bag.

☐ Create joyful songs or fingerplays to share with the children, such as this verse sung to the tune of "Frère Jacques":

> Ghosts and goblins,
> Ghosts and goblins,
> Halloween, Halloween.
> Today's the day for ghosts,
> And for little goblins,
> Halloween, Halloween.

a scary "skeleton" with a mask and costume may be greeted with sobs and tears rather than with joyful laughter. These young children are at an age where they are not quite sure whether or not a "real skeleton" walked in, and that uncertainty could cause traumatic reactions. However, if dressing up is shared in an atmosphere of play and fun, the children will have a great deal of enjoyment because they know they are safe.

You may wish to consider the suggestions for Halloween-related activities given in the box.

THANKSGIVING Because of their difficulty with time concepts, the historical aspects of Thanksgiving should be avoided with young children. But since the traditionally special meal is so widely accepted, having the group prepare and share it can be a very meaningful activity. However, try to stay away from celebrating the meal after dressing the children in feathers, Pilgrim's hats, buckskin vests, and other time-worn paraphernalia. This practice often leads to unwarranted stereotypes and confusion about the holiday itself.[10] Let them participate in the preparation of their meal by helping to make the stuffing and to place it into the turkey. They can also make cranberry sauce, prepare applesauce, dice the vegetables, and bake the bread. After the food has been prepared, the entire class can sit together and eat the meal. During the meal, the teacher can lead conversations emphasizing thankfulness and friendship. Other appropriate Thanksgiving-time activities are described in the box.

HANUKKAH Hanukkah is an eighty-day Jewish holiday that comes in either November or December, on the twenty-fifth day of the Hebrew month *Kislev*. It is a solemn festival celebrating religious freedom for the Jews. Traditional components of the celebration include:

THANKSGIVING-TIME ACTIVITIES

☐ Arrange a trip to a turkey farm. Examine turkey feathers. Note how they differ from feathers of other birds.

☐ Read stories or sing songs with special Thanksgiving flavor. Creative movement can add to the fun; ask the children to strut like a turkey while they sing the "Gobble, gobble, gobble" of a song's lyrics.

☐ Involve children in creative art projects, such as making mosaics from seeds, grasses, or corn.

☐ Encourage children to portray Thanksgiving customs at the dramatic play corner.

☐ Discuss things that the children are thankful for.

☐ Direct the children to stuff a small, lunch-type paper bag with newspaper and to wrap a red pipe cleaner around the top. They should allow a portion of the cleaner to hang down. Then, using red tempera paint, they paint the turkey's head. Colored construction paper strips are glued to the back of the bag to form a colorful tail.

---

1. The *menorah*, a special candleholder with eight branches and a place for a smaller candle called the *shamash*. The shamash is lit first and is then used to light the other candles. Starting on the right and moving to the left, one candle is lit the first night, two the second, and so on until there are nine (including the shamash) in the menorah on the last night.
2. The *dreidel*, a four-sided top that is enjoyed by the children. There is one Hebrew letter printed on each side, collectively reading, "A Great Miracle Happened There," referring to the first Hanukkah when only one little jar of oil lit the holy lamp in the temple for eight days.
3. *Gelt*, coins often given as gifts to the children, one each night. Although Hanukkah often occurs during the Christmas season and gifts are exchanged for both celebrations, Hanukkah should not be referred to as the Jewish Christmas.

Some activities appropriate for Hanukkah are found in the Hanukkah activities box.

CHRISTMAS   Although this holiday has become overcommercialized and ostentatious over the past few years, children nevertheless look forward to this day more than any other day except, in some instances, to their

---

HANUKKAH ACTIVITIES

☐ Display a menorah, dreidel, or gelt along with pictures in a special area of the room.

☐ Invite a Jewish parent or a rabbi to share the traditions of Hanukkah with the children.

☐ Make dreidels from styrofoam blocks through which dowels have been inserted and held in place by glue. The four sides of the dreidel should have these symbols:

THERE
WAS
GREAT
MIRACLE

☐ Play a dreidel game by giving each child a number of nuts. Each child places one nut in the center of the group. Taking turns, the children each spin the dreidel. If the first symbol faces up, that child puts a nut in the center; the second symbol, the child gets half the nuts; the third symbol, the child gets nothing; and the fourth symbol, the child wins all.

☐ Visit a nearby Jewish temple or synagogue.

☐ Make potato *latkes* (pancakes) for a snack during Hanukkah. Latkes are traditionally eaten during Hanukkah.

☐ Use the dreidel in any classroom games normally requiring a spinner or dice.

☐ Use sponge prints to make Hanukkah decorations.

birthday. Naturally, the gifts and special holiday magic have a great deal to do with this extremely popular holiday. However, because the children in your preschool facility may be from various ethnic backgrounds or non-Christian homes, it may be wise to emphasize winter customs and the spirit of giving that accompanies Christmas-time, rather than its religious significance. Only if your school is affiliated with a Christian church-related organization should you stress the religious aspect of Christmas—but don't start too early. Having a tree for three weeks, for example, makes it hard for the children to wait and may overstimulate them to the point of frustrating the teacher. Some activities that can be used to enhance the holiday season are described in the Christmas-time activities box.

Some Spanish Americans or Mexican Americans celebrate *Las Posadas* beginning on December 16 as a re-enactment of Joseph and Mary's trip to Bethlehem. The celebration often includes the whole community in feasts, parades, and other festivities. Much of the celebration is like Christmas, but special customs characterize Las Posadas; chief among these is a nightly search of homes to see where statues of Joseph and Mary could be housed. Prearranged, such a home is found on the ninth night (Christmas Eve) where

---

CHRISTMAS-TIME ACTIVITIES

☐ Decorate the Christmas tree with creative ornaments made by the children. Stringing popcorn, using glue and glitter on pine cones (or styrofoam balls), or fashioning paper chains are tree decorating suggestions that have been used by preschool teachers over the years.

☐ Read fanciful stories (such as Moore's *The Night Before Christmas*) or sing lively songs (such as *Jingle Bells*) that reflect the spirit of the holiday season. Asking the children to prance like reindeer, flitter like snowflakes, or laugh like Santa adds to the joyfulness of such activities.

☐ Make special handmade gifts for parents or for janitors, cooks, and other support personnel in your preschool facility. For example, napkin rings can be easily constructed by most four- and five-year-olds. Cut paper towel rolls into

1-inch sections. Cut several 1-inch strips from construction paper, long enough to wrap completely around the sections. Have the children cut a bell, tree, or any seasonal design out of construction paper and glue it to the strip of construction paper. Then have them staple the paper strip to the roll and insert a seasonal paper napkin.

☐ Have a special Christmas party with class-made cookies, milk, and, perhaps, a scoop of ice cream. If desired, a parent may be asked to dress as Santa and entertain the children as they listen to stories or sing carols. Special inexpensive gifts may be shared.

☐ Visit a senior citizens' home or hospital. Sing one or two carols or perform a simple seasonal skit that will entertain those who are away from their normal home life during the holidays.

Seasonal themes can be effectively adapted to nearly all areas of the early child-hood curriculum.

coffee, punch, wine, tortillas, tamales, and other special foods are served. Special experiences designed to communicate the characteristics of Las Posadas include the following:

- Make *piñatas.* Fill them with wrapped candy or nuts and small unbreakable toys. Children are blindfolded, spun around one by one a time or two, and given chances to swing a stick to break the piñata.
- Invite a Spanish American or Mexican American parent to your classroom to explain Las Posadas.
- Prepare tortillas, tamales, or other traditional foods.
- Read stories of Las Posadas to the children (see Marie Hall Ets and Aurora Labastida, *Nine Days to Christmas* [New York: Viking, 1959]).
- Provide materials and costumes for the dramatic play area so the children can play out the events of Las Posadas.

VALENTINE'S DAY   This holiday is especially appropriate for young children because it deals with one of the most pervading attributes of the young child's life: love. The time-honored tradition of sending and receiving Valentine's Day cards makes this day especially valuable for studying the mail system. Valentines can be made by the children out of precut hearts for their parents and put into envelopes; the envelopes can be stamped and addressed to their parents by the teacher. Then, a trip to the post office, where the children can see the envelopes cancelled and routed into the proper channels can be a valuable field trip activity. Other appropriate Valentine's Day activities include:

- A Valentine's Day party where the children prepare heart-shaped Jello molds, cakes, or cookies for treats is always a happy experience. Valentines can be exchanged, but be sure that each child brings one for every member in the room. Since most of the children will be unable to read or write, it is not necessary to address the cards.

☐   Craft activities can be used to design a gift to take home for a parent or other member of the family. Provide heavy cardboard tracers for one large heart and one small heart. The children trace around the large shape onto white construction paper and around the small shape onto red construction paper to form the basic ingredients for a placemat. The red heart can be glued on top of the white heart, and the entire product decorated with glitter, stickers, or frilly paper.

EASTER   Usually signalling the coming of spring, Easter is a delightful time of the year for the preschool child. Buds can be seen popping out on trees, bulbs poke their way through the cold ground, and birds twitter as they build their nests. An awareness of these wonders of nature helps the child later understand the religious significance of Easter and Passover when and if those holidays are observed by his family. However, at this early period of their lives, children seem more concerned about the Easter Bunny, little chicks, and candy. Therefore, they should be given opportunities to enjoy the season through a variety of enjoyable activities in the classroom. See some suggestions in the Easter-time activities box on page 364.

OTHER SPECIAL DAYS   Patriotic days such as Columbus Day, Lincoln's and Washington's birthdays, Martin Luther King, Jr. Day, or other special cultural or ethnic observances stimulate an appreciation for our community or country. Teachers may focus on patriotic stories, songs, or special trips to parades or displays in order to stress the way in which the accomplishments of great people are observed.

Other special days such as Earth Day reflect different concerns. Cleaning the playground or planting a sapling may help the children become aware of the growing concern for the total environment.

Contemporary concerns demand that equal treatment of all ethnic groups and cultures represented in American society be stressed. Learning about the traditions of the many groups in the country helps foster greater interpersonal understanding as well as increased self-pride. It is imperative, then, that preschool teachers seize upon opportunities to share days that are important for different groups within the framework of the activities suggested earlier. The Chinese New Year, St. Lucia's Day, Tanabata, Mardi Gras, Kwanza, and other special days should be recognized and integrated into the school day. Often, children will experience difficulty understanding the significance of holidays they have never observed before, but it is still important to include a variety of holidays so children are made aware of and are exposed to other important celebrations. Creative teaching suggestions and further information concerning holidays can be easily found in teacher resource guides.

The basic content, then, for social studies comes from the six social sciences: history, geography, civics, economics, sociology, and anthropology. As a preschool teacher, you will have many opportunities to "teach" anthropology but, as you can see from our previous discussion, you will not be doing so at 9:30 in the morning under the heading of "anthropology period." Anthropology, like each of the other social sciences, is an area that can cohesively integrate other areas of the curriculum. In other words, it furnishes the content, or raw material, necessary for the child to be able to play purposefully with blocks, create an art project, or sing and listen to stories. Betty L. Broman explained: "The social studies are one of the two content areas of instruction (the other is science); therefore, whenever you are teaching a skill subject (language arts or math, for example) generally you are teaching social studies at the same time. Social studies is the 'glue' that bonds together the elements of the curriculum for young children."[11]

The present approach to teaching the content of social studies has been patterned after the time-honored "here and now" philosophy advocated by Lucy Sprague Mitchell[12] and the "object-oriented" practical philosophy of Caroline Pratt.[13] Repulsed by the historically popular technique of making the children memorize social studies facts about things they had absolutely

---

EASTER-TIME ACTIVITIES

□ Easter-time signals the beginning of spring and the reawakening of plant and animal life. Have the children plan their own flower or vegetable gardens, select the seeds, and look after the plants as they grow.

□ This is an excellent time to introduce pets to your classroom, if you do not yet have any. The care and feeding of pets is an important part of any child's preschool experience.

□ Color hard-boiled eggs with a food dye solution. Refrigerate the eggs. At an Easter party, the children can peel the eggs and eat them. Use the discarded shells for a group art activity—make a mosaic design with colored egg shells and glue.

□ Read or tell stories (*The Runaway Bunny* by Margaret Wise Brown [New York: Harper & Row, 1977]) or sing special Easter songs (*Peter Cottontail*).

□ Hatching chicken or duck eggs in a classroom incubator is both challenging and enjoyable.

□ Craft activities offer creative ways for children to make special Easter gifts for loved ones. For instance, you can poke a small hole with a compass into half of an egg shell. Have the child paint the shell with tempera paint and push a pipe cleaner through the hole, bending the inside end slightly to keep it in place. Then have the child place his flower(s) into an empty film container vase filled halfway with plaster of paris. When the plaster of paris hardens, the flower will stand rigidly in place.

no experience of, these educators sought to make the subject serve a real function in the school. Influenced by John Dewey, they argued that the first step in the education of all young children was to help them experience things for themselves. Mitchell's "here and now" philosophy, for example, stressed that anything that was given to the child outside the realm of direct experience and observation was dangerous. Therefore, she recommended "here and now," firsthand experiences for young children—trips, objects, and resource persons. Caroline Pratt stressed that the real function of the school was to provide the child with practical experiences (projects) that would serve to integrate all the subjects taught (this is similar to Broman's description of the role of social studies). Pratt felt that through useful activities and emotional support, the child would build a foundation of practical skills that would serve him all throughout his life.

Because of this stress on direct experience and involvement in the preschool social studies program, three direct contact sources are identified as essential for all teachers: *taking field trips, utilizing resource persons,* and *examining real things.*

FIELD TRIPS AND RESOURCE PERSONS

Field Trips

Field trips present an opportunity for students to observe people and places being studied and thereby clarify and extend major concepts. Field trips can be considered either highly concrete or highly abstract, depending

Field trips to new and exciting places provide young children with firsthand experiences essential for effective learning.

on the degree of participation the child experiences in the events being observed. If the child is encouraged to ask questions, manipulate materials, or participate in an activity, the trip can be considered a concrete experience. In most field trips, however, the child assumes the role of a passive observer, and the field trip assumes a more abstract character. The teacher should attempt to make a field trip experience as concrete as possible.

Field trips comprise some of the most exciting learning activities for preschoolers. These children have a tremendous need for direct experiences that help clarify their thinking and form sound foundations for later conceptual growth, and worthwhile field trips help provide such opportunities.

Your first field trip with a group of youngsters should be taken after they have been in school long enough to have become familiar with the teachers, the other children, and their surroundings. Once they feel safe in their "home" environment, they can be taken on short walking trips to places not far from the school. Always be on the lookout for inviting opportunities: a construction site, road construction, a neighborhood fair, community agencies, and the like. Special cues from the children themselves may help you choose these brief trips—firefighters in the dramatic play corner or construction workers "building" a house on the playground show interest in these areas. As increasingly longer trips are planned, there are special considerations that must be followed. The checklist in Figure 9-1 enumerates some of the special considerations involved in planning preschool field trips.

In addition to careful planning of all phases of a field trip, it is advisable to extend courtesy and appreciation by sending group-dictated letters of thanks to all persons involved—chaperones, resource people, bus driver, school nurse, and supervisor. Letter writing can be done in the early years by asking the children to express their thoughts to you. As the children dictate their thank-you message, the teacher may write it on a chart. If any of the children are able to write, they can copy the letter and send it to the designated person. A strong personal touch is associated with the letter when it is handwritten by the children.

One additional point worth remembering is that it is helpful to compile a schoolwide file of successful field trips. This file can be kept in the supervisor's office or in the teacher's room and referred to when desired. Information should be compiled in summary form and stored on a file card like the one in Figure 9-2.

Resource Persons

Resource persons are individuals either within or outside the school who may have certain expertise, experience, skill, or knowledge in a field of special interest to the class. Generally, children enjoy contact with outside visitors and the contributions and interesting materials they share. In studying topics related to the neighborhood or community, for example, much insight can be gained from persons who provide goods or services in the specific area—police officer, firefighter, farmer, delivery person, construction worker, doctor, nurse, newsperson, baker, industrial worker, store worker,

FIELD TRIP CHECKLIST

PRETRIP EVALUATION

☐ I am familiar with the location to be visited.
☐ This trip is suitable for the maturity level of my children.

TEACHER PREPARATION

☐ My supervisor has been notified of the trip.
☐ Administrative approval has been secured in writing.
☐ Parental permission slips have been signed.
☐ Transportation has been arranged.
☐ Proper supervision has been planned (a 1-5 adult-child ratio is ideal).
☐ Toilet facilities are present at the location to be visited.
☐ Clothing requirements have been communicated to the parents.
☐ Safety rules were communicated to the children:
  • Stay together in a group.
  • Walk with a friend.
  • Stay on the sidewalk.
  • Cross only with the green light.

TEACHER-CHILD PLANNING

☐ The children are familiar (but not too familiar) with where they are going.
☐ Points of interest have been shared.
☐ Individual and group responsibilities have been assigned.

THE TRIP

☐ All children can see and hear.
☐ I offer cues and comments to stimulate the children's interest.
☐ I am constantly aware of special problems or emergency situations.

FOLLOW-UP ACTIVITY

☐ informal discussion of the trip
☐ art projects related to the trip
☐ group experience charts
☐ creative dramatics
☐ bulletin board display

Figure 9-1   Checklist for preparing preschool field trips.

```
Place name:

Address:

Phone:

Name of person to contact:

Best time to call:

Admission charge:

Number of people accommodated:

Time required:

Experiences available:
```

Figure 9-2   Field trip information form.

craftsperson, lawyer, banker, clergy, government official, and so on. When introducing children to different cultures or ethnic groups, people with appropriate backgrounds can provide information and answer questions. As with field trips, careful planning is essential for a successful visit by a resource person:

1. Determine whether inviting a visitor is the best way to get the intended knowledge and information.
2. Determine whether the speaker's topic and style of delivery are suitable to the maturity level of the children.
3. Inform the speaker about such matters as the age level of the children, the needs of the children, the time allotted for the presentation, and the facilities available.
4. Follow-up and discussion related to the speaker's presentation should be provided. Discussion, reporting, art projects, dramatization, creative writing, and further reading are all suggestions for summarizing and extending the information.
5. A joint evaluation is, of course, suggested as a means of judging the effectiveness of the speaker and the audience.
6. A letter of thanks is highly recommended as a gesture of appreciation and gratitude.

Special speakers are often very willing to share their accomplishments with children. The problem is that teachers often do not know where to find them. Many teachers solve this problem by sending questionnaires home with their children. An example of such a questionnaire is given in Figure 9-3.

Many times, interested schools or parent–teacher organizations keep a centralized card file of persons from throughout the community who are willing to share their expertise, including those who can help break down stereotypes, such as senior citizens with special skills or hobbies, women carpenters, male nurses, and so on. The card file can be organized by subject listing, and all teachers can use it as a ready reference. Care must be exercised, though, in the way contributors are solicited as possible classroom speakers. The practice of sending request forms throughout the community, for example, is a questionable procedure since a small number of persons who have little or no immediate usefulness may volunteer. Undesirable public relations problems may result as these persons may never be called upon to speak. The safest approach seems to be requesting recommendations from other teachers, involved parents, and other school personnel. In this way, you will be able to select speakers that will inform and motivate your children about a variety of new jobs and experiences.

DEPICTIONS OF REALITY

Teachers cannot possibly expect to bridge the extreme gaps of time and space in order to expose their children to direct experiences as each social

```
Area of knowledge:
Preferred age level:



Name:
Address:
Phone:



Days available:
Hours available:



Is it best for us to visit you, or are you willing to come to our classroom?


```

Figure 9-3 Special speaker questionnaire.

studies concept unfolds. However, children can have experiences with reality when real objects and events, or their representations, are introduced to the classroom. Children benefit immensely when they are able to touch and personally examine items such as clothing, cooking utensils, food, tableware, games, and ornaments of a certain people, country, or region under study. In a unit on transportation, for example, children's concepts were enriched when they manipulated and observed models of animals, carriages, automobiles, trucks, airplanes, bicycles, and so on, which were displayed as representatives of major modes of travel.

Similar real objects or models can be viewed in or obtained from many sources. Perhaps the most valuable sources for these materials are parents or other interested people in the community. Many parents or other citizens are happy to lend mementos they collected on trips to various parts of the world. Also, you may wish to explore such possibilities as museums, industries, travel centers, worship centers, theatrical supply houses, or specialty stores. Your children will exhibit an increased enthusiasm for learning as they become involved with real things in realistic settings.

SOME FINAL THOUGHTS

Building on content from science and the social studies, children are ultimately led to increasingly sophisticated understandings of their physical and social worlds. The preschool classroom is an excellent context from which to investigate the basic concepts related to these fields and to develop necessary attitudes of respect and concern for their social and physical environments. Both areas are sensitive and complex—they present a formidable challenge to you because of their immense possibilities. Accept that challenge and try your best to develop a unique program that meets the needs and interests of those trusted to your professional charge.

NOTES

1. Carol Seefeldt, *A Curriculum for Child Care Centers* (Columbus, Ohio: Charles E. Merrill, 1974), pp. 176–177.
2. G. Craig, *Science for the Elementary School Teacher* (Boston: Ginn and Company, 1947), p. 60.
3. K. Wann, M. Dorn, and E. Liddle, *Fostering Intellectual Development in Young Children* (New York: Teachers College Press, Bureau of Publications, Columbia University, 1962), p. 53.
4. John Jarolimek, *Social Studies in Elementary Education* (New York: Macmillan, 1971), p. 258.

5. Katherine H. Read, *The Nursery School* (Philadelphia: W.B. Saunders, 1971), p. 315.

6. Carol Seefeldt, *Social Studies for the Preschool-Primary Child* (Columbus, Ohio: Charles E. Merrill, 1977), p. 125.

7. Vivian Edmiston Todd and Helen Heffernan, *The Years Before School*, 2d ed. (New York: Macmillan, 1970), p. 280.

8. Dorothy J. Skeel, *The Challenge of Teaching Social Studies in the Elementary School* (Pacific Palisades, Calif.: Goodyear, 1974), p. 21.

9. Mildred Parten, "Social Participation Among Preschool Children," *Journal of Abnormal and Social Psychology* 33, no. 2 (April 1932): 243–269.

10. See Patricia G. Ramsey, "Beyond Ten Little Indians and Turkeys," *Young Children* 34, no. 6 (September 1979): 28–51.

11. Betty L. Broman, *The Early Years in Childhood Education* (Chicago: Rand McNally College Publishing, 1978), p. 192.

12. Lucy Sprague Mitchell, *Young Geographers* (New York: John Day, 1934).

13. Caroline Pratt, *Experimental Practice in City and Country Schools* (New York: Dutton, 1924).

10

Creative Development: Encouraging the Spirit of Wonder and Magic

JACK AND JILL WENT UP THE HILL TO FETCH A PAIL OF WATER

ELL DOWN
YE HI

Copyright 1978,
The Register and Tribune
Syndicate, Inc

"I'm gonna fetch a glass of water."

Creative youngsters enjoy expressing their ideas in unique ways. (*The Family Circus* by Bil Keane courtesy of The Register and Tribune Syndicate, Inc.)

Joel enthusiastically turned to the easel to begin his favorite activity. He started to paint a warm, rich winter scene. His smiles and expressions of strong involvement indicated deep thought and careful planning—almost as if he were saying to himself, "This is a special picture because it is all mine." When it was completed, Joel stepped back to admire his work of art. With pleasure sweeping his face, Joel showed his picture to his best friend, Arthur. Both boys giggled and chatted as they surveyed the scene. All was going well until a strong voice intervened, "Whoever heard of a green sun? Do your picture over again and paint the sun yellow. I won't let you take home such a silly picture."

Later that day, Terri and Shana secluded themselves in a distant corner of the playground, participating in an activity that both seemed to greatly enjoy—expressing their thoughts to each other in spontaneous, colorful

language. "Look at that blue bird," said Terri, "wouldn't it be funny to see a green
checkered bird?" Shana laughed, "A green checkered bird? It would have to come
from a green checkered egg!" The two girls continued to talk using joyful similar
expressions. Their attention was focused on their surroundings, but their
thoughts were running off into highly fanciful directions. Their kindergarten
teacher, sensing the value of such imaginative thought as a means of developing
creative self-expression, listened to the children and encouraged their verbal
explorations. However, when it became time to move indoors, Mr. Carling
announced, "The fun is over now, girls. It's time to go in and do our reading."

Many children enjoy fanciful experiences like these. They love to participate in activities where their minds are allowed to wander—seeking to find
new relationships between the known and the unknown, experimenting with
knowledge in new ways, or producing something in their own unique, original manner. Adults, however, often become confused about such common
childhood endeavors and frown upon such originality with comments such
as, "Stop that *silliness*," or "Do it the *right way*." Such rigidity has a powerful
influence on the child's confidence as well as on his willingness to try something new. Joel, for example, may now hesitate to join the others in a group
finger-painting activity directed by the teacher because of the crushing experience he had. "What if I don't make a picture like my teacher wants?" may
begin to characterize his thinking whenever new projects or activities are
initiated.

Whenever children express their thoughts or actions in inventive, self-
initiated, original ways, we say that they are *creative* children. Creative think-
ers are those who produce truly unique reactions to their environment. The
reactions may be similar to those discovered by millions of children before
them, but the characteristic that makes any reaction creative is that it was
new to them. This may show up in infants as they discover different ways to
play with their toys or in adults as they seek to find an easier way to perform
a household chore. Each person has some unique way of meeting a situation,
but some people apparently feel freer to search for and express their unique
ideas than do others. E. Paul Torrance feels that a great deal of what contributes to a person's ultimate ability to exhibit open-ended, original thinking as opposed to rigid, closed-ended thinking occurs in the school:

> Creative imagination during early childhood seems to reach a peak between four-
> and four-and-a-half years, and is followed by a drop at about age five when the
> child enters school for the first time. This drop has generally been regarded as the
> inevitable phenomenon in nature. There are now indications, however, that this
> drop in five-year-olds is a man-made rather than a natural phenomenon.[1]

Some people argue that this phenomenon occurs because schools begin to
clamp down and limit the freedom of children during the kindergarten year.
"You're acting like a two-year-old," or "What do you think you are—a
clown?" and similar sarcastic put-downs often accompany adventuresome,
unique attempts at self-expression. Most children eventually conform to the

Young children have rich imaginations and love to express their thoughts in creative ways.

growing rigidity of the school structure, but a few are reluctant to change —they clearly keep a "bit of that child" within them as they continue to meet life's challenges in independent, adventurous ways.

The noted Russian psychologist, Kornei Chukovsky, believes that creative thought is extremely important since "without imaginative fantasy there would be complete stagnation in both physics and chemistry, because the formulation of new hypotheses, the invention of new implements, the discovery of new methods of experimental research, the conjecturing of new chemical fusions—all these are products of imagination and fantasy."[2] Sidney Parnes added these thoughts: "We must cultivate talent in the way soil nurtures a seed. It provides for the growth of the seed but it does not tell the seed what to become."[3] Arnold Toynbee warns Americans that a lack of emphasis on creativity in our schools could cause dire results:

If America is to treasure and foster all the creative ability that she has in her, a new and bright spirit of change has to be injected into her educational philosophy. The rather rigid egalitarian models of educational selection and treatment, which seem to me to be tenaciously held by the . . . majority of American people, will, I should press, have to be refashioned to include the creative talents of the coming generation. . . . New educational philosophies and new institutions of learning need to be constructed to provide an opportunity for creative individuals to enhance their talents in schools.[4]

Some highly creative people, including Einstein and Edison, were considered dunces by their teachers because they would not (or could not) conform to the inflexible patterns of thought expected by the teachers. V. Goertzel and Mildred Goertzel, in their study of over 400 eminent people, most of whom would be regarded as highly creative, estimated that 60 percent had serious school problems.[5] Those are only a few who had the persistence to "stick it out." But what has happened to the thousands of youngsters who surrendered their creative urges to conformity and, therefore, were never encouraged or allowed to make significant creative contributions to society? Teachers and parents should be highly concerned about such questions, as well as about providing encouragement and activity to help salvage neglected and wasted human resources. Let's explore more deeply the characteristics of creative behavior in preschool children.

CREATIVE BEHAVIOR OF PRESCHOOL CHILDREN

Perhaps the most significant studies of creativity in preschool children were those conducted by E. Paul Torrance of the University of Georgia.[6] His developmental and experimental studies were concerned with the characteristics of creative behavior in four- and five-year olds. You should be aware of these characteristics so that you are able to arrange your environment in ways that encourage such patterns in all children. A sketch of his tentative conclusions and exemplary excerpts follows.

Creative preschool children learn in creative ways. They enjoy experimenting, manipulating, and playing. They ask questions, make guesses, and offer their findings—sometimes quickly and emotionally, at other times tentatively and quietly.

Wilfredo always enjoyed participating in the various learning activities arranged about the room, and today was no exception. Moving to the science area, he quickly became engrossed in the manipulation of sound jars—glass containers filled to different levels with water. Each container, when struck with a small mallet, produced a different pitch. Wilfredo experimented with the various jars for some time until he discovered a pattern. Running to the teacher and asking her to come, he proudly announced, "Listen, here's the song we were singing before—I learned a song, I learned a song!" and plunked away at the first few notes of "Jingle Bells." "Oh, that's wonderful, Wilfredo," replied the teacher, "How did you learn?" "It was easy," he replied, "I just figured it out."

In similar ways, young children will always try to make sense out of their environment by seeking out things that are wrong or missing or by finding answers to things they don't understand. They are uncomfortable until they do something about inconsistencies in their lives. You will find these children saying, "I'll have to figure this out," when faced with situations such as finishing a puzzle, moving a heavy object, building with blocks, or watching snow melt.

Creative preschool children have amazingly long attention spans when involved in creative endeavors. Although many "experts" have established 15 minutes as the maximum attention span of a preschooler for one activity, Torrance found that creative youngsters were able to concentrate on creative tasks for as long as 30 minutes and, in some cases, for as long as 60 minutes at one time. For that reason, he recommends that children be allowed to continue with exciting activities even though the curriculum calls for something else. This point is illustrated in the following incident related by one of Torrance's students:

> A three-year-old on a walk with the class was shown a snail. Completely fascinated, he spent the remaining school time (one-and-one-half hours) observing and touching the snail, rather to my annoyance, but I let him alone while the rest of us went on with crafts. The child consequently became so interested in nature's small creatures that at age five he is quite an authority on small creatures. He approaches them stealthily and while looking for lizards practically looked a rattlesnake in the eyes. He immediately recognized it and retreated just as quietly and was unharmed.[7]

Reading this excerpt brought to mind the comments of one teacher who remarked about a creatively talented youngster in her room: "If that boy should live to be a man, and an opportunity given for the exercise of his talents, few names will be greater than his."

Creative children have a surprising capacity for organization. Although these children can tolerate disorder for short periods of time, they demonstrate a need for orderliness and have strong capacities for organizing their environment. They want things to be organized and have a real interest and talent for making sure they are.

> *The block building corner was the center of activity this morning for Gina and Yi-Ming, two exceptionally talented four-year-olds. They cooperatively created a block building that was to represent an indoor swimming pool, planning and coordinating their efforts all along the way. The combination of blocks was decided upon after great periods of discussion and deliberation. Once completed, both children stood back and joyfully examined their majestic creation. "Isn't it nice?" asked Yi-Ming. "Yep—and we did it by ourselves," answered Gina, "It looks just like the pool at the YMCA." "Oh, . . ." thought Yi-Ming out loud, "but where will the people go in? We forgot the door!" Gina examined the structure for a minute and then offered a suggestion. "We can't put it there," complained Yi-Ming, "the water will leak out. Let's think this out." Both children studied the structure, offered alternative solutions, and finally came up with a plan that met their satisfaction. "It sure pays to think," offered Gina as they finally approved their structure.*

Gina and Yi-Ming demonstrated a strong ability to organize their efforts in their team construction of a large building, as well as in their formulation of a solution to their problem situation. They recognized that they needed to act in an organized manner if they were going to accomplish their task and took almost as much pride in their ability to organize their problem-solving efforts as in their final creation.

Creative children are able to return to familiar things and see them in different ways and in greater depth. These children do not get bored when exposed to the same experience more than once. Surprisingly, they seem satisfied after the first experience, but are prepared to examine it more thoroughly the second time around.

Rose was most interested when her group visited the farm one day. They went into the barn and watched a number of hens sitting on their eggs. The teacher explained that the hen's warm body kept the eggs warm until they hatched, but that the chicks were not yet ready to be hatched. As the group moved on, the parent volunteer talked with Rose and answered many of the young girl's questions.

Upon returning home, Rose enthusiastically shared her new interests with her parents. Realizing her strong desire to observe the hatching of young chicks, Rose's parents arranged for a visit to the farm of a friend near the time when his eggs were to hatch. Rose, of course, was fascinated by the experience and stayed at the farm all day, watching the young chicks frolic.

Some adults hesitate to closely duplicate an experience for young children for fear they will be bored or inattentive. Creative youngsters, however, use a second experience to examine their recollections of the first more slowly and methodically. They can savor the first experience, extend it, and think more deeply about it.

Creative preprimary children learn a great deal through fantasy, and solve many of their problems of development through its use. Fantasy is one of the young child's favorite ways of thinking, and it should be developed and guided in the preschool setting. Unfortunately, adults often eliminate expressions of fantasy in school (especially in the primary grades) because they view it as psychologically unhealthy. However, imaginative role-playing, storytelling, artwork, and language play are quite normal childhood activities and are a part of creative learning.

Mrs. Hernandez enjoys watching her children paint and appreciates all of their creative expressions. The children feel comfortable with their teacher because they know she will never say, "That's not right," or "Do it this way." Ronnie, for example, is a careful, methodical painter who likes to make neat paintings. He carefully dips his brush into green paint and draws a long line. He then adds a few dots on each side of the green line and draws a circle. He then dips his brush into the red paint and dabs a small amount inside the circle. "All done," Ronnie proclaims as he carefully puts his painting aside to dry.

Tara, on the other hand, expresses her creativity in a bolder, less controlled fashion. Tara starts her picture by putting her brush into the red paint and smearing it in the center of her paper, making large, bold strokes. She then adds blue and yellow, slopping on each color so that a considerable amount overflows and overlaps. She intently and actively paints her picture until the entire paper is covered with one color or another. She is content throughout the activity to explore all the possibilities of the medium, but in a different way from Ronnie.

Mrs. Hernandez obviously realized that both children were experiencing cognitive insights and emotional release during the process of their artwork and allowed each to work individually. She knew that the creative *process* in which they were involved was much more important than the resulting *product,* so she allowed them to adopt a style that was most comfortable for them rather than imposing her own pattern. Likewise, we must encourage self-expression through art, music, creative dramatics, or language usage by allowing children to express their fanciful, personal thoughts in an atmosphere of freedom and acceptance.

Creative young children enjoy "playing" with words and seem to be natural storytellers. Children's art seems to be appreciated by many people throughout the country; we see it displayed on advertisements, book or magazine illustrations, even postage stamps. Their verbal compositions, however, are seldom as widely appreciated or attractively treated in publications and displays. Many imaginative stories are created daily by young children and deserve much more recognition than they now receive.

Several children in this four-year-old classroom were becoming interested in experimenting with word sounds and story construction. As Cindy and Dee played at the outdoor water table, for example, they verbalized, "Drip, drip, drip. Splishy splashy, splishy splashy. . . ." "Look, I'm making it rain." "Rain, rain, you're a pain." "Rain splashing . . . the clouds are bumping together . . . wet trees, wet sidewalks, a flood!" "Get out the raincoats and 'brellas."

Their teacher, Mr. Jackson, enjoyed listening to such creative patter and often offered thought-provoking comments designed to encourage further verbal exploration. "That's a very nice story," he offered, "I like it very much. What if it rained all over the world right now?"

"I like rain," said Cindy. "It's fun to run through the puddles. My dog runs with me—splish, splash, splish, splash."

"I'm afraid of the thunder," said Dee, "Kaboom . . . kaboom. . . ." Playfully, the two girls joined in shrieking laughter and ran to the porch roof for "cover."

There are many opportunities during the day to encourage such creative verbal self-expression. Perhaps the most important role of the teacher in these instances is to appreciate the children's expressions and listen to what they say. When they find that you value their creative endeavors, the children will enjoy expressing their thoughts and will eventually feel more comfortable using other avenues of creative expression, too.

One pitfall of encouraging creative verbalization should be emphasized at this point. Make a concerted effort to resist the temptation of requesting that the children tell you a story. Not all children can do so freely and asking them to express their thoughts at your request will be putting them in the position (sometimes frustrating) of trying to "please the teacher." Wait for them to want to express their thoughts—that personal interest in verbal expression can serve as a valuable pathway for finding creative delight, sharing thoughts with others, or for expressing emotions and fears.

ENCOURAGING CREATIVE THOUGHT

All individuals are born with some degree of creative potential and are subject to Piaget's suggestion that the basic goal of education should be to produce individuals who are capable of *creativity* (bringing new or original thinking to the solution of problems), *invention*, and *discovery*.[8] Some people may look at such a statement and respond, "Don't look at me—I'm as *uncreative* as anyone can be!" Such people view creativity in an unrealistic light —they think of it as a magical ability that allows someone to design a new invention, compose a best-selling song, or paint a masterful picture. The teacher of young children must see youngsters in a wider, fuller sense. In this view, creativity means any way of reacting to a situation that goes beyond the mere imitation of what someone else did in that situation. Earl C. Kelley explained: "Every person needs the chance to be creative. This does not mean that everyone should paint a picture or write a symphony. Creativity occurs whenever a person contrives a new way out of a unique dilemma. It is simply meeting the problems of living and inventing new ways to solve them. Most of us do this every day in a greater or lesser degree."[9]

Young children, because of their limited experiences, meet new problems daily. Whenever they develop original solutions to such problems, they are displaying some degree of creative thinking. Some children may display a higher degree of creativity than others, but no children are without some creativity. In infants, creativity may show up when the child invents a new way to play with a plastic ring; in toddlers it may be reflected in a new combination of words. Whatever the outward manifestation of the creative process, its essential feature is the ability to generate different ideas in the production of things or ideas. Of course, some children will possess more potential for creativity than others. We must not look unfavorably on those who do not—the less creative are valuable, too. Our main message here is to provide situations so that all children will be encouraged to bring out and nourish the creative potential with which they are endowed.

Even though creativity exists in all people, studies show that certain specific thinking abilities—*fluency, flexibility, originality,* and *elaboration*— account for the differences in the degree of creativity from one person to another. These four characteristics suggest a general description of creative thinking, but no one really knows for sure if this is correct. Because no one is yet sure about what creativity is, we are forced to say that creativity is a highly complex mental process. E. Riley Holman has prepared one of the most meaningful explanations of the four specific thinking abilities associated with creativity:[10]

Fluent thinking involves the production of a *quantity of ideas* in response to a specific problem. The focus is on the free flow of thought and on generating an unlimited number of relevant responses to that problem. For example, the young child who responds to the question, "What things are red?" with "apple, book, a car, a beet, a crayon, Santa's suit and shoes" is a more fluent thinker than the child who gives only "fire engine and an apple." Fluency is encouraged by giving students many opportunities to participate in open-ended learning experiences where their free-wheeling thoughts are valued.

Flexible thinking relates to the production of *different kinds of ideas* suggested in relationship to a specific problem. The focus is on variety and diversity of examples, not merely a great number of ideas, as with fluency. The flexible thinker is one who is able to shift his thinking so that different types of ideas are produced. For example, the child who indicates that a pencil may be used for several diverse purposes such as to write, hold up a window, tap on a drum, and lead a song is more flexible than the one who suggests that it may be used to draw, write numbers, write words, and write secret messages. Teachers can encourage flexible thinking by stimulating children to think about situations where many answers are possible and by appreciating their responses to those situations.

Original thinking is associated with the production of thoughts or products that can be judged as *clever or remote*. It is characterized as the production of ideas that are so far away from the obvious that they are considered unusual. For example, the child who, in response to the teacher, finishes the short sentence, "He opened the bag and found . . ." with "a giant spotted firefly." is more original than the child who suggests "an orange." Originality can be developed by encouraging students to bring something "new" into their normal classroom routines and by composing songs, poems, stories, or skits reflecting particular themes.

Elaborative thinking involves adding the necessary ingredients to a new response in order to actually develop it or *work it out in reality*. It may also involve embroidering upon a simple idea or response to make it more detailed or to outline the steps necessary to put an idea into operation. For example, the student who responds to the teacher's invitation to add more information to the sentence, "The cat sat on the porch," with "The lazy, black and white alley cat sat on the top step of the rotten, old porch" demonstrates greater elaborative ability than the one who says, "The black cat sat on the old porch." Elaboration can be encouraged by asking children to add detail to a simple idea to make it more interesting or by stimulating great amounts of verbalization.

Children exhibiting these creative abilities are apparent in the preschool setting—we can see a steady progression in their ingenuity, imagination, and mastery of ways to use things available to them. They first understand the ways in which materials can be used normally and then begin to explore ways in which they can shape new products or find new uses for products. The child does this with many things in his environment: plastic cups are not merely to be used for drinking liquids, they make wonderful scoops for the sand area, they can hold a pet hermit crab while its cage is being prepared, they can be used in pairs to simulate binoculars, and they can even be decorated with glue, sand, seashells, spangles, and pebbles, and sent home as colorful pencil holders. Paper clips, napkins, rubber bands, paper bags, straws, water, clay, paints, blocks, saws, hammers, leaves, twigs, rhythm instruments, ad infinitum—are all fuel for the child's creative engine. The teacher is the key that turns on that engine and encourages it to continue running.

Tests designed to measure children's creativity tend to measure the four basic thinking abilities. J. P. Guilford's *Unusual Uses Test* requires the children to propose unconventional uses for common objects.[11] For example, the child is asked to tell all the ways he can think of to use a brick, a light bulb, or a piece of paper. M. A. Wallach and N. Kogan use a variety of techniques, among which is asking children to describe various kinds of pattern drawings.[12] Figure 10-1 illustrates some of the patterns employed by Wallach and Kogan, as well as some of the more conventional and creative replies. These and similar tests may be useful to teachers who are interested in measuring the creative potential of their youngsters.

Teachers can and should encourage creativity in young children. Although all children will not become Mozarts, Michelangelos, Einsteins, or Curies as a result of their creative experiences, most educators believe that creative thinking is a valuable cognitive tool. Researchers have attempted to identify the conditions under which creativity seems to flourish in the schools and have come up with these general conditions:

1. Time limits are removed from activities in which children are deeply involved.
2. A free, open atmosphere is established where open expression is encouraged.
3. The children are allowed to share ideas and to stimulate one another's thinking.
4. Conditions where stress and anxiety are present are removed.

In order to establish such conditions, teachers apparently have to assume two important roles: (1) facilitator for the child's thinking and (2) arranger of classroom activities that encourage creative expression and free thinking.

Facilitating the Child's Thinking

The teacher must develop the skills of listening to the children and encouraging their deeper explorations into creative thinking. She can do this by asking questions that encourage children to go beyond the obvious, that help them see relationships among ideas, and to improve or combine ideas. The following list offers some idea-spurring questions that indicate interest in the children's thinking and serve to encourage deeper thought:

"What else can your boat do?"
"What might happen if people knew how to fly?"
"What if all the trees had red leaves?"
"If you were a bird, how would you tell me you are hungry?"
"Why do you suppose the ice melted?"
"In how many different ways could you use the light bulb to get my attention?"

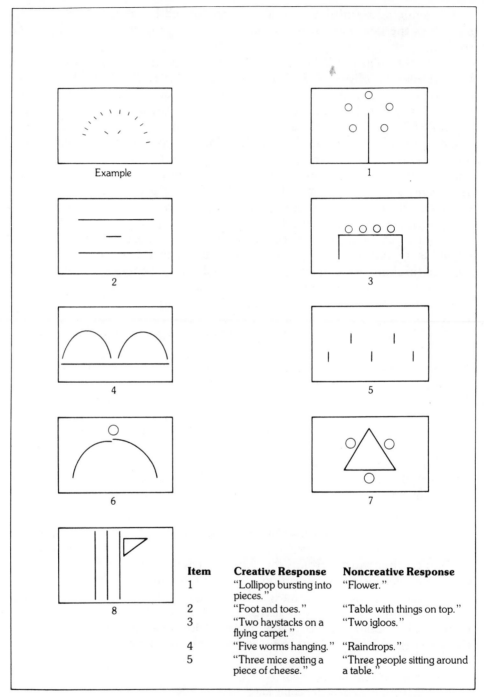

Item	Creative Response	Noncreative Response
1	"Lollipop bursting into pieces."	"Flower."
2	"Foot and toes."	"Table with things on top."
3	"Two haystacks on a flying carpet."	"Two igloos."
4	"Five worms hanging."	"Raindrops."
5	"Three mice eating a piece of cheese."	"Three people sitting around a table."

Figure 10-1 Stimulus materials to assess children's creativity. (From *Modes of Thinking in Young Children* by Michael A. Wallach and Nathan Kogan. Copyright © 1965 by Holt, Rinehart and Winston, Inc. Reprinted by permission of Holt, Rinehart and Winston.)

"Have you ever thought of a new way that this ball could be used?"

"Why is your painting like you?"

"Does the stop sign take the place of anyone?"

"What would you add to (or take away from) the story?"

"What would happen if we slept during the day and were awake at night?"

"What, instead of the shovel, could you use to dig in the garden?"

"How would you feel if you saw a fly as big as a cow?"

"If you had a chance to be any animal you wanted to be, which one would you choose?"

Notice that all questions deliberately went beyond the obvious and toward encouraging original ideas, many ideas (rather than only one), combinations of ideas, improvement of ideas, and free association among ideas. The ability to seize opportunities and ask questions like these is a sophisticated one that comes after a great deal of thought and practice. Be aware of the opportunities when they arise, for your children must be helped to experience the satisfactions associated with expressing oneself freely as a person, with confidence and approval.

Arranging Classroom Activities

Although each area of the preschool curriculum is ripe for creative endeavors, the areas of art, music, and play are often more closely associated with creativity than some others. Preschool teachers understand the value of these areas and make sure that children have many opportunities for free expression through art, music, and play.

ART

Art activities provide many opportunities for young children to release their creative abilities. They allow children to depict people or things in highly personal ways. Youngsters enjoy the possibilities presented by various art media and love to experiment with form and color or simply engage in sense-pleasure play without concern for the depiction of people or things. You may find, then, that some children are content to swish their hands pleasurably through finger paints, while others are more concerned with representing clouds, grass, the sun, or trees. Whatever the individual inclination, children revel in the use of paints, crayons, and paper.

To some adults, whatever the children do with art materials is messy —their scribbles or sensory activities seem to be only unimportant blobs or meaningless jumbles of line and form. These adults often fail to understand or appreciate beginning artistic expression, and often resort to supplying follow-the-dot books, coloring books, or dittoed forms to their children. Such materials hinder the creative freedom that youngsters seek and start them on the road to learning that there is only one correct way to express oneself artistically—the way identified by the teacher or adult. Viktor Lowenfeld emphasized the importance of creative, free artistic expression as opposed to a guided, form-oriented approach:

> It has been proved beyond any doubt that such imitative procedures as found in coloring and workbooks make the child dependent in his thinking; they make the child inflexible, because he has to follow what he has been given. They do not provide *emotional relief* [italics mine] because they give the child no opportunity to press his own experience and thus acquire a release for his emotions; they do not even promote *skills* [italics mine] and discipline, because the child's urge for perfection grows out of his desire for expression; and finally they condition the child to adult concepts which he cannot produce alone, and which therefore frustrate his own creative ambitions.[13]

So, by not allowing the young child to express himself freely with art media, we are stifling creative potential, as well as hindering the youngster's developing *emotional* and *skills* growth. The *emotional* aspects of free artistic production are well exemplified by teachers, executives, businesspeople, or other employees involved in nonphysical labor who find great emotional release and satisfaction in sewing, painting, building, or producing unique materials with their hands during their free time. Such activities help drain accumulated nervous tension, frustration, and anger, and present opportunities to experience the joy and pleasure associated with creating something unique. The young child finds the same values when activities such as pounding and shaping in clay help release emotional strains, and painting a picture with brightly colored paint results in feelings of happiness and accomplishment. The *skills* aspects of free artistic involvement are illustrated in many ways:

- □ *small motor skills:* cutting; pasting; holding brushes, crayons, and pencils
- □ *eye-hand coordination:* painting the chimney so that it rests on the roof; cutting along a line with scissors; squeezing glue from a container so that it lands on the needed spot; placing a sunflower seed at just the right place on a collage
- □ *problem-solving skills:* deciding what color to paint a flower; determining how large to make a tree; settling on the proper materials to use for a collage
- □ *language skills:* talking to others as they participate; listening to adults as new words or directions are communicated ("Pull the string through the hole in the end of the box."); observing his name written by the teacher on a finished project

Although creativity may be the major purpose for advocating preschool art experiences, teachers should be aware of the important benefits of free uninhibited artistic pursuits. Observations of children in artistic acitivty have

Children are free to express their creativity in a variety of art activities.

resulted in four distinct theories of the unique development of children's art. It is important that you know the theories because they form the groundwork on which we explain *how* children develop their abilities and *what* they portray in their finished products. Such knowledge helps you interpret the child's work, set realistic expectation levels for their work, and helps guide you in selecting and planning your teaching strategies and materials.

Developmental Approaches (Growing)

The *developmental theory*, perhaps the most popular theory of art development, is primarily associated with Viktor Lowenfeld and W. Lambert Brittain, who described children's growth in artistic abilities as progressing through a series of distinguishable, sequential stages.[14] The three stages of art development normally associated with preschool youngsters are the scribble stage, the preschematic stage, and the schematic stage.

THE SCRIBBLE STAGE (2–4 YEARS) The analogy that scribbling is to drawing as babbling is to speech illustrates the importance of this first stage. Before the age of two, the child is probably more interested in eating a crayon than drawing with it, but at about age 2 he begins to use it to scribble lines that are random and disorganized. As he matures, he moves to the *named scribble stage*, which can be described in the following anecdote.

Teodoro began his picture by putting two blobs of green paint on the easel paper. "Come see my tree," he proudly requested of the teacher. Although the painting was nowhere near the likeness of a tree, Teodoro nevertheless used this symbol to represent something he had thought about. In a short time, as he began a second painting, Teodoro again placed two green blobs on the easel paper, this time commenting, "This is my horse."

Adults are usually amused by this stage, as the child asserts that his scribbles are "mommy," "doggie," or "house." The child's interest in the process varies at this stage, and he often uses a great deal of paper for a few randomly scribbled lines.

After the named scribble stage comes the *controlled scribble stage*, a transitional phase where the children are beginning to exercise some control over horizontal, circular, and vertical motions. The child is able to make his lines and circles go in the desired direction, but he is as yet unable to draw the object he wishes to represent. It is at the end of this period that the child moves away from using art media for the sensory pleasures he experiences, and begins to use them in a more conscious effort to represent something.

PRESCHEMATIC STAGE (4–7 years)   At this stage, the child first begins to represent the objects he sees in his everyday world, mostly people. In drawing people, the child usually begins to draw the head as a roughly circular line that encloses marks standing for eyes, nose, and mouth— although these facial features are often out of their usual location. The child also begins to represent other objects during this stage, usually with lines and crude circles or rectangles.

SCHEMATIC STAGE (7–9 YEARS)   Although this stage has been identified as characteristic of the seven- to nine-year-old, Lowenfeld and Brittain tell us that it may appear in some youngsters by the age of five. During this stage, the child seems to place his major efforts toward the representation of a human figure. He adds ears and hair (scribbles at the top of the head), sticklike arms sticking out the side of the head and ending in a club or sunburst of fingers, a set of legs that grow straight down from the head, again ending in a club or sunburst of toes. When the torso first appears, it will look like a crude oval or circle with the legs sticking straight out. By the age of five, arms, legs, and torso may begin to take more realistic shape, usually represented by circles, ovals, and rectangles. Clothing and scenery may appear by this time.

Some educators believe that this interest in drawing the human figure is so significant that a child's ability to represent details in his picture can be used as a measure of intellectual maturity. Dale Harris revised and extended the Goodenough Draw-A-Man Test, and theorizes that increasingly sophisticated representations of the human figure indicate advanced levels of intellectual capabilities.[15] Such thoughts have become controversial today,[16] but nevertheless they point out the value of art as more than a single-dimensional activity.

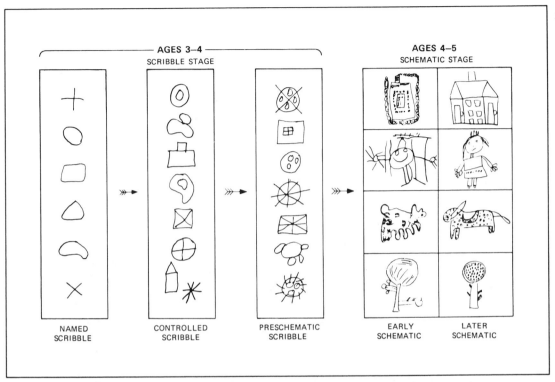

AGES 3–4
SCRIBBLE STAGE

AGES 4–5
SCHEMATIC STAGE

NAMED
SCRIBBLE

CONTROLLED
SCRIBBLE

PRESCHEMATIC
SCRIBBLE

EARLY
SCHEMATIC

LATER
SCHEMATIC

Figure 10-2 A chart depicting shape, design, and stages in the development of children's drawings. (Reproduced by permission of John Wiley and Sons, Inc., New York, N. Y., from *Development of the Child* by David Elkind and Irving B. Weiner, 1978.)

For an illustration of the artwork done by children during each of the developmental phases, refer to Figure 10-2.

Lowenfeld claimed that passage through each of the developmental stages is a natural phenomenon—that children must pass through one stage before they can attain the next. However, he felt that such movement could not be stimulated by outside teaching, but only by providing an open environment in which the children freely bring forth and exercise what they already possess. When given opportunities to do so, they naturally progress through the developmental levels. In effect, the children are left alone to draw what they like while the teacher acts as a guide and inspiring force. Any application of external standards or patterns is considered a negative force producing only inhibitions and frustrations. R. Kellog stated:

[The child is] a very experienced master of self-taught art. . . . In fact, Picasso said that adults should not teach children to draw but should learn from them. . . . Children left alone to draw what they like, without the interference of adult guidance, usually develop a store of gestalts, which enable them to reach the culminating stage of self-taught art. From there, if they are especially gifted, they may develop into great artists, unspoiled by the stenciled minds of well-meaning adults.[17]

This developmental philosophy of preschool art education dominated the early childhood curriculum from the time of Froebel until the 1960s. It was during that time that all developmental theories came under assault, and the concept of teaching art by providing a challenging environment while waiting for children to grow and develop through predetermined stages became unpopular. Also during that time many art educators followed a philosophy that emphasized the formal teaching of art skills, developing cognitive goals through art experiences, and advancing attitudes of art appreciation.

Sylvia F. Burns gives examples of some of the possible cognitive goals expected when activities are prepared with specific goals in mind:

Crayons: Initial color perceptions, use of small muscles, perceptual-motor development, space and shape relationships, pictorial representation of the child's world. Counting, matching, grouping of colors, whole-part relationships, use of crayons for rubbings (paint over with thinned tempera—scientific learning that some things do not mix).

Paint: More complex medium than crayons involving another approach to perceptual learning. A constantly changing medium good for scientific learnings: looks different wet than when dry, opaqueness can be covered over (What is underneath the visible color?). Variations in texture, fluidity, different textured effects depending upon brushes used. Can be mixed to change color, dripped into another color. Can be used on materials other than paper (Is the result the same?). Excellent vocabulary builder.

Paper collage: Size relationships, shape discrimination, whole-part concepts, arrangement (design). A two-dimensional experience for reading. Problem solving (choosing from offered materials). Beginning math (classifying, counting shapes).

Three-dimensional collage: Separating and putting together of items. Bringing together shapes and elements in the world (important for beginning reading). Sorting, comparing, seeing similarities in items, classifying items of same shape and/or material. Use of items in new ways (seeing alternatives). Problem solving (how to fasten).

Clay: Sensory-tactile perceptions via shaping, rolling, pulling, pounding. Representation of personal ideas and perceptions of things in the world. Concepts of mass, change, relationship of parts to whole, fractions (whole, half, quarter). Math (many, few, larger, smaller, more), may also be used for addition and subtraction.

Finger paint: Compare consistency. Motor development, change of form. Development of control (not confined to small area). Visual-motor coordination, figure-ground perception. Vocabulary builder.[18]

Programs reflecting such goals emphasize cognitive growth at nearly the total exclusion of traditional goals. However, today, early childhood educators have retreated from such a drastic swing and have "rediscovered" to some extent the ideas of Viktor Lowenfeld. H. J. McWhinnie explains: "Lowenfeld's . . . ideas have new meaning for the 1970's. Someone with his orientation is now needed to redirect art education towards a greater concern for the individual and social ends and move it away from the excess of concern with the cognitive goals and discipline centeredness."[19]

Cognitive Developmental Approaches
(Knowing and Growing)

This theory of artistic development is mainly influenced by Jean Piaget and his idea that children's art grows and develops in direct relationship to their abilities to understand the *permanent existence of objects*. This means that the child must be able to observe objects, fix them in his mind, and form mental images of those objects even when they are removed from his immediate environment before he can represent them through any medium, including art. If the child is able to evoke the past with such accurate images, then we say that he possesses the ability to conceptualize the permanent existence of objects (see Figure 10-3). The child who does not have this ability to understand the permanent existence of objects will not be able to form an accurate mental image of the object when it is removed from his environment—the object will cease to exist as it did before. So, according to Piaget, the child must be able to *think* about and *conceptualize* his experiences before he can be expected to *represent* them through any form or symbol—including artistic expression and language. Constance Kamii and Norma Radin state that "only after thorough sensory-motor acquaintance with real things does the child become able to reproduce actions in the absence of objects."[20] He

THE CHILD DIRECTLY OBSERVES AN OBJECT AND FORMS A MENTAL IMAGE.

THE OBJECT IS REMOVED FROM THE CHILD'S DIRECT LINE OF OBSERVATION.

THE CHILD IS ABLE TO FORM ACCURATE MENTAL IMAGES OF THE OBJECT EVEN THOUGH THAT OBJECT IS NO LONGER PRESENT.

Figure 10-3 The child who is able to conceptualize the permanent existence of objects.

Figure 10-4   The child paints a bellybutton even though he cannot see it.

must be able to internalize real things or actions before he is able to translate them into symbols.

Our discussion to this point has been directed mainly toward the cognitive half of the cognitive developmental approach. The "developmental" half adds that representation through artistic expression results not only from the child's ability to form mental images but also from his growing ability to understand *pictorial space relationships* such as:[21]

1. *The stage of synthetic incapacity*—The child neglects the size proportions, distance orientation, and perspective relationships. This stage is normally found to last up until the ages of six or seven and is accounted for by the child's inability to completely "pull together" all the elements involved in his mental images.
2. *The stage of intellectual realism*—The child represents what he knows rather than what he sees. For example, children will often draw a human figure completely clothed, but with a round circle placed on the shirt or blouse. Since the child becomes very sensitive to navels at this age (6–9 years) he paints his "bellybutton" even though he cannot see it. He knows it is there and feels compelled to represent it (see Figure 10-4).
3. *The stage of visual realism*—The child, beginning at age 9 or 10, begins to show a more complete understanding of spatial relationships. He draws only those objects or parts of objects that can be seen and shows a more sophisticated knowledge of size and space.

The educational implications of the cognitive developmental theory of art development are similar to those of the theory as it is applied in all other areas of the curriculum: (1) Provide the children with rich experiences so that their mental images can be more accurately formed (bringing content to the child's expression) and (2) furnish a wide variety of materials so that the children acquire skills in using the media. With a combination of these two considerations, the cognitive developmental art program is designed to offer a developmental sequence of experiences that relate to each other and that lead to increasing depth of skill and understanding.

Perceptual Approaches (Seeing)

This theory of art development was formulated by Rudolf Arnheim. It states that children draw what they *see* rather than what they *know* (as the cognitive developmentalists contend). For Arnheim, perception is the basis of artistic expression. He theorizes that children first draw whole images with very little detail because that is the way they first perceive what they are drawing—as perceptual wholes rather than as total images comprising a series of parts. Arnheim states: "It is evident that children limit themselves to representing the overall qualities of objects, such as the straightness of legs, the roundness of a head, the symmetry of the human body."[22]

When the child draws a human figure as a large round circle with stick-like arms and legs, it is because his visual judgment is fairly unsophisticated and this lack of sophistication is reflected in his filtered drawing. As the child's perceptual skills grow, however, he gradually includes more of what he sees. The child, then, grows in artistic ability as he re-creates perceived objects on sheets of paper and compares that representation to what he views. For example, the child may walk around a house and see all of its four sides. Then, he attempts to represent this multi-dimensional sight on two-dimensional paper. The immature child has great difficulty choosing which view he would like to represent and ultimately decides to show several views at once—he sees no problems in doing so (see Figure 10-5). However, once he grows in his perceptual powers, the child becomes dissatisfied with such

Figure 10-5   Representing a multidimensional object.

representations and attempts to alter or control his efforts more effectively. In this way, the child's *artistic development* (the growing ability to add greater detail and to form increasingly accurate representations) parallels the child's *perceptual development*.

Early childhood educators attempting to apply this theory to practice believe that if artistic development is to be encouraged, it must be encouraged through perceptual training, especially through activities that emphasize *visual discrimination* (refer to Chapter 7).

Psychoanalytic Approaches (Feeling)

This final theory of artistic development holds that children draw what they *feel*—that art is one of the primary means of expressing what is deep down inside. Children's art, then, is seen to be a reflection of emotions rather than a reflection of general growth and development, concept formation, or perceptual development. The theory suggests that if a child draws himself as a large circle with sticks for arms and legs, it is not because he is unaware of his other body parts; rather, the large, prominent circle represents a preoccupation with the womb, breast, or other emotion-laden object. Likewise, if the child represents a mother in a family picture as being disproportionately larger than the father, it is because the mother assumes central importance for the child rather than because the child has a perceptual problem. Interpretations can be readily made as the child draws a picture of his family room with an enormous television set, as he uses warm colors to paint a picture of his school setting, or as he aggressively splatters and heaps onto his easel paper blobs of angry reds after a discomforting situation on the playground.

The psychoanalytic theory of art development has influenced early childhood education over the years to a great degree, perhaps to an extent equal to the developmental theory of Lowenfeld. Many traditional preschool practices have been patterned after this thinking, with the idea that art materials allow for an effective release of the child's inner emotions, and provide valuable opportunities for the release of aggressiveness or built-up tensions. Katherine Read, perhaps the leading educational advocate of this theory of art development, offers this view of art in the preschool setting:

> Experiences in the graphic and plastic arts offer [an] avenue through which individuals release their feelings and find satisfactions. It is [an] avenue of expression which may serve as an outlet throughout the life of the individual. . . . The anxious attention on the *product* [italics mine] rather than the *process* [italics mine], the coloring books, and other "patterns" that were imposed on us have all served pretty effectively to prevent most of us from expressing ourselves through art. Yet art is an important means of expression and of draining off feeling as well as a source of satisfaction. . . .
>
> As we ourselves work with children, we must try to safeguard their use of art media as a means of self-expression. For every child, art can serve as an outlet for feeling if the process is emphasized more than the product. It does not matter that there are differences in ability just as there are in music. Given an easel, paper,

and paint, and no directions, every child will paint. For some children painting will remain an important avenue through which they can express feeling all through their lives.[23]

Read, therefore, advocates the use of free, unstructured painting as the major avenue of emotional release through art. Through such activity, she believes, we gain a great deal of insight into what children are feeling.

Theories of art development may at times be confusing because of their complex nature. So that you will be able to compare and contrast those discussed in this chapter with a minimum of difficulty, Table 10-1 has been prepared.

Table 10-1   Comparison of Major Theories of Art Development

Theory	Basis of Theory	Educational Implications
Developmental (growing)	Children naturally progress through developmental stages of growth in art.	The teacher serves as a guide and inspirer as the children freely experiment with a variety of art media.
Cognitive developmental (growing and knowing)	Children represent objects only as they are able to form permanent mental images of those objects. Their ability to reproduce such images progresses through developmental stages.	The teacher provides a wide variety of direct experiences and many developmentally appropriate tools and materials.
Perceptual (seeing)	Children draw what they see. They grow in their ability to represent objects as they grow in their perceptual skills.	The teacher provides opportunities for the children to draw or paint so that they are able to compare their representations with real things and begin to improve upon their efforts. Additional training in visual discrimination would be provided.
Psychoanalytic (feeling)	Children's art products reflect their emotions.	The teacher encourages extensive use of paints and various tactile materials such as finger paints and clay, with the goal of releasing children's feelings.

Your feelings regarding the merits of these theories bear an important relationship to the teaching strategies, activities, and materials that you will use with the children. They help you decide on the degree of guidance or freedom to give the children and on the kinds of activities the children seem ready to enjoy, and they make you aware of the kinds of products children are able to create. Whatever theory appeals to you most, however, you will certainly use many of the following popular suggestions for early childhood art activity.

Art Activities for Preschoolers

Teachers of preschool children are able to choose from a wide variety of suitable materials for their children. These materials can be used in a variety of creative ways. Remember that certain materials are more appropriate for some ages than for others.

Suggested Art Materials for the Two- to Four-Year-Old
- □ Pencils: kindergarten size
- □ Crayons of assorted colors and sizes
- □ Newsprint paper for drawing or painting (12″ × 18″ or 18″ × 24″)
- □ Finger-paint paper: 12″ × 18″ or 18″ × 24″
- □ Colored paper of assorted colors and sizes
- □ Brushes for easel painting (¼″ to 1″ width, round and flat bristle)
- □ Poster and tempera paint of assorted colors, liquid or powder form
- □ Paint containers: old cans or plastic containers
- □ Easels
- □ Smock or apron for each child
- □ Chalk of assorted colors and sizes
- □ Plastic modeling materials such as playdough, clay, salt and flour mixes
- □ Yarn of assorted sizes and colors
- □ Glue and scissors, paste
- □ Scrap materials for collages or texture experiences

Suggested Art Materials for the Four- to Eight-Year-Old
- □ Poster paint of assorted colors
- □ Brushes of assorted sizes, round or flat bristle
- □ Crayons and chalk of various colors
- □ Modeling materials: clay, playdough, and so on
- □ Paper: construction, drawing, finger-paint, easel, and so on
- □ Scrap materials for collages
- □ Easel painting supplies
- □ Glue, scissors, paste
- □ Magic markers or colored pencils
- □ Printmaking materials

EASEL PAINTING AND OTHER PAINTING EXPERIENCES Easel painting is perhaps the most popular of all preschool art activities. It pro-

Easel painting is enjoyed by nearly every preschool child, and is, therefore, one of the most frequently used avenues of creativity in early childhood facilities around the country.

vides the child with initial opportunities to explore and discover growing artistic abilities. Children enjoy painting at easels—some would probably prefer to spend most of the day drawing and scribbling. When first given opportunities to paint at the easel, the young child often engages in experiments with tempera or poster paints and a variety of brushes in sense-pleasure play, experiencing form and color with little concern for the depiction of objects. By about the age of four or five, experimental circular motions turn into heads and tree tops, while longer strokes become legs, arms, tree trunks, and horizontal lines. Such figures will not actually look as they appear to our eyes, but remember that young children are progressing through *first* experiences in depicting reality; this is a giant step in the development of their thinking abilities.

The easel painting area should be in a quiet, uncluttered part of the room near a sink or toilet facilities (important in the case of spills and other accidents). Newspaper or long sheets of butcher paper should be spread on the floor to catch drips and spills. Furnish small containers of creamy tempera paint (to be held within newspaper- or waxpaper-lined easel trays) and a variety of brushes for experimentation. Each child should know that he can paint when he wants to, so the easels should be available each day for painting opportunities.

In addition to preparing the easel area, your role includes helping the children get ready for their painting experiences. Help them into their protective smocks (usually old shirts or plastic aprons) and help them to use the brushes that feel comfortable in their hands. Encourage and assist the child during his efforts, making sure not to interfere unless a specific purpose can be achieved. For example:

Teacher: "You painted the whole paper green, Paul. It looks very pretty."
Paul: "I like green color."
Teacher: "I wonder how your painting would look if you added dots of another color."
Paul: "How do you make dots?"
Teacher: "Let me show you." *(On another piece of paper the teacher shows Paul how to use his brush to make dots.)*
Paul: "I want to make red dots." *(Paul experiments a bit with the red paint and makes some large, irregular dots. After some time, he proudly announces that he has finished his painting.)*

Such informal instruction opens the door to new possibilities for the child and helps him develop increasing creative skills. In the same way,

---

PAINTING ACTIVITIES

☐ *Ink blots:* Prefold paper; drop thick paint onto paper from tongue depressors; refold, open. Several colors may be used to produce interesting designs.

☐ *String painting:* Dip short lengths of string into bowls of paint and let them fall on paper. Paper may also be folded, then string pulled out while the paper is held shut with one hand.

☐ *"Block" printing:* Dip objects into bowls of paint and press or rub on paper. Objects may be spools, corks, sink stoppers, sponges, jar lids, small blocks, scrub brushes, potatoes cut in shapes, combs, Q-tips, and so on.

☐ *Dry powder painting:* Put dry powder tempera paint in dishes at the easel or on the table, and use wads of wet cotton. Dab the dry paint onto a paper that has been completely moistened with a sponge and water.

☐ *Textured paint:* Mix a textured substance with paint for different effects, adding a little glue to ensure sticking. Use salt (which sparkles when dry), sand, fine sawdust, coffee grounds, or soap flakes.

☐ *Spatter painting:* You will need small wire screens on wood frames, toothbrushes, pans of thin paint, and various designs to set under the screen on protective paper. Objects may be paper silhouettes, leaves, cookie cutters, or a variety such as keys, forks, spoons, scissors, tongue depressors, and so on. Dip the toothbrush into the paint and run it over the wire screen. The paint will produce an interesting effect on the object below.

☐ *Table painting:* Use bowls of paint and short-handled brushes for a

children can be led to experiment with thick lines, thin lines, circles, swirls, and various color combinations.

After the children have begun to feel comfortable with easel painting and have learned to control brushes and paint, you may wish to introduce other painting experiences, such as those that can be done at tables. Note the examples in the painting activities box.

DRAWING   In contrast to *painting* (a medium mainly emphasizing experimentation with form and color), *drawing* finds children attempting finer pictorial representations, most typically of people. Their ability to represent people was illustrated earlier; remember they pass through stages of scribbling and drawing until, by about the age of five or six, most children can represent people relatively accurately.

Your role in encouraging representation through drawing is essentially that of an arranger of the environment and stimulator of the child's thinking. Place *crayons, pencils, nontoxic marking pens,* or *colored chalk* on a large table along with an ample supply of drawing paper. As they are encouraged to experiment with these materials, children will add trees, houses, and flowers

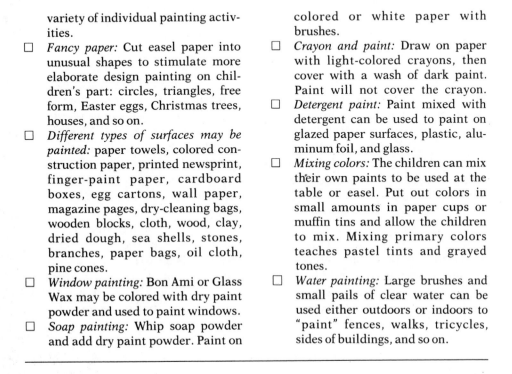

variety of individual painting activities.

☐ *Fancy paper:* Cut easel paper into unusual shapes to stimulate more elaborate design painting on children's part: circles, triangles, free form, Easter eggs, Christmas trees, houses, and so on.

☐ *Different types of surfaces may be painted:* paper towels, colored construction paper, printed newsprint, finger-paint paper, cardboard boxes, egg cartons, wall paper, magazine pages, dry-cleaning bags, wooden blocks, cloth, wood, clay, dried dough, sea shells, stones, branches, paper bags, oil cloth, pine cones.

☐ *Window painting:* Bon Ami or Glass Wax may be colored with dry paint powder and used to paint windows.

☐ *Soap painting:* Whip soap powder and add dry paint powder. Paint on colored or white paper with brushes.

☐ *Crayon and paint:* Draw on paper with light-colored crayons, then cover with a wash of dark paint. Paint will not cover the crayon.

☐ *Detergent paint:* Paint mixed with detergent can be used to paint on glazed paper surfaces, plastic, aluminum foil, and glass.

☐ *Mixing colors:* The children can mix their own paints to be used at the table or easel. Put out colors in small amounts in paper cups or muffin tins and allow the children to mix. Mixing primary colors teaches pastel tints and grayed tones.

☐ *Water painting:* Large brushes and small pails of clear water can be used either outdoors or indoors to "paint" fences, walks, tricycles, sides of buildings, and so on.

Many children enjoy painting or drawing at a table.

to their pictures of human figures. Because some children do not have opportunities to experience things beyond their immediate home environment, you may find those five- or six-year-olds getting stuck in a rut of drawing pictures only of people, houses showing all four walls, and tulips or "lollipop" trees. To move them away from such stereotyped production, provide them with a variety of experiences involving people, animals, flowers, buildings, and other kinds of places and events. Such experiences include trips to the zoo, farm, or areas of interest within the community; bringing animals to the classroom; or walking through the woods. During such experiences the child should be led to (1) notice apparent features of objects and (2) make creative interpretations of the objects they experience. The teacher can use questions or comments to stimulate thinking related to each of these areas. Questions like "Can you see the sunflower's seeds?" "Is the horse bigger than the dog?" "What color is the cake?" "Can you see the giraffe's long neck?" "Touch the flower. What does it feel like?" lead the child to observe more closely. To stimulate the child's creativity the teacher can ask "Did you ever imagine you were a spider?" "What would it feel like to be a tall tree?" "I wonder what the dog is trying to say." "How would you like to be able to fly like a bird?" "How would it feel to move as slowly as a caterpillar?"

This questioning-type approach offers the child an opportunity to rethink what he has experienced. This forces him to reconstruct the mental images needed to form the people, objects, or animals he wishes to draw.

But, to open up the child both to new experiences and to making a mental copy of those experiences is not all there is to the process of creative art. The child must *personalize* his association with the object, that is, he must transform it into an individually unique form that is free from any *standardized* expectancies. In effect, drawing activities should be motivated by varieties of direct experiences in which the children are led to think on levels that go beyond the mere recognition of objects. These creative thoughts should be directed toward the production of individually unique pictorial representations that demonstrate personalized awareness and increased insight.

Activities with crayon and chalk, other than drawing, are described in the drawing-related activities box.

TEXTURE EXPERIENCES   All children from their youngest years are fascinated by experimentation with different textures. Picture for a moment the infant who squeezes soft pudding between his fingers as he gurgles and laughs. This same attraction to sensory stimulation accompanies the child

---

DRAWING-RELATED ACTIVITIES

CRAYON ACTIVITIES

☐ *Crayon etching:* Cover paper with light-colored crayon, then cover light surface with dark crayon. Scratch through to light surface with edge of blunt scissors or tongue depressor.

☐ *Crayon leaf rubbing:* Place leaf under newsprint and scribble with crayon on top of paper to get impression of leaf. This can also be done with coins, string, pieces of paper, wire screening, burlap, and so on.

☐ *Crayon and paint:* Draw on paper with light-colored crayons; then cover with wash of dark paint. Paint will cover all but crayon markings.

☐ *Colored paper:* Using crayons on colored paper teaches children what happens when one color is applied to another.

☐ *Single colors:* Picking out one color to use for an entire picture offers a change from having a variety of colors to use.

☐ *Variety in diameter:* Wide crayons stimulate more extensive drawing; narrow crayons stimulate more detailed work. Using the entire flat side of crayon, after peeling paper, also adds variety.

☐ *Crayon stenciling:* Draw on cloth with a firm, even pattern of light, solidly applied color. Place material face down between two pieces of smooth paper and press with hot iron. Do not rub iron across paper.

CHALK ACTIVITIES

☐ *Wet paper:* Paper dipped in water permits chalk to slide more easily, gives more fluid motion to drawing, and makes colors more brilliant. Construction paper or paper towels may be used.

☐ *Wet chalk:* Chalk is dipped in bowl of water before being used on dry paper. The effects are similar to those of dry chalk on wet paper.

☐ *Buttermilk or diluted plastic starch:* Apply these liquids to wet paper. The chalk will stick to the paper after it dries.

☐ *Fixative:* This may be sprayed on dried chalk drawings or added to water for wet paper drawings. Prevents chalk dust from rubbing off. Common fixatives include hairspray, liquid starch sprayed from a bottle, or special fixatives purchased from school supply stores.

☐ *Chalkboard:* This large surface encourages expansive, sweeping motions. Children love to draw with chalk on the chalkboard.

throughout his preschool years as he seeks to experiment with various textures. Therefore, you should encourage children to explore textures as they become involved with a variety of art media. For examples, see the texture-experience activities box.

CUTTING AND PASTING Young children enjoy the prospect of using scissors, but may initially experience difficulty in manipulating them. For that reason, their first cutting experiences should not be directed to cutting out patterns or cutting along lines, but should be random explorations with varieties of materials—construction paper, cloth, string, newspapers, magazines, tissue paper, and so on—using blunt but sharp scissors. The children take special pleasure in the cutting actions and will not be overly concerned about the form of the final product at this stage of development (at about the age of three or four). These cutting activities help the children get used to handling scissors and help them develop the hand and finger muscles neces-

---

TEXTURE-EXPERIENCE ACTIVITIES

CRAYON RUBBINGS Place drawing paper over various textured surfaces such as sandpaper, a screen, the wall, floor, and so on. Rub a crayon over each surface and notice the different effects.

FINGER PAINTING Place finger paint directly on paper or on the table. Make a design by smearing the paint with the whole hand, fingers, palm, fingernails, or knuckles. A suggested procedure for organizing the finger-painting experience is:

1. Cover a table top with paper or oil cloth, if preferred. At the early stages of finger painting, your children may feel less frustrated by sliding, tearing paper if the paint is directly applied to the table.
2. Allow plenty of "elbow room" so the children can experience free rhythmic body movement.
3. Put on smocks or aprons.
4. Apply finger paint to the shiny surface of finger-paint paper, or directly to the table.

5. Encourage the children to experiment freely.
6. Children should help clean their area when they finish with their design.
7. Have the children wash their hands immediately and remove smock or apron.
8. The children may wish to take their paper home. If the design was made on the table, simply press a sheet of paper onto the still-wet table, and a print will be made.

For a change of texture, add sand, salt, coffee grounds, or fine sawdust to the finger paint.

For a variation in color, put powder paint in salt shakers and let children add their own color to uncolored finger paint. This will help them learn color names, color concepts, and the concept of mixing colors to create new colors.

You should wet the smooth side of finger-paint paper for best results. However, such paper is not necessary. Children may finger paint directly on formica-topped tables, or on large

sary for opening and closing the scissors. When these skills become fairly refined (at about the age of four or five) the child is ready to cut out something he has thought about. For example, Carlos had come to the cutting table from the creative dramatics area where he had been role-playing different scenes that fascinated him on a recent field trip. "I'm gonna make a punkin," he announced, and proceeded to cut out a figure crudely approximating an orange circle. The teacher held it up for the others to see and announced to the other children, "Maybe some of you would like to make pumpkins." Then she moved around the table and watched as several children gleefully cut out round, oblong, and other squiggly-shaped pumpkins. Whatever the final shape, though, the teacher was careful to praise and reassure each child for his cutting efforts.

As the children begin to cut out planned shapes, they soon will be interested in pasting things together. But, as with almost everything else in the preschool classroom, the young child needs to be guided and supported in his

---

pieces of oil cloth. A print can be made by placing newsprint on top of the design, gently rubbing, then pulling off. Results can be cleaned off quickly with a sponge.

A large work area is best for finger painting—the child can, thus, use rhythmic movements with arms and perhaps the entire body.

Be sure that you have help from aides or volunteers during this time— supervision and clean up will progress much more smoothly.

PLASTIC MATERIALS   These materials may be rolled, pounded, pinched, patted, and broken. Children first enjoy these materials (clay or playdough) for their sensory appeal, but eventually they become interested in manipulating and shaping them into recognizable objects. Recipes for plastic materials follow:

Cooked Dough
2 cups boiling water
½ cup salt
½ cup flour
¼ cup cornstarch; blend with cold
   water
   food coloring (optional)

Add salt to boiling water. Combine flour with cornstarch and water to make paste. Pour hot mixture into cold. Put over hot water in a double boiler and cook until glossy. Cool overnight. Knead in flour until right consistency, adding color with flour.

Uncooked Dough
3 parts flour to 1 part salt or
2 parts flour to 1 part salt
   a small amount of vegetable oil (for a
   smoother texture)
   food coloring (optional)

Mix flour and salt thoroughly. Add colored water, or add dry powder paint to flour and salt, mixing well before adding water. Add enough water to form dough into a ball. Knead on a floured surface until pliable but not sticky. One tablespoon alum may be added to each 2 cups of flour as a preservative.

(Tiger by Bud Blake courtesy of King Features Syndicate, Inc.)

initial efforts. First attempts that result in failure will be frustrating for these children, so careful guidance is a necessity. Children's first attempts at using paste will find them experimenting freely, much as they did with easel paint or finger paint. They will often apply globs of paste with their fingers to something they want to stick together with the idea that more paste ensures sticking. They quickly find out, though, that as their globs of paste dry and become hard, their objects fall apart. However, with your help, children quickly learn the proper amounts of paste to use and soon become interested in trying out a variety of different pasting media on different objects—trial-and-error learning that leads to careful observations of objects in their environment. There are commercially produced varieties of paste available, but you can also make your own. Two recipes for paste that you can use with preschool children appear in the box opposite.

PRINTING   The printing process involves using paint and a variety of objects to repeat a design over large pieces of drawing or butcher paper. The

Children enjoy the sensory appeal of clay and other plastic materials.

Young children should not be expected to cut out planned shapes until they have accumulated experiences with random cutting. These children have had those experiences and reflect confidence in their current task.

teacher prepares a printing area by first putting out several shallow pans and laying sponges or folded towels in the bottom of each. Then, she pours heavy paint into each pan so that a type of printing pad is formed. The children press their printing tools onto the pad and stamp their repeated designs onto a piece of paper. Some of the possible printing tools available for preschool youngsters are given in the printing activities box (p. 405).

PASTE RECIPES

Hobby Craft Paste

¾ c. water
2 T. light Karo syrup
1 t. white vinegar
½ c. Argo starch
¾ c. water
¼ t. oil of wintergreen

Combine ¾ c. water, corn syrup, and vinegar in a medium-sized saucepan; bring to a full boil. Stir cornstarch into ¾ c. water until smooth. Remove boiling mixture from heat. Slowly pour in cornstarch-water mixture, stirring constantly until smooth. If lumps form, smooth them out with the back of the spoon against the side of the saucepan.

Stir in oil of wintergreen. May be used immediately but will set to paste consistency in 24 hours. Store in covered jar. Keeps two months. Makes about 2½ cups.

Bookmaker Paste

1 t. flour
2 t. salt
¼ t. powdered alum
1 heaping tsp. oil of cloves
1 pt. cold water

Mix dry ingredients with water slowly, stirring out lumps. Use a slow fire. Cook over a double boiler until it thickens.

COLLAGES   The collage is a planned arrangement of one or several art media on one surface. Anything can be used to make collages: construction paper, drawn or painted objects, cloth scraps, or a variety of "junk" materials found in the environment. You may use a combination of such items or one item alone, but the goal is to create a collection of objects in a planned way. The following is a partial list of possible collage materials—use your imagination to think of ways they can be used.

Textured Materials

fur scraps	sandpaper	feathers
leather	velvet	cotton
felt	corduroy	pipe cleaners
burlap or sacking	seeds	acorns
corrugated paper	twigs	shells
egg carton dividers	pebbles	styrofoam
carpet scraps	dried flowers or weeds	

Patterned Materials

wall paper samples	linoleum scraps	catalogs
magazines	patterned gift-wrap	greeting cards
seasonal stickers	candy bar wrappers	stamps

Transparent and Semitransparent Materials

net fruit sacks	lace	metal screening
onion sacks	plastic wrap	colored cellophane
crepe paper	thin tissue paper	paper lace doilies

Sparkling or Shiny Materials

sequins	ribbon	Christmas tinsel
glitter	seasonal wrapping paper	mica snow
aluminum foil	paper from greeting cards	metallic paper

Shapes

buttons	cork	rubber bands
drinking straws	bottle caps	tooth picks
wooden applicators	keys	beads
spools	tongue depressors	fluted candy cups
scrap sponge	cup cake cups	gummed stickers
paper clips	macaroni, spaghetti	string
metal washers	heavy cotton rug yarn	old jewelry

Scattering Materials

sand	tiny pebbles	twigs
sawdust	wood shavings	salt
yarn	beans	popcorn
rice	seeds	eggshells

Guiding Art Activities

The teacher's role in guiding art activities basically involves two tasks: (1) arranging the environment with equipment and materials, and (2) supervising the work in a warm and friendly manner. While *arranging* the room for creative art activities, you should always remember that children grow best when they are allowed to explore freely and imaginatively in a stimulating and challenging setting. Such a setting has an adequate amount of space so that children are able to work comfortably alone or in small groups. Materials and equipment should be easily obtainable at the area where the work is being done. Children must be unhurried and free to plan and carry out special projects in their own ways. Some suggestions for designing art environments are given in the activities box on page 406.

There are a number of guidelines you should follow as you *supervise* the children during their creative art endeavors:

1. Offer encouragement and praise while the children work. Let them know how much you value their unique efforts. As you observe their work and talk to them about it, do not pressure them to describe what they are doing—they may be merely exploring with the art media and may not be able to express anything in particular about their product. You may wish to comment about the color, shapes, sizes, or design of the product and show an interest and appreciation toward the work, but refrain from forcing conversation when none seems constructive.
2. Avoid tactless, silly comments such as "What is it?" or "What are you making?" when the children are engaging in media explorations. How-

---

PRINTING ACTIVITIES

- *Food printing:* Cut potatoes, green peppers, corn cobs, celery, apples, or a variety of other fruits or vegetables across the center to get a variety of natural printing stamps. Special designs may be cut into solid vegetables such as potatoes or carrots.
- *Potpourri:* Use thread spools, hair curlers, cookie cutters, the round ends of paper towel rolls, forks, cotton balls, carpet scraps, bottle caps, and other common scraps to make effective printing tools.

- *Rolling pin printing:* Rolling pins, cardboard tubing, or metal cans are equally effective for this activity. Glue yarn or string to the rolling pin so that it is strongly attached. Dip this printing tool into the paint and roll it over a surface.
- *Sponge printing:* Dip various sponge pieces into the paint and stamp them onto a surface.
- *Button printing:* Glue a variety of buttons to dowel sticks and use them for printing.

ever, you can perfectly well lead off with the open-ended request, "Please tell me about your picture." Along the same line, refrain from being overly critical when children experience unavoidable accidents. Just as we would never admonish a house guest for spilling a drink by complaining, "Oh, you are so clumsy!" we must also never admonish children for their accidents.

3. Resist the use of patterns, outlines, or guides whenever possible. Of course, some special projects will necessitate the use of such structures, but excessive use of such materials limits the freedom of expression offered by unstructured art activity.

4. Help children and encourage their efforts, but refrain from fulfilling requests such as, "Will you draw a dog for me right here?" Do not allow children to become dependent on you—encourage them to think about ways in which they can accomplish their goal by themselves. Such requests for help from children usually come because of a desire to produce a "masterpiece" to please the teacher or parent. Let the children know that what they create should be pleasing to them and it is their own—not the teacher's.

5. Resist the temptation to recognize only the "best" works to be shown in a display area. Remember that your enthusiasm should be extended to all within your room, so an undue emphasis on the work of only a few children will soon discourage the rest.

6. Allow the children to take their productions home. Children often get frustrated when they are not allowed to share their artwork with their parents, so a question such as, "Do we get to take our pictures home

---

ACTIVITIES FOR DESIGNING ART ENVIRONMENTS

☐ An easel painting corner should be basic to nearly all preschool settings. Place newspapers or butcher paper on the floor of a cleared area of the room (to catch drips or spills); provide some small containers of paint, some brushes, and an easel; and make sure that smocks are available for protection.

☐ Arrange a large table that features a special *art center*—this in addition to the classroom easel area. Art center activities may include finger painting, collage work, cutting and pasting, or any other special individual or small-group project that can be done by the children as part of their daily planned program.

☐ Design a bulletin board or display area that can effectively exhibit the art creations of the children. Display the work at the children's eye level rather than at your own (see Figure 10-6).

☐ Play some soft music in the art area so the children can relax and think in comfort.

☐ Make handy various clean-up materials such as a sponge, water, or mops so that the children can easily clean up when they are finished or if there is an accident.

ON BULLETIN BOARDS OR OTHER WALL DISPLAYS

ON VARIOUS LEVELS OF DISPLAY BOXES

ON ORDINARY CLOTHESLINE WITH CLOTHESPINS

ON VARIOUS KINDS OF SHELVES

TACKED TO A BOARD AND LEANING AGAINST THE WALL

ON FREE-STANDING CORRUGATED CARDBOARD

Figure 10-6 Some ways of displaying children's art.

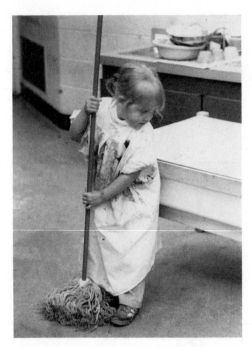

Arrange your art corner in a location where children can clean up inevitable accidents whenever they occur.

tonight?" should not go unheeded. Encourage parents to value their children's artistic development and to display their children's work in a prominent place in the home.
7. Print the child's name in the upper left-hand corner of his drawing or painting. In this way you tend to personalize his efforts while giving him opportunity to begin developing reading skills.

By providing appropriate classroom arrangements and by encouraging free, creative exploration, many values emerge from children's art activities. In such environments, we find a burst of individualism, self-expression, and confidence. Children naturally enjoy the sensory qualities of art and thoroughly delight in the satisfaction of producing unique products. The enjoyment of creating, the fascination of working with art materials, and the creative processes involved in art activity all help to support the incorporation of a strong art program in the preschool curriculum.

MUSIC

Listening to music, creating music, moving to music, and making music together should be joyous parts of the preschool curriculum. Children look forward to participating in music activities and should be given many opportunities to do so.

The primary aim of music in the preschool setting is not to develop musical talent per se, but to think of music as an *enjoyable* art form and a creative means of self-expression. The key word in the previous statement is *enjoyable*—every child should find music to be a rewarding experience and should never be forced to participate in a music activity he has no interest in. Such unfair demands eventually create negative attitudes toward this inherently pleasant childhood activity. As an example of what can be done to create negative attitudes toward music, consider the misguided kindergarten teacher who required each of her children to stand in front of the entire class and sing a memorized solo. This performance was evaluated by the teacher and used as the criterion for each child's report card grade in music! Contrast that musical program to this one:

In Ms. Carpenter's kindergarten classroom, music was looked upon as something natural and spontaneous—it could be expected to come at any time from anyone. Bea walked into school this morning and sang her favorite seasonal song to the aide: "Jingle bells, jingle bells, jingle all the way. . . ." Other children soon caught the pattern and chimed in, "Oh what fun it is to ride. . . ."

The aide sang along with the children and all ended the song with a great deal of laughter and excitement.

Ms. Carpenter welcomed such natural musical expression, but also provided regularly planned musical activities during the daily sessions. Such periods were always relaxed and comfortable, and the music was suitable for preschool children. On this particular day, Ms. Carpenter capitalized on the children's interest in "Jingle Bells" and planned group rhythm activities to accompany the song. First, Ms. Carpenter asked the children to think of themselves as Santa's reindeer. They were all to sit in a group and rest because it was Christmas Eve and Santa was about to begin his long, tiring journey to deliver presents to children all over the world. The twinkling sound of "Jingle Bells" on the piano signalled the children to stand in pairs, with one child (Rudolph) as the leader. As the twinkling music played, the reindeer pranced about as they pulled Santa and his sleigh on his merry rounds. They made small stops as Santa delivered his presents to each house, but quickly started again as Santa signalled the reindeer to prance and pull again. After about five such stops, Ms. Carpenter saw that some of the children were becoming tired, so slowly and at a lower pitch on the piano, she asked the reindeer to plod back to the North Pole where they all flopped down to sleep.

In addition to such planned and unplanned musical experiences, Ms. Carpenter provided many informal interludes during the session. Four keys on the piano signalled the start of rest time for those who were ready for it, a short lullaby accompanied back rubs for children ready for a rest period, short tunes signalled clean-up time or snack, and a record player was kept in a corner where children could slip on earphones to listen to favorite records.

Children enjoyed these pleasant musical experiences and looked forward to participating in them. Ms. Carpenter understood the importance of such nonthreatening activities and applied her knowledge to design pleasurable experiences that invited voluntary participation from each child.

Music can contribute in many ways to the growth and development of young children. Because you must be able to provide many types of opportunities for participation, guidelines and resources are presented in the following sections.

Singing

Children in the preschool setting are often uninhibited in the adult sense, and frequently enjoy opportunities to express themselves in spontaneous song. Because young children have such natural inclinations for song, they should all be provided with chances to develop their interest. How can we do this? Certain developmental cues can guide you in answering this question.

Children enjoy listening to others sing and sing spontaneously as they play. To encourage them, make singing an integral part of your daily routine. Sing melodious tunes whenever it is time for toileting, rest, play, or snack. Show the children that you enjoy singing and are not inhibited or embarrassed to sing in front of them. This *enjoyment* characteristic is the first necessary ingredient in your musical program—if you feel self-conscious in front of the children, you will likely make them feel the same way and they will suppress their desire to sing with you. It may sound surprising, but children will actually enjoy listening to you in much the same way you enjoyed listening to a parent, grandparent, caregiver, or teacher. So, instead of calling to a child who needs assistance, you may wish to sing something—for example, this

Children are absorbed by the enthusiasm generated by teachers who truly enjoy music in the early childhood setting. They often are encouraged to experiment with instruments after watching adults play them.

adaptation was sung by one teacher to the tune of "Twinkle Twinkle Little Star."

> Let me help you, Sally Mae,
> We'll get that shoe tied today.

You can compose simple lyrics to accompany other enjoyable activities. For example, this song (to the tune of "Clementine") was composed by a teacher during a cooking activity:

> Cut the carrots,
> Cut the carrots,
> Cut the carrots, one by one,
> Our soup needs lots of carrots,
> Isn't this a lot of fun?

One teacher adapted "Here We Go Round the Mulberry Bush" for clean-up time:

> This is the way we wash our hands,
> Wash our hands, wash our hands,
> This is the way we wash our hands,
> To make them nice and clean.

The most important advice for you in this phase of developing a singing program for young children is to have confidence in your musical ability and to lose your musical inhibitions. Children are not music critics—they are generally oblivious of your shortcomings and appreciate your efforts to make routines enjoyable. Their response to your efforts will be gratifying and professionally rewarding. Perhaps a personal note might convince those of you who remain skeptical.

Your author, for reasons not appropriate to detail here, always felt ill at ease in a singing situation—whether it was singing "Happy Birthday" or bellowing a tune in the shower. It was more painful for me to sing a song, for example, than it was to have a tooth pulled. So, whenever my family got together during a holiday, everyone joyously sang along while I quietly watched in envy. The same attitude accompanied my undergraduate education, as silent lip movements helped me to mask self-consciousness and survive in music methods class. However, when I walked into my first kindergarten class as a student teacher and saw the children react positively to my sex and size, I began to understand that personal inhibitions regarding singing would soon need to be overcome. At this point, I decided that the best way to do so would be to "sink or swim."

The opportunity presented itself on that first morning with the children—Jenny was having a birthday and her mother had sent cupcakes for all the children to share. Naturally, a group singing of "Happy Birthday" was in order and the cooperating teacher turned to me (perhaps sensing my feelings) and asked, "Would Mr. Maxim care to lead us today?" Swallowing hard, I managed to force out the response, "I would love to," all the while picturing a fog horn-voiced giant leading children in song. Needless to say, the children were more interested in Jenny's birthday than in my voice. You know, I never really noticed that they knew I was singing—and they loved it!

From that rewarding point on, I have found that, like it or not, I get involved in any excuse for singing: family gatherings, ballgames, birthday parties, and especially activities with children.

Like me, you may suffer from a bit of initial stage fright. However, if you face your responsibility maturely, the blending of voices in your classroom will convince you that your self-imposed constraints on your musical talents were both unnecessary and exaggerated.

As you sing to the children and praise them for their own spontaneous efforts, some simple songs may be slowly introduced.

Children enjoy singing songs that have simple, repetitive lyrics, unsophisticated melodies, and narrow, low melodic range. Group singing for preschoolers should be started when you sense that the children are ready for it. Such sessions should not be made part of a rigid schedule, but should arise whenever a positive reaction seems apparent. These following guidelines may help you as you plan activities to bridge the gap between spontaneous singing and group-oriented song:

1. First songs should be action songs—relatively fast-paced songs that involve some types of body movements. The standard action songs of "Eency Weency Spider" and "Where is Thumbkin?" are two such favorites. Another popular song is the following:

   If You're Happy and You Know It
   If you're happy and you know it
   Clap your hands *(children clap hands twice)*
   If you're happy and you know it
   Clap your hands *(children clap hands twice)*
   If you're happy and you know it
   Then your smile will surely show it
   If you're happy and you know it
   Clap your hands *(children clap hands twice)*

   Other verses could include: Pat your head;
   Stomp your feet; Touch your nose; Wave your hand;
   Give a cheer (Hoo-ray!); and so on.

2. Sing the song all the way through and invite the children to join in the actions. If the children wish to hear the song a second time, sing it again. However, do not *ask* if the children want to hear it another time— someone will say no. Some children will learn the words quickly and will soon join in. Do not insist that the others join in with comments such as, "Everyone sing now" (a sure way to quiet the children), or "Buddy knows

the words already—everyone listen to him sing" (a sure way to discourage anyone from learning the words). *Stay away from* the practice of singing a line over and over again until the children learn it and then moving from line to line until the entire song is learned—this type of dissection leads to certain boredom and eventual loss of interest.

3. Pick up the song again the next day and repeat the previous procedure. By this time the children should be fairly familiar with the lyrics, and many of them will join you as you sing. If the children have not begun to join you willingly by about the third day, there is no point in continuing to push it. Find another song that may attract the children.

Some beginning teachers feel that their inability to play an instrument is a handicap for teaching young children to sing. However, children do not need musical accompaniment to enjoy singing—as a matter of fact, pianos or other instruments often distract young children. Unless you are skilled enough to play an instrument by ear, children may be helped more by having no accompanying music than by having it.

Despite these cautions, there are two *chording* instruments that are fairly easy to learn and furnish delightful accompanying music for children's songs: the guitar and autoharp. The soft, simple chords produced by these instruments provide enjoyable backgrounds for songs. With the guitar, you will need to learn the finger positions required for basic chords, but you will need to learn only a *few* chords because children's songs are relatively unsophisticated. The autoharp is even more easily learned since it uses preset chords—as a matter of fact, three-year-olds often enjoy playing it. You only have to press down on a chord bar and strum the strings to produce the desired sound—the chord bar leaves the correct strings free while stopping all the rest. Each chord bar is marked on the autoharp and you need only press the right bar to play the accompaniment. Many books have chords marked for the teacher. They look like this:

```
   C         C         C         C
One lit-tle, two lit-tle, three lit-tle In-dians,
  G7        G7        G7        G7
Four lit-tle, five lit-tle, six lit-tle In-dians,
  C                   C         C         C
Se-ven lit-tle, eight lit-tle, nine lit-tle In-dians,
 G7     G7        C
Ten lit-tle In-dian boys.
```

As you can see, the song contains only two different chords, each repeated several times before the other is reintroduced. Only a few minutes' practice with a guitar or autoharp should make you ready to share this favorite song with your children.

Your responsibility in creating an environment for music in the preschool setting, then, is to establish an atmosphere of comfort and acceptance, and use music throughout the day. Children will enjoy your enthusiasm and appreciation for singing, and will themselves compose and sing simple tunes in their work and play. When you sense their strong interest in group singing, capitalize on it and share with them some appropriate, lively, action-oriented tunes.

Rhythmic Activities

Young children are conscious of musical rhythm and enjoy moving to the beat of musical selections. Evidence of this interest can be shown by observing children as they play in unstructured settings: they chant in rhythm as they swing or jump rope; experiment with words or sounds such as "quack-quack" or "bow-wow"; twirl in a circle while "dancing" to a favorite song; or sway and tap as a catchy tune is heard. These and many other forms of rhythmic movement can be easily seen in an environment of freedom and acceptance where children can express their feelings openly.

Like singing, rhythmic expression should at first be encouraged through spontaneous activity. Allow the children opportunities to move rhythmically in their own ways for short periods of time during the day. Often, children will do so if different kinds of music are played on the record player. You will find them clapping or tapping as they attempt to "keep time" to a regular beat. Other children will be content to twirl and move to the music. Still others will enjoy holding colorful scarves in their hands and allowing them to trail as they glide smoothly to the beat of the music. Such random bodily movements eventually become more controlled as children are exposed to planned rhythm experiences. These initial experiences should involve steady rhythmic patterns that are not necessarily from songs. For example, the

Youngsters enjoy the sounds of rhythm instruments and take pride in learning how to establish basic rhythmic patterns.

teacher may steadily beat on a drum or tambourine as the children walk in a circle. She may ask the children to alter their gait as the beating is either speeded up or slowed down. Other initial activities are described in the rhythmic activities box.

As the children gain opportunities to experience such creative rhythmic activities, they will begin to anticipate the prospect of using rhythm instruments. If the instruments are all brought out at one time, you will probably find that the children become too excited about them. It is best to simply introduce one or two instruments at a time so the children will have opportunities to experiment with them freely. Of course, there will be some "noise" at first, but if you alternate their use between the outdoors and indoors, most problems can be overcome. At this point, you should talk informally with the children about their instruments, focusing on the sounds emitted by them. You may identify the instruments for the children by using the appropriate terms—say "triangle," for example, instead of "clang-clang." As the children explore the instruments, you may help them discover the proper way to hold them. Have the child tap a triangle while holding it by one side as he had been doing and then tap it while holding it by the string. Don't say, "See, you were holding it wrong," but keep your comment open-ended, "Which way sounds better?" As the children become used to playing an instrument properly, they may be asked to furnish the rhythmic pattern in rhythm activities.

RHYTHMIC ACTIVITIES

□ Play the high-pitched piano keys in a spirited way as the children prance like elves or fairies around a circle. Then play some low keys in a deliberate way, and ask the children to march like giants around the circle. Other contrasting combinations include: hopping like grasshoppers and plodding like bears; flitting like bees and lumbering like elephants; and cavorting like ponies and trudging like rhinos.

□ Use even rhythms on the drum or tambourine during patterns of walking, marching, galloping, and skipping. (Skipping is a very difficult skill for fours and fives to acquire. Don't force a child to skip if he has difficulty doing so—give him help, but allow him the satisfaction of choosing his own rhythmic movement.)

□ Use some of the many excellent records that contain rhythmic tunes and encourage creative movement to music. Hap Palmer records are especially good for such activities, but there are several more that are as good.

□ Encourage the use of chants for children's actions, including jump rope chants. One popular jump rope chant follows:

Teddy Bear, Teddy Bear, go upstairs.
Teddy Bear, Teddy Bear, say your
   prayers.
Teddy Bear, Teddy Bear, turn out
   the light.
Teddy Bear, Teddy Bear, say
   good-night.

As such informal, creative experiences are provided for young children, they will slowly become able to manipulate the instruments properly and will gain sufficient control for group experiences. If you choose to group your children as a "rhythm band" you will at first need to develop sections of instruments. Those instruments most popularly used in preschool settings include *triangles, drums, rhythm sticks, cymbals,* and *bells.* Give each section enough time to work together so that they are able to coordinate their efforts. Rarely should you expect all sections to play together in unison—the responsibility of each section playing together is demanding for preschool youngsters. Only at the end, for one or two beats, should you expect all the children to play together. The following is a suggested procedure for organizing a rhythm band experience:

1. Choose a record with an appropriate beat, or select a suitable song to be played on a musical instrument.
2. Decide on the sequence in which each instrument will be played. For example, one teacher developed this plan for "Jingle Bells":

> Jingle bells, jingle bells *(bells only)*
> Jingle all the way *(triangles only)*
> Oh, what fun *(cymbals only)*
> It is to ride *(drums only)*
> In a one horse open sleigh. *(rhythm sticks only)*
> *(Repeat verse exactly as before.)*
> "Jingle bells!" *(everyone together)*

3. Develop cues with which to signal each group to enter the song. You may choose to hold up the instrument to be played, show the children a picture of the instrument, use a cue word such as "cymbals," or simply point to the next group to play.

The suggested rhythm instruments can be purchased from any of several school supply outfits. However, many teachers have found that teacher- or child-made instruments are often just as effective. Some of the many instruments you might make yourself include those found in the homemade instruments box (p. 418).

As the children gain increased coordination and skill in using these rhythm instruments, you will be able to supplement your total program in many ways. Poetry, music, creative movement, and musical accompaniment are only a few of the areas that can be more exciting when the children can supply their own music.

Recordings

Appropriate records of good quality should be available for use in the preschool setting. Such records can benefit your program in several ways: (1) they can be listened to for pure enjoyment; (2) they can be used as a guide for marching, dancing, or singing activities; and (3) they can be used to teach basic concepts. Several companies produce high-quality records for preschool youngsters.

Music activities can be used in many contexts during the preschool day. Singing, dancing, listening, moving, and playing instruments are all enjoyable activities for young children. Plan musical activities for your children, keeping in mind their level of development and their interests. Choose songs that are simple and activities that are active and involving. Don't be concerned about your personal musical talent—all confident teachers can provide a wealth of delightful musical experiences for young children.

PLAY

Play and childhood seem to go hand in hand. Children are constantly involved in play activities—experimenting with sounds as they bang together pots and pans, allowing their imaginations to run away as they sit in an orange crate "driving down the highway," or arranging a pile of blocks that will eventually represent the barn at a recently visited farm. Children receive many values from play activity, as it seems to dominate their day.

Play contributes to the development of every aspect of the child's growth we have discussed: social, emotional, affective, physical, cognitive, and creative (see Figure 10-7). In the following section, we discuss the viewpoints

Figure 10-7   The many contributions of play to the total development of the child.

expressed by various authorities relating play to areas of the child's development. The *social aspects* of play were discussed in Chapters 2 and 9, so only the various *forms* of play will be discussed here.

Different preschool programs in the country align themselves with one or more basic philosophies. You can easily identify these alignments as you observe the ways children are involved in their play. For example, preschool educators have traditionally believed that *free play* was an inherent right of children. Such traditional orientations saw children involved in free, active classroom activity that stressed John Dewey's basic philosophy of play: "A name given to those activities which are not consciously performed for the sake of any result beyond themselves; activities which are enjoyable in their own execution without reference to ulterior purpose."[24] Because of these

HOMEMADE INSTRUMENTS

WOOD CHIMES Hang different materials from a straight bar or a triangular wooden frame or a circular band of metal stripping so that they will strike each other when they are moved by the wind. For a variety of sounds, use different sizes and kinds of materials, such as nails, metal scraps, pieces of glass, strips of wood, dowels, pieces of bamboo, and pieces of pipe.

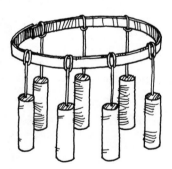

WOOD BLOCK TAMBOURINE You will need blocks of wood about ¾" × ½" × 6", bottle caps, and nails with wide heads. Remove the cork from the bottle caps. Place a bottle cap on the wood block and hammer a nail through the cap and partway into the wood block. Make sure the hole is wide

enough so the cap will slide freely along the nail. (Maybe make the hole in the cap first—with a larger-sized nail—then attach it to the wood.) Use as many nails and as many caps on each nail as desired.

NAIL SCRAPER You will need blocks of wood about 2" × 2" × 8" and nails of different sizes. Hammer a few nails into a block of wood so that they are all the same height. Leave a space and repeat the process with different sized nails—or use the same size, but hammer them in deeper. To play, run a large nail along the separate rows of nails.

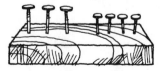

STRING GUITAR This is the most complicated instrument to make. You

orientations, "free play" was established as the rule of thumb for traditional preschool educators.

During the mid-1960s, however, cognitively oriented preschool programs emerged, signalling a change in the function of play. Almost apologetically educators of the period shied away from the term *play* and began to substitute phrases such as "exploring the physical properties of objects" when they established cognitive learning goals. These programs sought to structure children's play and pattern their experiences toward specific basic concepts. During this time, then, the emphasis changed from spontaneous, self-initiated play to structured play. Traditional educators openly criticized these ideas; they felt that excessive constraints were being placed on children and that their "play" was being replaced by "labor." Traditionalists ex-

---

will need a strip of wood about 2" × 24" × ¾", two screw eyes, 36" nylon fishline (squidding is best), two popsicle sticks, and a large nail for each one.

1. Insert a screw eye near each end of the wood strip.
2. About 1½" from each end of the wood strip, saw a ¼" deep groove across the strip for the popsicle stick.
3. Insert the popsicle stick sideways into the grooves, and tie the fishline between the two screw eyes.
4. Tighten the fishline by turning one of the screw eyes with the large nail.

5. Use as a rhythm instrument, or make several string guitars (each tuned to a different note).

DRUMS Use old coffee cans or large vegetable cans that can be obtained from the school cafeteria. Cover the open end with inner tube rubber as tightly as possible and secure it with heavy cord or wire. A drumstick is easily made with a dowel rod and piece of foam rubber at the end.

KITCHEN CYMBALS Collect discarded kettle lids (with knobs on top) and use them as cymbals.

RATTLES Some containers you might use are paper cups, plastic bottles, small plastic boxes and cans, wooden match boxes, and metal bandage cans. These can be partly filled with one or more of the following: dried beans, peas, grain, or seeds; table salt; rock salt; marbles; pebbles; feathers; sand.

(Many of these homemade musical instruments are based on the ideas of two creative teachers, Pearl Bailes and Mary Alice Felleisen.)

plained the differences between play and labor in basically this way: *play* is an activity in which there is no external end (the "process" is stressed); *labor* is the accomplishment of a predetermined material result (the "product" is stressed—there is no specific interest in the process).

By the mid-1970s, however, educators began to combine the two philosophies and view play in a new light—a common compromise Montessorian phrase "play is the child's work" described their beliefs. They began to view play as a valuable process that allowed children to grow toward desired products (goals). Although these educators have realized the value of play in developing cognitive skills, they reluctantly use the phrase in their program descriptions. They persist in using phrases such as "exploring the physical properties of a piece of soap," rather than "playing with a piece of soap." Sue Spayth Riley summarized the thoughts of many preschool educators today when she stated:

> Whatever it is called, or for whatever reasons, some educators feel disinclined to use the term; the fact remains that play is the very essence of childhood. . . .
>
> It is heartening to realize that the myopia of the early childhood academicians is diminishing. Some are finding the academic route a dead end, and are coming to an awareness of the tremendous potential of that most natural, spontaneous and self-directed activity of children—play. And whether they call it that or not doesn't matter too much.[25]

Leila P. Fagg summarized the various values of play in the preschool setting with the poem "Play Today?":

> You say you love your children,
> And are concerned they learn today?
> So am I—that's why I'm providing
> A variety of kinds of play.
>
> You're asking me the value
> Of blocks and other such play?
> Your children are solving problems.
> They will use that skill everyday.
>
> You're asking what's the value
> Of having your children play?
> Your daughter's creating a tower;
> She may be a builder someday.
>
> You're saying you don't want your son
> To play in that "sissy" way?
> He's learning to cuddle a doll;
> He may be a father someday.
>
> You're questioning the interest centers;
> They just look like useless play?
> Your children are making choices;
> They'll be on their own someday.

Figure 10-8 Developmental sequence of play.

You're worried your children aren't learning;
And later they'll have to pay?
They're learning a pattern for learning;
For they'll be learners alway.[26]

The activities described in the preceding sections of this text mostly reflect this current philosophy that play (the process) is an excellent medium through which to encourage growth in all areas of the child's development (the product). Play activities were described throughout this text as they contributed to all areas of development. The following are some of the typical stages children move through as they experience play activities. (See Figure 10-8.)

Sensorimotor Play

This is the earliest form of play, naturally found during infancy through about the age of two. During this time, the child's efforts are directed toward two major kinds of experiences: *sensory experiences* and *motor experiences*. Sensory experiences include:

1. *Sucking:* Infants will put almost anything to their mouth as they explore physical properties.
2. *Vocalizing:* Infants enjoy experimenting with their voices and delight in listening to the sounds made by others.
3. *Visualizing:* Infants gain great pleasure from gazing at and following moving objects. Their hands and feet infatuate them mainly because they are not really sure that these moving parts are actually part of their bodies and under their control.

Motor activities include:

1. *Gross motor activity:* Infants become familiar with the capabilities of their bodies through simple muscular explorations. As they gain experiences, infants often begin to imitate the actions of others and become motivated to acquire motor skills such as walking or running. Climbing on and in equipment of all kinds interests the toddler—the size or shape of the object to be climbed really does not matter.
2. *Fine motor activity:* Infants and toddlers enjoy collecting things that they get their hands on—often the goal of such activity is simply to gather as many objects as possible. Toddlers also begin to enjoy other play challenges:

☐ *Filling and dumping*—Toddlers spend a great part of their day filling cups, pans, wagons, or other containers with water, sand, beads, or the like. Naturally, what is filled must be dumped. Children will often spend a great deal of time simply filling and dumping material from the same container.
☐ *Building and knocking down*—Toddlers revel in experiences where they can build up objects such as blocks, boxes, or stacking rings, and then knock them over again. Often, toddlers build up a series of objects simply to knock them down again.
☐ *Manipulating*—Toddlers enjoy playing with puzzles or other objects that can be fitted together and broken apart again.
☐ *Exploring*—Infants, toddlers, and young children take pleasure in using their senses, especially touch, while finding out about the physical properties of objects surrounding them. For that reason, you will observe them squishing mud, spreading applesauce over their table, or exploring with finger paint, water, and sand.

Symbolic Play

As children move from toddlerhood, you will often observe changes in their play orientation. They begin to become more skillful with play materials and see play as a means for accomplishing some goal. At this stage, they

From infancy, children use play activity in increasingly sophisticated ways. *(Hi and Lois* courtesy of King Features Syndicate, Inc.)

begin to produce or construct things. They also start to move through the social orientations of play described in Chapter 8: observing someone else at play; playing alone; playing next to another child without interacting; playing next to another child while observing him from time to time; cooperating with other children.

Young children at the symbolic stage of play development continue to enjoy sensorimotor experiences, but their interests now include play orientations that reflect a growing comprehension of their environment. The children's imaginations begin to flourish at this point as they play different social roles. They turn to role-playing activities as they use dolls, cars, blocks, and other materials in more creative ways than they did before. These materials now provide the impetus for language play and dramatic play. Children may work with one or two others to play different social roles, for example. However, rules or plans do not affect their spontaneous efforts.

Games with Rules

Not until age 5 or 6 are young children able to make and accept rules to govern their play. The children still enjoy the sensorimotor and symbolic play activities experienced earlier, but they begin to realize that rules can be made to govern activities in which two or more children participate. In dramatic play situations, for example, the youngsters will differentiate the roles to be played by each child—mother, father, sister, or brother, if they should be playing house. In the earlier stages, these roles may have been identified, but no role differentiation would have been made—everyone would have done as he pleased. Likewise, motor activities such as puzzle making are done in a planned and deliberate way; simple competitive games such as tag or relay races are accepted with excitement; and group activities such as marching, singing, or parading are accepted and can be organized and carried through.

You can better understand the practical implications of these three developmental periods of play as you study the areas of the preschool curriculum that lend themselves to *creative play*. As you study the descriptions of these areas, recall the examples of play cited throughout this text. Such recollections will help you understand how central the role of play becomes in the total development of children.

Play Activities

DRAMATIC PLAY   Dramatic play involves the use of creative thinking while enacting roles or activities that are familiar to the children. By being involved in such a process, children are able to experience growth in all areas of development:

- □ *Social:* sharing and planning with other children
- □ *Emotional:* savoring pleasurable experiences and laying bare emotions such as anger, hostility, and aggression
- □ *Affective:* exhibiting likes and dislikes; exploring and expressing good and bad notions
- □ *Physical:* exercising muscular development and control
- □ *Cognitive:* expressing thoughts in play action (conceptual thought)
- □ *Creative:* bringing original thinking to the solution of problems encountered

The dramatic play area is a popular setting for young children. Various props encourage children to experiment at being mothers, fathers, babies, community members, teachers, animals, and so on—the list of possibilities is endless. Whatever the design of the dramatics area at any one time, the furniture and equipment should be child-size whenever possible. Many preschool classrooms contain a permanent housekeeping corner as well as a separate dramatic play corner that is changed periodically. The *housekeeping*

The housekeeping corner is a traditionally favorite area for dramatic play activity.

Children do not "pretend" during dramatic play—they actually *become* mothers, fathers, race car drivers, police officers, service station attendants, and so on.

corner generally includes a table and chairs; wooden kitchen equipment such as a stove, refrigerator, or sink; a wide selection of dolls; and cupboards containing cups, saucers, pots, spoons, pitchers, and so on. These materials do not need to be purchased—a little imagination turns orange crates into stoves or storage cabinets, and a little resourcefulness leads you to used and outgrown toys. The *dramatic play corner* offers children a wide variety of creative possibilities. Changeable items should be provided so that children can shift roles whenever they have such inclinations. In this area children can explore the lives of people in varying occupations and locations. For example, the following locations can be depicted with their equipment:

- ☐ *Ice cream store:* Ice cream scoops, empty ice cream containers, white aprons and caps, a table with chairs
- ☐ *Automobile repair shop:* Overalls, work caps, tools, hose for gasoline, miniature vehicles or crates to represent cars and trucks
- ☐ *Hamburger stand:* Aprons, caps, paper bags, napkins, fast food containers, pad and pencil, cash register, play money, trays
- ☐ *Hospital:* Doctor bag, stethoscope, bandages, doctor or nurse uniforms, bed, crutches
- ☐ *Tailor shop:* Table, measuring tape, variety of cloth, scissors, needle, thread, dolls to be fitted with clothes
- ☐ *Beautician parlor:* Hair curlers, aprons, shampoo and makeup bottles, hair dryer, old electric shaver, mirror

□ *Bakery:* Cookie cutters, bowls, baker's apron and cap, flour sacks, rolling pin, pie tins, cash register, toy money

Of course, these are only a few of the dramatic play situations youngsters can get involved in. Other creative possibilities for role-playing include: shoe repair persons, launderers, jewelers, service station attendants, firefighters, police officers, factory workers, secretaries, farmers, barbers, postal workers, race car drivers, and the like.

In addition to "prop corners," puppets are a pleasing medium for unstructured dramatization in the preschool classroom. Puppets can be the fancy, commercial variety or the imaginative, teacher-constructed variety. Some examples of teacher-made puppets are given in the puppet-making activities box.

PUPPET-MAKING ACTIVITIES FOR TEACHERS

□ *Puppet stages*—Large cardboard containers such as those used to pack appliances make excellent puppet stages. Cut out and decorate the side that faces the audience. Children may kneel inside and hide themselves from view as they manipulate the puppets.

□ *Sock puppets*—Take an old sock and turn it into an attractive hand puppet by sewing on buttons, yarn, and other materials.

SOCK PUPPET

□ *Box puppets*—Use an empty box for this puppet. Draw a face on a piece of paper and cut it in half at the

mouth. Glue the upper part of the face on the top half of the box and the lower part of the face on the bottom half. Operate the puppet by placing the hand in both halves of the box.

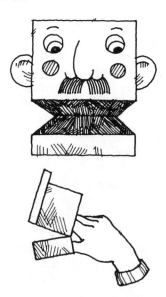

BOX PUPPET

Children often feel freer to express their thoughts through the puppet than they do on their own. Puppets are enjoyed by young children and help give meaning to their creative experiences.

BLOCK PLAY   Blocks are important additions to any preschool program. The block corner is as popular as the dramatic play area, and encourages much imagination. All preschools should be equipped with a wide variety of blocks varying in size, shape, color, and material of construction. Basic to most classrooms are the unit blocks, wooden shapes made in multiples of a basic unit: 5½″ × 2¾″ × 1⅜″. Unit blocks are durable, their natural wood color is pleasing to the eye, and the smooth finish makes the blocks pleasant to touch. They may be purchased as a complete set (over 750 blocks), half sets, or individual pieces. Each set of blocks contains many different shapes

---

☐ *Finger puppets*—Draw a head on a piece of drawing paper and leave a tab at the bottom. Tape the tab around the index finger as it forms a tube.

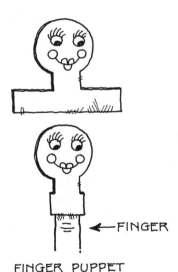

FINGER PUPPET

☐ *Food puppets*—Fruits or vegetables can be mounted on a stick and used in much the same manner as stick

puppets. Cloth or crepe paper may be used to make a "skirt" to cover the hand. Facial characteristics can be made from pins or cut with knives.

☐ *Paper bag puppets*—Draw the upper part of a face on the bottom of a bag and the lower part of the face on the side. Yarn may be glued on for hair.

PAPER BAG PUPPET

☐ *Stick puppets*—Draw and color a figure or face on a piece of cardboard and glue it to a tongue depressor or ice cream stick.

(*Tiger* by Bud Blake courtesy of King Features Syndicate, Inc.)

so that children at various levels of ability may use a set with success. Other kinds of blocks include:

- Large, hollow wooden blocks of various sizes and shapes that lend themselves to building large structures
- Boxes, boards, barrels, spools, five-gallon ice cream containers, milk cartons, and the like
- Tinkertoys, Lincoln Logs, and other plastic or wooden construction toys

Arrange the block corner in an area where the children are able to move freely and are safe from distractions or accidents caused by other children involved in unrelated pursuits. Place shelves or cabinets on the perimeter of the area and be sure that the children have a flat, steady surface on which to work—a carpeted area certainly would be inappropriate for building a tower, for example. Store the blocks in low cabinets so children can take them out and put them away without difficulty. Be sure that the children understand that all blocks are assigned a special position in the storage cabinet and that blocks should always be returned to that place.

Some children start at the block corner using only one large block, which represents to them a store, gas station, house, and so on. They often do this because they do not have the muscle control necessary to manage a two- or three-block structure. It would be appropriate for these children especially to start with cardboard boxes somewhat larger than the customary wooden blocks. By pushing, lifting, crawling into and out of, and carrying these boxes, the children begin to develop increased muscular control and confidence. Eventually, when the youngsters arrange the boxes to represent bridges, caves, tunnels, and other earthly or imaginative features, this random activity becomes more meaningful.

Once the child gains the control necessary for manipulating the smaller blocks, he may be ready to manage two- or three-block structures. When he reaches this point, you may wish to provide accessories such as toy vehicles, hoses, wagons, road signs, figures of people or animals, and other objects that encourage imagination and dramatic play. It is interesting to watch how the children's creative minds transform their block structures into super highways, city streets, or rural farmyards.

Children in any culture enjoy block play for all the pleasurable experiences such play contributes. Your role in maintaining an environment that encourages purposeful block play is critical. Basically, the role involves these responsibilities:

1. Observe the block area carefully. Your presence not only communicates an interest in what is happening, but it also helps to prevent unpleasant situations before they occur.
2. Provide support for the children engaged in block play. Encourage them to talk about their problems and accomplishments with well-timed questions such as "How can we get your gasoline station to stand?" or "How did you get it to stand up?"
3. Allow sufficient time for the block play. This amount, of course, should remain flexible and is usually determined by the children's interests and spans of attention.
4. Encourage the children to get their own blocks and to put them away when finished. You may wish to tape construction paper shapes on the block shelves so the children know where to put the different blocks. They can match their blocks to the block forms (think of the academic skills being developed through such a process!).

Block play and easel painting are recognized as perhaps the two most popular activities used by preschool teachers. One of the major reasons for this popularity is the realization of educators that block play, like dramatic play, integrates experiences in a total developmental context. Every

Building a representation of some real place with unit blocks is an activity that leads children to understand that places on the earth's surface can be represented by other means.

Some children prefer to begin block play by manipulating large cardboard boxes.

part of the child's growth is given an opportunity to flourish during block play, as the teacher guides and supports his efforts. For example, block play encourages growth in these areas:

1. *Social-emotional development.* Through dramatic play with blocks, the child is able to express feelings that otherwise may have been repressed. Also, joint ventures are commonly undertaken by the children in the block area, and the resulting give-and-take is a valuable contribution to social development.
2. *Physical development.* Lifting, pushing, pulling, grasping, stacking, and manipulating help muscular development.
3. *Cognitive development.* Concepts are developed as the children decide to place *one* block *on top of* another while trying to make their structure look like the model, or as children compare their creative structures among themselves ("My tower has *two more* blocks than yours").
4. *Creative development.* When the children use blocks of different sizes and shapes to represent physical or imaginary features, they are exercising their powers of imagination. During dramatic play, these features may be transformed into places where true-to-life adventures help stimulate and encourage powers of creativity.

WATER AND SAND PLAY   Perhaps no area of the preschool curriculum is so attractive to young children as the water and sand play areas. These areas provide relaxation, experimentation, sensory stimulation, conversation, manipulation, and, most of all, just plain fun. Anyone who has ever watched children at the beach can testify to the enjoyment children experience with sand and water. Water play should be carefully organized so that it is meaningful and successful for both the children and adults. One of the major concerns is that the children will become totally soaked before they complete their activity. However, if they are protected with full-length plastic aprons and are asked to roll their sleeves above the elbows, this worry can be resolved. Another major concern is water spilling onto the floor. If a sheet of plastic is placed on the floor, however, the possibility of damage to the room is significantly lowered. Finally, adequate measures for clean up should be a natural part of the water play routine. Provide sponges, mops, towels, and adequate storage space for the water play equipment. Help the children realize that they must assume their share of the responsibility if water play is to be a rewarding experience.

Suggestions for water play activities were given in Chapter 4, but children seem to enjoy experimenting and creating in these areas: (1) play with plain water, (2) play with water and soap (making bubbles or washing), (3) play with water and colors (tempera paint), and (4) play with water and various utensils (funnels, sponges, corks, boats, eggbeaters, cups, and so on).

The possibilities for water play activities are endless (refer back to Chapter 4). Allow frequent opportunities for such enjoyment—your delight and the children's pleasure will both be immeasurable.

The sandbox is another ideal area for informal creative play. As with water, the children find great sensory pleasure in manipulating the appealing material. Roads, airports, and cities are created by engineers and builders while cookies and cakes are created by cooks and bakers—all in the same sandbox. Imagination is allowed to flow during such activity—the children almost always accompany their construction with the "brrm, brrm," of a

Sand play is one of the ways in which children express their creativity.

steam shovel, a "whoosh" of a jet plane, or other more language-oriented dialogue. One boy, for example, made a circular arrangement of all of the leaves that had fallen into the outdoor sandbox and held them from blowing away with small amounts of sand. Sitting in the middle of his construction, he commented, "I'm an eagle and this is my nest." Small dump trucks, pails, shovels, road graders, animals, and other props also encourage children to dramatize and verbalize events within the sandbox environment.

OUTDOOR PLAY   The various dimensions of outdoor play were discussed in Chapter 4, but they need to be reemphasized at this point in order to stress the importance of this form of activity in fostering creative skills as well as developing physical skills. The playground equipment, like all the equipment contained in the classroom, encourages the children to exercise their imaginations. Jungle gyms become tiger cages from which captured tigers wish to escape; tricycles and wagons become buses and trucks taking people and products to various imaginative places; the sandbox is magically transformed into a beach or desert; and the storage shed turns into a safe hideaway for a band of dangerous desperados. All of these imaginative activities flourish on the playground and help the children create different characters and situations. Such situations help children give meaning to their past experiences, articulate their feelings and thoughts, and help give meaning and form to otherwise vague ideas.

The Teacher's Role During Free Play Activity

Although children should feel free to experiment and create, play time does not mean an unbridled "free-for-all" environment where anything goes. Realistically, it needs to be a rich experience for children—one in which there is a great deal of planning, guidance, and understanding. Some helpful advice regarding your role during play activities follows.

Use casual, noninterfering guidance. Remember that although the play process is providing the children with most of their learning, you must be ready to give support and guidance when needed. You act as a stimulant to the child in this regard as you introduce new materials, stimulate thought, and pull together random experiences into a meaningful whole.

Create an atmosphere of freedom. In order for children to enter freely into play activity, they must know that they have your acceptance and trust. You must remember that some children will have had more limited experiences with toys and play than others, so they must be allowed to approach materials at their own pace. On the other hand, some children will have had numerous opportunities for such experiences at home and will more quickly adapt to their use at school. Remember to begin where the children are, and encourage their entry into play when things become familiar to them.

Arrange equipment in an attractive and safe manner. A wide variety of materials is necessary in order to have an effective play atmosphere. If not arranged and kept in neat order, however, they can eventually become disorganized to the point of becoming unattractive. Children must understand that a great deal of responsibility for this organization is theirs. They should be warned that clean-up time is near and that "I'll help you put the truck in the shed if you bring it to me." Children can be encouraged to clean up and put things back in their original places through the use of a puppet or a catchy tune. Children are more than willing to help clean and organize the room—give them a chance and you will be richly rewarded by their willing cooperation.

Observe children by listening and watching. Your careful observation of children during play will tell much about their interests, abilities, emotional state, social adjustments, and all other areas of child growth and development. Such information can be used as an evaluative tool when you plan further individual and group experiences.

SOME FINAL THOUGHTS

Remember that preschool children are at the peak of creativity—they enter the preschool setting with curiosity and eagerness. Encourage their creative thought through all areas of the preschool curriculum, but especially in the areas of art, music, and play. Your own attitudes about the value of creative thinking will set the tone for creative endeavors in the classroom and determine whether or not the children can creatively reenact all that they hear, see, touch, smell, and taste. If we provide them with the avenues to interpret and express such sensations in imaginative ways, we allow them to grow and develop into beings whose creativity will be allowed to blossom fully later.

NOTES

1. E. Paul Torrance, "Adventuring in Creativity," *Childhood Education* 40, no. 2 (1963): 79.
2. Kornei Chukovsky, *From Two to Five* (Berkeley, Calif.: University of California Press, 1963), p. 116.
3. Sidney Parnes, quoted in *Igniting Creative Potential* (Salt Lake City, Utah: Bella Vista Elementary School, 1971), p. 110.
4. Arnold Toynbee, quoted in Calvin W. Taylor, "Introduction," *Igniting Creative Potential* (Salt Lake City, Utah: Bella Vista Elementary School, 1971), p. 13.
5. V. Goertzel and Mildred G. Goertzel, *Cradles of Eminence* (Boston: Little, Brown, 1962).
6. E. Paul Torrance, *Creativity* (Belmont, Calif.: Fearon, 1969), pp. 4–12.
7. Ibid., pp. 6–7.
8. Jean Piaget, "Development and Learning," in R. E. Ripple and V. N. Rockcastle, eds., *Piaget Rediscovered* (Ithaca, N.Y.: Cornell University Press, 1964), pp. 7–20.
9. Earl C. Kelley, *In Defense of Youth* (Englewood Cliffs, N. J.: Prentice-Hall, 1962), p. 140.

10. The explanations are taken from a yet untitled, unpublished manuscript by E. Riley Holman of West Chester State College, West Chester, Pennsylvania.
11. J. P. Guilford, *The Nature of Human Intelligence* (New York: McGraw-Hill, 1967).
12. Michael A. Wallach and Nathan Kogan, *Modes of Thinking in Young Children* (New York: Holt, Rinehart and Winston, 1965).
13. Viktor Lowenfeld, *Creative and Mental Growth* (New York: Macmillan, 1957), p. 18.
14. Viktor Lowenfeld and W. Lambert Brittain, *Creative and Mental Growth* (New York: Macmillan, 1970), pp. 91–187.
15. Dale B. Harris, *Chidlren's Drawings as Measures of Intellectual Maturity* (New York: Harcourt, Brace and World, 1963).
16. For example, H. J. McWhinnie, "Reviews of Recent Literature on Figure Drawing Tests as Related to Research Problems in Art Education," *Review of Educational Research* 41 (1971): 115–131.
17. R. Kellog, *Analyzing Children's Art* (Palo Alto, Calif.: National Principle Books, 1969), pp. 12–21.
18. Sylvia F. Burns, "Children's Art: A Vehicle for Learning," *Young Children* 30, no. 3 (March 1975): 201.
19. H. J. McWhinnie, "Viktor Lowenfeld: Art Education for the 1970's," *Studies in Art Education* 4 (1972): 8–13.
20. Constance K. Kamii and Norma L. Radin, "A Framework for a Preschool Curriculum Based on Some Piagetian Concepts," *The Journal of Creative Behavior* 1, no. 3 (July 1967): 314–324.
21. M. Brearly, *The Teacher of Young Children: Some Applications of Piaget's Learning Theory* (New York: Schocken Books, 1970). See also G. H. Luquet, *The Drawings of a Child* (Paris, France: F. Alcan, 1913).
22. Rudolf Arnheim, *Art and Visual Perception: A Psychology of the Creative Eye* (Berkeley, Calif.: University of California Press, 1969), p. 128.
23. Katherine H. Read, *The Nursery School* (Philadelphia: W. B. Saunders, 1971), p. 235.
24. John Dewey, "Play," in *A Cyclopedia of Education*, ed. P. Monroe (New York: Macmillan, 1913), p. 725.
25. Sue Spayth Riley, "Some Reflections on the Value of Children's Play," *Young Children* 23, no. 3 (February 1973): 147–148.
26. Leila P. Fagg, "Play Today?" *Young Children* 30, no. 2 (January 1975): 93.

11

Involving Parents
in the Preschool Program

"Miss Johnson thinks she knows my trouble.
What does 'hereditary' mean?"

Establishing and maintaining open lines of communication comprise very important components of sound teacher-parent cooperation. (*The Family Circus* by Bil Keane courtesy of The Register and Tribune Syndicate, Inc.)

"Why can't Curt read yet? Carver Johnson is learning to read in his school and Curt doesn't even know his alphabet yet. When is he going to learn to read?"

Curt's teacher took pride in her play-oriented, informal classroom. It was popular with the children and parents, too, so this parent's question was a difficult one to answer. The teacher realized that there is no complete agreement today about whether or not to teach reading formally in the kindergarten. It was impossible for her to rely on professional consensus to support her answer. Her major defense seemed to be that she based her program on the needs of the children in the program, and their needs indicated that they were not yet ready for formal reading instruction.

How would you communicate with this parent so that his anxieties and concerns were eased?

In the middle of free outdoor play, your supervisor hurriedly approaches you and asks you to come to her office to talk to an upset parent. Worrying that something has happened to a child in your group, you hurry to the office while the supervisor remains on the playground.

"What in blazes is going on in your school?" exploded Mr. Bates, the father of a child in your four-year-old group. "Yesterday Mike came home and told me that Roger punched him in the face. The thing I'm maddest about is that you stopped Mike from hitting him back. Now, I want you to listen to me carefully. . . . I'm a father who wants his son to settle his own problems like a man and not like a sissy. He has to learn to take care of himself and not to count on someone else to always help him. What are you trying to do?"

Remembering to keep your composure in this difficult situation, you decide to wait and not say things you might later regret. However, you know you cannot postpone this conversation until another day. What should you do?

It is now November and you have learned much from your first year of teaching. The children still have a long way to go, but you see they are gaining in school and they are a joy to work with.

Now, after a great deal of preparation, you are planning your first field trip—appropriately, to a turkey farm during the week before Thanksgiving. You send notes home to the parents of your four-year-olds, inviting them to join you, knowing that plenty of adult supervision is needed. Mr. Anderson, who regularly supports the activities of your school, answers promptly and volunteers to accompany you on the trip. It would be exciting, you think, if this original response carries over to the other parents. Your initial enthusiasm wanes as days go by and only three more parents indicate an eagerness to become involved in your project. You are thankful to those offering their help, but, at the same time, you are dismayed at the seeming lack of interest from the others.

This is a problem you did not expect before making your plans. How do you recognize the contributions of those offering their help? How do you encourage more participation in the future?

One of the things you felt was most important about the classroom environment was to arrange play materials so the children felt free to share things with each other. You have been working with the children for several months now and have found them generally cooperative in this regard—except for Bea. She is quite destructive and selfish—she throws materials, smashes toys, and abuses the equipment until some of it is either damaged or destroyed.

You didn't react immediately to her behavior, hoping that it would soon change. However, after mending or throwing away many items, and after exhausting your patience, you decide to inform her parents about Bea's behavior. However, you hesitate to set up a conference or a meeting because you have never before conducted one and are not quite sure of what to do should a confrontation occur.

How do you set up such a meeting so that Bea's parents are apprised of the situation in a positive, safe setting?

TEACHERS AND PARENTS

These situations are but a few of the many possible situations that involve you with the parents of your children. The success or failure experienced in such situations is directly related to the skills you bring to them. Teachers who have successfully developed such communication skills indicate that they were able to do so only after acquiring a background of basic knowledge about working with parents and applying this knowledge to experiences like those just described. It is understandable, nevertheless, that all the knowledge in the world will not alleviate your concerns about communicating with parents—and, in fact, some issues can be worked out best with experience. I can perceive some of the thoughts that may be going through your minds right now:

"What? Me give advice to parents? Why, I'm young enough to be their child. . . . Why would they listen to me?"

"How am I supposed to give advice to parents? I was never one myself, so how can I expect them to listen to me?"

"Tell a Spanish (Black, White, upper-class, lower-class, Chicano, and so on) mother how to raise her child? I don't know anything about their culture—how could I explain what she should do?"

These and similar concerns often seem to surface when teachers first begin to involve parents in the education of their children. These teachers understand the value of parental participation, but fear that they (1) might alienate parents by bringing up negatives about their children, (2) may not be able to offer solutions to parental problems, (3) might open themselves to parental criticism and anger (especially if they feel that the parents' experiences are more sophisticated than theirs), (4) will create a variety of other insecurities or anxieties during contact with parents. However, remember that parents often *want* help in raising their children—even those parents who seem to be able to answer the whats, hows, and whys of child rearing. The *unschooled parent*, of course, wants to learn the best methods of child rearing, and the *knowledgeable parent* often seeks professional reassurance of previously acquired information. Regardless of the type of program in which you work, participation with parents is essential for its success. Such participation can be found in many forms; the most popular of these are the ones described in the following sections.

Home Visitations

Many parents are afraid to come to school or they may feel uncomfortable if asked to meet out of their "turf." Recognizing this fact, some programs direct their teachers to visit the homes of their children so that parent contacts can be made in an environment of comfort and trust. All teachers might do well to accept this philosophy because such visits can help you gather important information, such as:

1. *Information about the child.* Casual observations and conversations can reveal facts about the child's interests, fears, attitude toward schooling, eating habits, comfort, cognitive stimulation, and other concerns.
2. *Information about the parent.* The home visit can reveal information about the parent, including attitudes about school, discipline techniques, educational background, perception of parent and teacher roles, and the like.
3. *Information about the family.* Home visits provide valuable cues regarding life style, roles of family members, sibling relationships, leisure-time activities, and other special characteristics.

Home visits are especially useful when they are arranged beforehand. Contact the parents so they will be able to cooperate in establishing a visitation time. When deciding the time with the parent, try to arrange it so the child is home when you arrive. You will be able to gain greater insight into the home life of the child if he is there when you visit. Most teachers try to arrange home visits with parents at three particular times:

☐ *Before the start of the school year.* These visits help to make the child, as well as the parent, feel more comfortable on the first day of school because they have gotten to know you first in their home in a relaxed social situation.
☐ *At regular intervals during the school year.* Some teachers organize three or four visits during the school year; others go so far as to schedule weekly visits. Regular visits help establish a sound historical view of the child's home activity during the school year and help maintain a continuing partnership between the parent and teacher.
☐ *On special occasions.* All too often, teachers make special home visits only when a severe problem arises in school. But the special home visit should be used more frequently for positive reasons. For example, a favorite toy or book can be brought to the children on their birthdays. Or, some teachers bring get well cards from classmates to the homes of sick children. Such visits help parents and children feel important, and they encourage them to feel secure as the year unfolds.

Initiating a home visitation program can sometimes be awkward because parents, as well as teachers, may feel negatively toward them. Doreen J. Croft suggested these reasons why parents may be reluctant to have teachers visit their homes:

1. The house is a mess, and the parents do not want the teachers to see their poor housekeeping habits.
2. Parents are fearful that teachers will judge them and get bad impressions.
3. Teachers are intruding on the parents' lives.
4. The family culture or way of life may be so different that the teacher would never understand it.
5. Parents' past experiences with home visits are all negative. If the teacher comes over, it's only because the child has been bad.

6. Parents do not see any real value in teacher visits.
7. Teachers try to change the parents and tell them how to be "better" with their children.
8. Parents are too busy to bother.[1]

On the other hand, teachers also sometimes feel that they are intruding on the parents, that they are "out of place" in the home (especially if it is ethnically, culturally, or socioeconomically different from their own), or that they are being forced to take time from their families or busy schedules. These concerns, however, will be minimized once you truly understand the values of home visits and appreciate the results they bring. If you find that home visitations can be made in your situation, here are some suggestions that may help change the attitudes of reluctant parents:[2]

1. Get acquainted with the parents on neutral territory, such as the school playground or a nearby park. These opportunities can result from group picnics or simply through informal meetings.
2. Establish a friendly relationship during such informal chats.
3. Be clear about your reasons for visiting the home. Tell the parents what you want to talk about and how long you want to stay.
4. Learn about the life style of the parents. By showing empathy and understanding, we establish trust and nonthreatening avenues of communication.

Sometimes parents open their homes to an entire class.

Parents become familiar with their child's surroundings as well as with the teacher during formal or informal visits to the early childhood facility.

School Visits

Parents should be encouraged to visit their child's school so they become familiar with the program and facilities, and also to let the child know that they are interested in his program. Such visits, however, should be carefully planned so that successful relationships have a better chance of developing. Parents should be made to feel comfortable and welcome at their child's school. Parents have many opportunities to visit, including:

☐ *Before the child enters school.* Invite the parent and the child to visit the school and become familiar with its facilities before the child enters. Make the parent and child comfortable in the situation by extending a warm greeting. As you orient the parent to your program, it may be wise to have a few favorite toys or books available for the child. In this way, both the parent and child begin to anticipate a successful preschool experience.

☐ *When the parent brings the child to school each day.* Often, both child and parent feel more assured when the parent is able to remain in the room for a short time after dropping off the child (this is especially true during the first week or so). It is the policy of many schools to ask the parent to stay with the child during the first day at school. In full-day programs, the parent usually stays only for the morning instead of for the whole day. If the adjustment to school seems comfortable, the same procedure may be repeated the second day; on the third day, the parent may stay one hour less. At this point, if all goes well, the child may be left for the entire day without the parent. In half-day programs, the same procedure may be used, except that the child may spend no more than two hours at the school on the first day. Every effort should be made to make this first experience as unstressful as possible for the parent as well as the child, for many parents are as negatively affected by separation as their children. Only when child, parent, and teacher feel secure can we introduce sound, meaningful experiences for all. Sometimes teachers react negatively to such close parent–child provisions and argue that a direct break is best for the child. When this happens, though, both parent and child may experience distress and communication between parent and teacher begins to break down. The situation gradually may lead to a poor home–school relationship. Cooperation and warm acceptance, then, should be extended to parents throughout the year as they drop off or pick up their children. A warm hello and a few personal words each day make the adjustment to school a success. An added value of such contact is that much can be learned about a home situation during either drop off or pick up time. One evening, for example, Gina eagerly asked of her mother, "Mama, did you get Daddy out of jail?" "Yes, Honey," she replied. "He's home now."

☐ *Regularly scheduled visits throughout the year.* These visits to the school, like all parent visits, are especially valued by the children. During the time they visit the school, parents are able to observe the classroom routine and watch the teacher work with their children. Such visits are usually scheduled with the cooperation of the parents so that the mutually agreed-upon time will be less disturbing to the children's normal routine.

Marian C. Marion recommends the use of a "parent-space" as a technique for making parents feel more welcome at their child's school. Her concept of a parent-space involves a special area in a room or the hall that could be reserved solely for the use of the parents. Marion explains:

> To create this "parent-space" [even] when a separate room is not available, all that is needed is a bulletin board, a small table and a chair or two. The space should be inviting—adequate lighting, comfortable chairs, a vase of flowers and attractive paper or burlap on the bulletin board. It should also be well defined. To do this, print with large letters on the board: PARENT'S BULLETIN BOARD. The parent-space should be readily visible when the parents enter the building. One school's parent-space is located near the area in which the children are received. The parents stop to read the board and any available material while their child is being checked in. If the parent-space happens to be separated from the classroom, a parent may stay to read or browse through books without interruption.
>
> Materials placed in the parent-space depend on the needs of a particular group of parents. If teachers want parents to stop, look at and read the materials they present, then the teachers themselves must stop, look at the needs of their parents and listen for clues to these needs. The clues are often given in casual comments made by parents in day-to-day conversation with the teacher; e.g., "I really have a hard time finding good books for Kim to read. I don't know if I pick the right ones." This mother could use some guidelines for choosing children's literature. Clues also come from the children; e.g., "I like play-dough. Can I take some home? My mom don't know how to make it." Perhaps a display of playdough and recipes is in order.[3]

Parent-spaces may also function in the following ways:[4]

1. *As an information center to announce vacations, tuition costs, parking information, and so on.*
2. *To introduce parents to activities in school that can be carried on in the home.* Such activities include finger painting, cooking, reading stories, and making puppets and other toys. Simple recipes or guidesheets can be included along with sample materials for the parents to manipulate.
3. *As a follow-up to parent meetings or study groups.* If your parents' interests on a particular subject were stimulated during a large-group meeting, you may wish to use the parent-space to display and/or check out additional material on the subject.
4. *To inform parents of personnel and activities in the classroom.* The parent-space can be used to advise parents of the various activities in which their children are involved during the day and to indicate which activities will be supervised by volunteers, aides, or the teacher.
5. *To inform parents of community events especially planned for children.* Information presented in a parent-space can extend beyond school matters to issues of community interest. Special free or inexpensive events sponsored by the Red Cross, local libraries, or recreation departments may be brought to the parents' attention. A check of your community may supply the names of these and other agencies that offer special programs for young children.

Parent—Teacher Conferences

Special individual conferences should be periodically arranged with your parents to discuss their children's growth, development, or special problem areas. During these conferences it might be a good idea to share items from the child's cumulative folder, samples of his artwork taken over a period of time, or results of special tests administered to the children. In sharing this information with the parents, it would be wise to follow these guidelines, many of which are based on the ideas of Katherine E. D'Evelyn.[5]

1. Help the parents feel comfortable by establishing a warm, friendly environment. Arrange chairs in a good conversational setting (don't sit behind a desk!) so that you and the parents enjoy equal status; serve coffee and doughnuts if possible; have an ashtray handy; and allow parents time to browse around the room upon entering.
2. Project a positive attitude toward the parents during the conversation. In order for conferences to be successful, recognize the parent as a valued person with his own needs and feelings. Accept parents' feelings, even though they may differ from your own.
3. Create a nonthreatening environment where parents are free to speak what they feel. Develop the skill of *active listening*, making it clear that all ideas are welcomed during the conversation. As you listen, look at the

person directly and let him know you are not only hearing the words being said but are truly aware of what is being said. You can communicate this feeling by: (a) *establishing favorable body language*—your facial expressions (smiles, frowns, looks of surprise, and so on) and posture (looking like you're at the starting gate waiting to get out, for example) communicate to the speaker the degree of your interest; (b) *rephrasing what was said*—by paraphrasing what the speaker said we invite the person to tell us more. For example, restating the parent's statement as closely as possible, "You don't feel that Julio should be playing with dolls," invites the speaker to go on from that statement to an elaboration of his feelings; (c) *feeding back feelings*—"You feel that Julio is becoming a sissy if he plays with dolls. . . . Would you like him to play outdoors more?" In this way, we acknowledge the parent's strong feelings and encourage him to tell us more.

4. It is a good idea to arrange for no interruptions during a conference. Nothing is more disturbing to the serious efforts of trying to think through a problem than to be interrupted at a crucial moment.

5. Responsibility for the success or failure of a conference rests primarily with you. Make an effort to establish rapport by: (a) expressing good points about the child, and (b) giving the parent the feeling that you are sharing with him the responsibility of meeting the child's problems.

6. Be as specific and direct as you can during the conference. Explain your program in easily understood terms, speak as clearly as possible, and show examples of the child's work to support your information and suggestions (but be careful about making comparisons with other children or other families).

7. If a parent gives what he thinks is the reason for a child's behavior, accept it, but lead the discussion on to the consideration of other possibilities. Remember that behavior is the result of many factors, rarely of only one.

8. If a parent suggests a plan of action for handling a particular problem, try to accept it. It is often more satisfying for parents to try their own ideas than to be forced into one of yours. A major goal in any parent counseling session is to get the parent to take the initiative. If the parent's plan fails, it is always possible to suggest others that may strike nearer to the root of the difficulty.

9. Help reassure the parents that they are part of a partnership with you and that you are willing to cooperatively plan for and carry through measures that are in the best interests of their children. Above all, don't communicate the feeling that you are trying to "teach" the parents how to deal with their children, but are there simply to work along with them.

10. Resist the temptation to assume an authoritative position should conflicts arise. Such a position gives parents the idea that you know best and that your ways must always be accepted.

11. Don't speak "educationese" at the conference. Educational jargon often creates a barrier between parent and teacher, so phrase your questions and comments in terms that are easily understandable by nonprofessionals.

12. Be ready to answer the questions most often asked by parents at conferences: "How is my child doing in his schoolwork?" "Does my child behave?" and "Does my child get along with the other children?"

13. Dwell on the positive aspects of the child's growth and development. Just as we all become affected by constant negative comments about ourselves, so do parents when they hear that their child is not doing well. This does not mean that you fail to tell parents about their child's shortcomings, but it does suggest that you let the parents know that you value the many positive virtues of their child, and that you want to help with any problem he may be having.

14. Approach the parent about helping to come up with a cooperative solution to the child's problem, if the child has one. Be sincere about such an offer as you jointly plan a positive course of action. Most parents sincerely want to do the best for their children, and if they are involved in such decisions, they will work more willingly toward solutions.

15. End the conference on a positive tone. Review the important points of the conference and let the parents know that you are looking forward to working with them in accomplishing mutual goals.

Following is a list of open-ended, nonthreatening questions that you may use during home or school visits, conferences, or other informal or formal contacts. This is just a partial list and may spur you on to developing others.

1. "How does _____ feel about school?"
2. "How does _____ help with duties around the house?"
3. "How does _____ get along with his brothers and/or sisters?"
4. "What special interests or skills does _____ have?"
5. "Have there been any sudden, upsetting experiences (illness, death, and so on) affecting _____ ?"
6. "Does _____ seem to enjoy participating in activities with other children?"
7. "How does _____ let you know when he's angry? happy? sad? interested? frustrated?"
8. "What do you and _____ enjoy doing most together?"
9. "What have you found to be the most successful way of controlling _____ 's behavior?"
10. "What do you think _____ should be doing in school?"
11. "What would you like _____ to be when he/she grows up?"
12. "What things do you do with _____ at home that you would like to see continued at school?"

Group Meetings

Many preschool centers plan regular large-group meetings (usually monthly) to bring together parents and teachers. Such meetings can be designed to introduce parents to the school program, to inform parents of new ideas in child rearing, or to present ideas relating to various other areas of interest such as fund raising enterprises or special activities. Some important guidelines to remember in planning such meetings include:

1. Plan the first meeting to familiarize the parents with your daily program. Rather than talking to the parents about the program and its policies, plan and develop a slide and tape presentation that shows its major characteristics. This will be a more meaningful experience and will hold the interest and attention of the parents more effectively (especially if their children are pictured in the slides).
2. Solicit help from the parents through a short questionnaire, or form a parent committee to make suggestions for future meetings. Repetitious meetings or topics in which few parents are interested soon lead to low attendance and a lack of interest. Some topics that have created enthusiasm among parents in our child-care program included: "preparing for the arrival of a new baby," "nutrition and your child's behavior," "teaching the preschool child at home," and "helping children cope with death."
3. Plan alternative sites for the meeting. Parents enjoy the school setting, but other successful group meetings can take place at dinner affairs, family picnics, swimming parties, and the like.
4. Encourage the parents to assume a major role in planning and carrying out the group meeting. By forming this "psychological ownership" of the meeting, the parents will be more interested in its success and will work harder to involve others.

Telephone Conversations

The telephone can be an extremely valuable tool for furthering positive parent–teacher relationships. Some parents, despite our most enthusiastic efforts, may remain somewhat timid about approaching the teacher at school. The telephone allows such parents to engage in dialogue with the teacher without facing the "threat" that a school setting may impose. Encourage these shy parents to telephone you, for this may be your only source of confidential information about their child.

You can further develop effective parent–teacher relationships with the telephone by calling the parent to convey a positive report. All too often, calls are made to report negative behaviors such as a child's uncooperativeness or tendency to destroy property. These negative calls should be done very infrequently—a face-to-face discussion is more appropriate in such circumstances. Calls reporting incidents such as the following help develop positive and confident relationships with parents: "Hello, Mrs. Dougherty. I thought you'd like to know about something that Kevin did today. He sat down at the drawing table this morning and wrote his name with crayon for the first time. Naturally, I praised him for his wonderful accomplishment, but I just wanted to let you know, too, just how happy I was. I'll make sure to send the paper home with Kevin." If positive attitudes are allowed to grow through such telephone calls, parents will soon feel openly comfortable to discuss their concerns and ideas with you.

Duplicated Messages

The importance of parent involvement in the child's education often leads preschools to prepare periodic messages, usually in the form of a newsletter, as a communication link between the home and school. Such newsletters serve three basic objectives: (1) They keep parents informed about routine classroom activity; (2) they help stimulate the parents' interest in the activities experienced by their children; (3) they provide suggestions that help reinforce and extend school learnings at home.

The content of preschool newsletters varies, but the following topics have been used successfully:

1. Names, addresses, and phone numbers of other children and their parents in the group
2. Suggestions for activities similar to those tried in school
3. Short lists of appropriate books for young children
4. Recipes for finger paints, playdough, paste, or food projects experienced by the children
5. Words to favorite songs or fingerplays
6. Short suggestions on topics such as dental health, thumb sucking, sleeping problems, fears, or personal grooming
7. Ideas for promoting reading, math, and other cognitive skills
8. Toy buying guides—especially around the Christmas season
9. Suggestions for activities that can be done during vacations, car trips, or other situations where children need extra stimulation
10. Information regarding fees, health services, the school calendar, school policies, and special activities planned for the school year

A sample newsletter is illustrated in Figure 11-1.

Parent Workshops

Special workshop sessions can be planned to introduce your parents to the techniques they can use to reinforce at home what has been done in the classroom. Some groups plan workshop programs in which parents are actually involved in manipulating the materials used by their children: finger paints, playdough, puzzles, and so on. The purpose of such activity is to help them understand the experiences their children are having in school and to help them organize similar experiences in the home. Other sessions may train parents to offer a wide variety of home-learning topics. One session included the sharing of basic parental skills, including those described in the following list:

```
                        PLAYTIME NEWSLETTER


                                        DID YOU KNOW?

      Playtime Bulletin Board       Did you know the dangers involved
                                    while your little child is a
                                    passenger in your car?  For exam-
    ┌─────────────────────────┐     ple:
    │ October 21 at 8:00 P.M.  │
    │                         │      • A 30 m.p.h. head-on crash ex-
    │ Parent-teacher meeting  │        poses your child to the same
    │ in all-purpose room.    │        force as a fall from a three-
    │ Slides will explain     │        story building.
    │ your child's school     │
    │ program.                │      • Holding a young child in your
    └─────────────────────────┘        lap is not an effective safety
                                       measure.  The child's weight is
    ┌─────────────────────────┐        multiplied by 10 to 20 times by
    │ October 23 at 4:00 P.M.  │       the force of a crash. A 20-pound
    │                         │        child may hit the windshield or
    │ Storytime at City Library.│      dashboard with the force of a
    │ Puppet show: "Pinocchio." │      400-pound weight in a crash.
    └─────────────────────────┘
                                    What can you do?  Besides spend-
    ┌─────────────────────────┐     ing hundreds of dollars for power
    │     October 24          │     windows or other optional equip-
    │                         │     ment on your car, make a $50
    │ The class will be going │     investment for a good child re-
    │ on an all-morning field │     straint.  It may be worth it in
    │ trip to the zoo.  Please│     the long run.
    │ have your child bring a │
    │ jacket to school.       │
    └─────────────────────────┘




                         TALK ABOUT FUN!

    Here's a game that we played in school.  The children enjoyed it very
    much so I thought you might like to try it at home.
```

```
                    Here's how:  The first person says "Ha."  The second per-
                    son then says "Ha Ha."  Then the first person (or the
                    third) says "Ha Ha Ha," and so on back and forth, each
                    player adding one more "Ha."  The "Ha's" must be said
                    WITHOUT LAUGHING (which isn't easy) and the player who
                    manages to keep a straight face the longest is the winner.
```

Figure 11-1 Sample format for a preschool newsletter.

1. Talk to your children—even infants love to hear your voice.
2. Listen to your children—they need to talk to you and know that you are interested in what they have to say.
3. Read to your children—a child who is read to is more eager to learn to read himself.
4. Take your child places—point out interesting things and give them exposure to a variety of new experiences.
5. Buy books for your children when you can afford them—a child who owns a few good books will be more interested in reading.
6. Praise your children when they do a good job—praise reinforces learning.

7. Keep your child in good health—provide plenty of rest, exercise, and good nutrition.
8. Show a genuine interest in your child—your attitude is usually the child's attitude.
9. Plan opportunities for nonpressured play—it gives your child an opportunity to try out new things in a safe manner.
10. Play with your children—provide appropriate playthings and a cheerful place to have fun.

Remember that your parents are probably your most important co-workers. The extent to which they effectively carry out educational practices in the home influences the rate and direction of your preschool program. Through on-site parent workshop sessions, you are able to inform parents of practical strategies for the home and thereby reinforce and extend the child's experiences and growth—the primary goal of a sound parent–teacher relationship.

Other Ideas

1. Acknowledge parents who are making valuable contributions to your program. Let them know their help is appreciated by thanking them publicly at a parent–teacher group meeting, sending them a special note, citing them in a newsletter, or holding a special thank-you party for them at the year's end.
2. Send a special "Smile-gram" to parents for their efforts with their children. See Figure 11-2.
3. Declare a special "Parent's Day" to let your parents know how much you appreciate their cooperation. American Education Week (usually the second or third week in November) would be a great time to send home thank-you notes from your entire class, hold a special thank-you party, or do a special art project just for the parents.
4. Take field trips to visit parents. Your class may be thrilled to see each other's parents in action—be they homemakers, mechanics, nurses, service station attendants, businesspeople, or bakers. Take pictures of your trip and mount them on a special career bulletin board. Be sure, though, that you convey the feeling that each parent's job is interesting and important. Some teachers adapt this kind of visitation experience by taking class trips to the homes of each child in the room. Parents normally enjoy activities like this, and often prepare simple snacks or activities for when the children arrive.
5. Inform parents of sources of good child-rearing information. County or state extension services often provide such materials, along with family service organizations and other agencies. A sample page of information from the Cooperative Extension Service of the Pennsylvania State University is presented in Figure 11-3. Other public service agencies that provide information about and services for children are:

SMILE-GRAM from Mrs. Turner

Dear Mrs. Thompson:

    Brenda did a much better job of recognizing her colors today because

of the help you gave her last night. Thank you for taking the time to

help Brenda and me.

                  Sincerely,

                  Joan Turner

Figure 11-2   Thank parents for their efforts.

American Red Cross	Easter Seal Society
Association for Retarded Children	Family Service Centers
Cancer Foundation	Hospitals
Center for the Blind	March of Dimes
Childbirth Education Association	Poison Control and Treatment Service
Children's Services	Salvation Army
Council for Exceptional Children	School District Offices
County Board of Assistance	Social Security Administration
Day Care/Head Start Programs	State Education Association
Department of Health	Welfare Offices

PARENTS AS PARTICIPANTS IN THE SCHOOL PROGRAM

Parents can add to the school program in many ways if they know you are interested in their help and that you welcome and respect their skills. There are two basic ways that parents can become involved in your program: (1) as volunteers in the classroom and (2) as decision makers in relation to certain policies and program concerns. Whatever the role of the parents, however, they must know that their efforts are sincerely wanted and appreciated—

COOPERATIVE EXTENSION SERVICE

The Pennsylvania State University

Chester County   Paul B. Dague Bldg., 235 W. Market Street   Telephone
Extension Service   West Chester, Pennsylvania 19380   215-696-3500

MARCH 1979

HOW THE EARTH-NATURE CLEARS THE WATER.
Place a piece of cotton in the hole of a flower pot—
add layers of charcoal and sand. Pour muddy water
into the pot. Allow it to drain into a glass. Talk
about how the water appears. How nature cleans water.

WALK THE LINE. Place a six or eight foot piece of
string or yarn on the floor. Stretch it tight, tying
the ends to chair leg if necessary. Have the child
walk on the line—first empty handed, then carrying
different objects.

MAKE A LEAF PRINT. Place a leaf under a piece of lightweight paper. Have the
child run a crayon back and forth on top of the paper. The impression of the leaf
will appear on the paper. Try other objects like coins, materials.

LET YOUR CHILD FEEL IMPORTANT. Do a hand print.
Have child lay hand on piece of paper. Trace around
it with a crayon. Put child's name on it. Hang it
up. Have child color it. Or, smooth out and flatten
enough play clay or dough to cover the palm of child's
hand. Have child press hand firmly into dough.
Allow dough or clay to harden.

Figure 11-3 County extension services are good sources of child-rearing
information. (Reproduced by permission of the Cooperative Extension Service, West
Chester, Pa.)

and, in fact, your program won't be as effective as you would like it to be without them.

Parent Volunteers

When you decide to encourage and accept parents as volunteers in the classroom, you must determine what their role is to be. In many instances, you will have both parents who are professionally competent and able to help with instructional-type activities, and parents who possess no particular professional skills but are willing to help with non-instructional tasks—make bulletin boards, ready supplies, help on field trips, and the like. Both groups must be accepted by you and given assignments suitable to their abilities and talents. Assigning professionally competent persons to do functions below those they normally do may be demeaning to that group; and unreasonable expectations may cause nonprofessionals to feel uncomfortable. If roles are defined to the parent volunteers and choices made available to them, they will almost without exception assume the one role best suited to their interests and abilities and be comfortable with it. (See Figure 11-4.)

Once parent volunteers have been accepted into your program, and their roles have been cooperatively defined, they must be totally involved in the classroom routine. The first step in this process is to plan an orientation session in which the following considerations are communicated:

1. the philosophy of the school
2. your personal philosophy of learning

Figure 11-4 Types of parent volunteers in the preschool setting.[6] (Text from *Parent Involvement in the Home, School, and Community* by George S. Morrison, 1978. Reprinted by permission of Charles E. Merrill Publishing Company, Columbus, Ohio.)

3. the school program
4. the policies of the school
5. methods of discipline and control, especially defining limits

When the parent enters the classroom for the first time as a volunteer, there are several things you should do:

1. Introduce the parent to the children and allow them to interact if there seems to be sufficient interest.
2. Ask the parent to observe only during the first day or so—this will help him understand the levels and types of classroom interactions and activities.
3. Make the parent feel welcome. Comment on special things that need to be pointed out and maintain a positive attitude throughout the day. As the parent's self-image is enhanced, he will gain increasing confidence in his ability.

Vivian Todd and Helen Hefferman offer these suggestions to parent volunteers working in the preschool setting.

The children come first: Help each child know that he has worth and dignity, that you can trust him and have faith in him. Some of the ways you can do this are:
1. Let the children take initiative whenever possible.
2. Avoid interrupting a child's activity; encourage him to finish what he wants to do.
3. Listen carefully when a child has something to tell you. Get down to his level by squatting or sitting. Mirror or enlarge what he says, but do not evaluate it.
4. Be generous in giving deserved praise.
5. Laugh with the children, not at them.
6. Use positive suggestions. Avoid "don'ts."
7. Talk with other adults only when necessary.
8. Discuss the children with other adults only in conferences, never in front of the children.
During easel painting: Display an interest in the children's work, but do not ask what they have made. They may not know!
1. Have only one child at each side of an easel at one time.
2. Encourage each child to put on a smock as a proper costume for painting. Some children may not paint if they have to wear a smock, so do not force this.
3. Encourage the child to replace the brushes in the correct cans.
4. Tell the child, "We paint on the paper."
5. Write the child's name on a corner of the paper. Add any interesting comments and the date.
6. Hang paintings to dry with clothespins on a rope between posts.
7. Let children who wish to, take paintings to their cabins; others may be saved for end-of-camp display.
During sand-and-water play: Provide sand or dirt and a dishpan filled with water for many kinds of activity much enjoyed by small children.
1. Provide small cans, boats, trucks, and shovels.

2. Allow children to explore as they choose, but help them stay within a limited area.
3. Encourage children to keep their clothes dry. Help them change clothes in case they get wet.
4. Join in their digging or be their guest to "eat" the cake they make.
5. Teach children that they may not throw sand or dirt at other children. You may say, "Keep the sand low," or "Sand hurts eyes."
During story time:
1. Join the group of children and show interest in the story.
2. Let a child who is disturbing others sit in your lap. If this is not enough, take him to a quiet place where you may read or look at a book with him, or just give him your attention in conversation.
During music time:
1. Feel free to participate with the children in singing, finger plays, and other musical activities.
2. Help children enjoy responding to music by enjoying it yourself.
3. Let some children respond with their whole bodies with rolling, swimming, or hopping movements; other children prefer to watch until they are ready to participate. Those who participate actively at some times may prefer to watch at other times.
4. Give a child disturbing the group your special attention with another activity in a diferent location. (See item 2 under "During story time.")
About your own child: It is not always easy for him to share you when you are working in his group. He needs your particular understanding attention as he gradually learns independence of you.[7]

George S. Morrison summarizes the impact of a sound parent volunteer program by stating these advantages:

1. The teacher becomes more effective and efficient when parents make materials, handle routines, or tutor children.
2. Children benefit from having social interactions with a wide variety of adults who bring rich cultural backgrounds, diverse skills, and different points of view.
3. The sense of self-worth through involvement is enhanced in the parent. As they are meaningfully involved, they gain increasing confidence in their child-rearing abilities.
4. Often, there is an enhanced relationship between the parent and child in the home as a result of involvement as a school volunteer.
5. Teachers become more empathetic toward the role of a parent. They can begin to see children from a parent's point of view.[8]

Parents as Decision Makers

A second major opportunity for parent participation is in the area of making decisions regarding the policies and curriculum directions of the children's school. This goal can be achieved in several ways.

PARENT ADVISORY COMMITTEES   Find three or four parents who are particularly interested in their children's school, who reflect a cross-

Parents can contribute to the success of preschool programs in a variety of ways.

section of the children, and who can work closely with you. Ask them to meet with you periodically to discuss relevant problems, preview upcoming activities, and advise you on possible directions of action on pertinent topics. This group can help set or review policy as it acts as a liaison between home and school.

AD HOC PARENT COMMITTEES   A popular technique in many preschools is to establish temporary parent committees, which are brought together to accomplish a single specific task and are then disbanded. For example, parent volunteers could be asked to design plans for a fund raising carnival to be held on the playground, to review a special piece of equipment for purchase, or to design and build a new area for storing art supplies. This one-time-only form of participation on an ad hoc committee is attractive to many parents, especially those who are too busy to make a long-term commitment.

PARENT COOPERATIVES   Parent interest and involvement in their children's education is the major reason for the growing popularity of cooperative preschools around the country. In a co-op, parents agree to work a certain amount of time per week in the classroom and to attend regularly planning meetings. Though they serve as an advisory group to the teacher, the parents normally assign the major responsibility for curriculum decisions and teaching techniques to the director or teachers. However, co-op parents do have a voice in determining how the school operates and what parent education activities are offered by the school.

Parent participation, then, should be encouraged and used in preschool programs. If done effectively, such participation can help the school and its teachers maintain a line of communication that keeps them in tune with the desires of the parents and keeps the parents informed about the successes and needs of their children. By maintaining two-way communication, we encourage the type of cooperation that helps create the best educational program possible.

A SELECTED PARENT INVOLVEMENT PROGRAM: PROJECT PARENT

Today, there are many unique parent involvement programs. To attempt to categorize them or even to present a representative sample of the various types is an impossible task. For that reason, one program that appears to have unique parent involvement characteristics has been chosen as an example: PROJECT PARENT. Note that its uniqueness was established only because its goals and methods were determined *after* the parent population being served had been studied.

Different from programs that seek to achieve only child-development goals, PROJECT PARENT[9] primarily pursues parent-development goals that naturally enrich the experiences of involved children. The fundamental objective of PROJECT PARENT is *to enhance the one-to-one parent–child relationship* through dynamic interaction of teachers, parents, and children in a multi-faceted program *designed to raise adult basic education skills in the area of parenting*. To achieve this objective, PROJECT PARENT was designed by the Early Childhood Program at West Chester State College to provide:

☐ a comprehensive understanding of the nature and responsibilities of parenting
☐ a fund of knowledge in the area of child development
☐ a repertoire of fundamental abilities for analyzing, supporting, and stimulating child growth and development.

Each participating parent is interviewed and pretested by Project staff members. Discussion of basic family information is directed toward the general health and specific likes, dislikes, fears, and habits of the child or children involved. Information about the parents is obtained through the Survey of Parent Attitudes, the Survey of Parental Evaluation Skills, and the KID Scale, that is, Knowledge of Infant Development. Finally, goals are established based on expressed parental concerns and interests. Each child's intellectual, social, and physical growth is measured through a pre/post test battery, including: the Peabody Picture Vocabulary Test (PPVT), the Slosson Intelligence Test (SIT), and the Vineland Social Maturity Scale.

Results of pretesting reveal developmental profiles that, in turn, form the basis for a prescriptive program for each child. Instructional materials and techniques are applied to formulate prescriptive programs covering perceptual and language skills development, as well as growth in self-concept. The prescriptive program is then thoroughly detailed and explained to each participating family, individually, by the Project's Parent/Teacher. Weekly cluster meetings, structured by the Parent/Teacher around specific topics, are the nucleus of PROJECT PARENT. Held in an informal environment, minimizing cultural and economic differences, these 90-minute meetings are extremely successful in achieving objectives. Each week, small clusters of about ten parents meet to "exchange notes" on the past week's successes and failures; get to know one another better and to learn . . . and, learn in interesting and varied ways. Following a general overview relating that week's topic to a child's overall development, the Parent/Teacher moves each cluster meeting through an audiovisual elaboration of the topic. A film, filmstrip, audio tape, or videotape is the great stimulator of cluster discussion. Questions, comments, shared experiences, even objections intermingle as participants' involvement deepens and their awareness grows. Older members help younger members, while the latter reveal fresh approaches to the former. Frequently, packages of crayons, construction paper, and so on are given to participants for home use. Occasionally, books, puzzles, lotto games, or toys are provided. These serve to increase the potential for positive interaction between parent and child. Intensity of learning in these cluster meetings makes them a key to the overall success of PROJECT PARENT.

Augmenting the work and accomplishments of cluster meetings, Project staff and the Parent/Teacher conduct monthly general project seminars in which ALL Project participants become involved. Also 90 minutes in length, each seminar is characterized by a presentation from a guest expert, or experts, on the topic at hand. For example, a Toy Workshop turns everyday household items into child-pleasing learning aids while stressing the parent's role as teacher.

Complementing cluster meetings and general project seminars, PROJECT PARENT features a third level of attention to its participants—the individual conference. Here, one-on-one discussions between parent and staff member delve into parent as well as child progress on the prescriptive program developed at the start of the Project. Difficulties with lessons are frequently resolved with alternate materials, while suggestions on instructional techniques are exchanged among participating families. But special problems are handled too. And, often these problems are resolved satisfactorily by Project staff members, or recommended specialists.

Before PROJECT PARENT could emerge as a functioning program, numerous steps were necessary, primary among which was the collection, organization, and adaptation of viable curriculum activities and materials. Thereafter, staff members recruited the Project's Child Development Specialist/Instructor (CDS/I), or as she came to be called, the Parent/Teacher.

Next, enrollment mailings, phone calls, and personal visits were conducted among all social service and community agencies within the immediate and surrounding areas. This helped assure the broadest possible participation.

In final preparation, prospective participants were contacted. Those having at least one child of 1½ to 5 years of age—a basic Project requirement —were interviewed. A random selection of those applying yielded a group of participants consisting of parents from 30 families. These parents ranged in age from 17 to 37 years; in educational level from high school to postgraduate; in income from low to high. They included the advantaged as well as the disadvantaged. One-third of the families consisted of teenage parents.

At the end of the posttesting, results showed significant growth on the parts of both parents and children. These results were shared with PROJECT PARENT participants with particular emphasis on areas of growth coinciding with previously expressed concerns and interests of the parents.

SOME FINAL THOUGHTS

Many strategies are available for preschool teachers to help them promote effective parent–teacher relationships. Because you will be working with unique individuals who prefer their own methods of interaction, some methods will work more successfully than others—there is no universal agreement about which ones are best in all situations. Through frustrating trial-and-error experiences, though, you will quickly be able to choose the best approach for the particular group of parents with whom you are working. To help you meet this goal, it would be a good idea to read about other parent programs—this will help you become familiar with parent involvement techniques other than those presented in this chapter. You might read the following:

- Doreen J. Croft, *Parents and Teachers* (Belmont, Calif.: Wadsworth, 1979).
- Mary Carol Day and Ronald K. Parker, *The Preschool in Action*, 2d ed. (Boston: Allyn and Bacon, 1977).
- Ira J. Gordon and William T. Breivogel, *Building Effective Home–School Relationships* (Boston: Allyn and Bacon, 1976).
- George S. Morrison, *Parent Involvement in the Home, School, and Community* (Columbus, Ohio: Charles E. Merrill, 1978).
- U. S. Department of Health, Education, and Welfare, Office of Human Development, Office of Child Development, Home Start, *A Guide for Planning and Operating Home-Based Child Development Programs*. DHEW Publication No. (OHD) 75-1080. (Washington, D.C.: U.S. Government Printing Office, June 1974).

NOTES

1. Doreen J. Croft, *Parents and Teachers* (Belmont, Calif.: Wadsworth, 1979), p. 50.
2. Ibid., pp. 50–52.

3. Marian C. Marion, "Create a Parent-Space—A Place to Stop, Look and Read," *Young Children* 27, no. 4 (April 1973): 221–222.

4. Ibid., pp. 222–224.

5. Katherine E. D'Evelyn, *Individual Parent–Teacher Conferences* (New York: Teacher's College Press, Columbia University, 1963).

6. George S. Morrison, *Parent Involvement in the Home, School, and Community* (Columbus, Ohio: Charles E. Merrill, 1978), p. 140.

7. Vivian Edmiston Todd and Helen Hefferman, *The Years Before School: Guiding Preschool Children*, 2d ed. (New York: Macmillan, 1970), pp. 574–575.

8. Morrison, *Parent Involvement*, pp. 150–152.

9. Russell A. Dusewicz, Project Director, PROJECT PARENT, West Chester State College, West Chester, Pa.

12

Putting It All Together: Creating a Challenging Preschool Environment

" If you think KINDERGARTEN is the pits... wait until you hit first grade!"

Planning an early childhood program that is challenging and rewarding is an extremely sophisticated professional skill. (*Dennis the Menace* courtesy of Field Enterprises, Inc.)

The true excitement of beginning teaching usually comes with the process of planning and selecting the equipment and materials for a given group of children, and in designing the actual physical facility. This process is an extremely sensitive one because the experience of spending time with teachers in the preschool setting is important for young children. Your children are probably leaving their homes for the very first time, and when they arrive in this strange, new environment, they are surrounded by new children (probably more of the same age than they have ever seen), new play areas, different toys, strange adults, unfamiliar toilet facilities, and a variety of other untried experiences. The children must be led into these new experiences by a trusting and knowledgeable adult, for such a person can give children a feeling of confidence and a spirit of adventure that is basic to an enthusiastic, emotionally safe introduction. One question that beginning teachers often ask is, "But what kind of experiences *should* I provide in order to make the environment as safe and as rewarding as possible?" This is extremely difficult to answer because there is no agreement today as to which approach to creating classroom environments is most effective. All the individuals or groups offering recommendations, however, agree on one basic guideline: The young child should be foremost in the minds of educators responsible for developing preschool programs. So, before any thoughts about the actual physical characteristics, teaching materials or strategies, and other features of the setting can be made, we must first consider the client.

FOUNDATIONS OF PROGRAM PLANNING

How do we view the development of the child? What theories of instruction best explain the learning process? These questions must be answered openly and honestly, for the decisions you make provide the foundation of your program (see Figure 12-1). Without a carefully formed view of the child as your foundation, your program stands a strong chance of falling and crumbling for lack of focus and well-defined design. However, if your foundation is strengthened and nourished in a sound, well-informed manner it will dictate the goals of the program: what is taught, the materials and methods used by the teacher, the scheduling of daily activities, and the ways in which the classroom is physically organized.

Preschool programs today are supported by a wide range of current opinions in the field of child development. Such programs take this information and turn it into basic program models that serve as guides for teachers developing their own programs. Currently, there appear to be three broad categories into which model programs fall:

☐ *Informal models*—These programs have evolved through the years from the early, traditional, child-centered preschools designed for middle-class children to today's informal settings for all children. The primary emphases of these programs today are the needs of the "whole child": (1) habits of health and personal care, (2) motor skills, (3) self-concept, (4) social and emotional development, (5) satisfactory behavior, and (6) language and intellectual development.

☐ *Skills-oriented models*—These programs emerged during the late 1960s and are primarily geared toward the formal, direct teaching of specific skills or information, especially in the areas of reading, math, and language. These programs are mainly teacher- or subject-oriented rather than child-centered; this means that the teacher directs the learning activities while the child participates in prescribed ways. Other develop-

Figure 12-1   The foundation of program planning.

mental processes are considered important, but the major purpose of these programs is to develop academic skills within a highly structured learning environment.

☐ *Cognitive developmental models*—These programs, which also emerged during the late 1960s, are concerned mainly with two areas: (1) the development of effective learning processes such as problem solving, concept formation, observation, experimentation, and manipulation with particular emphases placed on Piagetian tasks and language development, and (2) the acquisition of positive attitudes toward learning. The teaching strategies designed to meet these aims consist of teacher direction (sometimes formal and at other times informal) in activities, some of which may be highly structured and others more flexible. Because of this program flexibility, cognitive developmental programs range from high-structured approaches similar to the skills model to low-structured approaches similar to the child-centered informal model.

The philosophies of each approach have been discussed in detail throughout this text. A summary of each position is found in Table 12-1.

You will notice that there are many basic differences among philosophies in early childhood education—these differences affect the ways teachers prepare and use methods and materials of instruction. Within these separate models, the teacher must be fully aware of her unique role and of the expectations for the children. Once this awareness has been achieved, the teacher must be willing to carry through her responsibilities and prescribed functions enthusiastically. Successful program implementation, then, strongly depends on (1) an awareness of the teacher's role as prescribed by the model and (2) a willingness by the teacher to carry out that role at all times. Although there are differences among models, as listed in Table 12-1, certain characteristics are held in common. Eleanor Maccoby and Miriam Zellner summarized those common considerations:[1]

Table 12-1   Comparison of Three Basic Models of Preschool Programming

	Informal Models	Skills-Oriented Models	Cognitive Developmental Models
Objectives	Focus on social and emotional development, language skills, health and personal care, and intellectual abilities	Focus on academic knowledge and skills; also concerned about other areas of development, primarily personal and social behavior	Focus on development of Piagetian skills: sensorimotor, language, and cognitive; value social interaction as a tool to move child from egocentricity toward socialized behaviors
Source of child's motivation	Satisfaction of personal needs essential before learning can take place; personal needs include love and security; motivation mainly intrinsic	Motivation seen as capable of being manipulated from the outside through a reward system; such rewards can be material or social, but motivation seen as an aftermath (reward) rather than a precondition of learning	Child intrinsically driven toward seeking equilibrium; solving problems and gaining increasingly mature levels of logical thought seen as a motivation in itself
Learning environment	A balanced curriculum encouraging freedom and direct experience within well defined limits; learning activities based on developmental principles and adjusted to each child's interests and needs; teacher responsive to the child's intellectual, social, and physical needs; emphasis on an integrated project approach (such as cooking) where many learnings are encouraged	Very specific methods of classroom management and teaching; detailed methods and sequential skills development advocated; emphasis on programmed materials and teaching machines	Definite teaching strategies, but classroom free enough for exploration and discovery; materials designed to develop basic Piagetian skills such as classification, seriation, conservation, and problem solving

1. Individual differences among the children are recognized and dealt with as they enter the program.
2. Preevaluation is necessary in order to determine those individual differences.
3. Children's needs can best be met if they are properly identified and matched with the appropriate resources.
4. Children must be interested in school and motivated to learn before any behavioral changes can be expected.
5. Teachers must provide activities and experiences that lead to successful challenges for the children in their environments.
6. All children can experience success in any program provided that the activities are presented in such a way that they make sense to the children.

Perhaps, by now, you have begun to formulate some ideas that tend to influence you toward one particular program model or another. Such a decision requires deep thought and planning—you do not just appear in the room on the first day of school and "do what comes naturally." You must read, talk to other teachers, observe other classrooms, and study how others have organized their programs. A *good* program does not happen simply by chance. So, as you participate in professional field experiences or student teaching, make the most of your opportunities and begin to make choices about the type of early childhood program that appeals to you.

Observe and evaluate with a good program checklist as your guide, while you compare and contrast programs for young children. Ask for help from teachers at preschool centers or from your college instructors. They are all members of a team entrusted with your education and are as concerned about your professional education as you are about the education of the children you will teach. All early childhood professionals have a joint interest —the development of young children. Your commitment to this interest will be maintained and strengthened as you cooperate and share ideas with those in the field of early childhood education.

PLANNING PRESCHOOL PROGRAMS

The process of implementing philosophical decisions into actual program designs can be illustrated by comparing it to the process of planning a vacation. Assume that it is term break and an opportunity exists for you and a group of friends to visit any one of four possible vacation spots: Bermuda, Paris, the Florida beaches, or Vail, Colorado. Such a situation would probably involve a great deal of discussion as to the merits of each place, since individual interests and values would affect the final decision. Perhaps after a great deal of give-and-take some compromises could be reached among all members of the group and an eventual decision made. The teacher planning

Good early childhood programs differ in their philosophical orientations, but they all share one common characteristic: they attempt to provide the types of experiences best suited to the needs of their children.

her preschool program is faced with similar considerations. She does not simply choose one approach out of thin air and use it in her teaching. She is a member of a team—a team comprising *herself, parents, children,* and *administrators.*

☐ *The teacher.* You are an individual and have professional characteristics all your own. Your personality, your training, and your experience all influence the type of classroom practices you feel are most appropriate for your children. You must be true to these feelings and teach in a way that is most agreeable and most comfortable for you, for an uncomfortable or unappealing technique will most certainly result in artificiality and an unnatural style of teaching. Your children will sense the resulting feelings of unhappiness and will most likely respond to you and the classroom in a similar way. So, your knowledge of teaching methods and materials should be brought into the open and shared with others as the goals and techniques for your preschool program unfold.

☐ *The parents.* Parents looking for a preschool setting for their children often provide positive input into the strengths and weaknesses of the program. Encourage parents to share their ideas and to voice their concerns about what is being provided for their children. Parents are, in actuality, "consumers" who have a right to examine a program and make suggestions on the things that they would like to have provided for their children.

☐ *The children.* Remember that the children are the major reason why your preschool exists—the program is for them. Examine the backgrounds of your children, recall your knowledge of child growth and development, and think of all you know about the interests and abilities of youngsters as you plan your program. Keep these thoughts in mind, because the final program you choose should be affected by many variables directly affecting the children, including their families; whether they come from urban, suburban, or rural settings; whether they come from low-income, middle-income, or high-income homes; whether they speak English or another language; or whether or not they have had varieties of educational experiences before entering school. A good program respects these variables and is designed to promote areas that need to be strengthened and extended.

☐ *The administrators.* Although some preschools allow individual teachers sufficient freedom to plan and execute whatever program they desire, many require new teachers to accept the principles and policies established by the school itself. They desire this conformity because they want a coordinated program in which all involved are constantly aware of each other's responsibilities. Such programs range from those requiring strict teacher conformity to those allowing the teacher some degree of freedom within a basic curricular structure. Be sure to find out the type of teacher-freedom that is extended by the administration of the school you are considering for employment—if you are the kind of person who needs to follow a set curriculum and have the major plan of organization outlined for you, then you may feel awkward in a school that asks all teachers to assume full responsibility for planning and executing their own curriculum. Of course, the opposite is true for those of you who need freedom and openness in their planning.

Being a member of a team, then, implies that all members should have appropriate input into any decisions and, ideally, that such give-and-take will result in a decision that all can accept. Therefore, as you and your friends must choose one from among four vacation spots, the teacher and her teammates must choose from among the major philosophies of preschool education: informal models, skills-oriented models, and cognitive developmental models.

Goals

Once you have decided on the basic philosophy for your program, the next issue that arises is where you wish to go with it. To relate this decision to our vacation analogy, let us suppose that the group decided that Florida would be the most attractive and interesting place for you to go. You therefore established a major direction, but the decision-making process is still not finished. Your travel plans must now address the question of what you want to do once you get there. You must establish *goals*—what do you want to accomplish? Suppose the individuals involved in making the decision eventually choose these four major goals:

1. To visit Disney World
2. To swim, surf, and bask in the sun at the beach
3. To visit Cape Canaveral and other points of interest
4. To sample the entertainment at the various night spots

Of course, other possibilities for travel goals existed and were discussed in your group's deliberations—possibilities such as shopping, boating, fishing, jai alai, dog racing, and the like. But, after considering the variety of factors, your group eliminated those and settled on these particular four goals. If the group had not effectively planned the vacation in this way, you might have found yourselves fluttering from one activity to another when you got to Florida, and not really spending enough time at one to make it worthwhile, or you might have devoted so much time to one activity that you didn't have enough time for the others. In much the same way, the teacher must identify goals for her preschool program—statements that identify *what* she wishes to accomplish from the program she is developing so that it will operate as efficiently as possible. Before we examine goals of specific preschool programs, let's analyze the two major mistakes often made by teachers in stating such goals:

1. *Stating too many goals.* Some teachers list as many as 40 or 50 goals for their program. Such a figure is unrealistic and virtually impossible to accomplish. This is analogous to fluttering from one activity to another on your vacation trip and not spending enough time on any one activity to make it worthwhile.
2. *Stating goals too vaguely.* At times, the goals of a preschool program are stated in such a general way that they lack real meaning. This problem is analogous to the situation of saying, "I'm going on vacation to have fun." Such a statement lacks focus and would probably apply just as well to a trip to Antarctica as it would to a trip to Florida.

For most purposes, three to six well-stated goals, bearing directly on the chosen program approach, would be sufficient. Examples of goals for sample programs representing each of the three major directions of preschool programming follow.

Informal Programs
1. To help the children care for their bodies and establish healthful routines
2. To develop control of the large and small muscles
3. To help the children acquire effective patterns of speaking
4. To encourage feelings of friendliness, cooperation, and sharing
5. To develop an intellectual base necessary for successful learning

Skills-Oriented Programs[2]
1. To teach young children *academic skills* that will enable them to compete effectively in the public schools

2. To teach young children *social skills* that are necessary for successful adjustment to school
3. To train teachers, aides, and parents to use positive reinforcement to develop these skills

Cognitive Developmental Programs[3]

1. To help the child develop logical modes of thought through concept formation:
   a. to gain knowledge about himself and objects
   b. to see relationships between himself and things in his environment
   c. to group and order objects and events
2. To help the child develop the capacity to manipulate symbols and thus to act on and represent the environment

As you compared and contrasted the goals for each area, it is hoped that you understood that the illustrative programs described the goals for only *one* program under each heading and that even the various separate programs under each heading vary in their goal statements. Take, for example, two separate groups of students opting for a vacation trip to Florida. Obviously, their major direction is the same (program model) but their expected accomplishments (goals) may vary slightly (for example, swimming for one group and fishing for another). Likewise, teachers closely associated with each philosophy may disagree to some extent on exactly what they hope to accomplish.

Curriculum Organization

TEACHING TECHNIQUES   The types of learning experiences provided for the children should be closely aligned with the stated goals. For example, if we are to satisfy the four goals stated for our vacation trip to Florida, we must ask ourselves the question, "Now that we've determined where we're going and what we'd like to accomplish when we get there, what is the *best mode of transportation* to get us there?" In answering this question, we can examine the possibilities: airplane, boat, car, bus, bicycle, motorcycle, van, truck, pogo stick, walk, run, swim, balloon, hitchhike, crawl, or skip. Choices are numerous and varied—some are ridiculous and would never help us achieve our goals; others are more realistic and appear to be more reasonably suited to helping us accomplish the goals. In the same way, you must choose the most appropriate teaching strategies and materials as you move the children toward stated program goals. This analogy between the method of transportation for the Florida vacation and choosing appropriate techniques and materials for the classroom may appear trite; however, each day in thousands of preschool settings across the country, children suffer because their teachers fail to understand the obvious logic inherent in *choosing the most appropriate methods and materials for accomplishing any chosen goal.* Too often, approaches to teaching are chosen because they are "cute" or

You must decide whether it is more appropriate to guide young children through their learning experiences or to allow their free exploration into various learning activities. You also need to choose the most desirable learning materials to achieve your goals.

"gimmicky" and not because they were identified as valued strategies for accomplishing particular goals. Remember that your responsibility is to develop a professionally sound curriculum, and that such a project should result from effective, mature decision-making processes.

Theories of learning and development, as well as their practical applications to working with young children, were discussed and illustrated throughout this book. As you read through each section, you were asked to become a decision maker—you were asked to compare and contrast approaches to the education of young children and decide on the one, or combination of several, that appealed most to you. Now you are at the point where a commitment must be made. What should young children experience in the preschool setting and what is your role in that setting? Answers to this question may be arrived at using the kinds of if-then statements we used in making decisions regarding our Florida vacation. For example, we may have decided:

If we want to get to Florida as soon as possible to accomplish our goals, *then* an airplane might be the best mode of transportation to get us there.

If we've never before been to Florida and want to see the sights along the way, *then* an automobile might be the best mode of transportation to get us there.

If we'd like to join the numbers of others who are seeking to break unusual world records, *then* we'll try to see if we can hop all the way to Florida on a pogo stick.

In the same way, we must examine those techniques ("modes of transportation") that appear to be the best vehicle for accomplishing the goals we have identified as important for the children to be served. So, if-then statements may serve the same purpose in this decision as it did in the Florida vacation decision. For example:

If we seek to meet the needs of the "whole child" (social-emotional, physical, intellectual), *then* we must attempt to combine a trusting environment and informal experiences for learning. (Informal)

If the children need to develop sound reading, math, and language skills in order to be successful in their later schooling, *then* a highly teacher-directed, formalized approach should be the method of instruction. (Skills-oriented)

If the processes of problem solving and concept formation are valued, *then* the best classroom environment would be one in which there is student-centered activity such as observation, manipulation, and experimentation. (Cognitive developmental)

To illustrate how these approaches differ in actual preschool settings, consider these examples from the programs whose goals we identified on pages 466–467.

Informal Programs

Willie, four years old and an only child, is brought to school by his mother. After exchanging a few words with the teacher, Willie's mother leaves for home. Willie takes off his coat and hangs it in his locker. He looks around the room for a moment and then walks toward the art corner where he becomes engrossed in water color painting at the easel. He grabs a brush and covers the entire paper with bright, vivid colors. After three paintings, Willie leaves the easel and joins a group of children in the block corner. He finds that the children are playing with toy cars, the blocks serving as buildings on a street. The group soon has an argument over an accident, which the teacher sensitively handles. After this period of free play activity, the teacher calls the group together and guides individuals to interest centers dealing with topics in reading, writing, math, science, social studies, music, construction, and games. Jennifer is to begin with the science center where she will become involved in experiments with magnets. After she moves from the science center, Jennifer enters the math center where she and four other heterogeneously grouped children enjoy playing games centering on numbers. Following this learning center, Jennifer freely chooses to participate in a cooking activity led by the teacher and her aide. All through the cooking activity the teacher emphasizes concepts from different subject areas. For example, children use math skills to count and measure the ingredients, reading skills to learn new vocabulary and read the recipe, science while observing changes in matter, social skills while cooperating in special tasks, and language skills as they discuss each phase of the project. After making their no-bake cookies, the teacher asks the children to join together for snack time when they will eat the cookies and drink a glass of milk.

Following the snack time, children are given the choice of listening to a story (The Snowy Day) *read by the teacher or going out to play. Jennifer joins her friends on the playground and plays jump rope games for 15 minutes. Coming back into the classroom, Jennifer finds that she is just in time for a music activity, or, if she prefers, she can choose a free period at a learning center. She chooses to sing along in a seasonal song led by the teacher while other children become involved with drawing, puzzles, games, blocks, and the like.*

Jennifer and her friends find their classroom full of interesting activities. They are given free time to pursue activities in which they are particularly interested, and at other times, they are led by the teacher to activities identified as necessary for improvement in some area of development. The teachers constantly encourage children to succeed in what they undertake, and they accept each child as an individual. Continuous praise and reinforcement accompany the children's efforts: "You painted a very nice picture. I like it very much." Teachers encourage cooperative play and working as a member of a group. This informal program *is designed to help children develop in all areas, including beginning to learn academic-type skills.*

Skills-Oriented Programs

Vera, a five-year-old child from an urban ghetto area, comes through the door this morning to be warmly greeted by her teacher. "Good morning, Vera," says her teacher. "Good morning," replies Vera. "That was very nice, Vera," says the teacher, "I like the way you said good morning." Vera's program was designed to overcome the educational disadvantage that she reflected through scores attained on diagnostic tests. To ensure that such problems could be eliminated, her teacher designed a program that was structured so that Vera mastered one skill before she moved on to the next.

Vera is directed to a table where a trained aide is working with a group of four other children. The aide instructs the children to pick up their crayons and "circle the largest *ball" on a worksheet. Vera does her task correctly and is immediately given a bright red token, directly followed by the teacher's praise, "That was a very good job, Vera." After two similar tasks on the same worksheet, Arnold slams down his crayon and yells at the top of his voice. Ignoring Arnold, the teacher instead praises Vera because she is working so well. Picking up his crayon once more, Arnold reaches back and throws it across the table. Sensing that this potentially dangerous situation cannot be further ignored, the teacher calmly removes Arnold from the table to a chair that is isolated from the other children. "You threw a crayon at someone, Arnold, and we do not allow that in this room." After explaining the broken rule to Arnold, the teacher sets a kitchen timer for three minutes and allows Arnold to return after the three-minute period is over. Arnold's punishment is that he is not able to gain tokens for the period spent during "time out."*

Vera and the others in her group work with the aide for 15 minutes, after which they are free to exchange their accumulated tokens for special activities such as easel painting or puzzles. Vera chooses the easel painting and enjoys her activity for the next 20 minutes. For the rest of the morning, Vera works at learning tasks related to mathematics and reading, and is rewarded for her accomplishments all along the way with tokens and praise. After each 10 to 15-minute work period, Vera is given a chance to exchange tokens for special activities.

After completing her morning's work, Vera is helped with her coat and boots and waits for her older sister to pick her up. As she is ready to leave, her teacher says, "Good-bye, Vera. You were a very good worker today," and brings to an end another day in a behavioral skills-oriented preschool classroom.

Cognitive Developmental Programs

Sarah, a four-year-old, begins her day in the cognitive developmental program with a short planning period. In order to give children an opportunity to set goals and plan ahead, Sarah's teacher provides 20 minutes at the start of each day for the children to select the areas in which they would like to work. Each day, the children are free to choose from among four work time areas: the art area, large motor area, doll corner, or quiet area.

Today, Sarah chooses to start in the doll corner, then move to the art area, to the large motor area, and, if there is time, to the quiet area. Approximately 40 minutes of the morning is allotted to work time, so the teacher is on constant watch to encourage children to finish one task before they move to another. Sarah moves quickly to the doll corner where she is free to play in the company of an aide. The aide, serving as a guide for the child, uses language techniques during each learning experience: "The doll is near the table." "Is the chair far from the table?" "Find something that is near the shelf."

Sarah moves from the doll corner to the art area. She selects an easel and begins to make a series of lines. The aide stationed at this corner also uses language techniques while Sarah works. "The long green line is next to the bright red circle." Satisfied with her painting, Sarah hangs it up to dry and moves enthusiastically to the large motor area. This is one of her favorite areas; she enjoys equipment such as riding toys, hollow blocks, and boards. Again, an aide is near to stimulate language development by teaching spatial concepts such as up and down or above and below or by encouraging the children to verbalize their actions.

Although Sarah will not have time to join the teacher in the quiet area, she notices what the others are doing. The teacher has read a short story and is following it up with a discussion of the story's sequential events. She asks questions such as, "What was the first thing Harold did?" Then the teacher and the children cut out magazine pictures and place them in a sequence to tell a story. The sequences involve no more than four pictures. The teacher first discusses with the children what was happening in each picture, then asks the children to put the pictures together so they tell a story, and finally encourages those who were able to tell a story from the sequence of pictures.

After work time, Sarah and her classmates put away their materials and go to the bathroom. Even during this 15-minute clean-up period, the children are exposed to language as the teacher leads their work with comments such as, "All the big blocks go on the bottom shelf," and so on.

Following the clean-up period, the children are divided into groups for a juice time of approximately 30 minutes. This period again gives the teacher and her aides opportunities to extend language skills. When Sarah is being served juice, for example, she is asked, "Do you want more juice than Megan?" and, when the cookies are being passed, the teacher says, "Kelly is first, Jeanie is next, . . ."

A 20-minute activity time provides the children with a choice of staying indoors or going outdoors. Today, the teacher combines both an outdoor and *indoor activity for this period. The children are taken outside on the playground where they find a variety of leaves—some big, some little; some leaves with the same shape and some with different shapes. When they come back into the room, the children are asked to select a big leaf and a little leaf of the same shape from their assortment. After the children select their leaves, they place the big leaf on the gummed side of a piece of clear contact paper first, and then they place the little leaf in another spot. During this time, the teacher guides conceptual development by interjecting terms such as on, off, above, below, big, little, and so on. After the leaves are placed on the contact paper by the children, they are instructed to fold one side over the design. In this way, the leaves are encased in a folded piece of contact paper, and the entire project has resulted in a personal placemat for juice time or an attractive gift for a parent.*

Sarah's teacher, then, used informal activities during the day as one technique in furthering certain aspects of cognitive development. In addition, she provided specific times during the day when the children worked in small groups, investigating situations within a Piagetian framework. Today, the group activities focused on the Piagetian skill of classification. *Sarah joins a group of three other children in a corner where the teacher has prepared a large container of water and a variety of objects (sponges, wood blocks, fork, stone, rubber band, crayon, styrofoam, cups, and so on). The object of this activity is to encourage the children to experiment and classify the objects in the large group into two separate groups:* things that float *and* things that sink.

The final part of the cognitive developmental preschool day involves dismissal. Sarah is given her last bit of conceptual stimulation during this time—she is advised to "put the mitten on your hand."

These examples illustrate the fact that a rich variety of preschool programming exists today. Sometimes it is difficult to choose from among the alternative programs because there appear to be so many positive features associated with each approach. However, you must make a choice in a way that reflects the needs of your children and your conception of the teaching style that best suits you. Although this is difficult, it can be most rewarding —your creativity and professional skills are reflected in the smiles and sounds of delight of the children under your care.

To illustrate how important this phase of planning is, let me invite you to close your eyes for a moment and travel back to that wonderful time in your life filled with fantasy and imagination. Reach back and recall some of the exciting experiences of your own childhood—that vital period that should still be part of every teacher of young children. Riffle through the memories of bubble gum, playground swings, scraped knees, favorite pets . . . and the time an adventure led you to a secret corner of a dark closet which concealed a brightly wrapped gift meant especially for you! "I think I know what's in the box—but could it really be . . . ? I just can't wait to open it and see what it holds—just for me!"

Anticipating what the classroom environment will contain should be just as exciting for the young child as guessing the contents of a gift package. The experiences and adventures in store should be so interesting that they pro-

Each new day in the early childhood facility should be ripe for new adventures and exciting challenges.

duce intensive anticipation and the desire for extensive personal involvement in the challenging projects available. It doesn't take long, though, for the child's feeling of exquisite anticipation to be squelched by uninspired or poorly planned classroom experiences. Just as a poorly planned trip that results in detours, delays, stopovers, breakdowns, reroutings, or cancellations would affect our trip to Florida, so would an unimaginative, poorly planned classroom environment affect the extent to which educational goals are achieved. Besides *teaching technique,* then, two factors that affect curriculum organization are *classroom organization* and planning a *time schedule.*

CLASSROOM ORGANIZATION   Planning and arranging the children's physical environment is an important extension of your philosophy of teaching—the way you arrange the room and the materials you choose all reflect your feelings about the ways in which children grow and develop. Therefore, in order for the facilities to be of maximum benefit to the young child, they must be consistent with the philosophy and goals you have established for your teaching. Basic to any philosophy, though, is the recognition that *children are alike in many ways and different in many others.* For that reason, all planning should keep in mind the varying degrees of ability, creativity, curiosity, and interest that any group of children bring to their preschool experience. The preschool room is arranged and furnished with one general goal in mind: *to meet the individual developmental needs of all the children.* Much as car sickness, air sickness, or a variety of other individual problems may affect the mode of transportation chosen for our group vacation in Florida, so do individual differences in a preschool group affect the total success of a program.

Many buildings housing preschool programs were designed to provide rich environments for preschool children, but a large number of rooms (especially those found in churches, homes, or abandoned commercial buildings) were not designed with preschoolers in mind. There may be no low windows (if there are windows at all), no natural alcoves for a carpentry area, or no bare ground that can be turned into a garden plot. Such an environment may seem uninviting and hopeless, but with your ingenuity and creativity, you can meet the challenge and make the most efficient use of the usable space. Colorful, light paint or patterned walls can brighten the room; lamps add to its attractiveness and comfort. Low shelves or screens can be arranged to form the boundaries for a private dramatic play corner, carpentry area, or doll corner. Live plants placed on shelves or tables as well as in hanging baskets provide the children with both beauty and opportunities for experiences; large wooden or metal boxes filled with dirt and placed in a sunny area of the playground make splendid outdoor planters for vegetables or flowers. Don't be frustrated by the initial appearance of the place in which you will be teaching—it is professsionally very rewarding to make acceptable and comfortable a room that originally seemed frightful.

Most preschool teachers, regardless of their basic philosophy, prefer to divide their rooms into several basic areas, among which are:

1. art activity
2. block building and other large construction activity
3. dramatic play
4. books, records, and other language-related activity
5. manipulative toys, puzzles, and games
6. woodworking area
7. water and/or sand play
8. a large area for creative movement, dancing, storytelling, cooking, or other large-group activity
9. child-size tables and chairs for eating or individual projects
10. storage areas for clothing and other supplies

The way in which these areas are organized and maintained influences young children's acceptance of school and the learning process. The skillful teacher decorates and equips the room to provide continual motivation and a suitable climate for development. Of course, the preschool setting for three-year-olds would need to be somewhat different from that for four-year-olds; the setting for four-year-olds somewhat different from that for fives. Sample room arrangements for these three age groups are presented in Figures 12-2 through 12-4.

After you have studied these and other sample classroom arrangements, you must decide which is most closely aligned to your personal ideas of what best serves growing and changing children. As your personal plan begins to

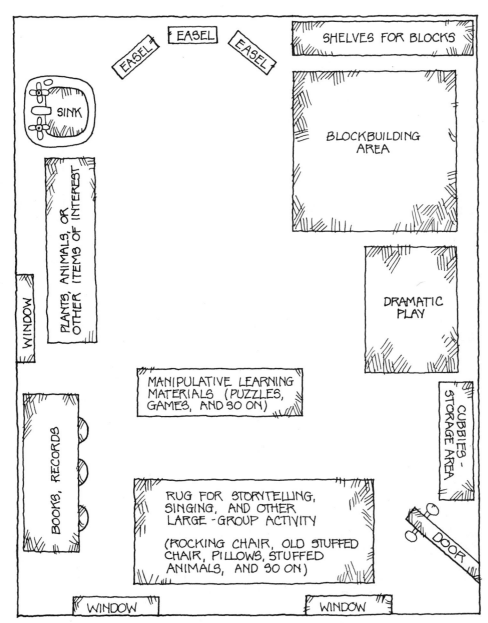

Figure 12-2 A sample classroom design for three-year-olds.

evolve, however, remember that any arrangement and selection of equipment and materials must contribute to the goals of the program. There are several key points to remember as you progress through this phase of decision making.

Have good reasons for choosing your room design. Consider the needs and strengths of your children and reflect these characteristics in the various

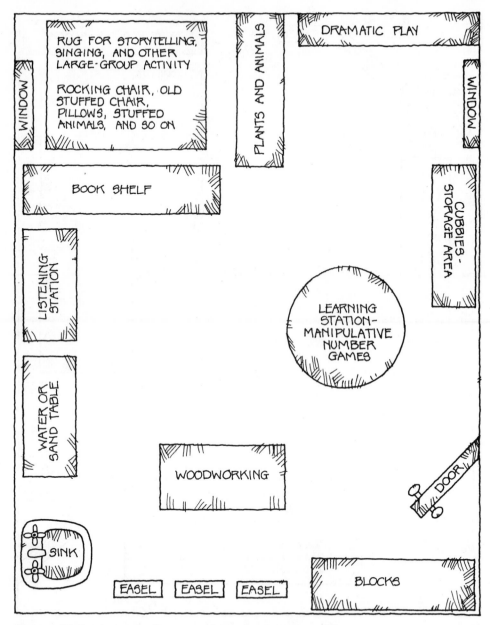

Figure 12-3   A sample classroom design for four-year-olds.

activity areas. It may be wise to draw different arrangements on paper before attempting to actually try them out—an admonition many teachers with sore backs would support.

Equipment utilization is multifaceted. Many different learnings often result from the use of one type of material. For example, an ice cream store

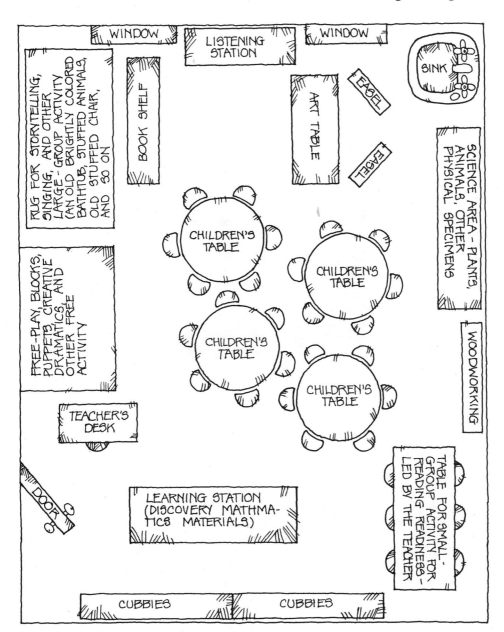

Figure 12-4 A sample classroom design for five-year-olds.

complete with signs can help the children with reading readiness, numeral recognition, color identification, language growth, creative expression, social skills, and a variety of other valuable learnings.

Toys and supplies should be conveniently stored so they are easily accessible to the children. Place them on low shelves so the children can easily reach

Isolated quiet areas encourage children to read, listen, or participate in other less physically active pursuits.

them, and place them as close as possible to the area in which they will be used. It is unnecessarily difficult to store blocks in one corner of the room and to locate the block play area in another.

Painting and other art activities should be located near a sink. This point is important not only for clean-up purposes, but also for the times when paints and pastes need to be mixed, spills need to be cared for, and the like.

Separate, as much as possible, noisy play areas from those areas requiring a quieter setting. It would be unwise, for example, to locate the library corner next to the woodworking center or the painting area next to the block corner. Children should be able to pursue individual tasks free from unnecessary disruptions or distracting stimuli. A quiet nook, isolated from the normal classroom routine, should be provided for the child who needs to be alone for a short period of time.

Furnish individual lockers (cubbies) where the children can store their belongings. Youngsters take comfort in knowing that a special part of the room has been designed for their personal use and will enjoy assuming responsibility for keeping it neat and orderly. The children should be provided with individual lockers (cubbies) in which they are able to store their wraps or personal belongings. These cubbies should be child-sized but still contain adequate space for the children to use them easily. Photographs with name labels help children identify their locations as well as provide them with practice in recognizing their own names.

Do not put all the equipment and materials out at one time. It can be dangerous to overstimulate young children with many new materials. The children become literally overwhelmed by everything around them and may demonstrate two basic behaviors: withdrawal from all activity because of too much stimulation too soon or uncontrolled darting about from one part of the room to another in an attempt to experience as much as possible in the shortest amount of time. Lori Fisk and Henry Lindgren illustrate this concern with the following example:

> Introducing a number of [classroom materials] all at once produces a situation in which children's cognitive systems collapse under an "overload of input," as my computerized friends and colleagues would say. Once, as a teenager, I babysat for a day, while the child's mother attended a conference. As she went out the door, she paused for ninety seconds and told me how to run the dishwasher, washing machine, clothes dryer, garbage disposal unit, and toaster oven. Before I could open my mouth to say, "Just a minute, you're going too fast!" she was gone, with a cheerful, "Have a good day!" Needless to say, I touched none of these household devices during her absence, since I was afraid that I would do something to break them. Children are of course less mature than teenagers and can absorb even less information if it is delivered all at once.[4]

Introduce only a few materials at the beginning of the preschool year and gradually add others as time goes by to maintain a comfortable, challenging environment.

Establish basic traffic patterns. Children need your guidance as they learn to move from one area of the room to another while pursuing activities of many kinds. They need to be informed from the first day on about the toilet facilities, storage areas, entrance doors, materials throughout the room, and

These children are preparing for a day at school by organizing their clothing and supplies in their individual "cubbies," or storage lockers.

how they are expected to move from one of these areas to another. Teachers use a variety of strategies for establishing basic traffic patterns. The following are some suggestions:

1. If there is an unusual amount of activity in one area, station yourself near so that you are able to aid children who need help.
2. Establish a handy path for the children to follow as they move from one area to another. Cut out colorful footprints and place them on the floor to direct the children from one area to another.
3. Mount close-up photographs of each child on tagboard cards and glue a clothespin to each card. A large tagboard sign depicts the various classroom areas. The pictures of the children are clipped to this sign to indicate the areas in which they are to work. The pictures are moved when the children are to change areas.

4. Draw and cut out symbols to represent each classroom area. String yarn or ribbon through the symbol, making a necklace. Make a number of necklaces for each center according to the number of children you wish to work there. Place the appropriate necklace around the children's necks to indicate which area they are to use during a specific period.

Make every effort to create a warm, friendly physical environment. Remember that, in many instances, you are providing the children with their first real educational experience and that the feelings they develop during this experience will most likely accompany them throughout the remainder of their schooling. For that reason, the rooms they enter should be friendly and alluring. This does not mean that an interior decorator has to design the room, but only that even the most unattractive room can be transformed into a more attractive one by painting, using colorful draperies, decorating with discarded store displays (such as animals, cartoon characters, story characters), exhibiting children's artwork, providing a small carpeted area, and a variety of other techniques.

To the beginning teacher, these suggestions may seem unattainable, since she may certainly ask, "But where can I get all of that? I can't afford it and the school won't buy it for me." That is a vital concern and one that must be addressed realistically. Understand, though, that you are not alone in your attempt to make the children's preschool experience a good one. Parents are often eager to contribute supplies; community agencies may be able to furnish used toys or furniture; maintenance workers can turn a drab room into a majestically colorful one with their skills; local stores and businesses often supply carpet remnants or old displays; and other groups are all eager to lend some support by offering free materials, equipment, or labor to help you achieve your goal. Encourage their honest interest and accept their willingness to help you transform your less than adequate facility into an attractive one. The following is a comprehensive list of free and inexpensive materials.

Millwork or Lumber Company: Wood "scraps" suitable for the carpentry table or art cabinet are given away by the box load. Sawdust is available as well as fascinating curls of wood created by planing. Leave a marked box and come back for it. Lathed scraps are available for purchase in some places and add special pieces for young builders. Button molds (used as wheels in the display) are available for purchase in 1", 1½", and 2" sizes.

Grocery Store: Boxes, boxes, boxes and a purpose for every size. Try a box corner for a table easel, a larger size for a puppet theater, a post office, or store, and of course, several for dramatic play of any sort desired by the children. Many cardboard displays disposed of by stores are suitable for various purposes in the classroom. Cardboard soft drink cartons are excellent for holding paint containers (prevent spilling at the table), and one painted white will be welcomed by your school "milkman."

Telephone Company: Empty telephone cable spools are wonderful additions to the outside play area. Small (3 ft. in diameter) ones make lovely doll corner tables. Stop a telephone man and put your name on the waiting list. On occasion, they may part with old instruments, but colorful, scrap telephone wire is always available.

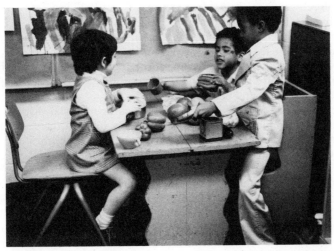

Teachers must use good judgment when selecting classroom materials designed to help achieve stated program goals.

Soft-Drink Companies: Wooden soft-drink crates are available at a minimal charge. Painted bright colors (children may do this in small numbers using left-over latex paint) they serve as excellent substitutes for the commercial hollow blocks. A set of casters on one will create a durable wagon for hauling blocks or friends. Set the casters in far enough to allow stacking. Wet strength fiberboard beer cases are excellent storage units. The children can easily handle them.

Ice Cream Stores: Ask at your favorite restaurant for their empty 3 gallon cardboard ice cream containers. Uses range from space helmets through spatter paint screen forms.

Gas Stations and Garages: Here you may obtain tires for playground swings, inner tubes to supplement materials at the carpentry table, and bottle caps from the drink machines. You may find a garage willing to cut the steering wheel from a wrecked automobile for the children to use in their play. Old tractor tires make fabulous bouncy sandboxes.

Wallpaper Stores: Wallpaper books of discontinued patterns are usually available on the first come, first served basis. Use textured sheets for easel painting. Those with fabric samples are especially nice. Precut samples make excellent puppet skirts.

Carpet Shop: Many carpet shops have samples of discontinued rug patterns available for 10¢ a piece. Larger samples cost more but can be used as rest mats. Here, too, you will find the soft foam underpadding pieces.

Tile Stores: Tile stores frequently have broken patterns of mosaic tile available for a minimal charge. Children enjoy matching, counting, and creating with these colorful squares. You can supplement by making parquetry boards on cardboard.

Boat Rentals and Marinas: At the beginning or end of the season, many rowboats or sailboats no longer "seaworthy" are destroyed. If you can find a truck and some help, they are yours.

Moving Companies: Overseas moving companies may occasionally part with a large, amazingly well-built packing crate for the cost of transportation. They make excellent play houses. It's worth a try. . . .

Print Shops: Print shops have assorted sizes of "scrap" paper. . . . Leave a box under the counter of [your] favorite print shop, and go to empty it every 2 weeks or so. Colored cardboard tickets, letter sheets, and all sorts of paper for collage can be obtained this way.

Builders and Road Construction: New construction offers at least the possibility of obtaining an unused sewer pipe for the playground.

Paint Shops: Paint color cards are fun color experiences and excellent collage. Old paint brushes are great for painting buildings with water. Cardboard paint buckets made the ball and bean bag game.

Fabric Shops or Departments: Stores that carry material dispose of the inner cardboard form which makes an excellent plaque for children's artwork. You may also find ribbon scraps to add to your art materials and fabric remnants if you don't get enough from sewing mothers.

Home: Dress-up clothes (maternity tops are ideal, need no hemming), ties, shoes (men's and women's), hats, costume jewelry. Old petticoats make lovely skirts, frilly nylon blouses, a bridal veil can be made by attaching old curtains to a clip hat. (Supplement by thrift shop sales.)

Empty food containers for store or building, paper towel rolls, empty detergent bottles, bleach bottles, cookie sheets for easy to clean finger painting, buttons, spools for bubble blowing, flashlight, yarn, scraps of material, empty egg cartons, aluminum pie plates, small juice cans and baby food jars for easel, newspapers for papier mache, magazines for cutting and pasting, scarves for dancing (dyed cheesecloth will work equally well) as butterflies, wind, kites; empty shoe polish bottles to refill with paint, cracker crumb container for sprinkling sand over glue patterns.[5]

You must also remain constantly aware of the new supplies that are being developed commercially for preschool youngsters. However, creative teachers have for many years transformed "junk" materials into some very creative and valuable classroom tools. One teacher designed and created these "junk" toys:

1. Stacked cans—Easy to do. Use assorted sizes and colors of cans and ask the children to stack them in sequential order.
2. Color lotto—Squares of construction paper mounted on cardboard and covered with clear contact. Children match the colored squares.
3. Parquetry—Floor covering samples used as pattern tiles for sorting and counting activities. Tiles are available in several sizes and can be used to create individual or patterned designs.
4. Sound shakers—Small plastic 30mm film containers filled with various materials—rice, beans, tooth picks, screws. Seal the lids. Which is loud, which is soft?

Choose only equipment that leads to the fulfillment of the basic goals of your program. Although some preschool programs require special equipment (for example, typewriters, programmed materials, videotape equipment) to achieve their goals, some basic supplies and materials are commonly found in most preschool settings. A listing of that basic equipment is presented below. As you read through the list, you should observe that it is a *general list* and not representative of all schools.

Infant Materials

mobiles	wall mirror	plastic bracelets
rocking chairs	yarn balls	household items
cribs	hand mirrors (safe)	pacifiers
rattles	bounce chairs	texture books
soft terry or sponge toys	small bathtubs	wind chimes
cradle gyms	green plants	music boxes
nesting toys	record player	

Art Area

easels	scissors	construction paper
paint	yarn	marking pens
brushes	drawing paper	aprons or smocks
clay	crayons	junk box (variety
paste	pencils	of materials)
	tablets	

Large Muscle Activity Area

balance boards	wheelbarrow	sandbox
wagons	trucks	ladders
tricycles	tractors	blocks
traffic signs	jungle gym	platforms
	tunnels	

Dramatic Play Area

furniture	puppet stage	dolls
puppets	variety of dress-up clothes	props

Library Area

books	catalogs	record player
chairs	homemade books	flannelboards
carpet	experience stories	pictures
	tape recorder	

Manipulative Area

dominoes	lotto games	blocks
beads	pegboards and pegs	table games (such as "Candy Land")
puzzles	Tinkertoys	
dressing frames	nesting toys	

Woodworking Area

hammers	vise	pliers
nails	wrench	saws
soft wood	planes	hand drills
screwdriver	nuts and bolts	workbench
screws	paintbrushes	sandpaper
files	paint (tempera or poster)	rulers

Water and Sand Play Area

plastic wading pool	water table with dishpan	squirt bottles
funnels	coffee pots	sponges
food coloring	doll clothes	detergent
various containers	construction equipment	straws

Music Supplies

piano	rhythm sticks	tape recorder
autoharp	bells	shakers
guitar	triangles	tambourines
record player	xylophones	handmade instruments
records	drums	

Science Corner

balancing scales	aquarium	magnifying glasses
magnets	terrarium	various materials to
seeds	animals	dismantle (such as
gardening tools	rocks	clocks, pencil
plants	seashells	sharpeners, old toys)
simple machines	compasses	

Choosing the classroom materials and deciding how to use them are only two of the three major decisions necessary for organizing the curriculum. The third, *planning the schedule of activity,* answers questions such as: "What should I have the children do first?" "How often should the children rest?" "When do I ask the children to change from one activity to another?" "Should I follow the same basic routine each day?"

PLANNING A DAILY SCHEDULE Planning the daily schedule as a framework for your curriculum is important for these reasons:

1. It provides a basic time structure into which you can plan activities.
2. It gives the children a sequential guide by which they can plan a series of classroom activities with minimal guidance from the teacher. John, for example, moved from the block corner to the bathroom to urinate. He washed his hands and sat down at the snack table with the other children. Following the snack, he headed directly to the carpeted area to hear a story from the teacher. At no time did John need to be told what to do—this basic sequence of events occurred each day and John had adjusted to the routine. Children need such established routine to feel safe and comfortable; they gain confidence in doing for themselves what is expected of them. A frequent cause of misbehavior or anxiety in young children is a quickly changing environment that is unplanned and unorganized.
3. It accommodates the parents who need to know when to arrive with their children, when to pick them up, when to arrive for a special event, or when to visit for a special purpose.

Sample time plans describing the difference between a full-day and half-day program were presented in Chapter 2. At this point, time plans reflecting the philosophical emphases of different programs will be illustrated, but for half-day programs only.

Informal Program

9:00–10:30 Free-choice activities—children are able to explore whatever games, toys, or equipment have been chosen for display. They may listen to records or play with blocks, puzzles, cuisenaire rods, and so on. These activities are selected to foster certain skills, concepts, or attitudes for that day, week, or month. The teacher or aide works with individuals or small groups on selected materials.

10:30–10:45   Snack time

10:45–11:00   Group time—this period is devoted to large-group activities such as singing, listening to a story, sharing, or participating in a group project such as cooking. These activities are designed to develop skills in all areas of the child's development.

11:00–11:30   Outdoor play

11:30   Dismissal

Skills-Oriented Program

8:00–8:30   Staff planning

8:30–8:45   Greeting

8:45–9:05   Instruction period 1—children are assigned to the reading, mathematics, or handwriting group.

9:05–9:30   Special activity 1—children exchange tokens acquired during the instructional period for art projects, puzzles, outdoor play, or games in which they might be interested.

9:30–9:50   Instruction period 2—children move to a group dealing with another skills area.

9:50–10:15   Special activity 2

10:15–10:30   Snack time

10:30–10:50   Instruction period 3

10:50–11:15   Special activity 3

11:15–11:30   Dismissal

Cognitive Developmental Program

8:30–8:45   Greeting as children arrive

8:45–9:05   Planning time—children select activities in which they would like to work.

9:05–9:45   The children work in self-selected areas: the art area, large motor area, doll corner, or quiet area.

9:45–10:00   Clean up—put away materials and equipment and use toilet facilities.

10:00–10:15   Juice time

10:15–10:45   Group time—teacher and aides work on special concepts with small groups of children.

10:45–11:10   Activity time: (indoors) music or circle games; (outdoors) playground equipment

11:10–11:30   Circle time—review what was done during the day.

11:30   Dismissal

As you compared and contrasted these daily schedules, it should have been apparent how the philosophy of the program dictates the amount of time spent on the various activities and, in particular, exactly what activities are provided for the children. Whatever the chosen direction, however, always keep the children in mind, for their interest (or lack of it) may require adjustments to the framework. The inflexible teacher who stops a child just before she "puts her baby to sleep" in the doll corner may have destroyed in one minute all the good things that had transpired in the previous 20 minutes. Certainly, an extra minute or two for that particular child would have made the activity a valuable learning experience. And extending an unpopular activity beyond its usefulness would be just as detrimental to your program as cutting off activities that are popular. By keeping a sensitive eye on the children and interpreting their reactions to daily activities, you can adjust the time blocks in your daily schedule and provide for the individual needs and interests of your children.

Up to this point in our program decision-making process, you have (1) identified a basic framework upon which to build, (2) formulated a set of goals to be achieved, and (3) chosen the teaching strategies and materials to help you reach those goals. Now comes the task of deciding which methods to use to judge how well your program has influenced the children's growth and development. That is, you are asking, "How effectively are my methods and materials helping the children progress toward the program goals?" The answers to this question comprise the last part of the decision-making process: *evaluation*.

Evaluating the Program

On our vacation to Florida, we may often hear two kinds of comments: "Wow, that was a lot of fun—I really enjoyed it," and "Let's go somewhere else—this is a bore." The experiences we have are constantly being judged as good, bad, or indifferent on the basis of how well they fulfilled our original expectations. Naturally, if the experiences are judged good, we are happy about our choices and satisfied with the trip. If the experiences do not meet our vacation expectations, we may feel negative or hostile, and our vacation goals may not be accomplished (see Figure 12-5).

In the same way, you should constantly look at the goals of your program to judge whether they are being accomplished in a successful and enjoyable manner. To do so, you must thoroughly understand the process of evaluation, for without such knowledge your teaching effectiveness and relations with the parents may be jeopardized. Before we examine the various evaluation processes, however, let's establish what evaluation is. *Evaluation* can be considered to be any formal or informal process by which teachers gather and analyze pupil data to determine whether changes should be made in the program to meet unique individual needs and interests more adequately. Many formal and informal techniques can be used to evaluate the progress of young children. These are discussed in the following sections.

Figure 12-5   Evaluation is a key feature of all planning experiences.

TEACHER OBSERVATION   Simply watching the children during the school day is perhaps the most popular technique for evaluating young children's skills, interests, understandings, feelings, emotions, or social abilities in the preschool. Data gathered during this type of evaluation procedure are normally recorded on one or both of these types of recording forms: (1) *anecdotal record forms* or (2) *checklists*.

Teachers often prefer to record short, but detailed comments about a child based on observations of his activity in the preschool setting. These comments, often jotted on 3″ × 5″ index cards, should describe only the child's behavior and not your interpretation of that behavior. For example, one misguided teacher made this comment about Arnie and included it in his permanent file: "Arnie caused a disruption in the block corner today by pinching Jerome. His social skills are much below the other children and may cause him problems in first grade." By recording your opinion, especially after experiencing some negative aspect of the child's behavior, you run the danger of stereotyping that child for the remainder of his school experience. How many times have we seen youngsters live up to the expectancies we establish for them (self-fulfilling prophecy)? If you must enter negative comments about children, balance them with positive comments so that future teachers will be aware of the child's strengths as well as his weaknesses. A sample anecdotal card for one child is illustrated in Figure 12-6.

These general suggestions should help you as you prepare anecdotal comments about individual children:

1. Record only the child's behavior and avoid making hasty judgments about that behavior.
2. Avoid stereotyping a child by predicting future behavior in terms of past experiences.
3. Refrain from viewing overconforming children too favorably and underconforming children unfavorably. One of the primary characteristics of highly creative youngsters is their inability to conform to normal routines or expectancies. We often shut off their creative potential by forcing them into patterns that destroy their originality and desire for uniqueness.
4. Record only the material that is useful. All too often, we teachers bury ourselves under mounds of observational data that lack focus. To make our observations useful, remember to select only those behaviors that describe a particular dimension of an individual's behavior.

Normally, anecdotal records are kept only for those few children who need to be observed for some special reason—temper tantrums or destructive behavior, for example. Whenever observations of all the children need to be made, *checklists* can be particularly useful. Checklists contain items that can focus on many areas of children's development and can be filled out in a much shorter period of time than can anecdotal records. A sample checklist is illustrated in Figure 12-7.

You are able to evaluate the progress of the young children under your care simply by observing them during regular routines and keeping a record of your findings.

```
┌─────────────────────────────────────────────────────────────────────┐
│                                                                       │
│   NAME      Johnny Smith                    AGE      4 yrs. 6 mos.     │
│                                                                       │
│   Monday (10-18-80)                                                   │
│                                                                       │
│       Worked for 20 minutes alone in the mathematics corner.  Johnny now │
│   recognizes the numerals 1-10 and can place the number of corresponding objects │
│   with each numeral.  He still becomes upset, though, when he leaves his mother │
│   in the morning.                                                     │
│                                                                       │
│                                                                       │
│   Wednesday (10-20-80)                                                │
│                                                                       │
│       Johnny worked at solitary activities again today and experienced a │
│   tantrum when asked to share a toy with another child.  He appears to be │
│   reluctant to work with others or to share his possessions with them. │
│                                                                       │
│                                                                       │
└─────────────────────────────────────────────────────────────────────┘
```

Figure 12-6 Sample anecdotal card.

WORK SAMPLES Many preschool teachers maintain folders containing work samples for each child. Naturally, not every piece of each child's work is kept for the folder, only periodic samples throughout the school year. Some teachers prefer to take weekly, bi-weekly, or monthly samples, which they date and place into the child's folder. In this way, the teacher can look at a child's former work and compare it to what he is now doing. This accumulation of work gives the teacher an idea of how well an individual is progressing and of what steps might be necessary to reinforce certain areas of development. Two art samples from one teacher's cumulative folder illustrate the progress of one individual in art (see Figure 12-8).

TESTS Many early childhood professionals agree that *subjective* means of evaluation (that is, anecdotal records, checklists, and work samples) are important, but they argue that more specific measures are necessary in order to give an unbiased view of the child's progress. Such specific measures, referred to as *objective* tests, are useful, but only if they are properly carried out. Helen Robinson explained some difficulties in testing young children:

> It is not easy to test young children. They react to the tester, the test situation, and to their inner needs with much less inhibition than older children or adults. Test results with young children are notoriously *unreliable*. You can get wildly different results on the same test within a brief period. The *validity* of many tests for young children is difficult to establish. The test may or may not measure what it purports to measure, and what it purports to measure may not be a valid indication of the child's development or learning. Children's self-concepts, for example, are a very relevant aspect of child development. So far, however, it has not been satisfactorily established that any of the instruments or procedures used for testing reliably reflect this construct.[6]

PRESCHOOL CHECKLIST

	Inappropriate for age	Appropriate for age
1. Visual acuity		
2. Visual discrimination		
3. Left-to-right sequence		
4. Auditory acuity		
5. Auditory discrimination		
6. Listens to stories		
7. Follows simple directions		
8. Articulates common sounds		
9. Uses appropriate words and sentences		
10. Conversations with others		
11. Large motor coordination		
12. Small motor skills		
13. Cooperates with other children		
14. Attends to personal needs		
15. Self-confidence (feelings of adequacy)		
16. Attention span		
17. Accepts limits		
18. Respects adults		
19. Recognizes numerals 1-10		
20. Distinguishes among the basic shapes		
21. Knows the eight basic colors		
22. Recognizes own name in print		
23. Interest in learning		
24. Respects classroom materials		
25. Curious about the environment		
26. Works independently		

Figure 12-7   Sample evaluation checklist.

Figure 12-8   Art samples from a cumulative folder.

Keeping these problems in mind, educators nonetheless find tests to be a valuable measure in determining to what degree their program goals have been met. Their procedure in doing so usually consists of administering a *pretest* as well as a *posttest*. The pretest measures the child's abilities as he enters the program, and the posttest gives an indication of how much he has grown as a result of it. Some means of continual evaluation is recommended for children who appear to have the greatest needs.

As with the tests themselves, the pre- and posttest procedure may have its shortcomings. For example, I can recall with horror observing the testing program designed for infants of low socioeconomic parents. During the pretest phase, the infants were kept waiting in groups of three or four with their parents while another child was being tested in a separate room. Naturally, feeding and rest schedules were disrupted as the infants were kept waiting for their turns, some for as long as one hour. The children became cranky and often cried as a result of the wait, but when they were separated from their mothers for testing, they became even more anxious and disruptive. I expressed my concern to the tester as to the reliability of the pretest since the infants were in such an unsettled environment. "Oh, don't worry," was the reply, "we want low scores on the pretest. We'll control the situation more effectively on the posttest and get greater positive results for the program than people would expect!" Testing, then, is open to many misuses, so whenever you need to use tests of any kind, be sure to do so in a professional manner.

There are many standardized, formal tests for preschool youngsters, mostly *achievement* or *intelligence* tests. *Achievement tests* are the type you probably remember most. They measure certain skills and abilities that result from instruction (reading, math, language, and so on). The type of achievement test that seems to be most popular among preschool teachers is the *readiness test*, a measure designed to indicate whether or not a child possesses the prerequisite abilities necessary to begin formal instruction. The most widely used readiness test is the Metropolitan Reading Readiness Test discussed in Chapter 6.

Intelligence tests are designed to measure a child's inherent ability for cognitive or creative functioning. (See samples of intelligence test-items in the test-items box.) The widely controversial IQ test is perhaps the most popular intelligence test. IQ tests have been roundly criticized in recent years for several reasons.

1. IQ scores reflect cultural bias because they were developed for the white middle-class youngster. This bias, then, accounts for one's score on the test.
2. IQ tests are used in ways to stereotype a child. Many educators have falsely used IQ scores to predict children's progress through school.
3. IQ scores were originally thought to be fixed throughout life and not affected by the child's environment. Surely, the experimentation of the 1960s put an end to this myth.

In recent years, educators have begun to seek a more comprehensive view of intelligence than merely a score on an IQ test. They have begun placing heavy emphasis on the processes of problem solving and creative thought. Tests of these processes assess the child's ability to think in logical, fluent, and original ways while solving unique problems.

Despite their problems, if they are used properly, achievement and intelligence tests can be effective measures of how well each child in your room compares to other children of the same age level. For example, you may find that the child's score of 105 on a reading readiness test places him at the 75th percentile. This means that when compared to all the children taking the test, he scored in the top 25 percent. Such information is important, but should not be used as the sole source of information about a child.

Formal tests, then, provide early childhood educators with important measures of intellectual and achievement levels if they are treated in a professional manner. The most appropriate professional use seems to be when such measures are utilized in conjunction with other evaluation techniques for the purpose of improving instruction.

CHILDREN'S SELF-EVALUATION   A final and less frequently used form of evaluation in the preschool setting is the process of children's self-evaluation. Often we are surprised at the reactions of children when they are given an opportunity to evaluate themselves and their day at school. Remember that children are not informed educational critics and cannot evaluate your pedagogical methods, but they are quite willing to let you know whether your routines and activities are pleasing or not. You can often gain important feedback when you informally ask questions such as: "What did you think about school today?" "What did you enjoy most this morning? Least?" "Show me that you can skip."

INTELLIGENCE TEST-ITEMS

AUDITORY PERCEPTION *Number and Syllable Recall:* Ask the child to repeat three series of two digits (example: 4–6, 3–8, and 9–2); then move to three series of three digits (example: 2–8–9, 7–1–3, and 4–5–9); and finally to three series of four digits (example: 3–5–1–7, 4–2–9–6, and 7–3–8–2).

The same procedure can be used as you ask the child to repeat 2 syllables:

a.   green car
b.   big boy
c.   cold ice

6–7 syllables:

a.   The dog barked at the man.
b.   The girl kicked the red ball.
c.   I jumped over the fence.

12–13 syllables:

a.   The little kitten was frightened by the big brown dog.
b.   We all played outdoors on the warm, sunny day.
c.   Jimmy kicked the big blue ball over the tall fence.

VISUAL MEMORY   Sit across a table from a child. On the table are six commonly used objects, such as a block, ball, crayon, scissors, clay, and toy horse. Tell the child you are going to play a game and that he must close his eyes. While his eyes are closed, you remove one of the objects. The child must identify the missing object when he reopens his eyes.

PERCEPTION   Have a set of beads that vary in size, shape, and color. Make a model for the child and ask him to repeat it.

VISUAL DISCRIMINATION   Prepare a set of about ten cards on which a picture at the top serves as the model the child uses to choose a matching picture from among three pictures at the bottom. Ask the child to find which of the pictures at the bottom is most like the one at the top. Pictures may vary in color, design, or position.

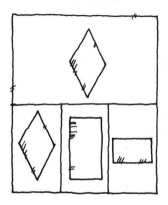

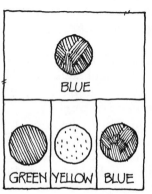

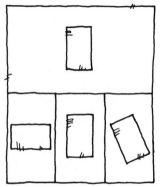

CONCEPTUALIZATION Three common tasks, each having to do with body concept, may be used to judge conceptual development.

a. Glue a picture of a person on a large sheet of tagboard and cut it horizontally into five sections. Ask the child to put the person together.
b. Draw a picture of an incomplete man wth the following parts missing: one ear, one eye, part of the hair, neck, one arm and hand, one leg and foot. Ask the child what is wrong with it.
c. Some tests prefer to ask the child to draw a complete person by himself. Judgments of conceptual maturity are made on the basis of how sophisticated the body is drawn.

SEQUENCING Have a set of cards picturing objects familiar to the child. Ask him to place the cards in line so that the one with the fewest red balls comes first and the one with the most red balls comes last.

VOCABULARY Prepare ten cards, each containing three or four pictures showing different relationships among the elements. Ask the child to look at each picture and decide which one shows what you said. For example, you may say, "The box is *under* the table."

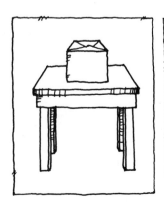

Some simple types of record forms can be used for student self-evaluation, especially if you are using learning centers in your classroom. They can gather information about how meaningful, interesting, enjoyable, or appropriate the children found the centers to be. Two special self-evaluation checklists are shown in Figure 12-9.

Obviously, most preschool youngsters will be unable to read the directions on the self-evaluation record forms. They were placed on the form simply to describe the kind of statement you may wish to read or say to the children as they respond. Because children's standards of appreciation may be much different from your own, these bits of feedback may offer valuable information to the wise teacher who welcomes and respects the opinions of the children she teaches.

The following lists describe ways in which the three philosophically different programs we have been discussing might evaluate their own effectiveness.

Informal Model

1. Observation
2. Anecdotal records
3. Teacher checklists
4. Metropolitan Achievement Test
5. Self-evaluation

Skills-Oriented Model

1. Progress Achievement Test
    The Behavior Analysis Model
    Department of Human Development
    University of Kansas
    Lawrence, Kansas 66044
2. Teacher checklists
3. Observation
4. Achievement tests related to the curricular areas

Cognitive Developmental Model

1. Stanford-Binet IQ test
2. Teacher checklists
3. Personality tests
4. Achievement tests
5. Tests of cognitive functioning (Piagetian tasks)

Sound, professional evaluation is a key to the success of preschool prorams. It tells us how the programs need to be extended and enriched in order to make each youngster's schooling experience personally rewarding and profitable. Every preschool educator should strive to formulate an evaluation plan that is consistent with the basic philosophy of the established program and to interpret the results of such feedback in ways that will ensure that each child's unique educational needs can be met.

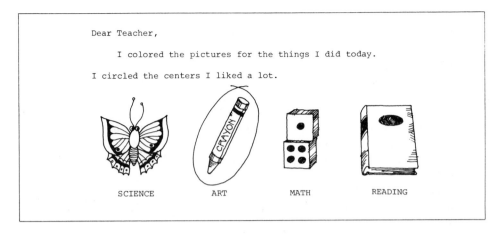

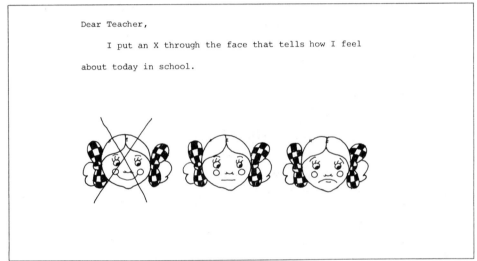

Figure 12-9   Two examples of self-evaluation checklists.

SOME FINAL THOUGHTS

Effective teachers are effective, logical decision makers. They must examine the current recommendations of early childhood professionals, weigh the consequences of each alternative form, and settle on a program that is satisfactory for the parents, the children, and themselves. This is a challenging task, and one that should be enthusiastically met by those who are ready to enter the field. Nothing can be as exciting and rewarding as molding and creating a personal program that dynamically grows and develops under your careful guidance. The true reward of developing such a program comes not from weekly paychecks or outstanding observation reports but from your tingling spine when, on the last day of school at the end of the year, a tearful group of youngsters announce, "I don't want to go home. School was so much fun this year."

The following list summarizes the major decisions necessary for effective program development. Examine it as you begin to design your personal plan for the parents and children you are to serve.

- *Philosophy:* How do I view the development of the child? What theory best explains the process of learning?
- *Goals:* What are the needs of the parents? The children? What do I hope to achieve?
- *Curriculum:* What is my role? The child's role? What materials and activities will be used? How will I arrange the classroom? How will I schedule the daily activities?
- *Evaluation:* To what extent did my program achieve its goal? How favorably do my children compare to others of the same age and background?

NOTES

1. Eleanor E. Maccoby and Miriam Zellner, *Experiments in Primary Education: Aspects of Project Follow Through* (New York: Harcourt, Brace, Jovanovich, 1970).
2. The skills-oriented descriptions are loosely based on: The Behavior Analysis Model, Don Bushnell, Jr., Project Director. Department of Human Development, University of Kansas, Lawrence, Kansas 66044.
3. The cognitive descriptions are loosely based on: The Cognitive Curriculum, David P. Weikart, Project Director. High/Scope Educational Research Foundation, 125 North Huron, Ypsilanti, Michigan 48107.
4. Lori Fisk and Henry Clay Lindgren, *Learning Centers* (Glen Ridge, N. J.: Exceptional Press, 1974), p. 58.
5. Jeanne Quill, *Beautiful Junk* (Washington, D.C.: Office of Child Development, U.S. Department of Health, Education, and Welfare, Project Head Start), pp. 2–3.
6. Helen F. Robinson, *Exploring Teaching in Early Childhood Education* (Boston: Allyn and Bacon, 1977), p. 531.

13

Providing for Children with Special Needs

Children from homes speaking nonstandard English present special challenges for the early childhood educator. (*Barney Google* courtesy of King Features Syndicate, Inc.)

Bob H., 14 years old, entered his sixth grade classroom on the first day of school in September anticipating another year of ridicule and failure. Able to read only at the primer level, Bob had been the favorite target of teachers' frustrations. In fact, Bob's new teacher (Mr. Bowles—his first year on the job) was warned by several colleagues and even by the elementary supervisor "not to worry because there's nothing that can be done for Bob anyway—he's pretty much of a lost cause." Perhaps because of a high degree of optimism or a strong sense of humanism, Mr. Bowles refused to accept their admonitions. Before planning a program for Bob, though, Mr. Bowles wanted to check the student's personal file. The file gave some useful information, but seemed heavily weighted with comments about Bob's academic failures. Mr. Bowles was not convinced, however, that he should think of Bob as a lost cause without first trying to help him.

Mr. Bowles greeted his children on that first day of school and, as they walked in, was particularly caught by Bob's physical maturity. Much larger than the other children, Bob seemed out of place in the room. For several weeks Mr. Bowles observed Bob's activities both with other children and with his school work. Bob seemed to get along with the others on the playground and at lunch but exhibited his strongest feelings during academic pursuits. Often these feelings came out as misbehaviors. Mr. Bowles immediately planned an individualized program for Bob in which he could work at his own level but without being subjected to materials below his maturity level; that is, Bob worked with manipulative materials and individualized practice sheets rather

499

than pages from a first grade arithmetic book. Mr. Bowles's observation also uncovered some interesting information—Bob was actually very skilled in some areas of his development, especially in the physical realm. Bob was an expert planner and builder, for example, and always assumed natural leadership whenever building situations arose in or out of the classroom. Also, Bob focused his library book selections on one area in particular: construction machinery. Mr. Bowles seized this discovery and used construction and construction machinery to motivate Bob in several curricular areas. As Bob experienced repeated successes and became motivated while being exposed to topics of personal interest by a teacher who was sincerely interested in him, despite previous circumstances, Bob steadily blossomed and grew throughout the year. By the end of the year, Bob's physical maturity was still far beyond that of the other children, but now his social, emotional, academic, and creative talents were growing, too.

Mr. Bowles kept in contact with Bob for the next few years until he took another teaching position in a distant state. His rewarding experiences with Bob were nearly forgotten until one day he picked up a newspaper from the town of his original position and focused on an advertisement with Bob's photograph prominently placed: "Bob H.'s Earth Moving and Excavation Company." If we measure success even in the most materialistic sense, Bob must certainly be near the top of all the students who were in Mr. Bowles's first sixth grade class.

What does all this mean to you, teachers who will be working with youngsters up through third grade rather than sixth? First, Mr. Bowles reflected a characteristic that should describe teachers at all levels, that is, he was primarily a teacher of children rather than a teacher of subjects. That means Mr. Bowles was aware of more than Bob's academic performance. He knew that intellectual development is only one area of the *whole child* and that children have strengths in other areas of development that should be addressed, too. He realized that we should accept the child at his present stage of development and capitalize on strengths to foster growth in areas that may need special attention. Second, Mr. Bowles realized that the preconceived stereotype of Bob that other teachers tried to communicate to him at the beginning of the year should not dictate how Bob would be treated that year. Mr. Bowles knew that negative statements are often made as an unconscious effort to cover up our own failures, not the child's. In addition, Mr. Bowles realized that all children must be treated fairly and given equal opportunities to excel; that just because some children may appear brighter or come from better homes, they should not be given greater opportunities than the "dull" child or the child from "the wrong side of the tracks."

Like Mr. Bowles, teachers throughout the United States at all levels of instruction are being made more sensitive to the special needs of children, especially those children who, because of certain limitations, either *personal* (conditions of the children themselves) or *environmental* (conditions in their surroundings), require some adjustment to their educational programs to help them approach their maximum developmental potentials more fully.

These children, often referred to as "children with special needs," encompass youngsters in two general categories: (1) those who may be described as *culturally different* and (2) those who may be described as *handicapped*. Although these categories often overlap, they are discussed separately in this chapter so that you will be able to better understand the special considerations that must be met to ensure optimal educational experiences for all children.

THE CULTURALLY DIFFERENT CHILD

Choosing a term that will identify children whose economic, social, or intellectual environment hampers their maximum developmental potential is a delicate task. Educators have often described these children as "disadvantaged," implying that lack of economic, social, or intellectual opportunities caused educational problems that prevented successful adjustment to and performance in school. When these children were compared to "advantaged" children, it was often found that they were behind in most areas of development—most seriously in academic development. Some blamed this lag on inadequate schooling, but others recognized the role of the home and community in meeting educational needs of young children. "Disadvantaged" youth, then, popularly became associated with two categories:

□ *Children from economically deprived families.* Numerous studies have shown that children from low-income homes have greater school-related problems than do children from homes with higher incomes. They may drop out of school earlier, adjust poorly to school routines, achieve at a lower scale, and generally underestimate the value of schooling.

□ *Children from minority groups or identifiable subcultural backgrounds.* The challenge is great today to provide equal educational opportunity to groups that have been, consciously or unconsciously, shortchanged by the American economic, social, and political system: Chicanos, Native Americans, and Blacks, as well as the residents of urban ghettos or rural slums, such as the Southern Appalachian whites. Research studies have shown that a great proportion of low school achievement can be directly associated with children from these groups.

Research evidence, then, indicates a high correlation between (1) low income and low achievement in school and (2) low school achievement and minority group or subcultural affiliation. Despite the popular use of the term *disadvantaged* to describe any child who, due to some damaging condition brought about by a social or economic cause, falls below the developmental levels of children at any particular age level, your author feels that the dangers inherent in establishing such a definition can unreasonably lead to stereotyped views of the children labeled in such a negative way. One danger is that we tend to forget that disadvantages are relative. Any person who tries to function in an unfamiliar milieu will be at a disadvantage. But perhaps the greatest danger is to imply that *all* members of any group be considered disadvantaged; that is, *not all* Black, Native Americans, Chicano, urban ghetto, Southern Appalachian, or migrant children should be generalized as being disadvantaged because of blemishes such as excessive materialism, racial hypocrisy, or selfishness found in *some* middle-class homes. To do so would be to create biases that are both incorrect and unfair. Because the term *disadvantaged* implied such a stereotyped definition for many years, I frown on its use and wish to substitute the phrase *culturally different* instead. I hope this phrase will not be interpreted as being negative and you will understand that, regardless of the term chosen, *severe economic and social hardships* are most likely to cause limited access to early educational opportunity rather than *membership in any particular ethnic or racial group*, and that those hardships seem to be more highly concentrated in some cultural and economic groups than in others.

Preschool programs, beginning primarily with the federally funded Head Start programs of the 1960s, carefully examined the needs of culturally different children and began to develop special teaching materials and instructional techniques, mainly to counteract the negative educational start these children may have received. The models were based on the following theories:

1. *The deprivation theory*—This theory states that the child who is deprived of quality experiences during the early years will not develop the processes necessary for normal acquisition of intellectual skills and abilities.
2. *The critical period theory*—This theory supposes that lack of intellectual stimulation during the early years causes some degree of permanent mental retardation.
3. *The cumulative intellectual deficit theory*—This theory observes that children from "disadvantaged" homes are greatly affected by their early lack of intellectual stimulation. This lack leads to an initial deficit that causes the child great difficulty in reaching newer, higher stages of development. Eventually, the child falls further and further behind children from "advantaged" homes.

Ornstein carefully examined the three prevailing theories and offered this critical response:

> It might be argued that the three theories constitute a scholarly mode for describing the disadvantaged in terms of being "stupid." Although the objective is to make the teacher aware of the intellectual factors related to learning, as well as to counteract the child's limited environmental stimulation with compensatory programs and proper teaching practices, the continuous listing of negative traits and supporting cognitive theories may be used to "alibi" the teachers' and schools' ineffectiveness. It may also be alleged that the social scientists themselves, by delineating these traits and theories, unwittingly contribute to the

teachers' acquiring negative attitudes about the disadvantaged students' inability to learn.[1]

Teachers, then, must understand low-income and culturally different children in order to avoid stereotyping them and translate those understandings into programs offering them equal educational opportunity. Without this understanding and without viable programs and quality teaching practices, any early educational disadvantages these children may have had will be perpetuated and exacerbated.

The educational problems of culturally different youth are varied and complex. They result from conditions in the home and community that affect learning in that they contribute to traditionally low expectations for educational success. Such conditions include dilapidated housing; poor hygienic practices; inadequate nutrition; low income; substandard medical care; illiterate parents; very little verbal exchange; paucity of educational experiences such as visits to zoos, museums, stores, and so on; poor attitudes toward education.

Improvement of these conditions cannot, of course, be assigned to the schools alone; a joint effort with the home and with community agencies is required. However, preschool educators are becoming increasingly sensitive to their responsibilities and are adapting their teaching methods so that culturally different youth are given every opportunity to learn and grow as much as possible. Some of the special adaptations and considerations are described in the following sections.

Language Factors

Perhaps the most damaging myth that has grown from studies of culturally different youngsters is the myth of "nonlanguage." Observations of these children in traditional middle-class-oriented classrooms led them to be described as "inarticulate" or "unresponsive," "not willing or able to communicate." However, many of these children came from homes where the language spoken was not the language of the school. They learned their subculture's rich language in the home or neighborhood, and freely expressed their thoughts with their peers. However, they frequently suffered damaging results when speaking in situations where standard English was expected. E. Brooks Smith, Kenneth Goodman, and Robert Meredith provide two examples to illustrate this point.

> A teacher noticed that one of her first-graders was unable to participate in the general discussion after the class returned from the trip to the zoo. She was, in fact, unable to answer the simplest question about the animals. She did not even seem to know the names of such common animals as lions, tigers, elephants, and bears.
> A few days later, the teacher tactfully raised the question with the child's mother during a parent–teacher conference. "You know," she said, "it would be very good for Mary if you and her father took her on trips to places like the zoo. She needs experiences like that." The mother was puzzled. "As a family we go on

many trips," she said. "We get to the zoo several times a year, as a matter of fact. It's one of the children's favorite trips."

Now it was the teacher's turn to be puzzled. "But Mary doesn't even seem to know the names of the animals or anything about them," the teacher said.

"Oh, she does know about animals," the mother explained, "but, you see, my husband is Old World Chinese. He is very anxious that our children learn to speak Chinese and appreciate their cultural heritage. So when we go on trips he insists that we speak only Chinese. Mary knows the Chinese names of many of the animals in the zoo. I'm sure she could tell you a lot about them in Chinese."

A second-grade teacher had prepared to introduce a story to her reading group. The children all lived in a housing project near the heart of Detroit. The story was about a squirrel. Assuming a lack of experience with squirrels, which she associated with suburban residential districts, the teacher had prepared a large cutout of a squirrel to show the children. "I'm thinking," she said, "of a small animal that likes to climb trees and has a bushy tail." Hands shot up and several children, bursting to answer, almost shouted, "I know, I know!" Triumphantly the chosen child said, "Squirrels! We got lots of squirrels where we live." "Really?" said the teacher in polite disbelief. "Who can tell me about squirrels?" She called on a black child, literally falling off the front edge of his seat in his eagerness to tell about his experiences with squirrels. "My daddy, he go huntin' for squirrel," he said. "Sometime he take me 'long." "Hunting?" the teacher said in a dull tone. "What do you do with the squirrels?" "First we skin 'em. Then we cook 'em," he said. "They goo-oood!" he added, drawing out the last word for emphasis. The teacher responded with a silent look of revulsion. An Appalachian youngster then said, "I know how to skin squirrels!"

Another boy spoke out without the teacher's permission. "My brother, he ten. He catch squirrel and tie tin can to they tail. Man, they sure fun to watch." "That's enough, Thomas," the teacher said coldly. "Class, open your books to page 37 and begin reading."[2]

Each vignette illustrates one of the two language problems common in today's preschool setting: (1) *bilingual children*, who have difficulty expressing their thoughts in expected school language and (2) *divergent children*, who have difficulty expressing their ideas and experiences in standard English. Teachers who are not sensitive to the needs of these groups can hurt and damage young children who are attempting to discuss their feelings and experiences. As rejections accumulate, children often retreat into the comfort of silence—hence, the label "nonverbal." Many children, then, who *seem* nonverbal in the school setting would be able to express themselves fluently if they were accepted by the teacher and were confident that neither their ideas nor their subculture's language would be ridiculed or rejected.

Making young children feel comfortable and wanted implies that teachers understand the language of their children. Sarah W. Zaremba compiled a list of basic words that English-speaking staffs could use easily with Spanish-speaking children. That valuable list is presented below. Pronunciation of the Spanish phrases is indicated by English words or syllables that can be pronounced in only one way. Syllables are divided by hyphens, and the accented syllable is always in capital letters. Practice reading some of the words aloud as you read through the list.[3]

English	Spanish	Pronunciation
Good morning.	Buenos días.	BWEH-nohss DEE-ahs
Good-bye.	Adiós.	ah-TH YOHSS
Thank you.	Gracias.	GRAH-s yahss
Please come.	Venga por favor.	VEHN-gah pohr fa-VOHR
Come tomorrow.	Venga mañana.	VEHN-gah mah-N YAH-nah
Come today.	Venga hoy.	VEHN-ga OY
Yes.	Sí.	SEE
No.	No.	NOH
I don't understand.	No entiendo.	noh ehn-T YEHN-doh
I understand you.	Le entiendo.	leh(ehn)n-T YEHN-doh
Please speak more slowly.	Hable más despacio, por favor.	AH-vleh mahss dehss-PAH-S yoh, pohr fah-VOHR
Please repeat.	Repita, por favor.	rreh-PEE-tah, pohr fah-VOHR
Where do you live?	¿Dónde vive usted?	DOHN-deh VEE-veh oo-STED
What is your name?	¿Cómo se llama?	KOH-moh seh YAH-mah
My name is —.	Me llamo —.	meh-YAH-moh —
Mrs. — will drive you.	La señora — le va a llevar.	lah seh-N YOHR-ah leh-vah-ah-yeh-VAHR
Let me help you.	Déjeme ayudarle.	DEH-hem eh ah-yoo-DAR-leh
Here is the bathroom.	Aquí está el baño	ah-KEE ehss TAH ehl BAH-n yoh
Wash your hands.	Lávase las manos.	LAH-va-seh lahss MAH-nohs
Soap.	Jabón.	hah-BOHN
Water.	Agua.	AH-gwah
Milk.	Leche.	LEH-cheh
Juice.	Jugo.	HOO-goh
Cracker; crackers.	Galleta; galletas.	ga YEH-ta; ga YEH-tahs
Where is your coat? sweater?	¿Dónde está tu abrigo? suéter?	DOHN-deh ehss-TAH too ah-VREE-goh, suh-EH-ter

English	Spanish	Pronunciation
What do you need?	¿Qué necesita usted?	KEH neh-seh-SEE-tah oo-STED
What are you planning to do with it?	¿Qué va a hacer con eso?	KEH va ah as-SEHR kohn EH-soh?
You haven't finished.	— todavía no ha terminado.	toh-dah VEE-ah nohah terr-mi-NAH doh
What's the rule?	¿Qué es la regla?	KEH ESS lah RREH-glah
Your mother is at home.	Tu mamá está en casa.	too mah-MAH ess-TAH enh KAH-sah
— is not feeling well.	— no se siente bien.	—noh seh see-EHN-teh bee-ehn
— is taking (child) home.	— va a llevar a (child) a casa.	— vah ah yeh-VAHR ah (child) ah KAH-sah
Sit down on the bus.	Siéntese en el autobús.	see-EHN-teh-seh en ell ow-toh-BUSS
The bus will come soon.	El autobús va a venir pronto.	ell ow-toh-BUSS vah a beh-NEER PRON-toh
After lunch.	Después de mediodía.	dehss-PWEHSS deh meh-dee-o-DEE-ah
Please ask.	Pídalo por favor.	PEE-dah-lo pohr fah-VOHR
Please tell him.	Por favor dígale.	pohr fah-VOHR DI-gah-leh
He's sorry.	El lo siente.	ELL LOH see-EHN-teh
Story time.	Es la hora de los cuentos.	ess lah OHR-ah deh lohs KWEHN-tohs
Please sit down.	Siéntese por favor.	see-EN-teh-seh pohr fah-VOHR
Listen.	Escuche por favor.	ehss-KOO-che pohr fah-VOHR
Walk.	Camine.	kahm MEE-neh
No running.	No corra.	NOH KOHR-rah
Speak softly.	Hable bajo por favor.	ah-ble BA-ho pohr fah-VOHR

Cardinal Numbers

English	Spanish	Pronunciation
One	Uno	OO-noh
Two	Dos	DOHSS
Three	Tres	TREHSS
Four	Cuatro	KWAH-troh
Five	Cinco	SEEN-koh

Six	Seis	SEH-eess
Seven	Siete	See-EH-teh
Eight	Ocho	OH-cho
Nine	Nueve	new-EH-veh
Ten	Diez	Dee-EHSS

Days of the Week

Sunday	Domingo	doh-MEEN-goh
Monday	Lunes	LOO-nehss
Tuesday	Martes	MAHR-tehss
Wednesday	Miércoles	mee-EHR-koh-lehss
Thursday	Jueves	hoo-EH-vehs
Friday	Viernes	vee-EHR-nehs
Saturday	Sábado	SAH-vah-dough

Knowledge of the primary language in which young children express themselves is necessary so you can tailor instruction to fit their needs effectively. Divergencies within the English language should also be understood by the teacher, for their original structure has special meaning to the group in which it is used. Such divergencies (dialects) result in different word forms, combinations of words, and pronunciations, and are often very difficult to understand. Consider these examples:

Jones scooped up the scorching grasscutter and shoveled it to Smith, the keystone sacker, who whirled and fired it to Brown, the gateway guardian, who nipped the runner by a half-stride. The twin-killing in the final stanza nailed down the win for Johnson, the Bluebirds' fireballing southpaw. (Baseball announcer)

My fellow citizens, it is an honor to be here with you today. When I embarked upon this campaign, I hoped it would be conducted on a high plane and that my opponent would be willing to stick to the issues. He has been inclined to be tractable instead—to eschew the use of outright lies in his description of me. I will not ignore these unvarnished fidelities no longer: his father is a Mormon who was secretly chagrined at least a dozen times by matters of a pecuniary nature. His son subscribes to a phonographic distributor and his great-aunt was an admitted sexagenarian. (Politician)

Now, Greta, outen the dog and don't forget to make the door shut after! (Pennsylvania Dutch dialect)

Tote the ball here, James, 'fo' I give you one upside the haid. . . . That be mine! (Black dialect)

Since Black dialect is the one dialect most popularly heard in preschool settings, let's examine some of its major divergencies from standard English. Even though the dialect differs markedly from standard English, you will find that it is a rich, sophisticated language in itself.

1. *Phonological divergencies*—differences in speech sounds between standard English and the dialect. Some of the common phonological divergencies found in Black dialect include:
   a. the disappearing *r*: *poor* = "po," *for* = "fo," *morning* = "monin'," *Paris* = "Pass."
   b. the disappearing *l*: *rule* = "roo," *oil* = "aw," *help* = "hep," *roll* = "ro."
   c. the difficult *th*: *birthday* = "birfday," *with* = "wif."
   d. dropping sounds at end of words (especially *t* and *d*): *mild* = "mile," *soft* = "sof," *fast* = "fass," *meant* = "men."
2. *Grammatical divergencies*—differences in sentence structure between standard English and Black dialect. Some examples include:
   a. the use of the verb *to be*: absence or presence of the verb *is* indicates permanence or temporariness of action. Thus, "He home" means that he is home for the moment; "He *be* home" means that he has been home for some time and is expected to remain there for a while.
   b. lack of verbal agreement: "They *is* our friends." "She *don't* live here no more." "He *has ran* faster then me." "Tom *seen* him yesterday."
3. *Vocabulary divergencies*—differences in the words used in standard English and Black dialect. Examples include: "Dig that deuce-and-a-quarter!" means "Look at that Electra 225!" "His jaws be set tight" means "He is very angry." "Those are cool vines, brother" means "That's a good looking set of clothes, friend."

Culturally different youngsters, then, may enter the preschool environment with a basic language characteristic: (1) they speak a language other than English (usually Spanish), or (2) they speak an altered version of standard English (usually Black dialect). Lack of facility in speaking standard English can, at times, create problems for these children and result in their having learning difficulties throughout their schooling if no special considerations are formulated. Several popular suggestions for approaching the problem of speakers of nonstandard English have been made over the years.

1. *Teach standard English to children prior to any other formal instruction.* Rapid drill and patterning provide young children with concentrated practice in standard English structure, vocabulary, and sound patterns. Proponents of this approach believe that bilingual education (the capacity to speak and think in two languages or dialects) should be "transitional," that is, children who do not speak standard English should be immersed in repetitive drill in the language as soon as possible, with classroom use of their native tongue kept at a minimum. As soon as these children have gained fluency in standard English, it is argued, they should be placed immediately into traditional English-only classes. This method is a refinement of the 19th century "melting pot" approach, where immigrant children were forced to learn standard English because no other language was allowed in the school. To use this approach in your teaching, review the behavioral position regarding language instruction in Chapter 8.

2. *Teach standard English, but don't force the child to ignore his culture's primary language or dialect.* In this environment, the child is encouraged to speak in his native tongue, while standard English is taught informally in an atmosphere of play and activity-centered learning. The child learns standard English as he hears and tells stories, looks at picture books, sings songs and says rhymes, and talks about daily activities. The emphasis is on the functional use of life experiences. Advocates of this position argue that children unfamiliar with both standard English and American culture learn them gradually while holding onto their own valued cultural and ethnic identities. In this environment, the adults and children speak in both standard English and the second language in the context of spontaneous learning experiences. To use this approach in your teaching, refer to the nativistic position regarding language instruction in Chapter 8.

3. *Teach standard English as a model.* This technique cuts across all preschool programs. Here, the teacher is the model for good language—she speaks carefully in standard English patterns. Common objects are labeled, actions are described, and language is used to describe actions and events during the day. Hearing standard English spoken by the teacher, it is argued, encourages children to imitate its use spontaneously.

The federal government has invested over $500 million to develop bilingual programs since the Bilingual Education Act was passed in 1968. Appropriations for programs set up under the act have increased yearly—$150 million was earmarked for 1979. Additional programs were developed under Title VII, Head Start, Follow Through, and under other public and private sources of funding. Bilingual education is a major area, and an issue of primary concern for early childhood educators today.

Being an issue in early childhood education implies that a basic controversy still exists on that topic. Basically, the controversy related to bilingual education involves these arguments:

1. Proponents of the English-only setting argue that current research studies show that bilingual children learn standard English in English-only settings more effectively than they do in settings where both languages are used. Also, the children score better on standardized English reading comprehension tests at later grade levels.

2. Proponents of the dual-language setting argue that their program makes children feel more comfortable in school and helps them develop a more positive attitude toward school-related activities. They feel that test score gains from English-only settings will be short-lived while the standard English learned in their natural life situations will have more permanence.

Despite the controversy over which teaching strategy results in most effective learning, most educators do agree that knowledge of childhood bilingualism and of the alternative techniques for teaching English as a second language is essential for a sound bilingual program. This knowledge, combined with a sincere respect for cultural diversities, is of primary importance in any program designed to understand and eliminate the learning difficulties of the child exposed to a new culture and new language.

Cognitive Factors

Related to language growth is the highly controversial topic of intelligence. The controversy centers on two viewpoints: (1) the belief that intelligence is primarily inherited and that efforts to improve it are largely fruitless; and (2) the belief that intelligence is largely a product of experience and that one can structure the environment to increase intelligence.

Arthur R. Jensen is the leading spokesperson for the first belief, a belief that educators today find unacceptable because of its strong racist overtones. Although I in no way support Jensen's ideas, I believe that all ideas (however unpopular they may be) should be shared in order to give learners an understanding of the dangers involved in looking at only one source of information.

Jensen contends that Black youngsters perform at a lower level on intelligence tests than their Caucasian counterparts because of genetic differences. He uses this argument to explain the lack of adequate standard-English speaking patterns among Blacks—that is, limited language comes from limited intelligence. Jensen believes that this limited intelligence results in Blacks' inability to learn conceptual material. He asserts that Blacks are able to learn through memorization but that material taught through problem solving and discovery is beyond their native ability. Consequently, Jensen believes that although programs can be designed to improve the *achievement* of Black youngsters, it is futile to expect growth in intelligence. Programs based on Jensen's premises would most probably find children being drilled in repetitive patterns until they can respond quickly and uniformly.

Jensen has been roundly criticized throughout the country for racism. Oscar Jarvis and Marian Rice summarize these feelings:

> Racist explanations [of intelligence] were developed in part to justify the institution of chattel slavery in the New World. As a slave, the Negro never participated in the total culture.... A hundred years after obtaining his freedom in the United States, he is still discriminated against in terms of education, housing, jobs, and social participation in the general culture. A genetic explanation of I.Q. differences, as reviewed by A. R. Jensen, simply does not take into account cultural history of the Negro in the United States.
>
> Negroes are disproportionately represented in the lower income groups. It is inevitable that differences in intelligence and achievement may appear as racial differences when the differences are primarily class differences.[4]

Jerome Kagan attacked the genetic view of intelligence with these comments:

Since middle-class children are more consistently encouraged than are lower-class children to learn to read, spell, add, and write, rather than to keep away from police or defend oneself from peers, the child's I.Q., social class, and school grades are all positively related. The I.Q. is an efficient way to summarize the degree to which a child has learned the vocabulary, beliefs, and rules of middle-class American society. . . . The child is asked to define the word "shilling" rather than the word "rap"; he is asked to state the similarity between a "fly" and a "tree," rather than the similarity between "fuzz" and "Uncle Tom"; he is asked what he should do if he lost one of his friend's toys, rather than what he should do if he were attacked by three bullies.[5]

These two major arguments attacking the genetic view of intelligence are directed, then, toward the social and economic limitations placed on Blacks and toward the cultural bias of intelligence tests. Still a third refutation of genetically fixed intelligence is based on studies by Benjamin Bloom that demonstrate that not only is IQ *not* fixed, but also that it can be altered with training, experience, and changes in teaching patterns. (See Chapter 1, pages 19–21.) Bloom's conclusions were that the long-term overall effect of living in a "deprived" as opposed to an "abundant" environment is 20 IQ points, and that providing early experiences is the key to raising intellectual levels.[6] This hypothesis found many supporters in the 1960s, and research evidence accumulated since then has convinced the vast majority of educators today that preschools can do a lot to prepare environments that provide experiences leading to changes in intelligence. Refer to Chapter 1 for a more complete discussion of this issue.

Based on today's accepted view, that the intelligence of all people can be altered by the environment, a number of innovative *compensatory* preschool programs have been developed. These programs were designed to provide the kinds of experiences and stimulating environments that could compensate for the social and economic conditions causing developmental lags, especially in the area of intelligence. Many of these programs, stimulated by Head Start and other federal, state, local, or private funding, showed positive results in achieving their goals. Some of the most popular model programs are:

Behavioral Approaches

Behavioral Analysis Model
Donald Bushnell, Project Director
University of Kansas

Academic Preschool (Distar®)
Wesley Becker and Siegfried Englemann, Project Directors
University of Oregon

Cognitive Approaches

The Cognitive Curriculum
David Weikart, Project Director
High/Scope Educational Research Foundation
Ypsilanti, Michigan

The Cognitively Oriented Preschool Experience (COPE)
George W. Maxim, Early Childhood Director
Educational Development Center
West Chester State College
West Chester, Pennsylvania

Informal Models

Bank Street Approach
Elizabeth Gilkeson, Project Director
Bank Street College
New York, New York

Tucson Early Education Model (TEEM)
Ronald Henderson, Project Director
University of Arizona

Factors Related to Self-Concept

A direct outgrowth of school performance and language ability is the child's self-concept. Should the child consistently experience failures in these two areas, his view of himself is likely to be diminished; repeated successes, of course, are likely to result in a good self-concept. Research has consistently shown that children from culturally different settings have low self-concepts in the school setting, primarily caused by lack of success. Even though these children come to school with the desire to succeed, continuous and cumulative failures cause a consistent lowering of their self-concept and a consequent drop in educational and personal aspirations. For these reasons, most current preschool programs evaluate the developmental levels of their children before entrance and establish learning tasks at which the children have high probabilities of success, rather than tasks at which they have low probabilities of success. Their methods of enhancing self-concepts generally fall into these categories:

1. *Helping children develop competence.* As mentioned previously, most children enter school with a drive to succeed. You can help them maintain this drive by establishing an environment in which they can experience success and do things for themselves—from putting a puzzle together to hanging their coats in the cubby.
2. *Giving sincere recognition and praise.* One of the most popular ways of enhancing a child's self-concept is to reward him with honest praise. Sincere appreciation of a job well done strengthens the child's character and motivates him to achieve new heights. A note of caution, however: A mechanical, free-flowing extension of praise is nearly as bad as extending no praise at all. Children may soon interpret constant gushy or flowery statements as insincere, and therefore meaningless. Nevertheless, children need encouragement, and praise must be given freely but honestly:

"I'm proud of you, Carlos, you learned a new word today." "You really tried hard this time, Lawrence, I'm sure you'll learn how to do it very soon." "I really like the way you cleaned the snack table today, Martha, you are a good worker."

3. *Respecting the child and his culture.* Often, prospective teachers of culturally different children suffer from prejudice based on lack knowledge. Only a small percentage of such teachers has ever experienced a culturally different childhood, and they find it difficult to empathize with the children or their parents. Ignorance of the causes leading to lack of opportunity often brings out feelings of fear, mistrust, and negative attitudes toward the capabilities of culturally different children.

Before working with culturally different children, therefore, you must examine your inner thoughts honestly for feelings of prejudice and fear. Your author, for example, who was brought up in a neighborhood that included many culturally different youngsters, had friends whose homes were dilapidated and torn—some even had dirt floors. Later, as part of my professional training, I took a course titled "Disadvantaged Youth." The course instructor had obviously never lived in a culturally different setting as a youngster. Before a trip to a rural "disadvantaged" home, she warned, "Be careful not to drink coffee or eat food while you're there. Remember that these people are not very sanitary." Predictably, to welcome us to the house, the mother offered coffee and a cake that she had baked especially for our visit. After hearing polite refusals from the others in my group (including the instructor), I eagerly answered, "I'd enjoy some" (remembering my friends' parents and the pride they took in their ability to cook). The mother's response, as you might suspect, was precious. My biggest reward of the entire visit, though, came when the father delivered a sign that indicated total acceptance of a visitor in a low socioeconomic rural home—he shared his hunting rifle with me. This experience is included to illustrate how preconceived ideas, even from respected professionals, can lead either to damaging or to improving self-concepts among the culturally different. And when you use a term such as *culturally different* to classify a child, think of who was actually culturally different in the vignette and what the resulting actions and words were. Can you apply such understandings to the children in your care?

Work toward understanding all children. Volunteer some time as a student assistant in preschool programs designed for the culturally different. Visit local community groups or neighborhood associations, talk to teachers of disadvantaged children, read about the particular culture in which you are interested, and observe culturally different children in their preschool setting or home environment. Be sure your feelings are not negative before you accept a position in a culturally different preschool setting. By experiencing the richness and pride reflected by people in all cultural groups, you will find that most of your feelings of apprehension quickly disappear. Children will soon sense your feelings and gain an impression of acceptance based on your words and actions.

As you keep in mind the positive ways to enhance self-concept, be aware, too, of the ways in which self-concept can be destroyed:

☐ *Through comparisons.* Comparing the efforts of one child with those of another frequently destroys a youngster's self-concept. This is done with comments such as: "Tina (a culturally different Appalachian child), why can't you learn to talk like Carol (an advantaged child)? I have a hard time understanding what you said."

☐ *Through giving too much or too little help.* Teachers often lower children's self-concepts by doing too much for them. Speaking for the child instead of waiting for him to talk, putting the coat on the child instead of having the patience to let him try, or standing by with a mop as the child carries a glass of water are only a few of the many ways by which we overprotect children and cause them to develop poor self-concepts. Of course, by not providing appropriate help and guidance, we risk the same results.

☐ *Through stereotyping young children.* Often we develop ideas and expectancies of others from hearing what other people say about them. Sometimes this happens when teachers say or think, "I'm just wasting my time with these children. How can I teach them when they *don't want to learn?*" "I don't know what I'm going to do with these children—they're so *lazy*." "Those children will never learn to speak well—they're just plainly *nonverbal*." Stereotypes like these are unfounded and tend to stick only because of unthinking people whose value orientations have been prejudiced by others insensitive to the differences brought about by lack of opportunity. Avoid making such comments for they will only strengthen negative views of the children and result in a low self-concept. Instead, think of the value of each individual and show confidence and respect for what each can do.

To summarize, the prospective teacher of young children must be aware of the conditions caused by social, economic, and cultural differences and how these differences influence major areas of performance in school. The areas of difference usually emphasized by educators are those relating to (1) language, (2) concept development, and (3) self-concept. Choosing teaching strategies in each area implies a knowledge of the effects of deprivation, an understanding of alternative instructional methods and materials, and a respect for the children being taught. Although this task responsibility is a challenging one, it can be one of the most rewarding of all.

THE HANDICAPPED CHILD

There are more than eight million handicapped children in the United States today, and the special educational needs of these children are not being met. More than one half do not receive appropriate services . . . and one million are excluded entirely from the public school system.—Introduction to PL 94–142 (1975)

Public Law 94–142

It was because of concerns like these that the Education for All Handicapped Children Act of 1975 (Public Law 94–142) was passed. Signed by President Ford in November 1975, PL 94–142 is primarily a funding bill; it offers fiscal support to states in return for their compliance with its provisions. The law requires state education agencies to be responsible for certain critical stipulations, including these:

By October 1, 1977

1. Each state must identify those children who are in need of special services, including mentally retarded, hard of hearing, deaf, orthopedically impaired, other health impaired, speech impaired, visually handicapped, seriously emotionally disturbed, and children with specific learning disabilities.
2. Each state must formulate a plan for the education of its handicapped children. The law stipulated that such a plan must provide handicapped children with the learning opportunities they need to become as self-sufficient and productive as possible in a "least restrictive environment" —an environment best suited to a handicapped child's special needs, but one that is as close as possible to a normal child's educational program.
3. Schools must develop an Individual Educational Program (IEP) for every child enrolled in a public school special education program. The IEP is a written statement jointly developed by a qualified school official, the child's teacher, the child's parents or guardian, and, if possible, the child. The written statement is to include these sections:
   a. an analysis of the child's present achievement level
   b. a listing of long- and short-range goals
   c. a statement of specific services that will be provided to help the child reach the goals
   d. an indication of the extent to which the child will become involved in regular school programs
   e. a schedule for evaluating the progress being experienced with the IEP and any recommendations for revisions that might be appropriate

By September 1, 1978

1. Each state must provide a *free* educational program to all handicapped children between the ages of *three and eighteen*. This program must provide an appropriate education that emphasizes special education and related services to meet each handicapped child's unique needs.
2. Again, an IEP must be prepared for each child.

By September 1, 1980

The law requires that, by this time, each state must provide a free, appropriate, public education for every handicapped child between the ages of *three and twenty-one*.

The particular characteristic of the law that interests early childhood educators is that it encourages the development of programs for preschool children by creating a *special incentive grant* for states that provide services to handicapped children aged 3 to 5. These special incentive grants can be up to $300 for each child served.

Obviously, this law makes new demands on all teachers, including both regular and special education teachers in public and private schools. Although the law calls for education of handicapped children in "the least restricted educational environment" it does not mention *mainstreaming*, that is, placing handicapped children in a regular classroom. However, in 1975 the Council for Exceptional Children (CEC), a leading recommending body for teachers affected by PL 94–142, officially described mainstreaming as necessary for handicapped children, not including children whose special needs are such that they cannot be satisfied in an environment that includes nonexceptional children. Their position identified the regular classroom teacher, alone or with help, as the optimal instructor for all students. Underlying this philosophy of mainstreaming is the recognition that when handicapped and nonhandicapped children have a chance to learn, grow, and play together, they grow in self-esteem, social skill, and understanding.

How do you fit into all of this? You should know as much as possible about PL 94–142 because every school district in the country is affected by it. As more and more handicapped children become integrated into the classrooms of public and private schools, regular teachers are more likely to provide appropriate educational experiences for them. To get ready for such an experience, you should:

1. Learn all about the handicaps with which you will be dealing.
2. Visit classrooms where handicapped children have been successfully mainstreamed.
3. Talk to teachers who have worked with handicapped children and gather useful suggestions from them.
4. Seek help from special education teachers who may have worked with children handicapped in ways similar to your children.
5. Attend special conferences, workshops, or other in-service training sessions designed to assist you in IEP writing and/or designing special learning materials and teaching techniques.
6. Talk to the child's parents and previous teachers. They can offer suggestions and advice as the school year progresses.
7. Seek special assistance through publications and nonprint media (speakers, films, and so on) from local, state, or national agencies.

Special Handicaps

It has been long agreed among early childhood educators that every child is unique and special. For that reason, all of education should be *special education* and all educational practices should be directed toward meeting each individual's unique needs. Some children, however, may possess certain extreme mental or physical difficulties that restrict them from reaching the same stages of development as other children. Such handicaps cause some children to differ markedly from the typical child at a particular age level and result in behaviors or characteristics that deviate in an extreme manner. The rest of this chapter will help you identify children with these special handicaps and will share ideas designed to help you develop skills in working with them. The charge of identifying children with special handicaps is a particularly difficult one, though. Philip Safford elaborates:

> One of the most difficult tasks facing the teachers of young children is that of determining which among the varying patterns of individual differences among children constitute "problems." A 4-year-old boy seems to be acting out themes of anger and destruction in his play with dolls. A 6-year-old frequently reverses the direction of certain numerals and letters of the alphabet as he learns to copy them from the board. A 3-year-old makes essentially no use of expressive language. Do such patterns of behavior indicate the presence of problems or handicaps, or are they within the bounds of normalcy, given the individuality of children's development?[7]

Such determinations can be effectively made by a sensitive, informed teacher who is aware of both the characteristics of typical children at various levels of development and the behaviors or characteristics of children having developmental difficulties. Early identification of developmental handicaps is extremely important, for the earlier they are identified, the easier it often is to improve or eliminate them. Nothing, however, can be done until the child is identified as needing assistance, and it is the adult working with early childhood youngsters who often sees the children enough to become aware of such difficulties. You have been presented with many descriptions of developmental standards throughout this book, and it is hoped that your ability to recognize the typical behaviors of children at various ages has been strengthened. Now you will be exposed to the characteristics of children who are developing so far from the normal patterns that they require certain adjustments to their environment.

MENTALLY RETARDED CHILDREN   Mental retardation is an extremely sensitive problem and one that has been defined differently by different educators throughout the years. Earlier systems classified mental retardation into levels such as *moron, imbecile,* and *idiot* in order to describe degrees of *feeblemindedness.* Certainly, you are aware of the derogatory nature of these labels and realize that their professional use is today condemned. Such labels usually were accompanied by feelings of hopelessness toward the child and a consensus that he was unable to benefit from any kind of education.

Fortunately, our view of mental retardation has now changed, although universal agreement has not yet been achieved. Many educators describe the degrees of mental retardation caused by brain injury or environmental factors according to performance on standardized tests of intelligence (IQ). The IQ, as discussed in earlier sections, is the most traditional yet the most criticized method of assessing children's intelligence. The IQ test was developed by Alfred Binet, a French psychologist attempting to identify slow learners in France in 1905. The test quickly reached the United States where Lewis Terman of Stanford University revised it for use in this country and gave it the name Stanford-Binet Test of Intelligence, the name it is known by even today.

Binet saw intelligence not as a single ability, but as a number of related factors that worked together. For example, he felt that as children grew older, their intellectual ability increased, but not necessarily at the same rate as their chronological age. To account for this difference, Binet converted scores on his test into a *mental age*, that is, the age at which a certain level of performance on his test would be considered chronologically normal. For example, a child of four would be considered normal if his mental age was also 4; however, a mental age of 2 for that same child would indicate a lag of two years below the norm.

The IQ, or *intelligence quotient*, is a formula designed to express this relationship between chronological age (CA) and mental age (MA). It expresses intelligence as the ratio of MA to CA multiplied by 100 to avoid the problem of using decimals.

$$IQ = MA/CA \times 100$$

Therefore, if a child's mental age is 24 months and his chronological age is 48 months, his IQ is:

$$IQ = 24/48 \times 100$$
$$IQ = 1/2 \times 100$$
$$IQ = 50$$

This tells you that the four-year-old child has the intellectual level of a two-year-old. An IQ of 100 is considered normal (average).

$$IQ = 48(MA)/48(CA) \times 100$$
$$IQ = 1 \times 100$$
$$IQ = 100$$

The *standard deviation* of IQ tests is 16; this means that we can categorize *normal* or *average* intelligence as the range of scores from 84 to 116. However, average intelligence is usually associated with IQ scores that fall within the 80–120 range. The American Association of Mental Deficiency (AAMD) examined the use of IQ scores to indicate mental retardation, and designed a classificational system to describe the levels of retardation for children falling below the normal levels of intelligence. Their work is shown in Table 13-1.

Table 13-1   AAMD Classification of Mental Retardation[8]

| | Intelligence Quotient Scores | |
| | | Wechsler Intelligence |
Level	Stanford-Binet	Scale for Children
Mild	67–52	69–55
Moderate	51–36	54–40
Severe	35–20	39–25
Profound	< 19	< 25

According to this system, degrees of mental retardation are identified solely through scores attained on two popular childhood tests of general intelligence. Samuel A. Kirk has also used intelligence test scores to classify levels of mental retardation, but has added a new dimension: explanations of potential growth within each level of retardation (see Table 13-2).

Many professionals today question the classification of young children into levels of retardation based solely on IQ scores. As a matter of fact, federal regulations now *prohibit* educational placement decisions (that is, placement

Table 13-2   Classification of Mental Retardation and the Potential for Growth within Each Level[9]

Level	IQ Score	Definition
Educable mentally retarded (EMR)	50–75/80	Unable to profit sufficiently from a regular program but has potentialities in (1) academic subjects, (2) social adjustment, and (3) minimal occupational adequacies.
Trainable mentally retarded (TMR)	25/30–49	Not educable in the traditional sense but has potentialities for training in (1) self-help skills, (2) social adjustment in the family, and (3) economic usefulness.
Totally dependent	25/30	Unable to be trained in total self-care, socialization, or economic usefulness, and requires almost complete care and supervision throughout life.

Mentally retarded youngsters find joy and happiness when provided with experiences designed to meet their special developmental needs. (© Nikolay Zurek/ Jeroboam)

in special education classes) solely on the basis of a single test of intelligence. Thus, you should be aware of alternative methods of determining to what extent mental retardation may exist in young children:

1. Observe the child for any characteristics or behaviors that are obviously immature for his chronological age.
2. Examine the child's cumulative records for information regarding the development of such skills as crawling, creeping, walking, and talking.
3. Evaluate the child's ability to remember things over a period of time.
4. Check the child's attention span and frustration level.
5. Examine the child's ability to get along with others and determine whether he is accepted or rejected by his peers.
6. Observe the child's interest in books or other learning-related materials.

The severity of mental retardation obviously varies widely—from the mildly retarded youngster who fits well into the normal daily routine to the severely retarded child who needs special care and understanding. Most preschool teachers are flexible individuals; normally they have little difficulty absorbing the mentally retarded child into the classroom or providing special educational services. Those who have done so usually followed general recommendations such as the following:

Recommendations for Working with Mentally Retarded Children

1. Initiate a systematic procedure for diagnosing the child's level of development, and plan a step-by-step program in which the child can experience repeated success.
2. Use as many direct experiences as possible.

3. Use manipulative, real learning materials so the child can experience as many sensory modalities as possible (hearing, seeing, touching, tasting, and smelling) in his learning. Don't rely on talking to the child!
4. Plan for patient repetition because the mentally retarded child needs more time than his normal counterpart to grasp ideas—be tolerant and understanding.
5. Provide constant reinforcement through reward and praise for each accomplishment.
6. Provide many opportunities for the child to speak. Piaget, Chomsky, and other prominent writers describe the interrelated development of language and intelligence and emphasize the importance of language as an evolving process of intelligence.
7. Encourage the child to persist and let him know that you like him and want to help him.
8. Be consistent in your behaviors. Mentally retarded children become anxious and frustrated when their authority figure fluctuates in her behavior patterns.
9. Respond to the child's questions and comments. The mentally retarded youngster will feel better about himself if he knows that his questions and comments are sincerely accepted by his teacher.
10. Be sure to avoid comparisons with the normal children in your classroom and eliminate a competitive climate. Help the child adjust to regular routines and get along wth the other children.

The key to an effective program for mentally retarded youngsters is your ability to individualize the program and to stimulate the child to learn with challenging tasks presented at his present ability level. With patience and understanding, these children are capable of doing many of the same things normal children can do, except on a slower and more delayed scale. The hypotheses of Bloom and Hunt (discussed in Chapter 1) during the 1960s enlightened educators to the fact that properly designed programs for preschool children can raise IQ scores by 20 or 25 points. If we go back to Tables 13-1 and 13-2, it is apparent that enriching environments during the early years can move children from the category of moderately retarded (Table 13-1) or educable mentally retarded (Table 13-2) to a low normal category (above IQ score of 80). Because of this and other evidence, early childhood educators have become convinced that planning educational experiences in terms of the child's developmental level rather than his chronological age is imperative. If this is done, there is no reason why mentally retarded young children cannot successfully adjust to and learn in regular preschool classrooms.

HEARING IMPAIRED CHILDREN The incidence of hearing problems in the nation's schools has been the subject of conflicting evidence over the years, especially among reports describing the hearing problems of preschool youngsters. S. R. Silverman and H. S. Lane, however, conducted an exhaustive study of hard of hearing and deaf youngsters and discovered that "of 18,926 children enrolled in public residential schools for the deaf in the

United States, 1028 were under the age of 6; of 15,370 children in public day schools and classes, 2453 were of preschool age; and of the 3686 children in denominational and private schools, 1646 were under the age of 6."[10]

Although total deafness is relatively rare in preschool classrooms (only 4 percent of all hearing problems result in deafness), mild or moderate hearing problems are found about as often as any other form of physical or mental handicap. The degrees of handicap are based on the extent of hearing loss as measured in *decibels* (db), standard units for measuring the volume of sound. Table 13-3 differentiates six classes of handicapped hearing in terms of extent of hearing loss, and describes the ability to understand speech within each category.

Although physical examinations and parental observations uncover some cases of hearing difficulty before the child comes to school, many mild or moderate hearing problems remain undiscovered until the child enters the preschool classroom. Thus, the teacher must be watchful of the children under her care so that possible hearing problems can be uncovered before complications accumulate. Symptoms of hearing difficulties include the following:[12]

1. Shows speech problems:
   a. reluctance to speak
   b. speech very loud, very soft, or very slow
   c. articulation (forms words or speech sounds) poor
2. Is unresponsive when spoken to; may often ask "Huh?" or "What?"
3. Watches the speaker's face while the speaker is talking
4. Cocks or turns the head toward a speaker
5. Has difficulty maintaining attention when spoken to
6. Complains about earaches or demonstrates actions that indicate pain in the ear

In keeping with the spirit of PL 94–142, you are responsible for helping *identify* youngsters with hearing impairments and for *planning* programs that provide least restrictive environments for them. This is not as threatening a situation for you as it may seem, for R. A. Stassen points out, "Of all handicapped pupils, those with amplifiable hearing losses are among the most potentially teachable."[13] The preschool setting should be the same for children with impaired hearing as it is for everyone else, except for the following recommendations.

Recommendations for Working with Hearing Impaired Children

1. Develop an attitude of readiness to listen. Use special signals to remind the child that you are about to speak. Encourage him to let you know when he's ready to listen to you.
2. Use the voice for getting the child's attention. Say the child's name when you wish to talk to him. Tapping him on the shoulder and similar measures only serve to bring unnecessary attention to the child's handicap.

Table 13-3 Levels and Characteristics of Handicapped Hearing[11]

Handicap Level	Amount of Loss	Ability to Understand Speech
No significant handicap	< 25 db	No significant difficulty with faint speech
Slight handicap	25–40 db	Difficulty only with faint speech
Mild handicap	40–55 db	Frequent difficulty with normal speech
Marked handicap	55–70 db	Frequent difficulty with loud speech
Severe handicap	70–90 db	Can understand only shouted or amplified speech
Extreme handicap	> 90 db	Usually cannot understand even amplified speech

3. Keep within close range when speaking. Turn toward the child so he can see your face. He is helped when he is able to interpret your lip movements as well as your facial expressions.

4. Use a normal conversational tone of voice. Speak in short sentences with a clear voice. Clarity is much more important than loudness, for increasing your volume will only single out the handicapped child and begin to label him as "different." Besides, clear speech is much easier to lip-read than is exaggerated speech.

5. Serve as a good speech model. Avoid overuse of gestures or overexaggerated lip movements or facial expressions. Children benefit more when they observe normal speech behaviors than otherwise.

6. Use frequent repetition. Talk to the hearing impaired child and repeat your words when it seems necessary. If you develop an accepting environment, the child will feel free to let you know when your words need to be repeated.

7. Encourage parents to expand your work in the home. Parental cooperation is essential to the success of any preschool program, but especially when special measures have been instituted to compensate for hearing handicaps.

8. Develop a favorable attitute toward the child. The single most important variable in working with the hearing impaired is an understanding teacher. You should treat the child as an able individual and be empathetic (not sympathetic) with his condition. Overprotection of such children is unnecessary; except for these few special recommendations they need to be treated like others in your room.

These hearing impaired youngsters have been mainstreamed into a regular class-room after being trained in the use of special hearing devices. (© Elizabeth Crews/ Icon)

Deaf children, of course, present a different situation from those who possess some degree of hearing. The ultimate goal, again, is to integrate the children into the regular classroom, but it is unlikely that they will make a good adjustment unless at least *some communicative* speech patterns have been developed in the home or in special school settings before the child comes to the regular classroom. W. M. Northcott believes that integration of the deaf into the regular classroom is not appropriate if these conditions are present:

1. The hearing loss was recently diagnosed and there has been no parent guid-ance to ensure transfer and maintenance of educational gains through home stimulation, and
2. The child is not yet aware that his hearing aid brings in meaningful environ-mental sounds, including speech, or that he must look at faces to gain under-standing from moving lips and facial expression.[14]

Once it has been determined that the deaf child can be mainstreamed, he must be placed in a situation where he can gain optimum benefit from his experience, much as any other child. This means that the major goal of his early preschool experiences should be *socialization.* Thus the child will have an opportunity to adjust to the room and to the other children. This is as much a benefit to the normal hearing child as it is to the deaf child, for he begins to understand and befriend the handicapped at an early age. Once the socialization process has begun, and the deaf child indicates an interest in formal learning, you may wish to contact hearing specialists or other resource persons for suggestions of supplementary teaching materials. However, special materials or methods should be used within the context of the regular classroom whenever possible so that the deaf child is generally treated like any other in your care.

Northcott observed hearing impaired children who were mainstreamed into regular classrooms and found that, even though these characteristics were not evident beforehand, the children had several features in common:

1. Active utilization of residual hearing and full-time hearing-aid usage, if prescribed
2. Demonstrated social, academic cognitive, and communicative (auditory and oral) skills within the normal range of behaviors of hearing classmates at a particular grade level
3. Intelligible speech and the ability to comprehend and exchange ideas with others through spoken, written, and read language
4. Increased confidence and independence in giving self-direction to the tasks at hand[15]

Children with hearing problems, then, are able to feel good about themselves, and can gain from the educational setting if they are integrated with normal hearing children. The sensitive teacher must look at these children with an understanding eye and match their unique needs with her program's resources. Except for following the special recommendations, the hearing impaired child should be treated as any other in your care.

VISUALLY IMPAIRED CHILDREN A physical handicap that is often found in the preschool setting is the inability to see clearly. Like the hearing impaired, the visually impared child is most often normal in all other areas of development, so he needs much the same kind of educational environment as the normal seeing child, except, of course, for certain special considerations.

Visually impaired children are normally classified into two categories (see Figure 13-1):

1. *The partially seeing:* children whose field of vision is 20/200 (that is, they can see at 20 feet what a normally sighted person can see at 200 feet) or better in the corrected better eye, but not greater than 20/70.
2. *The blind:* children whose field of vision is 20/200 or less vision in the corrected better eye.

Children with visual impairments exhibit distinct symptoms—you should be constantly alert to these. Some common symptoms include:[16]

1. crossed eyes (strabismus)
2. involuntary, rapid movements of the eyeballs (nystagmus)
3. squinting

4. rubbing the eyes
5. crusts, sties, or swollen lids
6. reddened or watery eyes
7. tilting the head to one side
8. pupils of uneven size
9. sensitivity to light
10. awkwardness in eye–hand coordination (in puzzles, dressing, and so on)
11. facial distortions while doing close work
12. avoiding tasks requiring good vision
13. complaints of pain in the eyes, headaches, dizziness, or nausea following close eye work
14. lack of interest in normally appealing visual experiences
15. tendency to regularly confuse letters, words, or numerals: 6 and 9, d and b, or bad and dad.

Like teachers of other handicapped children, the teacher of young children with visual problems must follow a number of special practices if mainstreaming is to be successful. The following suggestions have been recommended by Rose C. Engel:[17]

Recommendations for Working with Visually Impaired Children

1. The sense of touch helps to round out what the child hears.
2. "Puppy" is only a word until experiences of its wiggling, tail-wagging, cold nose, and wet tongue add meaning.
3. Listen and refuse a request if you need to but do not ignore it by not responding.
4. Many of the child's concepts are built and clarified by what he hears. Tell him where and why he is going before moving him. Talk about the type of flooring the child is crossing, such as "Now you are on the grass (cement, asphalt, tile, wooden floors)."
5. Thoughtfully arrange the environment for free movement with safety. Encourage independence.
6. Tell him what is going on. When you touch him, tell him who you are. Teach other children to identify themselves when touching him.
7. Let him make as many movements as possible by himself. Tell him to "come to your voice." Let him open doors with his own effort, when possible.
8. Hearing is the child's main channel for learning. Don't be afraid of a sensory overload on this channel for the visually impaired.
9. Give him opportunities to help others. He is so often on the receiving end.
10. Expect the standards of courtesy and waiting expected of others. A handicap is not to be used to take advantage of the rights of others.
11. Care for him rather than always taking care of him.
12. Adapt the environment or situation so that each child can be part of the activities enjoyed by others in the group.
13. Work for communication and praise the child for each success, remembering that receptive language always precedes expressive language.

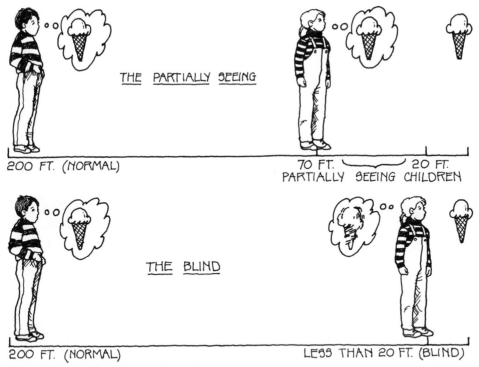

Figure 13-1 Categories of visual impairment.

14. Use a multisensory approach in teaching.
15. Be a good language model.
16. Use many kinesthetic experiences and sensory art activities to encourage manual dexterity and manipulation.
17. Physically take the child through what is expected before asking him to do it alone.
18. Encourage the child to verbalize his needs rather than anticipating them. In a situation where there is some problem in relation to another child, help him use a verbal rather than a physical approach.
19. Work with the child's parents and therapists. Parents are the prime educators of their children.
20. Listen! Give him time to talk by waiting for his response and try not to answer for him.
21. Respect the contribution and opinion of each child, including the visually handicapped child.
22. Use concrete experiences.
23. Repeat, but VARY, the situation to keep the child interested.
24. Encourage free physical movement.

With certain limitations, visually handicapped preschoolers—like children with normal eyesight—should be provided with an environment in which they can explore, discover, and manipulate. The teacher must respond

Blind children can be provided with regular academic or play activities when mainstreamed into preschool classrooms. The young girl is being helped to write while the young boy is being helped in the block corner by a child with normal vision. (*Left:* © Mitchell Payne/Jeroboam. *Right:* © Charles Harbutt/Magnum Photos)

to the children's interests and lead them to master special skills and abilities. If a young blind child can trust a teacher in such a setting, he will be able to move toward autonomy and increased skill with greater confidence.

In addition to the recommended teaching practices, you might contact a teacher or supervisor who has had special training in the field for other suggestions. Close cooperation among resource people, the classroom teacher, and parents can lead to special practices and procedures that will make the visually handicapped youngster's adjustment to the regular classroom a successful one.

PHYSICALLY HANDICAPPED CHILDREN Some children are born with a physical handicap; others acquire it after birth. The type and degree of each child's physical problem require the teacher to make appropriate adjustments within the context of the regular classroom. Since the special skills required to work with the wide range of physical disorders is a topic too broad for this text, the physical handicaps that appear to be most commonly found in preschool children have simply been listed and general suggestions have been made for meeting the affected children's unique needs. See Table 13-4.

Obviously, your chief role is to be aware of these conditions and try as hard as possible to design programs to fit the physically handicapped within the regular preschool setting. Be especially mindful that physically handicapped children suffer from many disadvantages brought about by their condition. Dorothy Rogers explains:

Physically handicapped children experience many disadvantages. For one thing, their developmental progress suffers, leaving them out of step with children of the same age. Blind children, for instance, are slower in learning to walk, eat, dress, and bathe. In addition, the physically handicapped individual is often an underachiever. The child with poor vision may not see the blackboard well; the crippled child feels isolated and hence can't relax and enjoy school activities. Teachers, although generally sympathetic with younger children, may be less tolerant of older ones. This intolerance is most common in the case of milder defects—notably of speech, hearing, or sight—that reduce academic achievement and reflect on the teacher's effectiveness.

Handicaps also impede social adjustment. A child lacking motor skills rarely plays an important role among peers. Activities are restricted, so one child grows envious, resentful, and withdrawn—sustained only by the successes of fantasy. Another may become anxious and angry, engaging in offensive aggression. After-

Table 13-4 Common Physical Handicaps in Preschool Children

Condition	Characteristics
Cerebral palsy	A nonprogressive condition in which the child is unable to control muscle reflexes voluntarily. The condition results from damage to the brain due to causes such as infection to the mother during pregnancy, insufficient oxygen during birth, Rh incompatibility between father and mother, birth trauma, or heredity. It can also result from brain injury or brain infection during the early developmental years.
Epilepsy	A convulsive disorder that often accompanies neurological disabilities such as cerebral palsy. Seizures, or "fits," characterize epilepsy. These seizures range from those in which the pupils constrict and dilate, the mouth froths due to an inability to swallow, respiration becomes irregular, and the body goes through a short period of quivering (the most dramatic type lasting up to two minutes) to the small seizure in which the child merely seems to be engaged in a daydreaming or staring spell (about 10 seconds).
Spina bifida	A condition caused by malformation of the spinal cord. The condition results in impaired mobility, usually paralysis of the legs. Other handicapping characteristics include mental retardation or lack of bladder and bowel control.
Amputation	Loss of any of the limbs through surgery. Artificial limbs are often supplied.
Paralysis	Brought about by a variety of neurological disorders, paralysis renders the child unable to control parts of his body, especially the limbs.

ward he feels guilty, but his efforts to "make up" are rebuffed. Still another child may, either consciously or unconsciously, use her handicap to gain selfish ends. In any case, her mood and attitude may make her such poor company that she becomes more rejected still—a vicious cycle. She may employ the handicap as an excuse to escape growing up or to take advantage of others and may even feel a masochistic enjoyment, feeding on the sympathy of others.

The handicapped child also suffers simply by being a child. Children are frequently insensitive to the feelings of less favored persons. They can be brutally frank, causing deep wounds. In one case, a lame child was called "Crip." In another instance, children mimicked a boy with a cleft palate, taking no pains to remove themselves from his hearing. . . .

The handicapped also suffer from societal attitudes toward them. While ostensibly heeding their welfare, people often feel pity or repulsion—or even an unconscious resentment that such people must be provided for. The handicapped, in turn, come to expect society's negative attitudes toward them, and they often acquire deep-seated inferiority complexes. Despite intermittent struggles, the majority are unhappy and often doomed to social isolation.[18]

Since the regular preschool classroom may be one of the first intensive exposures to normal children, the physically handicapped child should be made to feel comfortable by an understanding, helpful teacher. Again, be careful not to be overly helpful or to communicate pity. These children have come from hospitals or institutions where they have been exposed to therapy procedures encouraging self-help and positive self-concept. Your role is to build on this foundation by providing an accepting environment of warmth and tolerance. Kirk explains how the previous therapy received by the child can be supported and extended within the regular preschool setting:

1. Develop motor abilities in the child through special materials, special aids and supports for mobility, and through special methods provided by the physiotherapist, the occupational therapist, and the special teacher. In the school situation the teacher is the coordinator of the program even though specific prescriptions are given by the attending pediatrician or orthopedic specialist.
2. Develop language and speech, especially in the cerebral-palsied child, since this is one area where the majority are retarded or defective. This includes the ability to perceive oral language and to express it, to perceive visual stimuli and interpret them, and to express oneself in motor terms. The latter includes both speech and gestures. This phase of the child's development is assisted by a speech correctionist, the parents, and the special teacher.
3. Develop in the child the psychological factors of visual and auditory perception, discrimination, memory, and other factors considered intellectual. These functions are best developed through the school program which includes language usage, listening, planning, problem solving, dramatization, imagination and creative expression (through art and music media), creative rhythms, visual and auditory memory and discrimination, and perception. At this age level an environment with toys, sand tables, doll corners, and so forth, is provided so that the children will learn to respond to the attractions of the environment both physically and mentally. Through the addition of materials and the verbal and manual suggestions of the special teacher the children are helped to progress from one developmental stage to the next.

This physically handicapped child is grasping onto special hanging strings in order to encourage muscle growth through exercise. (© Jean-Claude Lejeune/Stock, Boston)

4. Develop social and emotional adequacy in the child at home and in the school by providing him with opportunities for acquiring emotional security, belongingness, and independence. The school situation is probably superior to the home in not overprotecting the child and in giving him opportunities to do things himself. The environment of the school which includes other children of the same age gives the child an opportunity to learn to interact with others, to share, and to cooperate. It offers him examples of activities which he can imitate, and at the same time the protection and help which he needs when he really needs it.[19]

If the child can learn to overcome problems related to physical handicaps at an early age in a regular preschool setting, chances are increased that he will accept the handicap and be willing to work toward the development of other assets. Such results are possible in schools for young children because the schools' flexibility allows them to meet unique individual needs and their desire to help enables each individual to grow toward his maximum potential.

LEARNING DISABLED CHILDREN *Learning disabled* is a term that has emerged during the late 1970s to describe any condition or set of conditions that prevents a child from functioning at the level of development normally expected for children at a particular age. These conditions may include perceptual disorders, motor disorders, mild brain damage, or "learning blocks" that affect learning in only one area such as reading or math. Although these children are not mentally retarded (often they are of average or above-average intelligence) and are essentially like all other children, they do have special educational needs.

The early diagnosis of learning disabilities is a primary responsibility of the early childhood educator, for the condition can best be remediated when discovered during the early years. A number of factors may lead you to suspect a learning disabled child (there are about 8 million learning disabled children in our schools):

1.   the inability to follow simple instructions
2.   the inability to repeat patterns and processes
3.   low levels of cognitive functioning
4.   confusion in spatial orientation—looking left when told to look right, and so on
5.   poor gross or fine motor control
6.   lack of established handedness
7.   poor appetite or cravings for certain foods

Although teacher observation is important for discovering learning disabilities in young children, resource personnel such as school psychologists should be contacted before a formal diagnosis is made. Once such a diagnosis has been made, however, an individualized enrichment program should be developed immediately with the aid of parents and other professionals such as reading specialists, pediatricians, or neurologists. The two learning disabilities most often uncovered in the preschool setting are *dyslexia* and *minimal brain dysfunction (MBD)*.

Dyslexia is broadly defined as any retardation in the development of reading, that is, reading at a level that appears to be below the learner's level of intelligence. It is often thought of as a neurological disorder causing the learner to see reversed letters or mirror images. For example, *saw* for *was* (reversal) or ʏod for *boy* (mirror image). To understand the extent of the problem, hold this page in front of a mirror, and try reading the next few sentences, or hold a mirror above Figure 13-2 and look only at the mirror as you attempt to complete the maze, going from start to finish by keeping a smooth pencil line. Although there are many other forms of dyslexia, these two (reversal and mirror image) are among the most common.

Many approaches have been suggested for treating the dyslexic. Since many educators feel that dyslexia is an outgrowth of failure to establish clear hand, eye, or foot preferences—a condition affecting the ability to read or write—most approaches focus on forms of patterning to encourage the establishing of *dominance* (handedness, eyedness, or footedness). These programs can be categorized into three major approaches: the Frostig program, characterized by materials involving various activities to promote visual perception; the Doman-Delacato approach, characterized by physical activity to overcome neurological problems; and the Fernald Tracing Method, emphasizing repeated tracing activities. Marianne Frostig felt that special edu-

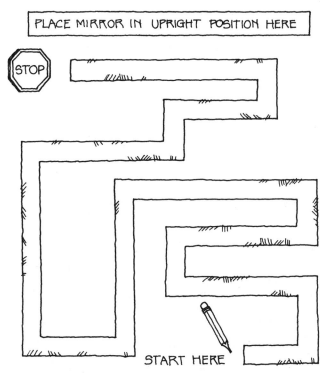

Figure 13-2   Illustration of dyslexic functioning.

cational intervention for learning problems should be directed toward the development of *visual perception.*[20] Figure 13-3 illustrates the types of patterning activities she developed. In this activity, the children are to focus their eyes on the separate paths of each feature pictured and to trace each with a pencil or crayon. Many other activities like this are provided in the Frostig materials.

The Doman-Delacato program is directed toward treating not the visible results of brain injury (learning disabilities) but the injured brain itself.[21] Robert J. Doman, Glenn Doman, and Carl H. Delacato knew that normal children develop by successfully accomplishing certain tasks at different ages; for example, successful attempts at crawling and creeping during infancy involve sending sensory nerve messages to the area of the brain governing those movements. Repeated successes gradually build up neurological patterns in that part of the brain enabling the child to make those and other related coordinated movements without much conscious planning. Hypothesizing that brain-injured children could be helped to activate brain cells in other parts of their brain to take over the functions of their dead ones (especially the ones governing patterned movements), the developers planned a group of patterning movements normally the responsibility of the damaged level of the child's brain. They felt that if these early developmental movements were repeated over and over (even with adults), the undamaged cells in the other parts of a brain would eventually receive the sensory messages

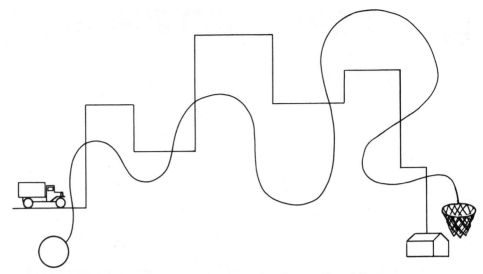

Figure 13-3   Sample work page from the Frostig Visual Perception program. (From *Frostig Visual Program*, copyright 1964. Published with permission from Follett Publishing Company, a division of Follett Corporation.)

that the exercises were feeding into it. Gradually, the child would be able to perform the movement patterns he once had been unable to perform. When the child exhibits the ability to crawl and creep in the Doman-Delacato program, for example, he is moved toward normal standing and walking, and eventually is patterned to improve other physical skills such as hearing, vision, manual dexterity, and, eventually, reading skills. A sample Doman-Delacato room is illustrated in Figure 13-4.

The Fernald Tracing Method is based on the idea of the efficacy of repeated practice.[22] It emphasizes the use of a patterned kinesthetic approach (touch and sight) to improve reading skills. The basic procedure is outlined below:

Stage 1
1. Child chooses words he wishes to know.
2. Word is written for the child with crayon.
3. Child traces the word while touching it, pronouncing each part as he proceeds.
4. Process is repeated until child can write it on his own.
5. He uses it in the story he is writing.
6. Story is typed when child is finished.

Stage 2
1. Same as stage 1 except tracing is no longer necessary.
2. Child learns word by looking at it, says it to himself, and writes it.
3. Each word *must* be pronounced as it is written.

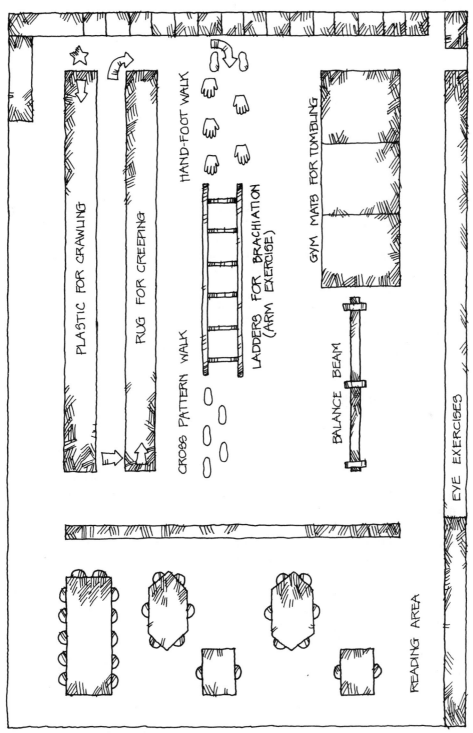

Figure 13-4 A sample Doman-Delacato room.

Stage 3

1. Child looks at printed word and says it to himself before writing it.
2. Child starts reading from books.
3. Permitted to read anything and as much as he likes.

Stage 4

1. Child begins to make relationships between words he knows and new words.

The early childhood teacher is important in the treatment of a dyslexic child. She must look for the symptoms of dyslexia and examine possible remediation procedures so that the young child can be provided with the program best suited to his needs. This program, whatever it may be, requires specialization—consultations with experts in the field are usually the most effective procedure.

Minimal brain dysfunction (MBD) is a general term characterizing a variety of learning and behavioral disorders commonly found in the preschool setting. Many of the characteristics associated with dyslexia can also be associated with MBD, except that MBD involves severe learning problems in *all* developmental areas, including reading and language. Characteristics of MBD include:

1. developmental lags—slowness in maturation
2. immature speech
3. poor visual-motor coordination
4. early cognitive failures
5. poor motor control—awkwardness or clumsiness

MBD can be *congenital* (inherited) or *acquired* (disease or accident causing injury to the brain). Your chief role is to make classroom observations and *refer* the suspected cases of MBD for further testing to appropriate specialists. As you can see, the signs of MBD do not differ greatly from those of dyslexia, and methods of diagnosis are similar. Some educators criticize educational literature for separating MBD from dyslexia in discussions of learning disabilities. Rather than enter into this argument, however, your author would only note that it is important to identify the learning disabled child and to search through various resources to try to find how this child can best be helped within the regular preschool setting.

Principles and practices for aiding the *seriously emotionally disturbed* and the *speech impaired* have been introduced throughout this book (see Chapters 3, 4, 8, and the earlier parts of this chapter). Note that in some truly exceptional cases you may seriously question whether you are able to offer sufficient help. Constant extreme behaviors such as rapid changes in moods or "blowing his stack" may indicate special needs requiring help beyond what you are able to provide. When this happens, feel free to admit your frustrations and seek the advice of a qualified professional. Behaviors in this category include those that: (1) are extreme and seemingly uncontrollable; (2) occur regularly; and (3) persist over an extended period of time.

MAINSTREAMING

Since our mission in early childhood education is equal education for all, the concept of mainstreaming physically and mentally handicapped children should be met enthusiastically by classroom teachers. In mainstreaming children aged six and younger, we build on all we know about the importance of the early years to all aspects of the child's development. There have been many suggestions for aiding the teacher in the process of mainstreaming preschool youngsters into the regular classroom setting. Some of the most popular recommendations are listed below:

1. View the child as a *whole child* with strengths as well as weaknesses. Avoid looking at the handicapped youngster as an "epileptic" or a "dyslexic," but rather as a child like any other child.
2. Learn all you can about the mainstreamed child's specific disability. Gain awareness of therapy techniques and become familiar with technical terminology.
3. Involve parents in dealing with their child both in the school and at home. They should learn what you are doing in school so that your practices can be reinforced and extended in the home.
4. Maximize interactions between the handicapped and the nonhandicapped children.
   a. Give simple explanations about a child's handicap, when needed. Youngsters are curious and will often want to know about a new child and will be satisfied by an open, honest explanation. ("Jeannie's legs don't work well so she needs a wheelchair.") Such a gesture on your part will set the stage for acceptance.
   b. Read books or tell stories about children with differences.
   c. Encourage the handicapped child to share strong capabilities. For example, the wheelchair-bound youngster may well help another child in a project demanding manual dexterity and soon gain that child's appreciation for outstanding manual skill.
5. Individualize your program. Start where the child is and plan a sequential program to encourage him to build one skill upon another. Build on continuous success rather than tearing down with repeated failures.
6. Make appropriate spatial and environmental changes in and around the school. Ramps may need to be built for physically handicapped youngsters, or grab bars may need to be placed in the bathrooms, for example.
7. Take special in-service training through workshops or seminars. Keep up on the current principles and practices of mainstreaming.

SOME FINAL THOUGHTS

The message is clear—the federal government has informed us that mainstreaming will be a characteristic of our educational system for years to come. The challenge is great, for mainstreaming is not easy. It requires changes in attitudes, behaviors, and teaching style. You will all be part of this movement, so it is important that you gain the skills and attitudes necessary for helping young children function effectively in society despite a handicap. What better place to start this process than in a warm, sensitive, understanding preschool environment?

NOTES

1. Allan C. Ornstein, "Who Are the Disadvantaged?" *Young Children* 26, no. 5 (May 1971): 267–268.
2. E. Brooks Smith, Kenneth S. Goodman, and Robert Meredith, *Language and Thinking in School*, 2d ed. (New York: Holt, Rinehart and Winston, 1976), p. 51.
3. Sarah W. Zaremba, "Spanish in the Preschool: A Bilingual Aid for the English-Speaking Staff," *Young Children* 30, no. 3 (March 1975): 174–177.
4. Oscar T. Jarvis and Marion J. Rice, *An Introduction to Teaching in the Elementary School* (Dubuque, Iowa: Wm. C. Brown, 1972), p. 491.
5. Jerome Kagan, "Preschool Enrichment and Learning," in *Revisiting Early Childhood Education*, ed. Joe L. Frost (New York: Holt, Rinehart and Winston, 1973), p. 199.
6. Benjamin S. Bloom, *Stability and Change in Human Characteristics* (New York: John Wiley, 1964), p. 88.
7. Philip L. Safford, *Teaching Young Children with Special Needs* (St. Louis: C. V. Mosby, 1978), p. 11.
8. From B. R. Gearheart and F. W. Litton, *The Trainable Retarded: A Foundations Approach*, Second Edition, 1979, The C. V. Mosby Company, St. Louis, Mo. Adapted from H. Grossman, ed., *Manual on Terminology and Classification in Mental Retardation*, 1977, Garamond/Pridemark Press. Baltimore, Md. Used with permission.
9. From *Educating Exceptional Children*, Second Edition, by Samuel A. Kirk. Copyright © 1972 by Houghton Mifflin Company, Boston, Ma. Reprinted by permission of the publisher.
10. S. R. Silverman and H. S. Lane, "Deaf Children," in *Hearing and Deafness*, 3d ed., ed. H. Davis and S. R. Silverman (New York: Holt, Rinehart and Winston, 1970), p. 385.
11. From *Hearing and Deafness*, Third Edition, edited by Hallowell Davis and S. Richard Silverman. Copyright 1947, © 1960, 1970 by Holt, Rinehart and Winston, Inc., New York, NY. Reprinted and adapted by permission of Holt, Rinehart and Winston.
12. Safford, *Children with Special Needs*, p. 62.
13. R. A. Stassen, "I Have One in My Class Who's Wearing Hearing Aids!" in *The Hearing Impaired Child in a Regular Classroom: Preschool, Elementary, and Secondary Years*, ed. W. H. Northcott (Washington, D.C.: Alexander Graham Bell Association for the Deaf, Inc., 1973), p. 3.
14. W. H. Northcott, "Candidate for Integration: A Hearing Impaired Child in a Regular Nursery School," *Young Children* 25, no. 6 (September 1970): 368.

15. W. H. Northcott, ed., *The Hearing Impaired Child in a Regular Classroom: Preschool, Elementary, and Secondary Years* (Washington, D.C.: Alexander Graham Bell Association for the Deaf, Inc., 1973), p. 3.

16. Dorothy Rogers, *Child Psychology*, 2d ed. (Belmont, Calif.: Wadsworth, 1977) and Samuel A. Kirk, *Educating Exceptional Children*, 2d ed. (Boston: Houghton Mifflin, 1972).

17. Rose C. Engel, *Language Motivating Experiences for Young Children* (Van Nuys, Calif.: DFA Publishers, 1973), pp. 10–11.

18. Rogers, *Child Psychology*, pp. 94–95.

19. Kirk, *Educating Exceptional Children*, pp. 258–259.

20. Marianne Frostig and D. Horne, *The Frostig Program for the Development of Visual Perception* (Chicago: Follett, 1964).

21. Carl H. Delacato, *The Treatment and Prevention of Reading Problems* (Springfield, Ill.: Charles C. Thomas, 1963).

22. Grace Fernald, *Remedial Techniques in Basic School Subjects* (New York: McGraw-Hill, 1943).

A Final Word
from Your Author

You are on your way to becoming a professional in the field of early childhood education. That is certainly an exciting prospect and one with a great amount of responsibility, for you are now at the point of your professional development where you are expected to make personal, informed decisions regarding the principles and practices you will use with any group of preschool children. The decisions you make and the ways in which you carry them through make you one of the most important factors in the future growth and development of each child with whom you have contact. This is a tremendous responsibility and one that must not be taken lightly. You will need to think and act on your own, without the immediate aid of Jean Piaget, B. F. Skinner, your instructor, your classmates, your textbooks, and other aids. Don't feel alone, though—every teacher must go through the process: "How do I do that?" "If only I had a chance to talk with my college instructor!" "Where can I get help?" And don't stop looking for answers to your questions or concerns. Make your future the brightest one possible by constantly growing in your field. Strive toward self-improvement and for increased professionalism. Although your career will be filled with hard work, your efforts will be rewarded with smiling faces and hugs aplenty. Best wishes for a long and fruitful career with young children.

As you progress through the approaching stages of your professional career, make every effort to keep up with what's new in the field. Look for magazines and professional organizations recognized as having a productive record in helping our young children. Some of the popular ones are listed on the next page.

PROFESSIONAL ORGANIZATIONS

National Association for the
Education of Young Children
(NAEYC)
1834 Connecticut Avenue, N.W.
Washington, D.C. 20009

Association for Childhood
Education International (ACEI)
3615 Wisconsin Avenue, N.W.
Washington, D.C. 20016

National Education Association
(NEA)
1201 16th Street, N.W.
Washington, D.C. 20036

Child Welfare League of America
(Day Care)
44 East 23rd Street
New York, New York 10010

Day Care and Child Development
Council of America
1401 K Street, N.W.
Washington, D.C. 20005

American Association of
Elementary-Kindergarten-Nursery
Educators
1201 16th Street, N.W.
Washington, D.C. 20036

Educational Resources Information
Center/Early Childhood Education
(ERIC/ECE)
805 West Pennsylvania Avenue
Urbana, Illinois 61801

American Montessori Society
(AMS)
175 Fifth Avenue
New York, New York 10010

MAGAZINES AND JOURNALS

Young Children (Journal of NAEYC)
National Association for the
Education of Young Children
1834 Connecticut Avenue, N.W.
Washington, D.C. 20009

Childhood Education (Journal of
ACEI)
Association for Childhood
Education International
3615 Wisconsin Avenue, N.W.
Washington, D.C. 20016

Today's Education (Journal of NEA)
National Education Association
1201 16th Street, N.W.
Washington, D.C. 20036

Day Care and Early Education
Human Sciences Press
72 Fifth Avenue
New York, New York 10011

Early Years
Allen Raymond, Inc.
P.O. Box 1223
11 Hale Lane
Darien, Connecticut 06820

Teacher
Macmillan Professional Magazines,
Inc.
262 Mason Street
Greenwich, Connecticut 06830

Instructor
The Instructor Publications, Inc.
P.O. Box 6099
Duluth, Minnesota 55806

Learning
Education Today Company, Inc.
530 University Avenue
Palo Alto, California 94301

Index

Credits

To the owner of this book:

I hope you have enjoyed reading *The Very Young: Guiding Children from Infancy Through the Early Years* as much as I enjoyed writing it. I'd like to get your reactions to the book so that I can improve it in future editions. Could you please take a moment to fill out this questionnaire? Thank you.

Your school: _____

Your instructor: _____

Department of: _____

Course title: _____

What did you like most about *The Very Young?* _____

What did you like least about it? _____

Was the entire book assigned for you to read? _____

If not, what parts or chapters were NOT assigned? _____

Was there anything that you found particularly difficult to understand?_____

_____

If you have any other comments, I'd be delighted to hear them.

Optional:

Your name _____ Date _____

May Wadsworth quote you in the promotion for *The Very Young: Guiding Children from Infancy Through the Early Years*?

Yes _____   No _____

Thank you for your help,

George W. Maxim

FIRST CLASS
PERMIT NO. 34
BELMONT, CA

BUSINESS REPLY MAIL
No Postage Necessary if Mailed in United States

Dr. George W. Maxim
Wadsworth Publishing Company
10 Davis Drive
Belmont, CA 94002

Education Editor